W9-AHD-999

Social Psychology

fourth edition
Social Psychology

JONATHAN L. FREEDMAN
Columbia University

DAVID O. SEARS
University of California, Los Angeles

J. MERRILL CARLSMITH
Stanford University

Prentice-Hall, Inc., Englewood Cliffs, New Jersey   07632

Library of Congress Cataloging in Publication Data

FREEDMAN, JONATHAN L.
   Social psychology.

   Bibliography:
   Includes indexes.
      1.—Social psychology.   I.–Sears, David O., joint
author.   II.–Carlsmith, J. Merrill joint
author.   III.–Title.
HM251.F68   1981   302   80–25934
ISBN   0–13–817783–X

Printed in the United States of America

10 9 8 7 6 5 4 3 2 1

Interior design by Jayne Conte
Cover design by Jayne Conte
Editorial/Production supervision by Joyce Turner
Manufacturing buyer: Edmund W. Leone

Prentice-Hall International, Inc., *London*
Prentice-Hall of Australia Pty. Limited, *Sydney*
Prentice-Hall of Canada, Ltd., *Toronto*
Prentice-Hall of India Private Limited, *New Delhi*
Prentice-Hall of Japan, Inc., *Tokyo*
Prentice-Hall of Southeast Asia Pte. Ltd., *Singapore*
Whitehall Books Limited, *Wellington, New Zealand*

Contents

ACKNOWLEDGMENTS

The authors gratefully acknowledge permission from the American Psychological Association to reprint the following tables and figures.

Tables 4–3, 5–6, 5–7, 5–10, 6–3, 6–4, 8–5, 10–3, 11–1, 11–5, 12–2, and 12–3.

Figures 5–5, 5–7, 6–2, 6–3, 6–11, 7–4, 10–7, 10–8, and 14–5.

Full reference material may be found in the References at the end of the book.

Preface

In the years since the last edition of this book was written, there have been some substantial changes in the field. Most of these changes are the result of typical cycles in a science in which certain topics capture the attention of people while other topics become temporarily of less interest to those working in the field. In social psychology it seems fair to say that some of the traditional areas such as group dynamics, leadership, affiliation and attitude change, though still of great importance, have received relatively little attention recently. In contrast, other traditional areas such as liking and attraction, aggression, and social perception have shown a resurgence. At the same time, interest has continued high in altruism and compliance and has grown enormously in attribution theory, environmental psychology, and sex roles. None of these shifts of interest mean that a particular topic is less important than it used to be, nor that some new topic is suddenly more important than it was. But there is no denying that in any given period of years, there is more research and progress on certain issues than on others.

In this edition we have increased coverage of those areas that are receiving more attention in the journals, and have reduced somewhat the amount of space devoted to traditional areas in which research is less active. In particular, we have added a new chapter on sex roles. This fascinating topic cuts across several fields of psychology including not only social, but also developmental and personality. Our chapter emphasizes the social aspects of sex roles but draws on work in other areas as well. To reflect the continuing and growing interest in social cognition, we have expanded coverage of attribution theory, social perception, and social cognition in general. In addition, liking, aggression, altruism, and environment are given more space than before, because there is a great deal of new research to discuss. Throughout the book we have added more material on the sociobiological approach to social behavior. Although this viewpoint has not yet had a major impact in most areas of social psychology, it has generated a considerable amount of discussion and is valuable mainly because it gives a new perspective on some traditional problems.

The major reduction in coverage is in the area of attitudes and attitude change, to which we devote one fewer chapter than in the previous edition. However, we feel strongly that just because issues are not receiving a lot of attention right now is not sufficient reason for reducing coverage substantially. The classic work on attitudes and group dynamics, for example, is still enormously valuable. There is no question that it is part of that body of knowledge to which all students in social psychology should be exposed. Therefore, while expanding coverage of the new areas in response to trends in the field, we have not shortchanged the traditional areas. In some instances we have compressed the material somewhat, but generally we have maintained full coverage.

A revision of a textbook consists in part of bringing it up to date by including research that has been conducted since the previous edition. Of course we have done this, and there are a great many references to very recent work. On the other hand, we have not dropped classic references just because new ones were available, nor added new ones just so we could boast about the number of recent citations. This text is not an encyclopedia of studies in social psychology, nor is it a list of the table of contents of recent journals. The point of the text is to present what we know in the field as clearly and comprehensively as possible, to discuss unresolved issues where appropriate, and to explain the findings using the best theories that are available. Through all of this, however, we have tried to keep in mind that this is a book for introductory students in social psychology. They do not want and do not benefit from long lists of references, from descriptions of ten studies to make a single point when one or two would suffice, nor from a presentation of every possible explanation of the same finding. We have tried to make the information in social psychology easy and accessible while at the same time making it interesting and relevant to the students' lives.

As before, we have tried to simplify without oversimplifying. The concepts and knowledge of social psychology should be within the reach of all college students and we have tried to accomplish this. On the other hand, this is by no means a simple text in the sense of being "low-level." In our opinion, it contains the material that students at any level, any kind of school should know about the field; and it presents the material in such a way that any student should be able to understand it while the best students should still be challenged by it. This is the material we teach in our classes at Columbia, UCLA, and Stanford and also the material we would teach anywhere else. Indeed, we recommend the book to graduate students for a thorough review of the field. Thus, it is comprehensive and rigorous but, we hope, easy to read and interesting.

The material for this book is drawn from a wide variety of sources. Rather than limiting ourselves to laboratory experiments conducted by social psychologists, we included many different kinds of research done by people in many different disciplines. Indeed, we tried to use any source that seemed appropriate and scientifically rigorous. In addition to laboratory experiments, we relied on findings from field experiments, correlational field experiments, surveys, observational work, and archive data. This research was conducted by social psychologists, of course, but also other psychologists, sociologists, anthropologists, ethologists, political scientists, and biologists. It is all grist for the mill, all knowledge about social behavior as long as the work itself is done well.

In preparing this edition we received help from many people. Our special thanks to Shelley Taylor who worked with us on the social perception and attribution chapters, and to Anne Peplau who worked on the sex roles chapter. We feel that these three chapters are immeasurably better because of the advice and guidance we received from these two outstanding psychologists. At Prentice-Hall, John Isley the psychology editor, got reviews of the work, discussed the plans for revision, and generally supervised work on this edition. Joyce Turner, production editor, took charge of all the details of turning the manuscript into a finished book, and did a fine job on this. And Robert Mony did an exceptional job of copyediting, one of the best we have ever seen. We are grateful to all of these people.

We would also like to thank the following colleagues for their constructive comments on our manuscript:
Robert Arkin, University of Missouri; John Burns, Arkansas State University; David K. Dodd, Saint Mary College; Jerald Greenberg, Ohio State University; M. Kian, Edinboro State College; Richard Lippa, California State University; C. A. Lowe, University of Connecticut; Elaine C. Nocks, Furman University; Letitia Anne Peplau, University of California, Los Angeles; Charles F. Seidel, Mansfield State University; Annette S. Thompson, Hood College; Glenn White, University of Arizona.

Finally, let us repeat and enlarge somewhat on a note from the previous edition. When it was published, there was a great deal of turmoil in the field of social psychology. Many people seemed concerned about a lack of progress in the field, about the direction it was taking, and about the general issue of whether it was appropriate to do research on social issues. Although many of these concerns still exist, it seems to us that morale among social psychologists is higher than it was and that there are fewer complaints about what is being accomplished. In response to some of the earlier concerns, there has been a shift to more applied research and perhaps more attention to important issues. Progress is always going to be slow in a discipline that deals with as complex matters as social behavior, but we feel confident that the decade of the eighties will be even more productive than the 70s and that the field is going to go through a period of increased vigor and growth.

Social Psychology

Introduction and Theories

* Mike Goldberg; Stock, Boston.

Social psychology is the systematic study of social behavior. It deals with how we perceive other people and social situations, how we respond to others and they to us, and in general how we are affected by social situations. Social psychology includes all areas of interactions between people such as affiliation, attraction and liking, aggression, conformity, communication, altruism, and influence of various kinds. It is concerned with how groups affect their members and how groups act as units. Recently, two problems have attracted considerable interest. One is how sex roles develop and how they affect people; the other is how the environment—including such factors as noise, architectural design, heat, and crowding—affects us. In addition, a great deal of research has focussed on the principles and rules by which people interpret the social world, perceive others, and try to make sense of what is happening around them. Social psychology tries to answer any and all questions about how people affect one another and how they behave in social situations. Not all of these questions have been answered fully—far from it—but the job of social psychologists is to ask the important questions and then to look for answers.

Of course, many fields other than social psychology also deal with these problems. Sociologists, urban geographers, anthropologists, and members of various disciplines of psychology are concerned with social behavior and social problems. Much of their research overlaps. Sometimes it is almost identical; sometimes it is quite different. But in order to understand certain complex issues, we need research from many points of view, using a wide range of techniques and approaches.

In order to get some sense of how different disciplines and subdisciplines approach social behavior, let us consider one example and discuss briefly the kind of research that has been done in the various fields. One of the most serious problems facing the country today is the extremely high crime rate. Over the past twenty years, the rate of violent crime has risen sharply. This increase has been most dramatic in urban areas, but suburbs and small towns have also seen greatly increased crime. Researchers have spent a great deal of time and energy trying to explain criminal behavior, and in particular, to understand its recent sharp rise. The approaches to this question differ greatly from field to field.

One approach, typical of sociologists, economists, and to some extent urban specialists, is to look for broad social explanations. The economist points out that crime is closely related to income level. Poor people commit many more crimes than more affluent people. And, according to some views, they do so simply because they need money and commit crimes to get it. Some of these crimes involve violence, some do not; but they are all motivated by economic need. To support this position, a sociologist or economist might note that murder (usually a noneconomic crime) is much less related to income level than car theft or robbery. So, the explanation of criminal behavior in general, and the increase in crime rate in particular, is that people are experiencing greater economic need than they used to, or that relative to others, they are worse off than they were.

Sociologists and demographers (those who study population trends and patterns) have related crime rate to social factors such as race, population density, and especially age. It is well established that violent crime against strangers is committed mainly by young people. (Many acts of violence occur between family members—child-, wife-, and even husband-beating, spouses killing each other, and so on; these are not especially crimes of the young. However, violent crime has risen most sharply in situations outside the family.) Since the percentage of the population aged fourteen to twenty-five has increased dramatically over the past twenty years, the rise in crime rate could be due entirely to the age shift in the population. There are more people in the age group that commits violent crimes, so there is more violent crime.

These explanations are made at the broad, general societal level; they do not discuss individual psychological mechanisms. Surely economic factors are a major reason why people commit crimes, and surely young people tend to commit most of the violent crimes. Improve the economic conditions of the poor and crimes will be reduced; wait until the baby boom generation grows up, and the crime rate will drop. Most sociologists would add factors such as racial tensions, immigrant problems, peer group effects, urban structure, and so on; but the level of explanation is still broad and general.

Psychologists deal with the problem of rising crime quite differently. They ask two additional questions: First, they want to know why some people commit crimes when others, in seemingly identical social situations (same income, age, race, and so on), do not. Second, psychologists look for the basic mechanisms that explain why certain factors lead to criminal behavior. Within psychology itself, different subdisciplines look for answers in different places.

Developmental psychologists and clinical psychologists who are interested in criminology focus on an individual's background to understand why that person has become a criminal. They are concerned with individual differences that lead to crime. How was the person raised? What kind of discipline did his parents employ? Were they divorced? Did they fight? Thus, one line of research would compare the incidence of criminal behavior among children whose parents were divorced with those whose parents stayed together. Perhaps "broken homes" tend to produce children who do not learn to behave properly, who become angry at the world, or who do not learn the usual cultural values and morals. A developmental psychologist would thus try to get information on the family background of delinquent and nondelinquent children. Better yet, he would follow the lives of a large group of children over a period of many years and relate their criminal or noncriminal behavior to their family background.

To investigate the role of parental discipline and other family factors is more complicated. It is very difficult to find out just how parents treat their children, whether the parents fight between themselves, and generally what a family's interpersonal relations are like. Just asking parents does not always yield trustworthy information, because most people are reluctant to tell a researcher that they regularly beat their children, or that they and their spouse have a terrific fight at least once a week. But this is a crucial line of research that may eventually tell us how child-rearing practices affect an individual's adult behavior and personality. One long-term study of this kind, for example, suggests that consistent discipline, imposed mainly by giving and withdrawing love rather than by physical force, produces children who are less likely to be involved in criminal acts. However, because of the difficulties just mentioned, we are far from sure of this relationship.

Social psychologists have also been involved in this kind of family research but generally their approach is quite different. Whereas other subdisciplines in psychology may ask what social factors, kinds of treatment in childhood, or other experiences affect criminality, social psychologists ask why a particular situation or factor leads to an act of aggression or violence at a particular time. Social psychologists may ignore for the moment the characteristics an individual brings to the situation and instead consider what factors increase or decrease the chances that an individual will be aggressive. In other words, they focus on the mechanism or process that leads to aggression. For example, one basic principle of social psychology is that when people are frustrated, when they want to do something and are prevented from doing it, they become angry and aggressive. This relationship between frustration and aggression is one explanation of why crime or any kind of aggression occurs. It has been tested in laboratories and in the outside world. This particular relationship can explain not only why someone commits an aggressive act in a certain situation, but also why economic and racial factors may lead to crime. It might be argued that people who are poor and who are discriminated against are frustrated; they cannot buy what they want, cannot get good jobs, cannot live in the way they would like. This frustration may be at the root of much crime. In other words, poor people do not commit crimes just because they want money or possessions—this is part of the motivation, but often only a small part. These frustrated people are also angry at society in general, and they take out this anger by violent and aggressive acts, many of which have little or no chance of producing any economic gain. The teenager who robs someone of ten dollars and then beats him up is acting not so much from a desire for money, but out of frustration and anger. Thus, the frustration-aggression relationship explains criminal behavior at quite a different level from that of sociology or economics. It deals more with psychological processes and internal mechanisms in its attempt to explain why social factors such as poverty lead to crime.

The other approaches are worthwhile and, indeed, are essential if we are going to fully understand complex social problems such as crime and aggression. And there is, of course, considerable overlap among disciplines in the kind of studies that are done. The point is that a single question—Why does crime occur?—can be asked and answered in many different ways; and the focus can shift from general to specific explanations, and from sociological to psychological processes.

THEORIES IN SOCIAL PSYCHOLOGY

Just as one single issue can be studied by several disciplines with differing viewpoints, so the same phenomenon can be approached in different ways depending on one's theoretical orientation. Students are often introduced to psychology through the major comprehensive theories of human behavior popular in the earlier part of the century. Almost everyone has at least heard of *psychoanalytic* theory and Sigmund Freud; of *behaviorism,* and John B. Watson, E. L. Thorndike, Clark Hull, and B. F. Skinner; of *Gestalt* theory and the European psychologists Köhler and Koffka. Each of these schools arose from the work of one or two charismatic individuals who often inspired a fierce sense of loyalty to their own ideas and equally fierce attacks on the supposedly grievous errors of other schools. They competed vigorously for supporters, a competition that at times took on the aspects of a moral crusade.

These schools of thought had the ambition of creating general theories of human behavior. They modeled their theories on those of the physical sciences, hoping to generate theories as detailed, universal, and complete as atomic theory in physics. Their goal was to explain and predict all human behavior.

Naturally many of these theories were applied to the problems of social psychology and began to structure its research. Social psychologists also soon began to disagree violently over competing approaches. But this phase did not last very long. The problems of social psychology quickly turned out to be sufficiently complex that it was hard to fit one general, simple theory to them. By the mid-1950s, when social psychology really began to flourish and expand, most of the original combatants had been replaced by more pragmatic researchers with more modest (or perhaps more practical) goals. Their ambition was to pose and verify *middle-range theories*—theories that attempted to account for certain specific phenomena such as attitude change, or aggression, or interpersonal attraction, but did not pretend to account for social behavior in general.

Most research in social psychology today therefore deals with one phenomenon, such as aggression, without referring to others, such as social perception. Social psychology is a bit like the outposts in the Far West of the frontier days: it is composed of little areas of order and civilization that have been carved out of a vast wilderness, but that seemingly have little to do with one another.

Social psychology, however, has more unity than that. Our approaches to a wide variety of different problems have been guided by a few general (and often rather simple) basic ideas that may be traced back to earlier general theories, just as today's interstate highways often follow the routes of eighteenth- or nineteenth-century frontier trails. The present controversies are often modern versions of old feuds. So we think that today's research in social psychology can be understood better if one understands its theoretical roots, even if these roots are usually implicit rather than explicit in the research itself.

The next section briefly presents a few of these core ideas. We do not intend to be comprehensive or detailed in presenting them. Rather, we want to convey their essence and particularly the contrasts between them, so that we can refer back to them in explaining controversies in later chapters. We will be simplifying in order to make the contrasts clear. As will be seen in succeeding chapters, each of these basic approaches applies, in one form or another, to most areas of social psychology. We will take them up again later on when they are relevant to more specific issues.

We shall apply each of these approaches to the specific problem of rising crime that we discussed earlier. Let us suppose that a policeman catches a high school dropout, Herbert, coming out of the rear door of a liquor store at 3 A.M., with a bag full of money. The store, like everything else in the neighborhood, has long since closed. The policeman shouts at Herbert to stop and put his hands up. Herbert turns, pulls a pistol from his pocket, and shoots the policeman, wounding him in the leg. Herbert is apprehended and ultimately sent to jail. The statistics predict that his stay in jail will not be productive or happy, it will be costly for society, and the chances of his committing further crimes are fairly high. Like many problems of social psychology, Herbert's situation merits our analysis because it is, from all points of view, an unfortunate situation.

Let us consider how four major theoretical approaches would view this event and explain it. The most general approaches that influence social psychology are the genetic-physiological, learning, and perceptual-cognitive, with a fourth, incentive-conflict, being in a sense a combination of the last two.

GENETIC-PHYSIOLOGICAL THEORIES

McDougall, Freud, Lorenz, and others have stressed the influence of innate characteristics on human behavior. Human beings are born with many genetically determined characteristics that distinguish them from other animals and from each other. There is no question that to some extent **genetic characteristics** play a role in determining behavior. At the simplest level, these characteristics limit the behavior humans are capable of and the stimuli they respond to. Humans cannot fly, they can eat meat, they are quite strong and fast relative to many other animals, but are weaker than many other animals, and so on. Humans are also intelligent, have language (or the capacity to develop it), have wonderful memories, and live long lives. They have excellent hearing and vision, but respond to only a limited range of sounds and light. Humans also mature slowly, being quite helpless as babies; and until they have lived at least six years or so they are unable to fend for themselves. (Goats, in contrast, can walk almost at birth and can manage by themselves soon after.) The list of important innate characteristics could be much longer, but clearly all of these qualities affect the kind of animal we are and our social behavior.

In addition, differences among people affect their behavior. Some are much bigger and stronger than others; some are smarter than others; some have better vision and finer coordination than others. Some of us are female (and can give birth to young), others are male and cannot.

The question then, is not whether any of these innate characteristics affect our social behavior—clearly they must—but how big a role they play and just what difference they make. For example, it has been suggested (by McDougall and Lorenz among others) that humans have an instinctive tendency to be aggressive. They argue that built into the organism, present at birth, and unalterable, is an aggressive impulse. In slightly different terms, Freud's psychoanalytic theory also proposes an innate drive toward destructiveness (though Freud thought it could be channeled into nondestructive behavior). The notion that **aggression** is instinctive does not help us much in understanding why Herbert robbed the store or shot the policeman, except to say that such aggressiveness is natural. It does not tell us why Herbert fired the gun whereas others might not have; nor why Herbert is a criminal and the policeman is not. But this view does provide one way of looking at human behavior that greatly emphasizes the role of genetic factors.

A somewhat different approach emphasizes the innate differences among people. Without taking a stand on whether everyone has an instinctive tendency to behave aggressively, this view says that some people are, for genetic reasons, more aggressive than others. For example, it has been argued that people who have a particular type of genetic structure (specifically XYY chromosomes instead of the more usual XY or XX) are likely to become criminals. Although there is as yet little evidence to support this idea, it would obviously be a partial explanation of criminal behavior. Perhaps Herbert has an extra Y chromosome (all XYY people are males), and that is why he is so violent. Similarly, this approach can rely on other physiological factors such as hormonal imbalance, brain defects, and so on to explain aggressiveness. (It is well established that damage to certain parts of the brain, especially the hypothalamus, can produce uncontrolled aggressiveness in animals.) The general idea is that the causes of all behavior, including social behavior, can be found in the physiology of the person—in the genetic structure, in innate characteristics, in physical characteristics that develop after birth, or in temporary physiological states of arousal, hormone production, brain stimulation, and so on.

The genetic-physiological approach has had relatively little impact on social psychology. Although innate characteristics and physiological processes doubtless affect social behavior to some extent, most social psychologists believe that these factors play a small role in social behavior. They generally assume that few instinctive or innate behavioral mechanisms exist in humans. And even if they do, their effect is relatively small and uninteresting. Similarly, with a few exceptions, social psychologists believe that physiological processes have little direct effect on human social behavior. However, both genetic and physiological factors are being investigated more fully, and they may become more influential in social psychology in the near future.

LEARNING THEORIES AND BEHAVIORISM

Until recently, the dominant theoretical approach to social psychology in the United States and Canada emphasized the role of learning. In a phrase, the idea was that prior learning determines behavior. This notion became popular in the 1920s and was the basis for behaviorism. Pavlov and John B. Watson were its most famous early proponents, a role filled later by Clark Hull and B. F. Skinner. Neal Miller and John Dollard applied the principles of learning to social behavior, and more recently

Albert Bandura has extended this application in an approach called *social learning theory.*

The core idea of the learning approach is that a person learns certain behaviors in any given situation, and when presented again with that situation, the person tends to perform the same behaviors. When a hand is extended to us, we shake it, because that is how we have learned to respond to an extended hand. When someone says something nasty to us, we may be nasty back or may try to make the other like us, depending on what we have learned to do in the past. So, perhaps Herbert shot the policeman because he had learned to behave aggressively, and even violently, in situations when challenged by authority.

There are three general mechanisms by which learning occurs. One is by **association,** or classical conditioning. You will remember that Pavlov's dogs were taught to salivate at the sound of a bell after many training trials in which they were presented with meat every time it was rung. After a while they would salivate to the bell even in the absence of the meat, because they associated the bell with meat. We learn many things by association, such as attitudes. For example, the word "Nazi" is generally associated with a series of horrible crimes or with disparaging descriptions. Thus we learn Nazis are bad, because we have associated them with awful things.

A second learning mechanism is **reinforcement.** People learn to perform a particular behavior because it is followed by something pleasurable and need-satisfying (or avoid behavior that is followed by unpleasant consequences). A child learns to approach her mother when she is hungry, because she has learned that mother provides food. A boy learns to retaliate against insults in school by fighting with his tormentor, because his father praises him for sticking up for his rights when he does it. Or a junior professor learns not to contradict the department chairperson in an open faculty meeting, because each time he does, she frowns and looks angry and snaps a rebuttal back at him.

The third major learning mechanism is **imitation.** People often learn social attitudes and behaviors simply by observing the attitudes and behaviors of role models. A little boy may learn how to chop wood by watching his father do it. Children and adolescents may develop quite elaborate packages of political attitudes simply by listening to what their parents say, particularly at election time. Imitation may occur without any external reinforcement at all, though some writers hypothesize that it works because the individual rewards himself (or herself) for accurately copying the role model.

The learning approach has three features in particular that set it off from the other core ideas in social psychology. First, the causes of behavior are supposed to lie mainly in the *past learning history* of the individual. Perhaps in Herbert's previous encounters with the police, they had been rough, rude, antagonistic, suspicious, and unsympathetic. Perhaps he had been reinforced in the past for responding violently to con-

United Press International.

FIGURE 1–2 One of the most powerful mechanisms of learning is imitation. In particular, children tend to imitate adults, especially their parents and others with whom they are close.

flict situations, and nonviolent responses had not brought him satisfaction as often. Or perhaps his father often acted in a violent way himself, so Herbert had learned to imitate a violent role model. The learning theorist is especially concerned with past experience and somewhat less with the details of the current situation.

Second, the causes of behavior tend to be located mainly in the external *environment* and not in the individual's subjective interpretation of what is happening. Learning approaches emphasize the events previously associated with a stimulus, or the past reinforcement contingencies

operating on a response, or the role models a person has been exposed to. All of these are external to the individual. Learning approaches are less concerned with such subjective states as emotions (for example, whether Herbert was fearful, angry, calculating, or whatever) or perceptions of the situation (for example, whether or not he expected the policeman to attack or shoot him).

Finally, the learning approach usually investigates *overt behavior* instead of psychological or subjective states. It focuses on Herbert's overt act—shooting the policeman—instead of emotional states such as his possible fear, anger, or guilt. The learning approach deals mainly with why Herbert behaved violently, rather than in some other way such as fleeing, obeying, freezing, or arguing.

In recent years, most learning theorists have begun to incorporate more cognitive processes in their models, so that we now have what might be called learning-cognitive theories, not just learning theories.

PERCEPTUAL-COGNITIVE THEORIES

Another influential approach in social psychology grew out of the **Gestalt** psychology that was originated in the 1920s and 1930s by German psychologists such as Koffka, Köhler, and Wertheimer. It was later applied by Kurt Lewin and Fritz Heider and more recently, by Leon Festinger, Harold Kelley, and others to social phenomena. The main point is that people are not simply passive agents in their dealings with the world. Rather, people organize their perceptions, thoughts, and beliefs into simple, meaningful form. No matter how chaotic or arbitrary the situation, people will impose some order on it. And this organization, this perception and interpretation of the world, affects how we behave in all situations, and especially in social situations.

This is easy to see in terms of our perceptions of the world around us. Put this book down and look around. First you will notice that you tend spontaneously to group and categorize objects. Instead of seeing objects individually, you see them as parts of a group. You see a row of books as a group, not as so many individual books. You see other students reading in the library mostly as a group of students. You experience that pile of dirty dishes by the kitchen sink as an oppressive heap, not as individual dishes.

Second, you will also notice that you immediately perceive some things as standing out (*figure*) and some as just being in the background (*ground*). Usually colorful, moving, noisy, unique, nearby stimuli are figures, whereas bland, drab, stationary, quiet, common, faraway stimuli are ground. Our perception spontaneously groups things and highlights some objects at the expense of others.

You can see how strong these organizing tendencies are if you try to resist them. Try to see the world around you as composed of unrelated, ungrouped, individual objects—for example, that each book and each shelf and each dish and each fellow student is an individual entity instead of being part of a common group or category. Look at a crowd of students walking across the campus and see how difficult it is to look at each one individually for very long; after a while, it is much more comfortable to see them as a group.

In addition to this perceptual organization, we impose a structure on other aspects of the world. We do not merely observe what is going on around us and within us, but we interpret what we observe. We make judgments and try to interpret our feelings and other people's feelings; we try to figure out why others are acting the way they do, what their intentions and motives are, and so on. For example, if someone says something complimentary to us, we have to decide if they really mean it or are merely saying it so we will give to their favorite charity. Our interpretation changes the whole situation and our response to it.

Cognitive-perceptual theories form the basis of **attribution** theory, which deals primarily with our perceptions of causality in the world. They are also central to the theory of **cognitive dissonance,** which con-

FIGURE 1–3 Expectations and attitudes determine our reaction to a situation. Are the police here being kind and understanding or are they causing trouble for an innocent person?

©Sepp Seitz 1980; Woodfin Camp & Associates.

cerns how we change and rearrange the world to make it seem consistent. And they are the basis of the work on social perception, which attempts to describe the kinds of organization we impose on our judgments of other people.

The processes of organization and interpretation are particularly important for social psychology because of their implications about how people perceive things and situations. Herbert does not perceive merely the individual parts of the policeman—his eyes, hair, clothes, and so on. Instead, he perceives the whole person—a policeman whose job is to arrest criminals, or perhaps, who is prejudiced against people like Herbert. Herbert will also go beyond what he can actually see and impute meaning to what is going on. He may see the policeman as threatening, as biased, as cruel. He may stereotype the policeman as being like other policemen (as Herbert knows them). And Herbert will respond to the policeman and the situation in general according to his own view of them.

Cognitive-perceptual theories differ from learning theory in a number of ways. They are essentially ahistorical, because they focus on the organization and interpretation of the moment. They are concerned with how Herbert perceives the situation, not with his upbringing or past experience with the police. Their primary focus is on internal states, not on overt behavior or the real environment. How Herbert interprets the situation and why he interprets it that way are more crucial than what the situation actually was or what Herbert actually did.

INCENTIVE-CONFLICT THEORIES

A final approach in social psychology views human behavior as a simple function of the incentives for various alternative acts. The main question is how much the person has to gain or lose by any given behavior. Go back to Herbert. Let us say he has the choice of fleeing, surrendering, or shooting. He expects that if he flees, he probably will be chased and probably shot, which adds up to a considerable negative incentive. If he surrenders, he is sure to go to jail, which is also a negative incentive. But he may reason that by shooting the policeman, he will be able to get away, and with the money too, which is both an absence of negative incentives and a strong positive incentive. So an **incentive** analysis simply considers the pros and cons of any given behavior, and from that predicts how a person will behave.

Usually an incentive analysis simplifies the situation and winds up considering conflicts between two possible behaviors. It simply considers whether the incentives attached to each behavior are positive or negative, and how positive or negative they are. So an *approach-approach* conflict involves two behaviors, each of which has only positive incentives—for example, two men ask you out for dinner on the same evening, and you like them both and would enjoy spending the evening with either. An *avoidance-avoidance* conflict involves two negative alternatives—for example, going to the dentist and spending hundreds of dollars for new fillings, or letting your teeth gradually rot away. Finally, the *approach-avoidance* conflict concerns some behavior that has both positive and negative incentives attached to it. Going to visit a senile grandparent in an old-age home is a kind and affectionate act, but it may also prove embarrassing and boring.

There are, broadly speaking, three different versions of incentive theories that we will run into in later chapters. One is a rational choice, or *exchange theory,* approach. This suggests that people make fairly rational calculations and pick the more favorable alternative. Numerous normative theories generate predictions about how decisions ought to be made, and offer useful baselines for comparing how decisions actually are made. Economists usually rely on some version of exchange theory to predict economic choices by individuals, firms, and governments.

A second version of incentive theory places more emphasis on need satisfaction. It views the individual as having certain needs or motives and behaving in such a way as to satisfy those needs. This form of incentive theory emphasizes a person's specific, unmet needs. For example, a person may have a strong need to see herself as a highly moral individual, so she may go out and work actively in a political campaign to root out a corrupt mayor. Or another person might fall in love with a girl who constantly is able to meet his esteem needs by telling him all the time how smart and handsome he is. A basketball player may take a swing at his opponent because his frustration at being elbowed and held all night long has built up and an aggressive act reduces that frustration. Herbert may have tremendous amounts of frustration and anger stored up in him, perhaps from a father who beat him, his inability to get a good job, and the disrespect he is constantly encountering because he never finished school and sounds barely literate when he speaks. His shooting of the policeman could be understood as a way of satisfying his need to express his anger.

A third version of incentive theory emphasizes field forces and views people as behaving in response to all the forces pressing upon them. This is clearest in Kurt Lewin's field theory. The idea is that all forces acting on a person come either from inside the person or from the environment. A person's behavior is therefore a function of where those forces push him, in almost a physical or geographical sense. Herbert was trying to get away from the liquor store, so his internal forces were moving him away. The policeman was an external obstacle, blocking his movement. Herbert therefore shot the policeman in order to move past the obstacle.

Note that the incentive analysis, like the Gestalt approach, is largely ahistorical. It deals with the relative advantages and disadvantages of possible responses in the current situation. It deals with the performance of various responses, not the learning of habits. The causes of behavior, then, lie in the immediate situation surrounding a person. An incentive analysis, like attribution theory, is very much concerned with internal states. Our perceptions of the situations, our positive or negative feelings about them, our expectations about the consequences of alternative acts, our hopes and fears, all are central to an incentive analysis. On the other hand, these expectations are based largely on learning and so past experiences are important. The three versions vary somewhat in how much motivational power they assign to the incentives or forces that operate on a person. One version of incentive analysis depicts a rather calculating, almost scientific chooser, another a person driven by internal needs and heedless of the environment, or using it for private purposes, and the last someone tossed and turned both by the environment and by personal needs. But all three versions have the same situation in mind: a person being confronted with a choice between alternative behaviors, and having to decide on the basis of how much he or she stands to gain or lose from each.

SUMMARY

1. The theoretical approaches we have described are by no means contradictory. Rather, each emphasizes one aspect of the causes of behavior without necessarily negating other aspects. Thus, the genetic-physiological approach looks for causes in innate characteristics or physiological mechanisms. Although the other approaches pay little attention to such factors, they would certainly include them if it were necessary. For example, learning theorists or cognitive psychologists would accept that the behavior of people who are hungry or tired differs greatly from that of those who are not, or that the social responses of a person with specific brain damage are far different from those of a person with normal brain function.

2. Learning theories stress a person's history; they analyze current behavior in terms of what a person has learned in the past. Learning theories tend to be mechanistic; they understate the role of intellect, of thought, and complex perceptual processes. Traditionally learning theorists have viewed people as entities with no expectations or beliefs, who respond automatically to any current stimulus.

3. The cognitive approach is probably now the most influential in social psychology. However, some cognitive theorists have absorbed a great deal of learning theory, while others stick mainly to cognitive and perceptual processes. In either case, no one denies that both present cognitive processes and past learning history determine social behavior. That is, a person's past experience influences his interpretation of any current situation and shapes his responses to it; but the interpretation and perceptual view of the current situation are major determinants of how the individual responds.

4. Finally, incentive theory combines learning and cognitive theories, but emphasizes rational choice. This approach is probably more influential among sociologists than among social psychologists, but it is implicit in much of social psychology. Incentive theorists believe that, all else being equal, people act so as to maximize their gains and minimize their losses. How they make such decisions, and how often they actually have to make them are complex questions. In a sense, a combination of learning and cognitive-perceptual processes provides the individual with a framework in which to behave—that is,

how to interpret a situation and give the appropriate response. The person will then behave according to the laws of incentive theory.

As we shall see, all of these approaches help us understand social behavior. Each approach seems to be especially useful in explaining certain social phenomena. Throughout the text, we shall discuss any particular theory that seems relevant and useful. But one should keep them all in mind, because they are all necessary for a full understanding of social behavior.

SUGGESTIONS FOR ADDITIONAL READING

ARONSON, E. *The social animal* (3rd ed.). San Francisco: W. H. Freeman, 1980. A brief, well-written introduction to the some of the most interesting aspects of the field. Not complete, but entertaining.

DEUTSCH, M., & KRAUSS, R. M. *Theories in social psychology.* New York: Basic Books, 1965. Still the best coverage of theories, though getting quite out of date.

HENDRICK, C., & JONES, R. A. *The nature of theory and research in social psychology.* New York: Academic Press, 1972. Not as strong as Deutsch and Krauss, but more current.

Methods

2

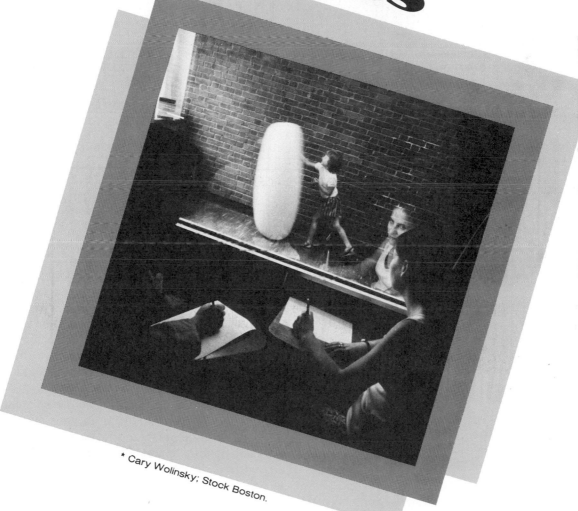

One of the most fascinating aspects of social psychology is that we all know a lot about social behavior even without having studied it systematically. We live our lives surrounded by other people and we observe how they behave. We are familiar with so many social situations that we have some idea how people behave in almost all social contexts. We think about ourselves and others, wonder why we acted the way we did at certain times, question other people's motives as well as our own, and in general have a great deal of experience with the topics and issues that are part of social psychology. Most other scientific disciplines are very different. No one who has not studied them knows much about nuclear physics, high-pressure chemistry, or laser technology. Daily experience tells us almost nothing about plant biology, biochemistry, or earthquakes. Thus, we come to physics, chemistry, biology, and geology in almost total ignorance; whereas we come to psychology, and to social psychology in particular, already knowing a great deal about the field and certainly having had experience that is relevant to it.

Much of what is taught in social psychology will therefore be somewhat familiar. It fits in with what you already know from your own experience and should be relatively easy to relate to and to learn. One of the exciting aspects of the field is that you do not have to take years of courses before you are equipped to deal with the most serious problems. Almost from the beginning, you can work with advanced and current research, and can discuss the very latest findings.

On the other hand, this familiarity with the field has its problems. Often you will feel that you already know much of the material. You may wonder why you are studying the field and why people are doing all this research when the facts are obvious. You may also sometimes feel that a particular finding is wrong because it is not consistent with your own experience. The difficulty is that our personal experiences are not always good indicators of how people generally behave. In addition, our observations of what happens are usually quite casual. We are not systematic, we do not write down each incident, describing it in an objective, unbiased way. Thus, we form impressions of how people behave that are sometimes correct and sometimes incorrect. For example, consider the following statements:

When we are anxious, we like to be with other people.

Advertisements that try to make people afraid backfire and are less effective than ads that do not arouse fear.

If it is in their own self-interest, people in groups will cooperate rather than compete, and raising the stakes increases the amount of cooperation.

The more you pay someone to make a speech against his own beliefs, the more he will change his mind to agree with the speech he makes.

In choosing friends and lovers, the most important principle is that opposites attract.

People who live in cities have higher rates of mental illness than people in small towns.

You may not agree with some of these statements, but it is fair to say that they all sound plausible. At least some people would agree with each of them. Yet, research has demonstrated that all of them are either false or oversimplifications.

We need systematic research because often we cannot trust our own impressions or those of others. This may be because we perceived incorrectly, because we were biased and misinterpreted what happened, because we saw correctly but remember it wrong, or because we saw a very unusual group of people or situations. In sciences such as chemistry or physics, you would not trust your casual observations of the operation of weights, levers, and gravity—you would not even want to trust Newton's. If all he had done was notice an apple falling down rather than up and he had then decided that there was a force called gravity, you would not be impressed. It is the careful research supporting his idea that makes us believe in Newtonian mechanics. And, of course, even more careful work demonstrated that there were errors in this theory, and modern physics has corrected them. Casual observations, even by very careful people, cannot replace systematic research in any field.

If someone says he has decided that men are smarter than women because almost every man he has met has been smarter than almost every woman, you would certainly question his conclusion and his data. How many men and women has he met, where did he meet them, are they representative, and how did he decide how smart they were? It would not be enough for him to say that he has met thousands of people and that he is very good at telling how smart they are, you would want some proof, some hard facts. Show me the numbers! That is exactly what systematic psychology does. It collects data in such a way as to rule out any sources of bias, to make sure the people are representative, and to keep track of the "numbers" so we do not rely on memory or general impressions.

This is also true when we are dealing with theories. It is easy to make up a theoretical explanation for almost anything. People have suggested at one time or another that criminals are genetically different from non-criminals, that economic factors are the major cause of crime, that criminals have a "criminal" conscience, and that crowding causes crime. These are all plausible theories of criminal behavior and we could construct many more. But these and any other theories are generally useless unless they are right, by which we mean that they fit the facts. And the only way to know this is to collect the appropriate data. Some social psychologists (for example, Gergen, 1978) have urged their colleagues to concentrate on making up theories and not to worry too much about data. Fortunately this is a minority view, since obviously a theory must stand or fall eventually on how well it can account for the evidence. A theory without data tells us nothing; on the other hand, data without a theory are difficult to understand and to fit into the rest of our knowledge. The ultimate goal of psychology, indeed of any science, is to have theories that explain the known facts in a particular realm. Such theories help us understand, appreciate, and cope with the world.

THE BEGINNING OF THE RESEARCH: THE QUESTION

Systematic research requires following a certain method of investigation—that is, posing a question in the right way and then using the right methods to make the data meaningful. All research begins with a question we would like to answer. What makes people like each other? How does fear affect affiliation? In what ways do people in groups behave differently from people alone? Why are crimes committed? We then design a study that can provide information which helps us answer the question as directly as possible. Of course, this is not always easy. In fact, the main difficulty of research is taking a problem that may be extremely complex and finding some way to get an answer. As we shall see, this often involves great ingenuity and patience, and even then any one study or series of studies may not give us a firm conclusion. That is why psychologists do many studies on the same problem, each designed to answer one part of the question or to narrow down the possible answers.

Theoretical Research

Before discussing how one goes about designing a study, it is important to know what kind of question one has. There are two basic kinds of questions: those that are directly related to a theory and those that are not. **Theoretical research** starts with a deduction from a theory. We have a theory and want to know if it is correct. To do this, we focus on some prediction that the theory makes and then see if the prediction comes true. For example, Einstein's theory of relativity predicts that light will be bent by a large body. To test this, the light from a star was observed at a time when it passed very close to the sun. Sure enough, the deviation was exactly as had been predicted. In the same way, though less dramatically, social psychologists test predictions from theories that relate to social behavior. Social learning theory predicts that a child will be more aggressive after watching someone being rewarded for being violent. So children are shown films in which people behave violently and are rewarded, and then the children are given an opportunity to be aggressive themselves. As predicted, these children are more aggressive than others who do not watch violent films or who see people being punished for acting violently. Social comparison theory, which we discuss in the next chapter, predicts that people will want to be together when they are unsure of their emotional reactions. So, people are made afraid, given an opportunity to affiliate, and we see that they affiliate more when they are afraid than when they are not.

In each case, the research began with a specific derivation (prediction) from a theory. The major goal of the research is to evaluate the theory. If the prediction comes true, the theory is supported; if the prediction is incorrect, the theory is either totally wrong or at least wrong in some detail. We would then go back and discard the theory or alter it to make it consistent with the new finding.

Empirical Research

Research that is not directly related to a theory is usually called **empirical research.** Instead of testing a specific prediction, the experimenter is interested in a variable such as fear, or a particular phenomenon such as persuasibility. He usually has no clear hypothesis as to the effect of the variable or the specific factors that affect the phenomenon. Empirical research, therefore, is not designed to see if a specific hypothesis is correct, but rather to gather information about the variable or phenomenon in question. The major difference between empirical and hypothesis-testing research is that empirical work tends to deal with many variables at once and to have many dependent measures in order to collect more data on the general problem.

For example, a study designed to investigate the factors involved in criminal behavior might obtain information on the age, sex, ethnic background, family experiences, physical health, and personalities of many people and see how these relate to whether the individuals had committed any crimes. Of course, these variables were not chosen at random. The experimenter has some ideas about what might be important and what probably is not. Age and family experiences are more likely to relate to criminal behavior than eye color or blood type. And in some instances, the psychologist will have a specific hypothesis to test, such as that children from divorced families commit more crimes. He has no specific theory, but he might have a hunch worth investigating.

Actually the boundary between theoretical and empirical work is often vague. A clear hypothesis, even if it does not fit in with a general theory, makes the work empirical in one sense, but the research is conducted just as if it were related to a theory. The essential difference is that when a particular theory is involved, the results of the research will either support or not support the theory. Even the absence of an effect tells us something about the theory. In contrast, with empirical work, the results merely show that some variable is related to some other, or that one hypothesis appears to be correct. Negative results (that is, no effect) tell us only that one person's hunch was wrong, and this does not usually fit into an existing body of data.

Basic and Applied Research

Another major difference between types of research is the extent to which the experimenter is interested in a particular, concrete situation or problem. The factors that produce crime can be investigated from a theoretical point of view (such as social learning theory) or from no specific theory. But whatever the position, the research can deal with a specific, real problem or with an issue in more general terms. Research on crime may concentrate on the effects of frustration on aggression, of child-rearing practices on juvenile delinquency, or perhaps of learning and imitation on violent behavior. Generally, this would be considered **basic research** because it focuses on a general issue not specifically tied to an actual situation in the world. The answer to any of these questions will tell us something about crime and may have application, but that is not the immediate intent of the research.

In contrast, the research may start with a specific, existing problem; it is then usually called **applied research.** One example is the research on how violence on television affects the behavior of viewers. The question is whether watching violent television programs causes people, especially younger viewers, to commit violent acts themselves. In this instance, the question is relevant to various theoretical and basic issues, such as the effects of imitation and learning, whether observing violence can reduce aggressive feelings, and so on. But unlike basic research, the emphasis is on the particular problem—how TV affects crime, and not on more general issues. It may be that the effects of television are quite different from the effects of any other form of communication, and that the research has no general value except for what it tells us about TV and crime. But someone doing applied research is relatively unconcerned about the broader issues. At least for the moment, the emphasis is on the immediate problem and how to solve it.

Clearly, both basic and applied research are important. The former should reveal general principles that will apply to a wide range of situations and problems; the latter should help solve existing problems quickly. It is essential that basic and applied researchers work together. Unfortunately, in the United States applied research has often been considered to be of lower status and less important than basic research. In recent years, government agencies that provide most of the financial support for research have begun to shift their interest largely to applied research, and to ignore basic research. These distinctions are unfair and unrealistic. Basic research almost always grows out of a concern with existing problems and must necessarily be related to them; and applied research has to start somewhere and relies on principles from basic research. Thus, the ideal arrangement is for each type of work to take ideas from the other. Basic research should take into account solutions that have been found to real problems; applied research should use general principles from basic research. In this way, basic and applied research complement each other, working back and forth between specific issues and more general propositions.

RESEARCH METHODS

Regardless of the original question, the next step is to decide what research method to use. Although the variations in study design are virtually unlimited, there are two basic varieties—correlational and experimental. Each has advantages and disadvantages. As we shall see, the type chosen depends largely on the problem being studied and the goals of the research.

Correlational Research

Correlational research consists of observing the relationship between two or more variables. It asks the question, when variable *A* is high, is variable *B* also high (a positive correlation), low (a negative correlation), or is *B*'s value unrelated (no correlation)? Height and weight are positively correlated, because tall people tend to weigh more than short people; the temperature on a given day and the amount of clothing worn tend to be negatively correlated—that is, people usually wear less clothing on hot days.

ADVANTAGES A correlational study is an efficient way of collecting a large amount of data about a problem area. For example, we could collect thirty personality variables about a large number of people and twenty different measures of behavior. Then we could see which personality factors correlate with which behaviors. In this way, we can discover a large number of relationships and interrelationships in a relatively short time. In contrast, it would take many experimental studies to investigate the effect of each personality factor on each behavior. For this reason, correlational studies are often used in empirical research; they make possible the efficient collection of large amounts of data.

Correlational techniques also sometimes enable us to study problems to which experimental methods may not be applicable. For example, much of the research on the effects of crowding on people has involved correlations. It is impossible experimentally to place individuals in high-density situations for very long periods of time. Since being in a crowded situation for ten years might produce very different effects from being in it for only four hours or even twenty days, the experimental work, although useful, is limited. Therefore, investigators have turned to statistics collected in actual situations. Data on the population density of various cities and parts of cities are available, as are data on crime and mental illness in those areas. By correlating measures of density with measures of crime and mental illness, it has been possible to get some indication of the relationship between density and pathology. Naturally, this raises all the problems of correlational studies, particularly the problem of making causative statements and ruling out other variables such as income; but it has the great advantage of providing some evidence on the effects of density over much longer periods of time than would have been possible in an experimental design.

DISADVANTAGES The major weakness of correlational studies is that they leave the cause and effect relationship ambiguous. If a study indicates that people who are more afraid affiliate more than those who are less afraid, this does not necessarily mean that high fear leads to greater affiliation. It may be that affiliating increases fear rather than the other way around. Those who affiliate tend to get frightened; those who do not affiliate become less frightened. Therefore, we find a relationship between affiliation and fear. In other words, the direction of causality (does fear lead to affiliation or does affiliation lead to fear) is unknown.

This is not always a serious drawback in a correlational study. In many cases we can be fairly certain of the direction of causation. The science of astronomy is based on correlations, and yet there is little doubt about most of the directions of causality. When the moon is in particular positions, there are high tides on earth. We assume that the moon is causing the high tides, rather than the high tides causing the moon to be in that position. First-born children who are anxious affiliate more than later borns. Obviously, if there is any causal relationship between these two factors, it must be birth order causing greater affiliation—not the other way around. No matter how much you affiliate as an adult, it cannot affect the order of your birth.

A more serious ambiguity than the direction of causality is the possibility, in all correlational studies, that neither variable is directly affecting the other. Rather, some other unspecified factor may be affecting both of them. This problem of attributing causation is especially obvious in the research on the relationship between crowding and crime in the cities. As we shall see, the finding is that there is a substantial correlation between the two—higher densities are associated with higher crime rates. But what does this mean? One possibility, of course, is that crowding causes crime. Another possibility—the opposite—is that crime causes high density. Choosing between these is not too difficult in this case. *If* one causes the other, it is more plausible that living under high-density conditions makes people commit crimes than it is that people move into areas because there is a lot of crime there.

However, it is even more likely that neither relationship is correct and that some other factor is producing the correlation. Crowding is strongly associated with income level—poor people tend to live under more crowded conditions than do rich people. Crime is also strongly associated with income level; poor people commit more crimes. Now we can see that the relationship between crowding and crime may be due entirely to the fact that both of them are associated with income level. Poor people live in high-density areas and commit more crimes. Therefore despite the correlation between density and crime, density itself may have no effect on crime rate.

Experimental Research

In the experimental method, we compare two or more conditions that differ in exactly specified ways. In chemistry, an experiment might consist of adding 1 cc. of a substance to one beaker, and 2 cc.s to another beaker; or adding 1 cc. to one and nothing to the other; or 1 cc. to one and 1 cc. of a different substance to the other. Then the differences between the reactions in the two beakers would be observed. The great strength of this procedure is that any difference in reactions must be due to the difference in what was added. To put it in more formal terms, the **independent variable** (what was added to the beakers) must have caused the difference in the **dependent variable** (the chemical reactions). In social psychology, experiments consist of exposing people to different conditions and seeing if there are any differences in their responses. The crucial elements in an experiment are: (1) the independent variable is deliberately controlled by the experimenter, or perhaps by some external force; (2) subjects are randomly assigned to a condition with nothing varying except the independent variable; and (3) the dependent variable is then measured.

RANDOM ASSIGNMENT The most important element in an experiment that distinguishes it from any other kind of research is the **random assignment** of the subjects of the study. Subjects must, as far as possible, be identical when they enter the experimental conditions. Ideally, we would use sets of identical twins and put one of each pair in one condition and one in the other. Since sets of identical twins are not abundant, we accomplish our goal by deciding by chance which condition to put each subject in. This can be done by flipping a coin, cutting a deck of cards, or more commonly and more precisely by using a set of random numbers.

The idea behind random assignment is that nothing the subjects bring to the experimental situations should determine which group they are in. If the assignment has been made purely by chance, no systematic differences should arise between the experimental groups. If the subjects are assigned on any other basis, the groups might differ in some way unrelated to the experimental conditions. Suppose that in testing the effect of violent and nonviolent television programs on aggression, you asked subjects which kind of programs they wanted to watch, and assigned them according to their choices. Then, after having subjects watch either violent or nonviolent TV for some period of time, you might find that those who watched violent programs were more aggressive. But you could not conclude that the programs made them more violent, because they might have been more aggressive in the first place. It would be no surprise to find that more aggressive people liked more violent programs. Thus, the "experiment" would be meaningless. It is possible to conclude that differences in aggression are due to the type of program only on the basis of a random assignment of subjects to the programs.

Similar problems occur if subjects are assigned to conditions on the basis of something they do or some attribute they have, even if they do not choose the condition themselves. We would not assign subjects who arrive early to one condition and those who arrive late to another, or even subjects who sign up on weekdays to one and weekend subjects to another. We do not know how these groups differ, but the possibility exists that they do—and any experimental results might be due to that difference.

It would also be incorrect to put subjects who understand the instructions in one condition and those who do not understand them in another. This is a tempting method of assignment, because often one condition is more complicated than another and we would like to be certain that everyone understands the instructions. But obviously, the groups would then differ in intelligence or interest in the proceedings, and such differences might affect the results. It can also happen that subjects are randomly assigned, but some subjects do not understand the instructions and must be eliminated from the study. If the instructions in one condition are more difficult and more subjects in that condition do not understand them and are therefore eliminated, there is no longer random assignment. There has been some self-selection. The less bright subjects in the difficult condition have decided (not intentionally, perhaps, but just as surely) not to participate. Thus, the other condition, in which even the less bright had no difficulty with the instructions, has on the average less bright subjects. Any time something a subject does or an attribute of his determines his condition in a study, random assignment has been lost.

One way of conceptualizing random assignment is this: Before an experiment begins, no one can specify any characteristic on which the subjects in one condition differ from those in another. They are, as far as anyone can tell, identical, except that some have been put in one condition and some in another. When assignment has been random, we can be certain within the confidence limits established by statistical tests that the two groups do not differ in any systematic way. Any differences between the two, say, in intelligence, would be due entirely to chance. There is a possibility that one group would be more intelligent on the average than another group. But the likelihood of this happening has been well established by statisticians, and the statistical tests we conduct on the results obtained are based on the likelihood of differences occurring by chance.

We apply a statistical test to the difference so that we state exactly what that chance is. We might find that only one time in a hundred would the two groups have differed that much simply by chance. This makes us believe that the results are probably due to our experimental manipulation. Thus, as long as we are certain that the subjects have been randomly assigned to conditions and that the experimental manipulation differed only in the way we intended, we can be confident that the differences that appear are due to the manipulation and not some unknown factor. This ability to specify the particular aspect of the situation that produced an effect is the major advantage of the experimental method.

DISADVANTAGES The major limitations of experimental research derive from difficulties involving the independent variable. Experiments tend to involve a restricted range of a variable, because it is difficult to produce strong emotions or to expose subjects to extreme conditions. For example, some subjects can be made more afraid than others, but none of them will be terrified. Some subjects can be frustrated more than others, but they cannot be terribly frustrated because it is impractical and unethical to do this deliberately. Some can watch more violent TV than others, but we cannot ordinarily make people watch only one kind of program, at least not for very long. Thus, we are restricted in the kinds of procedures we are willing and able to use, and the strength of the variable tends to be relatively low.

The experimental method generally cannot be used to study the effects of natural occurrences or the most important events in people's lives. Air raids, floods, and surgery do not strike people entirely at random. People are not poor, they do not live in cities, and they are not divorced purely by chance. Thus, any research on the effects of these kinds of variables must be correlational rather than experimental.

Finally, the experimental method is inefficient for collecting large amounts of data on many variables. Since experimenters must produce each factor, they are usually limited to one or two at a time. They could not vary twenty factors at once as is often done in correlational studies.

Correlational and experimental work complement each other. There are many cases in which both methods are useful. In general, correlational studies are particularly effective in the collection of large amounts of data; they provide us with ideas and hypotheses, which can then be studied in more detail experimentally.

Since the experimental method allows us to conclude that a particular variable is the cause of a particular effect, it enables us to test a hypothesis about how one variable affects another. It is therefore useful primarily in pinning down and specifying in detail relationships between variables, and in explaining such relationships. For example, during wartime, people tend to cluster together more than during peace. This might suggest that fear leads to affiliation. But greater affiliation might be due to other factors. Note that the greatest clustering occurs in air raid shelters, which are naturally small and which people occupy, not to be together, but to be safe from bombs. The bombs make the people afraid, so they go to bomb shelters—which are invariably crowded. Perhaps they would prefer to be alone and safe rather than with others and safe, but since the shelters are limited in number, they have no choice. The suggestion that fear leads to affiliation must accordingly be tested in more controlled situations—in an experiment in which two or more levels of fear are produced and affiliation measured. In other words, correlational work can produce data on which a hypothesis is founded, and experimental work can test the hypothesis.

FIELD AND LABORATORY RESEARCH

The next step is to decide where research should be done. Although most research in social psychology during the last ten or fifteen years has been conducted in the laboratory, some has always been conducted in the field, and the amount of field research now seems to be increasing. Both experimental and correlational research can be done in either the laboratory or the field, and each setting has advantages and disadvantages.

Field Research   ADVANTAGES Research in the field tends to deal with real people in real situations, as opposed to experimental subjects in relatively unreal situations in the laboratory. Accordingly, field research tends to minimize suspicion by the subjects, so their responses are more spontaneous and less susceptible to the kinds of bias that suspicion produces.

The researcher in the field can often collect data from types of people who cannot be attracted to an experimental laboratory. It has often been said that American social psychology is based on college sophomores, because they are the ones who are most available for experiments in laboratories. Field research can collect data from a wider variety of subjects and thus adds to the generality of the findings.

FIGURE 2–2 One method of collecting information on attitudes and values is door-to-door interviewing. Many of the large polling organizations specialize in this procedure.

    Another advantage of work in the field is that we are sometimes able to deal with extremely powerful variables and situations that could not be studied in the laboratory. This is particularly true of correlational work, because experimental field work is limited by the same kinds of factors that limit it in the laboratory. With correlational work, we can, as mentioned previously, observe people in extreme situations—when they are waiting to be operated on in a hospital or huddled together in an air raid shelter. This advantage sometimes applies to field experiments when the manipulation is done not by the experimenter but by some natural event that just happens to affect people randomly and therefore fits the criterion of an experiment.

DISADVANTAGES The major disadvantages of field research stem from the lack of control over the situation. It is generally extremely difficult to assign subjects to conditions randomly, to be certain that they are all experiencing the same thing, to get accurate measures on the dependent variable, and so on. A great many random events and conditions enter into a field study and often obscure the effects of the variables in which we are interested.

In particular, it is difficult to find pure manipulations of the independent variable and pure measures of the dependent variable. The experimenter must find or arrange circumstances that produce specific differences—and no others—between conditions. Even if one could find a situation that would, for example, produce two levels of frustration, it is exceedingly difficult to be certain that the two conditions do not differ in other ways. In the laboratory one could design a pure procedure that would accomplish this; in the field it is much more difficult. If subjects have been randomly assigned to conditions, the experiment can conclude that any difference in their behavior is due to the experimental manipulation. But if that manipulation is not pure (e.g., not just differences in frustration), the interpretation of the effect is ambiguous. Yes, it is due to the manipulation, but does that mean it is due to fear or to some other variable? Similarly, measurement of the dependent variable is often elusive in the field. The experimenter must not only produce differences in frustration but must also obtain a measure of aggression in the same setting. If there is an ideal independent manipulation, it is highly unlikely that it would be accompanied by a convenient method of assessing its effect.

With sufficient ingenuity and hard work, it is sometimes possible to find or arrange appropriate situations, but they are few and far between. The world is generally not set up to facilitate the study of a specific problem that happens to occur to psychologists. They may therefore find that field research does not lend itself to the problem in which they are interested.

Laboratory Research

ADVANTAGES The advantages and disadvantages of laboratory research are mirror images of those of field research. The major advantage of work in the laboratory is the control over the situation that it affords. Experimenters can be quite certain what is happening to each subject. If they are doing experimental work, they can randomly assign the subjects, subject them to the exact experiences necessary to study the problem, minimize extraneous factors, and go a long way toward eliminating random variations in the procedure. Even when variations do occur, experimenters can at least be reasonably certain that they know exactly what happened. Similarly, they have great control over the dependent variable and can measure it in considerably more detail and in a more uniform manner than in the field. Therefore, the laboratory is the ideal place in which to set up a situation designed to study a specific problem.

DISADVANTAGES The problems with laboratory work center around two aspects of the situation—the fact that subjects know they are being studied and the limitations on the kinds of manipulations that can be used. Whenever someone knows he is a subject in an experiment, there is always the possibility that he is not behaving naturally or spontaneously, that he is trying to please or displease the experimenter, that he is behaving in the way he thinks he should, that he is not accepting the experimental manipulation because he is distrustful, and so on. Any of these effects could produce bias in the results or obscure relationships and effects that actually exist. Although there are ways of minimizing these problems, as we shall discuss in detail below, they always exist to some extent.

The kinds of manipulations that can be used are limited. Laboratory research usually deals with low or moderate levels of variables. Subjects cannot be terrified; they cannot be made terribly sad; they cannot be made hysterical with laughter. In most cases this simply means that the effects are less strong than they would be if the variables were more extreme, but that the basic relationships are the same. However, it is a serious weakness when there is reason to believe that high levels of a variable would produce different effects from intermediate ones. In the work on the relationship between fear and attitude change, for example, it has been suggested that very high levels of fear would interfere with attitude change, whereas lower levels increase change. Since laboratory work never deals with extremely high levels of fear, this possibility has never been adequately tested. In most cases, however, the main problem created by this limitation is that it makes it more difficult to find the effect of a variable even though the effect exists.

A relatively minor disadvantage, mentioned previously, is that laboratory work tends to deal with a limited population of subjects. The vast majority of laboratory studies involve college students or perhaps children at a university nursery school. This problem is not inherent in the laboratory method. With sufficient ingenuity and a little hard work, it should be possible to attract a wide range of subjects to experimental laboratories, particularly if the laboratories are not located on college campuses. Perhaps anyone who agrees to take part in a psychological study is unrepresentative of the population. But psychologists can, at least, try to employ a wide variety of subjects.

Field and laboratory research do differ in the ways we have described, but these differences have been exaggerated to a large extent. It is possible to obtain considerable control of variables outside the laboratory, and it is possible to make laboratory situations extremely realistic.

BOX 2-1
FROM THE LABORATORY TO THE REAL WORLD

Psychologists have conducted a great many studies on how people play games and bargain with each other. Virtually all of this research has been conducted in the laboratory, and the question becomes whether any of the findings become are applicable to real world situations. For example, the research on bargaining indicates that making small concessions in response to the other

BOX 2-1 Research may offer some insights into how to bargain effectively. Taking a strong stand and rejecting one alternative may cause the other person to offer an especially good deal.

Irene Springer

players' concessions generally produces more concessions and rapid solutions. Another bargaining tactic that seems to work is to start with a very strong position in order to convince the other person that he will have to make concessions to you. This seems plausible, but there is always the possibility that in a natural setting the other person would become so annoyed by the strong position that he would become even tougher himself or that bargaining would break down entirely.

It is nice to be able to report that at least one study (Cialdini, Beckman and Caccioppo, 1979) demonstrates that this particular strategy does work in the real world setting of a new car showroom. This study compared two procedures in bargaining for a new car. In the first, the buyer indicated interest in a car, asked for a price, rejected that price and asked for a second price. In the second procedure, the buyer first indicated interest in an entirely different car and rejected the price for that price as too high. He then turned to a second car and followed the procedure just described.

In all cases, the sales person reduced the price of the car somewhat after the first price had been rejected. However, the second procedure resulted in lower prices. The sales person started off with a lower price for the second car than he did when the buyer immediately indicated interest in that car; and lowered the price more than he did in the first condition.

Thus, in buying a car and perhaps anything else, it seems to help first to take a strong stand by indicating the price is so high that it discourages you from even persuing a particular item, and then turning to a second item and bargaining for that. This probably demonstrates that you are a tougher bargainer, and perhaps also that you are less anxious to buy the particular car you eventually bargained for. Whatever the particular mechanism involved, the study showed that the results of research in laboratory bargaining situations are at least somewhat applicable to the real world.

The basic issue is not where the experiment takes place but how realistic it is. If the subjects know they are in an experiment, there tends to be a loss of realism. Field studies tend to be more realistic, or are easier to make realistic, than laboratory studies, but the distinction is one of degree. The important distinction is between realistic and nonrealistic studies, and realism can be produced either in the field or in the laboratory.

RESEARCH TECHNIQUES

Archive and Cross-Cultural Studies

Two other kinds of research are special cases of the field and laboratory types. The first is the so-called **archive study,** in which the investigator does not collect the data himself but uses data that are already available in published records. In most cases this is actually a kind of field study, with the main difference being that someone else has done the hard work. An example of the use of archives is the study described in Chapter 7 on the relationship between cotton prices and lynchings in the South. The investigators started with the hypothesis that frustration leads to aggression and then argued that a drop in cotton prices would produce frustrations, which would, in turn, produce an increase in aggression in the form of lynchings. The data on cotton prices and on the number of lynchings were readily available in statistics collected by the United States government and others, and the investigators simply looked up these data and ran correlations between the two variables. Similarly, the studies of the relationship between population density and crime relied entirely on data that were already available.

Since there is rarely any random assignment of subjects to experimental conditions, archive work is almost always correlational—but it can be very informative. The major problem with using archives is the difficulty of finding data with which to test the hypothesis. However, a vast amount of data collected for other purposes can be fruitfully used to study a variety of problems. Included in this is all the work done by psychologists both within and outside the laboratory; the accumulated data are generally available to other psychologists. Thus, reanalysis of previous work is one way of conducting research.

Cross-cultural work can be done in the field, in laboratories, or even by the use of archives. The only requirement is that data be collected in more than one culture. This type of research has two purposes. First, it allows for greater generality of findings if they hold in more than one culture. There is always the suspicion that a particular relationship between, say, fear and affiliation may hold in the United States but not in Japan. If we want to consider this relationship a basic process in human social interaction, we naturally want it to hold for all populations. Cross-cultural work is one way of testing the limitations and generality of any particular finding.

Another, more sophisticated use of cross-cultural work is in studying the importance of variables that differ in two societies. One of the basic hypotheses we discuss in this book is the relationship between frustration and aggression. This relationship could be tested by observing whether societies that are high in frustration exhibit more aggression than those low in frustration. Of course, observing only two societies would not be particularly useful, because they would differ on many variables beside frustration. Just as correlational studies on individuals need fairly large numbers to produce meaningful results, so do cross-cultural studies. The research must assess frustration and aggression in a large number of societies and see whether high levels of frustration generally tend to be associated with high levels of aggression. In this way, the extraneous, incidental factors present in each society become less important, and the relationship between frustration and aggression emerges.

Naturally, cross-cultural work can also tell us how societies differ.

Any time different results are found in different cultures, we have discovered something about each culture. We have, for example, found that Norwegians conform more than the French in a particular situation. We may not know why they do, we may not know whether or not it is due to the particular situation, but we know that in the limited set of circumstances, there is more conformity in Norway than in France.

Observational Research

A research technique that is being used more and more is direct observation of behavior. Social psychologists are always asking subjects how they are feeling, finding out how much someone contributes to charity, or having subjects vote for the leader of a group or play a game. All of these are legitimate, useful procedures. However, it is also possible simply to watch what people are doing either in a natural setting or in the laboratory. For example, in studying group behavior, you can observe the interactions and note what everyone says, how often they talk, how often they look at or touch one another, and so on. With children, you might observe the number of fights, sharing, talking, and playing with toys. The psychologist need not introduce any specific measure; instead, the natural behavior of the subjects is recorded. It is the same technique ethologists (people who study animals in their natural habitat) use to discover the behavior of animals. They obviously cannot ask a lion how often he fights or a chimp whether he uses tools. So, of necessity, ethologists have had to observe what the animals do. In the early days of social psychology, this was a common technique for studying human interactions. Then there was a long period in which observations of this kind were not used much. Now they are coming back, and that is a very favorable trend.

Observational research is usually quite difficult and tedious. Researchers must first construct a rating scale on which to record the behaviors. In doing this they must face the fact that they cannot record everything. There are an almost unlimited number of individual behaviors and pieces of behavior in any group interaction. For example, even talking is enormously complex. It is easy to record how often someone talks and what that person says; but each act of speaking also involves the pitch, amplitude, and speed of the utterance, the tone used, the number of pauses between words, and so on. People who study speech can spend hours analyzing a two-minute speech. Moreover, when talking, an individual uses very complicated facial and bodily gestures. Thus, unless you are going to focus entirely on speech, you must decide what aspects of communication you are most interested in.

Similarly, even a simple interaction can be described briefly, as A hit B on the head, or in lengthy descriptions of bodily stance, strength of the blow, gestures, preceding and following actions, and so on. In other words, the first task of the observer is to decide what actions to record. Next, a simple method of recording them must be devised so that various observers will agree on what happened. For example, a category called "acted friendly" would not be useful because it is often difficult to decide whether or not an act is friendly. Instead, observers use more specific categories, such as "smiled at other person," "offered to share toy," "helped up from ground," and so on. Then it can be decided later that all of these are indications of friendliness. Much of the difficulty with observation in research and in the real world is that we disagree on what a particular behavior means. A well-designed rating scale minimizes disagreements.

The importance of observational research is that it allows us to describe in some detail how people act in relatively natural settings. We record their actual behavior and do not have to rely on complex measurement methods that might make the situation less natural. When children fight in a schoolyard, we can conclude with some certainty that aggression is being expressed. When someone in the laboratory gives an electric shock to another subject after the experimenter has told him that is his job, it is less clear that true aggression is involved. We need the controlled laboratory research, but the observations are more true-to-life and help us relate the laboratory work to the real world.

RESEARCH ETHICS

After an investigator has decided what kind of study to do and where to do it, he faces the most difficult decision—how to do it. In designing any research, and particularly any that involves humans, ethical considerations must be taken into account. The social psychologist wants to discover how people behave in social situations. To do so, he must expose subjects to certain conditions and observe how they respond. But he must be concerned about their privacy and about the conditions to which he exposes them.

Privacy

An individual's right to privacy must be respected and cherished. As the president's panel on privacy and behavior research stated, every individual must be allowed to "decide for himself how much he will share with others his thoughts, his feelings, and the facts of his personal life." The social psychologist must guard the individual's privacy and at the same time pursue his research. Although this is a complex, personal matter, certain guidelines should be observed. The president's panel has listed several that are particularly important.

"Participation by subjects should be voluntary and based on informed consent to the extent that it is consistent with the objectives of the research." Ordinarily, individuals should not be subjected to experimentation unless they have agreed to it, and, whenever possible, this agreement should be given after they have heard exactly what is going to take

BOX 2-2
THE USE OF DECEPTION IN RESEARCH

It is sometimes difficult to conduct a study without employing some degree of deception. Subjects may simply not be told the true purpose of the study, or they may be deliberately deceived about an important element in the situation. Even in the simplest research subjects are rarely told the specific hypotheses that are being tested. In a learning study in which subjects are given a list of words to memorize, the experimenter will not tell them that the major hypothesis is that words early in the list will be recalled better than those in the middle of the list. If the subjects knew this, it might affect their behavior and make the results questionable. This is even more true in most social psychology studies, where the reactions of the subjects are more complex and more likely to be affected by their understanding of the purpose of the research. Knowing that the experimenter was interested in how aggressive they are would make most subjects act nonaggressively; knowing that they are deliberately being frustrated would make the frustration take on extra meaning that would make it difficult to interpret any results. Thus, with a few exceptions, a certain amount of deception is almost always practiced in psychology research. At the very least, subjects rarely can be informed ahead of time of the exact nature of the hypothesis being studied.

More extensive deceptions may involve the nature of the experimental manipulation or the dependent measure. For example, a confederate of the experimenter might insult the subjects to make them angry in order to see how this affects aggressiveness. Subjects would be allowed to believe that the other person was another subject who was simply being nasty. If the subjects knew that it was all an act, they would probably not feel insulted in the first place, and their responses would be different from what they would have been in reality. Similarly, the subjects might be given a chance to deliver electric shocks to another person, with this being the measure of aggressiveness. Actually, no shocks would be received, but the subject must be led to believe they are real; otherwise their behavior could not be called aggression in the usual sense of the term. Again, the subjects are deceived in order to make the results meaningful.

Although most social psychology research cannot be accomplished without some deception, many people feel that deception of any kind is unethical. They feel that it demeans the subjects and should never be used. A more moderate position that is endorsed by most research psychologists is that deception should not be used if at all possible, or be used only after considering its possible harmful effects on the subject according to the principles discussed in the text.

place during the course of the study. The experimenter has an obligation to tell a potential subject as much as possible about the study before asking him to participate.

Often, however, it is not possible to tell a subject everything about the study. This is typical of research in social psychology. Studies of impression formation, in which subjects are given a list of adjectives and asked to form an impression of the person, can be conducted with subjects who know all about the purposes and procedures of the work. But virtually all the other studies described in this book require concealment of certain aspects of the investigation. In some experiments, such as the similarity and liking work, only the purpose and specific hypotheses need be concealed. In others, such as the Asch conformity study, both purpose and details of procedure must be concealed. The experimenter must give as much information as he can, but the president's panel did not feel, nor do we, that research that requires concealment must cease. Instead, the panel added: "In the absence of full information, consent [should] be based on trust in the qualified investigator and the integrity of his institution." In other words, the individual may volunteer for a study without knowing everything about it because he trusts the investigator and the institution responsible. In essence, he is putting himself into their hands, because he believes they will do nothing to which he would object if he could be told. This is a legitimate and meaningful form of consent, but it places a particularly heavy burden on the investigator to be worthy of that trust.

"In some research, however, soliciting consent at all . . . destroys experimental purpose." If you wanted to observe conditions under which people who thought they were alone would break a rule, clearly telling them that you were watching would make the results meaningless for the original question. If you are interested in the factors that cause people to offer help voluntarily to someone in need, telling the purpose of the study would probably destroy it, because the subjects would be self-conscious about their own behavior, would realize that you thought they should give help, and the help would no longer be purely voluntary. In fact, informed consent may sometimes eliminate effects even when there is no obvious reason why it should. For example, Gardner (1978) reported that he successfully replicated the results of previous research on the effects of noise (to be discussed in chapter 14) several times over a period of years. However, he then instituted the informed consent rules, continued his research, and suddenly was no longer able to produce the standard results. Apparently, in this and probably in many other situations, calling subjects' attention to the focus of the study changes the results.

Thus, sometimes the only feasible way to conduct research is without informed consent, and with appropriate safeguards this is allowable. It should be used only when it is the sole way of conducting the research, when the work is important enough to warrant an invasion of privacy (no matter how slight that invasion is), and particularly when there is minimal possibility that the invasion of privacy will produce unpleasant consequences for the subject.

A distinction should be made between personal, private information about an individual and public information. Information about an individual's finances, sexual behavior, or even preferences for movies is personal. An individual's behavior when he is angry or frustrated is also quite personal. Research designed to obtain such information must carefully observe the guidelines on privacy. In contrast, whether someone crosses the street when the light is red, is willing to post a sign for safe driving, or smokes cigarettes is relatively public information. Almost anyone can obtain this information merely by watching the individual's behavior in public. Although an investigator should always be careful about the right to privacy, collecting public information of this sort need not be done under such strict guidelines.

In summary, the guidelines for the protection of privacy are to obtain informed consent if possible, to obtain consent based on trust if some concealment of purpose is necessary, and to conduct research without consent only when there is no other way to do it and there is minimal danger of causing distress.

Experimental Conditions

Another ethical consideration perhaps even more complicated than that of privacy concerns the conditions to which the subject is to be exposed. The determination of what should be done rests largely with the individual investigator. This is as it should be, because ultimately it is his responsibility. However, all universities now have a special committee to provide some supervision for the experimenter. Certain guidelines apply to all research in social psychology.

It is obvious that nothing should be done to a subject that has any likelihood of causing lasting harm. It may seem somewhat foolish to mention this, but unfortunately, it is sometimes lost sight of. Medical research, for example, has often exposed willing or unwilling humans to drugs, viruses, and other agents that could conceivably cause great harm. There have been lawsuits over such practices, and they are better controlled today. But the researcher is in conflict; his goals are noteworthy—he wants to save lives, discover a cure for cancer, in social research perhaps discover how to prevent war—so he may think some risk of harm to a subject is justified. We feel that, at least in social psychology, this is not so. A subject, even with his permission, should not be exposed to potentially harmful conditions.

After this criterion is satisfied, the problem becomes subtle and more difficult. Is it allowable to cause subjects some pain or distress if it is not lasting or extreme? We feel that it is, but only if stringent criteria are met. The experimenter must consider all the ways of studying the problem that do not cause distress. Often the same problem can be studied without aversive conditions, and if so, they must be used. If this is not possible (for example, the study involves reactions to pain or frustration), the experimenter must decide whether the importance of the problem warrants the use of procedures that will cause distress. While such procedures may not cause lasting pain or distress, there must be ample justification for exposing someone to an unpleasant experience. A replication of earlier work, a small point in a larger problem, or a slight extension of a previous finding would be less justification than a test of an important theory, a possibility of discovering a new relationship, or a major extension of previous work. The greater the distress the procedure will cause, the more justification, in terms of the importance of the work, is needed to use it.

Assuming that no other procedure is possible and the problem seems important enough, the experimenter must next give careful attention to the procedure to be used and the setting in which it will be used. Two issues are involved: first, conditions produced in the laboratory that are similar to those the person is likely to encounter in normal life are always preferable to unique conditions. Being threatened with an injection may be frightening, but it is a usual occurrence in the world—we all get injections. In contrast, being threatened with total isolation for five hours is also frightening, but it is not a usual occurrence—most people never face this threat. The advantage of the natural situation is that it is more likely to produce valid results that are comparable to behavior in the real world. More important from an ethical point of view, it is less likely to cause distress that individuals cannot handle or that will produce a lasting impression on them.

Second, the subjects should have volunteered to be in the study. As stated above, they need not necessarily be told everything that will happen, but they should know that they are in an experiment and should have freely given their permission. In other words, only someone who has given informed consent or consent based on trust should be exposed to distressing conditions. Subjects who have not given consent should be exposed only to conditions that have a minimal chance of causing distress.

One general rule that many psychologists use in evaluating research is that the subjects should leave the study in essentially the same state of mind and body in which they entered. That is, participation in the study should have no substantial effect of any kind that carries over once the subject has finished. Another way of stating this important consideration is that the study may be pleasant, interesting, and enjoyable or even mildly unpleasant, boring or tedious, but the subjects' state of mind, knowledge of themselves, and general attitude should not be altered by the experience. This guideline, if followed closely, would assure that the subjects would not be harmed.

We should add that providing the subjects with information about themselves, even if accurate, should also be avoided. Unless the study is specifically described as one in which the subjects will learn about themselves, the psychologist should not assume that giving information is justified. Many people who object to research without informed consent and to any deception seem to feel that it is good to give subjects personal information, because they are learning from the experience. But the subjects may not want that information. It may be useful but it may also be disturbing. Surely, telling subjects that they are uncreative or neurotic (even if true) is more likely to upset them than to benefit them. If subjects ask a psychologist to test them for neuroticism, they presumably want that information; but if they volunteer for a study, they probably are not expecting, nor do they want, information about their mental health.

These ethical considerations impose considerable restrictions on social scientists, but they need not prevent them from doing legitimate research. With sufficient ingenuity and care, they can study virtually any problem and still safeguard the privacy and well-being of their subjects.

DESIGNING THE STUDY

With these ethical considerations in mind, the investigator must design and conduct a study. As an example of this process, we shall now discuss in detail the design and execution of a laboratory experiment.

The investigator has a problem she wants to study. She must set up a situation in which one or more variables (the independent variables) are experimentally manipulated and in which subjects are randomly assigned to groups in such a way that the groups differ only in terms of these independent variables. Everything about the situation must be identical for the groups except the one variable in which she is interested. Then the experimenter must measure one or more responses (the dependent variables) in order to see what effect the independent variable has. She must take her measurements in such a way as to minimize the subject's suspicion. Only then can she elicit responses that reflect, as much as possible, the way subjects would respond if they were in a similar situation that occurred naturally.

The Independent Variable

The first step in the process generally is to decide on the specific way to manipulate the independent variable. The psychologist starts with a variable that is defined on a conceptual level. For example, she hypothesizes that high fear leads to an increase in affiliation. She may or may not have a detailed definition of *fear* in her mind, but she must have a fairly clear picture of the variable. Let us say she defines *fear* as the internal feeling produced by the anticipation of pain or harm from a known source. This conceptual definition may sound impressive, but it is very general. The experimenter's big problem is deciding on the particular way in which she is going to arouse fear. According to the definition, she must set up a situation in which the subject is anticipating harm from a known source, but the definition says nothing about the specific conditions under which this should be done.

CHOOSING A MANIPULATION There are several criteria for a good manipulation of this sort. Ideally, it should work on all subjects. The more uniformly the method works, the stronger is its effect and the more likely it is to produce significant and meaningful results. Therefore, the psychologist wants to use something that everyone or almost everyone is afraid of.

A second point is that social psychologists typically deal with several levels of a particular variable rather than simply its presence or absence. An affiliation study would probably involve high- and low-fear conditions rather than high- and no-fear conditions. There are two reasons for this.

First, and more important, is the necessity of making the conditions as similar as possible in all respects except the one that differentiates them in terms of fear. This is difficult to do unless we use almost identical terms when describing the situation to both groups of subjects. For example, if we told one group of subjects that they were going to be given electric shocks and did not mention this to the other, the two groups would differ in many ways. They might differ in terms of fear (the variable we are interested in), but they would also differ in feelings about the experiment and the experimenter, in their curiosity about the study and so on. Also, we have talked longer to one group of subjects than to the other, and although we cannot be sure what effect this would have, it is potentially important. In contrast, we could tell both groups that they are going to be shocked but make it more frightening for one than the other by varying the description of the shocks. We could tell one group that the shocks will be severe and painful and the other group that they will be mild and not painful. This would make the conditions virtually identical except for the few words necessary to produce the difference in fear. Then, any differences in the behavior of the two groups would be attributable to fear level and not to extraneous variables.

The second reason for dealing with two levels of a variable rather than its presence and absence is that it is generally not possible to be certain that a particular internal state is entirely absent. Even if the external conditions would not ordinarily arouse fear, many subjects may be afraid simply because they are in an experiment or because they are people who are always somewhat frightened. Similarly, even someone who has just eaten may be slightly hungry, even someone who has just slept twelve hours may be tired, and so on. Thus, from a conceptual and practical point of view, it makes little sense to think in terms of the total absence of a variable—instead, we talk in terms of less and more.

ETHICAL AND PRACTICAL PROBLEMS With all these considerations in mind, the experimenter eventually chooses a manipulation. She might decide to tell the subjects that they are going to be handling snakes. Many people are afraid of snakes and some snakes are dangerous, so this should arouse a considerable amount of fear. The problem with this manipulation is that many subjects are, in fact, not afraid of snakes as long as the snakes are not dangerous. Thus many subjects would not be at all afraid and the manipulation would not be successful. We could, of course, say they are poisonous snakes or perhaps giant anacondas. The few subjects who believed it might be terrified, but it would probably raise considerable skepticism among most subjects and they would feel no fear.

Another possibility might be to lock subjects in a room and simulate a fire that, presumably, would be threatening to engulf the building. If this were done convincingly, the subjects would probably be exceedingly frightened. However, in addition to obvious ethical problems, there are several difficulties with this technique. First, many subjects probably would not believe there was a fire. To make the fire believable would require elaborate apparatus, shouting people, firemen breaking down doors, etc. But most important is the virtual impossibility of finding a comparable situation for the low-fear or control group. A small fire might be thought to arouse less fear than a large one, but if the fire is dangerous, the subjects will be afraid; and they will probably be just as afraid of burning to death in a small fire as in a large one. If there is no fire, the conditions are so different that it might be hard to compare them. Certainly any difference between the high-fear (fire) subjects and the low-fear (no fire) subjects would be difficult to attribute entirely to the amount of fear they felt.

Finally, this manipulation would make it extremely difficult to maintian good control over the situation and collect reliable measures of the dependent variable. In a study that used essentially this manipulation (French, 1944), uncontrollable events occurred. A group of subjects were put in a room at the top of an old building at Harvard, ostensibly to discuss a problem. Soon after the experimenter left, smoke began coming under a door in the room. The subjects soon discovered that all the doors were locked, and at this point they presumably should have been very frightened. Unfortunately (or perhaps fortunately), human beings do not usually take this kind of situation lying down. Several groups included varsity football players, and they broke down the door, terminating the experiment. Other groups managed to break into the closet from which the smoke was pouring and discovered the smoke machine. Still others convinced themselves that it was an experiment and calmly went about discussing the problem, ignoring the smoke that was beginning to fill the room. If the investigators had been studying responses to crisis situations, these would be interesting results. However, they were attempting to study a specific dependent variable (organization). When this is the aim of an experiment, crisis situations often make it difficult to exert sufficient control so that dependent measures can be collected.

ELECTRIC SHOCK One manipulation that has been widely used in social psychology experiments has been found to arouse fear in most subjects, enables the experimenter to produce several levels of fear conveniently, and also minimizes the amount of suspicion the subjects might feel. This is the anticipation of electric shocks. For most subjects, electric shocks are particularly frightening, partly because they rarely experience them and partly because they know that electric shocks can be extremely painful. Thus almost all subjects are frightened by the threat of receiving them. Yet electric shocks are not so strange and unfamiliar that subjects are being exposed to a situation likely to harm them.

Moreover, it is extremely easy to manipulate the amount of fear shocks arouse by describing them in different terms for different conditions. All the subjects would presumably be somewhat afraid, but the more painful they expected the shocks to be, the more afraid they would be. In this way all the subjects could be given almost identical instructions, and yet the intensity of the fear could be manipulated conveniently by changing a few words in the description of the shocks. The high-fear group could be told: "These shocks will hurt, they will be painful. . . . It is necessary that our shocks be intense. . . . These shocks will be quite painful, but of course, they will do no permanent damage." A low-fear group could be told: ". . . very mild electric shocks. . . . What you will feel will not in any way be painful. They will resemble more a tickle or tingle than anything unpleasant." If the instructions are delivered convincingly, they should arouse relatively little suspicion, because even sophisticated subjects know that psychologists often use electric shocks. Also the experiment can be described as, say, a study on responses to intense stimuli.

CHECKING VALIDITY There are obviously many other ways of arousing fear that could be adapted for this type of study. It is desirable to vary the independent variable in more than one way in different studies so that we can be more certain that we are dealing with fear and not some other emotion. If the findings on fear and affiliation, for example, are based entirely on the anticipation of electric shocks, someone might argue that they are not the result of fear but something specific to electric shocks. By manipulating fear in many ways, all of which are consistent with our original conceptual definition of fear and finding the same results, we increase confidence in our interpretation of the findings in terms of fear rather than in terms of the specific manipulation.

Another way of increasing confidence in the interpretation of the independent variable is to provide some sort of independent check on the manipulation. On the face of it, telling subjects they are about to be shocked should arouse fear. The more vivid the description, the more fear it should arouse. The possibility always exists, however, that the manipulation did not arouse fear, that for some reason the subjects were not worried about electric shocks, or perhaps that the two groups did not differ in the amount of fear they felt. If we know that there is some response or behavior that is highly correlated with fear, by measuring it we can provide an independent verification of the presence of fear. For example, we could take measures of the subjects' blood pressure and pulse rate. Although physiological measures are generally poor indicators of the presence of fear, they do tend to be correlated with it. The greater the fear, the higher should be the blood pressure and pulse rate.

If we find that the subjects in the high-fear condition actually do have higher pulse rates and blood pressure than those in the low-fear condition, our confidence in the effectiveness of the manipulation is increased. We are not absolutely certain that it is fear we are producing, but we do know that we have aroused some internal state differentially in the two conditions and that fear is one of the likely possibilities. Another kind of check on the manipulation is a self-report from the subjects. We can ask the subjects how frightened they feel, how nervous, whether or not they are nauseated, and so on. If the high-fear subjects report that they are more afraid than the low-fear subjects, and particularly if the two groups do not differ on irrelevant feelings such as nausea, it becomes highly probable that the manipulation really was affecting fear levels.

Thus there are two ways of pinning down the meaning of the experimental manipulation. One is to use many different kinds of fear manipulations, all derived from our conceptual definition of it. If the different manipulations produce the same effect on the dependent measure (for example, if in all cases the high-fear group affiliates more than the low-fear group), we can be quite confident that it is fear that is producing the effect. The other way is to provide a direct check on the manipulation, either by the use of self-reports or by some other variable that we know from previous research to be highly correlated with fear. Unfortunately, neither of these approaches is particularly easy in most instances. A great deal of care is required to be certain of our interpretation of the manipulation, and much of the controversy in social psychology revolves around different interpretations of the same experimental manipulation.

The Dependent Variable

The original problem was to study the effects of fear on affiliation. We have decided how to manipulate fear; we must now decide how to measure affiliation. We want to do it in such a way that there is a minimum of ambiguity in the meaning of the dependent measure because we would like to be absolutely certain that it is affiliation we are studying. Also we must minimize the possibility of biasing the subjects' responses. We want them to respond spontaneously, with the responses being due to the experimental situation and the independent variable.

In the case of affiliation, our first criterion for a good dependent measure is not particularly difficult to meet. There are relatively few possibilities for measuring affiliation. They all are variations of allowing the subjects a choice of affiliating or not affiliating and observing which they choose. The particular way in which the choice is presented would depend in large part on making it fit in with the experimental manipulation of the independent variable and the whole setting of the study. But there is no great difficulty in assessing the desire to affiliate.

Dependent variables other than affiliation, however, are often more difficult to measure. In studying the effect of modeling on aggression, for example, the experimenter is faced with a considerable problem in finding a good dependent measure of aggression. He can observe whether the subject punches someone, draws a knife and stabs him, or performs other violent acts. These are clearly aggressive behaviors and would be excellent, unambiguous indications of aggressiveness. Fortunately for our society, but perhaps unfortunately for the experimenter, the likelihood of any subject committing a violent act such as these is virtually zero. Therefore, the investigator must depend on subtler indications of aggressiveness. He could ask a subject to make comments about another person and then code these comments in terms of their aggressive content. But many people would not consider it aggressive behavior to make negative comments about somebody else when asked to do so by an experimenter. Even delivering an electric shock to another person might not be considered aggressive if the experimenter has told them that this is part of the study. In other words, it is quite difficult to find a dependent measure that fits the conceptual definition of aggression, is feasible, and is unequivocal. Considerable ingenuity is necessary to design such a measure. The same is true of many other variables that are important to social psychologists.

Often experimenters cannot find a perfect measure of the variable they are interested in. For practical or ethical reasons, they are forced to resort to somewhat equivocal measures. Other interpretations of the measure are possible, and therefore the experimenters cannot be certain their results reflect the variable they are investigating. One solution to this problem is to use many different measures of the same variable. If the measures all produce the same results and are all designed to tap the same variable, they can have increased confidence in the meaning of the findings. Any one measure of aggression might be interpreted in a variety of ways, but ten different measures of aggression that produce the same results, even if each of them separately could be interpreted in several ways, make it more likely that the variable measured is aggression.

Having many measures also reduces the possibility that the results are due to some characteristic peculiar to a given measure. For example, delivering electric shocks carries with it a variety of meanings and connotations, not all of which the experimenter can know. Therefore, results based only on giving electric shocks are to some extent confused with characteristics of that particular behavior. If, on the other hand, the same results are obtained from delivering electric shocks, making negative statements, taking money from another person, slapping someone across the face, and drawing nasty pictures of someone, it begins to appear that they are not due to any specific characteristics of any one measure. The results appear regardless of the measure of aggression, so we have considerably more confidence in them.

This does not mean that experimenters always use more than one measure in an experiment or even that it is essential to have experiments that use different measures. Occasionally they find a measure that is very compelling, that has few alternative interpretations, and that just about everybody will accept as an adequate measure of a particular variable. But most of the time it is helpful to have a variety of measures of the same variable, if not in the same experiment, at least in different experiments. In this way experimenters can increase both the generality of the results and their confidence that they involve the variable in question.

This, then, is the basic procedure for conducting an experiment in social psychology. A hypothesis is formed, an independent variable is chosen, the manipulation is constructed, the experimental situation is designed, and a dependent measure is selected. Generally, a considerable amount of pretesting is necessary to work out the exact method of manipulating the independent variable, smooth out the procedure, and make as certain as possible that the dependent measure is appropriate to the situation. When the pretesting has been completed and the type of subjects selected, the experiment is ready to be run.

BIAS

Up to now we have been talking about aspects of the experimental method that are more or less general to all kinds of research. The choice of setting (laboratory or field) is not unique to social psychology, although it is more important in this area than in most others. The difficulty of manipulating the independent variable and of choosing a dependent measure is common to virtually all fields of science. In addition, there is one problem that, although not unique to social psychology, is particularly relevant and troublesome in this field—bias due to the experimenter or the subject.

Experimenter Bias

As we discuss in Chapter 9, subjects in a study are extremely susceptible to influence by the experimenter. They do virtually anything he asks. This is true even if he does not make any direct request. If he implies, consciously or otherwise, that he would like the subjects to respond in a certain way, there is a tendency for them to respond in that way. If, for example, the experimenter would like the subjects in one condition to be more aggressive and those in another condition to be less aggressive, subjects in the two conditions may differ in the way he expects simply because explicitly or implicitly he communicates his wishes. Moreover, the experimenter may not have made any deliberate attempt to influence the results. On the contrary, experimenters are aware of this problem and try to be as neutral and consistent as possible. But subtle cues tend to be picked up by the subjects and influence their behavior.

Many studies (for example, Rosenthal, 1966) have shown powerful effects produced by the experimenter's expectations and desires. In school settings, students a teacher thinks are bright do better than students the teacher thinks are less bright—even though the students do not actually differ in intelligence. This is even true of rats in a simple learning situation with identical rats: if an experimenter is told the rats are smart, they do better than if he is told they are dumb. Perhaps experimenters tend to handle the "smart" rats somewhat more gently and to encourage them somewhat more than they do the "dumb" rats. If an experimenter's expectations can have an important effect on such fairly simple, noninteractive behavior as learning in rats, obviously they can have an even more dramatic effect on complex social processes.

There are two solutions to the problem of bias. One is to keep the experimenter ignorant as to the experimental condition of the subject. This is usually referred to as keeping the experimenter "blind." If she does not know which experimental condition she is dealing with, there is no way for her to affect the conditions differentially. Although she may behave differently from one experimental session to another and these differences may affect the way the subjects respond, she cannot systematically behave one way for one condition and another way for another. This guarantees that randomness still prevails, because the experimenter cannot make the variations in her procedure anything other than random. She can, of course, try to guess what condition a subject is in, and if she wants or expects one condition to produce more aggression than the other, she may behave in differential ways to subjects she thinks are in the two conditions. But since she does not know who is in what condition, her differential behavior cannot produce systematic differences. In other words, as long as the experimenter is totally blind (i.e., ignorant) as to the condition subjects are in, any differences in the way they are treated are randomly distributed between the various conditions.

In many experiments, however, it is impossible to keep the experimenter blind as to the subjects' condition. Typically, the experimenter himself must deliver the experimental manipulation in one way or another. He tells the subject to expect severe or mild shock, he brings the subject a Coke, he knows how many confederates are present in a conformity situation, and so on. The experimenter is the main source of instructions and manipulations, and his skill is generally necessary to make certain that the manipulation is effective. Even in these cases, however, some degree of blindness can be introduced into the experiment. For example, two experimenters can be used, with one of them delivering the experimental manipulation and the other collecting the dependent measure, thus keeping the person who collects the dependent measure blind to the experimental condition. It is not quite as good as having an experimenter who is totally blind, because the first experimenter might communicate in some way what he wanted the subject to do later or might affect in some way the later behavior, but the procedure should substantially reduce bias.

A second solution to the problem of experimenter bias is to standardize the situation in every way possible. If everything is standardized and there are no differences between conditions other than those that are deliberate, there can be no bias. This is usually not easy to accomplish, but various procedures can maximize the amount of standardization between conditions. In the extreme case, a subject might appear for an experiment, find a written instruction on the door telling her to enter, have all instructions presented on tape, and complete the experiment before she meets a live experimenter. In this way, every factor in the situation would be absolutely standardized, and experimenter bias would be eliminated.

This degree of standardization is rarely feasible. Most manipulations require the presence of at least one live person. Experiments concerning guilt depend on another person being hurt in some way, and that person's presence should make the arousal of guilt stronger. Tape recordings do not allow any procedural variations, which might be necessitated by variations among subjects. A live experimenter can repeat instructions if they have not been understood, emphasize aspects to which the subject seems to be responding, and increase the strength of the manipulation by these variations. In addition, most manipulations are more forceful when delivered by a live experimenter, simply because people respond to other people more strongly than they respond to impersonal tape recordings. But even this is not always true. Being told by a tape recording that he is going to be given severe electric shocks might be very frightening for a subject—even more so than hearing the same thing from a live experimenter. But this is a special instance. Generally, a live experimenter has more effect than a recorded or written message.

Another problem with taped instructions is that the situation becomes somewhat unreal. As we have already discussed, many experiments suffer from a lack of realism, and the careful experimenter exerts considerable effort to make the setting more realistic. Written or taped instructions tend to make the situation more unusual and magnify this already serious problem. The subject tends to be more suspicious and less spontaneous, and the results become less valid.

These drawbacks do not mean that written or taped instructions are impossible—on the contrary, they are often useful—but at least part of the manipulation usually has to be conducted by a live experimenter. Nevertheless, the more standardization that can be introduced, the more likely it is that experimental bias will be eliminated.

In actual practice, the solution to the problem of bias is usually a combination of the two procedures we have described. As much as possible, the experimenter is kept blind as to the subjects' experimental conditions; also as much as possible, instructions are standardized by the use of tapes or written materials. It is often impossible to eliminate completely the possibility that some bias has crept into a study, but experimenters must take this into account and do whatever they can to minimize the likelihood that there is any.

Subject Bias

An even subtler source of bias in a social psychology experiment is the subject's desire to give the "correct" response in the situation. Most subjects want to give the socially acceptable response, in part because they want to impress the experimenter. They feel that if they give the "correct" response, the experimenter will be more favorably impressed than if they give an inappropriate response. This feeling could be minimized somewhat by having the subject respond anonymously so that the experimenter would not know how she behaved in the situation. Unfortunately, this does not solve the problem entirely. Most subjects want to impress not only the experimenter but also themselves. They want to think of themselves as good people and therefore do what they can to behave in the right way. As long as a subject is thinking about these considerations, it is virtually impossible to eliminate this kind of bias, though the procedure described in Box 2–3 may work.

For example, if an experimenter were interested in the effects of

---

BOX 2–3
THE BOGUS PIPELINE

Jones and Sigall (1971) devised an ingenious procedure for minimizing subject bias. The general idea was to construct a situation in which subjects would give their true opinions, feelings, and attitudes regardless of what the experimenters wanted or might think of them. In other words, the situation was constructed to make the subjects ignore any concerns they might have had about being nice to the experimenters, impressing them, or even looking good to themselves. To the exent that the subjects were able to respond honestly, the situation was designed to elicit their real opinions.

The method was to tell the subjects that they were hooked up to what was essentially a fancy lie detector that could tell their true opinions from a variety of physiological measurements. Electrodes were attached to the subjects' arms and legs. A very impressive-looking piece of machinery with moving dials stood in the room emitting all sorts of whirring noises. The machine actually measured nothing. The subjects were then asked to respond to a few questions just to check on the machine's accuracy. These questions were selected to make it appear as if the subjects' true feelings could be known, but actually the experimenters knew them from a questionnaire they gave the subjects earlier. Thus the subjects discovered that the machine did, in fact, give the right answers. Then the subjects were asked to respond to other questions, including the ones the experimenters were really interested in. Under these circumstances, the subjects had no reason to lie and so gave honest answers, even if the answers were unpleasant or uncomfortably revealing.

---

frustration on aggression toward whites and blacks, he might frustrate a subject and then give him an opportunity to aggress against either a white or a black. If this were done in a straightforward manner, most subjects would be aware that the experimenter was interested at least in part in differential aggression toward whites and blacks. At this point, every subject would have some feelings about the appropriate or most acceptable behavior. Most white college students would probably think that it is wrong to be prejudiced and, in particular, that it is bad to aggress more against a black than against a white. These subjects live in a social environment in which bigotry, discrimination, and prejudice are considered wrong by most people. Clearly the socially acceptable and desirable response would be to treat the white and the black equally or even to bend over backward and aggress more against the former than against the latter. However, in this case the subjects are responding in the way they think they should, not necessarily in the way they would in a natural situation. In fact, many white subjects may feel considerable prejudice against blacks and may have a tendency to aggress more against them than against other whites, but their knowledge about what is socially acceptable behavior interferes with this spontaneous behavior and causes them to respond differently.

This kind of bias is almost impossible to eliminate entirely but can be minimized in a variety of ways. The goal is to produce a situation in which the subjects respond spontaneously without worrying about the correctness of the response. The basic tactic is to disguise the dependent measure or to distract subjects from its importance. One way of doing this is by not telling subjects that they are being observed. In field research, within the ethical limits described above, people sometimes are not told that they are subjects in an experiment. They are approached and their behavior may be measured, but nothing is said about a psychological study. For example, we could observe how white salespeople in a store treat black and white customers on a particularly busy, hard day compared to an easy day. If frustration leads to aggression, the salespeople should be nastier on the hard day, and even more so to blacks than to whites if that aggression is directed at people differentially.

In the laboratory, disguising the measure and distracting the subject are somewhat more difficult. As we discussed previously, experiments can be set up so that the crucial measure is taken after the subject thinks the experiment is over. Another tactic is to make the subject think that he is an experimenter rather than a subject. The subject is told that he is to act as an observer or to assist the experimenter, but in the description of his role not much emphasis is placed on observing his behavior. This distracts him from the main emphasis of the experiment and tends to make him behave more spontaneously. A third tactic is using unobtrusive or so-called nonreactive measures, in which the subject does not know that a measure is being taken. We could count how many cigarettes he smokes or how often he blinks as measures of stress, or observe whether he chooses a task that requires sitting with other people as an indication of desire to affiliate. All these techniques reduce the possibility of the dependent measure being affected by the subject's view of what is socially desirable instead of his natural inclinations.

As a final note, we should emphasize that social psychology is, in general, a probabilistic science. Its findings and predictions are stated in probabilistic terms. We will see that high fear leads to greater affiliation than low fear. This does not mean that all people who are feeling high fear affiliate more than all people who are feeling low fear. It does not even mean that all people affiliate more when they are afraid than when they are not afraid. In other words, it does not apply to every person nor to all situations. It does mean that greater fear *tends* to cause people to affiliate more than low fear. More of the people who are feeling a high degree fear affiliate than do those who are feeling a low degree. There is a greater probability that a particular individual who is afraid affiliates than that a particular individual who is not afraid does so. Similarly, a communication from a high-prestige communicator *tends* to produce more attitude change than one from a low-prestige communicator, but not everyone who reads the high-prestige communication changes more than everyone who reads the low-prestige communication. In addition, some people may actually change more as a result of a particular low-prestige communication than a high-prestige communication. For a variety of reasons, any given individual might be influenced more by a communication from a nursing student than by one from a Nobel Prize winner. But *most* people are influenced more by the high-prestige communication. If all we know is that one person received a high-prestige communication and another received a low-prestige communication, our best prediction is that the former is influenced more.

A great deal of the variation in most situations has not been fully explained by social psychology. We have found that some percentage of the variance in affiliation is due to the amount of fear the individual is feeling. Many other factors, such as birth order and some we do not know about yet, also affect the amount of affiliation. Therefore, we can now say that high fear *tends* to produce an increase in affiliation. In discussing liking (Chapter 6), we say that proximity, similarity, and rewardingness explain a considerable amount of the variance. Someone who is close by, who is very similar to us, and who is rewarding *tends* to be liked more than someone who does not have these qualities. But someone who fits all these criteria is not necessarily going to be a friend.

This does not mean that the findings of social psychology are false or imprecise. It means that we have not yet specified all the factors that affect any given behavior and that the factors we have discovered do not affect all individuals equally in all conditions. However, these factors do affect behavior in the ways we have described, so we are able to understand and predict behavior better because of the research.

SUMMARY

1. Although we all know a great deal about social behavior from our daily observations and experience, some of our impressions are incorrect. Systematic reseach is necessary to be certain which of our intuitions are right and which are wrong, and also to make discoveries about how we behave in social situations.

2. There are two types of questions with which to begin research. One kind is directly related to an existing theory. Theoretical research is designed to test the theory, to compare two theories, or to assess the limits and exceptions to a theory. The other kind of research is empirical. It starts with a general question that is not directly related to a theory and tries to discover new relationships or to test a hunch or intuition.

3. A second distinction among types of research is between basic and applied. Basic research deals with fundamental questions, general principles, or theories. Applied research is directed toward answering a question related to a specific problem in the world—how to reduce prejudice, sell toothpaste, or design housing.

4. There are two basic types of methods in social psychology—experimental and correlational. Correlational research asks the questions: are two or more variables related? If one variable is high, is the other also high; or is the other consistently low? Correlational research can deal with a great many variables at once, and can investigate factors that cannot usually be manipulated in the laboratory, such as very high fear, poverty, or social class. But correlational research does not allow us to make causal inferences—we do not know if *A* caused *B*, *B* caused *A*, or some third, unknown variable caused both. Experimental research consists of comparing two situations that differ in only one deliberately varied way. If there is any difference in behavior, it is due to that one variable. This provides great control over the situation and allows causal statements.

5. Research can be done in the laboratory or in natural or field settings. The former provides more control, the latter is closer to the real world and often permits a greater range of intensity in the variables studied.

6. Archive research uses existing data; cross-cultural studies compare more than one culture; and observational research involves careful, systematic observations of behavior.

7. Social psychologists face many ethical problems in doing their research. They must be careful to guard the safety of subjects, to respect their privacy, and to ensure that their research produces no harmful effects on anyone involved.

8. In designing a study, the key questions are how to manipulate the independent variable and to measure the dependent variable. Moreover, great care must be taken to avoid the effects of experimenter and subject bias. The experimenter can unintentionally affect the results, or subjects can give results that they think are "correct" but are not what they would have done spontaneously.

SUGGESTIONS FOR ADDITIONAL READING

CARLSMITH, J. M., ELLSWORTH, P. C., & ARONSON, E. *Methods of research in social psychology.* Reading, Mass.: Addison-Wesley, 1976. An excellent, thorough discussion of methodology.

JONES, E. E., & SIGALL, H. The bogus pipeline: A new paradigm for measuring affect and attitude. *Psychological Bulletin,* 1971, 76, 349–64. This article presents the technique discussed in box 2–3.

HENDRICK, C., & JONES, R. A. *The nature of theory and research in social psychology.* New York: Academic Press, 1972. Another discussion of research methods.

Attachment and Affiliation

3

Lionel J. M. Delevingne; Stock, Boston.

Human beings are gregarious animals. Almost all people spend their lives in close contact with other people. Moreover, this contact is not limited to close family members. It is rare for someone to live with his or her family away from all other members of the species. On the contrary, most of the world's human population lives in large groups, surrounded by hundreds, thousands, or millions of other people. Some other animal species also live in very large groups—herds of gnus, zebras, and gazelles; schools of sardines and shrimp; and, of course, vast colonies of ants and bees. But none of these social groupings can compare in complexity and few in size to ours. Certainly the enormous progress we have achieved and the changes we have caused on earth are both due in large part to the fact that we seek out other people and interact with very large numbers of them in extraordinarily complicated ways. This tendency to spend time with other people, to affiliate, is the beginning and the cause of social psychology and is therefore an appropriate place to begin discussing social phenomena.

INFANT ATTACHMENT: THE BEGINNING OF AFFILIATION

The human tendency toward **affiliation** begins very early in life. Almost all infants form attachments to one or more adults. By attachment we mean that the infant responds positively to the presence of that adult, wants to spend time with her (or him), feels better when close, seeks out the adult when nervous or frightened, and is less nervous when the adult is around. Moreover, almost all parents also become attached to their children. Parents want to be close to them and draw closer to their children when frightened. This attachment causes the child to do what it can to be close to the parent; and the parent reciprocates. Together this causes them to spend time together, or to affiliate.

Two general explanations are usually given for why this attachment develops: the innate, or genetic, explanation; and the learning explanation. Though the two are by no means contradictory, they emphasize quite different mechanisms. Let us consider how each applies to attachment.

Innate Factors

One important school of thought in developmental psychology holds that infants and parents become attached primarily because this tendency is built into the human organism. Neither parent nor child needs to learn to affiliate or to become attached. Indeed, it is virtually impossible for normal parents and children to avoid becoming attached to each other because various specific mechanisms almost guarantee that it will occur. Bowlby, one of the leading proponents of this point of view, argues that attachment is genetically determined because it is essential for the survival of the child. Obviously, infants need to be taken care of and protected; they need to be watched so that they do not harm themselves; they need to be kept warm and comfortable and so on. And when children are old enough to move around, it is important that they not wander too far from their parents because otherwise they may injure themselves or get into dangerous situations or even simply get lost. The mutual attachment between parents and children keeps them close and maximizes the likelihood that children will get the attention they need and therefore survive.

The genetic explanation of attachment holds that certain behaviors and responses of the infant and the parent are wired in at birth, and that these cause the attachment to form. For example, all infants cry, and almost all parents tend to come when their babies cry. The crying acts as a signal to the parent that is very difficult to ignore. If babies did not cry (and a few do not), it would be extremely difficult for parents to know when they were needed, and they would therefore not appear as regularly.

Similarly, infants tend to smile quite a bit. But they do not smile randomly. At the beginning, they tend to smile at all sorts of things—bright lights, strange sounds, almost anything that is novel but not too intense. However, their smiling gradually changes and becomes more social in nature. By four months, infants are smiling mostly at social stimuli—at people or even pictures of people (Ambrose, 1969; Spitz & Wolf, 1946). And, most important, babies smile most regularly at the faces of familiar adults. Thus, quite early in the child's life it tends to greet its parents (usually the most familiar adults) with a smile; and the parents respond

Paul Conklin; Monkmeyer Press.

FIGURE 3–2 A baby's smile delights its parents, who smile in return. This interaction may be one basis for the formation of attachment.

with pleasure to this greeting. As we all know, almost nothing is more rewarding than having a baby smile at us, especially if the baby favors us with more smiles than it gives to others. Thus, the parent is drawn to the baby by the smiles, while the baby becomes attached in part because the parent comes in response to crying and in order to receive these smiles.

According to the genetic view, the development of attachment is a two-way street. Both parent and child play a role. Clearly, if the parent for some reason is not drawn to the child, does not come when it cries, does not like to see it smile, the child may not become attached. But it is equally true that some children do not elicit attachment. They do not cry normally or do not stop crying when held; they do not smile; they do not react to the presence of the adult. This behavior makes it much harder for the parent to become attached to the child (Bell, 1968). Thus, when a parent seems not to care enough for a child, it is not always the parent's "fault"; it may sometimes be because the child is not responding normally.

The Learning Explanation

An alternative view holds that attachment is due to learning and follows all the usual rules that govern the learning of any behavior. The child becomes attached to the parent because the parent feeds and comforts the child; the parent becomes attached to the child because the child rewards the parent. Many of the behaviors described above may be involved. For example, when the child cries, the parent comes because he or she knows that crying usually means that the child needs something. The parent arrives, gives the child food, or changes its diaper, or whatever. The child stops crying. Both have been reinforced by the interaction. The child feels better because it is no longer hungry or uncomfortable; the parent feels good because the child has stopped crying. Similarly, the parent is reinforced by the child's smile because it is always nice to have someone smile at you. Thus, just as an adult may learn to love another adult who provides reinforcements, so the child learns to love its parent if the parent provides the attention and care it needs; and the parent learns to love the child if the child reponds to this care with positive reinforcements in the form of smiles, hugs, lack of crying, and so on.

BOX 3-1
SECURE VERSUS INSECURE ATTACHMENT

An important line of research in developmental social psychology suggests that children differ in the quality of the attachment they form, and also that this difference, which appears early in life, remains quite consistent as the child gets older. Ainsworth distinguishes between what she calls secure and insecure attachment (Blehar, Lieberman, & Ainsworth, 1977; Stayton & Ainsworth, 1973). A child with secure attachment gives a more positive greeting when its parent appears after being away, follows the parent around more, and seems to engage in more exploratory behavior when the parent is present. However, the secure child cries less than the insecure one when the parent leaves the room. In other words, it seems as if secure attachment consists of being happy when the parent is around and wanting to be close to the parent, but not being too upset with the parent is gone, presumably because the child is confident that he or she will return. In contrast, the insecure child might be described as clingy; it stays overly close to the parent, cries as soon as the parent leaves, and is not necessarily comforted by the parent's return. Obviously there is a full range of attachment, and every child demonstrates some insecurity at times; but there are general patterns.

It also appears that a child who is securely attached at one year (i.e., shows the pattern of behavior described above), tends to be securely attached several years later; and children who are insecurely attached at one year, tend to remain insecurely attached later (Waters, 1978). Naturally, as with all personal characteristics of this sort, there are substantial changes over time. Some who are secure will become less secure; some who are insecure will become more secure. But it is impressive that the research finds substantial stability in this complex behavior pattern over several years.

The learning (or as it is sometimes called, social learning) approach has little specific to say about the formation of attachment. Rather than detailing the exact mechanisms involved, it outlines the kinds of processes that will produce attachment or any other behavior. It is important to note that the two approaches are not necessarily inconsistent. The learning explanation can rely on the same behaviors as are described by the innate explanation. The major difference is in emphasis. Bowlby, Ainsworth, and other proponents of the innate approach claim that attachment will form more or less regardless of conditions. No specific experiences are necessary; reinforcements are not essential; as long as the baby and parent are normal, and the situation allows normal interactions, attachment will occur. In contrast, the learning explanation requires that parent and child receive reinforcements from each other and seems to envision a more chancy, less directed sequence of events.

In addition, the two approaches stress different factors and make somewhat different predictions regarding the effect of certain responses. For example, the learning approach puts considerable emphasis on direct reinforcements such as food and comfort, whereas the other approach downplays the importance of feeding and emphasizes social interactions.

FIGURE 3–3 The young monkey preferred a cloth "mother" to one made of wire, even though the wire mother provided nourishment and the cloth mother did not.

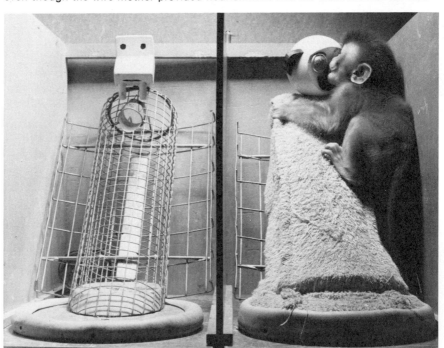

Courtesy Harry F. Harlow, University of Wisconsin Primate Laboratory.

Although the evidence is still sketchy on this point, it seems to favor the innate theory. Harlow and Zimmerman (1959) showed that monkeys became more attached to warm, cuddly mothers (actually made of cloth) that did not feed them than to cold, wire mothers that offered food. Also, learning theory should predict that the more quickly a parent responds to a child's crying, the more the child should be reinforced for crying and therefore, the more it should cry. Yet, the research indicates that when parents come promptly in response to crying, the babies actually tend to cry less (Ainsworth et al., 1972; Ainsworth & Bell, 1977).

In our opinion, the controversy between the two approaches will never be resolved in favor of one or the other. Clearly, many innate behaviors of the child contribute to the formation of attachment. The child does not have to learn to cry or smile or feel good when comforted, and all of these responses are important for producing an attachment bond between parent and child. On the other hand, there is no question that seeing a child smile or hearing it stop crying in response to your presence is reinforcing, and that without this reinforcement, you might not develop a typical strong attachment to a child. Indeed, as mentioned above, when the child does not respond to the parent's presence, attachment may not develop. Thus, one could say that certain innate behavior patterns help produce attachment, and that the mechanism by which they operate is through mutual reinforcement of parent and child.

THEORIES OF AFFILIATION

Parent-child attachment is probably the beginning of human affiliation. However, adult patterns of affiliation are much more complex and involve many different factors. Theoretical explanations of why adults affiliate are similar to theories of attachment, but focus on different issues. In addition, theories of affiliation must account for a wider range of behavior. They must explain why virtually all people affiliate, why they affiliate even when they are mature, and eventually why particular factors increase and decrease the tendency to affiliate in any given situation. At the moment no single theory of affiliation fully accounts for the phenomenon, but each of the following theories helps answer the questions just posed.

Instinct

Early social psychologists such as McDougall believed that gregariousness is a human instinct. Just as ants collect in ant colonies by instinct, and baboons build elaborate social structures, so people live together in groups. They do this not because they think it is good or right or even useful; they do it without thinking, just as a baby sucks on a nipple or is afraid of heights.

Humans are born with many genetically determined characteristics, and it is conceivable that among them is a tendency to seek out and to congregate with other human beings. If this were true, a child who had been raised in total isolation with a minimum of stimulation would be expected to affiliate with other people as soon as she was given the chance. It would not be necessary for a child to have any experiences after she was born in order for her to be an affiliative creature; she would affiliate even if she received no rewards or comfort from others.

Although there may be considerable truth in this idea, it is almost impossible to test. One way to do so would be to raise a child in isolation and study her later behavior. Obviously we cannot and would not do this kind of experiment; and even if we could, it would not be a perfect test. Total isolation is not a normal environment for a human baby and would probably have harmful effects that would obscure any natural tendency to affiliate.

Although we cannot test the idea directly, we can easily conceive of reasons why humans might have developed an affiliative instinct. Because of natural selection, any characteristic that increases the chance of the animal surviving (that has high survival value) should over many generations become dominant. Assuming that the characteristic is genetically determined in the first place, those animals that have it will survive and breed more and their offspring will tend to have that quality. Since there will be more of their offspring than of those without the quality, eventually all or most animals of that species will have the quality. Under most circumstances, people who are gregarious will have a better chance of surviving and breeding than those who are solitary. This must have been true many thousands of years ago when our forebears were fighting a primitive world. There was strength in numbers. The group provided some protection and an increased opportunity to get food by hunting in groups, and so on. Moreover, once young were born, they needed protection that could not be provided by a solitary woman or even a small family. Thus, it is highly plausible that people who congregated in large groups managed to live longer and to produce more children who survived infancy. If this tendency to affiliate is determined in any way by genes, it is likely that people who are alive today have inherited some genetic tendency to affiliate.

Keep in mind that this does not prove affiliation is genetically controlled. It may simply not be genetic in nature at all. The point of this argument is mainly to demonstrate that an explanation in terms of genetics is possible and even plausible. But, as we shall see, whether or not affiliation is instinctive, there are many other reasons why people want to be together.

Innate Determinants

Closely related to the idea that affiliation is instinctive is the obvious fact that we are gregarious because our other innate characteristics make it absolutely essential for our survival. We cannot survive alone; therefore, most of us spend time together.

Dependence on others is most evident when we are very young. Unlike most other animals, a human baby is virtually helpless for a long period of time. His early dependence on his parents for food and protection makes it necessary that he live with others for many years. Whereas most animals, even mammals, nurse for only a short time and can then forage for food on their own, the human baby is unable to feed itself for several years. It is conceivable that in a mild, protected, rich environment a child could stay alive after he was one or two years old, but under normal circumstances this would not be possible. He needs food, he needs protection from predators, he needs some kind of shelter, and so on. Similarly, a mother is extremely dependent on other humans for protection, particularly while she is taking care of her baby. Although it is possible for a solitary woman to survive even while nursing her child, under most circumstances she is dependent on at least one other human for protection and food.

Thus people are gregarious, by necessity, for the early years of their lives. If the parent and child did not stay together, the child would die. In this sense our innate characteristics, particularly our early helplessness, do cause us to affiliate. At a certain stage in life, however, we cease to be absolutely dependent on others. We no longer need them to give us food or protection. We could, in terms of our innate needs, become solitary. In our modern society a person could live in a penthouse apartment, have food delivered, watch television, read newspapers that were delivered with the food, and lead a safe, secure, comfortable, solitary life for many years. Or she could live on an isolated farm and accomplish the same thing without any help from others.

Occasionally someone does. There are cases of people becoming hermits, living alone, and, as far as we can tell, surviving perfectly well. But these are unusual, deviant cases. There are very few voluntary hermits, and those that do exist are generally considered somewhat crazy, certainly eccentric, and objects of curiosity. They are rebelling against perhaps the most universal characteristic of human beings, the tendency to be gregarious. Solitary confinement is almost always considered a severe punishment. Although it seems that our gregariousness is to some extent innately or instinctively determined, we are still left with the question of why people affiliate when they no longer need to.

Learning

One answer is that people learn to affiliate just as they learn anything else. The child depends on others for essentials such as food, warmth, and protection, and each time one of these basic needs is satisfied by someone else, the child learns something. By the simple process of association, other people become connected with rewards and the child learns to consider people positive aspects of her environment. In addition, because the child is rewarded when she is with other people, the act of associating with people is reinforced. She learns that when she needs something, seeking out other people usually leads to satisfaction. Thus, she has learned to affiliate with others; it has become a customary part of her daily life.

This learning affects an individual's behavior throughout life. As an adult, she no longer requires other people in order to survive, but still associates with them because she has learned to. Thus, as children learn all sorts of habits that shape their lives, so they learn affiliation. And because all children in all cultures to some extent must learn to affiliate, it becomes a characteristic of all people.

Satisfaction of Needs

It is also true that we have needs other than those that are necessary for personal survival—needs that only other people can satisfy. For example, although the solitary life leaves an individual with some means of sexual satisfaction, it denies us the outlet of sexual intercourse with other humans. In addition, the needs for achievement, love, appreciation, comfort, respect, and power, although not innate, are sought by most people, and these needs are extremely difficult to satisfy in isolation. Thus, although someone could stay alive in isolation, most people have acquired through early social learning many needs that can be satisfied only by others.

SPECIFIC CAUSES OF AFFILIATION

Instinct, innate characteristics, learning, and the satisfaction of needs are all explanations of why people affiliate. They are, however, general answers that do not allow us to specify much about the forces that control affiliation. If we say that animals eat because they have a need to eat or because they have learned to eat, we are correct but we do not learn very much about eating. On the other hand, if we say that animals eat when they have been deprived of food for four hours or when their blood-sugar level is low, we have specific knowledge about hunger and eating and can control the amount an animal will eat.

This distinction between general and specific explanations is also applicable to affiliation. Social psychologists have tried to determine the factors that increase or decrease the tendency to affiliate. We want to discover specific conditions that produce more affiliation and those that produce less in order to gain a more detailed understanding of the nature and causes of affiliation. We begin with the premise that almost all people have a tendency to associate with others. But we know there are times when this need is felt strongly, times when it is weak, and even times when people prefer to be alone. The question is: What factors increase and decrease affiliation?

Fear and Affiliation

A report of the most systematic attempt to study the causes of affiliation was published in 1959 by Stanley Schachter. In order to gain insight into factors that might increase affiliation, he began observing what happens when people are not allowed to affiliate. If affiliation is satisfying a need, this need should become very important when a person is denied the source of its satisfaction.

A study of case histories of people in total isolation—members of some religious orders, people who had been shipwrecked, volunteers for isolation experiments—did show some similarities. Almost all accounts of long-term isolation included descriptions of sudden fearfulness and feelings resembling anxiety attacks. Within limits, longer isolation produced greater fear and anxiety. Although it is impossible to conclude anything definitive from this observed relationship because many other explanations are also plausible, it does suggest that fear and affiliation are closely linked. If isolation produces fear, affiliation may reduce fear. Thus, Schachter was led to the specific hypothesis that persons with high fear would affiliate more than those with low fear.

To test this hypothesis, we must examine individuals who differ in their amount of fear. One method of investigation would be to study individuals who differ in the amount of fear they are experiencing in life situations. However, such people almost certainly differ on dimensions other than degree of fear. For example, although airplane pilots who are about to make their first solo flight are probably more afraid than pilots who have flown for years, they also differ in length of experience, probably in age, and certainly in attitude toward flying. Any differences found in affiliative tendencies might be due to factors other than the amount of fear they are experiencing. By using controlled situations, we can select people who are similar and experimentally manipulate their degree of fear, making some more afraid than others. Then, when the subjects are given an opportunity to affiliate, the amount of affiliation they exhibit can be compared and any differences attributed to the degree of fear that had been aroused in them. This is what Schachter did, and his experiment has served as a model for almost all the subsequent work in this area.

When a subject arrived for Schachter's experiment, she found an experimenter in a white laboratory coat, surrounded by electrical equipment of various sorts. The experimenter introduced himself as Dr. Gregor Zilstein of the department of neurology and psychiatry and explained that the experiment concerned the effects of electric shock. In order to make some subjects more afraid than others, the experimenter used two different descriptions of the electric shock.

Instructions designed to arouse a considerable amount of fear (high-fear condition) described the shocks in ominous terms. Subjects were told, "These shocks will hurt. . . . In research of this sort, if we're to learn anything at all that will really help humanity, it is necessary that our shocks be intense. . . . These shocks will be quite painful but, of course, they will do no *permanent* damage" (italics added). By continuing at some length in this vein, the experimenter communicated the notion that the subject was in for a very frightening and painful experience.

In the low-fear condition, by contrast, every attempt was made to make the subject feel relaxed and at ease, while minimizing the severity of the shocks. For example, the subjects were told, "I assure you that what you will feel [i.e., electric shock] will not in any way be painful. It will resemble a tickle or a tingle more than anything unpleasant." Thus, although both groups of subjects were told the experiment would concern electric shock, one group expected a painful and frightening experience, whereas the other group expected a mild and unthreatening experience. As shown by questioning the subjects, the result was that the former group was more afraid than the latter.

Following the arousal and measurement of fear, the experimenter told the subjects there would be a ten-minute delay while he prepared the equipment. He explained that there were a number of other rooms in

FIGURE 3–4 One reason for affiliating is to comfort each other. This can occur when people are frightened (as in the research described in the text) or sad, as in this picture.

United Press International.

TABLE 3–1
Effect of Fear on Affiliation

Condition	PERCENTAGE CHOOSING			Strength of Affiliation[a]
	Together	Don't Care	Alone	
High fear	62.5	28.1	9.4	.88
Low fear	33.0	60.0	7.0	.35

[a] Figures are ratings on a scale from -2 to $+2$.
Source: Adapted from Schachter (1959).

which the subjects might wait—comfortable rooms with armchairs, magazines, and so on. The experimenter continued that it had occurred to him that perhaps some of the people would prefer to wait with other subjects in the experiment and for these there was a classroom available. Each subject was asked to indicate whether she preferred to wait with others, alone, or had no preference. She was also asked to indicate the strength of her choice. In this and most subsequent experiments on this topic, the choice and rating of the intensity of subjects' desire to affiliate were the basic measures of the tendency.

The results of Schachter's study are shown in Table 3–1. The answer to the question of whether highly fearful subjects want to affiliate more than subjects with low fear is yes. The greater the fear, the greater the tendency to affiliate.

Now that we have found a relationship between fear and affiliation, the next step is to explain it. Why do fearful people affiliate more? There seem to be at least two explanations—fear reduction and social comparison.

FEAR REDUCTION

We have seen that isolation appears to increase fear, which in turn leads to an increase in affiliation. One probable explanation of this increase in affiliation is that people affiliate in order to reduce their fear. Schachter's first experiment did not test this explanation directly, but some support for it was provided in a subsequent study (Schachter, 1959). Subjects were told that if they chose to wait with others they could either not talk at all or talk only about things unrelated to the experiment. The purpose of this restriction was to make it more difficult for subjects to reduce fear by reassuring one another. To the extent that high-fear subjects were affiliating in order to reduce fear, there would be less preference for waiting together than there had been when talking about the experiment was allowed. That is just what happened. Restricting

BOX 3-2
BIRTH ORDER

Even when high fear is aroused, some people have stronger needs to affiliate than others. Is there any systematic reason for this? An important, although supplementary, finding in Schachter's study of affiliation is that birth order is an important determinant of a person's desire to affiliate. First-born children and only children when afraid have a stronger tendency to affiliate than do later-born children. In fact, the tendency decreases progressively for the later-born children; those born second show a greater tendency to affiliate than do those born third, who, in turn, show a greater affiliative tendency than those born fourth, and so on. As shown in the figure below, this progression is maintained regardless of the size of the family. The affiliative tendency of someone born second in a family of six is about the same strength as that of someone born second in a family of two. In other words, the order of birth, not the size of the family, is the determinant. Why should birth order have this effect on affiliation?

Theoretically, the effect might be caused by some innate difference between first and later borns, but there is no evidence of such genetic differences. Most psychologists feel that the way children are brought up is crucial. One possible analysis is as follows. Parents are more concerned about their first child than about later children. When a first-born child falls, her mother runs to comfort her. Therefore, the first-born child soon learns that when she is uncomfortable, her mother is a marvelous source of comfort. Eventually the child learns that people in general provide comfort. With later children, parents become less concerned about the trials and tribulations of growing up. They learn that children are surprisingly resilient and their misery mostly transient. Moreover, the parents are a little tired of oohing and aahing over every scraped knee, and they now have two children to care for and not so much time for each. Therefore, the affiliative tendency of the second child is reinforced less than that of the first child. The second child learns less that other people are a source of comfort and thus he learns to depend less on other people. By the time the third child is born, the parents are quite calm about raising children. They have even less time for a third child, so she learns even less, and so on. Thus, the earlier a child is in the birth order, the more she learns to depend on other people as sources of comfort when she is afraid.

This difference between first and later borns seems to affect many aspects of their lives. For example, first borns tend to seek psychotherapy (another person) more than later borns, while many more later borns become alcoholics (drinking is a nonpersonal "solution"). Also fighter pilots, who must face danger alone, are very likely to be later borns.

To summarize: When people are afraid, they vary greatly in the ex-

BOX 3-2 First borns, when afraid, affiliate more than second borns, who, in turn, affiliate more than third borns, and so on. This holds true regardless of the size of family—order of birth, not number of siblings—determines affiliation.

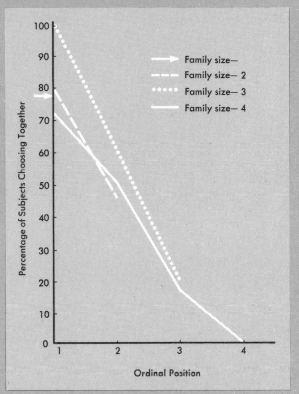

Reprinted from The Psychology of Affiliation by Stanley Schachter with the permission of the publishers, Stanford University Press. © 1959 by the Board of Trustees of the Leland Stanford Junior University.

tent to which they seek other people as a means of reducing their fear. One factor that affects this is birth order. First borns seek others when they are worried, and the tendency decreases progressively for the later born.

This finding on the effect of birth order provides additional support for the conclusion that one cause of affiliation is the desire to reduce fear. Although the birth-order effect could be interpreted in other ways, it seems that first and later borns differ in their dependence on others in reducing fear. The first borns are more dependent and show the effect of fear on affiliation more strongly.

discussion reduced the desire to affiliate. The result supports the idea that fear reduction is one reason why people want to be with others.

<table>
<tr><td>

Fear Versus Anxiety

</td><td>

The situation is complicated somewhat by the distinction between **fear** and **anxiety.** Although people generally use the two terms more or less interchangeably, psychologists use them to refer to quite different feelings. Freud suggested that being afraid of a realistic object or source of injury is different from being afraid when there is no real danger. He called the former *realistic anxiety* or *object anxiety,* and we shall call it *fear.* He called the latter *neurotic anxiety;* today, it is generally called *anxiety* to distinguish it from fear.

Someone being charged by a lion, advancing under enemy gunfire, or balancing on a narrow precipice while mountain climbing feels fear. He is in real danger and experiences the normal reaction to it. A person may be worried by a tiny mouse, upset at meeting new people, or nervous about standing on a wide ledge with a high protective fence. And there are times when he feels a sense of dread and becomes nervous and afraid but cannot connect the emotion to any specific object or situation. In all these instances there is no danger, he cannot be harmed, and yet he may experience a reaction similar to fear. This is anxiety.

According to Freud, anxiety is aroused by unconscious desires—sexual, aggressive, or otherwise—that people have but consider unacceptable. For example, men may unconsciously wish to be submissive, to act like children and be babied and taken care of by their mothers. But modern society puts pressure on men to be assertive, dominant, independent. Most men assume the role society dictates; they deny to themselves and others that they have the childish feelings. Then, when men are exposed to a situation that arouses these desires, they have a tendency to feel uncomfortable. However, because they are denying their needs, they do not know what is bothering them. Another example is the latent homosexual who feels uncomfortable in a communal shower. He is unaware of his homosexual feelings, but the situation arouses sexual feelings that he denies. He is, in a sense, afraid of his feelings, and it is this fear that we call anxiety. Stimuli that arouse hidden, unacceptable feelings produce anxiety.

Accepting this conceptual distinction, it is clear that Schachter's study of affiliation involved fear, not anxiety. Almost everyone recognizes that electric shocks can cause pain and harm and it is realistic to be frightened of them. Thus, we have been careful to state the original finding as high *fear* produces greater affiliation than low *fear.* This distinction is important because the reaction to anxiety is different.

Most people have learned that being with others usually reduces fear of something realistic. Other people reassure them, they realize that the others are going to experience the danger also, and there is strength in numbers. When our worry is unrealistic, however, associating with others

</td></tr>
</table>

is less likely to help and may even make things worse. The others presumably are not feeling anxious, because there is nothing real to worry about; therefore, we cannot talk freely about our worries. The others would be surprised, we might be embarrassed, and the interaction might increase rather than decrease anxiety. Even if we could talk to others, it would be more difficult for them to reassure us because they would not understand the real cause of our discomfort. Because associating might increase anxiety by producing embarrassment, a high-anxious subject would try to conceal rather than reveal his feelings. Accordingly, he should want to be alone more than a low-anxious subject.

To test this hypothesis, Sarnoff and Zimbardo (1961) conducted a study similar to Schacter's, with one important difference—both fear and anxiety were tested. One group of subjects was told, as in Schachter's experiment, that they were going to receive electric shocks; some members of this group were told the shocks would be quite severe (high fear), whereas others were told the shocks would be mild (low fear). Another group was put in a situation designed to arouse anxiety. They were told they would have to suck on a variety of objects. Some in this group were told they would have to suck on breast shields, rubber nipples, and other emotionally laden objects. The subjects were undergraduate men who felt reasonably mature and adult. On the premise that being asked to suck on infantile, ludicrous objects would arouse oral anxiety and would make them feel uncomfortable and foolish, these subjects were considered high anxious. Other subjects were told they would have to blow on relatively acceptable, innocuous objects such as whistles. This was expected to produce little or no discomfort, so these subjects were considered low anxious. The point was that neither anxiety group had anything realistic to be afraid of. Then the four groups—high and low fear, high and low anxiety—were given the measure of affiliation described previously. They had to indicate their preference for being alone or with others while waiting to go through the expected procedure.

The results are shown in Figure 3–5. As before, those anticipating severe shocks (high fear) wanted to wait together more than did those expecting mild shocks (low fear). However, as predicted, anxiety produced the opposite effect. The high-anxious subjects wanted to wait alone more than did the low-anxious subjects. The higher the anxiety, the *less* the desire for affiliation.

This complex finding was repeated by Teichman (1973) using a somewhat different manipulation of fear. Instead of directly threatening subjects with electric shock, the experimenter produced different levels of fear by varying how ominous and frightening the general situation appeared. In the high-fear condition, people wore white lab coats, acted impersonally, were surrounded by impressive recording equipment, and the subjects were told that various physiological responses would be measured. In the low-fear condition, everything was less formal, warmer, and less frightening. High and low anxiety were varied using the same pro-

Source: Adapted from Sarnoff and Zimbardo (1961).

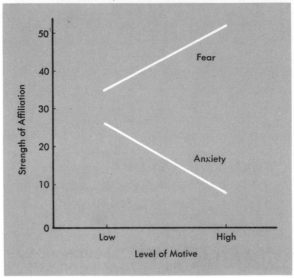

FIGURE 3–5 The desire to affiliate depends on the particular emotion that is aroused. High fear produces more affiliation than low fear; but high anxiety produces less affiliation than low anxiety. Note that the overall level of affiliation is higher under conditions involving fear than under those involving anxiety.

cedure as Sarnoff and Zimbardo employed. As before, there was more affiliation with high than with low fear, and with low than with high anxiety.

Although the effect of anxiety was originally discussed in complex Freudian terms, the explanation appears to be simply that the situation is potentially embarrassing for the subjects. That is, they are not undergoing any profound anxiety, oral or otherwise; they are merely worried about looking silly in front of other people.

The explanation in terms of potential embarrassment is given direct support in a study by Fish, Karabenick, and Heath (1978). Once again high and low fear and high and low anxiety were compared, and subjects affiliated more under high than low fear but less under high-anxiety conditions. The additional twist to the situation was that the subjects either did or did not expect to be observed during the fear- or anxiety-arousing tasks. The important finding was that when subjects were going to be watched in the anxiety situation they had much stronger preferences for waiting alone than when they were not going to be watched, whereas those who were frightened showed a small increase in wanting to wait with others. The authors interpret this result as showing that the anxiety manipulation really involved the threat of embarrassment. Only when the people expected to be observed did the situation bother them to the extent that they wanted to be alone. Thus, Sarnoff and Zimbardo were probably mistaken in talking about high and low anxiety affecting affiliation. Rather, the key issue in this research is whether or not the people feel they may be embarrassed by what they are being asked to do; and it is this embarrassment that causes them to avoid affiliation.

We thus have two distinct findings: Fear leads to increased affiliation. Anxiety or threat of embarrassment leads to decreased affiliation. In social psychology, making this kind of distinction aids in understanding a social phenomenon—in this case, affiliation. We can now make a more precise explanation of the relationships involved. Other people are a source of both comfort and embarrassment. When we expect them to provide comfort, we seek them out; when we expect embarrassment, we avoid them. Associating with others seems generally to decrease fear, so when fear is heightened, people seek others as a means of reducing it. But being around other people can increase anxiety, so when anxiety is heightened, people avoid affiliating.

SOCIAL COMPARISON

The analysis of affiliation in terms of fear reduction is only a partial answer. Schachter's original finding can also be explained in terms of Leon Festinger's theory of social comparison (1954). This important and influential theory contains two basic ideas: People have a drive to evaluate themselves; and in the absence of objective, nonsocial criteria, they will evaluate themselves by comparison with other people.

Everyone wants to know how good they are at whatever they do. Is she a good tennis player, a fast runner, a talented writer, a graceful dancer? We want to know if we are smarter, less smart, or similar to most other people; whether we are attractive compared to others and so on. Sometimes there is a fairly obvious objective criterion for evaluation. For example, if you get a perfect score on an exam or as a marksman, you know that you are doing very well. But most of the time, there is no such convenient criterion. How does a runner know if he is fast? Is a five-minute mile good? How about a mile in four minutes ten seconds? Forty years ago, the four-ten mile would have been superb; today, because others are running faster, it is less outstanding. Is a man 5 feet, 10 inches in height short or tall? In the United States, he is about average; in Japan, he would be tall; among the Watusi in Africa, he would be short. Only by comparison with those around us, can we evaluate ourselves.

An example of self-evaluation by comparison with others can be seen in the experiences of high school students who enter college. In high school they were the brightest ones around and they and everyone else considered them quite exceptional. But in college many of the freshman class had been outstanding high school students. Each must now compare himself to an essentially all-star high school group. Most discover that they are not so outstanding after all, that in this new group they are just average. Their own intelligence has not changed—the comparison group by which they evaluate their intelligence has. They feel that they adequately evaluate their abilities only by comparing themselves to the people around them. When these people change, their evaluations of themselves change.

This is especially true when feelings and emotions are involved. Because there are rarely objective criteria to indicate if one's feelings are appropriate to a situation, other people are the only source of information. In fact, to a large extent individuals define an appropriate reaction as the one most people have. Should one be afraid of a huge but harmless snake? By any realistic standard, the answer is no. But most people probably are somewhat frightened of a five-foot snake, regardless of its potential danger. Because the typical reaction is fear, most people would consider feeling fear to be more appropriate than not feeling fear. In fact, someone who was not frightened by such a snake would generally be considered rather odd. Thus, the so-called normative response is considered correct; anything else is, in a sense, wrong.

The appropriateness of any emotional reaction, therefore, can be ascertained only by seeing what others are feeling. This can apply to the type of emotion and also to the strength of the emotion. People clarify and evaluate their reactions by comparing them with others' reactions. When we are uncertain about our feelings, we try to clarify them. Accordingly, when other people are the only useful source of information, we compare ourselves to them. Thus the desire for social comparison is another possible reason for affiliating. And, the more uncertain an individual is about her feelings, the more she will want to affiliate with others in order to reduce the uncertainty. How does this explain the greater affiliation with high fear?

When subjects are told they are going to be given a severe electric shock, they naturally become frightened; we have seen that this leads to greater affiliation than if they were less afraid. One reason for this heightened affiliation is the subject's desire to reduce her fear and her expectation that being with other subjects will accomplish this. However, though they know it is appropriate to be afraid, they are not sure how afraid they should be. Should they be terrified, moderately scared, or only slightly worried? They are in a state of some uncertainty as to what the appropriate emotional reaction is. In contrast, mild shocks arouse only a slight reaction in the first place and subjects are pretty sure this is about right. Therefore, according to the theory of social comparison, high-fear and uncertain subjects should have strong needs to affiliate in order to find out what others are feeling and thereby to evaluate and clarify their own reactions. Low-fear subjects experience little uncertainty and little need to affiliate.

FIGURE 3–6 People compare themselves to others on many different dimensions. Here the emphasis seems to be on looks and hair style.

Hunger

This explanation in terms of social comparison is supported by the finding that the arousal of needs other than fear reduction can also increase affiliation. Whenever someone has a strong need, he tends to be uncertain about how he should be feeling. This uncertainty leads to a desire for social comparison and thus to affiliation. For example, Schachter (1959) demonstrated that a high degree of hunger causes people to want to affiliate more than a low degree of hunger. Subjects were called the night before they were to take part in the experiment and told that it would involve the effects of particular kinds of food deprivation on sensations. One group of subjects (classified as high hunger) was asked to fast for approximately twenty hours by omitting breakfast and lunch on the following day, and one group (medium hunger) was asked to fast for six hours by omitting lunch. A third group was also asked to omit breakfast and lunch, but when these people arrived for the experiment, they were presented with an array of foods and told to eat as much as they wished. The subjects in this group, who were then not at all hungry, were classified as low hunger.

All the subjects were put in individual rooms. The experimenter explained that the study actually involved four different tests. They were

TABLE 3–2
Effect of Hunger on Affiliation

	PERCENTAGE OF SUBJECTS CHOOSING	
Condition	Together	Alone
High hunger	67	33
Medium hunger	35	65
Low hunger	30	70

Source: Adapted from Schachter (1959).

called binocular redundancy, visual diplacity, auditory peripherality, and aural angular displacement, all meaningless terms made up just for this study. Each subject would take part in only one test. Two of the tests, the first and third, would be administered to two subjects at the same time while the second and fourth would be given to one subject at a time. In addition, before each test there would be an adaptation period during which the subjects would wait either with the other subject, if they chose the first or third test, or alone. The subjects then ranked the tests in the order in which they would like to take them. Thus, if they wanted to wait with another subject, they could choose test one or three; if they wanted to wait alone, they could choose test two or four.

The results, shown in Table 3–2, indicate that high hunger increased the preference for being with another subject. Of the subjects in the high-hunger condition, 67 percent chose a test in which they would wait with another subject; only 35 percent in the medium-hunger condition and 30 percent in the low-hunger condition chose one of those tests. Because moderate hunger is not a particularly unusual experience, it did not produce great uncertainty and did not lead to strong pressures toward affiliation for social comparison. By contrast, twenty hours of hunger, being unusual for these subjects, led to considerable uncertainty about feelings and therefore produced strong pressures toward affiliation for the purpose of social comparison.

Affiliation with Whom?

A more direct effect of the drive for social comparison can be seen when we examine whom the subjects want to affiliate with. One of the basic hypotheses of the theory is that people wish to compare themselves with others similar to them. The more similar they are, the stronger the drive for social comparison. For example, if a student is worried about a test and feels the need to find out how worried it is appropriate to be, does he want to talk to another student or the teacher? In most cases, another student. It would not help at all to find out that the teacher is not worried, because the teacher does not have to take the test. Moreover, the student wants to compare himself to others who are similar in ability. A better student may not be worried, but that would tell the poorer student very little about what is appropriate for himself. In comparing, he prefers some-one as close as possible to himself in ability, diligence, concern for grades, and so on. Such a student would give him the best information about how he should be feeling.

This leads to a clear prediction in terms of affiliation. To the extent that people affiliate for reasons of social comparison, they should have a stronger desire to affiliate with people who are similar to themselves than with people who are dissimilar. When they are concerned about evaluating their own emotions, they should particularly desire to affiliate with someone who is in their own situation.

Several studies have tested this prediction. Schachter (1959) used his standard procedure in which subjects were threatened with severe shock and then asked whether they would like to wait alone or with others. But for this experiment, the people with whom the subjects could wait were either other subjects who were waiting to take part in the study or students who had nothing to do with the experiment but who were waiting to talk to their advisers. In other words, one group of subjects was given a choice of waiting alone or with people who were similar to them; the other group was given a choice of waiting alone or with subjects who were quite different from them.

The results strongly supported the prediction from the theory of social comparison. Under high fear, subjects showed a strong preference for waiting with other subjects who were similar to them but did not want to wait with subjects who were different from them. However, in some sense the choice the subjects were given was not really fair. After all, there could have been considerable reluctance to walk into a room of students who were waiting to talk to their advisers, who may have known one another, and who certainly knew nothing about what the subject was doing.

A better test of the hypothesis was provided in a study by Zimbardo and Formica (1963), in which subjects were given the choice of waiting either with people who, like themselves, were about to take part in the study or with others who had just completed the study. The results of this test are more convincing because the people with whom the subject could wait were identical in both conditions, except that those who were about to take part in the study were presumably in the same emotional state as the subject making the choice whereas the others were in a different emotional state. Once again, the results supported the social-comparison hypothesis. Subjects showed a greater preference for waiting with those who were about to take part in the study than they did for waiting with those who had already been through the procedure. The more similar the others, the stronger was the drive to affiliate. Schachter has summarized these results: "Misery doesn't love just any company, it loves only miserable company."

However, fear and anxiety appear to affect somewhat differently whom people affiliate with. One study (Firestone et al., 1973) replicated

TABLE 3–3
Fear, Anxiety, and Type of Companionship

TYPE OF COMPANIONSHIP	AROUSED EMOTION	
Others	Fear	Anxiety
Similar	67%[a]	37%
Dissimilar	45%	66%

[a] Percent choosing to wait with others rather than alone.
Source: Based on Firestone et al. (1973).

the Schachter and the Zimbardo and Formica results for fear but got exactly the opposite with anxiety. Using the standard techniques, they aroused either high fear or high anxiety. Then, as in Schachter's study, subjects were told they could spend some time either alone or with other people. For half of the subjects, the other people were subjects in the same study; for half, they were people waiting in a room for some entirely different purpose. The results are shown in Table 3–3. You can see that frightened subjects wanted to wait with people like themselves and avoided being with others who were different, but anxious subjects did the reverse—they sought out dissimilar people.

© 1965 United Feature Syndicate, Inc.

Drawing by Charles Schulz.

A comparable result was reported in a study involving the amount of eye contact subjects would tolerate (Ellsworth et al., 1978). First, subjects were made either fearful or anxious (in this case concerned about being embarrassed), and then each subject waited with another person. This person either looked at the subject or looked away while they were together. The frightened subjects, who supposedly should want social comparison, preferred the person who looked at them. Obviously, it is easier to compare yourself with someone who is paying some attention to you and not entirely ignoring you. In contrast, the subjects who were worried about being embarrassed preferred the person who looked away and thus minimized the chance for social contact. Moreover, all of these results held mainly when the person was appropriate for social comparison.

These findings make sense if we take into account both motives—social comparison and the reduction of negative feelings. The fearful subjects seek out others to compare their levels of fear and perhaps also to reduce that fear; the anxious subjects avoid similar others because they think that will embarrass them and make them even more anxious since the others will know what they have just done or are about to do. On the other hand, perhaps they feel that being with irrelevant people will reduce their anxiety, the notion being that sitting with these other, normal people, will provide a contrast with the weird activities they are involved in. Whatever the exact explanation of these findings, this experiment does suggest that the characteristics of the group are very important. We still are uncertain what the effect would be if the members of the group were close friends rather than strangers. It might be that any negative or even strong feeling would cause most people to seek out their friends rather than be alone. For the moment, we do not know.

The Role of Uncertainty

The central assumption of the social comparison analysis is that uncertainty produces a need for comparing oneself to others. The more uncertain people feel about their reactions, the stronger should be this need for social comparison. Because the need for comparison leads to affiliation, the implication is that increasing uncertainty increases the desire to affiliate. A series of studies by Harold Gerard investigated this relationship between uncertainty and affiliation.

Gerard argued that merely arousing fear, as Schachter did, is not a very powerful way to make people want to compare themselves with others. The subjects in Schachter's experiment may not have been sure how frightened they should be, but they must have been sure that what they were feeling was appropriate (assuming they were frightened). In terms of the theory, the important factor influencing the strength of the desire for social comparison and consequently the drive toward affiliation should be the degree of uncertainty as to the appropriateness of one's feelings. When a person is extremely uncertain as to how she should be

Although we usually think of affiliation in a positive way, it can sometimes have negative or even frightening effects. People affiliate partly to reduce fear and partly for social comparison. Problems can arise when the group with whom a person affil-

BOX 3-3 The mass suicide at Jonestown may have been due in part to strong attachment to the leader, plus isolation from other influences.

United Press International.

iates has a distorted view of the world. Then, the person may find that his fear has been reduced, but he is surrounded by people with strange ideas. Since he *is* surrounded, and since the other people do make him feel good, he tends to accept these distorted views. While he may doubt them at first, they become strengthened by the fact that everyone around him shares them. He may thus come to accept such distorted views, no matter how unrealistic they are, and also to feel that he has no place in any other group, since now only this group shares his views. Thus arises a whole group of people who share similar ideas and views, who reinforce each other, who refuse to leave the group, but who are in a sense crazy.

It is quite possible that these mechanisms played a role in the Jonestown disaster, in which hundreds of people committed suicide because they accepted the distorted views of the leader and did what he ordered. The same dynamics may be at work in many fringe religious cults, in which members feel accepted and wanted by the group, take on its views, and then consider nonmembers as outsiders. Once they have joined and accepted the deviant views, the members have only other members to turn to for social comparison, since naturally everyone outside is different (i.e., they do not accept the views of the group). In terms of social comparison, once you have accepted a certain group as appropriate for comparison, you tend to judge yourself against them. Even if the group has strange, distorted, or crazy ideas, you may have no way of judging them and will tend to accept them as correct.

feeling, the drive for social comparison should be very high; the more certain she is that what she is feeling is appropriate, the weaker should be the drive for social comparison and the less the tendency to affiliate.

One critical factor affecting the degree of uncertainty is how much the person knows about her own feelings and the feelings of others. Thus, the more information she has about these feelings, the less the need for social comparison and, accordingly, the less the desire to affiliate. Gerard and Rabbie (1961) tested this hypothesis. The basic design of their experiment was similar to Schachter's. However, before the subjects chose to wait either alone or with others, some of them were given information about their reactions and those of the other subjects and some were not. In this way, the subjects' degree of uncertainty was manipulated directly, so that its effect could be clearly observed.

The procedure for informing the subjects of their reactions was quite ingenious. Each subject was seated in a separate cubicle, and electrodes were attached to his ring finger and forehead. The experimenter explained that these measuring devices gave an accurate picture of the subject's "emotionality," that is, recorded how afraid he was. Subjects in one condition were shown four dials, supposedly corresponding to the subject being tested and three others. The subject saw that he registered 82 on a

100-point scale and that the other subjects were registering 79, 80, and 81, respectively. Thus, he learned what he and the others were feeling and that they were all feeling about the same amount of fear. In another condition, the subjects were shown only their own rating, and in a third condition, they were given no information. Then all the subjects were asked to state their preference for waiting alone or with others.

The analysis of uncertainty in terms of social comparison implies that the desire to affiliate should be affected by the degree of uncertainty people feel about the appropriateness of their own reactions. Because they are concerned about how they compare with others, when they know their own and others' reactions and also that they all are experiencing about the same amount of fear, there should be little uncertainty. When they have either no information or information about only their own reaction, there should be considerable uncertainty. As shown in Table 3–4 the results agreed with these expectations. The subjects who had been given information about themselves and others showed the least preference for waiting together, whereas the other groups did not differ appreciably in their desire to affiliate. In other words, removing uncertainty—and therefore the need for social comparison—reduced the tendency to affiliate. This finding strongly supports the theory that one reason for affiliating is social comparison.

Uncertainty is also affected by the ambiguity of the information the person has about his own feelings and those of others. We have seen that the amount of information is an important determinant of affiliation. In addition, the more difficult it is to understand the information, the more uncertain the person should be and the greater should be his tendency to affiliate in order to reduce this uncertainty. In another study by Gerard (1963), subjects were shown dials that either wavered wildly or remained steady. Thus they had either clear or ambiguous information about fear levels. If one knows how afraid he is and how afraid others are, there is little to be gained by social comparison and therefore little need to af-

TABLE 3–4

Information, Fear, and Strength of Desire to Affiliate

Condition	STRENGTH OF DESIRE TO AFFILIATE[a]	
	High Fear	Low Fear
No information	66.80	54.53
Information about self	70.50	64.12
Information about self and others	55.09	47.67

[a] Figures are ratings on a scale from 0 to 100.
Source: Adapted from Gerard and Rabbie (1961).

TABLE 3–5

**Desire to Affiliate Related to Arousal and Knowledge
About the Arousal**

CONDITION	STRENGTH OF AFFILIATIVE TENDENCY
Placebo—no arousal	4.7
Caffeine—informed (Aroused and told what produced it)	4.5
Caffeine—misinformed (Aroused but not told what produced it)	5.4

Source: Adapted from Mills and Mintz (1972).

filiate. If the information is vague (and a rapidly oscillating needle on a meter is vague), there is good reason to affiliate—to find out what this vague information means. The study showed that with steady dials, subjects who knew their own and others' scores had little desire to affiliate; with wavering dials, however, even subjects who knew their own and others' scores had a strong need to affiliate.

The effect of uncertainty on affiliation was demonstrated in a particular elegant way in a recent study by Mills and Mintz (1972). The idea was to produce a physiological arousal by the use of a drug and to tell some subjects what had caused the arousal and not to tell others. Presumably those who knew that they had been aroused by the drug would feel little or no uncertainty about their emotional state, but those who did not know would feel uncertain as to what they were feeling and why. Therefore, those who knew that the drug had caused the arousal should feel little uncertainty and should not have a strong tendency to affiliate. Those who were aroused and did not know why should be quite uncertain and should have strong tendencies to affiliate. As you can see in Table 3–5, this is exactly what was found, once more supporting the notion that uncertainty is a major cause of the desire to affiliate.

All this evidence indicates that the need for social comparison is one reason why people affiliate. The major factor affecting the strength of this need seems to be the degree of uncertainty. The more uncertain they are about their feelings, the more they can gain by comparing themselves to others and, consequently, the greater the desire to affiliate.

THE EFFECT OF AFFILIATING

We have explained the effect of fear on affiliation in terms of two quite different mechanisms: the frightened person wants to affiliate in order to reduce his fear; he also wants to affiliate in order to compare his feelings with those of other people to discover if his feelings are appropriate. A somewhat separate but obviously related question is whether or not these two processes actually occur when affiliation is permitted. That is, does the individual become less afraid and does he compare his emotions?

If fear reduction is a rational reason for affiliating, waiting with other people should reduce fear even if the others are also afraid. If social comparison is a strong motive for affiliating, we would expect subjects to notice what others are feeling and to be concerned about the appropriateness of their own feelings. To the extent that their own feelings are different from those of the others (i.e., are inappropriate), subjects should tend to modify their feelings to make them less different. If everyone in the group does this, the feelings of the various members of the group should become more similar.

An experiment designed to test these two hypotheses was conducted by Wrightsman (1960). People who were very frightened were allowed to wait together or were forced to wait alone, and measures of fear level were taken before and after the waiting period. It was found that waiting in a group reduced fear more than waiting alone, with this applying particularly to first-born subjects. The group also showed a strong tendency toward uniformity of feeling.

McDonald (1970) also demonstrated the fear-reducing effect of waiting with others. However, this occurred primarily for first-born subjects and surprisingly was most strong for those first borns who said that they would prefer to wait alone but were forced to wait with others. Despite these somewhat perplexing findings, this study does provide more evidence that, in general, highly fearful subjects who wait in groups become less fearful. Thus both fear reduction and social comparison apparently do operate when people affiliate under conditions of high fear.

SUMMARY

1. Attachment between parent and child begins very early in the baby's life. Its development depends on the behavior and responses of both child and adult.

2. One theory is that the tendency to develop attachment is innate; it is wired into the organism because it is essential for the survival of the child. Attachment, according to this view, operates so as to keep parent and child close, thus providing the comfort and protection the child needs.

3. An alternative view is that attachment is learned, much like any other behavior or response. It is not innate, but may be due in part to the existence of innate behavior patterns that tend to produce reinforcements for the parent and child.

4. Affiliation may be instinctive, but there is no evidence to support this idea. On the other hand, our innate characteristics, especially the infant's long dependence on others for survival, forces us to affiliate.

5. Learning and the satisfaction of specific needs must also play a role in producing affiliation.

6. When people are afraid, they affiliate more. One reason for this is that people expect affiliation to reduce their fear. This is especially true of first borns who rely on others for relieving their fear more than do later borns.

7. Fear increases the desire for affiliation, but anxiety reduces it.

8. Another explanation of the effect of fear is that people are uncertain how they should be feeling, and they affiliate in order to compare their reactions with those of others. This tendency to evaluate ourselves by comparison with others is an important psychological principle called social comparison. A high degree of hunger also causes affiliation for purposes of social comparison.

9. According to the theory of social comparison, people should prefer to compare themselves to others who are similar to them. The research supports this prediction.

SUGGESTIONS FOR ADDITIONAL READING

BELL, R. Q. A reinterpretation of the direction of effects in studies of socialization. *Psychological Review*, 1968, 75, 81–95. A very influential article that points out the contribution of children to the parent-child bond.

BOWLBY, J. *Attachment*. New York: Basic Books, 1969. A full presentation of one point of view of how and why attachments are formed.

HARLOW, H. F. The nature of love. *American Psychologist*, 1958, 13, 673–85. This is the easiest discussion of Harlow's work on love, attachment, and motherhood among monkeys.

SCHACHTER, S. *The psychology of affiliation*. Stanford, Calif.: Stanford University Press, 1959. The major work on affiliation by a psychologist. A fine example of systematic research on a particular, important issue.

Social Perception

4

Jan Lukas; Rapho/Photo Researchers, Inc.

Affiliation is determined to some extent by one's expectations about interactions with other people and by one's knowledge of them. As we have seen, high anxiety reduces affiliation because one expects the interaction to be embarrassing; and high fear increases affiliation only if the other people are in a similar emotional state. Since our knowledge of and expectations about others are determined in part by impressions we form of them, it is appropriate now to consider the phenomenon of **person perception.** A glance at someone's portrait or at someone passing on the street gives us some ideas about the kind of person he is; even hearing a name tends to conjure up pictures of what its owner is like. And when two people meet, if only for an instant, they form impressions of each other. With more contact, they form fuller and richer impressions that pervade their entire relationship. These impressions determine how they behave toward each other, how much they like each other, whether the two associate often, and so on. First impressions are not only the beginning of social interaction, they are one of its major determinants. Consider the following situations.

A murder trial hinges on the testimony of one witness. The jury's belief in this witness, which will determine their decision, depends almost entirely on the impression they form of him in his brief time on the witness stand. They examine his face, his features, his clothes, the quality of his voice, and his answers and try to decide what kind of person he is.

Two freshmen who are destined to be roommates arrive at college and meet for the first time. Each one's personality—how easy he is to get along with, how nice he is—will have an enormous effect on the other's life. In the first few minutes of their meeting, they try to form an impression of each other, because they know they will be spending a great deal of time together during the year. They try to find out as much about each other as they can so they can behave accordingly.

People use whatever information is available to form impressions of others—to make judgments about their personalities, to adopt hypotheses about the kind of persons they are. This chapter deals with this process of social perception—with the kinds of information on which it is based, with the factors that affect it, and with the question of whether or not it is accurate, and the source of biases in it.

FORMING IMPRESSIONS

One important and apparently universal tendency is that people form extensive impressions of others on the basis of very limited information. Having seen someone or even her picture for only a few minutes, people tend to make judgments about a large number of her characteristics. Although ordinarily individuals are not overly confident of opinions formed in this way, they are generally willing to estimate the other's intelligence, age, background, race, religion, educational level, honesty, warmth, and so on. They would also tell us how much they thought they would like the other person if they could get to know her better and how much they like her at the moment. We shall discuss the accuracy of these first impressions below; for the present, it is important merely to note that people form impressions quickly on the basis of very little information.

Consistency

Moreover, given a few pieces of information, people tend to form consistent characterizations of others. In this respect, person perception is different from other kinds of perception. When people look at a house, a car, or any other complex object, they usually get a mixed impression. A house is large, is attractive, needs painting, has a nice dining room, is cold and unfriendly, and so on. In viewing a house, they do not force themselves to conclude that the whole house is warm or attractive. Objects do not have to be consistent. But there is a tendency to view another person as consistent, especially in an evaluative sense. The other person is not seen as both good and bad, honest and dishonest, warm and frightening, considerate and sadistic. Even when there is contradictory information about someone, he usually will be perceived as consistent. The perceivers distort or rearrange the information to minimize or eliminate the inconsistency. This may also happen to some extent when people perceive objects, but it is particularly strong in person perception.

Naturally, people do not always form consistent impressions of the other person's personality. There are times when two pieces of information about an individual are so contradictory that most people are unable to fit them into a consistent pattern. In such a situation, some may succeed in forming a pattern. Others, unable to resolve the inconsistencies between the contradictory qualities, end up with a relatively unintegrated impression. However, there are strong tendencies toward forming a unified impression of another person, even though the attempt to do so is not always successful.

Evaluation

The most important and powerful aspect of first impressions is **evaluation.** Do we like this person or dislike her? How much do we like her or dislike her? Our immediate impression may be composed of other dimensions, but they tend mainly to be parts of an overall warm, lukewarm, cool, or cold response.

Put more formally, the evaluative dimension is the most important of a small number of basic dimensions that organize these unified impressions. This was shown in work by Osgood, Suci, and Tannenbaum (1957) on the so-called **semantic differential.** Subjects were given a list of word pairs denoting opposite ends of various dimensions and were asked to indicate where on these dimensions they felt particular concepts, persons, objects, and ideas fell. The list consisted of such dimensions as happy-sad, hot-cold, and red-blue, and the items the subjects had to place ranged from mothers to boulders.

When the subjects' responses were collected, Osgood and his associates analyzed them to see if any clusters of adjectives emerged that could be considered basic dimensions on which all things had been described. They found that three dimensions accounted for a large percentage of the variation in all descriptions. By determining where subjects had placed a particular item on the dimensions of *evaluation* (good-bad), *potency* (strong-weak), and *activity* (active-passive), the experimenters needed little additional information in order to describe that item fully. To a large extent, all other dimensions (e.g., brave-scared, polite-blunt) were aspects of these major dimensions and not separate attributes.

This phenomenon is most dramatic when applied to the perception of people. Impressions of people can also be described in terms of the three basic dimensions, but one dimension—evaluation—accounts for most of the variance in them and appears to be the main distinction made. Once we place someone on this dimension, much of the rest of our perception of him or her falls into place. A favorable or unfavorable impression in one context, at one meeting, extends to all other situations and to other seemingly unrelated characteristics.

Later research has used much more sophisticated mathematical techniques, but it has mainly supported these early results: evaluation is by far the most important underlying dimension of person perception. But it has also led to the identification of two distinct dimensions of evaluation in common use. Rosenberg, Nelson, and Vivekananthan (1968), using

TABLE 4–1
Social and Intellectual Traits Used in Evaluation of People

EVALUATION	SOCIAL	INTELLECTUAL
Favorable	Helpful	Scientific
	Sincere	Determined
	Tolerant	Skillful
	Sociable	Intelligent
	Humorous	Persistent
Unfavorable	Unhappy	Foolish
	Vain	Frivolous
	Irritable	Wavering
	Boring	Unreliable
	Unpopular	Clumsy

Source: Rosenberg, Nelson, and Vivekananthan (1968), p. 290.

a procedure called multidimensional scaling, found people evaluated others in terms of their *social* and their *intellectual* qualities. Some of the traits which were most common are shown in Table 4–1.

These results suggest that people do evaluate others in a slightly more complex fashion than implied above. At least they sometimes think in terms of separate interpersonal and task-related qualities. However, this distinction does not alter the basic point: people think primarily in terms of liking and disliking when they perceive other people—that is, evaluation is the main dimension in person perception.

The Averaging Principle

How do people form an impression of someone when they have many pieces of information about him? What is the process by which these impressions are formed? The two main competing approaches emphasize either learning or cognitive factors. The learning approach, in its simplest form, suggests that people combine information in a rather mechanical, simple-minded fashion. People tend to reflect the stimulus situation in a fairly straightforward manner and not give much thought to it. If someone hears mainly favorable things about a person, she develops a favorable impression of him. If she hears mainly unfavorable or lukewarm things, she develops that kind of impression instead.

As applied to impression formation, this has evolved into an **averaging principle** (Anderson, 1965). The way it works is this: Traits can be rated in terms of how positive they are. For example, sincerity is generally considered an extremely favorable quality, and accordingly, people usually assign it the maximum value (+3); determination is only moderately favorable (+1); dishonesty is very unfavorable (−3). The question is how people combine these traits to form an overall evaluation. If an individual is known to have one highly positive trait, and one slightly positive trait, how positively is she rated? The averaging model suggests that someone who is rated sincere (+3) and also determined (+1) would receive an overall evaluation that was approximately an average of the two traits—that is, he would be considered moderately positive (+2). Thus, discovering a new trait that is only slightly positve in someone, when we already know she has a highly positive trait reduces the overall evaluation, even though both pieces of information are positive.

Norman Anderson, in a series of careful and precise experiments (e.g., 1959, 1965), produced strong evidence to support the averaging model. He found that when a piece of information that is only moderately favorable is combined with a previous evaluation that had been based on very favorable information, the overall evaluation did not increase and could even decrease. Similarly, two strongly negative traits produced a more negative evaluation than two strongly negative plus two moderately negative traits. To make an even better fit with the data, he later used a weighted averaging model (1968). He presented data showing that people form an overall impression by averaging all traits but giving more weight to polarized (highly positive or highly negative) traits.

This body of research as a whole indicates quite convincingly that the major principle accounting for impression formation is the weighted average. Researchers in this area share a broad consensus that an averaging principle is the dominant, though probably not the only, principle at work in impression formation. The averaging principle has the additional advantage of simplicity, or parsimony, so it is to be preferred, everything else being equal. But some important exceptions to it occur where more complex principles are required. And most of these are derived from the perceptual-cognitive approach.

Exceptions to the Averaging Principle

The perceptual-cognitive approach, in contrast, assumes that people form coherent, thoughtful, impressions. They do not just mechanically average incoming information, but arrive at some meaningful gestalt that makes organized sense out of the full input. Each piece of information is taken as an aspect of a coherent whole, rather than as simply another isolated trait. For the most part these two approaches do lead to the same predictions about impression formation. But there are some differences.

CENTRAL TRAITS One difference concerns whether or not certain traits imply more about an individual than do others. The learning approach simply assumes that all traits are plugged into the same averaging process at whatever value they have. The perceptual-cognitive approach assumes that some traits are inherently more meaningful than others. For example, the pair of traits warm-cold appears to be associated with a great number of other characteristics, whereas the pair polite-blunt, under most circumstances, is associated with fewer. Traits that are highly associated with many other characteristics have been called **central traits.**

In a classic demonstration of their importance, Asch (1946) gave subjects a description of an individual that contained seven traits—intelligent, skillful, industrious, warm, determined, practical, and cautious. Other subjects were given exactly the same list except that *cold* was substituted for *warm*. Both groups of subjects were then asked to describe the individual and also to indicate which of various pairs of traits he would most likely possess. The portraits elicited from the two groups were extremely different; substituting *cold* for *warm* made a substantial change in the subjects' impression of the other person. In another condition, instead of the warm-cold pair, Asch used polite-blunt. He found that substituting *polite* for *blunt* made considerably less difference in the overall picture formed by the subjects.

A later study by Kelley (1950) replicated this result in a more realistic setting. Students in psychology courses were given descriptions of a guest lecturer before he spoke. The descriptions included seven adjectives similar to those Asch used: half the students received a description containing the word *warm,* and the other half were told the speaker was *cold;* in all other respects their lists were identical. The lecturer then came into the class and led a discussion for about twenty minutes, after which the students were asked to give their impressions of him. The results are shown in Table 4–2. As in the Asch study, there were great differences between the impressions formed by students who were told he was warm and those who were told he was cold. In addition, those students who expected the speaker to be warm tended to interact with him more freely and to initiate more conversations with him. Thus, the different descriptions affected not only the students' impressions of the other person, but also their behavior toward him.

CONTEXT Another difference stems from the fact that the context also affects judgments. The contribution of any given attribute to our overall impression of a stimulus person will depend on the rest of the information we have about him. Knowing that someone is "intelligent," generally quite a good attribute, will not have as favorable an impact on our impression of a "cold, ruthless" person as it will on our impression of a "warm, caring" person. The context is different, and so is the impact of the trait. These context effects are closely related to the tendency to form consistent impressions. Good traits go together. Someone who is warm is also seen as positive in other respects, thus producing a consistent picture. They cause a person's traits to be distorted to produce consistency within an impression. This does not mean we only perceive people as good or as bad. But it does mean that we distort incoming information in that direction.

The mechanism producing such context effects is a matter of some debate. Anderson (1966), consistent with his learning approach, suggested that the influence of the context on the value of the new attribute is an

TABLE 4–2

**Effect of "Warm" and "Cold" Descriptions
on Ratings of Other Qualities**

	INSTRUCTIONS[a]	
Quality	Warm	Cold
Self-centered	6.3	9.6
Unsociable	5.6	10.4
Unpopular	4.0	7.4
Formal	6.3	9.6
Irritable	9.4	12.0
Humorless	8.3	11.7
Ruthless	8.6	11.0

[a] The higher the rating, the more the person was perceived as
having the quality.
Source: Adapted from Kelley (1950).

average of the value of the new attribute standing alone and the value of
the context. In this example, suppose "intelligent" is a +2 when it is considered all by itself. And suppose the joint value of "cold, ruthless," is −4.
Then, in this context, "intelligent" would be an average of the two, or
about −1. On the other hand, if the value of "warm, caring" is +4, you
can readily see that "intelligent" would come in around +3 in that context. Anderson describes this effect of context as a *generalized halo effect.*
As you can see, he does not assume much deliberate thought; the new attribute merely mechanically absorbs some of the good or bad feelings
associated with the context.

Asch (1946), on the other hand, worked mainly out of the perceptual-
cognitive approach. To him the whole is more than a mechanical average
of its parts. The perceiver creates a meaningful whole out of whatever information he is given, and the whole will change with different information. So any given attribute will have different *meaning* if it is placed in a
different context. Wearing only a bikini has quite a different meaning in a
symphony concert hall than it does on a summer beach, and would be
evaluated quite differently, even though it, and both contexts, are all
quite pleasant. In other words, Asch says a new attribute undergoes a
shift-of-meaning when it is placed in a new context. "Intelligence" in a
cold, ruthless person could be threatening, potentially hostile, and
destructive. In a warm, caring person, "intelligence" might be expected to
contribute to empathy, to insight, and to the ability to give to another person.

A good bit of research has been done on these two different explanations for context effects. One way to approach the controversy is to determine whether in fact the attribute shifts meaning in different contexts.
Hamilton and Zanna (1974, 1977); did find that the connotations of a par-

ticular trait changed when placed in different contexts. For example, in a positive context the word "proud" bore the connotation of "confident." In a negative context, it connoted "conceited." Similarly, Wyer (1974) found that the evaluations of these connotations also reflected the context. To use the example above, the quality ("conceited") of the original trait ("proud") implied by a negative context itself bore a negative evaluation. Such studies show that contextual effects are partly determined by a **shift-of-meaning** phenomenon, consistent with Asch's applications of a Gestalt approach.

THE NEGATIVITY EFFECT Another exception is that positive and negative traits are not treated exactly alike. Although people average available traits to arrive at a complete impression, they weight negative information more heavily than they do positive information. That is, a negative trait affects an impression more than does a positive trait, everything else being equal. This has been termed the **negative effect.** It follows that a positive impression is easier to change than a negative one (Hodges, 1974; Warr, 1974). Subjects are more confident of evaluations based on negative traits than of those based on positive traits (Hamilton & Zanna, 1972). And it also follows that the averaging principle does not hold for negative traits quite as well as it does for positive traits. This difference is particularly noticeable with the more extreme negative traits. Instead of simply being averaged in, the way moderately negative (or any positive) traits are, they seem to have a "blackball" effect: one extremely negative trait produces an extremely negative impression, no matter what other traits the person possesses (Anderson, 1965). When we are told that a prominent public leader is "a crook," our evaluation of him becomes quite negative, regardless of what else we know about him. But if we are told he is "impatient," we will just average that mildly negative quality in with whatever else we know about him.

There are two main explanations, at the moment, for this negativity effect. The first is based on the figure-ground notion we discussed earlier in connection with the perceptual-cognitive approach. As we will see below, positive evaluations of other people are much more common than negative evaluations. Negative traits, being more unusual, are therefore more distinctive. In a simple perceptual sense, then, a negative trait is *figural;* it stands out the way an unusual deformity or bright clothing or something of unusual size stands out. People may then simply attend more to those negative qualities and thus give them more weight in arriving at an overall impression. The second is a *cost-orientation* notion, based on an incentive theory approach (Kanouse & Hanson, 1972). The idea is that people are more concerned with costs than benefits when they make a decision. As a result, they scan the alternatives more carefully for their defects than for their assets, and take possible defects more seriously in making the decision. Your boyfriend might be very nice, and your parents like him, but if you think you might want to throw up every morning when

ELECTING A BAD PRESIDENT: A COSTLY ERROR

The negativity effect implies that voters are influenced in their decisions more by whatever negative things they might hear about each candidate than by the positive things. Lau (1979) used the reasons that survey respondents offered as to why they might vote for or against each presidential candidate as indications of the amount of positive and negative information they had about the candidate. Consistent with the negativity effect he found that the amount of negative information each voter had was more important than the amount of positive information in determining liking for the candidate.

He went on to explore the two standard explanations for the negativity effect. The figure-ground hypothesis would imply that negative information should be relatively more important for those who perceived a positive political world (trusted more politicians, thought they were competent), for whom negative information would therefore be more unusual, and *figural.* By the same reasoning, positive information should be relatively more impor-

tant for those who perceived a negative political world. The cost-orientation hypothesis suggests that when potential costs and gains are high, people are more strongly motivated to avoid costs than to approach gains. So Lau hypothesized that negative information would be relatively more important than positive information to those who cared about the outcome of the elections, than to those who did not care.

Lau found strong support for the cost-orientation hypothesis in explaining negativity in the evaluations of presidential candidates. When he examined congressional elections, he found stronger support for the figure-ground hypothesis. Lau suggests that when potential costs and gains are fairly high, as in electing a president, cost orientation is probably the best explanation for negativity. But when the potential costs and gains are much lower, as in electing only one of 435 congressmen, negativity is probably best explained by the perceptual (figure-ground) model.

you have to look at his ugly face, you probably will decide against marrying him. Either way, the negativity effect seems to be a fairly reliable one and depends in part on the more uncommon nature of negative traits and evaluations.

CUES IN IMPRESSION FORMATION

Both the averaging and the perceptual-cognitive approach assume that information comes in to us in piecemeal fashion, which we then combine into a consistent impression. But what is the nature of these inputs?

That is, what cues do we use to form an impression of another person? There are three main categories of cues: the *person* himself or herself, the person's *behavior,* and the context or *situation* the person is in. The quarterback on the football team has a reputation, perhaps as a pinpoint passer, a slow runner, and a good leader. Perhaps you see him play in the first game of your freshman year, and he completes a string of six straight passes in the last quarter, including a decisive touchdown to help the team in a come-from-behind win. It is an important game against a highly rated opponent. So you use all this information in forming your impression. You combine your knowledge of his reputation as a player with your perception of his behavior in the game, in a pressure-packed situation, and come away from the game thinking he is a potential all-conference star.

All of this is fairly straightforward. You focus on information that is relevant to the judgment you want to make, and come to a reasonable conclusion. This simple classification covers most of the cues people do use in impression formation. However, a couple of categories of cues warrant a little more discussion, because people are often not aware of how much they are really influenced by them.

Physical Appearance

One of the first things we notice about another person is his or her physical appearance. Potentially this could involve a great many things. Only certain aspects of appearance have been shown to influence an impression markedly, however (Fiske, 1978). A person's physique is important—its size, type, and health. Extremes of height and weight are quickly noticed. Handicaps attract much attention, and unfortunately, tend to stigmatize the person, as we shall see later. Facial features, including pupil size and mouth curvature, also affect impressions. Hair color is particularly noticeable. Impressions are also influenced by various aspects of the persons' grooming such as fashionableness of clothing, cosmetics, glasses, body odors, and breath odors. Overall, physical attractiveness proves to be one of the most important factors in first impressions, though it becomes less important as people become better acquainted, as we will see in Chapter 6.

The classifications of age, sex, and race, represent even broader determinants of physical appearance, and are enormously important in forming first impressions. Most people have stereotypes about men, women, older people, younger people, whites, and blacks, and even of specific combinations of these characteristics. For example, they may think of men as being strong, of older people as being wise in experience but often not very "with it," of blacks as having good senses of humor, and so on. When people give the physical appearance of belonging to one of these groups, there is a tendency to attribute these stereotypical qualities to them. Again, further acquaintance with the person can override this initial impression (or if you like, prejudice, because it really is

Peter Menzel and Tim Carlson.; Stock, Boston.

FIGURE 4-2 Although it is usually a mistake to assume that appearances tell us much about people, it is difficult to avoid forming very different impressions of the two people pictured here.

pre-judging). But it is undeniable that our group membership, insofar as it influences our physical appearance, has a powerful influence over impressions others have of us. We will discuss this more in Chapter 12.

Indeed, a successful book, *Black Like Me,* was written on just that premise, by a white man who spent several months traveling around the country in blackface posing as a black man. It documents in exquisite and poignant detail the radical difference it makes in one's reception by strangers whether they believe you are white or black. As an exercise, you might try to imagine your reaction if some olive-skinned acquaintance of yours, whom you had always thought to be "white," should tell you she is in fact "black." Or suppose she tells you she has an artificial leg, or that she is really over 40, even though you thought she was the age of most college students. How would your impression change?

Nonverbal Communication

In making judgments of other people, language, what the person says, is a particularly important source of information. But it is generally accompanied by a whole set of much subtler cues that may influence our impressions, but of which we are usually not aware. These are called *nonverbal communication,* or ways in which we transmit information without using language. A variety of kinds of nonverbal communication have been identified, some of which use speech, and others, movements of the body.

PARALANGUAGE Variations in speech other than the actual words and syntax, or **paralanguage,** carry a great deal of meaning. Pitch of the voice, loudness, rhythm, inflections, and hesitations, also convey information. Parents can often tell whether their baby is hungry, angry, or just mildly cranky by how it cries. Dogs bark in different ways and each means something different to someone familiar with the animal. And, of course, the significance and meaning of adult speech depend in part on these paralinguistic factors. A simple statement such as "You want to go to medical school," can mean entirely different things depending on emphasis and inflection. Say it aloud as a flat statement with no emphasis, with an inflection (rising voice) at the end, and it becomes a question. Then say it with added emphasis on the first word and it turns into a question as to whether or not the person addressed is qualified. These variations are often crucial in conveying emotions.

The short phrase "I like you" may indicate almost anything from mild feeling to intense passion depending on paralinguistic characteristics of how it is said. In fact, these variations are so important that they often must be added to written language. Using our earlier example, to show that someone thought medical school was an unlikely choice the sentence might read "'You want to go to medical school,' he said sarcastically (or disbelievingly)," or "'I like you,' she murmured passionately." Without these clues, the statements are difficult to interpret unless you know what is intended from the whole context.

Another line of rather sensitive observation of social interaction has been conducted by Starkey Duncan (1972; Duncan & Fiske, 1977) on the course of two-person conversations. When you think about it, a conversation involves quite a bit of coordination; people have to take turns, not interrupt, give feedback in ways that don't disrupt the speaker, and so on. How do they manage all that? Certainly they do not do it through direct verbal communication; people rarely say, "OK, now I'm done, it's your turn," or "Shut up, you've talked long enough, let me talk now" (though of course they do when desperate enough). Instead, Duncan argues that a number of very specific nonverbal cues tip people off as to when to take their turn in the conversation. A pause in the speaker's flow, a turn of the speaker's head toward the listener, and a drop in pitch or loudness in the final syllables of a word all were associated with yielding the floor to the listener. In addition, while one person is speaking, a listener who is not ready to take his turn engages in "back-channel communication," presenting signals that cue the speaker to continue. This may consist of "yeah" or "uh-huh," head nods, or smiles (Brunner, 1979). All of these provide feedback to the speaker on several levels at once.

One of the difficulties in studying paralanguage (and most other kinds of nonverbal behavior) is that variations are ambiguous. We all agree on the meaning of words. We all know what "medical school" refers to, and with some variations we know that when someone says he "likes" you, he is making a statement of positive feelings. But people differ considerably in the meanings they attach to paralinguistic variations. For some people a pause may be for emphasis, for others it may mean uncertainty; higher pitch may mean excitement or lying; loudness can be anger, emphasis, or excitement. The particular meaning depends on the context (if the speaker talks louder and makes a fist at you, it is anger), and also on individual habits and characteristics of the person. Thus, the problem of interpreting paralinguistic cues is enormous. We cannot conceive of a dictionary of such cues because they do not have specific, fixed meanings. Rather they depend on all the other factors we have mentioned.

GESTURES In recent years there have been many popular books dealing with gestures, or **body language** as they are sometimes called. These books have suggested that you can tell exactly what someone is thinking or perfectly interpret what they say by merely observing their bodily movements and posture. An open palm is an invitation, crossed legs are defensive, and so on. Unfortunately, these books are generally not based on scientific research and should be read with healthy skepticism. No one has constructed a reliable dictionary of gestures. Even more than with paralanguage, the meaning of gestures depends on the context, the person doing the action, the culture, and probably other factors also. An open palm is not always an invitation, as would be obvious to anyone who thought of the familiar gesture of putting up your hand palm out to mean "stop" not "go," or the reverse gesture with the palm in and the fingers moving toward the body to mean "come" or "enter."

However, this is by no means meant to deny that bodily gestures and posture carry information; clearly they do. They range from straightforward, direct gestures to very subtle ones. There are many bodily movements that are generally accepted and which convey specific information or directions. The gestures for "stop" and "come" are examples, as are pointing and gestures for "sit down," "yes," "no," "go away," "goodby," and various obscene gestures that have well-known meanings. In a sense all of these gestures are sign language for words. But it must be remembered that they are meaningul mainly when the context is well understood, and especially when the culture is.

EYE CONTACT Eye contact is an especially interesting form of nonverbal communication. As with other forms of nonverbal communication, the meaning of eye contact varies greatly and depends on the context; but in nearly all social interactions eye contact does communicate information.

To begin with, eye contact is used to regulate conversations. Typically, a speaker looks away as he starts talking and looks up just before finishing. Looking away seems to prevent the listener from responding or interrupting while looking up signals the end of a thought and allows the other to talk (Kendon, 1967).

Eye contact also indicates interest or the lack of it. Hollywood movies often have a couple staring into each other's eyes to portray love, affection, or great concern. Certainly we are all familiar with eye contact held for a long time, as a means of demonstrating attraction for someone. An otherwise casual conversation can become an expression of romantic interest if one of the speakers maintains eye contact. Conversely, avoiding or breaking the contact is usually a sign that the person is not interested. Indeed, when someone does not make eye contact during a conversation, we tend to interpret this as an indication that he or she is not really involved in what is going on. No matter how attentively someone answers questions, nods at appropriate times, and carries on the conversation, lack of eye contact means he is not interested in what we are saying.

However, there are obvious exceptions to this general principle. Lack of eye contact can sometimes mean that the person is shy or frightened. In addition, someone who is conveying bad news or saying something painful may avoid eye contact. And avoiding eye contact can be a way of respecting someone's privacy when discussing an intimate subject.

FIGURE 4-3 Leaning forward and gazing into the other's eyes usually implies strong attraction. We would be surprised if he were not in love, or at least, very fond of the person facing him.

When people have feelings they are embarrassed about, they do not like to be the focus of a direct gaze. In a study by Ellsworth and colleagues (1978), female college students were told they would have to discuss questions "about rather intimate personal areas of your life, things that college students usually do not like to talk about." Each then had to wait with a confederate who either stared directly at her 75 percent of the time, or one who just glanced at her once. By far most subjects preferred the gaze-averting confederate. Other subjects who were not expecting an embarrassing conversation did not prefer the gaze-averted confederate. The direct gaze apparently threatened the embarrassed girls.

Moreover, eye contact can be used to threaten. In several studies, experimenters stared at or did not stare at people who were walking past a street corner. Those who were stared at walked across the street faster than those in the no-stare condition. Similarly, when the experimenters stared at people in cars, they drove through the intersection more quickly, or stopped before the intersection, or averted their eyes (Ellsworth et al., 1972; Greenbaum & Rosenfeld, 1978). In another experiment, someone stared at a subject who was in a position to act aggressively toward the starer. Subjects who were stared at were less aggressive than when there

WHAT'S IN A SMILE?

Smiling, for example, might most obviously be thought to reflect the underlying emotion of happiness or joy. Anything that makes people happy ought to make them smile. Alternatively, smiling might be a communicative act—it might have little or nothing to do with the person's underlying emotion, but might instead be a gesture of friendliness. Kraut and Johnston (1979) observed a large number of people in ordinary interaction to test this contrast. They found that bowlers smiled when engaging in social contact, such as looking at their friends, but not when avoiding social contact, such as looking at the ground. However, their smiling was only weakly related to happiness; they smiled 30 percent of the time after a spare or a strike, and 23 percent of the time otherwise. In another set of observations, the researchers checked whether the smiling of pedestrians is caused by being with friends, and therefore by engaging in social interaction, or by the happiness caused by good weather. As this table shows, the weather had very little effect.

Percent of Pedestrians Smiling

	GOOD WEATHER	BAD WEATHER
Social interaction	61%	57%
No interaction	12%	5%

Source: Kraut and Johnston, 1979.

Being with friends, however had a strong effect. So it would seem that smiling is part of social interaction—a nonverbal technique of communication—more than an intrinsic sign of happy emotions.

was no staring (Ellsworth & Carlsmith, 1975). Apparently prolonged eye contact can be interpreted as a threat and causes people to escape or act in a conciliatory manner.

It is perhaps not surprising that eye contact can have two seemingly contradictory meanings—friendship or threat. In both cases, eye contact indicates greater involvement and higher emotional content. Whether the emotion is positive or negative depends on the context. Once again, the nonverbal communication has no fixed meaning and therefore must be interpreted by means of other information about the other person and about the situation.

CONFLICTING CUES How do people reconcile conflicting verbal and nonverbal cues from another person? A particularly important area of such conflcts is when people are lying or otherwise trying to deceive observers. Police, judges, and jurors are constantly trying to learn the truth from people who try to mislead them. A number of studies have been done to determine how good people are at detecting lying, and what cues they use in detecting it.

Many people are able to tell when others are lying, at least at better than a chance level. Not surprisingly, they can detect the fact of lying better than they can figure out the nature of the liar's true feelings. The cues people use in detecting lying fall into two categories. First, they listen closely to the content of the person's statements, particularly implausible or self-serving statements. Second, they notice paralinguistic cues.

For example, it may be possible to tell when someone is lying by noting the pitch of their voice. Several studies (Ekman et al., 1976; Krauss et al., 1976) indicate that the average (or more technically, fundamental) pitch of the voice is higher when someone is lying than when he or she is telling the truth. The difference is small and one cannot tell just by listening. However, electronic vocal analysis reveals lying with considerable accuracy. In addition, shorter answers, longer delays in responding, and more nervous, less serious answers all are characteristic of people perceived as liars or of people instructed to tell lies (Apple, Streeter, & Krauss, 1979; Kraut, 1978).

Aside from speech content, some observers feel that gestures are a truer indication of feeling than words. Ekman and Friesen (1974) argue that people attend more to what they are saying than to what they are doing with their bodies. If they are trying to deceive someone, for example, they may lie verbally in a calm way but reveal their true emotions through nonverbal cues. In Ekman's terms, there is *nonverbal leakage,* in which true emotions "leak out" even if the person tries to conceal them. For example a student may say she is not nervous about a test, but will bite her lower lip and blink more than usual, actions that often indicate nervousness. A young man waiting for a job interview may attempt to appear calm and casual, but will cross and uncross his legs continually, straighten his tie, touch his face, play with his hair. As a result, he will in fact come across as a nervous wreck.

In general, people are perceived much more accurately when visual information is available as well as such purely verbal messages, as a typed transcript (Archer & Akert, 1977). Visual cues are especially valuable when they conflict with what a person is saying (de Paulo et al., 1978).

On the other hand, as we have said repeatedly, there is nothing magically or unambiguously communicative about nonverbal cues. Most of them can communicate a variety of messages depending on the context. A touch on the arm by an attractive acquaintance means something quite different from the same touch made by a derelict in a subway station. Being tapped on the shoulder by your boss may mean something still different. A smile on the face of a bully as he moves in on a helpless prey means something quite different from the smile on your girlfriend's face when she sees you walking across the campus. Nonverbal cues can be highly informative, but only when they are solidly embedded in a familiar context, in which we know the role of the other person, have some notion of his or her general goals, know the norms for the situation, and so on. When we do not have a known or familiar context, as for instance on a first visit to a foreign country, we frequently feel lost and can make very little sense of nonverbal cues.

ACCURACY OF JUDGMENTS

How accurately do people usually perceive others? One argument is that people must be reasonably accurate in order for society to function as smoothly as it does. After all, we interact with other people hundreds of times every day, and most of these interactions seem to require accurate judgments of others. Since most interactions proceed without serious conflict or mistake, person perception must be fairly accurate.

It is generally no more difficult to judge the height of a man than it is to judge the height of a bookcase, a car, or a camel. The same is true of weight, color, and even attractiveness. We make these kinds of judgments about the external attributes of all objects and we make them fairly accurately. Similarly as long as the appropriate cues are provided, it is fairly easy to make judgments about somebody's role. We recognize that the woman standing behind a counter in a clothing store is a salesperson and we ask her how much a particular item costs. The man in the blue suit with the gun strapped to his side is a policeman and we treat him accordingly. The man rushing down a platform toward a train is obviously in a hurry and we get out of his way to make it easier for him to catch the train. The contexts in which we see the people enable us to make accurate assumptions about their roles and sometimes even their emotions and feelings.

But where person perception is unique and difficult, is when we try to infer individuals' internal states—feelings, emotions, and personalities. The bookcase obviously has none of these; the car has them only in advertisements and fantasies; perhaps the camel has them, but we usually do not worry about camels. However, we do attempt to make judgments of the internal states of human beings. We look at people and perceive them as being angry, happy, sad, or frightened. We form an impression of another person and think of him as warm, honest, and sincere. We also make judgments about such internal characteristics as a person's attitudes toward various issues. We guess whether he is a Republican or a Democrat, religious or nonreligious, an environmentalist or not.

Under most circumstances, judgments of internal states are extremely difficult. The internal state cannot be observed directly—it must be inferred from whatever cues are available. Therefore, we must restate our aim in studying the accuracy of judgments and the cues on which they are based. We are interested primarily in determining the kinds of judgments individuals can make of internal states and the cues on which these judgments of emotion, personality, and attitude are based.

How a person is feeling—whether he is happy or afraid, horrified or disgusted—is a type of judgment we often make. Therefore, much of the work on the accuracy of person perception has focused on the recognition of emotions. It began in 1872 when Darwin asserted, on the basis of his evolutionary theory, that facial expressions universally conveyed the same emotional states. Such universal signals would have great survival value for *homo sapiens,* a very social animal.

Are there such universals—that is, particular facial expressions or body postures for each emotion? Does everyone who is feeling a particular emotion have the same facial expression, or are there great variations among people in how they manifest the same emotion? Is it possible, for example, that one person's expression of disgust is another person's expression of contentment? (See Figure 4–4.)

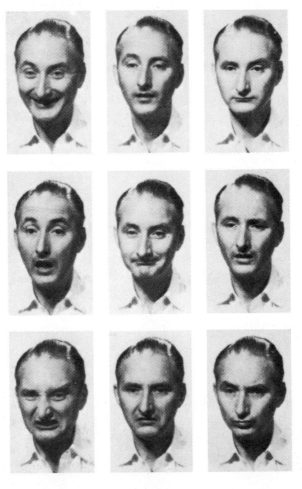

FIGURE 4–4 Examples of stimuli used in the study of the perception of emotions. The photographs illustrate expressions posed to portray the emotions listed. (You might try to identify them before looking at the key below.)

Top (left to right): Glee, passive adoration, complacency. Middle: Amazement, optimistic determination, dismay. Bottom: Rage, mild repugnance, puzzlement. (From Hastorf et al., 1966.)

Experimenters have studied quite actively how accurately people can make inferences about emotional states. The basic procedure is to present a subject with a stimulus representing another person and ask the subject to identify the other's emotion. For some studies, trained actors portrayed a number of different emotions, and pictures were taken of their expressions. One picture was chosen for each emotion. These were then shown to subjects, who were asked to indicate what emotion was depicted. Some of these pictures are shown in Figure 4–5. Other studies have used different stimuli such as real people or disembodied voices.

Given this wide range of techniques, it is perhaps not surprising that the results have also been varied. Early studies seemed to indicate that people could not judge emotions at better than a chance level. However, later studies have shown that subjects can discriminate among groups of emotions, even if they cannot discriminate perfectly between each individual emotion. Woodworth (1938) suggested that emotions can be arranged on a six-point continuum, with confusion between any two emotions being inversely related to the distance they are from each other. The six groups of emotions are

1. love, happiness, mirth
2. surprise
3. fear, suffering
4. anger, determination
5. disgust
6. contempt

Apparently people are quite adept at distinguishing emotions in categories that are three, four, or five points apart—they rarely confuse happiness with disgust or contempt with surprise. But they are much poorer at discriminating emotions that are closer on the continuum and find it almost impossible to discriminate emotions in the same category or only

FIGURE 4–5 The people pictured here have very different expressions on their faces and appear to be experiencing different emotions. Yet they were all in the same photograph, which was taken while they were witnessing a rally. They may, in fact, be feeling different emotions. On the other hand, they may simply be expressing the same emotion in different ways.

one group away. There is also some evidence, collected by Thompson and Meltzer (1964), that even on this continuum some emotions are more consistently identified than others. Happiness, love, fear, and determination tend to be relatively easy to discriminate, whereas disgust, contempt, and suffering are much more difficult.

It now appears that Darwin was approximately correct after all. At least at this rough level, a given facial expression does seem to convey approximately the same emotion throughout the world. Ekman and Friesen (1971) conducted a study on recognition of emotion from facial expressions with natives of New Guinea who had seen no movies, understood neither English nor Pidgin, had not lived in any of the Western settlement or government towns, and had never worked for a Caucasian. Presumably these subjects had had no visual contact with conventional Western facial expression of emotions. Each of these subjects was given a brief story depicting an emotion, such as, for "sadness," "His child has died, and he feels very sad." Then he was given one photograph that Western observers overwhelmingly agreed depicted that emotion, and two pictures depicting other emotions. On the average, adults chose the "correct" picture more than 80 percent of the time. Children were only asked to choose between one correct and one incorrect picture, but they averaged 90 percent correct. This does not prove there are no cultural differences in the facial expression of emotion, but it does provide evidence of universals that transcend cultural boundaries. In particular, happiness, anger, and interest can be detected with high levels of agreement both within and across culture; and fear, sorrow, and shame are also recognized at a significant level.

There are some necessary qualifications to these findings, however. Cultural norms do differ substantially in amount of emotional expression. Swedes tend to be relatively impassive, while Italians are quite expressive. Sometimes norms forbid honest expression, as for instance a disgusted reaction to someone with a terrible deformity, or a woman's anger at being belittled by her male superior at work. As we have seen above, though, sometimes the body, rather than the face, will nonetheless "leak out" these emotions. On the other hand, most of these studies use photographs and hence provide no information about the context the person is in, which should make recognition of emotion much more difficult. As we will see in the next chapter, judgments of others' emotions (as well as of our own, surprisingly) are substantially influenced by any information we can get about the person's situation. Not that everyone experiences the same emotion in any given situation, but it helps to know what the situation is.

Another concern has been with accuracy of judging more permanent personality traits, rather than just transient emotional states. Here the research is fairly discouraging, for a number of reasons. First, it is easy to identify some biases that observers are subject to; and second, many studies have serious methodological problems (Cronbach, 1955). It is also very difficult to measure personality traits, so there is a problem in identifying a proper criterion for accuracy.

Moreover, some influential psychologists (e.g., Mischel, 1979) now feel that personality traits usually apply to a fairly limited range of situations. That is, they concede that we do have unique, idiosyncratic dispositions that make us regularly react in our own distinctive way to any given situation. But they argue that these are not very constant from one situation to another. We may judge the truth a little when it comes to income taxes or to getting served alcoholic beverages before coming of age, but never steal our roommate's money that is just lying around, or cheat on examinations. So it would not make sense to talk about a *general* trait of honesty or dishonesty; we would have to talk about dispositions that are specific to particular situations. This disparity causes some considerable inaccuracy in detecting personality. So for the moment, social psychologists believe that perceivers may be able to detect others' transient emotions more accurately than their stable personality dispositions.

EVALUATIVE BIASES

What are the main sources of bias or inaccuracy in person perception? Some are based in the judge's evaluations of the target person. As we have seen, evaluation is the dominant dimension in person perception, so it is not surprising that it also introduces some distortions and inaccuracies in several different ways.

Halo Effect

As we said earlier, most judgments of other people tend to be evaluatively consistent. The stimulus person is seen as likable or not very likable. Then their other qualities are partly deduced from this decision. This is called the halo effect because one who is labeled *good* is surrounded with a postive aura and all good qualities are attributed to him. The converse (what should be called a "negative halo" or a "forked-tail" effect) is that one who is labeled *bad* is seen as having all bad qualities.

A good illustration of these effects is provided in a study by Dion, Berscheid, and Walster (1972). Subjects were given pictures of people who were either physically attractive, unattractive, or average. They then rated each of the people on a number of characteristics that have nothing to do with attractiveness. As you can see in Table 4–3, the attractive person was rated highest and the unattractive person lowest on almost all characteristics. Just because they looked good and therefore had one

TABLE 4–3

The "Halo" and "Forked-Tail" Effects Illustrated by Ratings of Attractive, Unattractive, and Average Persons

TRAIT ASCRIPTION[a]	ATTRACTIVE STIMULUS PERSON	AVERAGE STIMULUS PERSON	UNATTRACTIVE STIMULUS PERSON
Social desirability of personality	65.39	62.42	56.31
Occupational status	2.25	2.02	1.70
Marital competence	1.70	.71	.37
Parental competence	3.54	4.55	3.91
Social and professional happiness	6.37	6.34	5.28
Total happiness	11.60	11.60	8.83
Likelihood of marriage	2.17	1.82	1.52

[a] The higher the number, the more socially desirable, the more prestigious an occupation, and so on, the stimulus person is expected to possess.
Source: Dion et al., (1972).

positive trait, they were perceived as having other positive traits (conversely, those who looked bad were perceived as having other bad traits). We will consider some of the implications of the halo effect in Chapter 6.

Assumed Similarity

There is a strong tendency for people to assume that others are similar to them. This is particularly true when they are known to be similar in demographic features such as age, race, national origin, and socioeconomic status, but also occurs when they differ considerably on these characteristics. If one likes large parties, one tends to assume that other people like large parties; if one is aggressive, one assumes other people are also aggressive; and so on.

There are two related results of the phenomenon of **assumed similarity.** First, the individual rates another more similar to himself than he actually is; he distorts the other's personality to make it more like his own. For example, Schiffenbauer (1974) found some evidence that varying the subject's own emotion, by playing either a comic or a disgusting tape, would affect the subject's judgment of others' facial expressions in photographs; the subject would tend to interpret others' faces as expressing the emotion he himself was experiencing. Second, this distortion usually is so great that his rating of the other person corresponds more to his own personality (as he sees it) than to the other's personality (as the other sees it). As we shall discuss in more detail below, this means that perception of another person is often influenced more by what the rater is like than by what the person being rated is like.

Another result of this tendency is that people are more accurate in rating others who are similar to them, not because they are more perceptive with such people, but because they always rate people similar to themselves, so when they finally find one who is, they are naturally correct. Paradoxically, perhaps the most interesting implication of this phenomenon is that one's rating of others may be as good a measure of one's own personality as it is of the other person's. It may actually be a better measure of one's personality than is one's own self-rating because one is less likely to be concerned about concealing faults or exaggerating strengths. Therefore, if we want to find out what someone is like, the best procedure may be to ask him to rate other people.

This may be a special case of the more general fact that the perceivers' states of mind, and their current life situation influence their judgments of others to some extent. As early as 1932, Bartlett showed that men who were liable to be drafted into the military rated pictures of military officers as more threatening and indicating greater command ability than did men who were not draftable. Murray (1933) had girls judge photographs of faces after some had played a frightening game. Those who had played the game judged the photographs to be more menacing than those who had not played the game. And in 1957, Feshbach and Singer found that subjects who were frightened because they were expecting electric shocks perceived other people as more fearful than did subjects who were not frightened. Thus, as might be expected, perceivers' needs and feelings greatly influence their perceptions of other people—they tend to project their own feelings onto others and to be more sensitive to particular characteristics because of their own emotional state.

Positivity Bias

There is also a general tendency to express positive evaluations of people more often than negative evaluations. This has been called the *leniency effect* or sometimes the **positivity bias** (Bruner & Tagiuri, 1954; Sears & Whitney, 1973). Ratings of stimulus persons in laboratory studies are consistently positive, on the average, whether the subject knows the person or not. Similarly, public opinion polls show that political leaders are consistently rated positively more often than they are evaluated negatively, as Sears (1976) has shown. In the Gallup polls done in the United States over the period 1935 to 1975, 76 percent of the 535 persons and groups asked about were evaluated favorably. Similarly, in surveys done during the 1960s and 1970s throughout the United States by the University of Michigan Survey Research Center, 76 percent of the 50 politicians asked about were evaluated favorably. And in California during the same period, the California Poll found that 84 percent of the 263 politicians asked about were evaluated favorably. Positive evaluations of other people also are rated as more pleasant, are learned more readily, are expected in the absence of any specific information about them, and are expected to result from any changes in interpersonal relationships. When change in an impression does occur, it generally occurs toward more positive evaluations, everything else being equal.

There are a couple of plausible hypotheses about why people get evaluated so leniently. One general possibility stems from what Matlin and Stang (1978) call the "Pollyanna principle." They suggest that people feel better if they are surrounded by good things, pleasant experiences, nice people, good weather, and so on. So even when their houses are falling down, they are sick, people are terrible to them, and the weather is dismal, they will evaluate their situation favorably. So, most things get evaluated "above average" most of the time, pleasant events are thought more common than unpleasant ones, good news communicated more frequently than bad news, pleasant words recalled more accurately than unpleasant ones, and so on.

Sears, on the other hand, contends that there is a special positivity bias in our evaluations of fellow human beings, based on the assumed-similarity phenomenon. People identify with those they evaluate, and therefore evaluate them roughly as they evaluate themselves. They assume the other person is like themselves, so they are more generous than they would be to impersonal objects. If the positivity bias operates specifically in the evaluations of people, then it should not show up as strongly when impersonal objects are being evaluated. That is, there should be a positivity bias in person perception, but not in object perception.

The problem with testing this idea is that usually the stimuli themselves are so different it is hard to compare them. You could compare the evaluations of a rock with evaluations of one's mother, but they differ in so many other ways that it would be difficult to attribute any difference in evaluation just to the fact that one is an impersonal object and the other a person. To try to make this object versus person comparison in a fair way, Sears turned to evaluations of professors. UCLA uses a standard form for evaluating instruction, which has comparable items for the evaluation of the instructor (a personal stimulus) and for the evaluation of the course (an impersonal object): "What is your overall rating of the instructor" and "What is your overall rating of the course?" Presumably, both sets of ratings concern approximately the same experience—a specific course the student took. But in one case, mostly the impersonal aspects of it were being rated; i.e., the books, exams, class meetings, as well as the instructor. In the other case, only the personal aspect of it was rated in the person of the instructor.

Confirming the positivity bias, 96 percent of a sample of professors in the 1974–75 school year were rated positively (i.e., above "average"). And the personal stimulus, the instructor, was rated higher than the impersonal object, the course, in 74 percent of the cases (in 7 percent they were equal, and 19 percent of the time the course was rated higher). So perhaps simply being a specific, concrete human being, with whom we can identify and empathize, seems to make us give people a little break when we evaluate them.

Other biases are inherent in our cognitive processing mechanisms. Although human beings clearly have a greater capacity for processing information than other animals, it is not infinite. We can absorb only a limited amount of the stimulation we are bombarded with every minute; and when we need to retrieve it from our memory, we cannot get it all back in a flash. So any analysis of human cognitive processes must start out by acknowledging our limited processing abilities.

To compensate for these shortcomings, we use a series of shortcuts. These generally make person perception more efficient, but they also can lead to biases. They have been partly anticipated by the discussion of the perceptual-cognitive approach in the first chapter. One is that when confronted with other people as stimuli, we impose *structure* and *meaning* on them as we form impressions. We do not simply absorb all the information we can get about them; rather, we take in information selectively, then classify, categorize, relate, and organize it into a meaningful whole. Second, the nature of that structure is partly dictated by the nature of the person being observed. However, we tend to pay special attention to the *salient* features—the vivid, prominent aspects of the perceptual field, instead of giving equal attention to everything. Put another way, figural aspects of the person get more attention than does the ground. Third, human beings are lazy perceivers (McGuire, 1969), or somewhat more charitably, they are *"cognitive misers"* (Taylor, 1980). When we perceive other people, we try to cut corners and save effort. We do not try to perceive or remember all possible bits of information; we do only what is necessary to get a clear impression of what is going on. To this end there are a number of cognitive shortcuts we all use, and they will be described below.

Schemas

Perhaps most important, preexisting cognitive structures organize the processing of new information. Our perceptions of new information are biased to make them consistent with the original structure. For example, if we think someone is "warm," we are more likely to talk to him and interpret his behavior as reflecting that warmth. First impressions, stereotypes, expectations, prior attitudes—all influence the processing of any new information we might receive about people and their behavior. To put it another way, our processing is to some extent "theory-driven" rather than "data-driven"; we see other people as we expect to, as our theories would lead us to, rather than simply in terms of what they actually are and do.

Many terms have been used to describe such cognitive structures but probably the most common is **schema.** This refers to an organized, structured set of cognitions, including some knowledge about the object, some relationships among the various cognitions about it, and some specific examples (Taylor & Crocker, 1980). A good example would be a schema

FIGURE 4–6   Once we recognize this as a cocktail party, our perceptions of people are affected by our knowledge of standard cocktail party behavior.

about a "cocktail party." We know that cocktail parties usually are held in the late afternoon or evening, usually in someone's home, they have a number of guests and usually a host and a hostess, they have some food and a lot of alcoholic drinks (all of which are more likely to be prepared and served by the host and hostess than by the guests), and that normally the people interact by standing and talking to each other rather than by watching some common event (like a singer) or sleeping or running in circles around the living room. Our schema might include a couple of memorable parties we went to. In short, we have a clear, well-developed, somewhat abstract picture or cognitive structure in our minds about a "cocktail party."

PERSON SCHEMAS Schemas can be about different things. There are *person schemas,* which are structures about people. They can focus on particular people. For instance, our schema of Abraham Lincoln might include such elements as his being deliberate, honest, serious about his duties, and concerned for oppressed people. This is a schema because in our view they are all related to one another. That is, we perceive them all as aspects of a basically decent and conscientious personality, not unrelated traits he just happened to display from time to time.

One specific version of a person schema is a schema you have about yourself, or a *self-schema*. For example, Markus (1977) investigated the extent to which people had schemas of themselves as independent or dependent, by determining whether or not they would apply to themselves such adjectives as individualistic, unconventional, assertive, cooperative, timid, or moderate.

Person schemas can also focus on particular kinds or types of people. For example, our schema of an "extrovert" might include such elements as "spirited," "outgoing," "enthusiastic," and "self-assured" (Cantor & Mischel, 1977). Sometimes this type of schema is described as an *implicit personality theory*, because it seems to be a theory about what traits go with what other traits, and which ones do not go together. Someone might feel that "warm" goes with "happy" but not with "calculating." So, on overhearing someone say that Suzi is "warm," the person would infer that she was probably happy and not very calculating, even in the absence of any more information about her. An implicit personality theory, then, is this web of presumed relationships and nonrelationships among traits.

To some extent, such a "theory" is widely shared among people with a common background. One very general example was given earlier in discussing the two types of evaluative dimensions—the social and intellectual. The reason that two such dimensions can be systematically distinguished in people's judgments is that most perceivers share a common implicit personality theory—namely, that "helpful," "sincere," and "popular" go together, and that "scientific," "determined," and "reliable" go together (see Table 4–1).

On the other hand, as might be expected, people also have their own very personal and idiosyncratic implicit personality theories, in addition to whatever they share with people like them. Put another way, different people organize their perceptions of others along different dimensions. For example, one person might always describe others in terms of their degree of sense of humor, physical attractiveness, warmth, honesty, and intelligence. Someone else might consider these characteristics to be relatively unimportant and instead would emphasize the degree of the individual's diligence, aggressiveness, religiosity, and athletic prowess.

Then there are *role schemas*. These represent the organized, abstract pictures we have of people in a particular role, such as cowboy, professor, receptionist, or devoted lover. If our schema for "devoted lover" includes elements such as always understanding, always supportive, never angry, never childish, and always concerned first and foremost with the other person's happiness, we could be in trouble, because not too many people will live up to that schema. Similar problems sometimes arise between college students and faculty, when each has a schema for the other's role that does not take into consideration other aspects of the other's lives. A faculty member's schema about students may include constant interest and attention to the course, while the student's might include endless patience and consideration on the part of the professor. But students sometimes are sick, and unable to pay good attention in class. Faculty members may have arguments with their husbands, and therefore behave irritably toward innocent students.

Another social schema is the **stereotype** which attributes specific traits to a particular group of people. For example, an early study by Katz and Braly (1933) found white college students checking "superstitious," "lazy," and "happy-go-lucky" as the most common traits of Negroes, and "scientifically minded," "industrious," and "stolid" as most common for Germans. You might expect a student who is in the Beta fraternity to act like other Betas, or a black football player to act like other black football players, or people from Boston or Texas or Iran to resemble each other. All these involve having a particular schema for the personality and behavior of members of a group. We will take up stereotypes in some detail in Chapter 12.

EVENT SCHEMAS People also have schemas for events, or standard series of events, like the one described above for a cocktail party. Plainly having a baby, taking a shower, taking a final exam, or playing a basketball game would all be quite different. Sometimes such schemas are called *scripts* (Abelson, 1976). A script is a standard sequence of behavior over a period of time. For example, one script might be called "ordering-for-a-group-in-a-Chinese-restaurant." Everyone sits down, and the waiter brings the menus. Several people try to talk at once, giving their favorite dishes while others say they never know what to have and would someone else just please decide. Then people go through the menu section by section haggling over which soup to have, bargaining away their favorite beef dish (which no one else wants) for sweet-and-sour pork (which at least one ally does), and finally appointing the most self-confident and brash person to communicate the whole negotiated package to the waiter. The essence of a script is in its boundedness in time, its causal flow (early events cause later ones), and in its being a simple, coherent, perceptual unit.

Another example of schematic processing is the structure that people impose when they perceive others' behavior. In theory, human behavior is usually considered to occur in a continuous and uninterrupted flow; indeed, it has been referred to as a "behavior stream" (Newtson, 1973). But people cannot absorb everything at once. They need to decide what to pay attention to in order to form an impression of another person or an experience. They therefore tend to perceive behavior in coherent, meaningful chunks of action that are marked off by **breakpoints.** For example, imagine watching an outfielder break into a run at the sound of the bat hitting the ball; he dashes to the outfield wall, leaps up, catches the ball, lands on his feet, sets for a throw, and then throws the ball to the third baseman to stop the baserunner. Newtson argues that we perceive such a flow of activity as a sequence of separate behaviors, not as one continuous act. Breakpoints thus occur between the separate actions and mark where one ends and another begins.

Breakpoints seem to be inherent in any stream of behavior; they are not necessarily imposed on it by the perceiver. Perceivers agree on where certain breakpoints occur in films of someone in action, and perceive the same breakpoints again when shown the film five weeks later.

When instructed or motivated to do so, observers can pick up finer, or grosser, segments of behavior. A baseball coach will perceive more separate acts in an outfielder's play than will a spectator attending her first baseball game. The spectator will simply think, "The centerfielder made a nice catch." The coach, on the other hand, will think, "Did he get a good jump on the ball? How fast is he? How is his timing? How is his catch—does he have 'soft hands'?" And Newtson's research shows that when people are instructed to make finer distinctions, they develop more confident impressions of the stimulus person. Put another way, the more breakpoints we perceive in a person's stream of behavior, the more information we receive, and the stronger and clearer the impressions we develop.

When do breakpoints occur? Some ingenious research has tied them to changes in behavior, specifically to changes in the movement of different parts of the body (Newtson, Engquist, & Bois, 1977). Breakpoints also occur when the state of objects associated with the person changes. For example, breakpoints would be perceived when a baseball's trajectory is suddenly interrupted by the outfielder's glove, disappears from view, then suddenly flies through the air back toward the infield.

The more general point, then, is that we do not simply swallow the other person's behavior whole when forming an impression. Rather, we absorb meaningful, structured chunks of it. And the chunking process is partly imposed on the flow of behavior by the perceiver's own experience, expectations, and needs, and partly by inherent variations in the salience of various aspects of the behavior and associated objects. So the perceiver is partly imposing an artificial structure, and partly reflecting the truly variegated nature of the stimulus person's behavior.

SCHEMATIC PROCESSING Schemas are important because they help us process an enormous amount of information quite swiftly and economically. Indeed schemas make processing more efficient at virtually every stage. For example, a schema aids recall. Memory works best when we can bring back some schematic representation of past events or people, because the schema will bring many details along with it. To illustrate this point, Snyder and Uranowitz (1978) presented subjects with an extended case study of "Betty K," and then described her as either living a heterosexual life style or a lesbian life style, to evoke one schema or the other. Memory for the details of the case study was fairly strongly affected by this simple variation. The subjects tended to forget details that were inconsistent with stereotyped beliefs about heterosexual or lesbian women.

Schemas help us interpret information and draw meaningful inferences from it. A schema can help us fill in missing information when we have not gotten all the data. If you had been worried about whether or not your girlfriend spent last night with your rival, you were probably reassured when she called you from her grandmother's house this morning. The schema for her visiting her grandmother involves getting there for early dinner (the grandmother likes to cook and eats at 5:30 P.M.) not going out after the grandmother goes to sleep (at 8:30), and staying overnight there. You can fill in the rest, and relax.

A schema can help solve problems because it tells us what information to use. Ajzen (1977) asked subjects to predict the grade-point average of several students. He presented them with information about each student that either fit the usual schemas about the determinants of GPA (IQ, the number of hours spent studying each week), or was irrelevant to those schemas (dollars earned each week, number of miles lived from campus). The information relevant to the schemas was used much more heavily.

Schemas also provide normative expectations for what should happen. These expectations in turn can determine how pleasant or unpleasant we find a particular situation. Suppose a white person with a fine record applies to medical school but is rejected and is replaced with a black student with an inferior record. This violates the white student's expectations and is likely to make her quite angry. The same would apply to blacks who have worked hard to become educated, but still are unable to find jobs at their level of expertise. This sense of deprivation relative to expectation has been cited as one of the causes of ghetto riots and other forms of social insurrection (Sears & McConahay, 1973).

Because schematic processing is so automatic, it can make us more efficient at dealing with routine tasks. After being in college for a couple of years, you probably no longer have to think very much about what study habits to use. You know about how often to go through your textbook, how many notes to take on it, how much to underline or highlight it, how far before the final examination to start reviewing, and so on. You have a schema for studying-for-a-final-exam. The schema saves you a lot of time, energy, indecision, and anxiety. Perhaps the whole process was more complex when you were just starting college—it is for most freshmen—before it became routine.

Schematic processing can be triggered simply by the attempt to form an impression of another person. David Hamilton (1980) has conducted a series of studies that compare subjects operating under an *impression set*, who are instructed to form an impression of the stimulus person, with subjects operating under a *memory set*, who are just told to try to remember what they can about the stimulus person. He has consistently found that the impression-set subjects recall more information about the stimulus person than do the memory-set subjects, even though the latter were told explicitly to try to remember as much as they could. He interpreted this finding in terms of schemas—that is, the impression set induces perceivers to use various "person-relevant schemas" that help them organize and recall material better.

In later work, Hamilton tested this interpretation directly by building certain consistent schemas into the descriptions of the stimulus person. Indeed, when the impression-set subjects were later tested for recall of information about the stimulus person, they turned out to cluster their memories of it around these schemas. Srull and Wyer (1979) similarly found that explicitly activating certain categories of personality (like kindness or hostility) made them more central in the impression formed from later behavior by the stimulus person. Put another way, later information tends to be organized by whatever schema is dominant at the time.

Of course in this research the schemas are artificially induced by being built into the stimulus materials. Hamilton assumed that in real life our impressions of a new person are initially organized around very general, abstract schemas (like Extrovert or Athlete or Flirt). Later, as we get to know the person better, we develop a specific schema for that person (as most of us have for Abraham Lincoln or Jesus Christ or Jane Fonda).

The same gains in cognitive processing are likely to hold for self-schemas as for other kinds. They facilitate the processing of information, improve memory for specific behaviors, help people to predict their own performance, and help maintain the stability of their own self-images (Markus, 1977). For example, processing speed is often enhanced by a relevant schema. Markus (1977) contrasted subjects with self-schemas as independent or dependent people with subjects that had no such schema. She then read them sentences about certain independent or dependent behaviors. People with such self-schemas were able to indicate more quickly than those with none whether or not the behavior was typical of them. Not all research finds that schemas speed processing up. In some cases evoking a schema slows things down by introducing a more complex mass of information (Taylor & Crocker, 1980). But in general, information processing is speeded when a self-schema is relevant.

In fact, people may have stronger schemas about themselves than about other people. For example, Rogers and associates (1977) found that people recalled a list of traits better if they were asked to think about them in relation to themselves than if they just tried to learn them in the abstract. In later work (Kuiper & Rogers, 1979) they found that people could rate themselves more easily, and more confidently than they did other people.

LIABILITIES OF SCHEMATIC PROCESSING Schematic processing has some liabilities. A schema may be imposed on the basis of skimpy and preliminary information. Furthermore, real evidence about something may be rejected because it does not fit a schema, as often happens with stereotypes. For example, a teacher may believe that blacks are not as intelligent as whites. Yet on the midterm exam a black student gets the best grade in the class. The teacher decides that the student has cheated, instead of accepting evidence that violates her preexisting schema.

Schemas also may prevent you from recognizing a new situation. If a woman is used to behaving in a passive, dependent, giggly, little-girl manner to her father, she may respond that way to her husband as well. Her husband, however, may want her to be more independent, serious, and grown-up. She may continue to apply the father-schema to other men, inappropriately.

Implicit personality theories can also lead to errors, since there is a strong tendency for people to infer from the presence of one trait in an individual that he has various other traits. Knowing someone is intelligent causes most people to expect him also to be imaginative, clever, active, conscientious, deliberate, and reliable. Knowing someone is inconsiderate leads most people to expect him also to be irritable, boastful, cold, hypocritical, etc. But these inferences are not derived logically from the given trait; they are based on the individual's assumptions about personality. Intelligence does not necessarily denote activity, nor does inconsiderateness denote irritability. The tendency to make these assumptions is sometimes called the *logical error,* because people see certain traits as going together and assume that someone who has one of them also has the others.

This reducing of complex processes to schematic routines has been called the "mindlessness of ostensibly thoughtful action" by Langer. When people first approach a task, they are attentive to all the details of it. As they become more practiced the task becomes more automatic, and they are no longer consciously attentive to the details; the task becomes a whole schema, or "mindless." But schemas may prevent people from making necessary adjustments in their performance. In several studies Langer has shown that overlearning a task can have detrimental effects, if one's ability is later questioned (Langer & Imber, 1979). It is difficult to concentrate later on an automatic, overlearned task.

The same errors and biases regarding schemas of other people are likely to accompany self-schemas as well. Yet there are some new ones, too, that are specific to the self. People are likely to explain things in ways that enhance their own self-esteem. Hence they tend to exaggerate their own importance. For example, Ross and Sicoly (1979) showed that people consistently exaggerated their own contribution to shared activities. Their studies involved married couples' estimates of relative contributions to joint activities, college basketball players' estimates of their own roles in recent games, and recent college graduates' estimates of their own contribution to their bachelors' theses. And as we will see in the next chapter, people also tend to take excessive credit for successes and deny blame for failures. They exaggerate how many people behave in the same way they do, have the same personal problems, and have the same personality traits and opinions (Ross, Greene, & House, 1977). They also exaggerate how much control they have over events in their lives (Langer, 1975).

These egocentric biases could be obviously motivated by the desire to maintain high self-esteem. But they also could be created partially by simple cognitive factors. For example, aspects of the self are more familiar (or "available," to use a term to be introduced shortly) than are aspects of other people, and so they are easier to fit into a strong schema.

Quite a lively controversy has developed over this contrast between motivational and cognitive explanations for such biases (see Nisbett & Ross, 1980), though it is most likely that both are important.

In short, schematic processing has the advantage of speed and makes events comprehensible and predictable. It has the disadvantage of leading to erroneous interpretations, inaccurate expectations, and inflexible modes of response. But even this resistance of schemas to disconfirmation sometimes prevents irrational and destructive change. If you have a strong schema about your star pitcher's ability, and about the role of chance variations in baseball, you will not bench him just because he loses the first three games of the season. And if your schema for intense relationships includes occasional fights, you will not split up from your boyfriend just because you have a fight two nights in a row.

Cue Salience

We have described many cues that people are sensitive to in others, and use from time to time in impression formation. But clearly people do not use all the cues potentially available to them. They form meaningful impressions quickly and cannot possibly check out every detail of the other person's make-up, hair color, posture, tone of voice, and so on. So how is it possible that people can both be so quick to form impressions and be sensitive to so many different aspects of the other person and the situation?

Cognitive theory has put forward some clear explanations. According to the figure-ground principle, people direct their perceptions to those aspects of the perceptual field that stand out. These figural stimuli thus dominate an individual's perceptions. Therefore, in impression formation, the most salient, prominent, vivid cues will be utilized most heavily. If a student appears in a wheelchair the first day of class, everyone else in the room is likely to form an impression that is most heavily influenced by the fact of the person's physical handicap. Clothing, hair style, and perhaps even age, race, and sex will all be secondary. Later in the semester, other aspects of the person will become more salient, but initially the wheelchair stands out.

What determines the salience of one cue as opposed to another? A number of clearly specifiable conditions make cues stand out. *Brightness, motion,* or *novelty* are the most powerful conditions, according to Gestalt principles of visual object perception (McArthur & Post, 1977). A girl in a bright red sweater stands out in a crowded classroom, and her sweater is the most salient aspect of her. The student who gets up in the middle of a class and leaves halfway through the lecture draws our attention away from almost any other aspect of the person. A student in white robes and a turban is a novel stimulus, and we may notice very little else about him.

What makes a stimulus is also likely to be more salient if it can be imagined more vividly in *visual* form. Words, sentences, numbers often do not have the same impact as pictures which seem to be especially vivid in memory. For example, "Susan had her left leg bitten off by a shark and died from loss of blood" has more impact than "Susan died in an accident in Hawaii." Vivid details and concrete specificity, then, contribute to salience. So does emotional impact. Something that evokes extreme emotion is usually more easily retrieved than something that does not. Something that has happened to us or to someone we know, has more salience than something that has happened to a complete stranger. Things close to us in space or time are more salient than things distant. A series of rapes in our neighborhood has more of an impact on us than an equivalent series in Rio de Janeiro or Uganda. Something that happened this morning is more vivid than something that happened three years ago (Nisbett & Ross, 1980).

In general, anything that makes a cue *unusual* in its context makes it more salient, more likely to be attended to, and more heavily utilized. A novel cue is unusual in the time dimension; it is unlike anything that preceded it and so attracts our attention. Men with long hair were novel in the mid-1960s, and so were openly gay men or women in the mid-1970s. Impressions of them were heavily influenced by their hair and sexual

FIGURE 4–7 The person who is different in some way, stands out and captures our attention.

Ellis Herwig; Stock, Boston.

preference, respectively. Loud noises are distinctive and attract attention; we probably notice very little else about a waiter who drops his tray in a restaurant. We are more likely to describe a redhead in terms of hair color than we would a brunette. Behavioral violations of social norms are also unusual, salient, and dominate first impressions. We notice little else about the appearance and behavior of a flasher or a murderer or someone who stands only six inches away when talking to us on the sidewalk. The main thing we notice about someone smoking on a bus, in a theater, or in the no-smoking section of an airplane is her smoking, not her scintillating personality.

Another way to make the same point is to think of the *extremity* of a cue in its normal distribution in the population. The wheelchair, exciting behavior, white robes, red sweater, red hair, and smoking behavior are all extreme in the normal distributions of paraphenalia, classroom behavior, clothing, hair color, and behavior in non-smoking areas.

Why do salient stimuli have a greater impact on our impressions and judgments? There is some tendency for them to be learned more firmly to begin with, but not a very strong one. Rather, they seem to be retrieved more readily from memory later on, long after first contact with them. This greater availability in memory has been called the *availability heuristic* (Kahneman & Tversky, 1973); that is, something that is particularly available in our memory tends to have a disproportionate influence over our judgments. So, for example, we may draw conclusions about the way the courts treat murderers on the basis of our memory for one particularly vivid and flagrant case we read about in the newspapers. Generally speaking, memories are more available for either of the reasons we have been discussing: because they fit our schema (e.g., the courts always let hardcore criminals off too easily) or because they are salient (vivid, emotionally arousing, and so on).

Objective Self-Awareness

Just as we observe other people and form judgments of them, we also look at ourselves. We are aware of our own behavior and values; we evaluate our own performance; and we wonder how others are reacting to us. However, the degree of attention we pay to ourselves varies greatly from moment to moment. Sometimes we are involved in the environment: we are noticing other people and what is going on around us, and are quite unaware of our own behavior. On these occasions, we act spontaneously with little concern for how we may be appearing to others or what our actions may reveal about us. At other times, we become extremely attentive to ourselves, fully aware of every thought and action. This is sometimes called being *self-conscious*, in the sense that we look at ourselves as if we were someone else. A series of studies has demonstrated that the degree of self-consciousness can have dramatic effects on our behavior.

Duval and Wicklund (1971) proposed a theory of what they called *objective self-awareness*, which is the state of observing oneself as if one were an object. Under some conditions we look at ourselves the way we look at other people. We "stand back" and observe our own behavior, taking the point of view of an outside observer. According to the theory, such a state makes us more concerned about looking "right" or behaving "correctly." The definition of what is right in a situation is based either on one's own personal values and standards, or the standards that are set by the particular situation. The original explanation of these effects was that a strong self-evaluation process is automatically activated under a state of high objective self-awareness. According to this view, people become self-critical by comparing themselves to the standard (whether internal or external), with the main emphasis being on evaluation of their own behavior. A somewhat different view is proposed by Carver (1979), who explains the effects in terms of increased salience of the standards, and not any evaluation process. That is, the individual who is self-aware becomes more attentive to particular values, he compares himself to these values, and his behavior tends to be affected by them. The primary difference between these two ideas is that Duval and Wicklund picture the individual in a negative state because he is evaluating himself against standards that he is usually not completely satisfying. Carver, on the other hand, sees the person merely comparing his behavior to the standard but not necessarily becoming involved in positive or negative evaluations. It seems likely that the latter view is more generally right, though under some circumstances self-awareness will arouse self-evaluation also.

Thus, the implication is that people who are high in objective self-awareness, who are self-attentive, will be more likely to conform to standards they consider appropriate. For example, under most circumstances, males in our society think that it is wrong to hurt females. When males were asked to deliver electric shocks to women in a presumed learning experiment, heightened self-awareness caused them to give fewer shocks (Scheier et al., 1974). But when the experimenter specifically made a point of saying that giving shocks was the expected behavior in the situation, high self-awareness caused more shocks to be given (Carver, 1974).

SUMMARY

1. People tend to form highly consistent impressions of others, even with very little information.

2. The evaluative dimension is the most important organizing principle behind first impressions. People seem to decide first how much they like or dislike another person, then ascribe characteristics to them that fit this pleasant or unpleasant portrait.

3. There are two rival points of view about how people process information about other people: the learning approach, which has people essentially averaging information in a quite mechanical manner; and the Gestalt approach, which has people forming a coherent, meaningful impression that incorporates everything they know about the stimulus person.

4. We use a wide variety of cues in arriving at impressions of people, including physical appearance and nonverbal cues (voice inflection, gestures, body language, and eye contact).

5. Our judgments of other people are not always very accurate. In particular we have a hard time judging people's emotions from their facial expressions. We can tell fairly easily if their emotion is a positive or a negative one, but we have difficulty telling which positive or negative emotion is being experienced. Nevertheless, there do seem to be some universal connections across cultures between certain emotions and certain facial expressions.

6. Various identifiable perceptual biases distort our judgments of others: the halo effect (we tend to think a person we like is good on every dimension), the positivity bias (we tend to like most people, even some who are not so likable), and assumed similarity (we expect others to be like us).

7. We tend automatically to organize and structure the various separate bits of information we receive about other people. Certain cognitive structures called schemas help us organize this information. Schemas make information processing more efficient and speedy, aid recall, fill in missing information, and provide normative expectations. However, they sometimes fill in erroneous information or lead us to reject good but inconsistent evidence. They sometimes result in biased impressions.

8. Our attention is particularly drawn to perceptually salient stimuli, such as those that are bright, moving, novel, or unusual. Salient stimuli have a disproportionate influence over our impressions, and they can distract us from more valid information.

SUGGESTIONS FOR ADDITIONAL READING

ANDERSON, N. H. Averaging vs. adding as a stimulus-combination rule in impression formation. *Journal of Experimental Psychology,* 1965, *70,* 394–400. This gives the flavor of averaging research, using trait adjectives about hypothetical stimulus persons.

ASCH, S. E. Forming impressions of personality. *Journal of Abnormal and Social Psychology,* 1946, *41,* 258–90. This is the classic statement of the Gestalt approach to impression formation, and indeed to social perception in general.

EKMAN, P., FRIESEN, W., & ELLSWORTH, P. *Emotion in the human face.* New York: Pergamon Press, 1972. The best treatment of how people judge emotions from facial expressions.

HALL, EDWARD T. *The hidden dimension.* New York: Doubleday, 1966. An original statement by one of the pioneers in the study of nonverbal communication.

NISBETT, R., & ROSS, L. *Human inference: Strategies and shortcomings of social judgment.* Englewood Cliffs, N.J.: Prentice-Hall, 1980. An elegant and outspoken treatment of social cognition, especially cognitive biases in person perception.

SCHNEIDER, D. J., HASTORF, A. H., & ELLSWORTH, P. C. *Person perception* (2nd ed.). Reading, Mass.: Addison-Wesley, 1979. A paperback that pursues the material in this and the next chapter in more detail.

TAYLOR, S. E., and CROCKER, J. Schematic bases of social information processing. In Higgins, E. T., Hermann, P., and Zanna, M. P. (eds.), *The Ontario symposium on personality and social psychology,* Vol. 1. Hillsdale, N.J.: Erlbaum, 1980. The most complete discussion of schematic processing in social psychology.

TAYLOR, S. E., & FISKE, S. T. Salience, attention, and attribution: Top of the head phenomena. In Berkowitz, L. (ed.), *Advances in experimental social psychology.* Vol. 11. New York: Academic Press, 1978. Pp. 249–88. The many ways in which salience affects person perception.

Attribution Theory

United Press International.

In the previous chapter we saw that our perception of another person's traits is central to all our perceptions of him. If we see another person as "warm," a whole series of connected perceptions fall into line. Moreover, as will be seen in later chapters, these first impressions have a great deal to do with how we like and behave toward that person. But this does not answer the question of how we perceive the traits of another person. How do we know that that person is a "warm" person? Indeed, how do we form judgments about a whole series of other dispositions in another person? How do we decide that the person is intelligent, or a good curve-ball hitter, or an anti-Semite? And how do we come to conclusions about other, more transient mental states, such as intentions of moods?

The perception of people often involves inferences about internal states. When we are thinking about a person, we are concerned about motives, personality, emotions, and attitudes. We must make such inferences on the basis of limited information, because we have access only to external cues such as facial expressions, gestures, what the person says about his internal state, what we remember about his behavior in the past, and so forth. We do not have direct information about his internal state; we have only the indirect information given by external cues.

THEORETICAL APPROACHES

The study of these inferences has become one of the most active research areas in social psychology. It has been organized under several theoretical approaches, which have been called *attribution theory*. An *attribution* is the inference an observer makes about the internal state of an actor or of himself on the basis of overt behavior.

Heider's Naïve Psychology

Theorizing about attributions began with Heider (1958), whose concern was with phenomenal causality. That is, he was interested in how people in everyday life figure out what causes what. Like most in the perceptual-cognitive tradition in social psychology, he postulated two strong motives in all human beings: the need to form a coherent understanding of the world and the need to control the environment. One of the essentials for satisfying each motive is the ability to predict how people are going to behave. If we cannot predict how others will behave, we shall view the world as random, surprising, and incoherent. Without the ability to predict others' behavior, we would not know whether to expect reward or punishment for our work performance, a kiss or punch in the jaw from our friend.

Similarly, there is no way we can have a satisfactory level of control of our environment without being able to predict others' behavior. We need to be able to count on a salesperson's giving us a pair of slacks, rather than calling the police if we give her the right amount of money for them. We need to be able to count on that big truck not suddenly doing a U turn into our front bumper as we inch along Fifth Avenue. We need to be able to count on getting veal scallopini and not pigs feet when we order in a restaurant. So a key factor in controlling our environment is being able to predict how others are going to behave in it. To be able to do this, we need to have some elemental theory of human behavior. So Heider proposed that everyone, not just psychologists, invests considerable energy in searching for causal explanations for other people's behavior. And he suggested that the result was a **naïve psychology**—that is, a general theory of human behavior held by each ordinary person.

The key element in such a naïve psychology is the ability to identify what others' stable, underlying dispositions are. To predict how they will behave, we need to be able to form a judgment (even if it is only a snap judgment) of their personalities, motives, emotions, and attitudes. If our daughter looks unhappy, we need to know whether she is hungry and peeved because her mom and dad spent a little too long (from *her* point of view!) in bed, or because her stomach is upset and she is about to lose all those cookies she was gobbling in the meantime. Is old Mr. Hodgkinson being anti-Semitic by refusing to take our $97,000 or even our $99,500, for the house he has listed at $99,500? If so, we should just forget it. Or, does he just want to bargain, so we should hang in there? Is that blonde we cannot get our mind off just playing a little hard to get, and we should continue to chase her; or is she really uninterested, and should we just give up? In order to predict and control our environment, we need to make all kinds of judgments about others' internal dispositions.

The central issue in most perceptions of causality is whether to attribute a given act or event to *internal* states or to *external* forces. A person is generally perceived as acting either because of some internal state or because of some external force. The blonde wants to know whether we are motivated primarily by an overwhelming and undiscriminating internal sexuality (we will go out with any female), or by the uniqueness of her, an external object. A student who is failing a course wants to know whether it is because he is not smart enough or doesn't work hard enough (internal causality), or because the professor's lectures are ambiguous, the text is set at a level too difficult for the class's background, or the tests are unfair (external causality). Debates rage in school board meetings, academic conventions, courtrooms, and legislative halls about whether black children do less well in school than white children because of inferior native endowment and low motivation (internal causality) or because of racial discrimination, insensitive middle-class white teachers, inferior facilities, and unstimulating peer groups (external causality).

So the major question is whether to make an external attribution or an internal attribution. External attributions would ascribe causality to anything external to the actor, such as the general environment, the specific person being interacting with, role constraints, proffered rewards or threatened punishments, luck, the specific nature of the task, and so on. Internal causes include personality traits, motives, emotions, moods, attitudes, abilities, and effort.

A second important, but subsidiary, issue in perceptions of causality is whether the cause is *stable* or *unstable*. That is, we need to know whether or not the cause is a relatively permanent feature of that external object or of the internal dispositions of the actor. Some external causes are quite stable, such as rules and laws (the prohibition against running a red light, or against breaking the throwing arm of an overly successful opposing quarterback), occupational roles (professors are called upon to give lectures year in and year out), or the difficulty level of certain tasks (it is always hard to hit a curveball, and always easy to get our daughter to laugh by tickling her). But some external causes are quite unstable: in competitive sports it is hard to judge how much of an obstacle the opposing player or team is because they are not always playing at exactly the same level of proficiency. A certain baseball star could be brilliant one day, and the next he might not be able to get a ball over the plate. So his performance would not be a stable external cause of the performance of the batters against him. Similarly, certain jobs vary a good bit in the external demands they place on the jobholder. Being a general places quite different external forces upon a person in wartime than in peacetime, and even quite different demands depending on the sector of combat.

An illustration is Weiner's typology for simple achievement tasks, shown in Table 5–1. One usually attributes a student's success or failure at a particular task to one or more of four possible causes: ability, effort,

TABLE 5-1

Classification Scheme for the Perceived Determinants of Achievement Behavior

	LOCUS OF CONTROL	
STABILITY	Internal	External
Stable	Ability	Task difficulty
Unstable	Effort	Luck

Source: Weiner (1974), p. 6.

luck, or task difficulty. And these causes fall quite neatly into the internal-external, stable-unstable categories, as the table shows.

Finally, the importance of the stable-unstable distinction relates back to the original motivation that people have for causal attributions. If an outcome is attributed to a stable cause, it will be given more weight in determining predictions for the future. Valle and Frieze (1976) had subjects judge a hypothetical applicant for a position as a life insurance salesperson. They asked the subject to explain why he had sold so much insurance in the past and to estimate his prospects for the future. When the subjects attributed past performance to stable factors, such as ability or personality, it was more highly associated with their projections for the future than was the case when the explanations for past success had to do with unstable factors, such as luck, unstable effort, or the particular season in which the sales took place.

BOX 5-1

PAROLE DECISIONS

People base their predictions about their own future outcomes, or other people's, on attributions for past behavior. Carroll (1978) got members of the Pennsylvania Board of Probation and Parole to fill out questionnaires after parole release hearings. He found the board members tended to release prisoners on parole more often if unstable attributions were made for the original crime, such as being high on drugs or alcohol, or the influence of bad company, and so on. Stable attributions more often led the board to deny parole. You might give some thought to what these might be, and to what kinds of evidence such a board might need to change them into unstable attributions, so that parole would be granted.

The Principle of Invariance

How do we arrive at such causal attributions? There are two simple principles: First, Heider suggests we generally use the *principle of invariance.* We normally assume that any given behavior could be determined by a variety of causes. But we tend to look for an association between a particular effect and a particular cause, across a number of different conditions. If a given cause is invariably associated with a particular effect in many different situations, and if the effect does not occur in the absence of that cause, then we attribute the effect to that cause. Suppose our boss tells us she likes our work whenever she has just returned from a vacation, and she criticizes us all the rest of the time; we attribute her behavior to whether or not she has recently had a vacation. Suppose our department chairman hires beautiful women for secretaries but always opposes any qualified woman for a faculty position; we attribute his behavior to his sexist attitudes. Suppose the local NBA team always loses to the Boston Celtics and always beats the Detroit Pistons. We attribute its performance to its ability level (moderate), and the ability level of the opposition (high and low, respectively).

This principle of invariance is, of course, exactly the same as the scientific method that scientists use. A scientist also arrives at a judgment of causality by seeing that a particular factor is associated with a particular effect across a number of different conditions. If a scientist finds, for example, that objects invariably fall from higher elevations to lower elevations, no matter whether they are feathers or cannonballs, no matter whether they dropped from the top of a building or waist height, he concludes that there is a general causal factor—namely, gravity. Similarly, as naïve psychologists, ordinary people observe the behavior of others and look for regular, invariant effects that follow a particular stimulus. In that way they arrive at an attribution to the critical cause.

Kelley's Cube Theory

Harold Kelley has generated the most comprehensive theory about how people apply the principle of invariance. He assumes that "The effect is attributed to that condition which is present when the effect is present and which is absent when the effect is absent" (1967, p. 194). That is, the effect is attributed to the factor with which it covaries. If the team always wins at home and loses on the road, we attribute the winning or losing effect to the home-road factor.

More specifically, people look for the simultaneous occurrence of (or covariation between) the causes and effects across three different dimensions: (1) stimulus object (2) actors (persons), and (3) context. Because people are assumed to check across these three independent dimensions, this can be called a **cube theory.** People look for regularities amidst all this information. If they see that a particular event occurs invariably with a certain set of conditions, they know what cause to attribute the event to. In Heider's terms, they are looking for that invariable effect given a certain

FIGURE 5–2 Our attributions about the cause for this man's behavior depend on whether he acts and dresses this way only when he is entertaining in the street or whether he does it all the time.

set of conditions or, in Kelley's terms, the regular covariation of conditions that determines whether or not the effect occurs.

This sounds complicated, but it is really a simple idea. It is easiest to grasp with a simple example. Suppose our friend Mary shows up at work one day, and tells us that she had gone out to a local night club the night before. She tells us they featured a comedian. She had laughed hysterically at his jokes, and in fact thought he was the funniest thing she had heard in years, and we should definitely go see him. Our dilemma lies in trying to figure out why she laughed so hard at the comedian. If the cause was that the comedian really is very funny, then we should definitely follow her advice. But if it was just something unusual about Mary, or about the situation that night, we would not be so likely to go. That is, we try to decide whether her behavior is caused by something specific to the stimulus object (the comedian), to the actor (Mary), or to the context (the people she was with, the drinks, etc.).

Kelley's theory suggests we solve the dilemma by checking each dimension in turn. This involves answering three questions for ourselves: (1) Does Mary always laugh at *any* comedian, or did she really laugh unusually hard at this one? (2) Have we heard the same report from others, or is Mary the only one who laughed at this particular comedian? and (3) Did she laugh during each of the three shows she stayed through, or was it just the people she was sitting with and the drinks she had during one of them?

Kelley's theory then leads to three different kinds of information that people use in trying to arrive at a causal attribution: (1) *Distinctiveness* information. Does the person act in this manner only in regard to this stimulus object, and not in regard to other objects? That is, is Mary's reaction distinctive to this particular object? (2) *Consensus* information. Do other people act in the same way in this situation? Did other people like this comedian as well? (3) *Consistency* information. Does this person consistently react the same way at other times or in other situations? This, then, is the process Kelley hypothesizes to occur when we attribute a given effect to a given cause. We quickly review our store of information along these three dimensions. The review may be implicit and automatic rather than deliberate and conscious, but still we review what we know.

For an external attribution to be made—that is, for the comedian's comic ability to be the true cause of Mary's laughter—all three tests have to be passed in the appropriate manner: high distinctiveness, high consensus, and high consistency. Her reaction has to be distinctive to this comedian and not to others; other people have to like the comedian; and she has to like the comedian consistently in this and other situations.

McArthur (1972) has made the most systematic study of predictions from Kelley's cube theory. She gave subjects a very simple hypothetical event, varied the kind of consensus, distinctiveness, and consistency information available to them, and then measured their attributions. The three main predictions and the results are shown in Table 5–2, using this same example. The first case is the same as the one just cited and promotes an attribution to the object itself, since it passes all three tests. Everyone else was also laughing, she didn't laugh at any of the other performers, but she always laughed at this one. So he must be a funny comedian. Mostly, the subjects saw it that way too; given this pattern of information, 61 percent attributed her reaction to the comedian (the other 39 percent made other attributions). The second example leads the observer to make a person attribution: Mary laughs at any comedian and always

TABLE 5–2

Why Did Mary Laugh at the Comedian?

| CONDITION | AVAILABLE INFORMATION | | | MOST COMMON ATTRIBUTION |
	Consensus	Distinctiveness	Consistency	
1	High—everyone else laughed too.	High—she didn't laugh at anyone else.	High—she always laughs at him.	Stimulus object: The comedian (61%)
2	Low—hardly anyone else laughed.	Low—she always laughs at comedians.	High—she always laughs at him.	Person: Mary (86%)
	Low—hardly anyone else laughed.	High—she didn't laugh at anyone else.	Low—she has almost never laughed at him.	Context (72%)

Source: Adapted from McArthur (1972).

laughs at this one—but hardly anyone else did. Mary must be a laugher (86 percent). The third case leads us to think there is something special about the situation: she didn't laugh at anyone else, she has almost never laughed at him before, and hardly anyone else laughed. Something unique must have happened. And 72 percent did attribute her laughter to the particular circumstances.

The Discounting Principle

The other main principle in making causal attributions is more obvious but very important. Kelley calls it the *discounting principle:* "the role of a given cause in producing a given effect is discounted if other plausible causes are also present" (1972, p. 8). That is, we make less confident attributions, and are less likely to attribute the effect to any particular cause, if more than one cause is likely. An insurance salesperson is very nice to us and invites us to dinner, but we may not be able to make a confident attribution about why he is so friendly. We could take him at his word and attribute his behavior to his real liking for us. More likely, we may discount his behavior and attribute it partly to liking and partly to his wanting our business. Of course, if we have no money to buy insurance, we may not do any such discounting.

FIGURE 5–3 Although the fact that they are in the military may cause to make attributions about these people's attitudes, we know that they are parading and carrying guns because they are required to do so. Thus, we discount other explanations of this behavior.

F. Siteman; Stock, Boston.

Two studies by Thibaut and Riecken (1955) provide a clear demonstration of the discounting principle. In the first experiment, the subject induced both a high-status and a low-status person to comply with his request. Then he was asked why they had complied. The idea here is that a low-status person should be perceived as responding primarily to external pressure (a request has been made by a more powerful person), whereas the high-status person would be seen as responding to some combination of external pressure (a request has been made of him, but it is not very compelling because it has been made by a less powerful person) and internal preferences (the request could be ignored if the high-status person did not want to comply). And indeed the actual results came out just this way. When the subjects were asked to indicate why the other people were influenced, in almost all cases they reported that the high-status person "had wanted to anyway." Yielding by the low-status person was more often attributed to the pressure put on him. Thus the locus of causality was more internal for the high-status than for the low-status person. This is what the discounting principle would lead us to expect. When the behavior is perceived as being caused by a mixture of internal and external forces (as was the case with the high-status complier), then we tend to divide up our attributions accordingly.

Perhaps the most common dilemma we are faced with is whether to attribute some behavior purely to an internal cause, or discount it and make an attribution to some combination of internal and external causes. In a second study, for example, Thibaut and Riecken showed that a strong person who performs a helpful act is perceived as nicer and as a better person than a weak person who performs the same act. Being helpful when strong portrays more internal causality; being helpful when weak is probably some combination of internal (being a nice person) and external causality (being forced to be helpful or suffer the consequences).

WHEN ATTRIBUTIONS ARE MADE

When do people engage in this attributional process of asking "Why?" Though human beings are supposedly a curious species, they do not go around asking Why about everything that happens. They do not wake up in the morning and ask why the sun comes up, why the boxer on TV is wearing boxing gloves, or why the bus they are riding in is still stopped while the green light has changed to red. Indeed most natural events and human acts probably do not inspire us to much cognitive effort searching out the correct causal attribution. As we saw in the last chapter, human beings tend to be miserly with their cognitive resources; they take many shortcuts and avoid cognitive work in a wide and creative variety of ways. And we cannot be very precise about the conditions under which people do undertake the search for causes, because they have not been researched very thoroughly as yet. But something is known.

Perhaps most important, people tend to be especially curious about causality when something unexpected happens. Explanations for the sun's and moon's movements are sought more around the time of an eclipse than normally. Newspaper readers, government officials, and social scientists want answers when there is a sudden, unexpected outburst of racial violence or student unrest than when the status quo is humming along as usual.

Bad, painful, unpleasant events also inspire the search for causal attributions. Bulman and Wortman (1977) poignantly document the efforts of paraplegics crippled by spinal cord injuries to analyze why it had happened to them. Most of the injuries were the result of unavoidable accidents, but still they wanted some more definite explanation. The assassination of John F. Kennedy inspired not only the Warren Commission's official explanatory effort, but a horde of amateur assassination buffs investigating alternative explanations. A wealthy family victimized by alcoholism funds research on alcoholism; and the Kennedy family, with one mentally retarded child, funded research on that disorder at an extraordinarily generous level. In intimate relationships, conflict triggers both partners to search for the root causes of the conflict (and often angrily to exchange competing explanations; see Orvis, Kelley, & Butler, 1976; Orvis, 1977).

Dependency also seems to motivate a search for causes. Berscheid and co-workers (1976) assigned one subject to be the date of another subject for up to a five-week period. This assignment increased the search for information about the prospective date, and increased efforts to make inferences about the date's traits. Whether dependency increases attributional search because it simply raises the stakes of any interaction, or because it makes some unpleasant, threatening event more likely, is unclear. And it may be that a temporary reduction in power raises more questions than does a chronic state of dependency and powerlessness. Revolutionary activists have always had a notoriously difficult time getting slaves, peasants, serfs, or other permanently downtrodden groups to question their status.

ATTRIBUTIONS ABOUT OTHERS

When attributions are made, how are they applied to judgments about the causes of others' behavior? In particular, when do we infer that another person's act reflects his real dispositions such as traits, attitudes, moods, or other internal states? Sometimes clearly they do not. A prisoner of war often may say things contrary to his real attitudes. Or a boy may try to act cheerful and happy in school the morning after his girlfriend jilted him. On the other hand, sometimes a POW expresses real, heartfelt criticism of his own nation's war effort, with which he may disagree. This certainly happened in the Vietnam War with some American soldiers and airmen. And the boy may have some genuine sense of relief, if his affair had been depressing him for a long time. So how can we tell when to infer an internal state that corresponds to the act, and when to infer some other cause?

The *discounting principle* suggests that we typically observe the person's act and then subtract out the environmental force. We use our own past experience to determine how this environment normally affects normal people. For example, we assume that hostages under armed guard are not making completely honest statements about their own attitudes; rather, we assume they are mostly acting under coercion, and any statement they make is mainly caused by these strong environmental forces. Most research on this problem has dealt with attributions about another person's expressed opinions. How do we know when to attribute a statement of opinion to a real attitude (an internal attribution), rather than to external forces? Social psychologists certainly know that people often give false opinion statements to others, succumbing to conformity pressures to avoid social disapproval. We discuss this in detail in Chapter 8. And apparently ordinary people take this into account when they make attributions.

The discounting principle would lead us to expect that when external forces are strong, a person's stated opinion is not necessarily perceived as an accurate reflection of a true underlying attitude. On the other hand, when external forces are weak, the expressed opinion tends to be trusted as reflecting the internal attitude. And this has generally been found. Jones and Harris (1967), for example, presented subjects with essays written by other students, in several conditions: the essays either supported Fidel Castro or opposed him (at a time when most college students and other Americans opposed Castro), and were supposedly written in some cases on an assigned side, and in other cases with free choice of position. With free choice, of course, the observers readily inferred that the writer's expressed opinion was the same as his true underlying attitude. This can be seen in Table 5–3. With free choice, the pro-Castro and anti-Castro speeches are seen as reflecting underlying pro- and anti-Castro attitudes, respectively. Even when the writer was described as having no choice of position (strong external forces), the observers still generally felt the written position reflected the underlying attitude. However, they were less confident this was so. The writer might hold the position advocated in the essay, but the subject was not as sure, because of the strong external forces operating.

A second factor in making attributions about others' attitudes is our *expectancy* about them, based on any additional information we might have about them. We know our friend has long been a supporter of black liberation movements in South Africa. So when we have dinner with her and her parents, we still infer that she is a strong supporter of the movement, despite the fact that she seems to be nodding agreeably at her parents' conservative statements. We have past information about her at-

TABLE 5-3

Attitude Attributed to Writer

CONDITION	SPEECH DIRECTION	
	Pro-Castro	Anti-Castro
Experiment 1		
Choice	59.6[a]	17.4
No choice	44.1	22.9
Experiment 2		
Choice	55.7	22.9
No choice	41.3	23.7

[a] A high score indicates a pro-Castro position attributed to the writer.
Source: Jones and Harris (1967), pp. 6, 10.

titudes, that gives us an expectancy about what she really believes. We use that information, along with our perception of her current overt behavior (which seems to be somewhat anti-movement) and the external forces (she does not want to get into an argument with her parents), to give us a confident attribution.

To test this, Jones and associates later (1971) did another experiment, much like the ones just described, directly varying this additional information about what attitudes the essay-writer might reasonably be expected to have. The essay writer again either had or did not have free choice about the position taken in the essay; this time on the subject of legalization of marijuana. But this time the subject also had direct information about the writer's usual political and social attitudes, in the form of a prior attitude questionnaire with items on various freedom and civil liberties issues. Again, choice led to perceiving the overt position as being the writer's true position, whereas no choice led to less confident attributions. But, when the position taken by the essay was expected from the writer's other attitudes, the observers confidently inferred that the writer really believed it, whether or not choice was present. This is shown in Figure 5-5. Put another way, observers confidently felt that overt behavior reflected a true underlying attitude (1) when there were no external forces (the free choice condition) *or* (2) when there were strong external forces but the overtly taken position was consistent with expectancies about the writer's overall sociopolitical attitudes.

In general, then, observers do attribute overt behavior to internal dispositions in the absence of clear external forces, or when they have other information about the person's past behavior that allows them to discount the role of the external forces. When Ted Kennedy makes a pro-civil-rights speech to an NAACP convention, we attribute it to his true pro-civil-rights attitudes. To be sure, there are strong external forces—the NAACP certainly wants to hear him support civil rights. But we know that

Patricia Hollander Gross; Stock, Boston.

FIGURE 5-4 Since they are wearing uniforms and were therefore in the army, their protest carries different meaning than if they were people who had not served in the military. Would the protest carry a still different significance if they were neatly dressed in fancy uniforms?

FIGURE 5-5 Attribution of attitude as a function of expectancy, choice, and essary direction (strong essarys only).

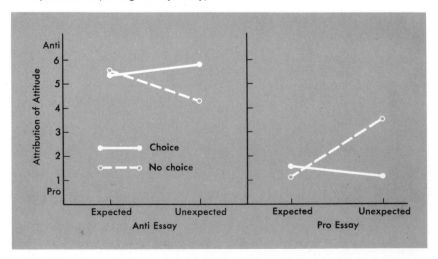

he has been a strong supporter of civil rights in the past, so we attribute his speech to his true attitudes, not to the forces represented by the audience.

SELF-PERCEPTION

One of the most provocative hypotheses in attribution theory is that people arrive at perceptions of their own internal states in the same way that they arrive at perceptions of others' states. This work proceeds from the general assumption that our own emotions, attitudes, traits, and abilities are often unclear and ambiguous to us. So we have to infer them from our overt behavior and from our perception of the environmental forces surrounding us. In other words, we try to attribute causality for our acts using substantially the same data, and the same attributional processes that we use in attributing causality for other's acts. This work has been especially active with respect to attitudes and emotions.

Attitudes

Conventionally, psychologists have assumed that people determine their own attitudes by reviewing the various cognitions and affects in their consciousness, then expressing the result. But Darryl Bem (1965) assumed that we receive only minimal and ambiguous internal cues to our attitudes, just as we have no direct access to the internal cues in others. So we must infer our own attitudes by self-observation rather than introspection. In other words, people come to know their own attitudes by inspecting whatever external cues are available, and then making the appropriate attribution. Bem does not hold that people never use internal evidence, but his theory does suggest that to a surprising degree people rely upon the external evidence of their overt behavior, and the conditions under which it occurs, to infer their own true attitudes.

The direct evidence for this theory involved studies that manipulate the individual's overt behavior, and then measure his report of his internal dispositions. If the self-perception process is working, he will report different dispositions depending on his overt behavior. For example, Salancik and Conway (1975) subtly manipulated subjects' perceptions of their own religious behavior. Some subjects were induced to report a lot of religious behavior, whereas others were induced to report very little, even though both groups actually engaged in the same amount. The way experimenters induced such differences in reports of behavior was by manipulating whether the subject said he or she did the behavior "occasionally" or "frequently." For example, to induce the subject to report a high level of proreligious behavior, he was asked if he "occasionally" read a religious newspaper or magazine, attended a church or synagogue, and consulted a minister about personal problems. To induce the subject to report a low level of proreligious behavior, he was asked if he "frequently" did each of these things. Since most college students, even those who are rather religious, do these things at most "occasionally," they tended to agree when asked if they did them "occasionally"; they therefore seemed (to themselves as well as to others) rather religious. On the other hand, the other subjects tended to disagree when asked if they did them "frequently," so they would seem rather unreligious. One group of subjects therefore maintained that they engaged in religious behaviors, while the other group denied it. And sure enough, when later asked about their own overall religious attitudes, in the form of the question "how religious are you?", the first group, which had been induced to describe themselves as engaging in religious behaviors, said they were more religious.

We shall discuss most of the research related to this idea in Chapter 11, because there we discuss how overt behavior controls internal attitudes. For the moment, the important point is that even attitudes, which are usually considered to be internally determined, may to some extent be affected by attributions based on overt behavior.

Emotions

The major theorist concerned with the self-perception of emotions is Stanley Schachter. Traditional theorists of emotion proposed that we recognize what we feel by considering our physiological state, our mental state, and the external stimulus causing these states. But recent evidence indicates that many, if not all, emotional reactions are biochemically similar—perhaps identical. Since their internal physiological characteristics are indistinguishable, we need other information to explain our emotions. So Schachter suggests that we arrive at perceptions of our emotions from (1) physiological arousal (which is more or less undifferentiated) and (2) an appropriate cognitive label, such as "angry" or "happy." To arrive at an appropriate cognitive label for our ambiguous feelings of arousal, we review the situation and/or how we are behaving, and from that we infer what our emotion must be. The experience of any given emotion therefore increases with generalized arousal and with attribution to some appropriate emotion-arousing stimulus. This emphasizes the importance of external cues concerning both our own behavior and the environment.

With this as a starting point, Schachter conducted a series of studies on the interrelationship between physiological and social factors in emotion. These experiments varied the availability of an internal attribution for physiological arousal, hypothesizing that when no internal attribution was available, arousal would be attributed to emotion-arousing properties of the external situation. In the first, Schachter and Singer (1962) varied (1) whether or not subjects were given an arousing drug (epinephrine), and (2) cognitive labels attributing the resulting physiological arousal either to the drug, or to the subject's own emotion. The drug epinephrine, in appropriate quantities, produces the kind of physiological arousal that is generally associated with emotions but that does not resemble any particular emotion. Some of these subjects were told that the drug would produce a noticeable physiological arousal—such as more rapid heartbeats—and others were not. Thus, some of the aroused people could attribute their internal state to the drug, whereas others were unable to. A final group of subjects was not given epinephrine and so was less aroused physiologically. All subjects were then placed in a situation in which a confederate of the experimenter pretended to be experiencing a particular emotion. Half the subjects were exposed to someone behaving in a euphoric, elated way; half were exposed to someone acting very angry. The euphoric confederate made paper planes and flew them around; started a small game of basketball using crumpled papers and an old wastebasket; sang, danced, hopped around, and in general presented a zany, light-headed attitude. The angry confederate made nasty remarks, had an unpleasant expression on his face, muttered to himself, and generally presented a disgruntled, annoyed picture. The question was, how did the subjects react?

Those who had been aroused by the drug and had not been informed of this (the "external attribution condition") became more euphoric in the euphoria condition and more angry in the anger condition than the other groups. When there was arousal and no irrelevant cause to which to attribute it, the subjects presumably interpreted their arousal as being caused by an emotion-arousing situation—the same situation causing the other person's behavior. When he was happy, they became happy; when he was angry, so were they. But when aroused subjects could attribute their arousal to the drug (in the "drug attribution" condition), they were relatively unaffected by the other person's behavior. They knew that their physiological state was due to the drug and therefore did not interpret it as emotional arousal. The procedure and results of this experiment are shown in Table 5–4.

The key element here is that when the person was both aroused and placed in a situation with no other attribution, he "caught" the salient emotion from the external situation. That is, in the absence of any alternative, he attributed his arousal externally to the situation's capacity for producing either euphoria or anger. Consequently, he acted in a more euphoric or angry way. In the other condition, where arousal was attributed to the drug, no such emotion was aroused. In short, what was important for the experience of emotion was first of all the *arousal,* and second the *cognitive label* or the attribution made for the arousal. When the label attributed the arousal to the drug, the subjects acted as if they experienced no particular emotion. On the other hand, when they did not know that the drug was responsible for their arousal, they took their cues about their emotions from the external environment.

A number of further studies have used this same general approach, and most of them have gotten approximately the same results. Some have not (e.g., Marshall & Zimbardo, 1979). On balance, the phenomenon iden-

TABLE 5–4

The Schachter-Singer Experiment

SEQUENCE / CONDITION	STEP 1 Given Arousing Drug	STEP 2 Told It Would Be Arousing	STEP 3 Confederate's Behavior	STEP 4 Presumed Attribution for own Arousal (Unmeasured)	STEP 5 Own Behavior (Measured)
Drug attribution	Yes	Yes		Drug	Calm
External attribution	Yes	No	Euphoric or angry in all cases	Situationally; induced emotion	Euphoric or angry
No arousal	No	No		None	Calm

Source: Adapted from Schachter and Singer (1962).

tified by Schachter and Singer seems reliable, though no single experiment by itself is adequate to confirm the point.

MISATTRIBUTION The Schachter-Singer experiment led to a series of what have been called **misattribution** studies. The idea was to give the subject a neutral pill (or some other neutral stimulus), and then get him to misattribute some normal everyday emotion to the pill and thus reduce his experienced emotionality. The model for such misattributions was the "drug attribution" condition in Table 5–4. When a person attributes his experienced emotionality to a drug, he does not attribute it to environmental events (as in the Schachter-Singer experiment) or to his own real emotions (as in the experiments to be described next). As a result he does not perceive himself as "really" emotional; he thinks his subjectively experienced arousal is just caused by the drug.

In one such experiment, Nisbett and Schachter (1966) gave all subjects an ordinary sugar pill. Experimental subjects were told the pill would produce physiological symptoms, such as hand tremors and palpitations; control subjects were told it would produce only nonphysiological symptoms. Finally, all subjects were administered painful electric shock. The hypothesis was that the experimental subjects would attribute their physiological reactions after the shock to the pill, rather than to the shock itself, and so would think the shock hurt less. The control subjects, having no basis for an attribution to the pill, would blame their reactions on the shock itself. And indeed it was found that these control subjects found the shock more painful than did the experimental subjects.

Such misattribution studies hold arousal constant and vary the attribution (or cognitive label) applied to the arousal as a way to change behavior. Schachter's general theory can also be tested, however, by manipulating the person's perception of his own arousal, holding constant the attribution, and then seeing if behavior changes. To test this idea requires giving random false feedback to subjects about their own arousal. Valins presented heterosexual male subjects with slides of nude females, and after each slide provided faked feedback to the subject about rate of heartbeat. Each subject was wired to fake electrodes and told that his own heartbeat was played into his earphones. After each slide, some subjects heard increased heartbeats, which they thought were their own, and others heard what they thought were irrelevant sounds. Valins found that subjects rated nudes as more attractive when they had been accompanied by their own supposedly increased heartbeat. Also, after the experiment was over, subjects were allowed to take some slides home. They mostly took slides that had been associated with increased heartbeat. This was evidence that people infer their own internal subjective states (in this case sexual attraction to a particular woman) on the basis of what their bodies tell them (or, in this case, what they thought their bodies were telling them), and not necessarily on their perceptions of the external stimulus itself.

Another example is from a study by Cantor, Zillman, and Bryant (1975). They had heterosexual male subjects ride an exercycle vigorously enough to reach a high level of physiological arousal. Physiological arousal based on this kind of exercise tends to last longer than the person really realizes. So a few minutes later, the subjects no longer felt aroused but objective indicators of arousal showed they were. Female nudes shown at this point were rated as more attractive than those rated immediately after the exercise (when they presumably attributed their arousal to the exercise) or at a still later point (when there was no remaining arousal to be misattributed to the nudes).

If normal emotions could be so easily changed by misattributing them to a sugar pill or a new stimulus, then perhaps harmful emotions could be reduced in the same way. It could be a useful kind of therapy if disruptive and maladaptive emotions could be dispensed with through a "reattribution" treatment. Storms and Nisbett (1970) tried this with insomniac patients. The patients were given placebos (harmless sugar pills) before going to bed. In the arousal condition, they were told the pills would cause physiological arousal; in the sedation condition, they were told it would actually reduce arousal. As expected, arousal subjects got to sleep more quickly, because they attributed their jumpiness and restlessness to the pills rather than to any emotional preoccupations. On the other hand, the sedation subjects actually got to sleep later than usual, because they were still jumpy and restless after taking a supposedly relaxing pill. They could only infer that their emotional problems and worries were even worse than usual. Once again the point is that reattributing one's normal emotional arousal (insomnia anxiety) to something external to the emotion itself (in this case the drug) reduces the emotional experience, with the beneficial behavioral consequence of reducing insomnia.

On the other hand, a study by Kellogg and Baron (1975) not only failed to replicate these findings, but actually found the opposite: Subjects given a pill that was supposedly arousing had more trouble sleeping. Since this was a very careful study, it raises the possibility that the original result is not correct, or that this particular misattribution effect occurs only in certain, limited circumstances that we are not yet able to specify. In other words, although the Storms and Nisbett study produced fascinating results, we should be very careful about accepting them until they have been repeated by other experimenters. However, we should also keep in mind that the effect we are talking about here—actually reducing insomnia—is very large and dramatic compared to the effects of most brief experiments done by social psychologists. Thus, it is perhaps not surprising that the effect is difficult to demonstrate and may occur only under restricted conditions.

In general when these "misattribution" or "reattribution" studies were first done, they gave some promise of providing a new therapeutic tool for dealing with disruptive anxieties, fears, depressions, low self-esteem, and other seemingly neurotic emotions. A variety of other studies have tried to apply reattribution therapies to public speaking anxiety, test anxiety, depression, and other unwanted emotions. Some have been successful and others have not (Berkevec and Glasgow, 1973; Koenig, 1973; Nisbett et al., 1976). One unavoidable problem is that it relies on deceiving the subject (or patient), which may be neither ethical nor practical in the long run. It is probably too early to judge how powerful the technique is for therapeutic purposes.

SOME LIMITATIONS The most extreme forms of this self-perception viewpoint would seem to argue that we get almost no information about our own attitudes and emotions by introspection; that outside observers know as much about our own internal feelings as we do. This is almost surely too extreme. First of all, this self-perception process works mainly when there is a good bit of ambiguity or uncertainty about our internal states. People do have attitudes that endure from one moment to the next and are not based entirely on current behavior. They do not decide about whether or not they like steak on the basis of whether or not they have recently eaten steak. They have real feelings toward steak and it is those feelings that determine their responses. Israelis have certain attitudes about Nazis, and bigots have certain attitudes about minorities, which they are quite clear about regardless of their most recent behavior. When we are slapped in the face, we do not have to wait to see if we strike back to know if we are angry. When our girlfriend says she no longer loves us, we know we feel hurt no matter whether tears come or not. If a male subject is shown a whole series of beautiful nude females, it may be fairly easy to alter his preferences among them based on false feedback. But it strikes us as unlikely that the same subject, shown a nude Miss July and a nude hippopotamus, and given false feedback that his heartbeat had accelerated more for the hippo, will seriously think he desires the hippo and will want to take her slide home.

A second limitation is that this self-perception process seems to work best when the person does not care very much about what response she makes. When it really matters, then people seem to monitor their own attitudes and emotions more carefully, and are less influenced by external cues. To test this idea, Shelley Taylor (1975) ran an experiment like the Valins nude-slides study—except that this time *female* college students were presented with pictures of full-face color photographs of clothed *male* graduate students. She first had each of the women rate these pictures for attractiveness. Then the subject was given false feedback about her physiological reactions to one of the slides, by overhearing a confederate saying that she (the subject) had reacted more strongly to that slide than to any other slide. Half the time this false feedback of high arousal concerned a slide the subject had already rated as highly attractive, and half time it concerned a slide of a man the subject had rated as only medium in attractiveness. According to the self-perception idea, this false high-arousal feedback ought to boost the subject's ratings of the attractiveness of these slides.

But the critical variable was how important the attitude was, to test the notion that the self-perception process works best with relatively inconsequential attitudes. In the high-importance case, the subject was told she would be meeting some of the men whose pictures she had seen. In the low-importance condition, no such future meeting was mentioned.

When the subject expected to meet the man, she gave quite similar ratings both before and after the false arousal feedback. As shown in Table 5–5, one stimulus person became slightly less attractive, and the other slightly more so. False feedback changed initial attitudes more when no future meeting was expected, and so the ratings were not very important. In general then, people probably use external cues to determine their own attitudes most often under conditions of low involvement.

Finally, do people have as little insight into the causes of their own behavior as the self-perception theory implies? Bem's notion that people have little access to their own attitudes and emotions suggests not, but it does not address the matter directly. Nisbett and Wilson (1977) have taken the position that people often cannot report accurately on the effects of particular stimuli on their behavior. Note that this is contrary to the

TABLE 5–5

**Effects of False High Arousal Feedback on
Attractiveness Ratings**

CONDITION	INITIALLY HIGH ATTRACTIVE SP	INITIALLY MEDIUM ATTRACTIVE SP
Future meeting	−0.59	+1.17[a]
No future meeting	+1.09	+2.75

[a] A positive score means an increase in attraction.
Source: Adapted from Taylor (1975), p. 130.

general viewpoint expressed by the cube theory, which depicts people as reviewing the possible internal and external causes of their behavior rather systematically and sensitively.

While they may be unaware of the minor causes, people are certainly aware of the major causes of their own behavior. For example, do you know why you are reading this book? Do you know why you stopped at the red light while driving to school today? Do you know why you sit down in the classroom at the beginning of class, and get up at the end? Shout in your neighbor's ear, and then ask her if she knows why she jumped and looked at you crossly. On the other hand, it is probably hard to explain why you put your left sock on before your right sock this morning, or why you bought the leftmost tube of toothpaste in the drugstore rather than the one in the middle or the one on the right.

In short, people probably mainly use external cues to determine their own attitudes and emotions mainly when they have uncertain or ambiguous internal reactions, or when they have rather mild reactions because they really do not care much one way or the other. And people are probably not so sensitive to the causes of their own behavior when there is some real ambiguity about them, or when the situation is unfamiliar or unimportant, or when the causes really are quite subtle or hidden.

THE NAÏVE SCIENTIST?

By and large, all this research does seem to follow fairly well the pattern described by the principles of invariance and discounting, and Kelley's cube theory. People do seem to review what information they have about their own behavior, or the behavior of others, and attribute it to internal or external causes depending on the information available. If there is strong evidence of internal dispositions, an internal attribution is made. If there is evidence of no internal causes or just weak ones, with evidence of strong external forces, an external attribution is made. So where do some of the problems or limitations of attribution theory arise?

Attribution theory, particularly in Kelley's version, describes an essentially rational, logical process. In fact, Kelley draws an analogy between the naïve psychologist, the person in the street who tries to arrive at causal attributions for everyday events, and the systematic scientist, who applies the scientific method to achieve causal explanations for natural events. In that form, attribution theory assumes that people process information in a rational way, that they are fairly objective in assessing information and in combining it to produce a conclusion. But we know that people tend to be intellectually lazy (or at least cognitively miserly), and it is unlikely that they spend most of their waking moments diligently trying to ferret out the causes of things. Moreover, since psychologists themselves have such a struggle unraveling the causes of human behavior, ordinary people can hardly be expected to do much better. Furthermore people are far from being logical and rational. Indeed, most of this book, and most of psychology, is devoted to studying the irrational aspects of human behavior.

Kelley really offered the cube theory mainly as a starting point, and believed that in many ways the most interesting questions would arise about the departures from it; that is, about the errors and biases that people make as they try to establish causality. For that reason, we now turn to several biases that have been identified in empirical research. These can be grouped conveniently into two categories: cognitive biases and motivational biases.

COGNITIVE BIASES

Theorizing about cognitive biases comes generally from the perceptual-cognitive tradition, as discussed in Chapter 1. One application of this thinking to social perception has already been covered in Asch's view of impression formation (see Chapter 4). He, you will remember, argued that people spontaneously and automatically form coherent and meaningful impressions. People quickly see the parts in interrelation, form a complete impression even with only minimal information, and promote a structured impression. Heider and Simmel (1944) made a similar demonstration of how naturally and readily we create order and meaningfulness in simple perceptual relationships, by spontaneously perceiving causes and effects in them. They showed subjects a film that involved the movements of two triangles and a circle. These are shown in Figure 5–6. During the course of the film, these shapes moved around in various ways. For example, the large triangle moved toward the small one and contacted it vigorously. The subjects described the movements as if they were the movements of animate beings, whether they were instructed to do so or just asked generally to interpret the film. They mentioned such relationships as "chasing" and "fighting," and dispositions such as "shy" or

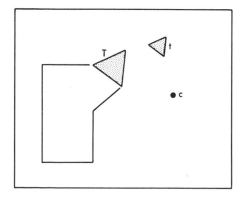

FIGURE 5–6 Geometrical figures used in the study of phenomenal causality.

Source: Adapted from Heider and Simmel (1944); Shaver (1975), p. 37.

"bully." The point of the demonstration was that people quickly arrive at causal judgments when they see even simple perceptual forms moving, and they attribute the movements to internal dispositions of the stimuli and to characteristics of the surrounding environment.

Bassili (1976) extended this research using computer-generated films depicting movement of abstract figures across a stimulus field. These figures moved closer or farther from each other (spatial contingency) and did so either moving right after one another or separated by more time (temporal contingency). Then he asked subjects to describe what they had seen. He too found that people talked about the intentions of the circles. The most important point, however, was that he showed temporal contingency to be crucial for the perception of an interaction between the figures. That is, one figure had to move immediately after the other for a causal relationship to be perceived. Spatial contingency was critical for determining the nature of that relationship. When they came closer together, relationships like chasing, following, and hitting were ascribed. When they did not move in concert with one another, such relationships were not perceived.

These two studies indicate how spontaneously we perceive causality even when the stimuli we are dealing with are simple abstract forms moving in simple spatial relationships. More important, they suggest that we arrive at causal attributions on the basis of rather simple perceptual gestalts—that an attribution is made on the basis of what makes a simple, coherent explanation. This implies that biases and distortions are likely to intrude when they can promote simplicity, and occur on the basis of simple perceptual relations like movement, precedence, similarity, contact, or proximity in general.

Salience

One way we simplify is to overreact to *salient* stimuli, as indicated in the last chapter. In particular, this bias leads us to perceive the most salient stimuli as the most causally influential ones. If something is in motion, or colorful, or loud, or novel, we are likely to see it as the main cause of whatever else is changing in the environment. The man who is running down the street is seen as causing the bank's alarm system to go off. The loud thunderclap is perceived as causing people to scurry for cover. The woman in the red dress is thought to cause people's heads to turn. Of course sometimes the most salient stimuli are in fact the strongest causes of people's behavior, so such attributions would then be accurate. Bias arises because the most perceptually salient stimuli dominate causal explanations even when they are not actually the most powerful causes.

In a most elegant way, Taylor and Fiske (1975) tested this simple idea, that whatever is perceptually salient will attract the dominant causal explanation. Two confederates served as "actors." They engaged in a conversation, facing each other. The ordinary subjects were "observers" sitting either behind the confederates or next to them. Each actor thus had observers both sitting behind him and facing him. Clearly, the actor and his behavior would be more salient for those who faced him than for those who sat behind him. But both actors ought to be equally salient for the observers sitting to the side, equidistant from the two actors. This arrangement is illustrated in Figure 5–7. The confederates then held a standardized five-minute conversation, chatting as if they had just met. They exchanged information about majors, common job plans, home towns, family, extracurricular activities, and the like. The conversation was carefully monitored to make sure that roughly the same conversation occurred in all experimental groups.

Then the subjects were asked for their causal perceptions: How much had each confederate set the tone of the conversation, determined the kind of information exchanged, and caused the other actor to behave as he did? The results are shown in Table 5–6. It shows that the more perceptually salient actor (the confederate the subject faced) was given the dominant causal role, and that the less salient actor (the one the confederate sat behind) was seen as less influential. Subjects sitting equidistant from both confederates, saw both as about equally potent. Thus Actor A was seen as most powerful by those facing him, while Actor B was seen as most powerful by those facing *him*—even though all subjects in reality were observing exactly the same interaction (and one in which both actors contributed about equally, in reality, according to the unbiased observers in the center).

This finding is quite general. The same authors replicated this study

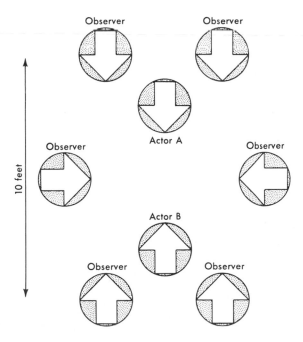

FIGURE 5–7 Seating arrangement for actors and observers, with arrows indicating visual orientation.

Source: Adapted from Taylor and Fiske (1975), p. 441.

This finding has also been applied to the effects of token integration, because the "token" black or female stand out to such a degree in a group that is otherwise all white or all male. So Taylor, Fiske, Close, Anderson, and Ruderman (1977) set up group discussions that were all white, had one black, or were evenly divided in race. The same tape recording was used in all cases, but each speaker was identified with a still slide as he spoke, and the race of the speakers was varied. Subjects who were exposed to this mixed-media discussion rated the speakers for amount of contribution to the discussion. The "solo" black stood out as talking more, being more influential, and giving a clearer impression than did the same speaker in either of the other contexts, where his race did not make him so salient.

using videotaped rather than face-to-face interactions. And Taylor and her colleagues (1979) found the same thing even under conditions they thought would reduce the importance of salience; e.g., when the perceiver was distracted, when impressions were assessed after a delay, when the conversation itself was very interesting, and when the perceivers themselves were involved in the discussion. In all these experiments, it should be noted, the real causes are held constant, only the salience is varied along dimensions irrelevant to the person's actual behavior. So it is reasonable to conclude that perceptual salience induces stronger perceptions of causal role among observers.

TABLE 5-6

Mean Ratings of Causal Role Attributed by Observers to Each Actor as a Function of the Observer's Seating Position

OBSERVER'S POSITION	ACTOR	
	A	B
Facing Actor A	20.25	15.54
Center	17.51	16.75
Facing Actor B	12.00	20.75

Source: Taylor and Fiske (1975), p. 441.

The most important consequence of this attributional bias is that people overestimate the importance of dispositional factors in others' behavior. Put another way, observers take too little account of external causes (contextual factors) in judgments of other persons' behavior. That is, we tend to explain other people's behavior as caused by their dispositions, and underestimate the causal role of the situation. This bias in observers is so common that Ross (1977) calls it "the fundamental attribution error."

Salience is the explanation for this overattribution to internal forces, according to Heider: "Behavior . . . has such salient properties that it tends to engulf the field;" that is, we pay so much attention to the person's behavior that we tend to ignore the situation in which it occurs. The behavior becomes figure and therefore stands out against the surrounding ground of the situation. And figural, or salient, cues are overused in causal explanations, as just demonstrated.

We have already seen one example of this fundamental attributional bias in the Jones and Harris (1967) study of attributions about the attitudes of people writing essays on Fidel Castro. Observers trying to determine the essay writer's true position paid much more attention to the writer's expressed position (that is, to his overt behavior) than to the situation (that is, to whether or not the writer had any choice about the position taken in his essay). This can be seen in Table 5–3. Quite a number of later studies have been done to determine whether this Jones and Harris result is typical. It is a very important one, because it is a key illustration of the principle that behavior engulfs the field, and thereby biases causal attributions in the direction of overemphasizing dispositions and underemphasizing the environment. In its original form, it made quite a strong statement: Even when subjects knew that the writer had no choice about the position to be advocated, they still perceived the position he advocated as his true position. That is, they ignored information about situational pressures, and attributed the behavior to the writer's true dispositions.

Later work has explored two possibilities. One is that observers might have been attributing the essay to the writer's true position because the essay was in fact rather strong and persuasive (having been prepared for the occasion by the investigators). Perhaps essays that were genuinely forced would seem unenthusiastic and less convincing, and would betray the lack of choice involved, so no internal attribution would be made. Snyder and Jones (1974) did five experiments, this time using essays actually written by students assigned to advocate a particular position. But again, the subjects perceived the position advocated as the true position of the communicators, even under no-choice conditions. Even with a deliberately drab, unenthusiastic, unforceful presentation, using a speaker who simply read a transcribed version of the talk, spoke in a monotone, and used no gestures, Schneider and Miller (1975) found that observer subjects took the no-choice speaker's position at face value, and felt that it represented his true opinion. Finally, with patently weak arguments, observers did no longer take the no-choice writer's overt position as his true one. Jones and associates (1971) presented subjects with weak essays on legalization of marijuana. The writer presented two arguments from each side, and then simply concluded that his side was right. In this case, the apparent position was not taken as the true position. In fact, the opposite side was taken as the true position.

A second possibility is that the real lack of choice involved in this

---

BOX 5-3
HOW TO SEEM SMART

One ingenious use of this fundamental attribution error made observers considerably overestimate other students' amount of general knowledge. Ross, Amabile, and Steinmetz (1977) set up pairs of Stanford students in a quiz situation. One was a "questioner," and the other a "contestant." In the experimental condition, each questioner was allowed to make up ten "challenging but not impossible" questions on any subject he or she wanted and then pose them to the contestant. Both then rated themselves and their partner for general knowledge. The questions that were made up were indeed fairly difficult (e.g., on the order of "What is the capital of New Mexico?"), and contestants only got four of ten

right, on the average. But the important finding was that contestants vastly overestimated the questioner's knowledge. Contestants rated the questioners as extremely well informed by comparison to themselves, while questioners rated both as about equal, as shown below. The fundamental attribution error occurs when observers take overt behavior too seriously and ignore the situation. These contestants apparently thought the questioners were really well informed since they had known the answers to seemingly hard questions. They ignored the artificiality of the situation—that is, the questioners were able to make up any question they liked and were obviously likely to make up questions they knew the answers to.

		RATING[a] OF:	
		Questioner's Knowledge	Contestant's Knowledge
RATING MADE BY:	Questioner	53.5	50.6
	Contestant	66.8	41.3

[a] Rating made on a 100-point scale.
Source: Ross, Amabile, and Steinmetz (1977).

situation was not emphasized enough. So, would clearer cases of no choice yield an external attribution? Miller (1976), for example, presented subjects with audiotapes or videotapes of speakers reading aloud essays that were described as being written by someone else. Still the read-aloud position was taken to be the speaker's true position. In one final experiment, Snyder and Jones (1974) first put the subjects through the no-choice procedure themselves, so they would appreciate just how little choice there was. And they were given the two arguments on which they were to base their own essay. The subjects were thus able to experience the fact that the essay-writer had no choice about either the position taken or the arguments used. In this case the effect disappeared. The position taken by the speaker was not taken as his true position.

All in all, it appears that the tendency to take a speaker's position as his true attitude seems amazingly resilient, even in conditions when he has no choice, is unenthusiastic, gives weak arguments, and is simply reading somebody else's speech. As long as the target person is presenting the material visually or orally, the behavior still seems to engulf the field. Only under the most extreme situational constraints, and with very weak arguments delivered in drab, written form, does the behavior-engulfing-the-field phenomenon disappear, and observers finally accept the causal role of external forces.

Why is this phenomenon so tenacious? Why do observers resist all information about the external constraints placed upon these speakers? Certainly part of the answer lies in the salience of the behavior. But why should behavior be attributed to the person rather than to the situation? Jones (1979), following Heider, contends that a person and his actions form a natural perceptual and cognitive unit. They are in a "unit relation" like those described in the last chapter. We think of the two as indivisible. It is "*his* action," not an independent event which temporarily seems to be in the same physical space as the actor. It is very hard to break a unit relation by detaching the two perceptually, so we naturally connect a person to his act, and perceive him as causing it.

Actors Versus Observers

One of the most provocative elaborations on the fundamental attributional error is that it holds for observers but not, apparently, for actors perceiving their own behavior. They instead seem to overemphasize the role of external factors. That is, as Jones and Nisbett (1971) put it, observers overestimate dispositional causes, while actors overestimate situational ones. A wife who gets angry at her husband at a cocktail party for spending too long in the corner talking to that blonde is likely to attribute his "offensive" behavior to him: to his lack of caring for his wife, his infidelity, his selfishness, his immaturity, and other such dispositions. He, on the other hand, is likely to attribute his behavior to some characteristics of the blonde, to her fascinating conversation or stimulating personality. So the observing wife makes internal attributions, while the offending husband actor makes external attributions.

This has proved to be one of the most interesting and widely researched of the various attributional biases. In one of its earliest demonstrations, Nisbett et al. (1973) asked male student subjects to write a paragraph on why they liked the woman they dated most, and why they had chosen their major. Then they were asked to write similar paragraphs for their best friend. These responses were scored for the extent to which the behavior was attributed to the actor's disposition (e.g., I need someone I can relax with, or I want to make a lot of money) or externally, to the aspects of the stimulus object (e.g., chemistry is a high-paying field). As can be seen in Table 5–7, external reasons are given for one's own behavior much more than for another person's behavior. And there is some tendency, though it is not as strong, to give internal reasons for a friend's behavior.

Jones and Nisbett offer two explanations for this actor-observer difference in attributions. One is that the participants have access to *different information* and therefore naturally come to different conclusions. For example, the actor has direct access to his own current subjective state—his intentions, attitudes, and emotions—all of which play some part in determining his behavior. The observer, of course, has only indirect access to them. And the actor has access to much more historical information than does the usual observer, concerning how he has responded in the past to similar situations, how his behavior has varied across situations, and what his previous attributions have been. In Kelley's terms, the actor has more consistency and distinctiveness information. With all this inside information about how his behavior has varied across situations, the actor should be more likely to attribute it to the unique characteristics of each particular situation, rather than perceiving himself as behaving uniformly due to some general predisposition. And in fact as would be expected from this differential-information hypothesis, observers have been shown to give the same attributions as

TABLE 5–7

Number of Stimulus Object and Dispositional Reasons Given by Subjects as Explanations of their Own and Best Friend's Choices of Girlfriend and College Major

Explanation	REASONS FOR LIKING GIRLFRIEND		REASONS FOR CHOOSING MAJOR	
	Girlfriend	Dispositional	Major	Dispositional
Own behavior	4.61	2.04	1.52	1.83
Friend's behavior	2.70	2.57	.43	1.70

Source: Nisbett et al. (1973), p. 159.

actors when they are given the same information as actors have. Eisen (1979) had actors provide consensus, distinctiveness, and consistency information about their own behavior. Observers given that information then gave substantially the same attributions as the actors did themselves.

The other explanation, and the one more actively pursued by most researchers, is that the difference is due mainly to *different perspectives,* or perceptual orientations. The observer is naturally focused on the actor. This special salience of the actor leads the observer to overattribute his behavior to his dispositions, as we have already seen. This is "the fundamental attributional error." But the actor is not looking at his own behavior. He is looking at the situation—the place, the other people, their expectations, and so on. The actor's own behavior is not very salient to himself. For this reason the actor will see the situation as more salient and therefore more causally potent. In short, whatever attracts attention also becomes perceived as the causal force in the situation, just as Heider and Simmel had suggested in their early studies of abstract forms. For the observer, the actor's behavior engulfs the field, and so it then attracts causal explanations. For the actor, on the other hand, the environment rather than behavior is most salient, and *it* attracts causal explanations.

Storms (1973) succeeded in showing that differential perspectives could explain the actor-observer difference in locus of perceived causality. He reasoned that the difference could be reversed by reversing point of view. If the actor's own behavior was videotaped and played back to him, he ought to perceive himself as the most salient object in the field and ascribe causality to his own dispositions. Similarly, if the observers see more of the situation to which the actor is responding, rather than just focusing on the actor, they ought to ascribe more causality to the situation rather than simply seeing the actor's dispositions as the major cause.

To test this hypothesis, Storms also set up a situation in which two strangers (actors) meet to get acquainted. Sitting at the other end of the table from them were two observers watching their conversation, each instructed to watch a specific one of the two actors. Both actors were videotaped. But on playback, one actor's behavior was shown and the other's was not (the experimenter said that one camera had not worked). Thus one actor saw himself, which should have increased dispositional attributions; the other actor saw just the same thing that he had seen during the conversation, namely, the other actor, this time on videotape. Similarly, one observer saw a videotape of the actor to whom *his* actor has been responding, and therefore should have been more attuned to the situational forces operating on his actor. The other observer saw simply a repeat of the same thing he had seen earlier.

The standard actor-observer difference came out when the subjects saw no videotape replay, and so had only their normal perception of the discussion to go on. It also did when they simply saw a videotape repeating what they had already seen. In both cases, the observers made more dispositional attributions than did actors. This is shown in columns

1 and 2 of Table 5–8. But the crucial condition was the one reversing the actors' and observers' perspectives. When actors saw their own behavior played back and observers saw a playback of the person to whom their actor had been responding, the actors became more dispositionally oriented and the observers more situationally oriented. That is, the effect reversed. This is shown in the third column of Table 5–8.

This experiment confirms the basic actor-observer prediction of Jones and Nisbett, that under normal circumstances actors make more situational attributions and observers make more dispositional attributions. But it also suggests that this difference occurs because of their different perceptual orientations or points of view. That is, they are receiving different current information from their respective perceptual fields. And when this perceptual orientation is reversed, so too are the causal attributions.

Regan and Totten (1975) added yet another wrinkle to this same idea. They reasoned that if the observer adopted a more empathic attitude and tried to think or see things the same way the actor did, then the observer ought to see the world the same way the actor does. That is, if the observer adopted the perceptual orientation of the actor, through empathy, the observer ought to make more situational attributions. Their subjects were shown a videotape of two women students chatting for about 7 minutes about their home towns, intellectual interests, and travel. In one case the subjects were given instructions such as the following: "Please try to empathize with the girl on the left side of the screen. Imagine how Margaret feels as she engages in the conversation. While you are watching the tape, picture to yourself just how she feels in the situation." They found that the empathetic view reversed the usual actor-observer finding. That is, when the observers had the normal observer set, they were inclined to give more dispositional than situational attributions. However, under instructions to empathize with the actor, this reversed slightly, and the situational attributions became more prominent, pre-

TABLE 5–8

Tendency to Give Dispositional, Rather than Situational Attributions

ATTRIBUTION	NO VIDEOTAPE	VIDEOTAPE— SAME ORIENTATION	VIDEOTAPE— NEW ORIENTATION
Actors' attributions for own behavior	2.25	.15[a]	6.80
Observers' attributions for actor's behavior	4.80	4.90	1.60

[a] The higher the number, the more dispositional relative to situational attributions.
Source: Adapted from Storms (1973), p. 169.

sumably just as they would have been for the actor herself. Similarly, observers who merely anticipate engaging in the same actions start giving actorlike attributions—that is, they start to use the situation to explain the actor's behavior, just as the actor does (Wolfson & Salancik, 1977). Presumably they are empathizing and identifying with the actor, and are already starting to see things from his perspective.

These studies give good evidence that the actor-observer effect can be produced merely by the different points of view that actors and observers have. Does this then invalidate the differential-information hypothesis? Probably not. It is more likely that each is most important under different conditions. The Storms and Regan-Totten studies, which supported the differential-perspective idea, used vivid, real-life group discussions in which behavior was very salient, and historical factors were less important since it was a novel situation with strangers. The Eisen study, which supported the differential-information idea, used private responses to personality items on a questionnaire as the behaviors. The subject's behavior was much less salient, but the task did draw a good bit on both historical information and on the actors' inner feelings about themselves. In general, when historical factors or internal states are crucial determinants of behavior, actors will have better information and will probably be more accurate attributors. But when the behavior itself or the external situation is very salient, the differential-perspective theory will account better for differences between actors' and observers' attributions (Monson & Snyder, 1977).

Underusing Consensus Information

One safeguard against the fundamental attributional error ought to be consensus information. If we know that almost everyone thinks that calculus is difficult, then we should not make a dispositional attribution for Susy's troubles with it. We should attribute them to a difficult situation.

Kelley's model of attribution assumes that consensus, distinctiveness, and consistency information will all be used about equally. None of these is regarded as inherently more informative than any other. Yet experiments comparing them have found that subjects do not use consensus information as much as they should. For example, in trying to explain why Mary laughed at the comedian, it makes little difference to most observers whether other people were laughing at him or not. In trying to explain why Ralph tripped over Joan's feet at the dance, most observers feel it is irrelevant whether or not other men have tripped over her feet in the past (McArthur, 1972, 1976; Nisbett & Borgida, 1975; Ruble & Feldman, 1976).

In fact, in one study (Wells & Harvey, 1977) subjects seemed so dedicated to making dispositional rather than situational attributions for others' behavior that they completely ignored information of extremely high consensus (e.g., that 73 percent of the people in that situation had done exactly the same thing). Rather, they concluded that those people were an unrepresentative group. In other words, instead of interpreting such standardized behavior as reflecting a very compelling situation, the subjects concluded the behavior was caused by something internal to the actors—the fact that so many people did the same thing was interpreted as reflecting that they were weird people!

A number of writers have noted the parallel between such indifference to consensus information and a comparable lack of regard for what is called *baserate information* (Kahneman & Tversky, 1973). That is, people seem to disregard the probabilities and easily get distracted by concrete details. We discussed this bias in the last chapter in connection with Kahneman and Tversky's notion of an availability bias. Similarly, Nisbett and associates (1976) have speculated that such indifference to consensus and baserate information derived from their abstractness. Possibly people simply take more seriously concrete, vivid, singular instances, and tend to ignore the more abstract, bland, statistical kinds of information.

One implication would be that consensus information influences attributions only in the absence of more direct, valid, and concrete information. Feldman and co-workers (1976) showed subjects videotapes of five persons, one of whom (the actor) was depicted choosing one of several pictured items. Immediately after his choice, the other four visible within camera range were asked whether or not they liked that one best too. Either they all responded positively that they did (high consensus) or negatively (low consensus). Then the subject was asked whether the actor's choice told more about the actor or about the pictured item. From Kelley's theory, high consensus should lead to a stimulus object attribution: if everyone likes it, it must be wonderful. Low consensus should lead to a person attribution: if only the actor liked it, it must be a special quirk of his. The other variation was access to direct information about the concrete objects the actor was choosing among. The subjects either were shown the same pictures shown to the actor or not. The results are shown in Figure 5–8. Consensus information has little or no effect when the subjects were exposed to direct information about the object in question. The same thing happened in a study by Hansen and Donoghue (1977), who varied whether or not the subject himself had personally engaged in the relevant behavior. Consensus information affected attributions only when the subject had had no personal experience with the act.

Under what conditions is consensus information more powerful? Three conditions seem clearest. One is when the consensus information itself is highly salient and vivid. In 1976, Gerald Ford ran television commercials in which several ordinary people were quoted, seemingly spontaneously, giving their reasons for supporting him. The assumption surely was that such vivid statements would be a more salient version of consensual support for him than some more statistical statement of a poll. A second is when consensus information does not violate a clear expectancy.

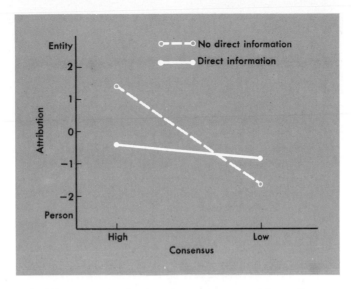

FIGURE 5–8 Attributions from consensus information.

Source: Adapted from Feldman et al. (1976), p. 696.

Perhaps you do not have enough information about the object to have a clear expectancy, so you use consensus to determine your attributions. Finally, consensus information may be more effective when organized by a plausible causal theory linking it to the event. If you believe that college football players tend to be poor students, your perception of P.E. 101 will be much affected by their performance. If they all get A's, you will perceive it as a "Mickey Mouse;" if they all fail, you will perceive it as very difficult.

MOTIVATIONAL BIASES

The other general class of attributional biases arises from people's efforts to satisfy their own needs and motives. All the preceding biases just discussed were analyzed as if people had only one kind of need—the need to predict and control their environments. This is a characteristic operating assumption of the perceptual-cognitive viewpoint, as we indicated in Chapter 1. But of course in reality people have many other needs—for love, for revenge, for self-esteem, for prestige, for material goods, and so on. Quite a lot would be left out of our account if these needs were ignored. And they prove to have quite a substantial role in biasing people's causal attributions.

Ego-Enhancing Biases

Perhaps the most common motivational bias in the attribution process is the *ego-enhancing bias*. This describes attributions that glorify the ego or defend self-esteem. Perhaps the simplest example and most common

WONDERFUL WINNERS AND VICTIMIZED LOSERS

A homey example of the self-serving bias comes from interviews by Kingdon (1967) with the winning and losing candidate in each of thirty-three races in Wisconsin for U.S. senator, U.S. congressman, state senator, state assemblyman, and five statewide offices. They were asked a series of questions about why they thought they had won or lost. The winners thought the most important factor was the characteristics of the candidates! The losers downplayed that factor and blamed the outcome on party label (the voters just voted a party line against my side), and on the voters' ignorance. The results are shown in the table below. In addition, 70 percent of the losers said the voters were "not informed," compared to 32 percent of the winners, while only 3 percent of the losers said the voters were "very informed," compared to 26 percent of the winners.

Even more impressive were the results from an open-ended question, "Could you summarize the major factors that have contributed to your wins and defeats over the years?" For the "wins," 75 percent of the respondents emphasized matters within their control: "their hard work, personal service to constituents, matters of compaign strategy, building a reputation, and publicizing themselves." For the "defeats," 90 percent of the respondents emphasized matters beyond their control, "the party makeup of the district, the familiar name or other unbeatable characteristics of the opponent, national and state trends, lack of money, or other uncontrollable circumstances" (p. 141). Only a few (10 percent) attributed their losses to internal factors such as laziness or mistakes in strategy.

Comparison of Winners and Losers on the Rank Which They Assign to Party Label, Issues, and Candidates' Characteristics

VARIABLE	MOST IMPORTANT		LEAST IMPORTANT	
	Winners	Losers	Winners	Losers
Election Issues	17	7	50	55
Characteristics of the Candidates	62	35	3	28
Party Label	21%	59%	47%	17%
	100%	101%[a]	100%	100%

[a] Rounding error.
Source: Kingdon (1967).

case is the taking of credit for success and the externalizing of blame for failure. We attribute our successes to internal causes such as our own ability, hard work, or general goodness. We blame our failures on external factors like bad luck, an oppressive political structure, a nagging wife or sexist husband, bad weather, and so on. A simple example comes from a study of college students' explanations for the grades they received in three examinations in a semester course (Bernstein et al., 1979). A and B grades tended to be attributed to internal factors such as ability and effort, whereas C, D, and F grades were attributed to external factors such as test difficulty and bad luck. Such biases can also be described as "self-serving."

The ego-enhancing bias has been the subject of a variety of experimental studies. Some focus on the subject's own personal achievement. In these studies, the subject is given a success or a failure experience, and then asked to evaluate the reason for it. Some have involved a teacher-learner situation, in which a subject has tried to teach a student something, while manipulating the student's success or failure. In most cases, subjects attributed their successes to internal causes and their failures to external ones (see Bradley, 1978; and Zuckerman, 1979, for careful reviews). And when the subject has a success experience, internal attributions such as ability or effort give the subject a more positive feeling than do external attributions such as task ease or chance (Reimer, 1975). So it is to the subject's advantage, in terms of self-esteem, to claim the credit for success internally rather than sharing it.

These differences become magnified with ego involvement. As a task becomes more important to individuals, they are more motivated to bias their attributions to salve their bruised egos. Hence high ego involvement exaggerates ego-enhancing biases, that is, it produces even more external blame for failure, and more credit for success (Miller, 1975). It should therefore also be more marked for actors than for observers. In terms of ego enhancement, the actor has much more to gain than does the observer by biasing his or her attributions. A number of studies have been done that show precisely this finding. One example is by Snyder, Stephen, and Rosenfield (1976). In this case, subjects were run in a game against each other. They were randomly assigned to win or to lose the game. And the subjects were asked to attribute the causes for their own winning and losing, as well as for their opponents' outcomes. The data are shown in Table 5–9. It can be seen very clearly that actors attribute their wins to internal factors such as skill and effort, whereas observers are more likely to attribute the actor's wins to easy tasks and to luck. On the other hand, losses are blamed by the actor far more on external factors like luck, whereas observers are more likely to give some credit to lack of skill and lack of effort. Taylor and Koivumaki (1976) show the same thing.

COGNITIVE INTERPRETATIONS Some authors (Miller & M. Ross, 1975; Nisbett & L. Ross, 1980) suggest that there might be cognitive instead of motivational reasons for these findings. While we have emphasized the role of ego enhancement, these critics argue that most of the subjects in these experiments have been much more used to success than to failure experiences (e.g., high school and college students receive few Fs) and therefore failure comes as a surprise to them. In Kelley's terms, a failure would be low in consistency, whereas a success would be consistent with past experience. And as we saw earlier, high consistency provokes an internal attribution, whereas low consistency produces an attribution to the situation. If I always perform this way, then it is me. If my performance departs from what I expect from past experience, then it must be the test, or luck, or something about the situation. So people might show a pattern of attributions that would appear self-serving, but have simply been made for cognitive reasons, without ego enhancement being a factor at all.

There are several problems with this argument. One is that most people do not have universally successful experiences. Their judgment of their success is normally determined by some subjective level of aspiration, not by some absolute standard. For example, most college students do not regard getting a C or D as a success experience, even though it is a passing grade. Some even feel disappointed by a B. Only one team wins the Super Bowl or the World Series or the NBA championship; and many of the others must feel they have failed. Most personal histories of success and failure are more complicated than this view suggests. Most people have experienced many failures as well as successes, and it is doubtful that anyone's past history leads him or her to expect success most of the time.

The way to test these theories is to hold expectancy for success or failure constant and then see whether people still engage in self-serving attributional biases. If so, some motivational forces must be at work. Ross and Sicoly (1979) did just that in a clever way. First they put subjects through a task that supposedly measured their "social perceptiveness." Then the subjects were led to believe they had either succeeded or failed at the task. Their attributions for these outcomes were predictably self-serving. But their expectancies for further success or failure were

TABLE 5–9

Attributions by Actors and Observers for Winning and Losing

ATTRIBUTION	ACTOR		OBSERVER	
	Actor Wins	Actor Loses	Actor Wins	Actor Loses
Internal (skill, effort)	8.13	0.56	3.54	3.00
External (luck, task difficulty)	4.25	4.74	6.00	3.38
Internal–external	+ 3.88	−4.18	−2.46	−0.38

Source: Adapted from Snyder et al. (1976), p. 438.

therefore fixed and known, since they had already gotten their outcomes. A critical variation was therefore introduced at this point: an observer randomly told the subject she bore either more or less personal responsibility for the outcome. That is, the observer told the subject that the outcome was more internally caused, or more externally caused, than the subject had claimed. No matter which it was, this new information was equally unexpected, since it departed by the same amount from the subject's judgment as already expressed. So expectancy was held constant. Finally the subject was asked how accurate this new feedback was. Ego-enhancing feedback (internal attributions for successes, and external for failures) was judged to be considerably more accurate than ego-deflating feedback. Self-serving biases, therefore, are present even when expectancies are held constant.

Another argument against a motivational basis for self-serving biases is that people seem to show such biases even when explaining someone else's behavior. It presumably does not boost our own ego to claim that others have been responsible for their own successes or blameless in failures. So perhaps cognitive factors, such as simple violations of expectation, are responsible in those cases. From our discussion of positivity biases in the last chapter, though, it should be clear that people also have a generous streak when it comes to other people. People tend to evaluate others more positively than negatively, giving a ''bonus'' of positive evaluation to other people, everything else being equal. Applying it to the question of self-serving attributions leads us to expect that perhaps people will extend some of the same generous rationalizations to others that they apply to themselves. And there is considerable evidence that they do. Taylor and Koivumaki (1976) asked subjects to explain three positive behaviors (paying a compliment to someone, talking cheerfully to another person, and having fun) and three negative behaviors (having a heated argument with someone, being rude to someone, and forgetting to do something) on the part of various persons: oneself, one's spouse, a friend, and an acquaintance. In all cases they found dispositional causality attributed much more often for positive acts than for negative acts. The data are shown in Table 5–10. It should be noted that the subjects were not *as* generous with friends and acquaintances as they were with themselves—presumably that is where the self-serving ego-enhancement came in—but they did extend some rationalizing help.

In a more realistic study, Ross and colleagues (1974) had real teachers actually teaching spelling problems to an eleven-year-old boy (a confederate), who either succeeded or failed. In this case the teachers tended to blame themselves when the boy failed, rather than blaming him. They may simply have been being generous to a young boy they scarcely knew. Finally, Karaz and Perlman (1975) found a positivity bias in explanations for race horses' performances like those in these studies of people. Subjects were shown videotaped horse races, in which the horse in question won or lost. Subjects attributed wins to the horse, and losses to a highly competitive field of other horses or to the circumstances of the race. So even a horse gets personal credit for its good performance, and does not get blamed for its poor performance.

The fact that self-serving biases seem to increase with greater ego involvement, and to be greater for actors than observers (though not absent for the latter), is consistent with the notion that they are based on motiva-

TABLE 5–10

Mean Ratings of Dispositional Causality

STIMULUS PERSON	POSITIVE ACT	NEGATIVE ACT
Acquaintance	6.41	4.74
Friend	7.41	3.92
Spouse	7.66	3.36
Self	7.57	3.31

Source: Adapted from Taylor and Koivumaki (1976), p. 405.

tional needs and not exclusively on cognitive mechanisms. There seems to be quite a strong tendency for attributions to be biased by self-esteem needs, especially in the case of taking credit for good events and avoiding blame for bad ones. But the confirmation or disconfirmation of expectancies is also an important factor in our attributions for success or failure. When something surprising happens, we need a new explanation.

IMPRESSION MANAGEMENT We should mention yet a third possible explanation for self-serving attributional biases. They may simply serve a self-presentation or impression-management function. That is, we may not really misperceive the causes of our outcomes at all. But when asked, we try to persuade other people that we are responsible for our successes and blameless in our failures, because then they will have a higher opinion of us. That is, our real perception of causality may not be distorted, but our need for personal self-promotion may make us try to mislead others. Bradley (1978) has argued that many of the studies showing self-serving biases can be reinterpreted in this vein. Orvis (1977) addressed this problem directly with his data on conflicts between intimate couples (see Box 5–5). This time he contrasted the causes the person actually believed to account for his or her misdeeds with the causes the person had communicated to the partner. He found substantial evidence for self-serving biases in both. That is, people really do believe their misdeeds are controlled by external forces more than by their own bad personality dispositions. But in addition to that, they argue more strenuously for such excuses than they really believe in them. In general self-serving biases are not merely "fronts" for impression management purposes, though they probably serve that function on occasion. At this point, all three interpretations remain viable, and indeed, probably all have some validity.

The Illusion of Control

We have seen in these last two chapters how people tend to distort the social world perceptually into a more orderly, organized, predictable, and sensible thing than it really is. They do it in many ingenious ways, using first impressions, schemas, scripts, attributional biases, and a wide variety of other cognitive mechanisms. But people do not only distort the world in predictable directions. They also distort it in more *controllable* directions as well. They systematically overestimate their control over events, and underestimate the role of chance or uncontrollable factors. Put another way, they too often attribute causality for events to themselves. Langer (1975) has called this "the illusion of control." Calling it an illusion may be a little strong; it is more like a systematic bias of modest magnitude than a total lack of contact with reality. But such a bias has been demonstrated in some interesting ways.

The typical experiment has led subjects to exaggerate their control over chance outcomes. For example, Langer got subjects to buy lottery tickets for $1.00 with the hope of winning up to $50. Half the subjects were allowed to choose their tickets from a box, while the other half were given their tickets. Later they were asked how much they would sell their tickets for, as an indication of how valuable they thought they were. Subjects who chose their tickets valued them at $8.67, on the average, as opposed to $1.96 for those given their tickets. The act of choosing apparently blinded the subjects to the fact that the lottery would be settled by chance, and that their choice made no difference at all in their prospects for winning.

While people do not always ignore the role of chance, they do tend to do so under some conditions more than others. Wortman (1975) attempted to specify the conditions for the illusion-of-choice phenomenon. She suggested that people feel they can control chance events only if they initiate the activity and know what they hope to attain in advance. In other words, they must feel that they started the ball rolling and that their will is controlling the event because they know what outcome they want. In one study Wortman put two different marbles in a can, and told her subjects that each marble stood for a different prize. Then subjects either chose a marble, or were given one, under conditions in which they either did or did not know which marble stood for the prize they wanted. They were not allowed to see which marble was which. Nevertheless, the subjects thought they were most responsible for the outcome when they were allowed to choose a marble rather than being given one, and when they knew in advance which marble stood for the prize they wanted. Then they could imagine having control over the outcome.

"A JUST WORLD" The illusion of control implies that people have more control over their fates than they in fact do. One consequence of this illusion is the tendency to blame the victim for what happens to him. A person who is involved in a traffic accident must have been driving carelessly. A woman who is raped must have been acting in a provocative manner and brought it on herself. Even the victims themselves blame the victim. For example, many rape victims blame themselves for being raped; they see themselves as having behaved in the wrong way, such as hitchhiking or leaving their apartment window unlocked (Janoff-

Bulman, 1979). Minorities who are discriminated against are often seen as being too pushy, unmotivated, or passive and are believed to alienate people with their demands; they therefore are seen as deserving their fates. Earthquake, tornado, hurricane, and flood victims are believed to have shown insufficient preparedness. There are many accounts of the guilt experienced by survivors of disasters and accidents, or by bereaved family members. They frequently dwell obsessively on the period before the incident, thinking of some way they could have averted the tragedy. They desperately imagine ways they could have controlled what is usually uncontrollable (Wortman, 1976). In short, people are presumed to control their environments and are seen as getting what they deserve, and deserving what they get.

To explain such observations, Lerner (1965) has offered the notion that we believe in a "just world": good people get good outcomes, and bad things happen to bad people. The key point is that observers make moral attributions to others' dispositions based on the events that happen to them. I attribute to you the characteristic of being a lousy driver because someone ran a red light and hit you at an intersection on the way to school. To test this notion, Lerner ran several experiments showing that subjects tended to derogate victims who had been picked at random to be given electric shock. Lerner suggests that we need to feel that we can control events. Therefore, to protect this sense of control, we blame people for the bad things that happen to them. If people in general are responsible for any disaster that befalls them, presumably any of us can avoid disaster by acting properly.

LEARNED HELPLESSNESS What happens when we are confronted with our lack of control? Seligman (1975) has identified a phenomenon he calls **learned helplessness,** which is based on the experience of a lack of control of the environment. He contends it leads to depression and even to death. It was first noted in experiments on animals. Animals that are given shocks they cannot escape from are later unable to learn how to escape when it is possible to do so. Animals who initially could escape from the shock (e.g., by pressing a bar) later have no trouble learning a new response that will help them escape. It is as if the initially helpless animals just give up.

A typical learned helplessness experiment on humans is very similar. Subjects are given problems to work out and then given feedback about their performance that has nothing to do with how well they did. In this sense, the problems are insoluble. The outcomes have been externally caused and are seemingly random. The subjects learn that they have no control over the problems; they have learned they are helpless. When tested later on easier problems, they prove much less successful than subjects for whom the feedback was contingent on performance—that is, those for whom the environment was predictable and controllable. In short, performance generally deteriorates following the insoluble problems. Seligman suggests that the deterioration occurs because no stable internal attribution has been formed; the subjects learn that what they do has no effect on the outcomes of their behavior.

This basic phenomenon has been expanded upon in a number of different ways. People can become "helpless" themselves just by watching others contend with insoluble tasks. That is, learned helplessness can work vicariously, through modeling, as well as through direct experience (DeVellis, DeVellis, & McCauley, 1978). The experience of noncontingent effects, of lack of control, can lead to physical symptoms as well as performance decrements. Pennebaker and associates (1977) showed that people who are unable to turn off aversive noise bursts are, compared to people who could control them, more likely to have watery eyes, congested noses, dizziness, flushed faces, and shortness of breath. And people who generally believe they can control the environment (who have a high "internal locus of control") are more disrupted in performance and more likely to get depressed during the experience (Pittman & Pittman, 1979).

Finally, it may help people to cope with adversity if they do retain their beliefs in their control over their life outcomes. Bulman and Wortman (1977) interviewed twenty-nine paraplegics in a rehabilitation institute who had been disabled in various accidents, ranging from being shot to being tackled in a football game. They were each rated by a nurse and a social worker on how well they were coping with the accident, in terms of accepting the reality of the accident and attempting to deal positively with the paralysis. The more they blamed another person, and the less they blamed themselves for the accident, the worse they coped. The authors suggest that "the ability to perceive an orderly relationship between one's behaviors and one's outcomes is important for effective coping" (p. 362).

AMERICAN INDIVIDUALISM A number of phenomena described in this chapter have been seen to reveal a pervasive bias toward perceiving internal or dispositional control of behavior. The fundamental attribution error overestimates internal control, especially in observers. Work on the illusion of control, the just world and learned helplessness, documents how people prefer to believe in internal control, and in fact are disrupted psychologically when they are forced to face their own helplessness and the randomness of much that affects their lives.

Why this bias toward internality? One possibility has been considered in some detail above. Perhaps, at a simple perceptual level, actors and observers alike tend to see an act as so thoroughly connected to the actor (in what Heider called a "unit relation") that they cannot easily attribute it to some external cause (Jones, 1979). Another possibility is that all human beings share a strong emotional commitment to the feeling of free will, and to feeling that they are free to act any way they choose. The illusion of choice or of control may be crucial to our motivational systems and feelings of well-being, for some adaptive reasons deriving from natural selection (Brehm, 1966; Monson & Snyder, 1977).

FIGURE 5-9 Because we seem to value independence and self-reliance, we have different attitudes toward this elderly man than we would toward someone who was merely sitting in front of a fire keeping warm.

A third possibility is that this bias toward internality is a cultural norm characteristic in particular of Americans. Many observers have noted how dedicated Americans are to individualistic values, to the beliefs that individual people can control their own destinies, are responsible for their outcomes, and so on. Poverty is due to the laziness and stupidity of the poor, wealth to the genius and hard work of the successful. The Horatio Alger myth is one of our hardiest. This individualism has been traced back to America's Protestant heritage (see, for example, McClelland, 1964; Sears & McConahay, 1973; Sniderman & Brody, 1977).

More interdependent cultures emphasize the collective and interpersonal causes of events, and not so much the free acts of individuals (Sampson, 1977). The tradition in the United States, on the other hand, is that individuals stand on their own two feet. Most Americans do not think of themselves as part of a larger social whole, such as an extended family or church or community. Other cultures emphasize the group nature of human life much more centrally. For example, in the United States, the decision to marry is supposed to be the free choice of the persons involved and is based on romantic love. In many other cultures such decisions are made collectively by family or kinship groups because marriages are thought to affect the whole community. So it remains for further research in other cultures to determine whether this emphasis on dispositions, free will and choice, and personal control is limited to our culture, with its strong tradition of Protestant individualism, or is a more general human characteristic.

SUMMARY

1. Attribution theory is concerned with how ordinary people explain social events. The causal explanations people give are treated in terms of being internal to a person (emotions, attitudes, personality traits, or abilities caused the event) or external to him (the people around him, the task he was working on, luck, the weather). Some causes are stable (intelligence, task difficulty); others are unstable (mood, effort, luck).

2. Theorists begin from the assumption that people are strongly motivated to explain the events around them. They do so by looking for invariance; that is, which causes are regularly associated with which effects. And they use a discounting principle; that is, to the extent that several causes are plausible, they will spread their explanations among them.

3. Kelley's cube theory suggests that people base their attributions upon three kinds of information: distinctiveness (is this the only situation in which the person does this), consensus (would other people do the same thing in that situation), and consistency (does he always do this in this situation).

4. Other people's personality traits and attitudes are normally inferred from their overt behaviors by considering the external forces operating on them at the time. If these forces are strong, attributions are shared between external and internal causes. If these forces are weak, internal attributions are made.

5. Attribution theory can be applied to self-perception as well as to the perception of others. That is, the same principles may account for how we infer the causes for our own acts and how we infer the causes for others' acts.

6. The internal cues we receive from our own emotional arousal states seem now to be more ambiguous and undifferentiated than has commonly been assumed in the past. Consequently, we infer both the nature and degree of our own emotional arousal by an attributional process that relies on evidence about our own behavior, external indications of our arousal states, and environmental conditions.

7. It is possible to manipulate people's perceptions of their own emotions through a process of misattribution. When their internal emotional states are ambiguous, they can reattribute their emotions to previously neutral stimuli, such as neutral drugs.

8. Under some conditions, we infer our own attitudes from our own behavior. However, such inferences seem to be most common when we are not especially involved in our attitudes and when they have little consequence for our future lives.

9. In its purest form, attribution theory describes a logical, rationalistic

mechanism for arriving at causal explanations. But several systematic biases have been discovered.

10. In general, people ascribe more causality to internal dispositions than they should and less to external forces. This has been called the fundamental attribution error. It is particularly true for observations of other people's behavior. Self-perceptions may indeed be biased in the opposite direction and overattribute causality to external forces. In both cases the bias seems due mainly to the relative salience of the behavior or of the situation.

11. People are quite heavily influenced by the need to give explanations that support or protect their own self-esteem; they do so by externalizing blame or taking credit for success. They also seem to extend this generosity to others, especially those who are close.

12. People seem to need the illusion of control over their environments. Their perceptions exaggerate their own level of control, and they become emotionally disturbed when they feel they have no control. They believe in a just world in which people get what they deserve, and which is based on the assumption that people can control their own outcomes.

SUGGESTIONS FOR ADDITIONAL READING

HARVEY, J. H., ICKES, W., & KIDD, R. F. (eds.). *New directions in attribution research.* Vols. 1 and 2. Hillsdale, N.J.: Erlbaum, 1976, 1978. Essays on almost every facet of attribution research by almost everyone who has made a major contribution to it.

KELLEY, H. H. Attribution theory in social psychology. In David Levine (ed.), *Nebraska symposium on motivation*, 1967. Lincoln: University of Nebraska Press, 1967. Still the best and most coherent basic statement of attribution theory.

KELLEY, H. H., and MICHELA, J. L. Attribution theory and research. *Annual Review of Psychology*, 1979, *31*, 1–79. An excellent recent review of the whole attribution tradition, coauthored by one of its principal originators.

JONES, E. E., KANOUSE, D. E., KELLEY, H. H., NISBETT, R. E., VALINS, S., & WEINER, B. *Attribution: Perceiving the causes of behavior.* Morristown, N.J.: General Learning Press, 1972. An influential early collection of theoretical statements on attribution theory. Includes excellent papers on the actor-observer effect, self-perception, negativity, and others.

MCARTHUR, L. A. The how and what of why: Some determinants and consequences of causal attribution. *Journal of Personality and Social Psychology*, 1972, *22*, 171–93. A representative early study of Kelley's cube theory of attribution. It uses a role-playing methodology that is typical of much (though not all) research in the area.

Liking and Attraction

6

Peter Vandermark; Stock, Boston.

In the previous chapters we discussed how people perceive other people. Now we turn to a basic dimension of interpersonal perception and interpersonal relations—that is, how much people like one another. We have already seen that the evaluative dimension explains a great deal of the difference in attitudes and perceptions. When we rate anything, whether a book, a house, or the president of the United States, how positive we feel toward the object is a key factor in our rating. This is particularly important when other people are involved, because the extent to which two people like each other is a fundamental determinant of their interaction. It affects practically every phase of their relationship—how much they choose to see each other, how close they stand, what they say to each other, how they treat each other, how much they are influenced by each other, and on and on. Among the first questions we ask ourselves when we meet somebody else are: Will she like me? Will I like her?

Note that we have used the word *like* rather than a more technical or neutral term such as *positively evaluate*. The reason is that we are concerned with something more than a positive evaluation of another person. We may positively evaluate a candidate for the presidency of the United States or a movie actress, but we are not friends with them. The distinction is, of course, not clear, for most of the factors that affect positive evaluation also affect more personal liking. However, we shall use *liking* because we are dealing not only with the question of why someone evaluates another person positively but also with why someone tends to like and become friends with another person.

We shall consider six major determinants of liking—proximity, personal qualities, familiarity, rewardingness, cognitive balance, and similarity. In each case, we shall describe the general effect of the variable but concentrate on trying to explain why it operates as it does and on specifying situations that magnify or minimize its effect. At the end of the chapter, we will take a look at the development of more intimate relationships, although they have been investigated less thoroughly.

PROXIMITY

Probably the best single predictor of whether two people are friends is how far apart they live. If one of them lives in Brazil and the other in China, it is almost certain they are not friends. If one lives in Chicago and the other in Phoenix, or even if they live on opposite sides of the same city, it is unlikely they are friends. In fact, if two people live only ten blocks apart, it is considerably less likely that they are friends than if they live next door to each other.

How Proximity Operates

W. H. Whyte (1956) conducted a study of friendship patterns in Park Forest, a suburban residential community. Almost everyone had moved into Park Forest at about the same time. Because all the houses were similar, the residents had chosen their homes and neighborhoods pretty much by chance. There were no "better" areas, no cheap houses—nothing in particular to distinguish the various parts of the town. Thus, the possibility was minimized that people in one area were in some way different from those in another before they moved into the community. It was almost as though a large group had been assigned randomly to houses.

For some time Whyte read the social column in the newspaper and kept a careful check on who gave parties, who was invited by whom, and, in general, who was friendly with whom. The patterns of association he found depended a great deal on proximity. Almost everyone at a baby shower lived within a few blocks of one another, and almost everyone who lived within the area was there. The same was true on the other side of town at an eggnog party. In the whole town there were practically no friends who did not live near one another. Similarly, there was a remarkable occurrence of friendships among people who lived close together.

This same kind of effect occurs in much smaller units than a whole town. A study by Festinger, Schachter, and Back (1950) investigated the patterns of friendship in a large housing development called Westgate West, which consisted of seventeen separate two-story buildings, each containing ten apartments (five on a floor). The layout is shown in Figure 6–2. This housing development was similar to Park Forest in certain respects. For one thing the apartments were almost identical. More important, however, residents did not choose where they were to live; they were

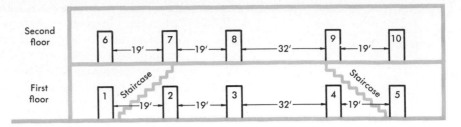

FIGURE 6–2 Floor plan of Westgate West. All the buildings in the housing development had the same layout. In the study, functional distance was defined simply as the number of doors away two people lived—the differences in distance measured by feet were ignored.

Source: Adapted from Festinger, Schachter, and Back (1950).

given apartments as the apartments became vacant. In other words, like Park Forest, Westgate West came close to being a field experiment—the residents were randomly assigned to a condition.

All the residents were asked, "Which three people in Westgate West do you see socially most often?" The results are shown in the graph in Figure 6–3. It is clear that residents were most friendly with those who lived near them. People on the same floor (top line) mentioned their next-door neighbor more often than their neighbor two doors away and their neighbor two doors away more often than their neighbor at the other end of the hall. Of nextdoor neighbors, 41 percent were chosen, whereas only 22 percent of those two doors away and 10 percent of those at the end of the hall were. Moreover, it should be noted that the distances were very small. People who lived next door were 19 feet apart (in case of the two middle apartments, 32 feet apart), and the maximum distance between two apartments on one floor was only 88 feet. But these differences, only a few extra seconds in walking time, were important factors in determining friendships.

In addition, people who lived on different floors (the bottom line of the graph) were mentioned much less than those on the same floor even when the physical distance between them was roughly the same. This was probably because it takes more effort to go up or down stairs than to walk down a hall. Thus, people on different floors were in a sense farther away than those on the same floor. The investigators referred to this phenomenon as *functional distance,* meaning that the probability people would meet was determined by the design of the apartment house plus actual distance. The closer people lived, as measured by either physical or functional distance, the more likely they were to be friends.

A similar study of a new college dormitory showed the same striking effects of proximity (Priest & Sawyer, 1967). Proximity had an enormous effect on simple recognition: floormates were more than four times as likely to be recognized than other dormitory residents. But even with recognition held constant, proximity enormously affected friendship.

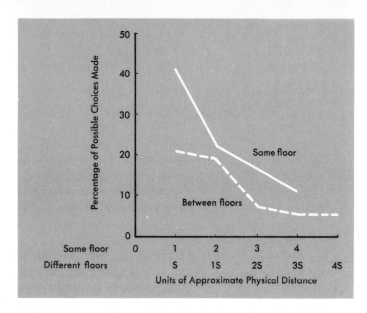

FIGURE 6–3 The relationship between functional distance and liking. The distance between people on the same floor and on different floors was closely related to friendship patterns—the closer two individuals lived, the more likely they were to be friends. Living on different floors (bottom line) reduced the likelihood of friendship because functional distance was increased.

Source: Festinger, Schachter, and Back (1950).

Among those who recognized each other, and even after almost a full academic year, roommates were twice as likely as floormates to be named as friends, and floormates were more than twice as likely as dormitory residents in general to be named as friends. So proximity did increase familiarity. But this increase in familiarity was not enough to explain the higher level of friendship among roommates and floormates. Proximity increased liking even aside from greater familiarity.

Another rather elegant demonstration of the effects of proximity comes from a study done in the Training Academy of the Maryland State Police (Segal, 1974). Trainees were assigned to seats in classrooms and to dormitory rooms by name in alphabetical order. Thus, the closer their last names were alphabetically, the more likely they were to spend time in close proximity, both in and out of the classrooms. After six months, each trainee was asked to name his three closest friends on the force. To an astonishing degree, the trainees' friends turned out to be those with names near theirs in the alphabet. Figure 6–5 shows how closely associated in the alphabet the friends' names were to each other. On the average, each person chosen as a friend was only 4.5 letters away from his chooser in the alphabet. So the mere fact of being assigned to a room and sitting

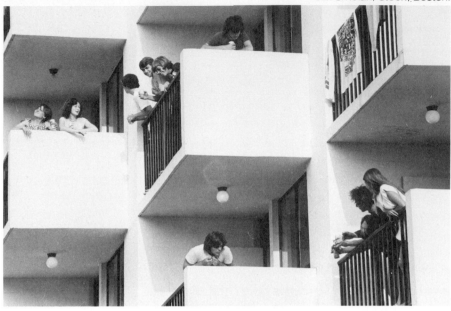

FIGURE 6–4 The social life on these apartment terraces shows the importance of function distance. Although the apartments themselves may be quite far from each other within the building, the terraces bring the people close together and allow the formation of friendships.

closer dictated friendship choice, even over a six-week period of getting to know the other trainees quite well.

This phenomenon is so strong and so common that it is one of the easiest to demonstrate. You can try it yourself by asking a student who lives in a dormitory to make a map of his or her dorm friendships. In almost every case the map will show that those who live near each other are much more likely to be friends than those who live far apart. In general, proximity produces increased liking.

Why Proximity Causes Liking

The simplest explanation of the effect of proximity is that people who are close are more *available* than those who are farther away. We cannot like or be friends with someone we do not know, and it is difficult to remain friends with someone we do not see fairly often. Obviously, we choose our friends from people we know; we also choose our enemies this way. Close relationships, either positive or negative, are generally with people we see regularly—and certainly with people we know. It is easy to show that both marriages and murders involve people who see each other a lot. At this level, the phenomenon does not sound very exciting. Naturally, we

Reprinted from Mady Wechsler Segal, "Alphabet and Attraction: An Unobtrusive Measure of the Effect of Propinquity in a Field Setting," JOURNAL OF PERSONALITY AND SOCIAL PSYCHOLOGY, *30*, No. 5 (1974), 654–57, Copyright 1974 by the American Psychological Association. Reprinted by permission.

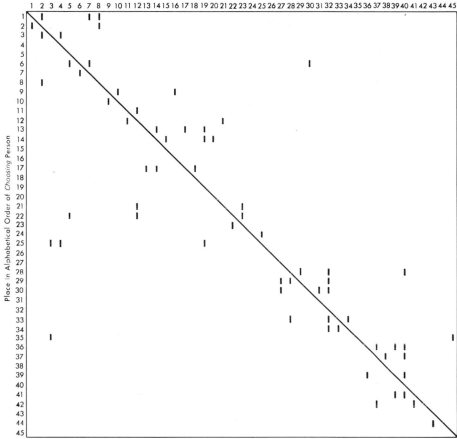

FIGURE 6–5 Matrix of friendship choices. People close in the alphabet tended to become friends.

are not going to become friends (or enemies) with someone we do not know. The closer another person lives to us, the more likely it is that we would know him well enough to become friends.

However, it is a mistake to explain the effect of proximity entirely on the grounds of availability. Although the residents of Westgate were somewhat more likely to see the people who lived closer, in terms of availability they would certainly get to know quite well people who lived only 38 feet away. The people downstairs were also available; it certainly was not beyond the strength of these people to walk downstairs if they wanted to make friends with somebody. Yet, there was a strong effect of

*"Do you really love me, Anthony,
or is it just because I live on
the thirty-eighth floor?"*

proximity. Why did sheer physical closeness or likelihood of seeing someone make such a difference in patterns of liking, even when other people were readily available as friends? Also, why did proximity lead primarily to positive rather than negative relationships? After all, we have to know someone to hate him just as we have to know someone to like him.

Some studies have suggested that *familiarity* with an object or person, by itself, will lead to greater liking. In one study (Zajonc, 1968), subjects were shown a number of Turkish words, and some of the words were shown many more times than others. (In other studies, nonsense syllables and Chinese words were used.) Afterward, the subjects were asked to guess the meanings of the words. There was a strong tendency for them to give positive meanings to the words they had seen more often. Although the findings from these studies are not conclusive, there does seem to be considerable evidence that familiarity leads not to contempt but to liking. We shall discuss this in more detail later.

Simple *interaction* with another person may increase liking. To demonstrate this, Insko and Wilson (1977) set up three-person groups. They then asked two of the subjects (A and B) to get acquainted while the third (C) merely listened, then they asked another pair (B and C) to get acquainted while the third (A) listened. A and C never interacted. Later they all rated each other. The pairs involved in direct interaction liked each other better than did the pair that did not interact, even though all concerned were present in the same room the whole time.

The expectation of *continued interaction* is another factor. As we will see later in this chapter, when an individual knows he is going to be in a particular situation, he generally tries to convince himself that it will be pleasant, or at least not too unpleasant. Similarly, if he expects to interact with someone else in the future, he tends to exaggerate the other person's positive traits and ignore or at least play down the negative ones. Presumably people try to convince themselves that interactions will be pleasant. When we decide ahead of time that another person is nice, we probably will like that other person when we actually meet. If the other person lives next door, we anticipate a great deal of contact with him and want this contact to be pleasant. Accordingly, people are strongly motivated to perceive their neighbors in positive terms.

Anticipated interaction also has other effects. In addition to deciding that the other person is very pleasant, we will go out of our way to be pleasant ourselves. In first meetings, and knowing there will be many other meetings, an individual will try to be especially nice, to avoid conflict, to promote a friendly relationship. As we shall discuss at greater length below, being nice to someone is a good way to make her like us. Thus, two people who are anticipating future interactions and therefore behaving nicely are likely to be friends.

Another possible explanation of the effect of proximity involves how *predictable* the other person's behavior becomes. The more we see someone else, the more we learn about him and the better we can predict how the other person will behave in a variety of situations. When we know fairly well how another will act or react to what we do, we are less likely to do something to annoy the other person—and vice versa. Each learns how to act to make interactions free of unpleasantness and therefore does not cause unpleasantness intentionally. Of course, two people can still annoy each other, but generally, they can avoid conflict. Although this does not necessarily make people friends, it does make it easier for them

TABLE 6-1

Proximity Increases Liking Only of Pleasant People

DISTANCE	CONFEDERATE'S BEHAVIOR		
	Pleasant	Neutral	Unpleasant
Close	12.25[a]	8.67	7.42
Far	10.67	9.00	9.08

[a] High numbers indicate high liking of the confederate.
Source: Schiffenbauer and Schiavo (1976), p. 279.

to be friends. Primarily pleasant interactions lay the groundwork for friendship.

An Exception to the Rule

Although proximity to other people usually makes us like them more, it does not always have this effect. The simplest exception occurs when there are initial antagonisms. If we form a dislike for another person at the first contact, there is evidence that proximity does not increase liking.

This hypothesis was tested by Schiffenbauer and Schiavo (1976). They placed a subject in a laboratory with a female confederate, and gave him or her some problems to solve. Depending on the experimental condition, the confederate then acted in a positive, pleasant way, by commenting favorably upon the subject's performance: "Yes, that was a very good strategy. It is a strategy only a very smart person would use." Or the confederate behaved neutrally: "No comments;" or in a negative, unpleasant way: "Yes, that was a very poor strategy. It was a strategy only a very dumb person would use." The other independent variable was proximity: The confederate sat closer (2 feet) or farther away (5 feet) from the subject. As can be seen in Table 6-1, proximity increased liking for the confederate when she was positive, but actually decreased liking when she was negative. So proximity probably increases liking for a beautiful, subtly perfumed woman; and decreases it for a garbage collector just off work. We shall discuss this distance effect further in the chapter on environmental psychology.

We saw in the last two chapters that a "positivity bias" exists. Most people evaluate most other people positively. So even if proximity produces liking only for positive, attractive, desirable people, then the positivity bias would ensure that proximity would increase liking most of the time—because most people are regarded by others as positive, attractive, and desirable.

Of course, proximity is not the only factor affecting liking. People do not always like their nextdoor neighbors; even roommates do not always like each other. A best friend can live down the hall or on the other side of town. Friends and marriage partners must be chosen from those available, from those we know. But among those who are available, we have a considerable amount of choice, and this choice is affected by a number of other important factors. So what other factors produce liking?

PERSONAL QUALITIES

We can all name a number of personal qualities that, at least in our society, tend to make people like other people. Other things being equal, there is a tendency to like people more if they are honest rather than dishonest, helpful rather than harmful, friendly rather than unfriendly, kind rather than cruel, and so on. Obviously many personal qualities determine liking, so all we can do here is mention some that have been most researched.

Warmth and Other Traits	"Warmth" is an especially important quality in determining liking. In Chapter 4 we discussed how central a trait "warm" is in determining an impression of another person, presumably because it is so crucial in helping us decide whether we like someone or not. One way warmth manifests itself is in our tending to like things, praise them, approve of them, rather than tending to dislike things, disparage them, say they are awful, and be generally critical. Folkes and Sears (1977) ran a series of experiments to test this hypothesis—that is, to find out whether or not "likers are liked best." They had subjects read or listen to survey interviews in which the interviewee was called upon to evaluate a long list of objects. In some cases the objects were political leaders; in others they were cafeteria workers, cities, movies, or freshman courses. In each case it was found that interviewees who expressed predominantly positive attitudes—that is, who said they liked most of the politicians, cities, movies, or courses—were liked better than those who expressed mainly negative attitudes. "Likers" were liked best. Folkes and Sears concluded that the explanation lay in the greater warmth communicated by mainly positive interviewees, because other analyses showed the effect was not due to any greater perceived intelligence, knowledge, or similarity of attitudes on the part of the more positive interviewees.

Some other traits that help generate liking have been identified in a study by Norman Anderson (1968). He compiled a list of 555 adjectives that are used to describe people. He then asked college students to indicate how much they would like a person who had each of these characteristics. (A sample of the adjectives is listed in Table 6–2.) One of the most striking results of the study was that the trait most valued by college students in the 1960s was sincerity. Of the eight top adjectives, six—sincere, honest, loyal, truthful, trustworthy, and depend-

TABLE 6-2
Likableness of Personality Traits

HIGHLY LIKABLE	SLIGHTLY POSITIVE TO SLIGHTLY NEGATIVE	HIGHLY DISLIKABLE
Sincere	Persistent	Ill-mannered
Honest	Conventional	Unfriendly
Understanding	Bold	Hostile
Loyal	Cautious	Loud-mouthed
Truthful	Perfectionistic	Selfish
Trustworthy	Excitable	Narrow-minded
Intelligent	Quiet	Rude
Dependable	Impulsive	Conceited
Thoughtful	Aggressive	Greedy
Considerate	Shy	Insincere
Reliable	Unpredictable	Unkind
Warm	Emotional	Untrustworthy
Kind	Bashful	Malicious
Friendly	Naïve	Obnoxious
Happy	Restless	Untruthful
Unselfish	Daydreamer	Dishonest
Humorous	Materialistic	Cruel
Responsible	Rebellious	Mean
Cheerful	Lonely	Phony
Trustful	Dependent	Liar

Source: Adapted from Anderson (1968).

able—related to sincerity in one way or another. Similarly, the adjectives rated lowest were liar and phony, with dishonest being close to the bottom. There seemed to be agreement among the subjects on which characteristics are desirable and which undesirable. Presumably, possessing the highly rated qualities increases the probability that one will be liked, whereas possessing those rated low reduces it.

Physical Attractiveness

Another simple but potent factor that affects liking is physical attractiveness. Other things being equal, people considered attractive are liked more than people not considered attractive. For example, Walster (1966) conducted a "computer dance," in which students were randomly assigned to each other as dates for the evening. They found that liking for the students' partner was closely related to the partner's attractiveness. Both men and women who were considered attractive were liked more. In general, physical attractiveness plays an important role in determining choices for dates and even for marriage partners. Stroebe (1971), however, found that physical attractiveness is less important when a marriage partner is being chosen than in dating. Apparently for long-term relationships, other factors are more important.

FIGURE 6–6 Although not all couples are this well matched in terms of attractiveness, there is no doubt that physical appearance plays an important role in romantic relationships.

THE MATCHING HYPOTHESIS However, if everyone agreed on who was most attractive, and everyone really went for those few, a monstrous traffic jam would result along with an untold amount of disappointment and resentment. This, however, does not happen. Usually people calculate the probability of success as well as measuring the attractiveness of their goal, and then try to maximize some combination of the two. In general this is called an **expectancy-value theory** of decision-making, and it argues that people try to maximize the product of value (in this case, the attractiveness of the potential date) and expectancy of getting it (in this case, the likelihood of actually going out with the person).

The implication is, therefore, that people should pursue the most attractive possible person only if the probability of rejection is quite low. In real life, the most attractive people are most in demand, and the chance of rejection is high. The expectancy-value theory argues, therefore, that people will go for the most attractive person they realistically can get. That would mean that less attractive people would go for less attractive partners than would more attractive people. In other words, it would predict that people would go for someone roughly similar in attractiveness to themselves.

Berscheid and associates (1971) call this the *matching* hypothesis because it suggests that people match their own attractiveness rather than simply pursuing the most attractive possible target. Their research included a staged computer-matching dance. In this realistic setting, they found *both* the general physical attractiveness effect *and* the matching effect. That is, the most attractive people were the most sought after the dates, but less attractive people did not go after them very much. On the average, most people sought out someone slightly more attractive than they were themselves.

Is the matching tendency caused by fear of rejection by the most attractive targets? The expectancy-value theory would predict so: the less attractive subjects ought to pick less attractive dates, for whom there is less competition, and so a better chance of acceptance. And in a simple experiment, Shanteau and Nagy (1979) found just that. They presented females with pictures of two males varying in attractiveness, with verbal labels indicating how likely he would be to go out on a date with them. Their choices were affected both by attractiveness and the probability of a date.

As a consequence of this matching process, people in general do naturally wind up with partners who are at about the same level of physical attractiveness as they are. For example, Silverman (1971) had male and female observers rate couples in naturalistic dating settings, such as bars, social events, and theater lobbies. Separate observers rated the attractiveness of each partner in a pair completely independently. On the average, the rated attractiveness of one dating partner was very close to an independent rating of the other dating partner (made by another observer). For 85 percent of the couples, the ratings did not differ by more than one scale point on a five-point scale. Murstein (1972) has found the same high level of correspondence in attractiveness among engaged (or "going steady") couples.

THE DOUBLE STANDARD In our society, at this particular point in history, physical attractiveness seems to be more important to men than to women. In choosing dates and marriage partners, men are more influenced by the physical attractiveness of women than the women are by the physical attractiveness of men. Several studies have found the frequency of dating in high school and college to be more strongly determined for women than for men by their own physical attractiveness (Berscheid, Dion, Walster, & Walster, 1971; Krebs & Adinolfi, 1975). In arriving at judgments of attraction, men use sex appeal and physical attributes more often than women do; women tend to use interpersonal qualities more (Morse, Gruzen, & Reis, 1976). Of course this could change rapidly. The effects of the women's movement are beginning to change many traditional behavior patterns, particularly sexual behavior. Women's sexual behavior has come to resemble men's, in terms of frequency and type of activity, overcoming the hallowed "double standard" (Hopkins, 1977). Perhaps women also are beginning to emphasize physical attractiveness as much as men in choosing sexual partners.

THE HALO EFFECT The halo effect (see Chapter 4) operates with physically attractive people also. Physically attractive people are perceived as having a cluster of other desirable characteristics, even when in fact they do not. An interesting problem, however, is just how far this goes. It is one thing to expect a beautiful girl to be warm (who wouldn't be, if everyone were always reacting to you as if you were wonderful?), but quite another to expect her to be highly intelligent, innocent of any crime she might be accused of, or especially qualified for high political office. A number of studies have explored the boundaries of the halo effect in physically attractive people. One representative study already discussed in Chapter 4 is by Dion, Berscheid, and Walster (1972). They presented subjects with photographs of students from a college yearbook: some of the students photographed had been judged by other subjects as highly attractive, some as average, and others as relatively unattractive. (Half the photos, and half the subjects, were of each sex). The subjects were then asked to rate those shown in the photographs on a number of dimensions. As shown earlier in Table 4–4, the more attractive students were rated as having a better personality, higher status, more likely to get married and to have a more successful marriage, and likely to be more happy. The only exception was that attractiveness was not expected to affect the student's future competence as a parent.

The converse also holds. Likable people are also perceived as being more beautiful. Gross and Grofton (1977) presented male and female subjects with photographs of undergraduate girls along with "personality descriptions" supposedly written by the girl's discussion partner. The descriptions were carefully tailored to describe the girl favorably or unfavorably. Then the girls were rated for attractiveness. The girls whose personality had been described in a favorable light were rated as being more physically attractive, as well, even though the photographs and descriptions had been paired at random.

In most of these cases, the halo effect may be based on very realistic expectations, rather than on some irrational whim. Perhaps an attractive person will develop a better personality over time, because his or her self-esteem is constantly being enhanced, and self-confidence built up. Maybe

TABLE 6-3

Perceived Quality of the Essay

OBJECTIVE QUALITY OF ESSAY	WRITER'S PHYSICAL ATTRACTIVENESS			TOTAL
	Attractive	Control	Unattractive	
Good	6.7[a]	6.6	5.9	6.4
Poor	5.2	4.7	2.7	4.2
Total	6.0	5.5	4.3	

[a] A higher score indicates higher perceived quality of the essay.
Source: Landy and Sigall (1974), p. 302.

an attractive person is likely to go further occupationally, because attractive people do in fact get promoted faster, and so on. Indeed, Goldman and Lewis (1977) showed that more attractive people also have more social skills. They had male students phone female students they had never met in another lab. The students chatted for five minutes, and then rated their phone partners. Independent observers also rated each student for physical attractiveness. The more attractive the students, the greater the social skills they were seen as having, even though their partners had only talked with them on the phone.

The halo effect has been shown to generalize into a number of areas quite irrelevant to physical beauty. Landy and Sigall (1974) presented male subjects with essays on the role and effects of television on society. The essays were supposedly written by a woman whose picture was attached to the essay. She was either attractive or unattractive. In addition, the essay was written well in some cases (clear, grammatical, organized) and poorly in others (ungrammatical, spelling errors, cliches). A control group got the essays without any picture of the author. As can be seen in Table 6-3, the attractive woman was thought to have written the better essay, regardless of whether it was objectively good or bad.

Other studies have found attractive people treated more leniently when they do something wrong. Dion (1972) found that transgressions committed by attractive children were viewed less negatively by adults than were the same acts committed by unattractive children. Similarly, Landy and Aronson (1969) found that subjects in a mock jury sentenced an unattractive defendant to more years in prison than they did an attractive defendant, given a crime described in exactly the same terms. Moreover, in two different studies they found that killing an attractive victim brought a longer sentence than killing an unattractive victim.

LIMITS ON THE HALO EFFECT But, as with all things, the attractiveness-based halo effect has its limits. Sigall and Ostrove (1975) hypothesized that jurors would actually be *more* punitive toward a beautiful defendant if her offense were somehow directly related to her

TABLE 6-4
Mean Sentence Assigned, in Years

OFFENSE	DEFENDANT'S ATTRACTIVENESS		
	Attractive	Unattractive	Control
Swindle	5.45	4.35	4.35
Burglary	2.80	5.20	5.10

Source: Sigall and Ostrove (1975).

attractiveness. So they gave mock jurors the details of a case, along with a picture of the defendant, either an attractive or an unattractive woman. The charge was either one of burglary, which could have almost nothing to do with the defendant's beauty, or swindling, which is something a beautiful woman might use her looks to get away with. Verifying this hunch about connecting crime to attractiveness, a control group, not shown the photographs but given the case materials, did in fact rate the swindler as probably more attractive than the burglar. And attractiveness did reduce the burglar's sentence, as in the other studies cited above. But the beautiful swindler was given a somewhat harsher sentence than the unattractive one. The results are shown in Table 6–4. Thus, it helps to be beautiful, as long as it does not appear that you are trying to get away with something extra because of it.

The halo effect conferred by attractiveness may also be weaker when the subjects actually interact with the stimulus person face-to-face, and thus get a more realistic and complete contact with the person. For example, Kleck and Rubenstein (1975) had male subjects interact in an extended interview with a female confederate whose attractiveness was experimentally manipulated through clothes and makeup. They found that the subjects liked the more attractive confederate better, but they did not attribute any especially socially desirable personality traits to her.

And physical attractiveness may help you more with the opposite sex than with your own. In one study, an essay was presented to subjects along with the picture of the alleged author. The essays attributed to the most attractive authors were rated highest in quality, but only by the opposite sex. The medium-attractive authors did best, according to their own sex (Anderson & Nida, 1978). In another study, fifth and sixth graders were told to try to get another child to eat a cracker coated with an unpleasant tasting substance. The most attractive children were the most successful—but only with the opposite sex. Attractiveness had no effect on their persuasive powers with their own sex (Dion & Stein, 1978).

We cannot understand liking without understanding that some people have likable qualities in greater numbers than do others. As important as these personal qualities are, however, they do not completely account for liking. Much depends upon the type of interaction two people have. Let us turn to familiarity, one of the most important aspects in human interaction.

FAMILIARITY

Some recent studies have suggested an interesting explanation of the effect of proximity on liking. The idea is that familiarity, all by itself, increases liking. For example, consider Parisians' reactions to the Eiffel Tower. When it was first constructed, they were outraged and thought it was a hideous, modernistic monstrosity on the landscape of their beautiful old city. Today it is a beloved monument, and in some ways even has come to symbolize Paris. Familiarity has thus bred liking.

This turns out to be a quite general phenomenon. To begin with, when a quality continuum in the English language has both negative and positive poles (e.g., good-bad, right-wrong, tall-short, beautiful-ugly), the word describing the positive pole is almost always used more frequently. Thus, *good* appears in books and newspapers more frequently than *bad*, *right* more frequently than *wrong*, and so on. This finding, by itself, is just a curiosity. Without additional research, there would be no way of knowing whether familiarity made the words positive, or vice versa. But the finding does suggest that familiar things may be or become more positive than unfamiliar things. In some way, familiarity is associated with being good.

As already mentioned, Zajonc conducted several experiments (1968) to demonstrate that familiarity by itself increases liking. He called this the "mere exposure" effect. His initial demonstrations of this phenomenon involved quite impersonal, nonmeaningful stimuli, such as nonsense syllables or Chinese characters. More directly relevant to our current concern, in another study by Zajonc subjects were shown pictures of faces. Some of the faces were shown as many as twenty-five times, others only one or two times. Afterward, the subjects were asked how much they liked each face and how much they thought they would like the person pictured. The results are shown in Figure 6–7. Familiarity appeared to have the same effect with faces as it had with words. The more often the subjects had seen a face, the more they said they liked it and thought they would like the person pictured.

Another ingenious demonstration that involves faces adds to our understanding of liking. Faces are not perfectly symmetrical; maybe our left eye is a little higher than the right, our smile is a little crooked, our hair is parted on the right instead of the left, and so on. Our friends see our face as it looks to an outside observer, and they certainly think of it as our "real" face. But we have another face, the mirror image of the one our friends see, and we see this face every morning in the mirror. Here the right eye is higher, the part is on the left, and so on. According to the mere

Zajonc, R. B., "Attitudinal effects of mere exposure," *Journal of Personality and Social Psychology,* 1968, *8,* p. 18. Copyright 1968 by the American Psychological Association. Reprinted by permission.

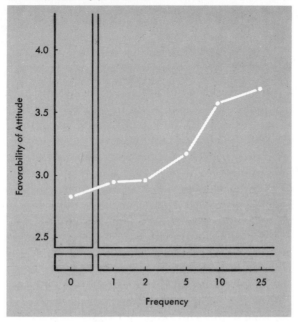

FIGURE 6–7   The relationship between frequency of exposure and liking. Subjects were shown photographs of different faces and the number of times each face was shown was varied. The more often the subjects saw a particular face, the more they said they liked the person pictured.

exposure hypothesis, our friends and lovers should like the real face best, while we ourselves should like the mirror image best. Mita, Dermer, and Knight (1977) showed just that. They got college girls to bring in their girlfriends and their lovers, photographed the girls, and then presented the pictures of the girls to all of them. Some pictures were true prints and others were made from reverse negatives. The girls themselves preferred the mirror image (by 68 percent to 32 percent). Their lovers and their girlfriends, on the other hand, preferred the true prints (by 61 percent to 39 percent, in each case). So each liked best the face he or she had seen the most.

The exposure effect is not limited to pleasant situations. It is no doubt true that the more we take our girlfriend out to eat in a restaurant with a pleasant atmosphere, the more we will like her. But what if all our rendezvous are in a grimy coffee shop? It turns out that familiarity increases liking in *either* positive or negative contexts. Saegert, Swap, and Zajonc (1973) varied the amount of exposure to other people in either pleasant or unpleasant circumstances. The subjects were all tasting a variety of substances, but half tasted pleasant substances such as Kool-Aid, and half tasted quite unpleasant ones such as vinegar, quinine, or citric acid. In either pleasant or noxious taste conditions, the people liked each other more when they had seen each other more. Thus, mere exposure increases liking regardless of whether the situation is positive or negative.

There are some limits on the "familiarity breeds liking" effect. First of all, a lot of repetition may cause boredom and a feeling of tedium, so liking may not increase much after a certain point. Hence it occurs most regularly when the stimuli are initially unfamiliar, and with some exposure rather than at extreme levels of repetition. Miller (1976) tested this idea by putting posters up in the commons area of a college dormitory. For the moderate exposure condition, 30 posters were put up (at 50-foot intervals) for two days. For the overexposure condition, 170 additional posters were put up for three more days. The dependent variable was the student's attitude toward the message featured in the poster. Miller found that moderate exposure increased liking for the message, but overexposure actually diminished it. However, there has not been enough research for us to know whether or not this is a typical result of high levels of exposure, and if it is, how much exposure is required for liking to start falling off. Most studies are done within relatively short periods of time, so they cannot test very adequately for satiation.

The mere exposure effect seems to be limited to stimulus objects that are inherently positive or neutral. That is, greater exposure to *negative* objects does not increase liking for them. Perlman and Oskamp (1971) tested this idea by presenting subjects with pictures of stimulus persons presented positively (as scientists or clergyman), neutrally (dressed in a sports shirt or suit), or negatively (as a janitor or in a police lineup). They found that increased exposure to positive or neutral pictures increased liking, but no such effect occurred for the negative pictures. The results are shown in Figure 6–8.

The general principle appears to be that exposure enhances liking when the object is intrinsically pleasurable or at least neutral, but not when it is strongly negative. To make this point graphically, Zajonc uses the example of seeing a particular man in handcuffs repeatedly over a period of weeks. After a while we become convinced he really is a criminal, rather than coming to love him. But even if an initial rating is only mildly negative, increased familiarity does have a strong effect. For example, in Zajonc's studies, many of the initial ratings were on the negative side of neutral, and he did get the familiarity effect. Thus, it appears that only a strongly negative initial evaluation or perhaps one that is anchored in some actual occurrence is not affected by the familiarity phenomenon.

Another exception to the general tendency of contact leading to lik-

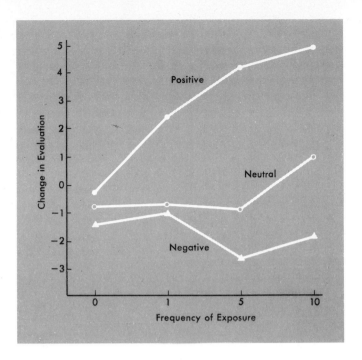

FIGURE 6–8 Mean change in evaluation of stimulus persons, as a function of frequency of exposure and picture content (positive, neutral, or negative). Positive scores indicate a positive shift in evaluations.

Source: Perlman and Oskamp, 1971.

ing occurs when people have conflicting interests, needs, or personalities. As long as they see little of each other, the conflicts are minimized. They may not particularly like each other, but they have little reason to dislike each other. When contact is increased, however, the conflicts are exaggerated and aggravated. Under these circumstances, they may sometimes dislike each other more as a result of closer contact.

Why does mere exposure increase liking? It is clear that exposure makes the person more able to recognize the stimulus. Learning improves the person's ability to identify and classify the stimulus. This improved recognition might itself make the person more positive; perhaps we fear and dislike the unknown. And certainly it is clear in many experiments that repeated exposure improves recognition.

On the other hand, some studies have shown fairly clearly that positive feeling is generated by exposure even in the absence of recognition or evidence of learning. That is, exposure produces more favorable affect even when the person remains essentially unaware of the stimulus (Moreland & Zajonc, 1979; Wilson, 1979). So it may be that we aquire more positive feelings about repeated stimuli even when we are not con-

One simple application of the mere exposure principle might be to political advertising. Millions of dollars are spent in political campaigns to influence voters. Do more dollars, and therefore more exposure, produce more votes? Grush and colleagues (1978) argue that the advertising dollar really works only under these same limited conditions—namely, lots of spending (so lots of exposure), numerous candidates (so it would be confusing without a lot of exposure), and previously nonincumbent, unknown candidates (so there would be no problem of satiation). Under other conditions, they predicted that voting would be controlled by amount of precampaign exposure (such as holding a prominent office or be-

ing an incumbent). And that is what they found. They investigated the primary elections for the U.S. Senate and House of Representatives in 1972. The amount of money spent by a candidate was the best predictor of success *only* in races with nonincumbents, who did not hold a major state office currently, with at least three candidates, and with relatively high spending. Otherwise the best predictor was the winner's precampaign visibility, in terms of incumbency, holding high-visibility office, or having a famous name. And only 19 percent of the races were in the first category, indicating some fairly stringent limits on how common mere exposure effects might be in real life.

sciously paying attention to them. For example, you may be growing to like the other people in your class even though you are not thinking about them or learning their names or learning anything about them.

REWARDINGNESS

People like others who reward them or who are associated with pleasant experiences. We like beautiful women or handsome men because we enjoy looking at them. Kind people reward others constantly and are therefore liked more. The same is true of people who are friendly, sincere, trustworthy, warm, and so on. Someone with these qualities is nicer to be with than somebody without them.

Simple Learning Principles

The effect of rewardingness can be explained in terms of simple learning principles. There are two versions of the learning idea relevant to liking. One is simple *association*: we come to like things and people that are associated with other good things, by a process of generalization of affect. We love that little Italian restaurant in Greenwich Village because it was there that our girlfriend told us how much she loved us. Perhaps we also love the girl because the food was so good!

This association notion is very important, very fundamental, and true most of the time. Yet, as with so much that occurs with people, its very truth and simplicity should not blind us to other processes that may reverse it on occasion. For example, someone with whom you spend a very painful or stressful time may wind up a close friend, even though by association the person should make you think of pure misery. For example, Kenrick and Johnson (1979) put subjects in a situation that involved very noxious, unpredictable bursts of loud noise. Their liking increased even though they hated the experience. People can be quite reassuring to each other in periods of stress and unhappiness, as we saw in Chapter 3.

A second version of the learning idea is that we come to like those who actively reward us. If somebody rewards us or we share a rewarding experience with him, the positive aspects of the experience or the reward are linked with the other person. He thus becomes more positive and we like him more. The **reciprocity principle** is perhaps the most important application of the rewardingness idea. We like people whom we know like us. If the only information we have about someone is that he likes us, we are predisposed to like him also. If he dislikes us, this feeling too will be reciprocated.

This effect has been illustrated in an experiment by Aronson and Linder (1965). They had subjects go through a series of brief interactions with a confederate who was posing as another subject. After each interaction the subject overheard an interview between the confederate and the experimenter in which the confederate gave his impressions of the subject. In one condition, the confederate was quite flattering and said at the beginning that he liked the subject. He continued to make positive statements about the subject after each of the interviews. In another condition, the confederate was critical. He said he was not sure that he liked the subject much and gave fairly negative descriptions of him. He continued being negative throughout the study. Afterward, the subjects were asked how much they liked the confederate. The results are shown in Table 6–5. (The third condition will be discussed later.) As expected, the subjects reciprocated the confederate's evaluation of them, liking him when he liked them and disliking him when he disliked them.

Of course, this does not mean that *all* likes and dislikes are reciprocal. Sometimes we like someone who dislikes us, and vice versa. But other things being equal, there is a strong tendency to like those who like us. Although there are various explanations for this phenomenon, as we shall see below, probably the main reason for it is that the nicest thing anyone can tell us is that he likes us. It is extremely rewarding, and we like those who give us this reward.

Reciprocity plays a much more important role in some kinds of relationships than others. For example, it is more important for mutual friendship than for mutual respect. One study used real-life groups (state

TABLE 6–5
Liking in Response to Another's Evaluation

CONDITION	LIKING [a]
Positive evaluation throughout	6.42
Negative evaluation throughout	2.52
Negative, then positive, evaluation	7.67

[a] Figures are ratings on a scale from −10 to + 10.
Source: Adapted from Aronson and Linder (1965).

policemen and football teams) in which members were asked to indicate which other members were their best friends, and which they respected most. Reciprocity turned out to be much more important for friendship than for respect. Among the state police, 35 percent of friendship choices were mutual, but only 1 percent of the respect choices were (Segal, 1979). It is hard to be friends with someone who doesn't want to be your friend, but it is easy to respect someone who may not even know you exist.

The Gain-Loss Phenomenon

Reciprocity is very important in liking, presumably because it controls one of the rewards most central to a human being: another person's affection. But Aronson and Linder, in the study described above, suggested a complication in the simplest version of the reciprocity principle. It is not always just the *number* of rewards another person gives you; sometimes it is whether they are increasing or descreasing. They argue that we like best those people who show increasing liking for us, and dislike most those who show decreasing liking. According to this **gain-loss principle,** we do not react as extremely to those who are more steadily positive or negative to us.

In Aronson and Linder's study, subjects heard a confederate making either positive or negative statements about them and the subjects generally reciprocated the confederate's evaluations. But the experiment included one other variation—a condition in which the confederate began by making negative statements about the subjects and became more and more positive in his descriptions throughout the course of the experiment. By the last few interviews, he was making as positive statements about the subjects in this condition as he did when he was positive throughout. In other words, some subjects heard a confederate who liked them at the beginning and continued to like them, whereas other subjects heard a confederate who did not like them at the beginning but ended up liking them. Although in both these conditions the subjects liked the confederate, they liked him even more when he began critically and ended positively than when he was positive throughout (see Table 6–5). Note that this is an exception to the simple reinforcement or reward theory, because the confederate delivered more total reinforcement when he was nice all through the experiment than when he was positive only toward the end.

There are two general explanations for the gain-loss phenomenon. Aronson and Linder originally suggested that the initial negative statements caused the subjects some anxiety and self-doubt, all of which are painful feelings. When the statements gradually became more positive, they not only were rewarding in themselves but they also reduced these previous negative feelings. Thus, the later positive statements were more rewarding than they would have been without the initial negative evaluations. The negative statements increased the need for positive evaluations, and this made them more rewarding when they finally came.

Another explanation offered by the authors concerned the manner in which the subjects perceived the confederate. When the confederate liked them immediately and continued to like them, the subjects may have doubted how honest or discriminating the confederate was. They may have said to themselves, "This guy likes everybody." On the other hand, when the confederate began in a negative way, he seemed to be the type of person who could say unpleasant things about others and who takes time to make up his mind about them. That is, the critic appeared more discriminating and perhaps more reliable. Then, when he said nice things about the subjects, his opinion carried more weight and was therefore more rewarding. The subjects might have thought, "This guy is pretty careful about making up his mind about people, but he likes me." The determining factor in the subjects' liking the confederate was how much they were rewarded by the nice things he said, and it is more rewarding to be praised by a careful, discriminating person.

A number of studies have followed Aronson and Linder in getting the gain-loss effect. Clore, Wiggins, and Itkin (1975), for example, presented videotapes in which an actress performed warm behaviors toward a male (facing him, smiling, nodding her head) and/or cold behaviors to him (frowning, looking around the room). The subjects were asked to rate how much the male in the videotape probably liked the woman. When she changed from cold to warm, she was thought more likable than when she was constantly warm; and when she changed from warm to cold, she was thought less likable than when she was constantly cold. This fits the gain-loss theory. But a number of other studies have obtained only the simpler pattern, that the warmer the better and the colder the worse, irrespective of any changes (Berscheid, Brothen, & Graziano, 1976). The best we can say now is that the gain-loss phenomenon does occur sometimes, but we cannot say exactly when.

Ingratiation

We can see that saying something nice about someone is almost always rewarding. The more he believes us and values our judgment, the more it is rewarding. To the extent that he distrusts us and does not value our opinion, it is less rewarding. We like people who say or do nice things for us, but the strength of our liking is determined by how much we trust the motivation behind the action and how much we value the action itself. In particular, there is an important distinction between *genuine* reciprocity and **ingratiation.** If we assume that the other person is being nice to us for ulterior motives, we do not reciprocate the affection as much as if we trust his behavior as being genuine.

E. E. Jones (1964) has conducted a series of studies on the ingratiation phenomenon. In one experiment, female subjects were given a standard interview in which they were asked about their backgrounds, values, and personal opinions. While they were answering these questions, they knew they were being observed by somebody sitting behind a one-way mirror. After the interviews, the observer told the subjects her impression of them. Regardless of the manner in which the subjects had acted, the observer always responded in one of three set ways—she gave neutral responses, responses that were as similar as possible to a subject's own self-concept, or positive evaluations.

In addition, subjects were given two different types of information about the observer. In what was called the accuracy condition, the subjects were told that the purpose of the experiment was to discover how accurately people form impressions of others. The observer in this condition was supposed to be a first-year graduate student in clinical psychology who was participating as part of her training. It was mentioned that clinical psychology students received special training designed to enable them to be objective and to prevent their own feelings from influencing their judgments. Subjects in what was called the ulterior-motive condition were told that the observer was a graduate student who had asked to take the place of the regular assistant just for the day, because she was hoping to use the subjects in her own experiment in exchange for serving as the observer. The experimenter remarked that the observer would be very grateful for the subject's cooperation but that the decision was up to the subject. In this condition no mention was made of the importance of accuracy, nor was anything said about special training in being objective. In other words, in one case the observer was an objective, disinterested judge; in the other case she was someone who wanted a favor and was under no special pressure to be objective. After hearing the observer's judgments of her, each subject was asked to rate the observer. It was made clear that these ratings would be confidential and would not be shown to the observer. The subjects rated the observer on a variety of scales, all designed to indicate how much they liked her.

To begin with, the findings showed a strong effect of reinforcement. The more favorable rating the observer had made of the subject, the more the subject liked the observer. The effect of the different instructions was very interesting. Regardless of the type of remarks the observer had made, the observer who had an ulterior motive was liked less than the one who was trying to be objective and accurate. Most important, the largest difference in liking between the accuracy and ulterior-motive conditions and the only one in which there was an appreciable effect occurred when the observer made consistently positive evaluations of the subject. Under these circumstances, it probably appeared that the observer who had the ulterior motive was not being honest but was making the statements in order to get the subject to agree to take part in her experiment. Therefore, she was rated lower than the objective observer.

Apparently it is nice to receive favorable comments from somebody even if we suspect the person's motives. But we will like the other person less if we have suspicions than if we do not. When a person has something to gain from us, when we are in a superior position, there is a tendency to perceive behavior as ingratiating rather than honest. The nice things he says do not have the same effect. In general, flattery does not make us like others as much as honest compliments do. Under some circumstances it may actually make us dislike them, presumably because we feel they are being dishonest and are trying to take advantage of us. In other words, although there is a general tendency to like someone who says nice things, the effect is not as strong when the compliments are seen as ingratiation.

It will be recalled that a very similar phenomenon was discussed in connection with attribution theory in the last chapter. When there are strong external forces (such as something to be gained by a particular statement), an observer makes an external attribution for the statement. So whether the insurance salesman says he thinks we need insurance, or tells us how wonderful a personality we have, we tend to discount the statement and attribute it to some opportunistic motive. This, then, is another example of how we regularly make attributions of *intent* about others' behavior, and that partly determines our own reaction to the behavior.

COGNITIVE BALANCE

It has often been observed that people like to be surrounded by those who generally agree with them. As a result, they like best people who agree with them most. In an effort to explain such phenomena, Fritz Heider, Theodore Newcomb, and others have proposed a theory of cognitive balance or, as it is commonly called, the **balance model.** The basic assumption behind this model (and other similar models which are discussed in Chapter 10) is that people tend to prefer consistency. They want things to fit together and to be logical and harmonious, and this holds for their own beliefs, cognitions, thoughts, and feelings. In particular, people want their feelings about other people and objects to be consistent.

The notion of balancing forces comes originally from Gestalt theories of perceptual organization. As we indicated in the last two chapters, people try to achieve "good form" in their perceptions of others just as they try to achieve "good form" or "good figures" in their perceptions of inanimate objects. Balanced relations between people "fit"; they "go together"; they make a sensible, coherent, meaningful picture. Thus the main motive pushing people toward balance is trying to achieve a harmonious, simple, coherent, and meaningful view of social relationships.

Forces toward Balance

The simplest situation that illustrates consistency in this context is one person's (P, for Person) feelings about another person (O, for Other) and both their feelings about an object (X, for some thing). For example, consider a student's attitude toward a teacher and both their feelings about busing school children for racial integration. If we limit ourselves to simple positive-negative feelings, there is a limited number of combinations of these elements. They are diagrammed in Figure 6–9 with the initials (P, O, and X) standing for the student, teacher, and busing, respectively. The arrows indicate the direction of the feelings. A plus sign means a positive emotion, and a minus sign means a negative one. Thus, the first diagram shows that the student likes the teacher and they both support busing.

On the left side of the diagram are four possible balanced situations —situations in which the relations among the elements are consistent with each other. When the student likes the teacher and they both support busing, the structure is balanced. It is certainly consistent when two people who like each other like the same things—their relationship is harmonious because they both agree. If the student likes the teacher and they both dislike busing, balance (harmony) also exists—neither likes busing, and they are united in opposition to it. Finally, if the student dislikes the teacher and likes busing while the teacher dislikes it, or if the student dislikes the teacher and dislikes busing while the teacher likes it, balance exists. In either case, they disagree about busing, but the student dislikes and would not want to have much to do with the teacher anyway, so there is no conflict. For convenience, notice that each of the four balanced structures contains an even number of minus signs (negative relations). Whenever there is one negative relation, another is necessary to balance it.

The unbalanced structures have an odd number of negative relations. They occur when the student and the teacher like each other but disagree, or dislike each other and agree, about busing. The imbalance of these situations may be less obvious; the inconsistency lies in the fact that we expect those we like to have similar likes and dislikes to ours and those we dislike to have different likes and dislikes from ours.

The second assumption of the balance model is that imbalanced configurations tend to shift toward balanced ones. It is this assumption that gives the model its importance. Unstable systems produce pressures toward change and continue this pressure until they are balanced; that is, the structures on the right side of the diagram will shift toward those on the left.

The change from imbalance to balance can occur in many ways.

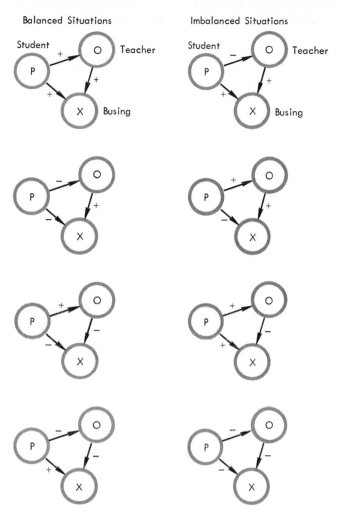

FIGURE 6-9 The balance model of liking. There are eight possible configurations of two people and an object. According to the model, the imbalanced structures tend to become balanced by a change in one or more elements.

Any of the relations may be altered to produce balance. For example, if both the student and the teacher like busing, but the student dislikes the teacher, balance could occur by any one of the following changes. The student could decide that he really does like the teacher or that he actually dislikes busing. Alternatively, he might distort reality by believing that the teacher is antagonistic to busing. Which mechanism is chosen depends on the ease of using it and on the individual doing the changing. We shall discuss this in more detail in Chapter 10. For the moment, the important point is that various possibilities exist.

The major implication of this theory is that people will try to impose or restore such perceptual order on social situations when they are ambiguous, or have become perceptually confused and chaotic. Numerous studies have presented subjects with hypothetical social situations such as "John likes his roommate Harry and Harry voted for Jimmy Carter." The subject is then asked to complete the triad: "How does John feel about Jimmy Carter?" The general finding is that people tend to develop balanced triads when they are initially incomplete or imbalanced.

Unit Relations

Heider, the originator of balance theory, makes a distinction between two kinds of relations that can exist in such triads: *sentiment* relations and *unit* relations. Sentiment relations involve feeling—liking or disliking the other person or the attitude object. Unit relations involve the perceived connectedness of objects. Objects that "belong together" comprise a unit. Most people would perceive me as having a unit relation with my dog, with my car, with my sister, with my typewriter, with my fellow Americans, and with the other people attending a lecture with me. In more formal terms, unit relations can be perceived because of the proximity of two objects, contiguity in time, similarity, physical kinship, nationality, ownership, or common fate. These are among the standard perceptual conditions inducing a coherent "good figure," as discussed in the first chapter. Heider actually specifies two main classes of unit relations: those that come about as a result of choice, and those that do not. If we see someone choosing an object (dating a particular person or buying a new red Chevy Nova), we are likely to perceive them as connected. We shall wait until Chapter 11 to discuss the effects of choice, since that is most commonly investigated in the context of dissonance theory; here we shall be concerned only with the effects of no-choice unit relations upon liking.

Most of the work on balance theory has involved sentiment relations. Forces toward balance move people toward agreeing with people they like, and disagreeing with people they dislike. But Heider also suggested that we balance our sentiments with unit relations. We feel a social relationship "fits" and makes a coherent, reasonable picture when people are connected to those they like, and disconnected from those they dislike. If unit relations are expected to be balanced with sentiment relations, when should this affect liking? The most obvious case is when we are in a unit relation with someone we dislike. Then our positive unit relation is imbalanced with our negative sentiment relation. Suppose that you hate your older sister. You are connected to her by virtue of being sisters. You certainly didn't *choose* her. But perhaps you feel oppressed and put down and infantilized by her. So what do you do? The prediction from balance theory is that you would try to balance your unit relation with your sentiment relation. This gives you two options: you could break off your relationship with her, claim she is no longer your sister, never see or call her, refuse to give her presents at Christmas, and so on. Or you could reevaluate her, see some of the good in her, try to avoid the unpleasant situations you get into with her, think she is after all your sister and part of your family and someone you love (warts and all), and generally change your sentiment from negative to positive. The issue comes down to which of those relations, unit or sentiment, you are more likely to change.

Often it is nearly impossible to break off the unit relation. It is hard to cut off a relationship with your sister. And when the unit is unlikely to change, but the sentiment is negative, the balance prediction is that liking will increase. Tyler and Sears (1977) conducted two experiments to test this idea. They reasoned that a unit relation occurs between two people when they expect to have to interact together. They presented subjects with stimulus persons that were either positive or negative (to induce positive or negative sentiments), then varied whether the subject would have to interact with the stimulus person or not. They predicted that anticipated interaction with negative stimulus persons would increase liking to restore balance, whereas liking would be unaffected by anticipated interaction with an already likable stimulus person.

In the first experiment, the subject was presented with a short essay supposedly written by a fellow student and with an attitude questionnaire supposedly filled out by the same student. The most important condition was designed to create a negative, disagreeing person. In it, the essay said this woman did not like most other college women because they were "silly and uninformed" about most issues. Moreover, the attitude questionnaire was carefully tailored to disagree with the subject on most current social and political issues. Then the subject was told either that she would have to have a discussion with this stimulus person, or that she would be having a discussion with someone else. Finally, the subject was asked how much she liked this person. The results were quite clearly in line with balance theory. As shown in Table 6–6, anticipated interaction

TABLE 6–6
**Effect of Anticipated Interaction on Liking
for Stimulus Person**

	STIMULUS PERSON	
	Pleasant	Unpleasant
Experiment 1: anticipating future interaction with stranger	+ 0.72	+ 3.95
Experiment 2: anticipating further interaction with present discussion partner	− 1.56	+ 3.78

Note: Entry is greater (or less) liking for stimulus person when anticipating further interaction, as compared to no further interaction, on a 24-point scale.
Source: Adapted from Tyler and Sears (1977).

substantially boosted liking for the obnoxious person. And anticipated interaction did not increase liking for the pleasant person very much.

The second experiment was designed to be more realistic. In it Tyler and Sears tried to see if the unit relation could swing liking for an obnoxious other person in a more positive direction, even when the subject had already had some direct contact with the stimulus person and thus had quite a clear impression of her. In this experiment they got confederates to act in an obnoxious manner in an initial discussion with the subject. They did this by, among other things, forgetting the subject's name, snapping gum, blowing smoke in her face, claiming the subject was saying silly things, and not looking at the subject when she was talking. Then anticipated further interaction was varied: the subject expected to talk for forty more minutes with the stimulus person, or with some other person. Finally, the subject was taken into a separate cubicle to fill out a questionnaire which, among other things, asked for liking ratings of the stimulus person. Again, the results supported balance theory, as shown in Table 6–6. Liking for the obnoxious stimulus person increased with anticipated interaction—although not as much as in the first experiment, presumably because the unit relation's effect had to overcome the strong and clear impression derived from the initial period of interaction. And in both experiments, liking for an initially positive stimulus person was not much affected by anticipated interaction, as balance theory would predict.

Other studies suggest that anticipated interaction increases liking in even more realistic situations. For example, in one study (Berscheid et al., 1976), subjects agreed to let the experimenters organize their entire dating life for a period of five weeks. Then the subjects were shown videotapes of various people, separated at random into those described as future dates and those as people they would not date. Prospective dates were liked better. And it did not matter whether they looked forward to five weekly dates with one person ("exclusive dating") or weekly dates with five people ("nonexclusive dates").

Unit relations also have been shown to affect liking in another way. The "halo" of a beautiful woman extends to a man who is thought to be in a unit relation with her, because of being her boyfriend or husband. Sigall and Landy (1973) manipulated the attractiveness of a female confederate by having her either tastefully dressed and made up, or wearing an unbecoming wig, no makeup, and unflattering clothes. When she met the subject, she was with a male stimulus person. She either described him as her "boyfriend" and held his hand, or she ignored him. The attractiveness of the confederate generalized to greater liking for the male stimulus person when he was described as her boyfriend, but not otherwise. In a later study, Bar-Tel and Saxe (1976) found similar results when man-woman pairs were described as being married, but not when they were described as unrelated.

There are two exceptions to the balance principle that ought to be kept in mind. They do not in any way invalidate it, but they do suggest some limits on it. First of all, balancing forces seem to occur mainly with positive relations between the two people involved. These are the top four situations in Figure 6–9, in which the person (P) likes the other person (O). When the person dislikes the other person, balancing forces seem to be relatively weak. Newcomb (1968) has described such situations as being "nonbalanced." He suggests that when we dislike someone, we simply become disengaged from the situation, and do not care much whether we agree or disagree with him. What the other person thinks and how it bears on our own attitudes are of little concern to us; we simply lose interest in her and she drifts out of our lives. This notion has been supported in several studies, which indeed find subjects simply to be less involved when triads include a negative P-O relation (Crano & Cooper, 1973), and balance not to be preferred very much to imbalance (Crockett, 1974). In other words, it is important that our friends agree with us, but it does not much matter whether or not our enemies do.

Second, the balance principle is not the only one that applies to these simple triads. People also tend to learn better, and like better, triads that embody positive relations between the two people. In Chapter 4 we referred to this tendency, in another context, as the positivity bias. And there is also some tendency for people to learn more readily, and like better, triads embodying agreement on the attitude issue. Regardless of whether a person likes another or not, agreement is preferred. In these ways, people seem to gravitate toward more pleasant, as well as toward conceptually and perceptually simpler, social relations.

This discussion of the balance model is, of course, greatly simplified. We have considered a system with only two people and one object and have ignored the multitude of other objects that are involved in any such structure, as well as the feelings of the teacher toward the student. But the basic principles work in more complex and realistic systems as well. Instead of busing, we could have included hundreds of things ranging from books to music, religion, politics, drugs, and law. Each item on which the student and teacher agree tends to make them like each other more; each item on which they disagree has the opposite effect. They may both like music, drugs, and law and dislike religion and books; but one may like the Democrats and the other the Republicans. Thus, they agree on five and disagree on one. Assuming for the moment that the topics are equally important and ignoring the possibility that their strength of liking and disliking for them may differ, this structure of items should tend to make them like each other. If their agreement were split four-two, the effect would be weaker; if they agreed on only one and disagreed on five, they would dislike each other. The more items they agree on, the more they should like each other.

The major implication of the tendency to seek balance for liking is that people like others who are similar to them. The student who likes busing but dislikes the teacher who also likes busing is faced with a conflict that might cause him to change his opinion and end up liking him. Similarly, if the student likes busing and the teacher dislikes it, the student will tend to dislike the teacher. Thus, if we meet someone about whom we know nothing except that he shares our love of skiing, or busing, or anything else, we will tend to like him.

The influence of similarity on friendship patterns is pervasive and important. In friendships or marriages or even simple likes and dislikes, there is a strong tendency for people to like others who are similar to them. Moreover, society generally assumes this to be true. Computer dating services are based almost entirely on this idea. In applying for a date, people list their interests and characteristics and the computer matches them with someone of the opposite sex who has similar interests and characteristics. Presumably this would lead to a better date than one chosen at random or one that does not take into account the importance of similarity.

The effect of similarity is seen most clearly with people who share gross cultural and demographic characteristics, attitudes, beliefs, interests, and backgrounds. Frenchmen like Frenchmen and Americans like Americans; elderly people tend to like other elderly people and young people like other young people. Such characteristics as national background, religion, politics, social class, educational level, age, sophistication, and skin color influence friendship patterns. Also influential are profession, intelligence level, talent in a given field, and probably even height, weight, physical agility, and strength. As we saw earlier in this chapter, there is some evidence for similarity in physical attractiveness influencing dating choices. In fact, on practically every dimension except perhaps personality characteristics (which we shall discuss at greater length below), people who are similar tend to like each other more.

One of the most important studies of similarity and friendship was done by Theodore Newcomb (1961). He took over a large house at the University of Michigan and ran it on an experimental basis. Students lived there just as they would have in any other dormitory except that they agreed to take part in the study and were questioned at periodic intervals. Newcomb had control over room assignments, and on the basis of information from tests and questionnaires he assigned some boys who were similar to each other to be roommates and others who were dissimilar to be roommates. He then intervened very little in their affairs. Under these circumstances, the effect of similarity proved to be powerful. Those roommates who were selected as being similar generally liked each other and ended up as friends; those who were chosen to be dissimilar tended to dislike each other and not to be friends. Thus, this study gave evidence that the computer dating services are correct in assuming that putting similar people together usually leads to a more successful, friendlier relationship than putting dissimilar people together.

The same effect has been observed in even more closely controlled situations. In laboratory experiments (Byrne, 1961; Byrne & Nelson, 1964), subjects were given a description of another person and asked how much they thought they would like him. The descriptions included his attitudes, opinions, and other characteristics. The important variation was that some descriptions made the other person seem very similar to the subject (with the same characteristics), whereas others made him seem very different. The results indicate that the similarity of the description determined how much the subjects thought they would like the other person. The more similar he was described, the more they liked him.

Similarity of values and attitudes produces greater liking even under what might seem to be unfavorable conditions. For example, Bleda (1974) gave subjects the usual questionnaire supposedly filled out by another subject. This stimulus person varied in similarity of attitudes to the real subjects. But in the attached sheet presenting other personal information, one stimulus person was described as maladjusted: she had recently had a nervous breakdown, had been hospitalized, and was seeing a psychiatrist. No such information was provided for the other stimulus person. But in both cases, similarity of attitudes was strongly related to liking. So we

---

BOX 6-2
SIMILARITY ⇌ ATTRACTION

Discovering similarities with someone clearly produces greater attraction toward them. But balance theory suggests the opposite also happens; when we like someone, we expect to agree with him about things we have not yet talked about. Similarity produces attraction, and vice-versa. But in real life sometimes the process flows only one way. For example, the University of Michigan interviewed a national sample of people of voting age in 1972, then reinterviewed them in 1974 and 1976. Granberg and associates (1979) found that attraction to President Nixon, as of 1972, determined perceived sim-ilarity of attitudes to him as of 1974. However attraction to President Ford, as of 1974, had no effect on perceived similarity to him in 1976. President Nixon was a well-known figure in 1972, and people had strong likes and dislikes about him. But the same was not true of the newly appointed President Ford in 1974; he had only been in office a few months and had not been well known before that. So whether similarity produces attraction, or vice versa, depends on the relative strength of each dimension. If one is weak and the other strong, the stronger will dominate.

FIGURE 6–10 Friendships can be based on virtually any kinds of similar interests. Here people are spending time together because they are all bikers, though they may have few other similarities.

tend to like people with attitudes similar to our own, even if in other ways they are not very attractive.

For similarity to affect liking, of course, the two people must discover they have similar values and attitudes. Yet in many first-acquaintance situations, those topics of conversation may not come up. When you first meet someone you find attractive, it is natural to be influenced most of all by how he or she looks, because that is what you first notice. Then you may learn something about their style of talking—whether they are talkative or more reserved, whether they use good grammar, have a wide vocabulary, or use the slang expressions you use. Often the initial conversation is so dominated by small talk that you never get around to talking about values, or goals, or how you feel about more general issues. But even if you do, other first-impression factors are of overriding importance.

Thus it is not too surprising that other variables—especially physical attractiveness—turn out to be more important than similarity in first-acquaintance situations. Kleck and Rubenstein (1975) had a female confederate and a male subject read off their attitude responses to each other, and then had the confederate interview the subject on a variety of innocuous topics about campus life. Attitude similarity did not affect the subject's rating of the social desirability of the confederate's personality

"You're the kind of man we need around here."

traits, her likability, or her desirability as a work partner. However, her physical attractiveness did affect most of these ratings. Similarly, Curran and Lippold (1975) set up a computer dating service and arranged for dates between college students. After the first date, the students rated each other. In two separate studies, the similarity-liking relationship was assessed, and in neither case was it very strong for either men or women. Again, physical attractiveness was a stronger influence.

Complementarity We have seen that people like others who share their attitudes and values. But is it also true that people tend to like others whose personalities are like theirs? This issue has created some controversy. Many studies of friendship and marriage have indicated that people tend to like and marry those who are similar to them in terms of personality. On the other hand, some studies have shown that there is a tendency for people to seek out those whose personalities complement theirs—that is, those who have opposite qualities. For example, a dominant person may prefer a submissive person. The question of whether similarity or **complementarity** in personality is the critical factor is quite complicated. The answer seems to be that both are important determinants.

As our discussion has demonstrated, under almost all circumstances similarity is an important consideration in liking and marriage. This applies to personality characteristics as well. Under most circumstances, a quiet, thoughtful, introverted person likes somebody similar to himself more than he does a loud and flighty extrovert. And the same is probably true of most important personality dimensions—aggressive-nonaggressive, stable-unstable, neurotic-nonneurotic, and so on. There is good reason to believe that friends tend to be similar on these types of dimensions.

But what kind of woman does a man who is extremely assertive, aggressive, and domineering marry? It would seem that if he married a woman who was similar to him, there might be an explosion. So one would think he would pick someone quite meek and submissive. It is easy to think of other examples that fit the need-complementarity hypothesis. Nevertheless, most studies do not support it in a very convincing way. They generally find that good adjustment and compatability are based on need similarity, especially in long-term relationships such as marriage. For example, Meyer and Pepper (1977) found, among couples married for up to five years, that marital adjustment depended more on similarity than complementarity. Even efforts to identify certain traits that elicit complementarity have not been very successful.

Another possibility is that complementarity may facilitate certain kinds of relationships and not others. For example, work relationships may generate complementarity because of the division of labor that often holds in job situations. Wagner (1975) found some evidence that camp counsellors liked each other best if they had compatible, complementary needs, such as one being dominant and the other being receptive to dominance, or one seeking aid and sympathy (succorance) and the other giving it (nurturance).

Our original question—of the relative importance of similarity and complementarity to liking—can be resolved as follows. The dominant determinant of liking is generally similarity. But sometimes, when two people have different roles, as in some marriage, friendship, and professional relationships, complementarity is important. In these cases, people tend to like others whose behavior fits their role. Since their roles are different, their behaviors tend to be complementary rather than similar. However, even with differing roles, the major determinant of liking in most relationships is similarity on dimensions such as cultural characteristics, socioeconomic class, values and attitudes, and so on.

INTIMATE RELATIONSHIPS

Most of the material on liking we have been discussing concerns only first-acquaintance relationships, or the beginning stages of more lasting friendships. Although that is an important stage in relationships, and certainly a very common level of relating to people, it is obviously not the only or the most important one. But it turns out that the factors we have discussed in this chapter play a major role in deeper, longer-term relationships as well. Take proximity, for example. A sociologist named Bossard examined 5,000 marriage license applications in Philadelphia in the 1930s and found one-third of the couples lived within five blocks of each other. Similarity of demographic characteristics is important too. Over 99 percent of the married couples in the United States are of the same race; 94 percent of the same religion, and so on (Rubin, 1973). Similarity of attitudes and values is another important variable. Kerckhoff and Davis (1962) found that couples who shared values moved closer to a permanent relationship over a seven-month span than couples who did not. Other studies mentioned above emphasize the role of similarity in marital adjustment. But it is important to consider more intimate relationships in their own right.

Social Penetration

How do people move from the first-impression stage, in which they develop a general feeling of liking based on similarity, attractiveness, seemingly desirable qualities, and so forth, to deeper and more meaningful

*"There's really not much to tell.
I just grew up and married the girl next door."*

levels of relationship? Altman and Taylor (1973) have developed a theory
about the process by which people gradually attain closeness and intimacy, a process they have called **social penetration.** It describes both the
overt interpersonal behaviors that take place, and the accompanying internal subjective feelings. Penetration occurs, in this view, along two
different dimensions; breadth and depth. *Breadth* refers to the number of
different areas of a person's life and personality that are involved in the
relationship, such as work, family, sexual behavior, hopes and fears,
financial life, and so on. *Depth* refers to the intimacy, or closeness to the
core of the person's being, at which the relationship exists in any given
area. For example, a casual acquaintance might be familiar only with a

INTIMATE AREAS

In studies done with college students, intimate personal levels are defined frequently in terms of sexual experiences, such as first experience, the kinds of activities preferred, previous partners, and so on. The details of one's interpersonal relations and self-concept are also viewed as very intimate, such as feelings about parents, things that make people proud of themselves and things they worry about most.

Less intimate levels include attitudes about religion or professors, future work plans, political attitudes, and matters of taste in such areas as hobbies, music, magazines, food, and summer activities. The following are some Harvard students' intimacy ratings in these areas, each on an 11-point scale.

	AVERAGE INTIMACY RATING
I. SEX	
1. My first sexual experience.	8.51
2. Feelings about my sexual adequacy.	8.13
II. INTERPERSONAL RELATIONS AND SELF-CONCEPT	
1. The things that I worry about most.	6.57
2. My feelings about my parents.	4.89
III. ATTITUDES	
1. My religious views.	3.46
2. My feelings about my teachers at Harvard.	2.13
3. My view of the Nixon administration.	1.55
IV. TASTES	
1. My likes and dislikes in music.	1.70
2. My preferences in food.	1.29

Source: Rubin and Shenker (1978).

person's approximate frequency of dating, and some idea of with whom; a real intimate might be familiar with some of the individual's more private anxieties, preferences, fantasies, and so on.

The theory of social penetration suggests (1) that social penetration processes proceed from superficial to intimate levels of exchange; (2) that interactions continue and expand to a given level of intimacy, and move to adjacent areas and slightly more intimate levels; and (3) that the pacing of penetration varies over time, and is highly subject to the rewards and costs of intimacy at whatever level, and in whatever area, it has already been established.

Generally, at first (the "orientation" stage) people scout out rather narrow areas of each other, assembling little tidbits of information at a rather superficial level. This is a cocktail-party level of getting acquainted. In this stage there is a strong effort at positive self-presentation, and an avoidance of any criticism of the other person. The second stage ("exploratory affective exchange") involves still relatively peripheral levels of the personality, but expands in richness into new areas and becomes more spontaneous. The flow of interaction becomes more synchronized and smooths out, becoming more friendly, relaxed, and casual. When it touches on even intermediate personal levels, however, exchange is still inhibited and based on stereotyped responses. The third stage, "affective exchange," characterizes close friendships or fairly extensive courtship relationships. The two people interact across many areas of the outer layers of personality, and are fairly free in praise and criticism. Many of the barriers to intimate areas have fallen, although some elements of caution and restrictiveness still hold. The people tend to be rather tentative and cautious in exploring truly central layers. Finally, the last stage ("stable exchange") embodies facile exchange in intermediate levels of intimacy, and both persons allow access to very private feelings and belongings.

Self-Disclosure

The disclosure of broader and more intimate aspects of personality is obviously the key to advancing social penetration. If we are willing to allow the other person access only to our most superficial and public selves, penetration cannot go very far. The intimacy (see Box 6–4) of self-disclosure depends on some fairly clear conditions. An obvious one is the closeness of the prior relationship between discloser and recipient. A less obvious one is proximity. If people have spent a good bit of time together in close proximity, they are more likely to disclose intimate material. Rubin and Shenker (1978) found that roommates were more mutually self-disclosing after a few months of living together than were hallmates, even though room assignments had originally been made largely at random. Similarly, Altman and Haythorn (1965) isolated navy recruits who were mere casual acquaintances together in pairs for a period of ten days. They found that isolation increased both the breadth and depth of self-disclosure.

It also helps if the two people are somewhat physically isolated from other people. For example, intimate self-disclosure occurs more readily in dyads (two-person groups) than in triads (three-person groups). Taylor and co-workers (1979) brought groups of acquaintances together in the laboratory in either twos or threes, and had them discuss problems of undergraduate life. The students later privately rated their discussions. They felt the discussions had been more intimate, and that they had learned more about the other discussants, when they had occurred in dyads than in triads. Intimate self-disclosure, therefore, seems to come easiest when the revealer feels safest with the recipient, with few or no other people in on the secrets. These then seem to be some of the conditions for intimate self-disclosure: a close relationship, a history of physical proximity, and current isolation from other people.

Self-Disclosure and Liking

But how does self-disclosure affect liking? The most influential early experimental work was done by Sidney Jourard. His initial hypothesis was that self-disclosure would increase liking, since it is a major mechanism for increasing penetration or intimacy with another person. He reasoned that having the self open to another person is intrinsically more gratifying than being closed up tight, and that this good feeling should generalize to the person to whom one was disclosing. And in turn, we should like a disclosing person more than a nondiscloser. To test this, Daher and Banikiotes (1976) presented subjects with stimulus persons (SPs) varying in intimacy of self-disclosure, and then measured liking for the SP. They used a long series of items about the self, to which the SP had supposedly responded. These items were graduated in intimacy of self-disclosure, so that they could be experimentally varied. The subject then read the SP's responses to these items, which were in multiple-choice format. The subjects liked better the SPs who gave more self-disclosure. A number of similar studies have also found that liking for an SP increases as he or she becomes more self-disclosing (Cozby, 1973; Jourard & Friedman, 1970). But it must be remembered that this self-disclosure was still at a rather superficial level. And the subject did not have to disclose anything about himself.

The social penetration thesis of Altman and Taylor leads us to expect a more complex relationship between self-disclosure and liking, in two ways. First of all, they argue that self-disclosure will lead to liking only if it is carefully paced. It must be slow enough that it does not become threatening to either person. If it races ahead prematurely into areas of great personal intimacy, it will arouse anxiety and defensiveness. Interpersonal barriers will go up, and it will have the effect of promoting distance between the people, rather than closeness. So someone who "comes on too strong and too fast" will be disliked rather than liked.

One example is a study by Kaplan and colleagues (1974). They varied both the formality of the interaction setting, and the intimacy of the subject's own self-disclosure. College male subjects were brought into the laboratory to be interviewed in one of three contexts. One was highly formal: the panelled and carpeted room was decorated with management and business journals, and the interviewer was supposed to be a business student. Then there was a medium-formality condition, in which the lab was stocked with psychotherapy literature and the interviewer was supposed to be a clinical psychology student. In the low-formality condition, decoration consisted of marital counseling and sexological literature, and the interviewer was a "human relations" student learning how to do sexual counseling. The questions answered by the subject were either highly intimate ("How often do you masturbate?" and "Would you describe any

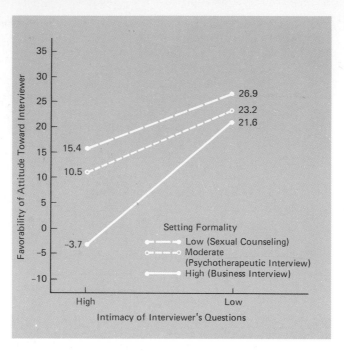

FIGURE 6–11 Interview setting formality and liking.

Source: From Kaplan et al., 1974.

things that you dislike about your mother?'') or nonintimate (''What are the kind of movies that you like to see?'' and ''How many hours of sleep do you need to feel your best?''). Ratings of attraction to the interviewer were obtained in an unusual way: After every question, the subject pressed a button indicating liking, ostensibly to give an ongoing measure of the ''interviewer's'' performance. The results are shown in Figure 6–11. Liking for the interviewer was highest in the informal setting with nonintimate questions—that is, for quite a modest level of social penetration between these two complete strangers. Liking was least for the formal-context interviewer asking intimate questions. Clearly, this person was probing at too deep a level, too fast. His demands for intimate self-disclosure were especially inappropriate given his own formality.

This example leads us to the second modification Altman and Taylor urge for Jourard's original hypothesis. This is that a *reciprocity norm* in self-disclosure determines liking. We like best people who self-disclose at about the same level of intimacy we do. Someone who discloses more intimate detail about himself than we do threatens us with a premature rush into intimate territory, and we want to put on the brakes. But if we are disclosing at a more intimate level than the other person, we are left feeling vulnerable and out on a limb. There is quite a bit of evidence that reciprocity of self-disclosure is a key factor in liking. In the Kaplan and associates study, the formal interviewer was asking for extremely intimate self-disclosure, but was providing none himself (or even promising any implicitly, as the "psychologist" and "human relations" interviewers might have been). And he was not liked.

But the most direct test of the reciprocity idea would involve experimentally manipulating the intimacy level of both persons' self-disclosures. Chaikin and Derlega (1974) videotaped two actresses' improvisations of a first-acquaintance encounter in a school cafeteria. They each were instructed to do it two ways: at a high and at a low level of self-disclosure. Then the experimenters presented the performances to subjects in each of the four combinations of self-disclosure: both high, both low, and high-low or low-high. In the high self-disclosure case, one woman told immediately of her relationship with her boyfriend "Bill," her first sexual partner, and of her parents' reactions; the other woman's high-intimacy disclosures concerned her mother's nervous breakdown and hospitalization, her fighting with her mother, and the possible divorce of her parents. In the low self-disclosure cases, they talked about the problems of commuting to school, where they went to high school, the courses they were taking, and so on. The main finding is that liking for both women was higher when they were at the same level of intimacy than when they were at different levels. Breaking the reciprocity norm led to less liking, but for different reasons. The woman who disclosed too little (relative to the other) was thought cold, whereas the more intimate normbreaker was thought maladjusted.

Demands for reciprocal intimacy of self-disclosure seem to be especially strong under two conditions. In the early stages of a relationship, we demand reciprocity for *nonintimate* disclosures. If you tell the stranger next to you in the lecture hall that you like this course, she is supposed to reciprocate with her reactions to it. In this opening stage of a relationship there is no norm for reciprocity about intimate matters. If she suddenly changes the subject, and tells you about her parents' rancorous divorce, you do not feel obligated at all to tell her anything intimate about your life; indeed, it may seem inappropriately intimate since she is a complete stranger. In the middle stages of the relationship, though, reciprocity about *intimate* details suddenly becomes very important. Suppose you sit next to her for several weeks, then go to the campus coffee house after the first midterm. If you then start telling her about your doubts about your ability in school, and your worry that maybe you should have gone to an easier college, you are putting yourself out on a limb and it is important that she make some reciprocal gesture, to show that she is interested in having a closer relationship too. If, in the midst of your disclosures about your secret fears, she suddenly starts talking about the weather, you may feel hurt and want to pull back to a less intimate level. So reciprocity at this stage is important for supporting tentative moves toward a closer relationship.

There is lots of evidence that people generally do not reciprocate sudden intimate disclosures by strangers. For example, Rubin (1975) found that people waiting in an airport responded *less* intimately to a student who provided intimate disclosures and then asked for reciprocation than to students providing more impersonal material. Their reluctance is partly due to feeling pressured into reciprocity, or "reactance" against loss of freedom (see Chapter 7). Archer and Berg (1978) found telling recipients it was perfectly all right to say anything they wanted—and thereby taking off the pressure to reciprocate—made them feel much freer to reciprocate with intimate disclosures.

A more gradual approach does not generate this reaction. For example, Davis (1976) set up an acquaintance exercise in which two people took turns disclosing to each other. He found that the average intimacy level increased through the exercise, as might be expected from our discussion of "penetration." More important for the reciprocity norm, he found that both the average level of intimacy and the rate of increase of intimacy were closely matched between partners. As one person became more intimate, or slowed down, so did the other. In a later study, Davis (1977) allowed the two discussion partners to talk more explicitly between turns about their feelings about the interaction itself. The intimacy of each partner's disclosures still was matched over the entire discussion, but the reciprocity norm was relaxed a little. Apparently they did not feel that both sides of every exchange had to be equally self-disclosing; instead, they came to a rough overall agreement that allowed an exchange to be unbalanced temporarily. Also, with more explicit discussion of the disclosure process itself, the two partners became more equal in taking the initiative. There was less tendency for one partner to take the lead, with the other following in reciprocation. And finally, because of the explicit attention to the process, they reached a more intimate level of disclosure more rapidly.

It would seem that young Americans today expect more closeness from self-disclosure in their intimate relationships than did earlier generations. Rands and Levinger (1979) asked college students and senior citizens to describe relationships characteristic of twenty-two-year-olds of their own generations. They found that today's young people expect pairs to be more expressive, to do more things together, to disclose both positive and negative feelings more openly, and to have more physical contact than the young people of two generations ago. Today's young also expect fewer sex differences, as for example in the female's initiation of social and physical contact. Although the senior citizens' memories may not have been completely accurate, at least they confirm some stereotypes widely held by social observers. For example, Altman and Taylor (1973) suggest that up through the 1950s, the middle-class norm emphasized a great deal of self-restraint, reserve, caution, and self-protectiveness about revealing intimate details. Close, intimate penetration was not allowed very much. Then a reaction set in, which was best characterized by such phenomena as encounter or test groups, in which perfect strangers were supposed to disclose at a very intimate level at their first meeting (see Box 6–5). Moreover, the "sexual revolution" meant that people climbed in and out of intimate relationships (as well as bed) much more often, freely, and intensively than they had in previous eras. Altman and Taylor offer some cautionary comments about this trend, suggesting that "instant intimacy" may prove illusory, as people give each other only superficial, stereotyped versions of their innermost feelings. And people may grow to mistrust intimate relationships, because they prove so transitory. In general, they caution us to remember that true intimacy comes slowly, that it comes only with trust and accumulated experience with the other person, and that it bears risks and costs. We therefore should not take intimacy too lightly or too much for granted, but treat it with respect and with care.

Romantic Love
One factor that clearly differentiates deep attachments from first impressions is romantic love. Unfortunately, it is one of the topics that social psychologists have been particularly negligent about studying. Perhaps they are in awe of its mysteries and do not want to meddle with it, for fear of discovering something mundane or demeaning about what is considered to be a beautiful phenomenon. Or perhaps their methodologies are

not appropriate for such a highly emotional, changeable phenomenon. Some psychologists, however, have begun to theorize about love and tie it in with some of the other theories we have presented.

First of all, all the factors that are important in liking are probably important in romantic love as well. Certainly proximity, warmth, physical attractiveness, rewardingness, and similarity would seem to be crucial ingredients. But some additional processes must also operate. The feelings in romantic love are much more powerful than are those in acquaintance or friendship relationships. In an effort to deal with these strange feelings, Berscheid and Walster (1974) have suggested that romantic love can be analyzed according to Schachter's (1964) two-factor theory of emotions we discussed in the last chapter. He theorized that any emotional experience consists of intense physiological arousal, plus the appropriate cognitive labeling. Romantic love, then, would consist of intense arousal, plus such labels as "this must be love," "the real thing," "she's all I can think about," or "he's the one for me." No one would be surprised by the assertion that positive emotional experiences, such as sexual gratification, excitement, and need of satisfaction, increase arousal and thus heighten the feeling of "being in love." But the theory also implies that even unpleasant emotional experiences should be arousing and, if properly labeled as part of "being in love," should enhance the experience of romantic love. So, fear, rejection, frustration, and challenge should all contribute to the feeling of love.

Not much solid research evidence is available to support this hypothesis, partly due to the fact that so little work has been done on it until recently. One attempt was made by Driscoll, Davis, and Lipitz (1972) who investigated the effects of parental interference on the relationships of married and dating couples. They found couples with high levels of parental interference reported *more* love than did couples with little interference. And increases in such interference over time were associated with even further increases in reported romantic love. They describe this finding, consistent with the Berscheid-Walster theory, as the "Romeo and Juliet effect," after that pair of "star-crossed" lovers seemingly cursed by the violent rivalry between the Capulet and Montague clans.

Another implication of this theory is that the "hard to get" woman, because she is so frustrating, ought to induce more love and be more attractive than one who produces less arousal because she is easier to get. In one series of studies, Walster, Berscheid, and Walster (1973) arranged for a female confederate to respond to calls under the guise of a computer date program. To one set of callers she responded that she would be delighted to go out on a date. To others, she agreed to go out only reluctantly. However, contrary to the theory, attraction to the woman did not differ in the two conditions. In another study, the confederate was a prostitute who suggested to half her prospective clients that she would take on any client; to the other half, she suggested she was quite selective and would only see a limited number. In all cases she then had sexual inter-

BOX 6-6

A RUSH ABOVE THE RAPIDS

By the misattribution theory, any strong emotional arousal should lead to greater attraction if its most salient probable cause is the attractiveness of another person. Hence Dutton and Aron (1974) had an attractive female interviewer approach solitary men either on a swaying suspension bridge looking down 230 feet to rocks and shallow rapids, or on a sturdy bridge 10 feet high. Presumably the suspension bridge created some substantial level of fear, and it could readily be misattributed to sexual arousal, given the attractive female interviewer. The suspension bridge did indeed produce more sexual themes in the projective tests the interviewer gave the subjects, and more followup phone calls to her (on the basis of her offer to explain the study further) than did the safe and sturdy bridge. Moreover, no such effects occurred with male interviewers. This study provides some support for the misattribution theory.

course with the client. Liking was measured by how much she was paid, whether or not the subject called back for a second appointment, and by her estimate of how much the subject liked her. Again, being "hard to get" aroused no more desire than being "easy to get." The same authors followed these studies with one testing a more refined hypothesis: that what is most attractive is being "selectively hard to get," rather than being hard to get in general. In this case, the same two conditions were used as in computer date situation. The "generally easy to get" woman said she was very eager to date anyone; the "generally hard to get" woman said she was willing but not eager to date anyone. The crucial condition was "selectively hard to get," a woman who said she was eager to date the subject but not anyone else who had called. And this, as might be expected, yielded the most attraction. But this finding is not very supportive of the original idea: it is not very negative, frustrating, or challenging to have a woman tell you she would be delighted to date you and is uninterested in any other man. Rather, she seems to have good taste and that is pleasing.

The idea that negative emotional experiences increase the experience of romantic love is certainly a popular myth. And it runs counter to the simple rewardingness idea we discussed earlier. But so far we can say little about whether or not it is true. Most studies of this phenomenon explain it in terms of simple reward or reinforcement. For example, when a strong negative emotion is aroused, such as fear or anger, a partner can be more reassuring and nurturant, and may be loved for that reason (Kenrick & Cialdini, 1977). Although it is provocative, the "emotional misattribution" theory for romantic love is still unproved.

SUMMARY

1. Simple proximity is one of the most important determinants of liking. Some of the reasons are that people who live or work near us tend to be more available for us to relate to, because anticipated continued interaction produces pressures to like someone, and because familiarity generally breeds liking.

2. Proximity does not tend to increase liking for intrinsically unpleasant, negative people. But most people are evaluated positively, as described by the positivity bias, so proximity increases liking most of the time.

3. Certain personal qualities produce greater liking, especially sincerity, warmth, and physical attractiveness. Each of these produces a halo effect, so that more attractive people are seen also as having a variety of other positive qualities, whether or not they do in fact.

4. Familiarity produces more liking, except in the case of clearly negative stimulus persons or other objects. Then familiarity produces less liking, if anything.

5. Rewardingness increases liking; we like people who provide valuable rewards for us. One of the most potent rewards is liking itself; hence we like those who like us (the reciprocity principle). We especially like those who like us increasingly over time.

6. The value of rewards (such as reciprocated liking) depends partly on our attribution of the other person's intent. If we perceive him as trying to ingratiate us, rather than genuinely liking us, we like him less.

7. The principle of cognitive balance is another important determinant of liking: we like people who agree with us, and dislike those who disagree with us. Therefore, similarity of values and attitudes is a crucial determinant of liking.

8. Moreover, we come to like those with whom we are connected through a unit relation; that is, those we will have a continuing connection with over time.

9. Whether similarity or complementarity in personality traits is more important is still quite a murky issue.

10. More intimate relationships develop through a process of "social penetration," in which the relationship gradually expands in breadth across each person's life, and deepens to more personal levels.

11. Reciprocity of self-disclosure is also a key determinant of liking. If one person discloses at a level of intimacy much greater than the other person does, it makes the latter uncomfortable and promotes distance. But if the first person's self-disclosure is too superficial, it simply perpetuates distance.

SUGGESTIONS FOR ADDITIONAL READING

ALTMAN, I., & TAYLOR, D. A. *Social penetration: The development of interpersonal relationships.* New York: Holt, Rinehart, & Winston, 1973. A provocative, short paperback on the development of intimate relationships. It embeds a description of experimental research in a larger theoretical framework, and contains thoughtful speculations about how people attain, and maintain, close and enduring relationships with each other.

BYRNE, D. *The attraction paradigm.* New York: Academic Press, 1971. A systematic and dogged effort to show how similarity produces liking in a wide variety of different situations.

DION, K., BERSCHEID, E., & WALSTER, E. What is beautiful is good. *Journal of Personality and Social Psychology,* 1972, *24,* 285–90. A classic study of the halo effect induced by beautiful women.

HEIDER, F. *The psychology of interpersonal relations.* New York: Wiley, 1958. One of the most influential books in modern social psychology. It develops the ideas of balance theory and of causal attribution, as they grow out of Gestalt theory. Also full of wise observations.

HUSTON, T. L. *Foundations of interpersonal attraction.* New York: Academic Press, 1974. A valuable collection of essays that summarize and speculate about research on attraction. Ranges from cognitive development, power, cross-cultural studies, similarity, and love, among others.

RUBIN, Z. *Liking and loving: An invitation to social psychology.* New York: Holt, Rinehart, & Winston, 1973. A most literate, readable, chatty paperback covering what social psychologists now think about liking and loving. Students find this one of the most interesting books in social psychology, perhaps because it ties research so closely to relationships between young people.

ZAJONC, R. B. Attitudinal effects of mere exposure. *Journal of Personality and Social Psychology Monograph Supplement,* 1968, *2,* 1–27. An impressive coordinated program of research developing the idea that "mere exposure" increases liking.

Aggression

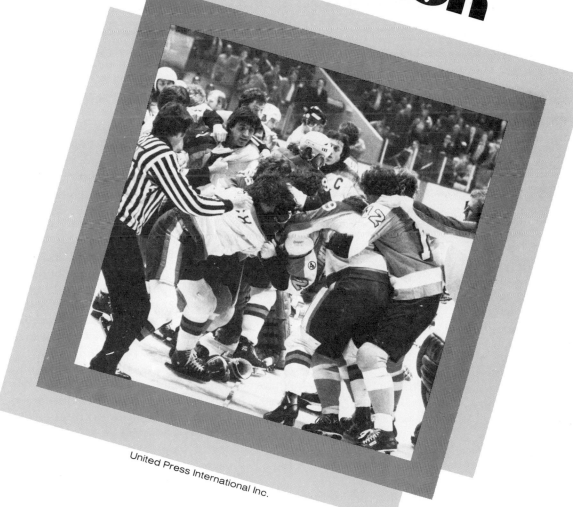

United Press International Inc.

In the previous chapter, we discussed the factors that cause people to like or dislike others. Clearly, liking is one of the most important aspects of interpersonal relationships. A closely related factor is how well we treat others. In a sense this is the behavioral counterpart of our feelings toward them. Treatment of others can range from very negative to very positive, but most of the research and interest have centered on aggression.

Although it might seem that everybody understands what aggression is, there is considerable disagreement as to what behavior should be considered aggressive. The simplest definition and the one favored by those with a behaviorist or learning approach is that aggression is any behavior that hurts or could hurt others. The advantage of this definition is that the behavior itself determines whether or not a particular act is aggressive. We merely have to ascertain whether an act was potentially harmful.

Unfortunately, this definition ignores the intention of the person who does the act—and this factor is critical. As indicated in Chapter 5, people normally come to some causal attribution about other people's actions, and aggressive acts are no exception. One of the first attributions they come to regarding aggression is of the person's intent. If a person tries to hurt someone, we ordinarily consider her to be aggressive; if she is not trying to cause harm, she is not being aggressive. Thus, the definition of aggression should be any action that is *intended* to hurt others. This conception is more difficult to apply, because it does not depend solely on observable behavior. Often it is difficult to know someone's intention, and thus we cannot judge whether she is being aggressive. But we must accept this limitation, for only by including intent can we define aggression meaningfully.

If we used the behavioral definition, some actions that most people consider aggressive would not be labeled as such because, for one reason or another, they are actually harmless. Suppose someone fires a gun at someone else, but the gun turns out to be either unloaded or loaded with blanks. The shooter was trying to cause harm, but in fact his act was harmless. It could not have hurt anyone because firing an unloaded gun or one loaded with blanks is not dangerous. Despite the fact that he was enraged and was trying to kill someone, by the behavioral definition, he was not being aggressive. In criminal law, attempts to injure another person are illegal, even if they are not successful. For example, conspiracies to commit a crime are illegal, and so are attempts at murder.

Ignoring intention also forces us to call some acts aggressive that are not, by the usual meaning of the term. If a golfer's ball accidentally hits a spectator, has the golfer committed an aggressive act? He has certainly done something that could cause harm. A golf ball traveling over 100 miles an hour is a dangerous object. In addition, he has in fact caused somebody a great deal of pain. Thus, the act fits one of the popular definitions of aggression: a response that delivers noxious stimuli to another organism. But surely no one would believe that the golfer was being aggressive. He was playing a game that, of all popular games, involves perhaps the least aggression.

Another category of pain-causing acts that should not be considered aggressive are those in which the ultimate goal is to help another person. Consider a dentist who gives his patient an injection of Novocain. Although an injection can be painful, most patients are grateful for it because it prevents them from feeling worse pain caused by drilling. Therefore, they would not consider the dentist to be acting aggressively when he provides them with the painkiller. Moreover, if the Novocain did not work for some reason, they would still not consider its administration an aggressive act, because the dentist was trying to ease their pain even though he was unsuccessful. Indeed, criminal law allows an exception in the definition of bodily assaults that allows doctors to operate on patients. We can see that ignoring intent would force us to call acts aggressive that, by common sense and any reasonable criteria, are not. We must therefore define aggression as behavior that is intended to hurt others.

But there is yet another distinction to be made. Normally we think of aggression as bad. After all, if an aggressive act results from an intent to hurt another person, it must be bad. But some aggressive acts are good. We applaud the police officer who shoots a terrorist who has killed some innocent victims and is holding others hostage. The important distinction here is between **antisocial** and **prosocial aggression.** The question is whether the aggressive act violates commonly accepted social norms, or supports them. "Prosocial aggression is aggression used in a socially ap-

Peter Southwick; Stock, Boston.

FIGURE 7–2 The distinction between anti-social and pro-social aggression is crucial in society. However, as shown here, it is not always easy to decide what is occurring.

proved way for purposes that are acceptable to the moral standards of the group'' (Sears, 1961, p. 471). Antisocial aggression is not. Unprovoked criminal acts that hurt people, such as assault and battery, murder, and gang beatings clearly violate social norms, so they are described as antisocial. But many aggressive acts are actually dictated by social norms, and therefore are described as prosocial. Acts of law enforcement, appropriate parental discipline, or following the orders of commanders in wartime are regarded as perfectly all right and even necessary. Finally, there is yet another category of aggressive acts, falling somewhere between prosocial and antisocial, which we might term **sanctioned aggression.** This includes aggressive acts that are not required by social norms, but which are well within their bounds. They do not violate accepted moral standards. A coach who disciplines a disobedient player by benching him is usually thought to be well within his rights. So is a person who in self-defense hits someone who is criminally assaulting him, or a woman who strikes back at a man who is trying to rape her. None of these things is required of the person, so none is prosocial. But they fall within the bounds of what is permitted by social norms, so they are not antisocial either.

The key to understanding the differences among antisocial, sanctioned, and prosocial aggression is in knowing what the relevant social norms are. That in turn depends, as will be seen in later chapters, on knowing what the person's reference groups are. Here it is enough to point out that it is usually easy enough to distinguish antisocial and prosocial aggression except in unusual cases. Most of the time we all agree on what is appropriate and what is inappropriate aggression. Occasionally we do not agree. In the 1960s, many blacks rioting in protest of discrimination and deprivation felt quite justified in their aggression, whereas most

---

BOX 7-1

WHO ARE THE WORST AGGRESSORS?

Something you might give some thought to: how common are these various types of aggression? Most of the terrible atrocities seem to have been committed as official acts of government. The murder of 6 million European Jews by the Nazis in World War II was by official order of the German government. The murder of more than 3 million Cambodians in the mid 1970s by the Pol Pot regime was by government order. Widespread torture of and violence against dissidents, such as that uncovered by Amnesty International in repressive regimes in Argentina, Chile, Iran, and the USSR, has all been by government order. The mass suicides at Jonestown in Guyana in 1979 occurred by order of the cult's leader, Jim Jones, and the norms of the cult were that everyone had to obey the leader.

The irony is that all these atrocities are examples of *prosocial* aggression. Each was committed by the legitimate leadership of the nation or group, and

supposedly for the broader social good. The Nazis claimed the noble goal of "purifying" the German race, leaders in Argentina and other nations wanted to restore "law and order," and so on. Sanctioned aggression can open the doors to much cruelty and barbarism too. Consider the near extinction of the American bison; although it was not caused by government order, it was certainly legal and was encouraged by the economic system. In contrast, there are, relative to these mass atrocities, few individual murders in any society at any given time. How much antisocial aggression do you see in everyday life? Is the most serious problem of civilized societies prosocial aggression or antisocial aggression? Crime is a major problem in the United States today. Yet the Founding Fathers felt in some respects that unrestrained governments as well as unrestrained private citizens could be highly dangerous. The Bill of Rights is a partial response to that fear. What do you think?

whites felt quite the opposite (Sears & McConahay, 1973). Members of youth gangs may feel retaliatory killings are justified, whereas most other people would disagree. Members of the Johnson and Nixon administrations felt the mass killings of North Vietnamese were justified because of the threat of communism, whereas antiwar protestors called them war crimes. But such dramatic instances of disagreement should not obscure the consensus almost all humans share about the vast majority of aggressive acts. Unprovoked aggression against an innocent victim is wrong. Killing is wrong except in certain very clearly specified cases. Aggressive acts in the service of social control, by duly authorized authorities, are permissible within certain boundaries. All over the world, and in all cultures, there is broad agreement on such general principles.

Our basic goal in this chapter is to explain why people are aggressive, and as usual we shall answer the question in terms of the factors that increase or decrease the effect. However, our discussion of aggression is somewhat more complicated than that of other subjects, such as affiliation, because it must consider two distinct phenomena—aggressive feelings and aggressive behavior. Generally when we feel like affiliating with others, we do so if others are available and they do not reject our company. The desire to affiliate usually leads to affiliation. But with aggression, as with certain other behaviors (e.g., sex), internal feelings are not always expressed openly. Whereas society welcomes and encourages affiliation, it discourages and condemns many, if not most, forms of aggression. Society can exist only if people control their aggressive feelings most of the time. We cannot have people hitting other people, breaking windows, or acting violently whenever they feel like it. Society places strong restraints on such expression; and most people, even those who feel angry much of the time, rarely act aggressively. We need to consider both the factors that increase aggressive feelings and the restraints that may prevent them from being translated into aggressive action. We thus have two questions—what produces aggressive feelings and what produces aggressive behavior.

SOURCES OF AGGRESSIVE IMPULSES

An aggressive impulse or feeling is an internal state that cannot be observed directly. We all experience anger, and virtually everyone at one time or another would like to hurt someone else. But these feelings are not necessarily expressed openly, and therefore aggressive impulses must be studied largely by asking individuals how they are feeling or by inferring the existence of their internal state from physiological measures or behavior, neither of which is a reliable indicator. Nevertheless, there has been a considerable amount of research on the factors that arouse anger. In discussing the question we shall consider three major factors—instinct, annoyance or attack, and frustration.

Instinct

It has been proposed by Freud, McDougall, Lorenz, and others that humans have an innate drive or instinct to fight. Just as they feel hungry, thirsty, or sexually aroused, so they feel aggressive. Although there are no known physiological mechanisms connected with aggressive feelings as there are for the other drives, aggression is considered a basic drive.

Freud argued that there were only two basic drives—the **libido,** which is constructive, sexual energy, and **thanatos,** which is destructive, aggressive energy. He suggested that all people have strong self-destructive impulses—death wishes, he called them—which sometimes are turned inward and sometimes outward. When these impulses are turned inward, they cause people to restrict their energies, to punish themselves, to become masochistic, and, in the extreme case, to commit suicide. When the impulses are turned outward, they are manifested in aggressive, warlike behavior.

As with other explanations in terms of instinct, the instinctual theory of aggression is difficult to evaluate. The ideal test would be to raise someone in complete isolation, being careful to eliminate all external stimuli that might arouse aggressive feelings. Then, if the individual acted aggressively when given the chance, the indication would be that aggression is, at least in part, instinctive. Since we cannot conduct this type of experiment, we rely heavily on investigations of aggressiveness among nonhumans.

Animals certainly do a great deal of fighting. They fight for food, to protect their territory, to defend their young, and so on. But one of the difficulties in evaluating this evidence is that our definition of aggressiveness may not be appropriate to much of this behavior. A lion that chases and kills a buffalo obviously intends to harm the buffalo. On the other hand, as far as we know, the killing is not done in response to anger or with intent to cause suffering. The lion must hunt for food and the buffalo happens to be its natural prey. Even if we do consider this aggression, it does not indicate the presence of an instinctive aggressive drive. The lion is hungry and kills in order to get food with which to satisfy the hunger. The instinctive drive is hunger, not aggression.

The same argument holds for fighting among members of the same species. They fight for mates, for territory, and for dominance. The first type of fight is motivated by sexual drives; the second, by the need for sufficient food supply. Battles for dominance are more complicated. Sex and hunger may be involved, because the dominant male usually has his choice of mates and the most desirable bits of food. Also, demonstrating dominance avoids unnecessary fights in the future, because the less dominant animals always give way before the more dominant. They fight only once to establish their positions and from then on coexist peacefully. Establishing dominance also facilitates the protection of the group, because it determines which animals will play what roles in defense. Thus, fighting for dominance serves many purposes and cannot be interpreted as evidence of instinctive aggressive impulses.

FIGURE 7–3 Animals attack and kill other animals for food. Their actions are certainly meant to harm the other animal, but would you consider this a form of aggression in the usual sense of the term?

However, the instinct notion does make one prediction that most other formulations do not—that aggressive impulses build up within the animals regardless of the external environment. If these impulses are not expressed, they continue to build up and the animals feel increasingly aggressive. According to the theory, a tropical fish swimming alone in an aquarium should feel gradually more aggressive, even if all its basic needs are satisfied. After, say, a week, the fish should be more likely to attack than it would have previously. On the other hand, if aggression is aroused only by external factors, the fish should not be especially aggressive, because it has spent a week swimming in a comfortable pool.

Konrad Lorenz (1966) observed tropical fish under a variety of circumstances similar to those just described. He reported that certain male fish normally attack other males of the same species but ignore other fish. If, however, all males of the same species except one are removed from the aquarium, the one remaining attacks fish of other species he had previously left alone. And if all fish are removed except a female of his own species, he will eventually attack and kill her. Lorenz interpreted this behavior as showing that fish have instinctive needs to be aggressive and that when the ordinary targets are removed, these needs cause them to attack whatever target is available.

Lorenz bases much of his argument for an aggressive instinct on the response to **crowding.** He claims that animals who are put in small spaces with many other animals of the same species will inevitably become aggressive. This response to a lack of space, often called **territoriality,** seems to suggest an instinctive aggressive response to a common life situation. However, as we discuss in detail in Chapter 16, the evidence for territoriality and for this aggressive response to crowding is questionable. This phenomenon does seem to occur among some species, but it is almost certain that it does not occur among humans. People do not consistently respond aggressively to a lack of space. Thus, responses to crowding should not be considered evidence for an aggressive instinct in humans.

The work by ethologists such as Lorenz and Tinbergen is fascinating. It indicates that many species respond instinctively to specific cues and have many instinctive drives. It does not, however, provide evidence concerning humans. The research relevant to humans has generally been done under less than ideal conditions, and definitive experiments have not yet been performed. Although some ethologists continue to be convinced that all animals have instinctive aggressive drives, most psychologists would now dispute this. Among animals relatively low on the phylogenetic scale, instinct plays an important role in producing aggression, but as one ascends the ladder, instinct probably becomes less and less important. In particular, there seems little reason to believe that humans have any instinctive impulses toward aggressiveness.

Annoyance and Attack

When we are bothered or assaulted by someone, we tend to feel aggressive toward that person. Imagine the reaction of a driver who is waiting for a traffic light to change from red to green when, before it does, the driver of the car behind him starts blowing his horn. Or that of someone peacefully reading the newspaper when somebody pours a glass of water down his neck. Or, finally, imagine a student's reaction when he expresses an opinion in a class and someone else disagrees with him and says he is stupid to hold such an opinion. In all these cases, someone has done something unpleasant to someone else. Depending on how the injured person takes it, he has been annoyed or attacked. It is extremely likely that he will become angry and feel aggressive toward the source of the attack.

Frustration

Frustration is the interference with or blocking of the attainment of a goal. If one wants to go somewhere, perform some act, or obtain something and is prevented, we say he is frustrated. One of the basic tenets in psychology is that frustration tends to arouse aggressive feelings.

The behavioral effects of frustration were demonstrated in a classic study by Barker, Dembo, and Lewin (1941). Children were shown a room full of attractive toys but were not allowed to enter it. They stood outside looking at the toys, wanting to play with them, but were unable to reach them. After they had waited for some time, they were allowed to play with them. Other children were given the toys without first being prevented from playing with them. The children who had been frustrated smashed the toys on the floor, threw them against the wall, and generally behaved very destructively. The children who had not been frustrated were much quieter and less destructive.

This effect of frustration may be seen in broader perspective in society at large. Economic depressions produce frustration that affects almost everyone. People cannot get jobs or buy things they need and are greatly restricted in all phases of their lives. The consequence is that all forms of aggression become more common. Evidence of this was presented by Hovland and Sears (1940) and confirmed by Mintz (1946). They found a strong relationship between the price of cotton and the number of lynchings in the South during the years 1882 to 1930. When cotton prices were high, there were few lynchings; when prices were low, the number of lynchings was relatively high. A drop in the price of cotton signified a depressed period economically. This depression produced frustration, which in turn led to more aggression. An extreme manifestation of the increased aggression was the increase in lynchings.

These examples illustrate the typical effect of frustration, but the original statement of the relationship between frustration and aggression was in more absolute terms. Dollard, Doob, and others at Yale began the work on this problem. They asserted: *aggression* is always a consequence of frustration. . . . the occurrence of aggressive behavior always presupposes the existence of frustration and, contrariwise, the existence of frustration always leads to some form of aggression" (Dollard et al., 1939, p. 1). It appears now that neither *always* in these assumptions is correct. Although frustration usually arouses aggression, there are circumstances when it does not. And, as we shall discuss below, factors other than frustration can also produce aggression.

Arbitrariness of Frustration

One important qualification is that arbitrary frustrations produce more anger and aggressive behavior than do nonarbitrary ones. If the frustration is perceived as being unintended, justified, mitigated by extenuating circumstances, or accidental, then apparently it does not make people as angry, and they are less likely to be aggressive. A hitchhiker on a cold, windy night feels frustrated when a car whizzes past him, but he feels differently if the car is a large sedan with only one occupant than if it is an ambulance rushing to a hospital. Although he is frustrated in both cases, he is angrier and more aggressive if it is the car that passes him than if it is the ambulance. A teacher who prevents her class from taking a trip to the zoo is frustrating their wishes. If she explains that the trip is a bad idea because rain is expected or because many of the animals are ill and will not be on view, less aggression will be aroused than if she offers no explanation or a poor one. A good reason for frustration minimizes aggressive feelings.

The key is that the victim must perceive the frustration or attack as intended to harm him if it is to instigate anger and aggressive behavior. That is, the victim must arrive at an attribution that his tormentor intended to frustrate or annoy him. This is easily understood in terms of attribution theory. If the victim attributes the frustration to some unavoidable circumstances, such as the ambulance racing to save someone's life, then it will not be attributed to some intent to hurt, and will not create so much anger. But if there are no such justifying external forces, and an internal attribution is made, the anger is much greater. Unjustified, arbitrary frustration does produce the most anger, attribution of blame, and aggression against the frustrator (Kulik & Brown, 1979). Retaliation following an attack is most likely when the attack is perceived as unjustified (Dyck & Rule, 1978). If you see the person as being forced into the frustrating activity or attack, you do not get as angry and aggressive. Suppose you have to pay a fine because of an overdue library book. You don't get angry at the student employee in the library; she is "just doing her job." In other words, you attribute her thwarting of you to the situational constraints of her role in the library: she does not intend to hurt you, she just has to enforce the rules.

This dependence of aggression upon perceived intent can be understood in terms of the dual role of physiological arousal and cognitive labels in generating emotion, as discussed in the last two chapters. The argument is that physiological arousal is fairly undifferentiated, so people have a hard time knowing what emotion they are experiencing simply on the basis of internal cues. When they are physiologically aroused, they look to the external environment for cues regarding which emotion they feel. If the environment gives them reason to think they are angry, they will experience anger, and this in turn will lead to aggressive behavior.

Perceiving another person as intending to hurt or frustrate you perhaps provides that cognitive label that this is a situation in which anger or aggression is appropriate. This analysis would suggest that the cognitive label affects angry impulses; we don't feel angry unless we see another person intended to frustrate us. On the other hand, it is possible that the cognitive label does not affect our feelings; just our overt aggressive behavior. We may feel angry when we are frustrated, whether the other person intended it or not, but we overtly express the aggression only when intent is clear, because social norms only justify aggressive behavior under those conditions.

So one possible interpretation of the effects of intent on aggression is that perhaps the person *feels* angry that the teacher won't take the class to the zoo, but restrains himself from overtly expressing it because he knows it would not be fair: who can go to the zoo when it is pouring cats and dogs? Put most generally, the issue is whether perceived intent increases anger arousal, or whether it increases only aggressive behavior without affecting the underlying emotion of anger.

To test this contrast, Zillmann and Cantor (1976) did an experiment that varied whether the subject was informed of mitigating circumstances before being provoked, right after being provoked, or, in a control condition, not informed at all of mitigating circumstances. The idea was that if intent affects angry feelings (as well as aggressive behavior), then informing the person of mitigating circumstances before provocation should prevent anger from being aroused. But if intent only affects aggressive behavior, then the early-informed victim will get angry anyway, but will not become aggressive himself.

The subject came into the laboratory and went through a long, complex series of events, which involved being hooked to physiological recording equipment, being shown slides of magazine advertisements and videotaped pictures of other students. During this time the subject interacted with two experimenters. One was rude and one was polite. During the course of the experiment, the rude experimenter constantly scolded both the subject and the polite experimenter: "Haven't you finished yet?" "Apparently you don't listen to instructions very well. You were told you had to sit still. This machine shows that you've been moving." The independent variable, mitigating circumstances for all this unpleasant behavior, was the polite experimenter saying "he's really uptight about a midterm he has tomorrow." In the "prior" condition, he said this before the rude experimenter insulted the subject. In the "after" condition, he said it afterward. In the third, control condition, he never said it.

The findings very clearly showed that the subjects never got very angry at the rude experimenter if they knew in advance why he was unpleasant. Both physiological measures (such as blood pressure and heart rate) and evaluations of the rude experimenter showed that the prior-to-provocation subjects were much less aroused and less angry than were either the control or the after-provocation subjects. What this means is that the subject's attribution about the cause of his tormentor's attacks affects his experienced emotion, anger, as well as his ultimate aggressive behavior. Being attacked when we know there are mitigating circumstances does not, at least according to this study, produce heightened angry emotions.

So it appears that in aggression, as in so many other contexts discussed in Chapter 5, the person's attribution is a key determinant of the response to frustration. If he believes his tormentor intends to harm him, he will respond much more aggressively than if he thinks it was an accident, or unintended. And if he knows from the beginning that there are external reasons for the harm done to him, he will not get as angry or as aggressive as if he finds out only later on.

A lot of annoying things happen to us all the time, of course, and only some of them come attached with "intent-to-annoy" attributions. This is not to say that we *never* feel angry unless there is some intent to annoy. Inanimate objects can create a great deal of anger: flat tires, snowdrifts, leaky faucets, burnt scrambled eggs, and rocks on which one stubs one's toe are not usually ascribed the human property of trying to harm us (though there are exceptions to everything). What it does suggest is that when no intent to harm is present, many frustrations and annoyances will make us less angry than common sense might suggest.

A good example is the effects of heat. Common sense certainly tells us we are more irritable and susceptible to becoming aggressive when it is too hot. Folk wisdom tells us that it is the heat of ghetto summers ("a long hot summer") that is partly responsible for riots and crime. In fact, one study showed that the ghetto riots of the 1960s occurred disproportionately often on days of above-average temperature (Carlsmith & Anderson, 1979). But high heat is normally not something we perceive as resulting from an intent to harm us. And a series of rather careful experiments has shown that heat, by itself, does not increase hostility or aggressive behavior. Nor does it make angry people any more likely to aggress. In fact, the opposite tended to happen: heat (averaging 94° vs. averaging 73°) tended to diminish the aggressive behavior of subjects angered by a confederate, and increase that among nonangered subjects (Baron & Bell, 1975, 1976). In yet another study, both groups showed less aggression when it was hot than when it was cold (Baron, 1972). Why heat has, if anything, a calming effect upon angry persons is not clear. But it certainly is possible that under oppressive heat, an angry person attributes his anger to the environment, rather than to an annoying confederate. And he may attribute the anger-arousing behavior by the confederate to the heat, and for that reason react less angrily to the confederate's apparently justified annoyance.

Nonspecific Emotional Arousal

Another source of aggressive behavior is generalized or nonspecific emotional arousal that is labeled as "anger." This notion follows from Schachter's two-factor theory of emotions just discussed. This view implies that arousal stemming from any number of sources might promote aggressive behavior, as long as it is labeled as anger. Loud noises (Geen & O'Neal, 1969), competitive behavior (Rocha & Rogers, 1976), or vigorous exercises all seem to increase aggressiveness when they occur in a situation that seems to call for anger. For example, Zillmann and Bryant (1974) did a study that varied nonspecific arousal by having the subject either pedal a bicycle ergometer for one minute (high arousal) or thread nickel-size disks with off-center holes onto a plastic-coated wire (low arousal). Verbal attack by a confederate was also varied, on the assumption that such verbal attacks would help the high-arousal subjects mislabel their feelings as "anger." These attacks came in the context of a modified "battleship" game. Finally, the subject was allowed to deliver loud, painful noises to the confederate each time the latter missed. As is shown in Table 7–1, the highest aggression was delivered in the high-arousal attack condition. Those subjects who were angry and exercised subsequently behaved more aggressively than when the exercise was not included. But arousal actually led to the *least* amount of aggression when there had been no provocation, when the subject had no basis for labeling his arousal as anger. Thus even arousal that is apparently irrelevant to aggressiveness or anger (like exercising, in this case) increases aggressive behavior, provided that it occurs in a situation that labels any arousal as "anger." A later experiment (Bryant and Zillmann, 1979) showed that this misattribution can continue to produce a high level of aggressive behavior, even after the emotional arousal has dissipated, as long as the cognitive label ("anger") holds firm. Arousing any kind of drive or emotion may increase the performance of a behavior even if it is irrelevant. But in order to produce ag-

TABLE 7–1
Mean Noise Intensity

	ATTACK	NO ATTACK
High arousal (exercise)	126.5	58.0
Low arousal (no exercise)	90.1	75.0

Source: Adapted from Zillmann and Bryant (1974), p. 789.

gression, it is necessary that the person somehow misattribute the arousal as stemming from anger, rather than from exercise, or the game, or the film, or whatever else is in fact arousing him.

AGGRESSIVE BEHAVIOR

Frustration, annoyance, and attack all tend to make people feel angry, and these angry feelings constitute one important element producing aggressive behavior. Ordinarily, the more angry a person feels, the more likely it is that he will act aggressively. But people often feel angry and behave peacefully, or at least are not overtly aggressive. It is also possible for people to act aggressively without *feeling* aggressive. Thus, the factors that control aggressive behavior are as important as those that arouse aggressive feelings in the first place. And the main mechanism determining human aggressive behavior is *past learning*.

To be sure, many animals respond aggressively to certain stimuli whenever they appear and these responses appear to be instinctive. If two male Siamese fighting fish are put in the same tank, they immediately attack each other and fight until one is badly mauled or dead. The presence of another male is sufficient to produce this aggressive behavior in each one. For our purposes, the important point is that it seems to be triggered automatically by the other's presence and was obviously not learned. There are countless other examples of similar reactions. Many animals have instinctive aggressive responses to particular stimuli—the presence of these stimuli immediately sets off a specific aggressive reaction. When the stimuli are removed, the aggressive behavior ceases. There is, however, little evidence that humans have this kind of instinctive response to external cues.

In contrast, a newborn infant expresses aggressive feelings in an entirely uncontrolled manner. Whenever she is the least bit frustrated, whenever she is denied anything she wants, she cries in outrage, flails her arms, and strikes out at anything within range. In the earliest days of life, an infant does not realize that other people exist and therefore cannot be deliberately trying to harm her. When she does discover the existence of others, she continues to vent her rage and probably directs much of it toward these people.

But by the time she is an adult, this savage, uncontrolled animal has her aggressive impulses under firm control and aggresses only under certain circumstances, if at all. This development is primarily due to learning. Anything which teaches a child that aggression is acceptable will increase her overall level of aggressiveness; anything which teaches her that aggression is wrong will have the opposite effect. However, most learning related to aggression is more specific than this. Individuals learn to aggress in one situation and not in another, against one person and not another, and in response to one kind of frustration and not another.

What we learn are the *social norms* concerning the expression of aggression. Sometimes these norms apply to the whole society; for example, we all generally share the view that it is wrong to kill another person except under some fairly extreme conditions (self-defense, executions, etc.). Sometimes they apply more narrowly to the social group we belong to; for example, upper-middle-class parents don't yell at their children as much as do working class parents, soldiers are supposed to shoot at the enemy in times of war but not shoot at anyone else, and they are not supposed to shoot anyone in peacetime.

These norms, and the learning of them, define whether aggression is good or bad, as already indicated. The distinctions between antisocial, sanctioned, and prosocial aggression are often quite subtle. But in-

---

BOX 7-3

THE ANGER OF THE "NEW URBAN BLACKS"

The 1960s witnessed an outbreak of violence by black people that had no real precedent in American history. Yet blacks were in most ways better off than they had been since being forcibly brought to this country as slaves more than a century earlier. Sears and McConahay (1973) analyzed this change as being due to changes in blacks' learning concerning expressed aggression. They identified a new generation of blacks, brought up in Northern cities in the post-World War II era, as having been socialized to a new set of norms. They called them the "New Urban Blacks," to compare them with the predominant prewar generation of blacks, who had been brought up in rural and small town South. The New Urban Blacks had grown up in an environment whose formal norms were racially egalitarian, unlike the earlier generation, which had grown up in a formally racially segregated region and era, since the North had generally not subscribed to the formal segregation

the South had. Moreover, the postwar era saw the desegregation of many major institutions, such as the armed services, educational institutions, and professional sports. Finally, the era of civil rights protest, in the late 1950s and early 1960s, provided models of aggressive blacks demanding their rights.

The "New Urban Blacks" were better educated, more politically sophisticated, took more pride in being black, and were more politically disaffected. Most important, they had more aggressive feelings about racial issues by the time of the ghetto riots. They were more sympathetic to the use of violence in achieving political aims, and more demanding of their rights. As a result, they themselves showed higher rates of active participation in ghetto riots than did older, Southern-reared blacks. Sears and McConahay concluded that the new ghetto norms promoted both more angry impulses and more overt aggression on the part of young blacks.

dividuals must learn them in order to function effectively in society. Those who never control their aggression will not be allowed to remain free; those who never use aggression are probably worse off than those who use it at appropriate times. Therefore, the critical problem in socialization is not how to teach children never to aggress but how to teach them when aggression is appropriate and when it is inappropriate. The impressive thing is how well almost all people do learn these complex norms. Almost everyone can tell us when aggression is all right and when it is not. Indeed, the few who cannot make at least the broad distinction are thought insane and are not held responsible for their actions.

Reinforcement

The first mechanism by which this learning occurs is reinforcement. When a particular behavior is rewarded, an individual is more likely to repeat that behavior in the future; when it is punished, he is less likely to repeat it. Just as a child learns not to track mud onto a rug, so he learns not to express aggression. He is punished when he punches his brother, throws stones at the girl next door, or bites his mother, and he learns not to do these things. He is rewarded when he restrains himself despite frustrations, and he learns this also. For example, in one study (Geen & Pigg, 1970) subjects were verbally reinforced ("that's good," "you're doing fine") for shocking a confederate. Other subjects in a control group shocked the confederate but were not rewarded for it. The reinforced subjects gave considerably more intense shocks than did nonreinforced subjects. We could give many other examples making the same point: Aggressive acts are to a major extent learned responses, and reinforcement is a major facilitator of aggression.

Imitation

Imitation is another mechanism that shapes a child's behavior. All people, and children in particular, have a strong tendency to imitate others. A child watches people eat with a fork or listens to them talking and tries to do the same. After a while, he also uses a fork and talks. This imitation extends to virtually every kind of behavior, including aggression. A child observes other people being aggressive or controlling their aggression, and he copies them. He learns to aggress verbally—to shout at people, to curse, and to criticize—and not to resort to violence—not to punch people or throw stones or blow up buildings. He also learns when, if ever, each of these behaviors is permissible. At certain times he should not aggress even verbally (e.g., when he disagrees with his parents), but at others, any kind of aggression is not only allowable but even necessary (e.g., when he is being attacked). Thus his own aggressive behavior is shaped and determined by what he observes others doing.

An experiment by Albert Bandura (Bandura, Ross, & Ross, 1961) illustrated this imitative learning of specific, aggressive behaviors. Children watched an adult play with tinker toys and a Bobo doll (a 5-foot,

Drawing by Charles Schulz; © 1965 United Feature Syndicate, Inc.

inflated plastic doll). In one condition, the adult began by assembling the tinker toys for about a minute and then turned his attention to the doll. He approached the doll, punched it, sat on it, hit it with a mallet, tossed it in the air, and kicked it about the room, all the while shouting such things as "Sock him in the nose," "Hit him down," "Pow." He continued in this way for nine minutes, with the child watching. In the other condition, the adult worked quietly with the tinker toys and ignored the doll.

Some time later, each child was left alone for twenty minutes with a number of toys, including a 3-foot Bobo doll. The children's behavior was rated as shown in Table 7–2. They tended to imitate many of the actions of the adult. Those who had seen the adult act aggressively were much more aggressive toward the doll than those who had witnessed the adult working quietly on the tinker toys. The first group punched, kicked, and hammered the doll and uttered aggressive comments similar to those expressed by the aggressive adult.

The children in this situation learned to attack a certain type of doll. They might also attack the same kind of doll in a different situation, and perhaps a different kind of doll, as well. Just how far this would extend—whether or not they would also punch their sisters—is not clear; but it is clear that they would be somewhat more likely to attack some things than

TABLE 7–2

Aggression by Children Witnessing Violent or Neutral Model

Condition	AMOUNT OF AGGRESSION	
	Physical	Verbal
Violent model	12.73	8.18
Neutral model	1.05	0.35

Source: Based on Bandura, Ross, and Ross (1961).

they were before. Through the process of imitation, these children showed more aggressive behavior.

Other studies (Baron & Kepner, 1970) demonstrate that modeling can not only increase but also decrease the amount of aggression. Subjects observed a model who gave a great many shocks to a confederate while other subjects observed a model who gave very few shocks. There was also a condition in which there was no model. Subjects who observed the aggressive model gave more shocks and those who observed the unaggressive model gave fewer shocks than when there was no model present.

Children do not imitate indiscriminately—they imitate some people more than others. The more important, powerful, successful, and liked the other people are, the more a child will imitate them. Also, the people they see most often are the ones they imitate most. Parents fit all these criteria, and they are the primary models for a child during the early years. Since parents are both the major source of reinforcement and the chief object of imitation, a child's future aggressive behavior depends greatly on how her parents treat her and on how they themselves behave.

This joint dependence on the parents for reinforcement and imitation produces an interesting consequence. Punishing a child for acting aggressively might be considered an effective method of teaching her not to be aggressive, but it often produces the opposite effect. Punishment should make the aggressive behavior less likely in the future. The child learns that she will be punished if she hits her sister, so she avoids the punishment by not hitting her. More generally, she will not be aggressive whenever she expects to suffer for it. She will not ordinarily start a fight with someone who is certain to beat her; she will not start a fight, even if she can win it, if she expects to be severely punished for it afterward. Parents are aware of this simple relationship and employ it to stop children from fighting.

As far as the parents are concerned, this tends to have the desired effect. A child who is punished for fighting does tend to be less aggressive— at home. Home is where the risk of punishment is greatest and therefore where the threat of punishment has the strongest inhibiting effect. Unfortunately, the situation is quite different when this child is out of the home.

"This will teach you not to hit people."

A child who is punished severely for being aggressive at home tends to be more aggressive outside than does a child who is punished less severely (Sears, Whiting, Nowlis, & Sears, 1953).

The explanation for this effect is that the child imitates her parents' aggressive behavior. When she is in a situation in which she has the upper hand, she acts the way her parents do toward her. They are aggressive and so is she. Thus, the punishment teaches her not to be aggressive at home, but it also teaches him that aggression is acceptable if he can get away with it. Regardless of what parents hope, children will continue to do what their parents do as well as what they say.

Aggression-Eliciting Cues

A third aspect of the learning approach is that people learn to aggress as a habitual response to certain cues, and such aggression-eliciting cues need to be present in the situation if anger is to be converted into aggression (Berkowitz, 1965). Any stimuli regularly and repeatedly associated with aggression take on this cue property, by a process of classical conditioning. Guns may do this, as may aggressively toned words ("punish," "hurt"), or the bully in the schoolroom or a police officer. A brawl is more likely to break out at a boxing match than at a tennis match. Atrocities against innocent women and children are more likely to occur in wartime conditions, such as at My Lai, than they are on market day in peacetime. Normally peace-loving, considerate people are capable of extravagant levels of violence in the presence of cues suggesting aggression. That is, the expression of aggression is to some extent controlled by the simple presence or absence of such cues.

In one study (Berkowitz & LePage, 1967) subjects in one group were made angry by being shocked by a confederate, while others were left alone and not made angry. They were then all given the opportunity to deliver shocks to the confederate. When the subjects sat down at a table to deliver the shocks, they noticed a gun or a badminton racket lying nearby. The measure of aggression was how many shocks the subjects delivered, and the experimenters found that angered subjects gave more shocks when the gun, rather than the badminton racket, was present.

Although this is a fascinating effect, later research has not confirmed it. Page and Scheidt (1971) found that the effect occurred only when subjects were both aware of what the experimenters were trying to demonstrate and were also trying to be cooperative. Even more damaging, Buss, Booker, and Buss (1972) repeated the original study almost exactly and did not notice more aggression when the gun was present. In four different experiments they tested the effect of having subjects fire a weapon before delivering shocks. They argued that if the presence of a gun should increase aggression, surely actually firing a gun would have an even greater effect. Yet they found that subjects who fired a gun were no more aggressive subsequently than subjects who had not fired a weapon.

BOX 7-4
HAIR-TRIGGER HONKERS

Another example of how aggressively-toned cues elicit aggressive behavior comes from a study by Turner, Layton, and Simons (1975). They drove a pickup truck around in a mixed business and residential area of Salt Lake City on a Saturday between 9 A.M. and 5 P.M. At stop lights they would wait for 12 seconds after the light turned green before they drove on. They measured how often the car behind them honked, as an indication of aggressive behavior. Again they varied the presence or absence of aggressive cues. The most aggressive had a .303 caliber military rifle in a plainly visible rifle rack in the rear window of the cabin, and a bumper sticker saying "Vengeance." In this condition, 60 percent of the cars honked. The middle condition had the rifle, plus a sticker saying "Friend" and 38 percent honked. The least aggressive had no rifle or bumper sticker, though the rifle rack was in plain sight, and only 27 percent honked.

The theory may still be valid, however, even if these "weapons experiments" were too artificial to support it. But the mechanism may be more complex than originally thought. In general, appropriate cues probably increase aggressiveness when they alter the subject's perception of the situation. If they cause the subject to feel that aggressiveness is more appropriate or more expected, this would certainly increase aggression. Also if the cue causes the subject to feel that the other person is a more aggressive person or more deserving of being aggressed against, that too would tend to increase aggression. For example, in the Berkowitz and LePage study the subjects were told that the gun belonged to the confederate, who was using it in another experiment. This may have suggested to the subject that the confederate was a violent person, lowered his estimation of the confederate, and therefore caused him to be more aggressive. In contrast, Buss and colleagues (1972) described the gun as belonging to the confederate, who was lending it to a friend and was not using it himself. This apparently was a crucial difference, probably because it did not make the confederate seem as violent a person.

Thus, we would conclude that humans are particularly affected by the presence of aggression-arousing cues when the cues produce a marked change in the perception of the situation. Much aggressive behavior is regulated in a very fine-tuned manner by the norms we have learned for particular situations. We honk at someone stopped at a green light but not a red light. We shoot a German soldier in March 1945 but not in December, after the war is over. An argument will lead to a brawl in a bar or on a playing field but rarely in an office building. A schoolboy will get into a fight with another boy but rarely with a girl or with a crippled child. Of course, some aggressive behavior is impulsive, and some is inappropriate to the situation, but the most impressive thing is how much aggressive *behavior* is controlled by the very complex, and often subtle, social norms developed by every human culture or subculture. Therefore it must also be controlled by cues that inform us about the norms for the situation we are in.

REDUCING AGGRESSION

Aggressive behavior has always been a major problem for human societies. Freud viewed aggressive impulses as constituting major problems for social control. Human beings have the capacity for great anger and for very destructive behavior, so it is as vital to understand what reduces aggressiveness as to know what causes it.

As described above, whether or not somebody aggresses in a particular situation is determined by two variables: (1) the strength of his aggressive impulses which in turn is determined partly by the degree of frustration of annoyance that produced it and partly by the extent to which the individual's interpretation of this frustration produce feelings of aggression; and (2) the tendency to express this aggression is determined by what he has learned about aggressiveness in general and the situation in particular.

This analysis, by itself, suggests some of the ways in whch human aggression can be minimized. One, the potential for frustration can be reduced. The Kerner Commission, for example, recommended a sweeping set of social changes after the ghetto riots of the 1960s to improve the treatment of blacks in our society, on the assumption that reducing their frustration would reduce the chance of further rioting. It is also possible for people to learn nonaggressive responses to attack or frustration. A hungry child can learn to deal with her frustrations in ways other than fighting or screaming. She can learn to make herself a peanut butter sandwich rather than pummeling her busy mother. These are essentially preventive measures. But there are other approaches to aggression reduction.

Catharsis

One ancient idea, following this kind of analysis, is that aggressive impulses can be reduced simply by expressing the aggression. Freud called this process the **catharsis** of aggressive feelings. In commonsense language, it involves "letting off steam" or "getting it out of your system." The core of the catharsis notion is that if a person feels aggressive, committing an aggressive act should reduce the intensity of his feelings. This, in turn, should make him less likely to act aggressively afterward. The idea is that aggressing is very much like eating. Whether or not someone eats is determined partly by how hungry he is and partly by the situation in which he finds himself. If he eats something when he is hungry, he reduces his hunger and will eat less later. If someone annoys us by honking his horn at us, we feel aggressive. If, at the next traffic light, we find ourselves behind his car and honk at him, this should reduce our aggressive feelings toward him.

The earliest version of the catharsis theory was Freud's, and it presupposed that we always have a reservoir of instinctual aggressive energy within us. No matter what the situation is, we have a certain amount of aggressiveness that we need to "get off our chest." The problem with this view is that it predicts reduction in aggressive drive following *any* expression of aggression. There is some empirical evidence that contradicts this: when nonangry people aggress, they often seem thereafter to be even *more* aggressive; they have built up steam instead of letting it off (Doob & Wood, 1972; Konecni, 1975).

With the later rise of the frustration-aggression hypothesis, it became more generally accepted that aggressive drives are not instinctual, but are instigated by situational factors like frustrations, annoyances, and attacks. The implication was that expression of aggression would produce catharsis only for those people who were frustrated or annoyed or angered to start with. This hypothesis suggested research to manipulate

Drawing by Jack Tippit; reprinted by permission, Parade Magazine.

J. TIPPIT

"Go ahead, Dad . . . release all that hatred and resentment. It's good to get it out of your system."

frustration and the opportunity to express aggression, and then measure the person's tendency to aggress even further. The prediction would be that angered people, when given the opportunity to express that anger, would show reduced levels of aggression later on. For nonangered people, however, expressing aggression would not reduce the aggression potential, because they would have no built-up reservoir of angry feelings to discharge.

EARLY FINDINGS   One way to test these hypotheses is to look at physiological arousal, as an index of angry feelings. Here most of the research is consistent with the catharsis analysis and predictions. To begin with, two studies (Hokanson, 1961; Hokanson & Burgess, 1962) provide evidence that expressing aggression decreases anger. In these studies, subjects were insulted by a low-status person, with the immediate effect being to increase their systolic blood pressure, indicating that the annoyance had increased physiological tension. We can interpret this as evidence that the subjects were made angry. Some of the subjects were then given an opportunity to deliver shocks to the experimenter who had annoyed them; some were not given this opportunity. Physiological measures showed that being allowed to express aggression resulted in lower systolic blood pressure—evidence that subjects who are originally angry will be less angry if they are allowed to express some aggression toward the source of their annoyance.

More direct evidence comes from behavioral studies of aggression. An influential early study of catharsis was conducted by Seymour Feshbach (1955). First, most of the subjects were angered by being insulted in class by their instructor. Then half the subjects were allowed to express aggression on a fantasy task—responding to four TAT cards (cards showing ambiguous pictures for which the subjects were to make up stories). The other half of this group did not respond to the cards, but all the subjects in an uninsulted group did. Afterward, their aggressiveness toward the instructor was measured, the results of which are shown in Table 7–3. The insulted subjects who were given the opportunity to express aggression on the fantasy task were less aggressive on the final measure than were the insulted subjects who did not do the fantasy task.

DIRECT EXPRESSION OF ANGER AGAINST FRUSTRATOR Later research has found, however, that catharsis is successful in reducing aggression only under a fairly restricted set of conditions. The clearest prediction of the catharsis approach is that angry people, engaging in direct physical aggression against their tormentors, should reduce the tendency to aggress against them later on. And this turns out to be the situation is in which catharsis effects are most easily observed. Perhaps the best demonstration is in an experiment by Konecni and Ebbesen (1976). First, the subject was insulted. She did an anagram task with the confederate, who finished her own problems quickly and then proceeded to insult the subject, criticize her for being so slow, and express doubts about her intellectual ability. Then some subjects were given the opportunity to aggress against the confederate, while others were not. Using a variant on the standard sham learning situation, the subjects were required to deliver "loud, but quite safe" blasts of noise to the confederate each time she made an error. Control subjects did not send any noise to the confederate. The dependent variable involved a "creativity test" in which all subjects were given a two-button box, one labeled "good" and

TABLE 7–3

Effect of Fantasy Expression of Aggression on Later Aggression

CONDITION	AGGRESSION
Angered:	
With fantasy task	21.17[a]
Without fantasy task	23.09
Not angered	14.92

[a] Figures indicate the amount of aggression on a scale from 0 to 36.
Source: Feshbach (1955).

the other "noise." The subject could administer either reward or punishment, depending on her feelings. The results clearly showed that delivering blasts of noise at the confederate reduced a subsequent tendency to do so. A similar study by Doob and Wood (1972), using shock rather than noise, found essentially the same thing: when the subjects were angered by a confederate, catharsis resulted from giving shocks to the confederate. In short, catharsis does seem to reduce the expression of aggression fairly reliably as long as (1) the person is angry, and (2) is able to express aggression in a fairly direct manner, and (3) is able to express aggression against the person who was responsible for his anger; i.e., his attacker, annoyer, or frustrator.

Why do these catharsis effects occur? The original theory viewed the person as filled with angry emotions that drained away as aggressive behavior was committed. An alternative explanation, however, is that the act of aggressing makes the person feel guilty or anxious and simply increases his inhibitions against further aggression. Hence the person might remain just as angry, but when clouded with guilt or fear of retaliation, he might not be as willing to aggress openly. It has been very difficult to distinguish between these lessened-anger and the raised-inhibitions explanations for what we have been calling catharsis effects. So this issue remains largely unresolved.

LIMITS ON CATHARSIS There are a number of clear limitations on the catharsis effect. One is that the person must be in an actively aroused, angry state for catharsis to work. Aggression committed by nonangry people seems to stimulate still further aggression. The Doob and Wood study (1972) showed that nonannoyed people actually increased aggression after shocking the confederate. Perhaps Freud was wrong: unless the person has recently been angered, there is not enough "steam" to "let off," and other processes take over, such as disinhibition or imitation. Their effect is to increase aggression. As Baron (1977) put it, catharsis may work in the heat of anger but not in cold blood.

Secondly, aggression against one's frustrator does not produce catharsis if the original frustration is perceived as not caused by that person. If the person is perceived as blameless, it does not help to aggress against him. That is, if someone frustrates you but you do not think it is his fault, expressing aggression back at him will not relieve your anger. Suppose you want to deposit a $20 bill in your checking account, but the bank teller, saying it is counterfeit and worthless, won't take it. You certainly feel frustrated, and you may get openly hostile, but you will not be able to reduce your angry feelings by yelling at the teller.

In a field study that makes this point, Ebbesen, Duncan, and Konecni (1975) took advantage of a marvelous opportunity when a large aerospace firm recruited several hundred engineers and technicians to work on a new contract for the Department of Defense. After nearly a year of successful work, the contract was abruptly canceled, and the company had no choice but to lay off about 200 disgruntled workers. To take advantage of the hostility caused by these layoffs, the researchers arranged for separation interviews with many of the workers. These interviews provided an opportunity for expression of aggression. They varied in focus, some concerned with the worker's feelings about the company, others with his supervisor, and still others with his own situation. After the interview, in an apparently unrelated action, the worker was administered a questionnaire on his attitudes toward these objects.

The interview did not seem to reduce these workers' anger. In fact, in general it had the effect of *increasing* aggression toward the supervisor or company, either relative to nondiscussed objects, or relative to the aggression expressed by nonangered workers (those not laid off, but interviewed anyway because they were leaving the company). Presumably no catharsis occurred because the layoffs were caused by a tormentor who was not explicitly discussed: the Department of Defense. The supervisor, company, and employee himself all were pretty much innocent victims. So this study is consistant with the earlier evidence that catharsis works only in response to intended aggression by a responsible agent. When it occurs in response to a frustrator who had no choice about it, there is no catharsis. This provides further evidence of how important causal attributions can be. Catharsis works only when an internal attribution is made to the frustrator or annoyer.

Evidence that other ways of expressing aggression produce catharsis have also been sought. One is *displaced aggression;* that is, aggression against someone other than your tormentor. Another is *vicarious aggression* against your tormentor; that is, aggression actually committed by someone else. In these cases, there are some studies that find cathartic effects (e.g., Konecni and Doob, 1972; Bramel, Taub & Blum, 1968), but other studies that do not (see Geen and Quanty, 1977). At the moment social psychologists simply do not know whether or not such situations produce a cathartic reduction in aggressive behavior, and if they do, what additional conditions would be necessary for them to do so regularly.

And if catharsis does not seem to work as well when the retaliator or target were not involved in the original aggravation, **fantasy aggression** may not be an especially reliable way to reduce aggressiveness either. Freud felt that hostile humor could serve as an indirect mechanism for releasing aggressive energy. When we are angry and hear someone tell a hostile joke (like a hostile ethnic joke), we vicariously engage in the expression of hostility and no longer feel so angry ourselves. To test this idea, a number of studies have aroused various degrees of anger, presented hostile (or unhostile) jokes to the subjects, and then measured their subsequent aggressiveness. The catharsis theory predicts that the angered subjects would show less aggression after being shown hostile jokes than after being shown nonhostile jokes, because the hostile jokes would help to siphon off their anger. Research testing this hypothesis has produced generally inconsistent results. Instead, other effects of humor have increasingly been hypothesized to reduce aggression, such as that humor distracts people from their frustrations and annoyances (Mueller & Donnerstein, 1977), or that it generates responses incompatible with aggressive behavior, such as laughter (Baron & Bell, 1974).

The question of fantasy aggression is also very relevant to the hot political issue of whether violence on television or in the movies affects aggressive behavior. If watching a crime movie actually reduced our aggressiveness, it would be quite an important matter, so we will discuss this issue in some detail later in the chapter. But from the above findings our suspicion must be that vicariously experienced aggression against some neutral person is generally not especially cathartic. Watching a boxing match may not really do much about the fact that your girlfriend is going out with your archrival at that very moment, and it apparently would not be likely to do much to relieve your anger, either.

THE RISKS OF CATHARSIS Finally, relying on catharsis as a way of reducing aggression is risky because it may have a number of undesirable side effects. There is the possibility of **disinhibition:** We all control our anger fairly tightly most of the time. But if it is once released, particularly when it seems to be socially approved, we will relax our inhibitions about further hostilities. So expressing aggression may lead to even more aggression. Geen and Quanty (1977) cite the reaction of a man who killed four people: "He said . . . he had a funny feeling in his stomach but after the first [killing] . . . it was easy" (p. 29). Aggression may be reinforced, if it relieves emotional tension (as it appears to), reinforced behaviors tending to recur more frequently. And aggressive behavior also may provide practice and cues for further aggression that would not have been present without it.

Another risk is that within any given sequence of behavior, aggression seems to escalate rather than to decline. That is, catharsis only seems to reduce aggression when there is some break in the action, a change in the victim, or some change in the mode of expression of aggression. So if you get into a fight, it is likely that the fighting will increase your aggression toward your opponent rather than decrease it. This has been a common finding with the Buss aggression machine, which has been used in so many aggression experiments. As the experiment goes on, the "teacher" almost always gives increasingly strong shocks to the "learner," no matter what conditions they are in. Goldstein, Davis, and Herman (1975) found the same thing with verbal responses, using the same teacher-learner situation. The subject was given a list of standard verbal responses from which he could choose, depending on whether the "learner" had made an error or not. The subject tended to give more and more intense punishments for errors. So for example, if the subject first responded to an error with "That's no good," he later would escalate with "You're a jerk," through "I never met anyone as dumb as you," to "Stupid son of a bitch." This *escalation phenomenon* appears to be another case of the disinhibition hypothesis. The authors suggest perhaps the same thing happened with the escalation of the bombing of North Vietnam in the late 1960s and early 1970s, and also in the case of the "battered child" syndrome. In these cases, the same behavior is committed over a period of time against the same victim, and it seems to escalate in intensity. It would seem that either a change in behavior or situation is required for catharsis to occur.

Fear of Punishment and Retaliation

It seems obvious that the fear of punishment or retaliation would suppress aggressive behavior. The kind of rational person described by incentive theories would certainly include such future consequences in his calculations about aggression, and avoid aggression if punishment seemed likely. Indeed, Bond and Dutton (1975) and Wilson and Rogers (1975), both using the shock-learning technique, found reduced shocking when the subject was told that later in the experiment the roles would be reversed, so he (or she) would be in the position of being shocked.

But as a general matter it turns out not to be so simple. For example, as noted earlier, children who are frequently punished for being aggressive turn out themselves to be more aggressive than normal. Perhaps it is because they model themselves upon an aggressive parent. Perhaps it is because frequent punishment generates a lot of anger itself. And sometimes harsh punishment produces disguised aggression that may escape punishment but expresses the anger. In any case, there is clearly no simple inhibition of aggression caused by harsh punishment of children's aggressiveness.

And fear of punishment or retaliation seems to spark **counteraggression,** that is more unreasonable and impulsive. When two people aggress against each other, an escalation on the part of one leads to increased aggression from the other. People who are attacked have a tendency to retaliate in kind against their attackers, even when retaliation is sure to provoke more attacks. One series of studies set up a situation in which subjects could avoid further attacks by responding to a first attack with nonaggression. But they did not; they continued to counteraggress following the first attack, even if it brought more attacks on them (Deverink, Schnedler, & Covey, 1978). It seemed that the subjects just wanted to get back at their tormentors, even when this deepened their own trouble. The only way to reduce aggression in such interdependent situations is for the initiator of the aggression to reduce the attacks. Only then will the victims follow along and reduce their own aggression (Epstein & Taylor, 1967; Kimble, Fita, & Onorad, 1977). Many lives have been lost on battlefields (and in palaces) because national leaders have felt that "national honor" demanded counteraggression, even though it almost guaranteed further retaliation and bloodshed.

The effects of anticipated punishment or retaliation are not simple. Sometimes they simply suppress aggression, as the person quite rationally wants to avoid future pain. But sometimes the threats are simply interpreted as attacks, and inspire even more aggression. And sometimes they convert direct aggression into something more covert, which may be just as harmful but harder to catch and punish. Punishment alone, therefore, does not control aggression.

Learned Inhibitions

Even if punishment, or threat of retaliation, were usually temporarily effective in suppressing direct aggression, it is too expensive to be a general solution to the problem. There are too many people in too many places for all to be monitored constantly. As it is, many people who commit serious crimes, such as murder, are never caught and punished. It is simply impossible to depend upon external controls to minimize violence, and anyway we would not want a society with such repressive control of individual citizens' behavior. So instead people must learn to control their own aggressive behavior, whether or not they are in danger of being punished. Just as people learn when aggression is desirable or permissable, so too they must learn when aggressive behavior must be suppressed.

AGGRESSION ANXIETY The learned inhibition of aggression can be called **aggression anxiety** (or *aggression guilt*). The person feels anxiety when nearing an aggressive response. Like a burnt child approaching a stove, he then backs off and suppresses the urge to aggress. Not everyone has equal amounts of aggression anxiety, of course. Women have more than men do. Children reared in middle-class homes tend to have more than children reared in lower-class homes. Middle-class norms are more forbidding of open physical aggression, and probably also urge more suppression of spontaneous outbursts of verbal aggression as well. It also appears that we are especially likely to grow up anxious about aggression if our parents use reasoning and withdrawal of affection as disciplinary techniques. If they use high degrees of physical punishment, we are likely ourselves to be relatively free about our own aggressiveness (Feshbach, 1970).

Aggression anxiety does not come only from early childhood training, though surely that is an important source. It also comes from the internalization of the norms of people important to us. All through our lives we are learning and relearning "the ropes," or the social norms of our immediate associates. Students learn not to curse their professors to their faces, and professors learn not to throw things at their students. We learn

---

BOX 7-6
WOMEN: REALLY UNAGGRESSIVE, OR JUST CLOSELY WATCHED?

In our society women generally behave less aggressively than do men (Frodi, Macauley, & Thome, 1977). Is this due to longstanding learned inhibitions, or is it due to external, situational controls—that is, do other people constantly suppress women's aggressiveness by monitoring their behavior closely and punishing female aggressiveness? Richardson and associates (1979) argued that if it were due to situational controls, a supportive situation would evoke substantial aggression, while even a silent observer would continue to inhibit the woman's aggression, because of the implied disapproval. In their experiment, each female subject was supposedly engaging in a competitive game with a man she could not see, and they were supposed to shock each other when they won. Over time the man (a confederate) delivered increasing shock. The female subjects did also—but only when working in complete privacy or with a supportive woman observer cheering her on. In the presence of a silent female observer, women's shocks remained low. The authors concluded that women are amply capable of retaliatory aggression—their learned inhibitions are not so strong as to prevent that. But their aggressiveness shows itself only in private or in a supportive atmosphere; it is monitored and enforced by the presence of others.

"No need to apologize. You had a job to do and you did it."

that it is all right to yell and scream at our children, but that it is not all right to beat them up. We can kill animals for sport or food, but we cannot kill each other or someone's pet animal. When you think about it, we all possess a great amount of information, with many finely graded built in distinctions, about what is and what is not permissable aggression. These learned inhibitions represent the most potent controls of human violent behavior we have; no police force could ever be numerous enough, far-sighted enough, or quick enough even to come close to them.

PAIN CUES Presumably people learn inhibitions against aggression in childhood. But what cues do they receive in adulthood that trigger these inhibitions? For example, what kind of restraints, if any, does the victim's reaction to aggression have on the aggressor's further violence? Signs of the victim's distress might arouse, vicariously, a similar negative emotional state in the aggressor: he might identify with the victim, have empathy for his suffering, and inhibit further attack. The experience of having been a victim does seem to inhibit aggression. In Bond and Dutton's (1975) experiment, using a shock-learning paradigm, the subject was supposed to be the teacher. But before the actual learning phase of the experiment began, the experimenter put half the subjects through the shock procedure themselves. The other half had no such experience of being shocked. The result was that subjects who themselves had been shocked gave consistently lower-intensity shocks to other subjects than did those with no personal experience. Still, since the intent of aggression is to hurt, the signs of pain in another person might simply reinforce the aggression, and increase it still further.

To test these possibilities, a number of studies have been done varying the *pain cues* transmitted by victim to aggressor. Baron (1971a), using the shock-learning technique, transmitted the supposed physiological reactions of the shock victim to the subject in the form of a "pain meter." This registered either "high" or "mild" levels of pain. The subject was angered in two ways: by having his own initial efforts at solving a problem criticized by the confederate, and by having the confederate shock him. But pain cues reduced further aggression, whether the subject had been angered or not. Then Baron (1971b) varied attitude similarity of the subject and victim, on the assumption that the subject would feel much empathy with a very dissimilar person. Even here pain cues only led to decreased aggression. Finally, Baron (1974) suggested that pain cues might increase aggression if higher levels of anger were used. This time, instead of just giving the confederate instructions to shock the subject to induce anger, the experimenter told him he could either shock the subject or deliver light flashes. The confederate then shocked the subject, totally incensing him, and arousing high levels of anger, as planned. This time pain cues did increase further aggression, at least in the angry condition. In general, then, signs of a victim's suffering inhibit further aggression, except in cases of extreme anger, when they are taken as signs of successful hurting.

DEHUMANIZATION For such reasons, it is often argued that victims become dehumanized when they are far away or anonymous to their attackers. For example, it was thought that it was easier to bomb North Vietnamese from the great heights of a B-52, or to order troops into battle from the distance of Washington, D.C., than to attack at closer, more personal range. Having the victim distant or anonymous supposedly makes aggression easier, because the pain cues are absent. Conversely, making him more human to the point that the attacker empathizes with his suffering, should reduce aggression.

A neat example of the dehumanization process occurred in the Turner and co-workers (1975) study involving the pickup truck that waited too long at a green light and got honked at (Box 7–4). The experimenters either left a curtain across the rear window open or closed it. In one case the victim (the driver who got honked at) was visible, and in the other case he was not. This produced big differences in honking. The visible driver was honked at 31 percent of the time, the invisible one 52 percent of the time. It is easier to aggress against someone we cannot see or identify in any very personal way. (Another example of this same phenomenon will come up in the next chapter, where we discuss Milgram's obedience experiment. It turns out to be much easier to give dangerous shocks to someone in another room whom we can't hear than to shock someone sitting right next to us.)

ALCOHOL AND DRUGS It is sometimes said that "the conscience is soluble in alcohol." Among the aspects of conscience that can be ignored when drinking, learned inhibitions against expressing aggression would seem to be prime candidates. Barroom brawls and murders by drunken husbands are legendary, and not just in Hollywood movies. An official tabulation shows, for example, that either the suspects or the victim or both were drinking in 41% of all solved murder cases in Canada in the period 1961–1974 (Statistics Canada, 1976). Alcohol was very likely to be involved when the suspect and victim were in a common-law relationship or close relationship (over 54% each), but much less likely if in a business relationship (30%), or had no relationship (36%). Such statistics raise the question of whether or not alcohol generally has a disinhibiting effect on aggression.

To test the effects of alcohol on inhibitions against aggression, Taylor and Gammon (1975) put each subject in a competitive reaction-time task against a confederate. Whichever one was faster was supposed to shock the other. Before they began, however, they were given either a high dose of alcohol (1.5 oz. per 40 pounds of body weight, which would be about three of four stiff drinks for the average subject), or a low dose (0.5 oz. per 40 pounds). As can be seen in Figure 7–4, the shock subject delivered more shock if he had drunk more alcohol (regardless of whether it was vodka or bourbon).

Not all studies show this relatively simple disinhibition of aggression resulting from alcohol. When the victim is more helpless, alcohol may actually depress aggression. And even in this experiment, the low dose of alcohol actually reduced aggression below the level shown by a no-alcohol control group. There are happy drunks and harmless, hapless drunks as well as obnoxious or angry drunks. Another disinhibiting drug, marijuana, has the reputation of not increasing aggression. No substantial amounts of experimental research have yet been done on it to allow an estimate of its effects upon releasing aggressive behavior. However, a careful review of the extensive clinical and field research on marijuana concludes that marijuana does not precipitate violence in the majority of those people who use it chronically or periodically. It does leave open the possibility that some people might have such weak inhibitions against aggression that marijuana would trigger their aggressiveness, but the research evidence on this point is too skimpy to draw a firm conclusion now (Abel, 1977). And other drugs, such as PCP ("angel dust") often trigger extremely violent reactions.

FIGURE 7–4   Mean shock settings as a function of type of alcohol and dose.

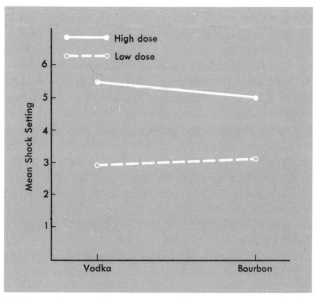

Source: Taylor and Gammon, 1975, p. 171.

Displacement

This brings us to a discussion of what happens to aggressive feelings when, for one reason or another, they cannot be expressed against the cause of the feelings. People are often frustrated or annoyed by someone but unable to retaliate against that person—he may be too powerful, not available, or they may be too anxious and inhibited to do it. In such a situation, they are likely to express aggression in some other way, one of which is called **displacement**—that is, expressing aggression against a substitute target.

When a man forbids his son to go to the movies on a school night, the boy feels angry and aggressive. He cannot attack his father because his father is too strong and because there are social inhibitions against it. Also, doing so would probably make it less likely that he would be permitted to go to the movies in the future. So he vents his rage on someone else. He has a wide range of people available. There is his mother, his older brother, his older sister, his younger brother, and a boy his own age who lives next door. All these people can be placed on a continuum in terms of their similarity to the boy's original source of frustration—his father. Although this similarity depends primarily on the boy's own view of the situation, let us suppose that he ranks them in the order listed, ranging from his mother to the boy next door. The question is, what determines which of these people he will select and how much aggression he will express?

The basic principle of displacement is that the more similar a person is to the original source of frustration, the stronger will be the individual's aggressive impulses toward him. Thus, as shown by the solid line in Figure 7–6, the boy's aggressive impulse is strongest toward his father and gets weaker as the person toward whom it is directed becomes less similar to his father.

When the only reason for not aggressing against the primary source of frustration is that he is not available, the aggression will be directed toward the next best person. Thus, if the boy cannot express his aggressive feelings toward his father simply because he left town, he would aggress against his mother—the person most similar to his father. Next would come his older brother, then his sister, and so on. The anger he feels toward his father is displaced to these people in the order listed.

The more complicated and probably more common situation is one in which aggression is not expressed because the victim has some reason for restraining himself. For example, the victim may feel too much anxiety to attack the father. The victim's anxiety operates in much the same way as does his aggressive impulse. Just as his impulse to hurt the source of frustration generalizes to other people, so does his anxiety about attacking the source. As with the aggression, the more similar the person is to this source, the stronger the anxiety felt toward him or her. This is shown by the dotted line in Figure 7–6. The boy is most anxious about his father, less anxious about his mother, still less of his sister, and not at all anxious about the boy next door.

FIGURE 7–5 We do not know what caused this display of aggression, but if displacement has occurred, it has not turned out too well for the bigger boy.

An important characteristic of the situation is that the anxiety declines faster than does the aggressive impulse, which means that eventually the two lines must cross. As long as the anxiety is stronger than the aggressive impulse, the individual will restrain himself; when the tendency to aggress becomes stronger than the anxiety, the individual will express his aggression. Thus, in our diagram, the boy would not attack his mother or his older brother because his anxiety toward them is stronger than his aggressive impulse. But his sister is just dissimilar enough to his father that he is not afraid of her and similar enough that the aggressive impulse is still quite strong. So because the boy is unwilling to hit his father, he makes a nasty comment to his sister.

In general, displaced aggression is most likely to be directed toward targets that are perceived as weaker and less powerful. One example comes from a learning situation in which women were insulted and angered by a co-worker and then were instructed to punish a child for errors (Berkowitz & Frodi, 1979). They tended to give the most punishment

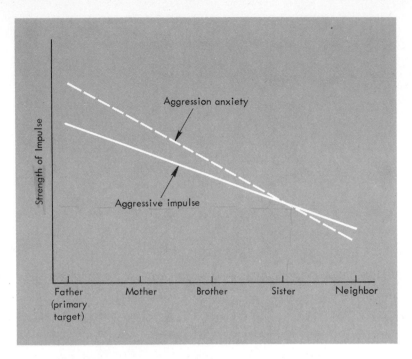

FIGURE 7-6 Feelings of aggression and anxiety are strongest toward the primary target. The strength of the aggressive impulse and of the anxiety decrease as the distance from the primary target increases. Since anxiety declines faster, at some point the aggressive impulse is stronger. The child expresses his anger at that target. The height at which the two emotions cross determines the strength of the aggression expressed.

to children who were physically unattractive or who stuttered. These children were more likely to be the targets of displaced aggression than were more attractive children or those who spoke normally.

The dimension along which similarity is determined need not be as simple as the one in our example. Much of the aggression in society may be due to displacement along complex and subtle lines. For example, many adolescents tend to have feelings of anger against their parents. Parents are the source of power in the family, they are the authority, and they must inevitably frustrate their children's wishes to some extent. Thus they arouse feelings of anger. In some cases, this anger is expressed directly against the parents in adolescent rebellion and breaks with the family. In many cases, however, it is displaced to other people who represent authority. Adolescents need not select those who are related to their parents by family ties or friendship. School administrators, trustees, teachers, the government, and so on fit the criterion and become likely objects for aggression.

Displacement may occur along a dimension of response similarity as well as along a dimension of target similarity. Imagine a president who gets angry at key members of the Washington press corps because he feels

BOX 7-8

FEAR OF BLACK RETALIATION MAKES
WHITES' AGGRESSION INDIRECT

One interesting line of research has shown how whites' aggression toward blacks becomes more indirect and covert when blacks later will have the opportunity to retaliate. The Donnersteins placed white subjects in the sham-learning situation, in which the "learner" was a black confederate. Then they tested how much the subject shocked the confederate, depending on whether their roles would later be reversed or not. Presumably, if the roles would reverse later on, the black might retaliate against the white. In several such studies, the Donnersteins (1972a, 1972b, 1975) found that potential retaliation markedly reduced the direct aggression performed by whites against blacks. In this teacher-learner situation, direct aggression was indexed by the intensity of the shock delivered by the subject when the confederate made an "error." Expecting to reverse roles increased the amount of reward given by the white subject to the black confederate for "correct responses."

But potential retaliation also had the effect of increasing covert, indirect, substitute forms of aggression against the black confederate. Indirect aggression was measured by setting the shock machine at one particular intensity, so the subject had no control over intensity, and then telling the subject he had to deliver shock for every error, so the subject had no control over whether to shock or not. But the subject did control the duration of shock; he could give either a quick one or a long one. The long one was a relatively disguised form of aggression; after all, the subject was just following instructions by giving the shock! And potential retaliation actually increased such indirect, relatively covert, disguised forms of aggression. So the black potential for retaliation against a white aggressor does indeed seem to reduce the white's direct aggression against him (and increase rewards given to him as well)—but it increases, instead, subtle and indirect forms of aggression.

Finally, it is interesting to note that all these effects occurred for black targets and not for white. Apparently the threat of black retaliation for white aggression is most potent. And it occurred much more toward a dissimilar black confederate (dissimilar in terms of attitudes and values, in the vein discussed in the last chapter) than it did toward a similar one (Donnerstein and Donnerstein, 1975). So the conversion of direct aggression into indirect aggression, because of threatened retaliation, occurred with dissimilar blacks, but not so much with whites or similar blacks.

they are misinterpreting his actions. He may be quite inhibited from attacking them directly, because he fears they will become even more unsympathetic to him, and make him even more unpopular than he already is. But he can attack them indirectly, by making snide comments about them behind their backs, by refusing to invite them to receptions at the White House, by reducing the number of telephones available to them in the press room, by refusing to call on them at press conferences, and so on. None of these responses is a direct act of aggression in response to the frustration he feels; rather, he displaces his aggression to subtler, more covert forms. In fact, there is a term for persons who habitually resort to such indirect forms of aggression: the *passive-aggressive personality*.

OBSERVED AGGRESSION IN THE LABORATORY

The catharsis theory suggests that expressing aggression reduces anger, and consequently the chance of further aggressive behavior. We have already discussed the most obvious, direct form of the catharsis hypothesis—namely, that direct aggressive retaliation (physical or verbal) against one's frustrator will reduce the level of future aggressive behavior. But, as indicated earlier, there is still one more version of the catharsis hypothesis. This is that our anger is reduced by observing other people's aggression, even when the target has nothing to do with the origins of our anger. The idea is that people experience the aggression vicariously and become less angry, just as if they were doing the actual aggressing. Aristotle originated this version of the catharsis idea in his discussion of the purpose and effect of Greek tragedy. Members of an audience experience a variety of emotions while viewing a play. For example, when the hero is insulted, they experience anger themselves even though they are not directly involved. This anger does not affect their behavior directly—they do not assault the insulter. Instead, they express their hostility empathically through the actions of the play's hero. According to Aristotle, this arousal and expression of emotion results in a purging, or catharsis, of the emotion, by which he meant that the viewers are less likely to experience this emotion in the future. If we watch a play depicting an endless string of invective and argument between people, like Albee's *Who's Afraid of Virginia Woolf*, we come out drained of any angry impulses ourselves.

This hypothesis is of great potential social importance. Many social critics have complained in recent years that violence on television or in the movies increases aggression among those who watch it. Many social psychologists feel the same way. Bandura's imitation theory, for example, suggests that media violence would lead the viewers to engage in imitative aggression. Berkowitz's conditioning theory suggests media violence presents cues that trigger habitual aggressive responses among viewers. Yet the catharsis theory makes exactly the opposite prediction; it predicts that watching aggression or violence done by others will actually reduce anger among those who are feeling angry. Which is correct?

The strongest early proponent of the catharsis theory in situations involving observed aggression was Seymour Feshbach. He did a pioneering experiment (1961) in which angered and nonangered subjects were shown either a violent boxing film or a neutral film. Measures of aggression taken after the film showed that watching the boxing film lowered the aggressiveness of angered subjects and slightly increased the aggressiveness of the subjects who were not initially angry. This study appeared to support the catharsis prediction. Observing others involved in aggression, like engaging in fantasy aggression yourself, can be a way of working through your own angry feelings, reducing your anger, and consequently reducing aggressive behavior. But this one demonstration of the anger-reducing capacity of witnessed aggression stands as an exception in the large body of laboratory studies done on aggression. Practically all the other laboratory studies have shown that watching others' violence actually increases subsequent aggressive behavior. These studies have typically followed one of two patterns.

Bobo Dolls

The imitation experiments done by Bandura using a Bobo doll represents one type. The point of these experiments was to demonstrate that young children can learn aggressive behavior by imitating the aggressive behavior of adults. Preschool-age children were mildly frustrated, and then they observed an adult batting a Bobo doll around. When the children themselves were placed in the room with the doll, they repeated many of the aggressive behaviors performed by the adult. The key theoretical notion in these experiments is that children learn specific aggressive responses by observing others perform them. It therefore follows that such vicarious learning should be increased when the adult's behavior is reinforced, and when the situation promotes identification with the adult model. So in these Bandura experiments, there was more imitative aggression (1) when the model was rewarded, (2) with a model of the same sex as the child, and (3) when the child had had a previous nurturant relationship with the model (e.g., when the model was a friend or teacher of the child) than when there had been no relationship between the two.

Movie Excerpts

The other important type of laboratory experiment was originated by Leonard Berkowitz and his students. These studies typically involved showing a brief film embodying violent physical aggression to college students who had either been angered (typically by insult) or not angered. The dependent variable was usually shock supposedly administered to a confederate, in a sham-learning situation. Most of these studies used a seven-minute clip from a boxing film starring Kirk Douglas called *The Champion*. Viewing the violent film generally produced more attacks on a confederate whether or not the subject himself had previously been attacked (e.g., Geen & O'Neal, 1969). In another study, subjects who were shown verbal aggression, in the form of a short film involving the insulting comedian, Don Rickles, subsequently showed greater overt aggressiveness themselves (Berkowitz, 1970).

Berkowitz's conditioning theory would predict increased aggressive behavior by viewers whenever the film presents aggression-linked cues. The more similar these cues to those present in the subject's immediate environment, the more likely would be an aggressive response. Hence inducing greater identification with the film aggressors also promoted greater behavioral aggression, as in the Bobo doll studies of preschoolers. For example, when subjects were told to identify with the winner of the boxing match, they displayed more aggression than did subjects who were told to identify with the judge or were not given any instructions about how to watch. Similarly, in another study the confederate was described either as a boxer or as a speech major. After watching a seven-minute clip from *The Champion*, subjects shocked the "boxer" confederate more than the "speech major" (Berkowitz, 1965). A confederate named "Kirk" got more shocks than one named "Bob" after seeing Kirk Douglas play the boxer who got beaten up in the film (Berkowitz & Geen, 1966). When the film presented justified aggression, by presenting the loser of the boxing match in an unfavorable light, more aggression was displayed (see Berkowitz & Rawlings, 1963; Berkowitz & Geen, 1967). In all these cases the model in the film presented cues that elicited aggressive behavior against the confederate. The more similar the subject to the filmed aggressor, or the confederate to the film victim, or the more justified the film violence, the more behavioral aggression shown by the subject.

The vast majority of these laboratory experiments have shown that observing aggression provokes greater aggressive behavior, not less. The catharsis effect simply does not occur in these experiments, except in rare instances. Whether one describes the effect as imitating, stimulating, activating, or triggering aggression, the result is the same: observing aggression in these laboratory experiments produces heightened aggressive behavior.

MEDIA VIOLENCE

It is an understatement to say that in recent years movies have begun to portray a great deal of violence. Fighting, beating, killing, and murder have always been common in Westerns and gangster movies. But movies in the 1970s escalated the amount of carnage as well as its vividness. People did not just die at a distance or clutch their stomachs and fall slowly to the ground. In these movies they actually bled and suffered; the bullet wounds gaped; blood pumped rhythmically from victims' bodies, rather than slowly staining their clothes. Television has also used quite a bit of violence in its programming. With the exception of talk, variety, doctor, and comedy shows, virtually all original programming for prime time television, as well as shows designed specifically for children, involve

© 1960 Punch; Rothco.

violence in one form or another. Westerns, police, gangsters, and spy shows, and most television movies include a full complement of fighting, shooting, and killing. Saturday morning cartoons feature more of the same. Although the violence on television is much less explicit and vivid than that in the movies, it is remarkably pervasive. All of which leads to the question of how this constant exposure to violence affects behavior.

Politics

The politics of media violence have become very important. As a result of congressional action, an enormous amount of money was made available for research on media violence in the late 1960s. A report was finally prepared for the Surgeon General of the United States Public Health Service, which had administered the research grants. This report concluded, rather cautiously, that:

> [There is] a preliminary and tentative indication of a causal relation be-
> tween viewing violence on television and aggressive behavior; an indica-
> tion that any such causal relation operates only on some children (who are
> predisposed to be aggressive); and an indication that it operates only in some
> environmental contexts (Surgeon General's Scientific Advisory Committee
> on Television and Social Behavior, 1972, p. 11).

This report immediately came under harsh attack, partly because some of the members of the committee that prepared it had been representatives of the television networks, and it was felt (quite understandably, not necessarily accurately) that they therefore could not be disinterested scientific observers (Cater & Strickland, 1975). Thereafter other reports were prepared, with widely varying conclusions (contrast especially Comstock, 1975, with Kaplan & Singer, 1976). But most of the criticism held that the commission had underestimated the effects of media violence.

This disagreement is understandable since much of the evidence is contradictory. As we have discussed in some detail, the evidence from laboratory experiments and some of the theoretical explanations suggest that viewing violence would, if anything, make the individual more violent herself. The child who watches someone get beaten up may learn that this kind of aggression is acceptable and even desirable in society (particularly if it is the hero who wins the fight). This could increase the child's tendency to behave aggressively in the future. On the other hand, viewing violence might possibly decrease aggressiveness if it allowed her to express aggressive feelings vicariously and thus produce a cathartic effect. But all the laboratory evidence suggests that only by behaving aggressively himself or by watching the source of his anger punished will the individual's aggressive feelings be reduced. Since this ordinarily does not happen on television, whatever aggressive feelings the child has should not be reduced and thus her aggressiveness should not decline. Just on the basis of laboratory experiments alone, then, we should expect media violence to increase aggressive behavior.

External Validity

Nevertheless, it is quite a long step from the typical laboratory study to the real-life situations to which we might want to generalize. These laboratory experiments must be judged, therefore, in terms of their **external validity** (Campbell and Stanley, 1963). *External validity* asks the question of *generalizability*. Do these laboratory findings hold up in other situations, with other populations, other measures, and other ways of manipulating the same variables? And, most important, do they hold up in the real-life situations that we are most concerned about?

One way to approach the question of external validity is to make explicit the situation to which we most want to generalize, and then see how closely it matches the experimental situations we have been studying. The concern about media violence has been expressed most about television, since it is piped free into the home and exposure is virtually uncontrolled (and nearly uncontrollable). Mostly the concern is that male adolescents (who are most responsible for violent crimes) will watch a great deal of violent television, then go out and commit violent crimes.

But laboratory studies of observed violence differ in some very important ways from this real-life situation. Consider the independent variables. The films presented to subjects are normally very brief, unlike television programs and viewing. And they are almost entirely composed of a single violent episode, like a few rounds from a boxing match, or an adult beating up a Bobo doll. In contrast, the normal child in real life spends up to four hours a night watching television and sees a number of different programs. And each program contains quite a mixture of romantic stories, humor, altruistic behavior, heroism, ordinary conversation, and all sorts of other human acts having nothing to do with violence. Even violent cops-and-robbers programs have humor, romantic entanglements, loyalty between cops, scenery, and other nonviolent matters. So instead of the brief, concentrated dose of exposure to violent models typical of experiments, television in real life presents children with a varied diet of all manner of possible behaviors to copy. Put another way, the experiments present the subject with a pure aggressive diet; normal television presents a much broader range of human behavior.

But the difference between real life and laboratory experiments is most evident in the dependent variable: aggressive behavior by the viewer. Most important, in all experiments the subject engages in aggression that is fully sanctioned, and often even prosocial. Never does an experiment measure aggression the subjects knows is wrong, or will be disapproved, or for which he will be punished or suffer any negative consequences at all. Children know it is perfectly all right to hit the Bobo doll; nobody will disapprove of them or think they are bad for doing it. Indeed, experiments that show the model being punished for hitting Bobo have produced markedly reduced imitative aggression. Most of the other experiments using somewhat older subjects have used a variant of the Buss shock-learning machine. The subject is told she is in a learning experiment and she is supposed to punish the victim for his errors. This is not socially disapproved, unsanctioned, or antisocial aggression; it is prosocial aggression. The subject has been instructed to shock the confederate to help increase scientific knowledge.

The concern about aggression in real life, in contrast, focuses exclusively on unsanctioned, antisocial aggression. We are worried about unprovoked assaults, armed robbery, assault and battery, rape, and murder. The concern is not about the media causing too much sanctioned or prosocial aggression. The concern about media violence has solely to do with antisocial, unsanctioned aggression—and that is never measured in laboratory experiments.

Laboratory measures of aggression differ from real-life violence in several other ways. There is normally no possibility of retaliation; indeed, where there is, aggression is reduced. Often the aggressive task is fun, novel, and a game; one writer has described Bobo-beating as "solitary aggressive play." A five-year-old playing with what is obviously a new toy is obviously a far cry from a gang of teenagers holding up a gas station and shooting the manager. Finally, in these experiments the aggression measure is taken immediately after exposure to the film. The reason is that any delay would obviously reduce the effect of the film. In fact, it is hard to imagine a seven-minute film clip having an effect that would last more than a couple of hours. Several studies have shown that the effects wear off very quickly, perhaps within a matter of minutes. But in real life, the boy does not rush out of his living room with a knife and attack the first person he sees. Most crime is committed quite a long time after the person has watched television. People who are roaming the streets are not home watching television; in fact, we might all be safer if they were.

So the external validity of these experiments seems rather poor. But

"I've had enough of it! Nothing but sex and violence!"

more important, they differ from real life in ways we know increase aggression. They are brief, almost purely aggressive in tone, the subject's aggressive behavior is measured immediately, and his aggression is completely "safe:" there is no chance of retaliation. And it is completely sanctioned (indeed, often encouraged or demanded). Since all these things have themselves been shown to increase aggression, they are likely to present an exaggerated portrait of the aggression inspired by violent films.

Field Experiments

One solution to these problems is to do experiments that come closer to matching the real-life conditions to which we want to generalize. To do this, we would want to maintain the experimental variation of exposure to violent, as opposed to neutral or nonviolent, films. But we would want to do it in the context of something more closely resembling the normal media diet of adolescents, and then observe their aggressive behavior in ordinary, day-to-day situations. Such studies are called **field experiments,** because they are done in the individual's natural situation, or in "the field." Only a few major field experiments have been done. Because the issue of media violence is so controversial and because both sides appeal to scientific evidence, we think it is a good idea to present some information about all the most important of these studies.

The first major study to investigate this problem in a realistic situation was conducted by Feshbach and Singer (1970). Boys in private board-

FIGURE 7–7 In our society most boys learn to play with guns at some time during their childhood. Whether this is due to violence on television is difficult to decide. Certainly, long before television existed, boys played with guns.

ing or state residential schools were randomly assigned to two groups: One group watched largely aggressive television programs such as "Gun smoke" and "The FBI," while the other group was limited to nonaggressive programs such as the "Ed Sullivan Variety Show" and "Bachelor Father." The boys watched only shows on the designated lists and could watch as much as they wanted as long as they spent at least six hours a week watching television. Various measures of aggressiveness were given before and after the six-week viewing period, and both peers and adult supervisors also rated the boys' aggressiveness.

The results showed that boys in the state schools who watched aggressive programs actually became less aggressive themselves. They engaged in fewer fights and argued less with their peers. The effect was the same but somewhat weaker for the boys in the private schools. This study thus indicates that, at least under some conditions, observing television violence under ordinary conditions might actually decrease aggressive behavior. The explanation offered for this effect follows from the catharsis notion, that the children identified with both the heroes and the villains in the programs, and thus did vicariously express some of their aggressive feelings through the violence on television. On the other hand, it must be noted that the effect could be due to the fact that boys who were limited to the nonaggressive programs might have been annoyed because they were not allowed to watch their favorite television shows. A very similar study by Wells (1973) found that violent vs. nonviolent television diets made very little difference. Despite these complications, these studies do attempt to test how ordinary television affects aggressiveness, and they do suggest that the effect may not be to increase it.

Another study was done in minimum security penal institutions for juvenile offenders both in the United States and Belgium (Parke et al., 1977). After a week of observation, the boys in four living cottages were shown a week of five violent movies (e.g., *Iwo Jima, Bonnie and Clyde*), and in four other cottages were shown five neutral films (e.g., *Lily, Daddy's Fiancée*). Then they were observed for an additional week. Boys in three of the four cottages shown the violent films did increase their aggressive behavior immediately after watching the film, though the effect had disappeared by the following noon. There was no effect in the other cottage shown violent films. There was no cumulative effect over the full viewing period.

Friedrich and Stein (1973) put nursery school children on a diet of twelve violent cartoons (*Batman, Superman*), or prosocial entertainment (*Mister Rogers*) or neutral films (e.g., about nature) for a period of four weeks. They were carefully observed by trained observers. They had three measures of aggression, and five others of good classroom behavior (rule obedience, delay tolerance, task persistence, cooperation, and prosocial behavior). The groups differed significantly on at most two of these eight measures, so the effect of the filmed violence cannot have been very great.

A somewhat different set of studies was done by Milgram and Shotland (1973). They prepared special versions of a prime-time television show—"Medical Center"—that included illegal (but nonviolent) acts. Three different versions of the episode were prepared. For example, in one, the protagonist smashes several charity-drive collection boxes, steals the money, and escapes to Mexico. Subjects viewed the program in a theater, and then were offered a free radio if they would show up at a downtown office a week later. At the office, though, there was a sign saying there were no more radios, and there was a charity donation box containing some money, including a $1 bill sticking partway out. Concealed TV cameras coded whether or not the subject took the dollar. But viewers of different versions did not differ. Seven experiments were done in this general style, and none of them showed any difference.

Each of these studies has its flaws. As was pointed out before, in the Feshbach-Singer and the Wells studies, the adolescent boys in the nonviolent conditions were deprived of their normal favorite programs. This frustration could by itself have increased their aggressiveness, thus eliminating any possible differences between the violent and nonviolent conditions. The Parke and associates study used a group-viewing situation in dormitories where boys in prison had been living together for some time. This was perhaps a little like watching movies in a fraternity (except with juvenile delinquents instead of college boys), and it evidently stimulated a good bit of rowdiness during and right after the movies, but this rowdy-group context is not the usual one for TV viewing in the home. The Milgram-Shotland studies were at the mercy of the idiosyncrasies of their specific versions of "Medical Center," and in most cases so little stealing emerged that it would have been hard for anything at all to influence it much one way or the other.

But all studies in social science are flawed. It is a myth that a perfect study can be devised. The minute we patch up one problem, another emerges (often created by the patch, in fact). The way to come to a conclusion about an important area of research is to look at the pattern of the data. The effects of these violent vs. nonviolent TV field experiments are not very dramatic. Feshbach and Singer get diminished aggression from the violent diet, but only in one set of schools. The studies by Wells, Friedrich and Stein, and Milgram and Shotland show no strong results. Parke and colleagues find increased aggression in three of four cottages, but it does not last and may be an effect more of group contagion than individual arousal. Milgram and Shotland get no differences in seven experiments. So it is difficult to see a very powerful effect of movie or TV violence on aggressive behavior leaping out at us from these field studies. Rather, observed violence in movies or television seems not to affect aggressive behavior much in real-life situations, one way or the other.

Other Possible Effects

The potential role of media violence is not limited to imitative aggression, however. A number of other questions can readily be raised. Why is there so much violence in movies and television? Is it because of some compelling interest that viewers have in violent content? Furthermore, watching violence may have effects other than allegedly stimulating violent behavior. We may become so accustomed to the sight of violence that it no longer offends us or shocks us. On the other hand, being confronted at close range with the vicious things that people do to each other may make us more resolved than ever to turn this into a peaceful world. It was argued that the comprehensive television coverage of the Vietnam War (the "first televised war") hastened public condemnation of the war and ultimately helped remove our armed forces from it. Some observers fear that the growing popularity and distribution of erotic literature, pictorial magazines, and movies over the past two decades provides yet another stimulant to violence, especially against women. In all these cases, research is so preliminary as only to be suggestive. But it is perhaps worth seeing what can be said at the moment about these other possibilities.

PUBLIC INTEREST IN VIOLENCE Is violence especially interesting and exciting to people? Apparently not for its own sake. Diener and

DeForb (1978) did content-analysis ratings of television programs for violence, drama, humor, and action. Then they compared these qualities with the relative popularity of various programs. They found humor and action were crucial determinants of popularity, but violence was not. Angry, aggressive people may prefer more violence in their films, however. Fenigstein (1979) induced subjects to have aggressive fantasies or to behave aggressively using the Buss teacher-learner procedure, and found they were more likely to want to watch film clips that featured violence, such as rioting at a rock concert, fist fights, and so on.

DESENSITIZATION TO VIOLENCE Media violence is also thought by some observers to desensitize viewers to any later real-life violence. The argument is that when you watch people being killed and maimed and beaten up on television, you become accustomed to the sight of violence, and it therefore no longer upsets you as much. Ultimately, it is argued, you yourself will be more willing to hurt other people, or at least you will be less likely to step in to prevent violence in real life.

The argument implies a two-stage sequence. It first suggests that the constant sight of media violence reduces our emotional response to it later in the real world. Then, second, this lower emotional responsivity should reduce our tendency to stop aggression in real life. There is a little evidence of at least short-term reductions in emotional arousal. Physiological arousal during violent films was reduced by exposure to a prior eleven-minute excerpt from a television police series (Thomas et al., 1977), or among children who are especially heavy television viewers (Cline, Croft, and Courrier, 1973). But is not yet clear that such exposure reduces the tendency to help stop aggression.

SPORTS EVENTS Some people argue that sports events help spectators relieve their everyday frustrations by allowing them to yell, cheer, boo, and root for their favorite teams. Sports events, they say, are cathartic because they allow people to reduce their tensions in a vicarious, playful manner that hurts no one. Others argue that the moblike atmosphere of sports events reduces people's inhibitions to aggression or leads them to imitate aggressive behavior (particularly in violent sports like hockey, boxing, and football). Sometimes terrible violence occurs after sports events. In Guatemala in 1977, for example, soccer fans of the losing team attacked the fans of the winning team with machetes and hacked five persons to death (Arms, Russell, & Sandilands, 1979).

To test whether sports events increase aggression in spectators, Goldstein and Arms (1971) and Arms and associates (1979) gave spectators paper-and-pencil tests of hostility before and after a football game, a hockey match, a professional wrestling match (all having a high degree of physical aggression), and a gymnastics meet and a swimming meet (neither of which present much aggression). On some tests, the watching violent sports seemed to increase irritability and hostility more than did watching the nonviolent ones. However, the effects were not very marked, and other explanations remain to be studied.

EROTICA   Another area of experimental research has concerned the effects of sexual arousal on aggressive behavior. The interest in this question derives partly from a concern that sexual content in films, books, and magazines makes men more violent toward women. But as a theoretical question it bears on the same underlying processes as do the effects of witnessed aggression: the stimulation of violent behavior by media content.

Freud originally felt sexual and aggressive impulses were closely allied, especially in men: "The sexuality of most men shows an admixture of aggression, of a desire to subdue. . . ." Presumably vicarious experiencing of sexual pleasure would serve as some catharsis of instinctual energy in general, and reduce the tendency to aggress. On the other hand, more recent theorizing follows Schachter's notion that such drives yield nonspecific arousal, which then is experienced more discretely and directed toward specific goals through cognitive labelling (Schachter & Singer, 1962, as discussed in Chapter 5 above). By this argument, an angry person who also becomes sexually aroused may thereby express even more aggression, if the situation fails to label the two sources of arousal quite distinctively.

These experiments have generally used some variant of the Buss sham learning procedure. A confederate makes the subject angry (or does not), the subject is exposed to some erotic pictures, literature, or films, and then is placed in the teacher-learner relationship with instructions to shock the original confederate.

What has generally been found? Exposure to erotica turns out to increase violent behavior, at least under one set of limited conditions: when subjects are (1) angry to start with, from insult or provocation, (2) the erotic materials are extremely explicit, realistic, "hardcore" pornography, (3) the predominant affect experienced by the subject is negative (e.g., disgust or distaste), and (4) the measure of behavioral aggression is taken immediately after the sexual arousal. For example, Donnerstein (and Barrett, 1978; Donnerstein and Hallam, 1978) had his confederates shock male subjects, then he showed them some hard-core black-and-white stag films depicting oral and anal intercourse and female homosexuality. Such subjects shocked the offending confederate more than did non-angered subjects, or subjects shown either no film or a neutral wildlife documentary. Similar findings were reported by Jaffe et al (1974), who used highly explicit literary passages (though their subjects were not first angered).

But the limitations on this increase in aggressive behavior are even more marked. First of all, all the experiments have been done with very short time delays between exposure to erotica and measurement of aggressive behavior. Usually the delay is no more than a few minutes. If the effects of sexual media are limited to that span, they surely do not constitute a major social problem. And second, there have so far been demonstrated marked sex differences neither in the subject's own response to erotica (though male subjects are, as always, more aggressive irrespective of circumstance) nor in the target: male and female targets receive about the same treatment (Donnerstein and Hallam, 1978; Jaffe et al., 1974).

Most important, though, almost any form of erotica less explicit than "hard-core" or "blue movies" seems not to increase aggression, and indeed often actually *reduces* aggression below normal levels (that is, below the levels of no-film or neutral-film control groups). For example, viewing still colored pictures of nude women or of sexual intercourse tended to reduce aggression below normal levels (Baron & Bell, 1977; Donnerstein et al., 1975). In at least one case, this reduction was greatest for previously angered subjects (Zillman & Sapolsky, 1977). There is some debate about why these forms of erotica have such different effects. One possibility is that the "hard-core" material may itself be rather frustrating, because it is too arousing for the etiquette of the psychological experiment situation. Or, the more common, milder "soft core" material may be distracting from the original anger-arousing provocation by the confederate.

Most likely, though, the more "hard core" material is inherently not very pleasant to most subjects. Indeed White (1979) has shown that college students find pictures of same-sex masturbation or mutual oral-genital contact much less pleasant than more common forms of pictorial erotica, such as conventional intercourse and love-making. And he argues, rather persuasively, that erotica decreases aggression when it produces positive feelings, though it may increase aggression somewhat when it produces negative effect. So presumably any erotic materials that depict sex in an ugly, disgusting way would be more likely to inspire aggression than would materials that are more artistic, and/or present acts that the subjects themselves feel comfortable looking at. Indeed he argues that any such pleasurable experience, whether or not it concerns sex, would have the same aggression-suppressing effect.

Of course, exactly what media content would give viewers a pleasant as opposed to a disgusted reaction will vary a lot depending on the person's own taste and background. For example, *Playboy* began showing female pubic hair and genital regions for the first time in the 1970's, sensing social norms had changed to make that acceptable and pleasurable to the bulk of its readership. But it later backed off from some tentative efforts to show acts of sexual intercourse. And in some cultures women are not even supposed to show their uncovered faces in public. So the exact content that yields pleasurable or negative feelings varies a good bit with social norms. The main point here is that aggressive reactions to erotica are the exception rather than the rule.

Conclusion

Laboratory studies seem quite generally to show that observed violence increases aggressive behavior. But these studies have been conducted in such a way that they may not be especially applicable to the real-life instances of antisocial violence that we are concerned with as private citizens. The film clips are not particularly representative of what is shown on television and in the movie houses today. The subjects tend to be preschool children and college students, rather than potentially criminal adolescents. The dependent variable is quite "safe," strongly approved aggression, indeed often playful aggression, instead of genuine harm to others. And the impact is measured immediately after exposure, rather than some hours or days later, as is presumably the case in real life. For all these reasons, we do not have much confidence in generalizing from these laboratory studies to crime in the streets.

The field experiments we have described come much closer to realistic replicas of real life. They have presented the typical movie and television fare of the day to male adolescents living in their normal life situations (though most of these have been in boarding schools, rather than living at home with their parents). They have measured genuine interpersonal aggression in a free, unconstrained atmosphere. However, these studies have generally shown that media violence has little or no systematic effect upon interpersonal aggression. Some show a modest, temporary increase in aggression. Others show a debatable decrease in it. But on balance there is no major impact one way or the other. Therefore, it seems correct to say that at the moment the field studies show media violence having little impact.

From a policy point of view, the question is whether the evidence is strong enough to urge the suppression of certain kinds of entertainment programs in order to reduce crime and violence. There are social conditions which we all know are terribly important in producing violence, such as unemployment, racial prejudice, poor housing, poor medical care (especially for people with mental health problems), the widespread availability of guns and alcohol, a highly mobile population that does not settle into tight little self-policing communities, and indifference to the welfare of children, among many other things. It seems to us that, at most, television and the movies could contribute only a small amount above and beyond such large social factors.

And we must be very careful about censorship of any kind. Today the government might decide that it is illegal to depict a knifing on television; tomorrow some censor may decide that it is illegal to depict an adulterous act, because people might imitate that; and the next day he may decide that it is illegal to depict protest demonstrations. Once the principle of censorship is accepted, it becomes harder and harder to draw the line. So it is no idle academic matter, this business of the effects of media violence upon interpersonal aggressiveness. We should recognize that no matter how passionately we feel about the issue, we must not take a stand until we have sufficient evidence. It is fair to say that most psychologists today believe that TV violence does generally increase aggressiveness. In our opinion the actual empirical evidence is weak and has not shown any role of media violence in increasing crime. Hence there is little evidence that will justify the imposition of restrictions upon entertainment programs.

SUMMARY

1. Aggression is defined as an action that hurts another person, and that is perceived as intended to do so.

2. Aggressive acts can be antisocial, prosocial, or merely sanctioned, depending on whether they violate or conform with social norms.

3. Aggressive feelings, or anger, need to be distinguished from aggressive behavior.

4. Instinctual bases for either aggressive feelings or behavior in humans, while sometimes asserted by ethologists and psychoanalysts, are not widely accepted by social psychologists.

5. The major determinants of aggressive feelings seem to be annoyance and attack, and frustration. Frustrations that are not attributed to intent on the part of the frustrator do not create as much anger. Generalized, nonspecific arousal states can result in experienced anger if they are accompanied with the appropriate cognitive labels.

6. Aggressive behavior has as its major determinant (other than angry feelings) the learning of aggressive responses. This learning can take place through direct reinforcement of aggressive responses, or through imitation, or the conditioning of aggressive behavior to certain eliciting cues.

7. Direct aggression against an attacker or frustrator can reduce aggressive feelings through the process of catharsis. However this too depends on perceiving the tormentor as the responsible agent.

8. Fear of punishment or retaliation can reduce aggressive behavior. However it may sometimes result instead in covert aggression, or actually increase aggression over the longer run.

9. Learned inhibitions of aggression are the most important control over it. Anxiety can be associated with the expression of aggression in general, or with its expression in quite specific contexts. Most people reduce their aggression when they see signs of pain in others. Such inhibitions can also result in the displacement of aggression to other innocent parties, and to the scapegoating of members of minority groups.

10. Observed aggression generally increases aggression in laboratory studies, whether they are done with small children, adolescents, or adults. It is especially potent in increasing aggression when the model is rewarded or when the observed victim is similar to the target of the subject's own aggression.

11. Field experiments of televised or movie violence, on the other hand, have not generally shown that it increases aggressive behavior in real-life settings. Therefore the laboratory studies of observed aggression should not be generalized to real-life situations. There is no good evidence yet that media violence contributes to violence and crime in our society.

SUGGESTIONS FOR ADDITIONAL READING

BANDURA A. *Aggression: A social learning analysis.* Englewood Cliffs, N.J.: Prentice-Hall, 1973. The definitive statement by the most influential spokesman for the social learning and imitation approach to aggression.

BARON, R. A. *Human aggression.* New York: Plenum Press, 1977. A thorough, readable, comprehensive treatment of aggression from a social-psychological perspective.

COMSTOCK, G., CHAFFEE, S., DATZMAN, N., McCOMBS, M., & ROBERTS, D. *Television and human behavior.* New York: Columbia University Press, 1978. A conscientious review of research on the effects of television, concerning aggression, politics, advertising, and other areas.

DOLLARD, J., DOOB, L., MILLER, N. E., MOWRER, O. H., & SEARS, R. R. *Frustration and aggression.* New Haven: Yale University Press, 1939. The original statement of the theory that frustration breeds aggression. As well as discussing their laboratory experiments, it ranges far into the larger social manifestations of aggression, such as criminality, war, and fascism.

FREUD, S. *Civilization and its discontents.* London: Hogarth Press, 1955 (first published, 1930). The classic exposition of how civilization must deal with aggressive instincts. One of Freud's most brilliant and influential critiques of society.

KAPLAN, R., & SINGER, R. Violence and viewer aggression: A reexamination of the evidence. *Journal of Social Issues,* 1976, *32,* 35–70. The most recent and most carefully argued review of the media violence research by two social psychologists skeptical of its capacity for inducing aggressive behavior in real life.

LORENZ, K. *On aggression.* Trans. M. K. Wilson. New York: Bantam Books, 1966. The most influential statement on aggression by an ethologist.

SEARS, D. O., & McCONAHAY, J. B. *The politics of violence: The new urban blacks and the Watts riot.* Boston: Houghton-Mifflin, 1973. A social-psychological analysis of the causes of ghetto riots.

SURGEON GENERAL'S SCIENTIFIC ADVISORY COMMITTEE ON TELEVISION AND SOCIAL BEHAVIOR. *Television and growing up. The impact of televised violence* (Report to the Surgeon General, U.S. Public Health Service, U.S. Department of Health, Education, and Welfare, Publication NHSM 72–9090). Rockville, Md.: National Institute of Mental Health, 1972. This was the report that created such furor.

Altruism and Prosocial Behavior

8

United Press International, Inc.

One night some years ago, a young woman named Kitty Genovese was walking along the street in a quiet neighborhood in New York City. Suddenly, a man came out of the shadows and attacked her. She struggled and screamed for help. After a short fight, during which she was badly injured, she managed to escape from her assailant and ran down the street shouting for someone to help or to call the police. Several minutes later, the man caught her and the struggle began again. It continued for half an hour, during which time she continually screamed and shouted, until finally she was killed. Her screams and the sound of the struggle were heard by at least thirty-eight people living in buildings near the scene. Many of these people came to their windows to see what was happening. Yet, not one person came to Kitty Genovese's aid, nor did anyone even call the police.

A recent newspaper article described a similar event with a somewhat different ending. A woman in Toronto was attacked by a man in an alley in broad daylight. As he attempted to rape her, she screamed for help. A great many people heard her cries and even watched the struggle from their windows, but for many crucial minutes no one offered help. Finally, two men driving by in a car heard the screams, stopped the car, and rushed into the alley. They pulled the attacker off the woman and held him for the police.

There are countless stories of this sort. Sometimes people help, sometimes they do not. We hear of individuals who are beaten, raped, and killed while those who could give assistance stand by; we also hear of

284

amazingly brave acts in which people rush into burning buildings to save children, jump into the water to rescue drowning men, and come to the aid of people who are being attacked. Clearly, human beings are capable of helping or ignoring others in distress. Why do people commit these acts of bravery and altruism? And why, sometimes, do they fail to give help when it is needed?

ALTRUISM DEFINED

Before trying to explain this kind of behavior, let us be clear about what we mean by **altruism** and **prosocial behavior** in general. An altruistic act is one performed to help someone else when there is no expectation of receiving a reward in any form (except perhaps a feeling of having done a good deed). That is, if you give to charity because you expect that charity to help you or because you want to impress the person who is asking or for any other concrete reason of this kind, it is not altruism in the pure sense. Your giving is still, obviously, an act that benefits others, but it is not altruism. Prosocial behavior is a broader category that includes any act that helps or is designed to help others. The distinction may not be important to the person who is helped, but the explanations of the two kinds of behaviors are quite different.

ALTRUISM IN OTHER ANIMALS

In *Sociobiology,* a book that has attracted a great deal of attention and stirred controversy, E. O. Wilson (1975) proposed that altruistic behavior in humans is genetically determined. In other words, just as Konrad Lorenz has suggested that aggression is built into the human system, Wilson says that altruistic tendencies are inherited. They are a part of "human nature," play an important role in our survival, and do not have to be learned. This, like Lorenz's argument, is almost impossible to test and actually has few implications for social psychology. If we accept this view, we would have to think of humans as more controlled by instinctive forces than we usually do, but at least some of those instincts would be positive rather than negative. This would fit in with the ideas of humanistic psychologists such as Carl Rogers and Fritz Perls, who have a highly positive, optimistic view of human nature. In any case, Wilson's suggestion is a valuable addition to the general explanation of human behavior in terms of instinct, since there is no reason to believe that only negative impulses such as aggression can be inherited. For our purposes, the important aspect of Wilson's work is that he points out many instances of animal behavior that could be thought of as altruistic. Remember that any act that benefits another with no expectation of

BOX 8-1

SOCIOBIOLOGY AND ALTRUISM

The argument in support of Wilson's idea that altruism is genetically determined is based on the standard notion of genetic selection. Any genetically determined trait that has high survival value (i.e., that helps the individual survive) will tend to be passed on. This happens because the individual with the trait is more likely to survive than one without the trait and produce more offspring, each of whom will tend to have the trait and will in turn be more likely to survive and reproduce, and so on. Eventually, individuals with genes that carry this trait will grow more numerous than those without those genes, and will come to dominate the species. Giraffes with genes that give them longer necks are better able to reach scarce food; they produce more young giraffes than those who have shorter necks; and after many generations we have giraffes with very long necks. However, necks that are too long are awkward and overly long-necked animals tend to die out. The species thus comes to be dominated by animals whose necks are just long enough for them to reach the food. Of course, this process takes many generations; and sometimes the environment changes in the meantime and a trait that was useful at one time becomes less useful later. But the principle that useful characteristics dominate less useful ones generally holds.

This principle is fairly easy to understand when it involves individual survival. Obviously, if an animal lives longer and is healthier, it will produce more healthy young and its genes will be carried on. Wilson's point is that the same principle can apply even when the particular individual's survival is threatened by genetically determined behavior. In the case of altruism, the tendency to help others has high survival value for the individual's genes but not necessarily for the individual. For example, imagine a bird that has fathered six chicks. Each of the chicks has exactly half of the father's genes. All together they have three times as many of the father's genes as he does himself. If the father sacrifices himself to save the chicks, his particular gene pool is still ahead of the game even though his individual genes die with him. Similar analyses can be done for other relatives who have varying percentages of the individual's genes. Clearly, the closer the relationship, the more justification for an altruistic act; but under some circumstances, there may be a biological justification for sacrificing oneself even for quite distant relatives. As Wilson points out, hive animals, in which all individuals share a high percentage of the same gene pool, should be more altruistic; and indeed, much of his evidence on animal altruism comes from bees, termites, and other hive insects.

Even though the biological justification for altruism is that it maintains one's gene pool, the actual behavior may include altruism that does not do this. An individual may have a genetically determined tendency to behave altruistically, and this genetic trait is due to the fact that over many generations such behavior maximizes the gene pool. But the individual may simply have a general tendency to be altruistic, without regard to the gene pool. Thus, on any given occasion, he may sacrifice himself to save someone who is not related at all and therefore shares none of his genes. In other words, even if altruism is genetically determined because of its biological value, it may still extend to situations in which it has no biological value but only value to society or to the other individual who is helped.

return is considered altruistic in the strict definition of the term. With that in mind, here are some of Wilson's examples.

In termite hives, the soldier termites will defend a nest against an intruder by putting themselves in front of the other termites and thus exposing themselves to danger (Wilson, 1971). Many soldiers die so that others may live and the nest survive.

When fire ants are attacked, those who have been injured are more likely to leave the nest than the uninjured, and the injured are also more aggressive in fighting the intruder. The injured ants are thus risking their own lives, and because an injured ant is less useful to the nest than an uninjured one, their behavior seems to be a form of self-sacrifice.

Among honeybees, workers will attack intruders by stinging them. When this occurs, the stinger stays in the intruder, thus killing the worker (Sakagami & Akahira, 1960). Once again, the worker bee dies and in so doing increases the hive's chance of survival.

Chacuma and other varieties of baboon have a characteristic pattern of responding to threats (Hall, 1960). The dominant males take the most exposed outside positions and may rush at an intruder. In addition, as the tribe of baboons moves away from the threat, the males will remain behind for a while to protect the rest of the group.

Among many animals, parents will sacrifice themselves when their young are threatened. This is most evident among birds, which have a variety of techniques designed to draw off or distract the threat. An impressive example is the female nighthawk, who flies from the nest as if she has a broken wing, flutters around at a low level, and finally lands on the ground right in front of the intruder but away from the nest (Armstrong, 1947; Gramza, 1967). Once again, an individual animal risks its own life to help another.

Animals of all kinds often risk their own lives for the benefit of others. Whether this is altruistic behavior in the same sense as a fireman rushing into a burning building is unclear. Perhaps an important factor is whether we believe the animal "knows" that it is risking its life or is simply acting automatically. A human being knows his life is in danger; a nighthawk probably does not. Yet, both are in fact performing an act that helps another with little or no possibility of reward to themselves.

FIGURE 8–2 Animals other than humans also help each other. Here one monkey is grooming the other, perhaps because it expects to be groomed in return.

These examples help put human altruistic behavior in perspective. We see that self-preservation is not the overwhelming motive we sometimes think it is. On the contrary, it seems natural for other animals and therefore at least as natural for humans to protect each other from harm and even to take risks doing so. Thus, in explaining altruistic behavior, we should not feel that it is a mystery but rather a reasonable behavior in the context of what we know of biology. The job of the social psychologist is to explain why altruism occurs at some times but not at others and to discover the critical factors that control this important behavior.

ALTRUISM AND BYSTANDER INTERVENTION

Much of the work on altruism has focused on the conditions under which people spontaneously help others. Interest in this question was stimulated by the kinds of incidents described at the beginning of the chapter, in which people who desperately needed help were not assisted by those who could easily have come to their aid. Latané and Darley (1970), who have done much of the work on this problem, refer to it as **bystander intervention.**

The Effect of Other People

One of the striking findings is that the presence of other people seems to reduce the likelihood of intervention. In one experiment (Latané & Darley, 1968), subjects were put in a room either alone or with other subjects. Smoke began to pour into the room through a small vent in the wall. Subjects who were alone in the room were very likely to report the smoke soon after noticing it. Of the subjects in this condition, 75 percent reported the smoke within six minutes of the time they first noticed it, and 50 percent reported the smoke within two minutes. In contrast, when more than one person was in the room, there was a strong tendency not to report the smoke at all. The number of people reporting the smoke ranged from 38 percent to as low as 10 percent.

In another experiment (Latané & Rodin, 1969), subjects also waited either alone or with others, and were given the opportunity to help a lady in distress. When the subjects arrived, they met a young woman who gave them a questionnaire to fill out and said that she would be working for a while in the adjoining room. She went into the room, shuffled papers, opened drawers, and made other noises for a few minutes; then she went into a carefully rehearsed act designed to make it appear that she had fallen off a chair and hurt herself. The subjects heard a chair fall loudly, the woman scream and then yell "Oh, my God, my foot . . . I . . . I . . . can't move . . . it. Oh . . . my ankle. I . . . can't get this . . . thing . . . off me." Of

"Hang in there, old man. There's bound to be a Good Samaritan along any time now."

the subjects who were waiting alone, 70 percent offered to help the victim in some way. When two strangers were present, only 40 percent of the groups went to the aid of the victim. When a confederate was present and deliberately did not help, only 7 percent of the subjects intervened. Once again, the presence of other people generally inhibited the tendency to intervene in this emergency.

Subsequent research has tried to pin down the specific reason for this effect. One plausible explanation is that when others are present, the subject feels that they will help and therefore he doesn't have to. Several studies (Schwartz & Clausen, 1970; Bickman, 1971; Ross, 1971) lend support to this notion. In Bickman's study, the subjects were in three different conditions—by themselves, with others who were also taking part in the study, or with others who were in the study but in another building. Subjects who were with others helped less than those who were alone, but if the others were in a separate building, it was just as if they were alone. In other words, if the other people were essentially irrelevant because they could not help, their presence did not matter. Ross varied whether subjects were alone, with two other adults, or with two children. As would be expected, the presence of children had much less effect than the presence of other adults, presumably because the children were less able to give help. The general idea is that each individual feels less responsible when other, presumably capable people are present.

The same argument suggests that we can increase the amount of help by making the individual feel especially responsible. In a study by Moriarty (1975), some subjects were asked to watch a suitcase or radio while someone was away; other subjects were not asked. When a confederate then came by and attempted to take the item, subjects who were asked to watch it were much more likely than the others to stop the theft (over 90 percent to only 20 percent intervened). In both conditions, many other people were present, but this had little effect on those who felt personally responsible. All this research indicates that the amount of help given depends on whether someone else who could also give help is present. If there is another person, each individual seems to feel less responsible and to have a tendency to wait for the other to give the assistance needed rather than offering it himself.

Individual Interpretation

Perhaps an even more important factor in these situations is how the individual interprets what is going on. It seems likely that our interpretation of the situation depends in large part on how other people are reacting. If someone yells "Fire!" in a theater and you see some people running for the exits, you assume that there must be a fire and you try to get out as quickly as you can. But if everyone remains seated, you will probably assume that the cry was a joke or a false alarm and you too will stay where you are. In other words, as we have discussed in terms of attribution theory, how we interpret the situation affects our behavior, and our interpretation is based in part on the behavior of others.

The same process operates in a bystander intervention situation. Suppose we hear someone crying for help from an adjoining room or outside the window. Although in retrospect it may seem obvious that the person really did need help, at the time it may not be so easy to decide. Perhaps it is a joke, perhaps a psychology experiment, perhaps the person is only slightly injured and is exaggerating, and perhaps there is no crisis at all. Even in the Kitty Genovese case, her need for help was probably not so clear to the people who heard her cries. It is quite common under these circumstances, especially when you cannot see exactly what is happening, to assume that it is a lovers' quarrel and that you should not intrude (Shotland & Straw, 1976). Perhaps that is unfortunate, but it means that the lack of help is often due to a misinterpretation of the situation, not to an unwillingness to help. When other people are present and sitting calmly, minding their own business, the individual may decide that the situation is less serious than he imagined. When three people in a room ignore cries of distress, perhaps (so the subject may think) no emergency exists. If other people are upset, we get upset; if other people are calm, we remain calm. And in the present context, if other people seem to have decided that a cry for help need not be answered, we have a tendency to draw the same conclusions.

Christy Park; Monkmeyer.

FIGURE 8–3 Sometimes people simply walk past someone who seems in need. However, in this case as in many others, there may be some doubt as to the need. Perhaps the man is drunk and would rather be left alone—a not uncommon occurrence in large cities.

Many studies support this interpretation. When the situation is so unambiguous that the subject must recognize the existence of an emergency, the presence or absence of other individuals has little effect. Piliavin, Rodin, and Piliavin (1969) observed what happened when a man collapsed on a New York subway train. The confederate who posed as the victim either appeared sober and carried a black cane, or pretended to be drunk. In the cane condition the victim received spontaneous help 62 out of 65 trials. The number of people in the subway car and their proximity to him had no effect at all. When someone seems ill and is obviously in distress, people appear to offer help whether or not there are others who could also give assistance. The "drunk" victim received help only 19 of 38 trials (the lower rate is presumably due to less concern for a drunk and some fear of getting involved), but even here the amount of help given was unrelated to the number of people present. A second study by Clark and Word (1974) found that help was given between 91 and 100 percent of the time when the situation was totally unambiguous, and the amount of help was unaffected by the size of the group. Only when ambiguity was introduced, in fact a high degree of ambiguity, did individuals who were alone help more than those in groups.

A study by Smith, Smythe, and Lien (1972) also lends support to the notion that a subject's interpretation of the situation is determined in part by how the other people behave. The authors report the typical finding that there was more helping when the subject was alone than when others were present. In addition, they found that the similarity of the other people to the subject was a critical factor. When the others were dissimilar, there was more helping than when the others were similar. This is what would be expected from an explanation in terms of normative behavior and social comparison theory. The subject's interpretation should be more influenced by people who are similar than by those who are not. When similar others sit and do nothing, it should reduce the subjects' tendency to help even more than when dissimilar others do not help.

The Expected Utility of Helping

One way of viewing a potential helping situation is in terms of how the individual perceives the **expected utility.** That is, how does the person view his possible gains and losses if he helps or does not help? Clearly, sometimes it is relatively easy to provide assistance, while at other times, helping may involve considerable costs in time, energy, and various complications. If someone asks you for directions, it is a trivial matter to stop for a moment and help out if you can. In contrast, if you are driving along a highway and you see someone stuck at the side of the road, it is much more time consuming to stop to help. In addition, in both situations the costs will depend in part on whether you perceive any possible threat to your safety. Does the person asking for directions look respectable, or is there some chance that you will be robbed? Is it a nice day on the highway, or is it raining? And so on. In every instance, the greater the perceived costs, the less likely you are to help.

BOX 8-2
AVOIDING HELPING

A request for aid often arouses mixed feelings in most people. On the one hand, they would like to help because it is a nice thing to do; on the other hand, they realize that costs are involved, costs that they would perhaps rather not assume. Indeed, one study (Paucer et al., 1979) demonstrated that people sometimes actively avoid a situation in which they will be asked for help. A table was set up in a passageway, and in some conditions it

George Malave; Stock; Boston.

Although there are benefits to helping, there are also costs. People often avoid a request for help because of the conflict between the benefits and costs.

held a box for donations to charity, while in others it did not. People tended to walk farther away from the table when donations were requested than when no donations were requested. Similarly, when someone was sitting at the table collecting donations, people avoided it more than when no one was there. And finally, when a handicapped person was sitting at the table, people steered farther away than when the person was not handicapped. In each case, the stronger the request for aid, the more people avoided the situation. Clearly, helping situations create some conflict, and people tend to minimize this conflict by keeping away. Presumably, it is easier not to donate when you are far away than when you are close.

There is also some cost to not giving assistance. You may feel guilty about not helping someone in need. Other people may see that you have not been helpful, and you will feel bad because they may thus have a poor opinion of you. You may have a general moral value that says you should help if you can, and not helping will make you feel that you have not been a good person. All of these considerations determine whether or not you offer help.

On the other hand, there is, of course, a positive side to the expected utility of helping. The greater the good you perceive you will do, the more likely you are to help. The more the person deserves to be helped, and the more help you are able to give, the better you may feel about offering assistance. For example, Gruder, Romer, and Korth (1978) had a female confederate telephone people and request aid. The woman's story was that her car had broken down and she needed to reach a service station. She had gotten a wrong number, and asked the person to call the station for her. In some cases she was in great need, in others less. Also, in some cases her problem was largely her fault because she said that she had forgotten to take the car in for service even though she had known it needed repairs; in others, it was not her fault—the car had broken down with no warning. The results were that people helped more when her need was greater and when she was not at fault, and therefore presumably was more deserving of help.

Several authors (Lynch & Cohen, 1978; Morgan, 1978) have applied a subjective utility model to helping situations and have found generally supportive results. Morgan and Leik (1979) have developed a complex model that includes the expected benefits to the intervener, benefits to the victim, cost of nonintervention and intervention, feelings of responsibility, and whether others can also help. Although as yet little evidence directly supports the total model, it seems likely that all of these considerations do affect the likelihood of helping. And, as Lynch and Cohen suggest, other variables in the situation may operate, at least in part, by changing the individual's perceptions of the expected utility. On the other hand, perceptions of utility do not fully explain helping decisions. The person who runs into a burning building to save a child is unlikely to be considering the expected utility of the action. People are not generally expected to risk their own lives for strangers, and there would be little social or personal censure for not entering the building. It is simply a brave act that is probably motivated primarily by basic emotions and by values having to do with human life, courage, and so on.

SOCIAL JUSTICE AND EQUITY

One of the factors that appears to affect altruism and prosocial behavior in general is a sense of justice and equity. People feel that each person should get what he or she deserves based on that person's effort, skill, and whatever other considerations they think are important. Homans (1961) called this a sense of **social justice** and Adams (1965) called it **equity,** but the two notions are essentially identical. If two people put the same amount of effort into a task, they should in principle receive the same reward. If one receives more than the other, inequity exists. People will generally try to restore equity by redistributing the rewards. In particular, the person who received more than his share may give some to the person who receives too little; or some third person, observing the situation, might be tempted to give to the one who suffered.

Presumably this is one of the motives behind charity, philanthropy, and social welfare programs. People tend to believe that every human being deserves at least some minimum share of the world's resources, and a person who has nothing is often given something to help restore equity. But we also believe that people who make an effort deserve more than those who do not, and this may explain opposition to public welfare programs that give assistance without regard to whether the individual is trying to get a job. In other words, in addition to a general feeling that everyone should be taken care of and given food and shelter, we tend to feel that some are more deserving than others, depending on the amount of effort or contribution they make.

This does not mean that everyone is always fair with everyone else, that greed does not exist in the world, or that people are not pleased when they get more than they deserve. The point is that, to some extent, people do feel pressure toward social justice, and they show some tendency to act to achieve it.

**The Evidence
for Equity**

A number of studies have demonstrated that people are motivated by considerations of equity. In several experiments (Berscheid & Walster, 1967; Berscheid et al., 1969), subjects played a game in which one, through no fault of her own, won a lot of money or trading stamps while the other one lost. At the end of the game, the winner (the real subject) was given an opportunity of returning some of the money to the other subject. Under these circumstances, there was a strong tendency to give back some of the winnings, even though they had been won legitimately. In contrast, when the winnings were equal, there was little tendency for the subject to give any winnings to the other player.

Schmitt and Marwell (1972) also found evidence for equity. When one member of a team was given two, three, or five times as much as his partner, he tended to give some of his money to his partner in order to make their rewards more equal. In addition, the overrewarded partner often chose to play a different game when he was assured that this would result in more equal partitioning of the rewards. In other words, not only did he give up some of his own money in order to produce a more equitable division, but he avoided the situation that produced the inequity in the first place.

Leventhal, Michael, and Sanford (1972) found that a subject who was asked to divide money among the members of a team gave higher rewards to better performers. But there was some evidence that, apparently in order to prevent conflict in the group, the worst performer was given somewhat more than he might have deserved and the best performer somewhat less. That is, the difference in rewards was somewhat smaller than performance would have warranted.

Several studies by Lerner show that quite young children sometimes follow rules of equity. At kindergarten age, children who play a game and can divide rewards seem to ignore equity and instead use what Lerner calls *parity*—that is, everyone gets the same amount regardless of his contribution to the game. But somewhat older children take into account each team member's efforts and give larger rewards to those who were more important members of the team (Lerner, 1974). In addition, those who contributed more seem to expect larger rewards. In another study (Long & Lerner, 1974), children who were overpaid for doing a job subsequently donated more to charity than those who were paid the amount they expected. An interesting feature of this result was that this difference occurred regardless of whether or not the donations were public. Apparently the children were contributing because they wanted to or felt it was the right thing to do, not in order to impress anyone.

People are also very concerned about receiving just treatment for themselves. If one member of a team is given all the money to divide, under most circumstances he will divide it equally. But if the amount of money he is given is less than he expected, there is a tendency for the individual to give himself more than he gives his teammates (Lane & Messé, 1972). Presumably, the person doing the dividing wants to make sure that he gets at least what he deserves. This is not exactly fair or equitable, but it does fit in some odd way with a sense of social justice (at least for himself). Similarly, if the person doing the dividing feels he is better at the task than his teammate, he will tend to take more than half of the available money, whereas if he is worse than his teammate he will actu-

There is evidence (Greenberg, 1978) that when the possible rewards are high, selfishness or even greed may enter into the division. With a low reward, subjects divided the money according to equity. But when rewards were high, and when the other person could not retaliate in the future, people tended to take more for themselves than they really deserved. In contrast, when retaliation was possible, people behaved generously toward the other person, sometimes giving more than the other deserved.

Miller (1977) explored the relative strengths of a justice motive and a desire for personal gain. Subjects were given varying amounts of money. Sometimes they were given enough so that they could give some away and still receive the amount they were supposed to get themselves; sometimes they received just enough to pay themselves fairly. In all cases, the other subject had not been paid enough. Miller found that people tended not to give money away if doing so would reduce their own payment below what they thought they deserved. On the other hand, if they could give away some and still have enough, they did so and especially liked that situation. In fact, they liked it more than when they received exactly the right amount themselves and did not give any to the other. Thus, getting just pay is nice and so is giving; but if you do both, that is best of all. People do want to be paid fairly, but they also like to be generous.

ally take somewhat less than half (Leventhal & Lane, 1970; Leventhal & Anderson, 1970).

Two studies have investigated individual differences in attitudes that involve social justice and equity. Greenberg (1978) divided subjects into those with strong and weak Protestant ethics, by which was meant a general feeling that people get what they deserve according to the amount of work they have put into a task. The high Protestant ethic subjects allocated rewards to make them fair according to the outcome of a game. If they won, they took more than half; if they lost, they took less than half. Moreover, if they considered that the game had been run unfairly for any reason, they redistributed the rewards to establish fairness. In contrast, subjects with a low Protestant ethic ignored both the outcome of the game and its fairness. In all cases, they kept exactly half of the rewards and gave away half. Both types of subjects were trying to be "fair," but obviously their personal definitions of fairness were quite different.

The degree to which one believes in a just world also plays a role in helping situations. Miller (1977) divided subjects into those with strong beliefs in a just world and those with weak beliefs. They were then asked to help in several different conditions. The victims were either unique—few others were in similar circumstances—or shared the same need with many others. The suffering of the victims was either brief (only during the Christmas season) or would continue for a year. The idea was that people who believed strongly in a just world would want to reestablish justice but would avoid futile actions. Assisting one person when thousands of others had the same problem was ineffectual in producing a just world; and helping for only a moment when the suffering would last a long time was also ineffectual. As predicted, those with a strong belief in a just world gave less help when the victim was one of many and when the suffering would last a long time, but gave more when the victim was unique and the suffering was brief. Subjects with a weak belief in a just world gave help at about the same levels regardless of uniqueness and duration of suffering. Once again, different attitudes toward justice and the world in general had a major effect on amount of helping.

Receiving a Favor

Another implication of the notion of equity concerns the effect of doing a favor for someone. Someone who does us a favor upsets the precarious balance of equity. While he has done something for us, we have not done anything for him. We owe him something. In order to restore equity, we must do a favor for him. We would be under considerable pressure to help if he made a request. Even if he asked us to do something that involved more effort than he exerted in doing us the favor, we would find it hard to refuse.

Berkowitz investigated this phenomenon in a number of studies (Berkowitz, 1968; Berkowitz & Daniels, 1964; Goranson & Berkowitz, 1966). In these experiments, a subject worked on a task and a confederate offered to help. Later, the subject had an opportunity to help the confederate on a similar task. A subject was more likely to offer help when he had previously been given help than when he had not been helped. In these experiments, the favor done for the subject was the same as the one he did for the favor-doer.

A study by Regan (1968) demonstrated a similar effect when the favors were different. College students were tested in pairs, one of each pair actually being a confederate of the experimenter. The study was described as dealing with perceptual and esthetic judgment. The subjects were put in separate rooms, shown a series of pictures, and asked to rate how much they liked each of them. After they had rated one series of pictures, there was a short break and the subjects were told they could do what they wanted as long as they did not talk about the experiment. At this point, the confederate got up, left the building, and returned several minutes later carrying two bottles of Coke. He handed one to the subject, saying "I asked him [the experimenter] if I could get myself a Coke and he said it was okay, so I brought one for you, too." The subject took the Coke, and the experimenter then gave them a second series of pictures to rate. In another condition, the experimenter went .out, returned with two Cokes, and handed one to the confederate and one to the subject, saying, "I brought you guys a Coke." In the third condition, no Coke was given to the subject.

After the second series of pictures was rated, there was another short break, during which the confederate asked the experimenter (loud enough for the subject to hear) whether he could send a note to the subject. The experimenter said that he could as long as it did not concern the experiment. The confederate then wrote the following note:

> Would you do me a favor? I'm selling raffle tickets for my high school back home to build a new gym. The tickets cost 25 cents each and the prize is a new Corvette. The thing is, if I sell the most tickets I get 50 bucks and I could use it. If you'd buy any, would you just write the number on this note and give it back to me right away so I can make out the tickets? Any would help, the more the better. Thanks (Regan, 1968, p. 19).

The measure of helping was how many tickets the subject agreed to buy. The data are shown in Table 8–1. When the confederate gave the subject a Coke and then asked him to do a favor, there was considerably more helping than when the experimenter gave the subject a Coke or no Coke was given. Helping in the latter two conditions did not differ appreciably. According to this study, it appears that having a favor done for us and then receiving a request from someone other than the person who did the favor does not make us more likely to comply with the request. But the study does show that one way of increasing helping is by doing somebody a favor. The recipient of the favor feels obligated to the favor-doer and is more likely to comply with a subsequent request by him than if no favor had been done.

The tendency to reciprocate a favor seems to be quite strong and universal. It has been shown to operate in many cultures, including the United States, Japan, and Sweden (Gergen et al., 1975). However, it is affected by various factors in the situation. For example, Greenberg and Frisch (1972) found that a larger favor was reciprocated more often than a smaller favor. In addition, when the initial favor was viewed as inten-

TABLE 8–1
Effect of Doing a Favor on Helping

CONDITION	NUMBER OF TICKETS BOUGHT
Confederate gave Coke	1.73
Experimenter gave Coke	1.08
No Coke	.92

Source: Adapted from Regan (1968).

tional, reciprocation was higher than when it was seen as somewhat accidental. Similarly, Goranson and Berkowitz (1966) showed that this effect depends in part on the individual's perception of why the other person helped him. In their study, the confederate either offered help voluntarily or was ordered to do so by a supervisor. When the help had been given voluntarily, subjects were more likely to reciprocate by helping the confederate than when the help was compulsory. Apparently, relatively little feeling of obligation is aroused when an offer to help is not made by choice. The study also suggested that the feeling of obligation is felt primarily toward the person who offered the help. Subjects who had been helped by someone tended to repay that person but showed considerably less tendency to offer help to someone else.

In addition to feelings of obligation, another possible explanation of the effect of doing a favor on helping is in terms of liking. Doing a favor is usually perceived as a friendly act. The recipient will tend to like the favor-doer more than he would like someone who did not do him a favor, and this liking may lead to greater helping. Yet, in Regan's study, liking was shown to have little effect on helping; and thus, for the moment, it seems that the effect of doing a favor is due primarily to feelings of pressure toward social justice and equity.

TRANSGRESSION AND GUILT

The idea that a feeling of guilt leads to expiation is probably as old as the concept of guilt itself. Guilt is aroused when we do something we consider wrong. When we feel guilty, we generally try to reduce our guilt. We can accomplish this in several ways: we can perform a good act to balance the bad one; we can subject ourselves to some kind of unpleasantness and thereby punish ourselves for our misbehavior (Wallington, 1973); or we can attempt to minimize the negative aspects of the guilt-arousing action.

The first two techniques make us more likely to comply with a request for help. If the request involves doing somebody a favor, performing a good act, or subjecting ourselves to unpleasantness or pain, agreeing would tend to reduce our guilt. Therefore, people who feel guilty should be more likely to give help than people who do not feel guilty. A number of experiments have demonstrated this.

Carlsmith and Gross (1969) conducted a study using a situation in which subjects gave electric shocks. Each subject was told that he was taking part in a learning experiment. One person would be the learner and the other the teacher. In all cases, the subject was the teacher and a confederate played the part of the learner. The subject's job was to press a button whenever the learner made a mistake. For one group of subjects, pressing the button sounded a buzzer and supposedly delivered an electric shock to the learner; for the other group, the button only sounded a buzzer. Thus, half the subjects were doing something quite unpleasant—shocking another subject. The other half were doing something innocuous—simply signaling when the other person made a mistake.

After a series of trials, the experimenter indicated that the study was completed and asked both the subject and the confederate to fill out a short questionnaire. While they were doing this, the confederate turned to the subject and, in a casual way, made the critical request. He asked the subject whether he would be willing to make a series of calls in connection with a campaign to save the California redwood trees. (In all cases, the confederate did not know which condition the subject was in.) The measure of helpfulness was whether or not the subject agreed to make any calls and, if he did, how many he agreed to make.

The results are shown in Table 8–2. Presumably, shocking the confederate made the subjects feel guilty, whereas delivering buzzes did not. If guilt increases compliance, subjects in the shock condition should have agreed to make more calls. This is what occurred. Those subjects who thought they had delivered electric shocks were more likely to comply than were those who delivered only buzzes.

Other studies involved other kinds of transgressions. In one study (Freedman, Wallington, & Bless, 1966), the experimenter told the subjects that it was extremely important that they not know anything about the test they were going to take, and the situation was set up so that virtually all the subjects said they knew nothing about it. Some of the subjects, however, had been told about the test by a confederate. Thus, these subjects were lying to the experimenter. Telling a lie and thereby perhaps ruining an experiment was expected to arouse guilt. It did. There was almost twice as much compliance among the "liars."

In another experiment by the same authors, the subjects sat at a table waiting for the experiment to begin. In some conditions, the table was specially prepared so that the slightest touch would tip it over and scatter index cards, which had been described as needed for somebody's thesis, all over the room. When the subjects tipped the table, they presumably felt responsible and guilty for mixing up the cards. In one

TABLE 8–2
Guilt and Helpfulness

CONDITION	HELPED	DID NOT HELP
High guilt (delivered shocks)	75[a]	25
Low guilt (delivered buzzes)	25	75

[a] Entries are percentages.
Source: Adapted from Carlsmith and Gross (1969).

control condition, the table was tipped by a confederate. In another, the table was stable and the cards were not scattered. Once again, there was more helping in the guilt than in either control condition.

This effect of guilt on voluntary helping was demonstrated in two very nice studies (Konečni, 1972; Regan et al., 1972). In the former, the subject was a pedestrian strolling along a street in Toronto. As he walked along, one of the experimenters suddenly dropped some index cards in front of him and gave the subject an opportunity to help pick them up. The measure of altruism was simply how many cards were picked up. In some instances the experimenter brushed against the subject and made it appear that this encounter caused the cards to fall. This was called a ''restitution'' condition because the subject had caused the harm but was being given an immediate opportunity to make up for it. In another condition the innocent subject strolling along the street ''ran into'' one of the experimenters, causing him to drop some books. The experimenter immediately picked up the books and walked off, obviously upset by the encounter. Subsequently a second experimenter dropped the index cards in front of the subject, who then had an opportunity to help him. This was called a ''generalized guilt'' condition because the subject had caused harm to one person and was given the opportunity of helping another. In a ''sympathy'' condition the subject watched as someone else bumped into the experimenter, knocking his cards down. The one who supposedly knocked the cards down kept walking, but the subject who had witnessed this sad event could help if he wished to. And finally there was a control condition in which nothing happened except that the cards were accidentally dropped in front of the subject.

The results are shown in Table 8–3. As before, it was found that subjects who had themselves caused the accident or who had caused an accident previously (the restitution and guilt conditions) helped considerably more than those in the control conditions. Unexpectedly, subjects in the sympathy condition who had merely watched someone else knock the cards down helped even more than those in the guilt conditions. But this condition is quite different from the others because it is the only one in which dropping the cards was clearly not the subject's fault. Someone ran

TABLE 8–3
**The Effect of Guilt, Sympathy, and Restitution
on Voluntary Helping**

	CONDITION			
	Control	Sympathy	Restitution	Guilt
Percentage helping	16	64	39	42

Source: Adapted from Konečni: (1972).

into him and knocked the cards down. He thus is a more pathetic victim and elicits help even though the subject feels no guilt himself.

The results of these and other experiments involving transgressions have been consistent. Regardless of the type of transgression—whether it consisted of lying, scattering valuable notes, delivering electric shocks, breaking an expensive machine, or taking something valuable from a partner—subjects helped more when they had transgressed than when they had not. The obvious explanation is that the transgression arouses guilt, which in turn leads to the increase in helping.

It is important to note that in most cases the effect was not caused simply by sympathy or compassion for someone who had been hurt. In Carlsmith and Gross's study, for example, there was one condition in which subjects did not push the button themselves but watched the confederate receive shocks. There was no difference in compliance between this group and one that merely delivered buzzes. And in the card-mixing study, when the table was tipped by the confederate rather than the subject, there was no more compliance than when the table was not tipped by anyone. Simply watching someone suffer does not usually increase altruistic behavior.

The research also shows that the person making the request need not be the one about whom the subject feels guilty. In some of these studies, the request was made by someone other than the person whom the subject had hurt. Even then, guilty subjects complied more than nonguilty ones. In addition, it appears that the request need not even benefit the victim. Subjects in several of the experiments were asked to do something that had nothing to do with the person they had injured. Once again, guilty subjects complied more than did nonguilty ones. This seems to indicate that the effect of guilt is not entirely specific to the person injured. People can reduce their guilt by doing a good deed for someone else. Thus, someone who feels guilty for any reason is more likely to comply with a request even when that request is not directly related to the cause of his guilt.

Some of the evidence suggests that although the subject would like to help his victim, he also wants to avoid contact with him. Guilty subjects have a tendency to comply less when the request involves associating with the victim than when they need not actually meet the person they injured. A guilty person seems to have two different motivations. On the one hand, he wants to make up for his guilty act by helping the victim or by doing something good for someone; on the other hand, he wants to avoid confronting his victim, probably because he is afraid of discovery or embarrassment. This implies that the effect of guilt is maximized when the guilty person can help without having to come into contact with the person about whom he feels guilty.

The Effect of Confession

An interesting aspect of the relationship between guilt and helping involves the effect of confession. One of the most common assumptions about confession is that it is good for the soul, by which we presumably mean that it is a form of expiation. This, in turn, implies that confession should reduce feelings of guilt. If confession does reduce guilt, it should also reduce helping. Studies by Carlsmith, Ellsworth, and Whiteside (1968) and by J. Regan (1968) supported this prediction. In the first study, subjects believed they had ruined an experiment because they used information they were not supposed to have. Some of them were allowed to confess what they had done; others were not given this opportunity; and a third group, who did not think they had ruined the study, served as a control. All the subjects were asked to volunteer for further experiments. The results are shown in Table 8–4. It is clear that guilt increased helping—those who used illicit information complied more than those who did not have the information. It is also clear that confessing, which reduced guilt, also reduced helpfulness—those in the guilt condition who confessed complied little more than those in the control group.

Regan's study, which used a different method for creating guilt, compared guilty subjects who were allowed to talk about what had happened, although not necessarily confess what they had done, with others who were not allowed to talk and with control subjects who had not transgressed. As usual, guilt increased helping, this time in the form of contributing money to an experimental fund. And again, those guilty subjects who talked helped less—they gave less money than did the guilty subjects who were not allowed to talk and the same amount as the controls. Presumably, talking reduced their guilt and they had no more reason to comply than did the controls. This work demonstrated that someone who is made to feel guilty and then confesses her wrongdoing helps less than if she is not given a chance to confess.

**Feeling Good
or Bad**

A possible explanation of the effect of guilt on helping is that the person feels bad and wants to do something in order to feel better. This suggests that anything that makes someone feel bad might increase the tendency to offer help. On the other hand, we also know that when we are feeling really good, we have a more cheerful view of the world and of our fellow humans and may accordingly be more likely to be altruistic. There is some evidence to support both ideas, but the second appears to be more

**TABLE 8–4
Guilt, Confession, and Helping**

CONDITION	NUMBER OF HOURS VOLUNTEERED
Guilt	4.33
Confession	2.67
Control	1.92

Source: Carlsmith et al. (1968).

powerful and consistent. In fact, feeling bad may sometimes increase helping, but at other times it may do exactly the opposite.

Probably the most impressive demonstration of the "feel good" effect is provided by Isen and Levin (1972), who arranged to have subjects find a dime in a public telephone. Subjects entered a phone booth to make a call, and some of them had the good fortune to discover a dime that had been placed there by the experimenters. Soon after leaving the booth, all subjects saw someone on the street drop some papers and had the opportunity to help pick them up. Whereas almost none of the subjects in the control (no dime) condition helped, virtually all of those who found the dime did help. Obviously it was not the 10 cents that mattered, but the warm glow produced by getting a free phone call. Similar results are produced by having people succeed or fail on tests (Isen, 1970; Isen, Horn, & Rosenhan, 1973; Weyant, 1978). Those who succeed are subsequently more helpful than those who fail. These and many other studies (including those mentioned in Box 8–4) indicate that under most circumstances feeling good makes people more helpful.

Another study (Isen & Levin, 1972) indicates that the good mood affects helping specifically and does not make people agree more to any request. Some students sitting in the library were given cookies by someone

BOX 8-4
MANIPULATING MOOD

In studying the effect of good and bad moods on helping, experimenters have devised many ingenious ways of affecting mood. Giving out cookies, leaving dimes in phone booths, and having people succeed or fail on tests all seem to induce appropriate moods. Some of the most interesting methods have involved merely asking people to think about positive or negative experiences. The procedure is to ask the subjects to concentrate very hard on an actual experience in their own lives that was either very sad or very happy (and presumably other kinds of moods could be used such as embarrassment, guilt, joy, and so on). The subject thinks of the experience, tries to picture it as vividly as possible, and does this for a few minutes. The evidence is that this procedure does affect mood and can increase or decrease helping, depending on the circumstances (Rosenhan, Underwood, & Moore, 1974; Kendrick, Baumann, & Cialdini, 1979). In a similar vein, Aderman (1972) had some subjects read statements describing good moods (elation, euphoria, satisfaction) while others read statements describing bad moods (depression, dissatisfaction). Simply reading about good moods increased helping relative to reading about bad moods. Finally, Fried and Berkowitz (1979) showed that music can affect mood according to whether it is soothing, stimulating, or aversive (as judged by experts). Soothing music increases helping when compared to other kinds of music or no music at all.

who walked around distributing them, and other students did not get the cookies. Then all subjects were given one of two requests: helping on a job that involved doing good for people or assisting in a rather mean study that involved disturbing people in the library. The results are shown in Table 8–5, which shows that those receiving cookies were more likely to agree to the nice request but considerably less likely to do the nasty favor. Apparently, when you feel good, you want to do good.

The effect of feeling bad is considerably less clear. We have already seen that feeling guilty, which is one kind of negative emotion, does tend to increase helping. However, other, less specific negative moods do not have this consistent effect. In a study by Isen (1970), subjects who failed a test were somewhat less likely to help than those who were not told how well they had done. The music study by Fried and Berkowitz (1979) that is described in Box 8–4 found that aversive music had no affect on helping. And two studies that manipulated mood by having subjects think about unpleasant events in their lives reported no effect on the rate of donations as long as they were anonymous (Rosenhan, Underwood, & Moore, 1974; Kendrick, Baumann, & Cialdini, 1979).

On the other hand, in one study (Kendrick et al., 1979), negative mood did increase helping when it occurred in public, and the same result was produced by failing a test in the study by Isen, Horn, and Rosenhan (1973). One explanation is that subjects who feel bad want to demonstrate to others that they are good people, and they can do this by performing a good deed in public. Exactly why a private good deed does not also counteract the bad mood is unclear. Perhaps the negative mood is related more to what others think of us than what we think of ourselves. In any case, positive moods consistently seem to increase helping in general, whereas negative moods seem to increase only public helping and not even this consistently.

Weyant (1978) has offered a resolution of these inconsistencies that is based in part on the perceived utility of the situation. The argument is that positive mood makes people genuinely interested in helping, whereas negative mood has mixed effects—people in a bad mood are actually less concerned with helping others than those in neutral moods, but are more

TABLE 8–5
Feeling Good and Helping

Condition	TYPE OF REQUEST	
	Do a Nice Job	Do a Mean Job
Cookies (feel good)	69[a]	31
No Cookies	50	64

[a] Percentage agreeing to request.
Source: Isen and Levin (1972).

concerned with making a good impression. This dual effect causes negative-mood people to offer help only when it will provide large benefits and is relatively easy to accomplish. When the required act will provide only small benefits or is difficult to do, negative-mood people will help less than control subjects. The study provided some support for these predictions. Positive mood (caused by success on a test) increased helping in all conditions; negative mood (caused by failure) increased helping when it was easy and had high benefit but the amount of helping was equal to or lower than that of a control group when the helpful act was seen as either less beneficial or hard to perform.

SUMMARY

1. Altruism is helping someone with no expectation of a reward. Other animals often put themselves in danger in order to protect another member of their species or family. It is suggested that altruism of this sort may be instinctive in animals and perhaps in humans as well.

2. Bystander intervention means coming to the aid of someone in distress. Research has shown that people are less likely to intervene when others are present and could help, and that this effect is due mainly to an interpretation of the situation based on what others are doing. If they do not help, it is assumed that help is not really needed or appropriate. There is also some tendency to feel less responsibility because others could help.

3. Social justice and equity lead to helping when someone is seen to suffer unfairly. People tend to act so as to reestablish equity. Doing someone a favor produces a sense of obligation so that the person is then more likely to offer help to the one who did the favor.

4. Transgressing a norm produces guilt, which in turn increases helping. If those who feel guilty are given a chance to confess, and thereby reduce guilt, their helping behavior is also reduced.

5. Feeling good is also likely to increase helping. There seems to be a "warm glow" that makes people want to share their good fortune. In contrast, feeling bad generally reduces helping unless the bad feeling comes specifically from guilt, or if the altruistic help is easy to do and is performed in public.

**SUGGESTIONS
FOR
ADDITIONAL
READING**

MACAULAY, J. R., & BERKOWITZ, L. (eds.) *Altruism and helping behavior.* New York: Academic Press, 1970. A series of articles for background information.

LATANÉ, B., & DARLEY, J. M. *The unresponsive bystander: Why doesn't he help?* New York: Appleton-Century-Crofts, 1970. Discusses research on this issue and presents some possible explanations.

WILSON, E. O. *Sociobiology.* Cambridge, Mass.: Harvard University Press, 1975. A fascinating account by a biologist of how genetic factors may affect behavior. Highly controversial and tough going, but well worth reading.

Conformity and Compliance

9

Omikron; Photo Researchers, Inc.

Five students arrived to take part in a study on perception. They sat around a table and were told that they would be judging the lengths of lines. They were shown a white card on which three black lines of varying lengths had been drawn and a second card containing one line. Their task was to choose the line on the first card that was most similar in length to the line on the second card. As shown in Figure 9–2, it was an easy task. One of the lines was exactly the same length as the standard, whereas the other two were quite different from it.

When the lines were shown, the subjects answered aloud in the order in which they were seated. The first subject gave his choice and each of the others responded in turn. Since the judgment was so easy, there were no disagreements. When all had responded, a second set of lines was shown, responses were given, and a third set was produced.

At this point, the experiment seems dull and pointless. On the third trial, however, the first subject looked carefully at the lines as before and then gave what was obviously the wrong answer. In the example in Figure 9–2, he might have said A rather than B. The next subject gave the same wrong answer, as did the third and fourth subjects. When it was time for the fifth subject to respond, he was quite disturbed. It was clear to him that the others were giving wrong answers. He knew that B was the line most similar to X. Yet everyone else said it was A.

Under these circumstances many people sitting fifth gave the wrong answer—they agreed with the others even though they knew it was incorrect. In fact, among these college students with good eyesight and

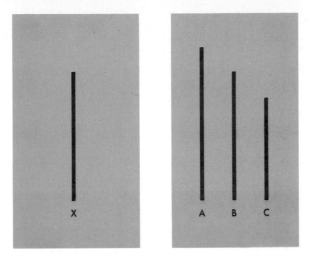

FIGURE 9-2 A representative stimulus in the Asch study. Subjects were shown the four lines simultaneously and asked which line was most similar in length to line X. When a number of confederates unanimously gave the incorrect answer (e.g., C), subjects conformed about 35 percent of the time.

presumably sharp minds, the incorrect answer was given about 35 percent of the time. Some subjects never gave the wrong answer, some did all the time; but overall they averaged about one wrong response in three. Of course, in this classic study by Solomon Asch (1951), the situation was staged. The first four "subjects" were confederates of the experimenter and were responding according to a script. But the real subject did not know this and gave the wrong answer rather than disagree with the others.

Residents of a northeastern city answered a newspaper ad asking for people to participate in a psychology study. They arrived in pairs and were told that the purpose of the study was to investigate the effect of punishment on learning. One of them was selected by chance as the "learner" and the other as the "teacher." The teacher's job was to read aloud pairs of words which the learner was supposed to memorize. Each time the learner made a mistake, the teacher was to administer punishment. He sat in front of a large, impressive "shock machine" containing a number of levers, each of which was labeled with the amount of shock it would deliver, ranging from 15 volts all the way up to 450 volts. Above the number representing voltage were labels describing the severity of the shock: "Slight," "Extreme intensity shock," and finally "Danger: Severe shock."

The learner was put in a chair in another room, his arm was strapped down to the chair, and electrodes were taped to it. He could not be seen by the teacher or anyone else; they communicated entirely by intercom. Before the testing began, the learner mentioned that he had a slightly weak heart but he was assured by the experimenter that the shocks were not dangerous. Then, the experimenter gave the teacher a sample shock. It was actually fairly severe and hurt considerably, but the teacher was told that it was a mild shock.

During the testing, the learner made a number of errors. The teacher told him he was wrong and delivered a shock. Whenever a shock was given, the learner grunted. As the level of shock increased, the learner's reactions became increasingly dramatic. He yelled, begged the teacher to stop shocking him, pounded the table, and kicked the wall. Toward the end, he simply stopped answering and made no response at all. Through all this, the experimenter urged the teacher to continue. "The experiment must go on. It is necessary for you to continue. You must continue." He also said that the responsibility was his, not the teacher's.

Under these circumstances, a large number of subjects dutifully delivered supposedly severe electric shocks. More than half of them continued to the end of the scale and administered the shocks labeled 450 volts. They did this even though the person they were shocking screamed for mercy, had a heart condition, and was apparently experiencing great pain. In this dramatic demonstration study by Stanley Milgram (1963), the "learner" was actually a confederate of the experimenter and did not receive any shocks. All of his responses, including errors, grunts, and groans, were carefully rehearsed and then tape-recorded to make them identical for all subjects. The "teacher," however, had no way of knowing that the situation was staged.

In both studies, people performed acts they would rather not have performed. In the study by Asch, the pressure on them was subtle. There was no direct command or even request—they were seemingly free to give any response they wanted, and were, in fact, specifically told to give the response they thought was correct. But there was great pressure from the group. Everyone gave the same response and the individual was strongly motivated to agree with the rest of the group. When someone performs an act because everyone else is doing it, we call it **conformity.** In the second example, the pressure to give the shocks was open and direct. The experimenter asked and then demanded that the teacher cooperate. When people do what they are asked—even though they would prefer not to—we call it **compliance** or **obedience.** Conformity might be considered a special case of compliance—giving into group pressure—but it is an especially important phenomenon that we shall consider separately.

The question of inducing people to behave in a particular way, especially against their own inclinations, might seem of interest primarily to heads of totalitarian governments or those who are trying to control others. Actually, the question is relevant to practically every phase of social life. We are constantly being urged to act in some way and we often do the same to others. We are asked to do homework, obey laws, pay taxes, drive carefully, save energy, give to charity, be courteous, support political movements and candidates, and get dental checkups. The socialization of children consists in large part of getting them to behave in ways that are consistent with the needs, laws, rules, and demands of society. In every case, some person or organization is trying to get others to perform some action when the others would just as soon not. What factors determine whether the act will be performed? Let us consider conformity in detail first before turning to the more general case of compliance.

CONFORMITY IN PERSPECTIVE

Human beings are remarkably diverse. Our behavior, attitudes, thoughts, feelings, and values have almost unlimited variations. We speak in hundreds of different languages, believe in hundreds of gods, a Trinity, one God, or no god at all. In some cultures, men take many wives; in some, they take one; and in a few, women take many husbands. In some cultures, pork is forbidden; in others, it is a delicacy. Almost every aspect of behavior—business, courtship, marriage, friendship, bargaining, communication—varies from culture to culture. The diversity is so great that members of one culture find it difficult to exist in another unless they have studied it carefully. They cannot eat the food, their sexual practices are considered unnatural, their manners rude, their every act foreign and wrong. They continually offend people and are offended themselves.

In contrast to this great diversity, however, people the world over have much in common. We are, after all, members of the same species; we have similar physical characteristics, needs, and abilities. Although we speak different languages, we all have language and use it quite similarly. Although we have different sexual habits, we all have family structures and prohibitions against incest. The exact forms of behavior may differ, but we do perform many of the same acts, play many of the same games, and have many of the same cares and problems. Thus, the huge differences among people must be seen against the background of basic innate, genetic similarites.

Moreover, within any subculture, the similarities tend to predominate. Just as fantastic diversity exists *among* cultures, great similarity exists *within* any given culture. Almost everyone speaks the same language and has the same values, the same behavior, and the same interests. In the United States, practically everyone likes hamburgers; in Japan, practically everyone likes sushi. The similarity of behavior and values is even greater in subcultures. The smaller the unit of society, the greater the similarity among its members. In the white, middle-class subculture in the American Midwest, almost everyone has similar attitudes toward marriage and courtship, behaves the same in business, and so on. Any outsider entering a different culture is immediately struck by the fact that everyone seems to be behaving similarly. From the outsider's point of view, it looks as though the people are all conformists.

FIGURE 9–3 Not everyone conforms to the norms of society. When someone deviates in some ways, it attracts a lot of attention. Unless this is what you want, some types of conformity are probably adaptive.

It is true, of course, that people in a culture do behave similarly. But it is important to note that, by and large, this kind of conformity is an adaptive and necessary phenomenon. Members of the society must be able to assume, to some extent, that others will behave in certain ways, will have certain values, will interpret behavior in particular ways, and so on. It makes life much simpler and allows society to operate. People can interact smoothly, interpret correctly what others are doing, and communicate easily. Perhaps the most dramatic instance of this is provided by language. If everyone spoke different languages or had different meanings for the same words, social interaction would be almost impossible.

Language is only one form of behavior that is shared by members of a society. They have an almost unlimited number of conventions and behaviors in common. For example, sexual relations tend to be highly ritualized and specific to a culture. How does one express affection for someone of the opposite sex without being improperly forward? How does a male communicate to a female that he wants to be friends but not lovers? These questions are difficult to answer, particularly in Western society but the answers that do exist depend largely on the rituals and customs of the society concerned. An arm around a waist, a light kiss, and holding hands are acceptable approaches in some societies but are improper in others. In some societies, these gestures between a man and a woman would indicate friendship; in others, they would be proposals of marriage. Not knowing these customs, or not following them, makes it difficult to make one's feelings and intentions known. By conforming to the norms of society, however, we can communicate our feelings unambiguously and avoid disastrous or embarrassing misunderstandings.

Similarity among the members of a culture is also due to similar backgrounds, experience, and learning. Children learn to do things in a particular way, to accept certain beliefs, and to develop certain motivations. To a great extent, all children in a society learn the same things. Then when they are adults, they behave in similar ways—not because they choose to, not because they even think about it, but because this is the way they learned to behave.

Conformity should therefore be considered within this context. Much of the similarity of behavior and beliefs that we see in society and that we call conformity is due to necessity and learning. Thus, although conformity usually has a negative connotation, there are often good reasons for people to be similar.

TRUE CONFORMITY

There are times, however, when people behave similarly in the absence of common learning or necessity. Often people who are free to behave in two different ways and who have no personal preference for either will do what they see other people doing. If, when driving behind a number of other cars, they see all the others turn left at a particular intersection, they would probably be strongly tempted to turn left, unless they had additional information about the correct route. When somebody on the street looks up, other people tend to look up also. If someone says that a Campbell's soup can twenty times its normal size is great art, someone else agrees and pays thousands of dollars for the privilege of having it in his living room.

Sherif (1935) provided a forceful demonstration of this kind of conformity. He took advantage of the perceptual effect known as the **autokinetic phenomenon**—a single point of light seen in the dark appears to move even though it is completely stationary. During World War II, pilots who were supposed to follow the lights of the plane ahead of them were bothered by this effect, because the lights seemed to move around in erratic and confusing ways. The pilots sometimes became disoriented and flew off course. Eventually the problem was eliminated by using lights that blinked, which prevented the autokinetic effect. Two important characteristics of this effect for Sherif's purposes are that it appears to virtually everyone and that is is extremely difficult for the person watching the light to estimate how far it moves. Typically, it seems to move erratically, at varying speeds and in different directions.

In Sherif's experiment, each subject was taken into a totally dark room and shown a single point of light. The subjects were told that the light was moving (since they were unfamiliar with the autokinetic effect, they believed it) and that their task was to estimate how far the light moved. The estimates varied enormously. Several subjects thought the light moved only 1 or 2 inches, whereas one thought it moved as much as 80 feet. (Apparently, this subject thought he was in a gymnasium, although actually he was in a small room.) In other words, the distance the light moved was quite ambiguous. Although the subjects had some idea how far it moved, they were far from certain because they had no guidelines, no background on which to base their estimates.

Into this ambiguous situation, Sherif introduced another subject who was supposedly also judging how far the light moved. This other subject was, in fact, a confederate who had been told to make his estimates consistently lower or higher than those of the subject. The procedure worked as follows: There was a trial during which the light presumably moved, the subject gave his estimate, and the confederate then gave his estimate. The same procedure was repeated for a number of trials. Under these circumstances, the subject soon began to make estimates that were more and more similar to those of the confederate than the ones he had made at the beginning. For example, if the subject began by estimating that the light moved between 10 and 15 feet and the confederate said it moved only 2 feet, on the second trial, the subject would tend to lower his estimate, and on the third trial, he would lower it more. By the end of the series, the subject's estimates were very similar to those of the confederate.

This was a situation in which the subjects were not sure of their positions. They had some information but it was ambiguous. They encountered somebody else who seemed quite sure of himself, even though they both seemingly had the same information. (The confederate gave consistent estimates over the course of the trials and therefore probably seemed much more sure of himself than the subject felt.) Thus, it was not simply a matter of the subject's conforming because they thought the other had more information. Rather, the subjects were influenced because someone said something different from them, because this other person kept saying it, and probably because this other person seemed sure of himself. This happened even though the subjects were told by the experimenter that the important thing was to give their own opinions because he was interested in the subject's perception of the situation.

This is quite a strong demonstration of agreement in the absence of a realistic reason, but it could be argued that it does not really show blind conformity. After all, the stimulus that the subjects were trying to judge was extremely ambiguous. The subjects had no idea how far the light moved, and were guessing when they gave their estimate. In contrast, the confederate seemed to have definite ideas about how far the light moved. It is true that there are large differences in the perceptual ability of individuals, and the subjects might have thought that the other person was better than they at judging how far a light moved in a dark room. Under these circumstances, it would be reasonable for subjects to go along with the other person or at least to use the estimates of the other person as a frame of reference within which to make their own judgments. In other words, although it appeared to be blind conformity, it may have been that the subjects had reason to conform.

This is the way Asch reasoned. He thought that once the effect of this frame of reference was removed, there would be little or no conformity. He felt that people are rational enough so that they would trust their own perceptions and beliefs when reality supported them and that they would accordingly remain independent even in the face of a group that unanimously disagreed with them. He constructed the experiment we described earlier and found a great deal of conformity—about 35 percent.

Although Asch's study used line judgments, others have found conformity with other physical stimuli, opinion statements, statements of fact, and logical syllogisms. Subjects have agreed that there is no population problem in the United States, because 6,000 miles of continent separates San Francisco from New York; that men are 8 to 9 inches taller than women on the average; and that male babies have a life expectancy of only twenty-five years. In other words, regardless of the type of stimulus and of how clear and unambiguous the correct choice is, when individuals are faced with a unanimous group opinion that differs from the correct one, the pressure exerted by the majority is strong enough to produce an appreciable amount of conformity.

It is important to keep the unambiguousness of the situations in mind if we are to understand the phenomenon. There is a tendency to think that the conforming subjects are uncertain of the correct choice and therefore are swayed by the majority. This is not always the case. In many instances, the subjects are quite certain of the correct choice and, in the absence of group pressure, would choose correctly 100 percent of the time. When they conform, they are conforming despite the fact that they know the correct answer.

These results are very clear. People do conform to other people—even when doing so means going against their own perceptions of the world in an unambiguous situation. They do not really accept what the others are saying; in most cases, they believe themselves to be correct. Nevertheless, when asked to respond, they give the same response the others give. This is what we mean by conformity. People have an opinion and all the information necessary to support it, and yet they express an opinion that conforms to the opinion expressed by others.

WHY DO PEOPLE CONFORM?

An individual in a confomity situation is under pressure from several sources. Most of the factors that affect conformity can be grouped into classes in terms of the kind of pressure they apply. There are those that determine the amount of trust an individual has in the group and in himself. These affect how much information the individual thinks the group's responses convey. Other factors in the situation affect the degree to which individuals want to be similar to the group or, stated differently, how much they are concerned about being deviant. In addition, various characteristics of the individuals determine their tendency to conform. Throughout our discussion of the variables that affect conformity, it will be helpful to keep these classes in mind. The operation of the specific variables can be most clearly understood in terms of these more general categories.

**Information
and Trust**

Other people are an important source of information. They often know something we do not; by doing what they do, we may gain the benefit of their knowledge. A thirsty traveler at an oasis in the Sahara Desert who sees Arabs drinking from one well and avoiding another would do well to drink from the well they are using. Similarly, someone waiting for his turn at a Coca-Cola machine who sees someone lose a quarter but then have success by using two dimes and a nickel would do well to try the small change before the quarter. And a student who does not know an answer on a test and copies from the person sitting next to him is also indulging in an adaptive bit of conformity. All these people are doing what someone else is doing because the other has or seems to have information they do not.

In a conformity situation, the individual initially holds one view and discovers that the group holds an opposing one. The individual wants to give the correct response. Therefore, the more he trusts the group or thinks it is a good source of information, the more likely he is to conform. At the extreme, if he thinks that the group is infallible, he will always go along with it, even though he might be quite certain of his own opinion. Similarly, if the group has vital information he does not have, conformity would he high. In either case, the individual would decide that he is mistaken and the group correct. The same mechanism operates in less extreme circumstances. The more confidence a person has in the group, the more shaken her own belief will be and the more she will conform. This does not necessarily mean that she is convinced by the group. It means her confidence in her own position is shaken enough so that she does not want to disagree. Therefore, the more the individual trusts the other members' opinions and distrusts her own and the more information she thinks their opinions convey, the more she will conform.

Fear of Deviance

The fear of being deviant is a basic factor in almost all social situations. We do not want to stand out as different; we want to be like everyone else. An individual faced with a group that disagrees with him is reluctant to be deviant. He wants the group to like him, to treat him well, and to accept him. He is afraid that if he disagrees with them, they might dislike him, mistreat him, and consider him an outcast. He tends to conform in order to avoid these consequences.

This fear of being deviant is justified by the group's response to deviancy. Almost any group exerts strong pressures toward uniformity, and someone who does not conform risks grave consequences. When someone disagrees with the rest of the group, various efforts are made to get him to conform. The most straighforward is trying to convince him that he is wrong and the group right. This was shown in a study by Schachter (1951), in which three confederates were included in a group—one of them consistently took a position deviant from that of the group, one started deviant and changed, and one took the same position as the group. Under these circumstances, the rest of the group spent a great deal of time trying to change the position of the two confederates who held deviant positions. They argued with the the deviates, presented reasons to support their own position, cajoled, and did whatever they could to change the deviates' stand to agree with the group's.

Being the object of such an intensive campaign is not pleasant. The deviate feels great pressure to change in order to please everyone and to stop the attacks. If he does change, he is accepted and treated much like any other member of the group. If he maintain his deviant position, eventually the communication to him stops. The group decides that it cannot influence him and begins to ignore him. In the study, the group liked him less than someone who agreed with the group and tended to ostracize and reject him. When the time came to assign jobs, the deviate was never elected to top positions, was never the leader. Instead he was given the worst jobs.

Similar negative consequences of being deviant were found in the study by Freedman and Doob that was discussed in Chapter 7 on aggression. A group of people who had never met before were brought together and given some information about each other. One of them was described as being different from the others, but just how he was different was not made clear. All the groups knew was that his personality was in some way different from theirs. The group was then asked to choose one of their members to take part in a learning study. Whoever was chosen would have the job of responding, and whenever he made an incorrect response, he would receive an electric shock. It was clearly an unpleasant position to be in. The group chose the deviate overwhelmingly for the job of receiving the shocks, or suffering. In another situation, the group had to choose someone to receive a reward of several dollars for taking part in a simple learning study. For this favorable position, the group avoided choosing the deviate and instead picked an average member. In other words, deviates are selected for painful, bad jobs and not for rewarding, good ones.

A group can also apply sanctions directly to a deviate. In a study at the Hawthorne plant of the Western Electric Company, observations were made of the behavior of a number of workers whose wages depended on their productivity. By working harder and accomplishing more, each worker could receive higher pay. However, the employees had developed their own standards as to the right amount of work to do in a day. Every day, after they had accomplished this amount of work, they slacked off. By working just this much, they earned a reasonable sum of money and did not have to work hard. Anyone who did work hard would make the others look bad and might cause management to increase its expectation of output. Thus, the group wanted to maintain its productivity at a fairly low average level.

In order to do this, the group exerted intense pressure on its members

© 1963 Punch; Rothco.

"I fear we must have misread the invitation."

to be sure they did not surpass the established level. To begin with, the group set up a code of behavior. A person should not work too much or else he was a "rate buster." Nor should a person work too little—that would make him a "chiseler." In addition, the group devised a unique method of enforcing this code. Anyone who worked too fast or too slow could be "binged." Binging consisted of giving the deviate a sharp blow on the upper arm. Not only did this hurt but it was a symbolic punishment for going against the group's accepted behavior. Any group member could deliver the punishment, and the person who was binged could not fight back. He had to accept the punishment and the disapproval it indicated.

Binging is merely a dramatic example of the kinds of pressure present in all groups that cause members to conform to the accepted opinions, values, and behavior. By persuasion, threats of ostracism, direct punishment, and offers of rewards, groups put pressure on individuals to conform. If they conform, they are accepted and treated well; if they remain deviant, they must face the consequences.

BOX 9-1
CONFORMITY AND SELF-AWARENESS

In Chapter 4, we discussed self-consciousness and self-awareness. People differ in how much attention they pay to their own behavior. Sometimes they concentrate on what they are doing—in particular on how they appear to others. On other occasions, people behave more or less spontaneously without caring much about how they appear to others. Clearly, the typical conformity situation—in which a group sits around waiting to hear your opinion—tends to produce a high degree of objective self-awareness—that is, seeing yourself as others see you. And high objective self-awareness makes you more likely to behave consistently with what you think are the values and attitudes of the other people. To some extent, someone in a state of high objective self-awareness accepts the values of the other people, or of society in general, and is influenced by these attitudes. Also,

and more important in terms of conformity, this concern about others' attitudes causes you to behave in such a way that they will form a good impression of you.

Thus, part of most conformity situations is a high degree of self-consciousness and a concern about being accepted. Moreover, anything in the situation that increases self-consciousness should also increase conformity. Having the other people present and looking at you should produce more objective self-awareness than having them in the other room, hearing your voice only over a loudspeaker. As would be expected, there is less conformity when others are not physically present and able to see you. Situations in which someone is on public view, such as being on television or in front of an audience, produce high objective self-awareness. Although there is no direct evidence, we should find more conformity under these circumstances than when the individual is less exposed to other people.

This concern about looking good to others, especially when you are in a state of high objective self-awareness, may affect behavior in a wide range of social situations, and in particular, many social psychology experiments. We mentioned in Chapter 2 that one difficulty with research is that subjects are often worried about making a good impression on the experimenter. Subjects may sometimes be so worried about this that they behave not in the way they feel but in the way they think the experimenter wants them to behave, or in the way that they think will make the best impression on the experimenter. It is very difficult to eliminate this tendency, though the bogus pipeline procedure, described in Box 2–3, is one attempt to do this.

The work on objective self-awareness, especially as it relates to conformity, indicates that any situation that focuses the individual's attention inward will increase her concerns about looking good. The experimental situation typically does just this, because the experimenter is obviously interested in how the subject behaves and is observing closely. Therefore, laboratory situations must usually increase objective self-awareness and lead to greater concern about looking good and to greater conformity than a more natural setting. People in natural situations may therefore be less conforming than they appear to be in laboratory studies.

The strength of the desire not to be deviant varies considerably from person to person and from situation to situation. Some people probably do not feel it at all or even prefer to be deviant; and in some circumstances, most people would probably like to be deviant. But for most people in most situations, there is a tendency to avoid it.

The conformity situation is, of course, perfectly designed to raise the individual's fear of being deviant. Everyone is taking one position and she knows that position is incorrect. She is already deviant in her own mind, but by going along with the group, she can avoid appearing different to the other people. Thus, she is in great conflict: on the one hand her own senses or intelligence tell her that the group is wrong; on the other hand, the group members all agree and she will stand out if she does not go along with them. The joint effect of fear of being deviant and lack of confidence in her own opinion will often cause someone to conform. The strength of these two motives varies considerably depending on the situation, and each of the factors we all shall discuss can be understood in terms of how it affects the two basic considerations.

Group Unanimity

An extremely important factor in producing conformity is the unanimity of the group opinion. When someone is faced with a unanimous group decision that he disagrees with, he is under great pressure to conform. If, however, a group is not unanimous, there is a striking decrease in the amount of conformity. When there is even one person who does not go along with the rest of the group, conformity drops precipitously to about one-fourth the usual level. This is true when the size of the group is small, and it also appears to hold when the group is quite large, up to fifteen people. One of the most impressive aspects of this phenomenon is that it does not appear to matter who the other nonconforming person is. Regardless of whether he is a high-prestige, expert figure or has low prestige and is not at all expert, if he does not agree with the group, conformity tends to drop about three-fourths (Asch, 1951; Morris & Miller, 1975).

In one study (Malof & Lott, 1962), white Southern students were put into the standard Asch situation and faced with unanimous majorities who gave incorrect responses. Then, a black student in the group broke the unanimity by disagreeing with the majority. The amount of conformity—for both prejudiced and nonprejudiced subjects—greatly decreased. In fact, the black student disagreeing with the group caused conformity to decrease as much as did a white student disagreeing. Apparently, the presence of someone else who disagrees with the majority always makes it easier for an individual to express his own opinion, regardless of his feelings about the other person.

Moreover, this effect is found even when the other disagreer gives the wrong answer. If the majority says A, another person says C, and the correct answer is B, the subject is less likely to conform than if everyone agreed on one incorrect answer. Simply having some disagreement within the rest of the group makes it easier for one person to remain independent despite the fact that no one agrees with him.

In a study by Allen and Levin (1971), subjects were presented with either a unanimous majority, a three-man majority and a fourth person who have the correct answer, or a three-man majority and a fourth person

Drawing by Handelsman; © 1972 The New Yorker Magazine, Inc.

"Well heck! If all you smart cookies agree, who am I to dissent?"

who gave a different answer but one that was even more incorrect than that of the majority. The subjects made three kinds of judgments—perceptual evaluations such as those used by Asch, information such as whether Hawaii was a state, and opinion items for which there was no actual correct answer but for which there were popular ones. The results are shown in Table 9–1. For all three items, the unanimous majority produced more conformity than either of the nonunanimous conditions. The effect was strongest for the perceptual items and weakest for the opnion items.

The fascinating finding was that for both perceptual and information items, there was practically no difference in amount of conformity when the fourth subject gave the correct answer from when the fourth subject gave an even more incorrect answer than the majority. Even when the dissenter gave an answer further away from the subject's own impression than that given by the majority, conformity was cut approximately in half. The results were somewhat less clear for opinion items. On these, when the dissenter agreed with the subject's opinion, there was a little less conformity than when he gave an even more discrepant answer; but even then there was somewhat less conformity than when the majority was unanimous.

A study by Wilder and Allen (1973) showed that the effect of breaking the unanimity works well on opinion items even if the dissenter is also wrong. In this experiment, one person either gave the correct answer or gave an answer that was at the opposite end of the scale from the incorrect majority. In other words, in the latter case, both the majority and the dissenter were wrong, but the subject's own opinion fell in between them. Under these conditions, any break in unanimity greatly reduced conformity compared to a unanimous majority.

Finally, Morris and Miller (1975) showed that the timing of dissent made a difference. When one person dissented after the majority had expressed its opinion, conformity decreased. But when the dissenter answered before the majority, conformity decreased even more. Ap-

TABLE 9–1

Conformity Produced by Unanimous Majorities, and by Majorities with One Dissenter Who Gives Either the Correct or an Even More Incorrect Choice

	TYPE OF JUDGMENT		
	Perception	Information	Opinion
Unanimous	.97	.78	.89
One correct	.40	.43	.59
One more incorrect than majority	.47	.42	.72

Source: Adapted from Allen and Levin (1971).

parently, when the subject heard the correct response at the beginning, the majority's incorrect position carried less weight.

The dramatic decrease in conformity when unanimity is broken seems to be due to several factors. First, the amount of trust in the majority decreases whenever there is disagreement, even when the person who disagrees is less expert or less reliable than those who make up the majority. Of course, this is in a situation in which the person himself is also disagreeing with the majority. That is, he initially holds an opinion different from theirs, and he discovers that someone else does also. The mere fact that someone else also disagrees with the group indicates that there is room for doubt, that the issue is not perfectly clear, and that the majority might be wrong. This reduces the individual's reliance on the majority opinion as a source of information and accordingly reduces conformity. Second, if another person takes the same position that the individual favors, it serves to strengthen his confidence in his own judgment. As we shall discuss in more detail below, greater confidence reduces conformity. A third consideration involves the individual's reluctance to appear deviant. When he disagrees with everyone else, he stands out and is deviant in both his own and the others' eyes. When someone else also disagrees, neither of them is as deviant as he would be if he were alone.

This last result should probably be taken as encouragement to speak one's mind even when he disagrees with almost everybody. In the story "The Emperor's New Clothes," for example, the whole crowd watched the naked emperor in his supposedly beautiful new clothes. However, when only one person had the strength to say that the emperor was naked, everyone else found strength to defy the pressures of the majority. After a while the majority had become the minority and perhaps even disappeared. Certainly, this is a strong argument for freedom of speech, because it suggests that even one deviant voice can have a sizable, important effect as long as there are other people who inwardly disagree with the majority but are afraid to speak up. It may also explain why in totalitarian states and some orthodox religions no dissent is allowed. Even one small voice disagreeing with the ruling powers could encourage others to do likewise. Then, after a while, the regime would be in danger of toppling. Perhaps it is dangerous to make too much of this one finding, but it does stand out as one of the most striking aspects of the conformity process.

Group Size

Suppose there were two people in a room and one of them said that it was very warm. If the room was, in fact, quite cold, the second person would be unlikely to agree with the first. He would feel cold himself and would assume that the other was mistaken or feverish. If forced to make a public statement on the temperature of the room, he would probably say he though it was rather cold.

If the room contained five people and four of them said it was warm, the situation would change markedly. Even if one person felt cold, he would be likely to doubt his own perceptions. After all, it is somewhat unlikely that all four of the others were feverish or mistaken. If he were asked how he felt, he might be uncertain enough to agree with the rest. He might say that the room was warm and then wonder what was wrong with him. When one person disagrees with you, he is feverish; when four others do, you must be sick yourself. Four people tend to be more trustworthy than one, in terms of both honesty and the reliability of their opinions; it is harder to mistrust a group than one person. Four people saying something offer better information than just one.

A series of experiments has demonstrated that conformity does increase as the size of the unanimous majority increases, at least up to a point. In some of his early experiments, Asch (1951) varied the size of the majority from two to sixteen. As shown in Figure 9–4 he found that two people produced more pressure than one, three a lot more than two, and four about the same as three. Somewhat surprisingly, he found that increasing the size of the group past four did not increase the amount of conformity, at least up to sixteen. Thus, he concluded that to produce the

FIGURE 9–4   Group Size and Conformity

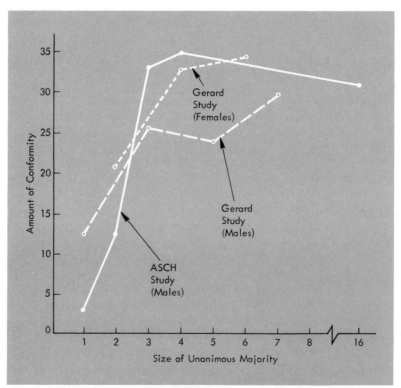

Source: Adapted from Asch (1951) and Gerard, Wilhelmy, and Connolley (1968).

most conformity, the optimal group size was three or four and that an additional increase did not have any effect.

Gerard, Wilhelmy, and Conolley produced somewhat different results in a later study (1968). They tested male subjects with unanimous majorities of one, three, five, and seven and female subjects with majorities of two, four and six. The amount of conformity with each size group is also shown in Figure 9–5. Conformity increased greatly when the group size was increased from one to three for men and from two to four for women. This is essentially what Asch found—the major effect of group size occurs when the group is increased beyond size two. Unlike Asch's results, however, the new data suggest that additional conformity is produced by still larger groups. Although there is a slight dip for men in groups with a majority of five, both males and females conform most when faced with the largest groups.

Using quite a different procedure and different measure, Milgram and associates (1969) produced similar results. The situation was very simple. On a very crowded street in New York City, a number of people played the old game of looking up in the sky to see whether anyone else would look up also. This time it was done as a deliberate experiment and careful observations were made of passers-by. The confederates stood and looked up at the sixth-floor window of an office building across the street. Either one, two, three, five, ten, or fifteen confederates stood around looking up at the window. The chief measure is what percentage of those who passed by actually stopped and looked up at the window also. When one person was looking up, only 4 percent of the passers-by conformed to his behavior; with five it went up to 16 percent; with ten it was 22 percent; and with fifteen it was 40 percent.

A similar effect was found by Mann (1977) in a study of queuing at a bus stop in Jerusalem, Israel. When two or four people lined up, there was little tendency for others to join the line. But when six or more were on line, newcomers generally also go on line; and the more there were on line, the more likely it was that other people would join it.

However, research by Wilder (1977) makes it clear that it is not simply the number of people that makes the difference. In this study, subjects heard the opinions of varying numbers of other people. The important difference between this and previous work was that these other people were sometimes expressing their opinions independently and were sometimes members of groups. For example, some subjects heard the opinions of four people who all belonged to one group, while other subjects heard the opinions of four independent people or four people who were members of two different groups. Wilder found that the number of people in a particular group had little effect on the amount of conformity; whereas the number of independent opinions, either from separate groups or from individuals, had a major effect on conformity. This may explain why increasing the size of a group above three or four adds little to conformity. Once the group is seen to be acting as a unit, the number of additional

Marc Anderson; Prentice-Hall, Inc.

FIGURE 9–5 Social pressure and the need for order often cause people to obey simple rules, such as lining up for a bus. However, it seems as if lining up sometimes depends on the number of people present.

individuals within the group does not matter. In contrast, adding entirely independent judgments from people outside the group might increase conformity.

Expertise of the Group

Another characteristic of groups that is relevant to conformity is the expertise of the members. How much do they know about the topic under discussion? How qualified are they to give information?

The more expert a group is in relation to an individual, the more he should trust them and value their opinion. If, in our example concerning room temperature, the other people in the room were ill with the flu or were just off the plane from Alaska, the individual would probably be inclined to discount their opinions and trust her own. She would be less likely to conform than if the others were neighbors who were in good health. On the other hand, suppose the scene was shifted to the wilds of northern Alaska, and the problem was to discover the right way back to camp. If the individual had a strong feeling that the correct route was to the left but the rest of the group disagreed with her, she obviously would be more likely to trust four natives than four neighbors from home. She would conform more to the natives than to her neighbors.

Similarly, when an acknowledged expert agrees with the group, conformity is increased (Crano, 1970; Ettinger et al., 1971). Although the evidence is rather meager, it appears that the more expert a group is in terms of the particular judgments being made, the more conformity will be produced.

Individual Self-confidence

The other side of the coin, of course, is that anything that increases the individual's confidence in her own ability will decrease conformity. One factor that has a powerful effect on confidence and, consequently, on the amount of conformity is the difficulty of the judgment to be made. The more difficult the judgment, the less confidence the individual tends to have and the more likely she is to conform to others' judgments.

If someone asks us to name the capital of our home state, we know the answer and are sure we know it. Even if four other people gave a different answer, we probably would trust ourselves more than them. We are unlikely to conform, at least not because of lack of confidence in ourselves, although we may still conform for the other reasons cited. However, if we are asked to name the capital of Sierra Leone, the question is more difficult. Even if we have some idea of the correct answer, we are probably less certain. Then, if four people disagree with us, we are more likely to trust them and conform. The same is true with any problem. As difficulty increases, our confidence decreases and we conform more.

Coleman, Blake, and Mouton (1958) presented subjects in a conformity situation with a series of factual questions that varied in difficulty. The correlation between difficulty and conformity was .58 for men and .89 for women. That is, the more difficult the item, the more likely the subject was to conform to an incorrect response.

Additional evidence supports the idea that this effect of difficulty was due to confidence. In a similar situation (Krech & Crutchfield, 1962), subjects were asked to indicate how certain they were of their judgments on several items. On those items the subjects were quite certain of, there was only 15 percent conformity; items that the subjects were fairly certain of produced 24 percent conformity; and when the subjects were somewhat uncertain, there was 36 percent conformity. It seems quite clear that as the subjects' judgments became less ambiguous, as the problems became easier, there was less conformity. Conversely, as the problems became more difficult and the subjects found it harder to make certain judgments, there was more conformity.

A related variable is how competent a person feels to make the responses. Obviously the question about Sierra Leone's capital would be easier for an expert on Africa than for a social psychologist. If a person considers himself a math expert, he would be more confident of his answers to math problems than if he were not an expert; this holds even if the problems are quite difficult for him. Someone with good eyes would be more confident in making visual discriminations than someone with bad eyes.

This means that you should be able to make someone feel more knowledgeable about some subject and thereby decrease conformity. Sure enough, several studies have demonstrated just this (Mausner, 1954: Snyder, Mischel, & Lott, 1960; Croner & Willis, 1961; Wiesenthal et al., 1976). In Snyder's study some subjects were given a lecture on art just before being asked to make artistic judgments; other subjects did not hear this lecture. As you would expect, those who heard the lecture and supposedly felt more expert than they had before conformed less. Similarly, Croner and Willis showed that people who were successful on a particular task tended to conform less on related items than did others who failed the task.

Group Cohesiveness

Another important dimension affecting conformity concerns the individual's relationship to the group. Do the members feel close to the group or not? How much do they want to be members of the group? The term **cohesiveness** has been used to include all these considerations. It refers to the total sum of the forces causing people to feel drawn to a group and making them want to remain members of it. The more the members like one another, expect to gain from group membership, feel loyalty, and so on, the more cohesive the group is.

Greater cohesiveness leads to greater conformity. When working for a valuable prize, a group produces more conformity than when there is no prize or a smaller one. A group that considers its task important or values itself highly produces more conformity among its members than one that puts less value on its task or itself. Moreover, group members conform more in a group with a lot of group spirit.

This increased conformity is due to the individuals' reluctance to be deviant. As we saw earlier, being deviant involves the risk of rejection. Someone who is deviant too often or on too important an issue may be mistreated and, in the extreme case, may be ejected from the group. The more a person cares about the group, the more serious his fear of rejection is and the less likely he is to disagree. The less he cares about the group, the less serious his fear is and more likely he is to disagree. If someone is a member of a small group of friends, he has a tendency to avoid being a minority of one on any issue. Fear of rejection or expulsion is at least one reason for this. If, however, he no longer likes the group or feels that it is restricting his social life, this pressure to conform decreases. The worst that could happen if he deviates is that he would be thrown out of the group. When this ceases to be a serious threat, there is less reason for conforming and he feels freer to be deviant.

Commitment
Another factor that influences conformity is the degree of an individual's commitment to this initial judgment or opinion. We can define **commitment** as the total force that makes it difficult to give up a position, that binds the person to his position. Typically, we think of commitment in terms of an individual's feelings of being bound. Does she feel free to change her opinion or does she feel, for some reason, that she cannot or should not change it?

There are many ways of producing commitment to an initial judgment. The subject can write it down, say it aloud in the presence of others, or take any action that establishes her opinion in her own or others' eyes. In the standard Asch situation, the subject feels little commitment to her initial judgment. She has looked to the stimuli and presumably made a judgment. But she has not communicated this judgment to anybody. She has not said it aloud, written it down, or in any way made it a concrete decision. She would not embarrass herself by changing; she would not be admitting that she was wrong or that she was a weak person. There is no reason for her to stick to her initial judgment except a belief that it is correct. Under these circumstances, maximum conformity occurs.

Once the subject expresses her opinion, she becomes more committed to it. If others know her initial opinion, they would know that she has changed. The rest of the group accordingly might feel that she is allowing herself to be influenced by group pressure, that she does not have the courage of her convictions, and so on. The individual herself would feel this way. On the other hand, if she has never made her feelings concrete in any way, she can tell herself that her initial judgment was only a first impression, that she was never sure of it, that she changed because she thought it over more carefully. Thus, once one commits oneself to a position, one is more reluctant to give in to group pressure and conforms less.

The degree of a subject's commitment to a first judgment was varied in a study conducted by Deutsch and Gerard (1955). Some subjects (no-commitment condition) saw the stumuli but did not make a public or private statement of their opinion until they had heard the judgments of the rest of the group. Others made a minimal private commitment by writing their answers down on a magic pad before hearing any other responses. (A magic pad is a familiar child's toy that has a piece of cellophane over a layer of graphite. When one writes on the cellophane, it presses into the graphite and the word appears. Lifting the cellophane causes the words to disappear.) In this condition (self-commitment, magic pad), the subjects wrote their responses on the magic pad, heard the others' responses, gave their own response, and then erased the pad. In a third condition (strong self-commitment), the subjects wrote their answers on a sheet of paper that they knew was not going to be collected and that they did not sign. Finally, there was a public-commitment condition, in which the subjects wrote their response on a piece of paper, signed the paper, and knew that it was going to be collected at the end of the study. Thus, the four levels of commitment were none; private, magic pad; private, written; and public.

TABLE 9–2

Commitment and Conformity

COMMITMENT	PERCENTAGE OF CONFORMING RESPONSES
None	24.7
Private, magic pad	16.3
Private, written	5.7
Public	5.7

Source: Adapted from Deutsch and Gerard (1955).

The results are shown in Table 9–2. Clearly commitment reduces conformity. Even the magic-pad condition, in which the subjects knew that no one would ever see what they had written, produced less conformity than the no-commitment condition. The stronger commitments reduced conformity even further. Interestingly, there was no difference between public and strong private commitment, perhaps because the latter produced such strong commitment that conformity was already at a very low level.

A somewhat different type of commitment involves the behavior of conforming itself. Someone who, for one reason or another, does not conform on the first few trials tends to become committed to this nonconforming behavior. Similarly, someone who does conform at the beginning tends to get committed to that behavior. An individual can be induced to conform from the start by giving him difficult discriminations. When he is subsequently given easier problems, he tends to continue to conform. If, on the other hand, he is given easy problems at the beginning and does not conform to the obviously wrong answers of the other people, he will continue to be independent even when he is later given difficult problems.

This is particularly true when responses are public. When others know a subject's response, they know whether or not he is conforming. This increases his commitment to a conformist or independent line. Thus, in a face-to-face situation, someone who conforms on early trials continues to conform, and someone who does not conform is generally independent throughout. In a non-face-to-face situation, this effect is less strong, and, in fact, there is a general tendency for most subjects to conform more on later trials. Commitment, therefore, can be to either a particular response (e.g., A is the right answer) or a type of behavior (e.g., conforming).

Characteristics of the Individual

Thus far, we have been talking about factors that vary with the group or the situation. These operate in much the same way for all individuals. In addition, there are variables that each person brings with him to a situation. There are enormous individual differences in how much people conform, even in the same situation. Some people conform on 100 percent of the trials; others conform on no trials. How do the conformers and non-conformers differ?

To begin with, although there are few controlled experiments on this variable, there appear to be differences in the amount of conformity shown by people of different nationalities. For example, a direct comparison of Norwegians and Frenchmen (Milgram, 1961) found that in a variety of situation and subjects, the Norwegians conformed more than the French. Exactly why this occurred is not clear, but it seems to be consistent with the traditional emphasis on individuality in French life and the strong sense of social responsibility and group identification found in Norwegian society.

In another study (Frager, 1970) Japanese students were found to engage in anticonformity more than American students—i.e., they deliberately took a minority position, even when it was wrong. Anticonformity was also related to alienation—to rejection of contemporary Japanese society, and nostalgia for the old days of Japan. Schneider (1970) found that both black and white children conformed more when the majority was white than when the majority was black. However in this study, as in others on the matter, there was no general tendency for black children to be more conforming than white children, despite the common hypothesis that racial prejudice forces blacks to be more submissive than whites. It seems likely that there are considerable differences among other ethnic groups and subgroups, with some tending to conform a lot and others tending to conform relatively little.

There are also great differences in the amount of conformity shown by different individuals within a society. A number of studies have been conducted on this problem, but, unfortunately, the results are somewhat weak and inconsistent. Other than ethnic and national differences, there are no individual factors that have consistently been shown to affect conformity. We tend to think that intelligence, education, feelings of self-esteem, and so on should make people more independent and reduce conformity. However, the evidence simply does not support these intuitions. One study (Stang, 1972) indicated that people with high self-esteem conformed less, but other work has failed to find this effect. For the moment, there does not appear to be a conformist type, nor are any particular personality characteristics clearly associated with a high degree of conformity.

COMPLIANCE AND OBEDIENCE

Conformity is a limited example of the more general issue with which we started this chapter—how to get people to commit an act they would rather not perform. Social pressure in the form of a unanimous majority is one way, and as we have seen, many factors determine the effectiveness of this pressure. But there are many other ways to produce compliance.

One way to produce greater compliance is to increase external pressure on individuals to force them to perform the desired behavior. The use of rewards and punishments is a familiar means of eliciting compliance. A parent who wants her twelve-year-old son not to smoke often uses threats or bribes. She threatens to revoke his allowance, give him a beating, or deprive him of his favorite TV program if he disobeys her. Or she may promise him a bigger allowance or extra TV if he obeys. A third alternative is the use of cajolery, reasoning, and argumentation. She can tell him the medical reason why he should not smoke, or that it is unattractive, or anything else she thinks will convince him. All these methods work. A person with acne who is offered $10,000 for giving a testimonial for a skin cream is more likely to agree to have his scarred face appear on television than is one who is offered only $1. Someone who is told that LSD may cause irreparable brain damage and psychosis is more likely to avoid taking the drug than is someone who is told that it will make him dizzy (assuming they both believe what they are told). Within limits, the more the reward, threat, or justification, the more the compliance.

Compliance can also be affected by modeling and imitation. As with many other behaviors, an individual will tend to do what he sees someone else do. In an aggression situation, if the other person behaves aggressively, he will tend to become more aggressive; if the other person is not aggressive, it will reduce his own aggression. The same kind of effects occur with compliant behavior. If the individual witnesses someone else being highly compliant, he will tend to be more compliant then he might otherwise have been. In contrast, if he witnesses somebody being noncompliant, he will tend to be less compliant than he might have been. This kind of effect has been amply demonstrated by Bryan and Test (1967), Grusec (1970), and others.

At least for compliance, however, the effects of modeling appear to be somewhat limited. White (1972) demonstrated that imitating someone who donated money produced a smaller increment in donations than when the subject actually went through the motions of donating the money himself. And Grusec (1970) showed that to be effective the model must actually engage in the behavior and not just talk about it. The situation was one in which subjects could either share rewards or not share them. There were three conditions—no model, a model who said that she would share her rewards but did not actually do it, and a model who did share her rewards. Those subjects who had witnessed a model sharing were more likely to share themselves than those for whom there was no model. But those who merely heard a model say that she would share did not themselves share any more than if there was no model present. In other words, as with many things in life, it appears to be not what the model says that has the effect, but what she actually does.

As might be expected, direct instruction by telling the subject how to behave also had a considerable effect on degree of compliance. For example, telling a subject that he should donate money and reminding him

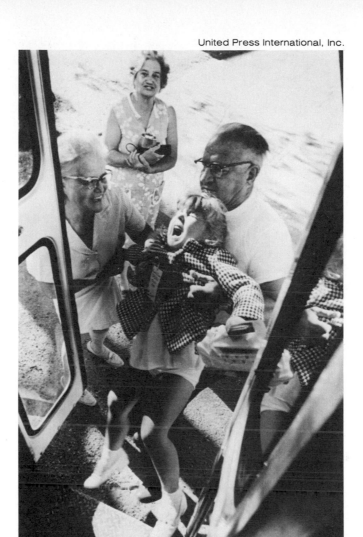

FIGURE 9–6 Sometimes getting children to obey is not easy. Most adults use gentle coaxing rather than more threatening measures. One more example of the limits of threats in producing compliance.

when he does not causes him to donate more even when he is later left alone (White, 1972). Similarly, telling a subject ahead of time that he must not enter a particular room inhibits him from subsequently going into that room to help someone who is in distress, whereas specifically telling him that he can enter the room naturally increases the likelihood that he will (Staub, 1971). When the experimenter specifically tells someone how to behave, it is to be expected that under most circumstances the subject will be more likely to behave in that way than if he had not been told.

The effect of direct instructions and social pressure varies considerably, depending on the circumstances. One way to maximize compliance is to place the individual in a well-controlled situation in which everything is structured to make noncompliance difficult. The individual is asked to do something and is free to refuse. However, refusal is made difficult because everyone expects him to comply. A familiar example of this phenomenon can be seen in a doctor's office. Someone is sitting quietly, enjoying a magazine while he waits to see the doctor. Then the nurse asks him to come into the doctor's office. He knows the doctor is still busy with two other patients and will not be ready to see him for another fifteen minutes. He would be more comfortable staying where he is, and there are no obvious threats for refusing the nurse or rewards for complying. Nevertheless, he walks docilely into the office and waits uncomfortably, this time without his magazine and maybe without his clothes—all because the nurse asked him to do so and the situation is set up so that is is difficult for him not to comply.

The phenomenon is even more clear in psychology experiments. Subjects find it extremely difficult to deny the experimenter anything. They have agreed to take part in a study. By doing so they have, in effect, put themselves in the experimenter's hands. Unless the experimenter deliberately frees them from this obligation, the subjects tend to agree to virtually any legitimate request. If a group of subjects are brought into a room and asked to eat dry soda crackers, they will do their best to eat as many as they can. After they have eaten several dozen and their mouths are parched and they are extremely uncomfortable, the experimenter can simply go around and say "Would you eat just a few more," and the subjects try to cram a few more soda crackers down their throats. They will do so even though they are given no justification, offered no direct rewards, and threatened with no punishments. Students have been reported to eat huge numbers of crackers in this situation.

The dramatic study by Milgram (1963) described earlier strikingly demonstrated this phenomenon. Many people dutifully delivered supposedly severe electric shocks to a man who screamed for mercy, had a heart condition, and was apparently experiencing great pain. Other work (Shanab & Yahya, 1977) has duplicated this research with Jordanian children aged 6 to 16 years old and gotten results similar to those of Milgram. Indeed, an even higher percentage (73%) administered the maximum level of shock. Neither age nor sex affected the results. The pressures of the situation, the urging of the experimenter, the lack of perceived choice (although, of course, they could have stopped at any time), and the acceptance of full responsibility by the experimenter made refusal difficult.

Any factors that make the individual feel more responsible for his own behavior or that emphasize the negative aspect of what he is doing will reduce the amount of obedience. In subsequent studies (1965), Milgram has shown that bringing the victim closer to the subject has a substantial effect. In the extreme case, when the victim is placed not in another room but actually right next to the subject, compliance decreases dramatically. Tilker (1970) supported this finding and demonstrated that reminding subjects of their own total responsibility for their actions makes them much less likely to administer the shocks. The results demonstrate that under these circumstances subjects feel enormous pressures from the situation and from the demands of the experimenter. Opposed to these feelings are the pressure of responsibility and concern for the welfare of the victim. As long as they can shift the responsibility to the experimenter and minimize in their own minds the pain the victim is enduring, subjects will be highly compliant. To the extent that they feel responsible and are aware of the victims's pain, they will tend to be less compliant.

The Hawthorne Effect

One of the most effective ways of exerting pressure on individuals to do something is to make them happy and to show them that we really care about them and want them to do this thing very much. This is probably implicit in most laboratory situations. The experimenter is sincere, presumably is dedicated to what he is doing, and talks individually to his subjects to tell him what he wants them to do. The subjects have put themselves in the experimenter's hands, feel that the experimenter wants them to perform the acts, are having a lot of attention paid to them, and find it hard to refuse any request that is even remotely reasonable. They feel obligated to the experimenter and therefore want to help him.

In a classic study (Homans, 1965), the purpose of which was to investigate the effect of various working conditions on rate of output, six women from a large department at the Western Electric Company's Hawthorne plant were chosen as subjects. The experiment took place over a period of more than a year. The women, whose job consisted of assembling telephone relays, worked in their regular department for the first two weeks (the first period) to provide a measure of their usual rate of output. They were average workers. After this initial period, they were removed from their department and put into a special test room identical to the main assembly room, except that it was provided with a method of measuring how much work each woman did. For the next five weeks (the second period), no change was made in working conditions. During the third period, the method of paying the women was changed. Their salary had previously depended on the amount of work turned out by the entire department (100 workers); now it depended only on the amount of work turned out by the six women. During the fourth experimental period, five-minute rest pauses were introduced into the schedule—one in the morning and one in the afternoon. In the fifth period, the length of the rest pauses was increased to ten minutes. In the sixth period, six rest periods of five minutes each were established. In the seventh, the company provided a light lunch for the workers. During the three subsequent periods, work stopped a half-hour earlier each day. In the eleventh period, a five-day workweek was established, and finally, in the twelfth experimental period all the original conditions of work were reinstituted, so that the circumstances were identical to those in which the women had begun.

From the point of view of the experimenters, this seemed like a good scientific way of testing the effect of various working conditions. Presumably the rate of work would be influenced by the conditions, so it could be determined which promoted work and which interfered with it. The results, however, where not what the company expected. Regardless of the conditions, whether there were more or fewer rest periods, longer or shorter work days, each experimental period produced a higher rate of work than the one before—the women worked harder and more efficiently.

Although this effect was probably due to several reasons, the most important was that the women felt they were something special, that they were being treated particularly well, that they were in an interesting experiment, and that they were expected to perform exceptionally. They were happy, a lot of attention was paid to them, and they complied with what they thought the experimenter (their boss) wanted. They knew that the main measure of their work was the rate at which they produced, they knew that this was what was being watched, so it did not matter what changes were introduced. They always assumed that the changes were for the good, that they were supposed to increase their work—therefore they worked harder. Each change stimulated their efforts further.

Limits of External Pressure

We have described a number of ways of increasing compliance. The most straightforward is to exert pressure on the individual, which can be done with threats, rewards, justification, or social pressure. He can also be exposed to a model who is doing what the experimenter wants, and the individual will usually imitate the model. A different approach is to place the person in a highly controlled situation designed to put subtle pressure on him and to make refusal difficult. It is important in this technique to give the impression that the subject is expected to comply, that the possibility of his not complying was never considered, that the experimenter is dependent on him, and that he, in essence, agreed to comply when he entered the situation. Another factor in this technique is the assumption of responsibility by someone other than the subject. The experimenter or someone else relieves the individual of personal responsibility, so he feels freer to do whatever is required. The consequences are not his concern, not his fault.

These procedures tend to increase compliance. However, they are not foolproof. Someone trying to elicit compliance often does not have large rewards, threats, or justifications at his disposal; and it is rare that he has sufficient control over the situation to produce the conditions necessary to make refusal difficult. In less ideal circumstances, people find it fairly easy to refuse even simple requests.

BOX 9-2
THE OVERJUSTIFICATION EFFECT: TOO MUCH REWARD

Although it might seem that the larger the reward the more effective it would be in getting someone to do something, this is not always true in the long run. It is probably true that greater rewards will be more effective, as long as one is willing to continue giving them. However, we often use rewards to get someone interested in some activity, to get them to comply in the first place, but then we withdraw the rewards and hope that they will continue the behavior. For example we might give a child an extra cookie for making her bed, or give a class a prize for finger-painting. Advertisers often provide small rewards in the form of prizes or coupons for trying their products. In all of these instances, those giving the rewards do not want to continue offering them. Instead, they hope that once having tried the behavior or product the people will learn to enjoy it. Their hopes may be misplaced, at least under some circumstances.

A series of studies has demonstrated that giving rewards can sometimes actually reduce interest in a particular activity (Deci, 1971; Lepper et al., 1973). For example, Lepper and associates (1973) asked children to play with magic markers, something that most children enjoy doing. Some of the children were promised and given a reward for doing this; others were promised nothing but given a reward; and others were neither promised nor given a reward. All of the children played with the markers. Later, the experimenters observed how much time the children spent using the markers in a free play period. They found that those who were promised the reward played with the markers significantly *less* than either of the other groups. Getting the reward for playing had somehow undermined their interest in the activity. Interest in the task is reduced most when the rewards are based on how well the person performs (Karniol & Ross, 1977; Harachiewicz, 1979).

The usual explanation of this effect is in terms of attributions that the children make about their own behavior. According to the view, the children who were promised and given a reward decided that they had played with the markers in part because they were going to get a prize. When the prize was no longer offered, the behavior seemed less desirable because its total value had declined. These children assumed that they had played with the markers because it was fun and because of the prize. Since there was also a prize, the play did not have to be as much fun as without the prize. Thus, it seemed like less fun. In contrast, those who played with no promise of a reward, were doing it simply for fun and therefore saw the activity as more enjoyable.

In terms of compliance, the implication is that rewards may sometimes backfire. If the activity required is basically uninteresting or even unpleasant, rewards will probably be helpful because they will increase the likelihood of compliance in the first place. And since the task is not enjoyable, there is no basic interest to undermine. But when the activity is inherently enjoyable or satisfying in any way, giving rewards may reduce the person's future compliance. If you think that children can learn to get satisfaction from cleaning up their rooms, rewarding them too much may reduce the chance of this occurring. Similarly, if we reward people for being altruistic, for helping others, or for being responsible citizens, we may make them less good citizens in the future unless we keep supplying them with rewards. Thus, the effect of reward is sometimes limited and may depend on the initial interest in the activity and whether the amount of the reward is too great for the particular action.

Sometimes the amount of external pressure that it is possible or appropriate to use produces less compliance than desired. The heroic soldier refuses to divulge the secret information even under torture; the typical nonheroic smoker refuses to give up cigarettes despite the real danger of cancer and heart disease; the letter writer refuses to use zip codes despite a variety of threats and cajolements from the Post Office. In these cases, increasing the amount of external pressure would increase compliance, but for one reason or another, it is impractical or undesirable to increase the pressure beyond a certain point.

REACTANCE In addition, increasing the amount of external pressure sometimes actually decreases the amount of compliance. Under certain circumstances, too much pressure causes the person to do the opposite of what he is asked to do. A series of studies conducted at Duke University by Jack Brehm (1966) explored this phenomenon, which Brehm calls **reactance.** The basic notion behind his work is that people attempt to maintain their freedom of action; when this freedom is threatened, they do whatever they can to reinstate it. Whenever increasing the pressure on an individual is perceived by her as a threat to her freedom of action, she protects it by refusing to comply or by doing the opposite of what is requested. We are all familiar with the child who, when told to do something, says "I won't," but when her parents say, "All right, then, don't," the child goes ahead and does what was requested. This kind of "countercontrol," or reactance, also occurs in adults.

The clearest demonstration of reactance is an experiment (Brehm & Sensenig, 1966) in which subjects had a choice of two problems to work on. The problems were essentially identical, but the subjects were told that some people were better at one and some at the other, and therefore the experimenter was giving them their choice. Into this simple situation was introduced the external pressure in the form of a note from another subject who was supposedly making the same choice in another room. In one condition, the note read, "I choose problem A." The other subject was expressing his preference, and this put some pressure on the subject to agree with the choice. In the other condition, the note read, "I think we should both do problem A." With this note, the other subject was not only expressing his preference but also directly trying to influence the subject's choice. Although the external pressure was greater in the second condition, it produced less compliance. In the low-pressure condition over 70 percent of the subjects complied by choosing the problem suggested on the note. In the high-pressure condition only 40 percent of the subjects complied—60 percent of them chose the other problem. Thus, by increasing the pressure on the subjects in such a way that they felt their freedom of choice threatened, reactance was aroused and the amount of compliance actually decreased. This study demonstrated that even when it is possible to exert more external pressure on an individual, it may not always produce the optimal amount of influence. It may sometimes boomerang and result in less influence than would milder pressure.

This effect has been shown in a variety of situations. It seems to work with both behavior and attitudes. Thus, although increasing the amount of external pressure is usually an effective way of increasing compliance, there are many situations in which it is necessary to find other ways of doing so. When the possible amount of external pressure would produce less compliance than desired, when increasing the pressure would arouse reactance and therefore decrease compliance, or when it is important to produce the desired behavior with little or no obvious pressure in order to maximize its subsequent effect (such as in attitude-discrepant behavior, discussed in Chapter 11), it is important to look for factors other than external pressure that affect the amount of compliance. It is these other factors that we shall deal with now.

OTHER FACTORS IN COMPLIANCE

In order to make an individual more likely to comply with a request rather than increasing external pressure on him, it is possible to expose him to some experience or situation that would have the same effect. Ordinarily such an experience would occur before the request was made (instead of at the same time), but it would increase subsequent compliance.

**The Foot-
In-the-Door
Technique**

Sometimes one's goal is to get someone to agree to a large request that most people ordinarily would not accept. One way of increasing compliance in such cases is to induce the person to agree first to a much smaller request. Once she has agreed to the small action, she is more likely to agree to the larger one.

This **foot-in-the-door technique** is employed explicitly or implicitly by many propaganda and advertising campaigns. Advertisers often concentrate on getting the consumer to do something, anything connected with their product—even sending back a card saying they do not want it.

Drawing by Charles Schulz; © *1957 United Feature Syndicate, Inc.*

The advertisers apparently think that any act connected with the product increases the likelihood that the consumer will buy it in the future.

A study by Freedman and Fraser (1966) demonstrated this effect. Experimenters went from door to door and told housewives they were working for the Committee for Safe Driving. They said they wished to enlist the women's support for this campaign and asked them to sign a petition, which was to be sent to that state's senators. The petition requested the senators to work for legislation to encourage safe driving. Almost all the women contacted agreed to sign. Several weeks later, different experimenters contacted these same women and also others who had not been approached before. At this time, all the women were asked to put in their front yards a large, unattractive sign, which said "Drive Carefully." The results were striking. Over 55 percent of the women who had previously agreed to sign the petition (a small request) also agreed to post the sign, whereas less than 17 percent of the other women agreed. Getting the women to agree to the initial small request more than tripled the amount of compliance to the large request. This effect was replicated in studies by Pliner, Heather, Kohl, and Saari (1974), and in a somewhat different setting by Snyder and Cunningham (1975). Moreover, Seligman, Bush, and Kirsch (1975) showed that the larger the first request, the greater the effect.

Why this technique has such a strong effect is not entirely clear. The most likely explanation is that people who agree to a small request get involved and committed to either the issue itself, the behavior they perform, or perhaps simply the idea of taking some kind of action. Any of these involvements would probably make someone more likely to comply with future requests.

Another explanation might be that in some way the individual's self-image changes. In the safe-driving experiment, for example, a woman may have initially thought of herself as the kind of person who does not take social action, who does not sign petitions, who does not post signs,

---

BOX 9-3
THE "LOW-BALL" PROCEDURE

The foot-in-the-door effect consists of first making a small request and then sometime later following it up with a larger request. This tends to produce greater compliance with the second, larger request than if only the larger request is made. A somewhat similar technique, called the low-ball procedure (Cialdini, Cacioppo, & Bassett, 1978), also increases compliance, though probably for quite different reasons. The low-ball procedure consists of first getting compliance to a small request and then immediately increasing the size of the request. For example, you might first ask someone to help you carry a small suitcase up the stairs, and when the other agrees, you might say, "Oh, I didn't mean that small case, I meant this trunk. You don't mind, do you?" The other never actually complies with the small request. Instead, the larger request is substituted for the small one, and often the person agrees.

Although the explanation for this effect is not entirely clear, it seems to involve the difficulty people have in rejecting a request once they have complied with it. Even though the request has actually changed somewhat, the person has agreed and has more difficulty backing out of it than if he were presented with the large request in the first place. For example, when asked to carry the big trunk, he could say that he was very busy or that he did not like moving, or he could offer any number of explanations of why he could not help. Once he has agreed to carry the suitcase, however, most of these explanations no longer work. He could still say that he had a bad back, but obviously he does have the time and does not hate moving (since he has already agreed to give the time and energy for moving the small case). In a sense, he is trapped. He has been tricked into doing something he might not do if he were asked directly. In contrast, the foot-in-the-door procedure involves no trick, but merely two straightforward requests. Apparently, the person agrees to the second request not because he feels trapped, but because his self-image has changed or because he enjoyed giving help the first time.

or, perhaps, who does not even agree to things that are asked her by someone at the door. Once she had agreed to the small request, which was actually difficult to refuse, she may have changed her perception of herself slightly. Since she agreed to sign a petition, perhaps, after all, she is the kind of person who does this sort of thing. Then, when the second request was made, she was more likely to comply than she would have been otherwise. Thus, performing the first action changes individuals' attitude toward either themselves or the action itself. In either case, this change makes them less resistant to performing a similar act in the future, even when the second request entails a much more extensive commitment. Some indirect support for this explanation is provided in one study (Zuckerman, Lazzaro & Waldgeir, 1979) in which giving money for complying with the first request eliminated the effect. Supposedly the money provided an external reason for compliance and the person had no need to change his self-image. This is consistent with the overjustification effect described in Box 9–2 and with the self-perception explanation of the foot-in-the-door effect.

We should note that sometimes the opposite technique from the foot-in-the-door also works. Two experiments have demonstrated that asking first for a very large request and then making a smaller one can increase compliance to the small one compared to asking only the small favor. In one study (Cialdini et al., 1975) some subjects were asked to contribute time to a good cause. Some were asked first to give a huge amount of time and when they refused, as almost all did, the experimenter immediately said then perhaps they might agree to a much smaller commitment of time. Other subjects were asked only the smaller request, while a third group was given a choice of the two. Although 16.7 percent in the small-request-only condition and 25 percent in the choice condition agreed, 50 percent who heard the large request first agreed to the smaller one.

This effect would be familiar to anyone who engaged in a bargaining situation with a used car salesman, a union, or management. The tactic is to ask for the moon and settle for less. The more you ask for at first, the more you expect to end up with eventually. Presumably, the idea is that when you reduce your demands the other person thinks you are compromising and the amount seems smaller. In a compliance situation such as asking for charity the same might apply—a quarter doesn't seem much money when the organization initially asked for a hundred dollars.

Clearly, both the foot-in-the-door and the reverse tactic work at times, but we do not yet know which strategy is better nor when each of them will operate. One difference seems to be that the reverse effect has been shown when the smaller request follows the large one immediately and is obviously connected; the foot-in-the-door works even when the two requests are seemingly unconnected.

Labeling

Closely related to the "self-image" explanation of the foot-in-the-door effect is the effect of labeling the individual's behavior. If you reinforce people's image of themselves by providing a verbal name or label, it tends to make them behave consistently with the label you provide. In a study by Kraut (1973), people were asked to contribute to charity and were then labeled either "charitable" or "uncharitable," depending on whether they had contributed. Other subjects were not actually called by the label. Later, they were asked again to contribute. The labels had the effect of making them behave the way they did the first time—those who had given the first time and were labeled charitable gave more than those who were not labeled; and those who had not given and were labeled uncharitable gave less than if they had not been labeled.

On the other hand, providing an inappropriate label may make people try to compensate for the label by behaving differently from what would be expected. Steele (1975) called people on the phone and said that it was common knowledge that they were (or were not) involved in the community or said something negative that was irrelevant to the community. He then asked them to help form a food cooperative for the community. As you can see in Figure 9–7, the labels (or as he termed it, "name calling") increased compliance compared to using no label at all. But the negative labels produced even more compliance than the positive one, presumably because the subjects felt that the label was unfair and they wanted to show that they were community-minded.

In both situations, the label seems to affect the person's image. Sometimes a label can solidify that image and make the person behave consistently with it; other times, the label can make the person worry about her image and try to do something to make it better. When we combine this research with that on the foot-in-the-door, it appears that cognitive elements, and especially what the person thinks of herself, play an important role in compliance.

FIGURE 9–7 Any kind of label increased compliance, but a negative label, especially an irrelevant one, increased it the most. (Based on Steele, 1975.)

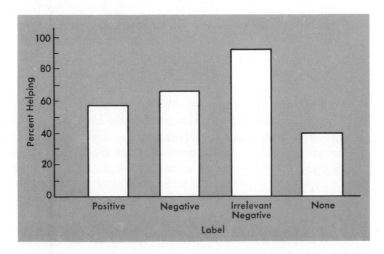

Motive Arousal People comply or obey for a variety of reasons. They are afraid of the consequences if they do not comply, they are seeking rewards if they do, they feel internal obligations that cause them to comply, and so on. In any situation, some of these reasons are stronger than others. Whether or not compliance occurs depends to some extent on whether the situation makes relevant the particular concern that at that moment is important to the individual. If the person is primarily worried about being punished, for example, a situation that involves the threat of punishment should be more effective in evoking compliance than a situation involving only rewards. Conversely, someone who is unconcerned about punishment but desirous of rewards would comply most in a potentially rewarding situation. This is analogous to the operation of other drives. If someone is hungry, food is a good incentive; if he is thirsty, water is better than food; and so on.

In a study by Carlsmith, Lepper, and Landauer (1969), some children were asked by a threatening adult to pick up 150 tennis balls. Some children picked up all of them, some picked up 40 or 50, and some picked up only a few. Overall, there was a considerable amount of obedience. Other children were asked to perform the same task by a warm, rewarding adult. Again, some of them picked up a lot of balls and some picked up only a few, but the average number of tennis balls picked up was quite high. Both threats and promises are reasonably successful means of inducing obedience.

The situation changed dramatically when some of the children were frightened and some were not. In the former condition, children had just watched a frightening movie, while the others had watched a happy, lighthearted movie. The frightened group should have been particularly concerned about being punished, about negative things happening to them. These concerns would be especially strong when the adult was someone whom they knew might punish them if they disobeyed him. If he asked them to pick up the tennis balls, they should obey him more (from fear of being punished) than someone whom they knew was a nice, rewarding person. In contrast, the children who had watched the happy movie should be relatively unconcerned about negative outcomes and more concerned about positive ones. The threatening adults should not impress them because they were not frightened. Instead, they would respond more to the nice adult because he would give them what they want—rewards. As may be seen in Table 9–3, this is what happened. The frightened children obeyed the stern, punishing adult more than the warm, rewarding adult, whereas the children who were not frightened obeyed the warm adult. This result was repeated by Lepper (1970) using a somewhat different situation. He found that subjects who were made anxious responded more strongly to punishment than to positive reinforcements while less anxious subjects showed the opposite preference, responding more strongly to positive reinforcements than to punishment.

TABLE 9–3

Motive Arousal and Compliance

MOVIE	STERN	WARM
Scary	108.5[a]	62.4
Happy	69.9	99.8

[a] Entries are the number of tennis balls picked up.

Source: Adapted from Carlsmith, Lepper, and Landauer (1969).

SUMMARY

1. Performing an act because everyone else performs it is called conformity. Performing an act when someone asks you to even though you would rather not perform it is called compliance.

2. Conformity is often adaptive because it is necessary to get along with others and also because other people's actions may give you information about the best way to act in a particular circumstance.

3. In controlled situations, when neither of the above considerations were relevant, there was still a great deal of conformity—about 35 percent in the Asch judgment experiments.

4. People conform because they use the information they get from others, because they trust others, because they are afraid of being deviant.

5. When the rest of the group is not unanimous, conformity drops sharply.

6. Other factors producing greater conformity are larger groups, expertise of the group, and a lack of confidence by the individual. Greater commitment to an initial position reduces conformity.

7. Compliance and obedience can be increased by the use of rewards, punishments, threats, and pressures from the situation. However, too much external pressure can backfire and produce reactance, a tendency to resist limitations on one's freedom of action that causes the individual to do the opposite of what is requested.

8. Compliance can be increased by first asking a small request and then a large one—the foot-in-the-door effect. Under some conditions, the reverse also increases compliance—a very large request followed by a small one.

SUGGESTIONS FOR ADDITIONAL READING

Asch, S. E. Effects of group pressure upon the modification and distortion of judgements. In H. Guetskow (ed.), *Groups, leadership, and men.* Pittsburgh: Carnegie Press, 1951. The classic study, still well worth reading.

Freedman, J. L., & Doob, A. N. *Deviancy.* New York: Academic Press, 1968. An experimental study of the effects of feeling and seeming deviant.

Milgram, S. Behavioral study of obedience. *Journal of Abnormal and Social Psychology,* 1963, 67, 371–78. A provocative experiment, though just what it means is certainly in question.

Attitudes and Attitude Change 10

If you want peace, prepare for war. Marc Anderson; Prentice-Hall, Inc.

What makes someone a Republican or a Democrat, a conservative or a liberal, a Protestant or a Catholic? Why are some people anti-Semitic, others antiblack, and still others not prejudiced at all? Why do people decide that one toothpaste is best or that drugs are horrible? What determines whether or not someone will change her mind about toothpastes or drugs? If someone is a Republican, how can we convince him to vote for a Democrat? Conversely, how can we prepare someone to meet an attack on her opinions so she will be able to resist the attack? These questions form the basis for the extensive work on attitude formation and change, which in a sense has been the central core of social psychology in the United States for many years.

In 1937, in the first textbook mainly devoted to experimental studies in social psychology, Murphy, Murphy, and Newcomb wrote: "Perhaps no single concept within the whole realm of social psychology occupies a more nearly central position than that of attitudes" (p. 889). Although interest in this problem has probably declined somewhat in recent years, social psychologists have devoted more time in the past forty years or so to the study of attitude formation and change than to any other topic. This is due, in part, to the great interest in interpersonal influence, since attitude change is one of the forms this influence takes. It is also due to an increasing emphasis on cognitive development and cognition in general. The work on attitudes therefore reflects both major concerns of social psychologists. By concentrating on how attitudes are developed and changed, we can gain insight into the process of social influence and cognitive structure and how these two phenomena affect behavior.

DEFINITION OF ATTITUDES

Each of the traditional definitions of **attitudes** contains a slightly different conception of what an attitude is or emphasizes a somewhat different aspect of it. G. W. Allport (1935) proposed that "an attitude is a mental and neural state of readiness, organized through experience, exerting a directive or dynamic influence upon the individual's response to all objects and situations with which it is related" (p. 810). He saw an attitude primarily as a set to respond in a particular way, and he emphasized its behavioral implications. Because this definition was much influenced by learning tradition, it also emphasized how past experience forms a person's attitudes.

In contrast, Krech and Crutchfield (1948, p. 152) defined an attitude as "an enduring organization of motivational, emotional, perceptual, and cognitive processes with respect to some aspect of the individual's world." This definition reflected their commitment to a cognitive, Gestalt perspective. Notice that it omits any reference to the origins of the attitude and is concerned only with the person's current subjective experience. Note also that it emphasizes organization; it views the person as a thoughtful and actively structuring organism. The person does not simply passively reflect his or her world. And finally, note there is no mention of overt behavior. The cognitive tradition emphasizes the person's subjective experience and is less concerned with how a person acts.

Today a third definition is more common. An attitude toward any given object, idea, or person is an enduring system with a *cognitive* component, an *affective* component, and a *behavioral* tendency. The cognitive component consists of beliefs about the attitude object; the affective component consists of the emotional feelings connected with the beliefs; and the behavioral tendency is what Allport referred to as the readiness to respond in a particular way. For example, a student's attitude toward Robert Redford might include the knowledge that he is a man, blond and blue-eyed, very handsome, an actor, and a good skier; feelings of attraction and liking; and the behavioral tendency to see all his movies. This is the definition that most social psychologists today seem moderately content with and the one we shall use throughout our discussion.

Before considering the definition of attitudes in more detail, it is important to distinguish between attitudes and *facts*. Although it is difficult to draw a sharp dividing line between the two, the main distinguishing characteristic of attitudes is that they involve an evaluative or emotional component. A scientist believes that it is 252,710 miles to the moon or that human beings have forty-six chromosomes. He also has a complex collection of other facts about the moon and chromosomes. But under most circumstances, he does not have any emotional feelings toward either—he does not think that the moon is good or bad, he does not like or dislike chromosomes. In contrast, he has a collection of facts about Robert Redford or poison gas, but he also *does* have emotional feelings about these.

Attitudes have a behavioral component although not every husband who feels mistreated will express it in such a dramatic fashion.

We distinguish facts from attitudes mainly by the presence or absence of an evaluative component.

As a result, facts and attitudes function differently. The crucial difference is that attitudes, once established, are much more resistant to change than are beliefs in "facts." The scientist who believes that humans have forty-six chromosomes in most cases has no strong commitment to that belief or strong feelings about it one way or the other. Not so many years ago, scientists were convinced that humans had twenty-four chromosomes. Then somebody discovered that there were forty-six. Those who originally believed we had twenty-four chromosomes probably changed their opinion quite readily when they saw the evidence. Certainly high school and college biology students, who were in no way involved in the controversy, changed their "knowledge" almost instantaneously. Unless someone was involved with the research, he had no reason not to change his mind when the new research results appeared.

This is different from the way people react when their attitudes are concerned. As we shall see, attitudes more often are highly resistant to change, do not generally respond to a few new facts, and are more complicated in this respect than facts. People do not change their attitudes without putting up a fight and being exposed to a considerable amount of pressure. The presence of the evaluative component seems to change the dynamics considerably; it makes the attitude-change process much more difficult.

Cognitive Complexity

Thus we conceive of an attitude as a collection of thoughts, beliefs, and knowledge (cognitive component), and as including positive and negative evaluations or feelings (affective component), all relating to and describing a central theme or object—the attitude object. This knowledge and feeling cluster tends to produce certain behaviors. Figure 10–2, which is a schematic representation of a hypothetical person's attitude toward smoking cigarettes, is one example.

Around the central object are clustered the cognitions related to it in the person's mind. These cognitions describe the object and its relations to other objects. The relations can be many and varied. The surrounding cognitions may be simple descriptions or characteristics of the core object—in our example, cigarettes are smoky, taste of nicotine, and are expensive. Or, they may involve causal links to the core object cigarettes are likely to cause lung cancer and heart disease, they cut down on your wind, they offend people in elevators, they relax you in a social situation or when studying, your parents don't like them but your roommate does, and so on. In Figure 10–2, the causal links to other objects are indicated with a line, and the sign by the line indicates whether it is a positive or a negative relationship. Cigarettes *are* dangerous (the person thinks), they *help* reduce discomfort, and they *facilitate* studying. These are all positive links. On the other hand, her parents *do not* approve of them. That is a negative link.

For simplicity we have shown only a few of the multitude of cognitions that an individual could have regarding cigarettes. And a number of other factors are not included in the structure. For example, each cognition can vary in importance (e.g., the fact that cigarettes are expensive is probably less important than the fact that they are dangerous). The picture can get quite complex and include a great many cognitions that vary in the nature of their relationship to the core and in their evaluative component. So this picture is an oversimplification of attitudes in real life. For

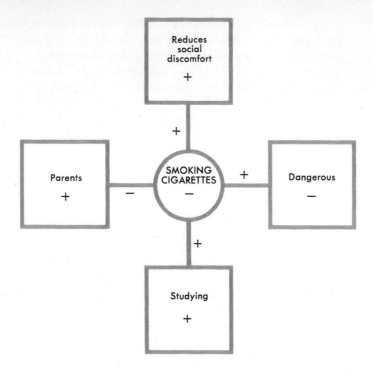

FIGURE 10-2 Schematic representation of an attitude toward smoking cigarettes. The core object is surrounded by a cluster of cognitions, which are all related to it. The individual's overall evaluation of smoking cigarettes is determined in part by its relationship to the separate items in the cluster.

example, just think of the Pandora's box opened up by the fact that these cognitions are related to one another and to many others, rather than existing in a vacuum. The thought that cigarettes help studying is meaningful only when an attitude toward studying is considered. And then attitudes toward studying can bring in attitudes toward parents, teachers, a future career, and so on. So the real cluster would contain all the person's thoughts in connection with cigarettes.

Evaluative Simplicity

Next, there is the **affective,** or evaluative, **component.** Many of the separate cognitive elements themselves have positive or negative feelings connected to them, and the central object does too. In Figure 10-2 positive and negative evaluations of the elements and central object are indicated by plus and minus signs, respectively. The individual has a strong negative evaluation of cigarettes. She dislikes and is afraid of them. This is shown in the diagram by the minus sign in the central circle. The evaluations of the related objects are shown in the boxes. The person likes her parents, likes to have social discomfort reduced, and likes studying to go easier. But she does not like danger.

Most attitudes tend to be as evaluatively simple as they are cognitively complex. Even in thinking about Robert Redford, most people most of the time do not consider all the things they know about him. They do not remember many details of his movies or his personal life; rather, they simply have a positive attitude, consisting mainly of feeling attracted to him. Or in thinking about hard core drugs, most police officers do not think of the scientific facts they once were told, or the preaching against drugs in childhood. Rather, the drugs are illegal, and the people they see on drugs are pathetic and abhorrent, so they simply hate drugs. The multitude of cognitions exists in their minds and may have some influence on them, but by and large, their attitude, particularly the evaluative component, is less complex.

There have been many demonstrations of the evaluative simplicity of most attitudes. At the everyday level of interpersonal relations, this simplicity can be seen in person perceptions, as described in Chapter 4. Our impressions of other people quickly tend to become evaluatively consistent. No matter how much we know about them, we tend generally to like them or to dislike them. They may have a few qualities that do not fit into our overall evaluation of them, but our impressions tend mostly to be consistent.

At the more remote level of attitudes about public affairs, people have less information, and in many areas their attitudes are not highly interrelated (Sears, 1969). But on the most important issues, their attitudes are strikingly consistent even when the manifest content covers quite a broad range. On racial issues, for example, white Americans tend to have highly interrelated attitudes. If they are opposed to government action to promote school integration, they are also likely to be opposed to civil rights demonstrations, affirmative action programs, busing of school children for integration, and so on.

Finally, Anderson and Hubert (1963), among others, have shown that attitude change can persist long after the content that produced it is forgotten, the affective component being more durable and central than the cognitive component. And while the structure of an attitude is complex, one important part of it—the part consisting of affects or feelings—is often very simple.

This evaluative simplicity, even in cases of considerable cognitive complexity, is extremely important. For example, both police officers and drug users know a great deal about drugs, have much complex information on them, and understand a variety of interrelationships between drugs and other aspects of the world. And each of these pieces of information to some extent influences their general feelings toward drugs and has a substantial effect on their behavior. Knowing what drugs look like, how much they cost, where they can be obtained, the difference among various kinds, and so on, affects the activities of both the users and the narcotics squad. Nevertheless, the relatively simple evaluative component of the attitude is the major determinant of behavior. Although the details of users' and police officers' behavior toward drugs is influenced by the knowledge they have, the general direction of their behavior is influenced primarily by their overall evaluation—whether they consider drugs to be positive or negative.

Thus, two facets of attitudes must be kept in mind. First is the evaluative simplicity, even in the presence of cognitive complexity. Second is the interrelationship of all elements of the attitude; each element can affect the total attitude and every other element.

THEORETICAL FRAMEWORKS

Now that we have a general view of an attitude, we can consider the theoretical frameworks within which attitudes have been studied. As with other areas of social psychology, the main theoretical approaches outlined in chapter 1 have been applied in one form or another to research on attitudes. The conditioning approach sees attitudes as habits, similar to anything else that is learned; principles that apply to other forms of learning also determine the formation of attitudes. The incentive theory holds that a person adopts the attitude that maximizes his or her gains. Each side of an issue has its costs and benefits, and the individual will adopt the side on which the net gains are greater. Finally, the Gestalt approach, as reflected in cognitive consistency theory, asserts that people seek harmony and consistency in their attitudes, and between their attitudes and their behavior. It particularly emphasizes acceptance of attitudes that fit into the person's overall cognitive structure. These approaches are not necessarily contradictory or inconsistent. They represent different theoretical orientations and differ primarily in the factors they emphasize when explaining attitude formation and change.

Conditioning and Reinforcement

The conditioning and reinforcement model is most closely associated with Carl Hovland and others at Yale University. The basic assumption behind this approach is that attitudes are learned in much the same way as other habits. Just as people acquire information and facts, they also learn the feelings and values associated with these facts. A child learns that a certain animal is a dog, that dogs are friends, that they are good; finally, he learns to like dogs. And he learns this attitude through the same processes and mechanisms that control other kinds of learning.

This means that the basic processes by which learning occurs should apply to the formation of attitudes. In developing an attitude, the individual acquires information and feelings by the processes of *association, reinforcement,* and *imitation.* Associations are formed when stimuli appear at the same time and in the same place. If a police chief, a parent, or a television reporter shows us a dirty, broken-down man and says the word *drug*, we form an association between the negative image and the word. Conversely, we may be exposed to positive things that can become associated with drugs: a friend says they are good, or we see a movie in which someone on drugs seems to be having a pleasurable time.

Learning the chracteristics of an object, a person, or an idea is obviously an important aspect of developing an attitude. Although the studies described in the chapters on person perception and liking were conducted in a somewhat different context, many of them illustrate this effect. For example, Norman Anderson conducted experiments in which he listed a number of attributes of a person and then asked subjects to state their impression of that person. As you will remember from Chapter 4, the subject's final attitude was roughly an average of the listed characteristics (warm, friendly, intelligent, ambitious, courageous, and so on). Having learned the characteristics, the subjects, in a sense, also learned an attitude.

This process applies to things as well as to people. Individuals learn the characteristics of a house, a country, an idea, a bill pending before Congress, or anything else. An attitude consists of that knowledge plus some evaluative component based in part on that knowledge and in part on other factors (which we shall discuss later). The simplest factor in attitude formation is thus the association between the object and other words or qualities.

Learning also occurs through reinforcement. If one takes a drug and has a pleasant experience, the act of taking the drug is reinforced and one will be more likely to take the drug in the future. Similarly, if you say "Drugs are great" and someone else applauds you for making the statement, positive attitudes toward drugs are reinforced.

Finally, attitudes can be learned through imitation. People imitate the behavior of others, particularly if those others are strong, important people. As we shall discuss below, they often find they have learned contradictory values from different people and are under great stress to resolve the conflicts. As you know, many students find college confronts them with ideas and values different from those they had previously learned from their families.

Association, reinforcement, and imitation are the major mechanisms in the learning of attitudes. As a result, learning theories have dominated the research on the *acquisition* of attitudes. The learning approach to attitudes is relatively simple: it views people as primarily passive. They are exposed to stimuli, they learn by means of one of learning processes or another, and this learning determines the attitude in question. The final attitude contains all the associations, values, and other bits of information the individual has accumulated. A person's ultimate evaluation of, say, drugs depends on the number and strength of the positive and negative elements previously learned.

**Incentives
and Conflict**

The theory based on incentives and conflict views the attitude situation in terms of an approach-avoidance conflict. The individual has certain reasons for accepting one position and other reasons for rejecting it and accepting the opposite position. He thinks drugs are dangerous; he knows they are illegal; and he wants to finish college and get into law school. These considerations produce a negative attitude. However, he believes drugs are exciting, and he knows many of his friends take them. These considerations tend to give him a positive attitude. According to the incentive theory, the relative strength of these incentives determine his attitude. If his initial attitude were negative, it would become more positive only if there were greater incentive for taking this new position than for maintaining the original one.

This view is similar to the learning approach in that the attitude is determined more or less by a sum of the positive and negative elements. The difference is that the incentive theory emphasizes what the individual has to gain or lose by taking a particular position. Whether or not his friends would like him, how enjoyable the experience is, etc. are the critical considerations. When there are conflicting goals, the individual adopts the position that maximizes his gains. It differs from the conditioning approach in that it ignores the origins of the attitude and treats people more as deliberate, calculating, active decision makers, and less as passive reflectors of the environment.

A common version of incentive theory is the *expectancy-value* approach (Edwards, 1954). This approach assumes that in making decisions, people try to maximize subjective utility. The subjective utility of a decision alternative is the product of (1) the value of a particular outcome times (2) the probability that this alternative will produce that outcome. Suppose a person is trying to make up her mind about a proposed law banning homosexuals from teaching school in her city. One of her strong positive values is allowing people to choose their own sexual life styles, and she perceives the law as interfering with that. This gives her strong negative incentives about the law, pushing her away from it. A second value she has is of letting children go through school with the "right" influences on their sexual development. But she does not see the law as being likely to promote this because she thinks gay teachers do not try to turn children into gays, any more than spinster teachers try to discourage them from marriage. This second expectancy-value combination, then, gives her only a weak positive incentive for voting for the law. Hence, on balance, she votes against the law.

Incentive theories tend to depict people as rational and calculating. People are described as adopting positions that are best for them. Even the so-called irrational incentives served by attitudes turn out to benefit the person; they make the person feel better. So while incentive theories of the expectancy-value sort have helped to predict attitude change and have provided normative guidelines for the attitudes people rationally "should" have, they tend to overestimate how thoughtful and deliberate people are.

Cognitive Consistency

The major framework for studying attitudes is **cognitive consistency** theory. Actually, there are a number of somewhat similar theories associated with Lewin, Heider, Abelson, Festinger, Osgood, and others. The theories differ in some important respects, but the basic notion behind them is the same. They begin with the assumption that people seek consistency among their cognitions. An individual who has several beliefs or values that are inconsistent with one another strives to make them more consistent. Similarly, if his cognitions are consistent and he is faced with a new cognition that would produce inconsistency, he strives to minimize the inconsistency. The cognitive consistency theories grow out of the Gestalt tradition; they depict people as striving for coherence and meaningfulness in their cognitive structures.

BALANCE THEORY There are basically three variants on the cognitive consistency idea; these variants specify consistency pressures between different components of attitudes. The first is **balance theory,**

which involves consistency pressures among certain evaluations or *affects* within a simple cognitive system (Heider, 1958). As indicated in Chapter 6, such a system consists of two objects (one of which is often another person), the relationships between them, and an individual's evaluations of them. There are three evaluations: the individual's evaluation of each of the objects and of the relationship of the objects to each other. The system is balanced only when either one or three of these relationships is positive. That is, a balanced system is one in which you agree with a liked person or disagree with a disliked person. Imbalance exists when you disagree with a liked person or agree with a disliked person. If Joe loves Susan, but she smokes cigarettes and he hates cigarette smoke, the triad is unbalanced (one negative).

According to balance theory, imbalance creates a pressure to change in order to restore a state of balance. Change can occur in different ways, which we will discuss more later on. Here it is enough to say that balance theory uses a *least effort* principle to predict the effects of imbalance. People will change as few affective relations as they can, and still produce a balanced structure. So our friend Joe may decide to put up with cigarette smoke, perhaps deciding it is not so bad after all; or he may diminish his affection for Susan; or he may try to persuade her to give them up. Each would involve only one change. But he will probably not change his mind about cigarettes *and* persuade her to stop smoking *and* give her up, even though that would also create balance. The less effortful change is preferred.

Research on balance theory has generally supported these predictions: people do adjust imbalanced systems toward balance, and in ways that minimize the number of changes that must be made. One qualification is, however, that balance pressures seem to be much weaker when you dislike the other person than when you like him or her. Newcomb (1968) calls such situations "nonbalanced," rather than "imbalanced." His idea is that we simply do not care very much whether we agree or disagree with someone we dislike; we just cut off the relationship and forget about the whole thing.

Aside from this, perhaps the main value of this research is that it describes the notion of cognitive consistency in extremely simple terms and provides a convenient way of conceptualizing attitudes. The balance model makes it clear that in a given situation there are many ways to resolve an inconsistency. It focuses our attention on one of the most important aspects of attitude change—the factors that determine which of the various modes of resolution are adopted.

AFFECT-COGNITION CONSISTENCY A second version of the consistency approach is that people also try to make their cognitions consistent with their *affects.* That is, our beliefs, our "knowledge," our convictions about the facts of the matter are determined in part by our affective preferences. Not only would a National Rifle Association enthusiast *like* a new governor less if he supported gun control, but the enthusiast will come to have different *beliefs* about the man; he may think of the governor as being gullible, soft, wishy-washy, not very bright, a liberal, a man who doesn't pay much attention to the genuine needs of his constituents, and so on. In other words, the enthusiast changes his cognitions to make them consistent with his affective preferences.

Rosenberg (1960) provided a striking demonstration of the cognitive changes created by a change in affect toward an attitude object. He obtained from white subjects a comprehensive description of their attitudes toward blacks, racial integration, and the whole question of relations between blacks and whites. He then hypnotized the subjects and told them that their attitude toward blacks moving into their community was the opposite of what it had previously been. If the subject had previously been strongly against integrated housing, he was told that he now was in favor of it (or vice versa). That is, Rosenberg changed the subject's affect toward integrated housing. And the important point is that the affective change occurred without supplying any new cognitions or changing any old ones, since it was done by hypnotic induction. The subjects were then awakened from their hypnotic trance and questioned about their current attitudes about blacks and integration.

Rosenberg found that the change he had produced under hypnosis in this one affect was followed by many dramatic reversals in the subjects' cognitions relevant to integration. They came to believe housing integration was necessary to remove racial inequality, that it was necessary to maintain racial harmony, that it was the only fair thing to do, and so on. Thus, these ramifying cognitive changes tended to reduce the imbalance that had resulted from the induced affective change. As the theories of cognitive consistency would predict, the pressures toward reducing inconsistency resulted in a variety of cognitive changes.

DISSONANCE THEORY A third implication of cognitive consistency theory is that *attitudes* will change in order to maintain consistency with overt *behavior*. The main formal theory here is cognitive dissonance theory, first proposed by Leon Festinger in 1957. As originally proposed, dissonance theory focused upon two principal sources of belief-behavior inconsistency: the effects of making decisions, and the effects of engaging in counterattitudinal behavior. Such inconsistencies produce cognitive dissonance, which may be reduced in a number of different ways, the most interesting of which is to change attitudes so they are no longer inconsistent with behavior. We will not discuss this theory further here, because the next chapter will spell out its predictions and describe some of the ingenious research it has led to.

Attribution theory has also been applied to belief-behavior inconsistencies. Conventionally, psychologists have assumed that people determine their own attitudes by reviewing the various cognitions and affects in their consciousness, then expressing the result. However, Bem (1965) has argued that people know their own attitudes not by inspecting their insides, but by inferring them from their own external behavior and their perceptions of the situation. In other words, people infer their own attitudes in the same way that they infer other people's attitudes: by inspecting whatever external cues are available, and then making the appropriate attribution. The implication is that changing behavior may lead to the person's inferring that his own attitudes have changed. If I suddenly find myself studying my biochemistry every night, I infer I must really like it (as long as an internal attribution is made!). We shall also discuss research related to this idea in the next chapter. For the moment, the important point is that even attitudes, which are usually considered to be internally determined, may to some extent be affected by attributions based on overt behavior.

The other theories of attitude change described it as resulting from quite a different type of situation. In those cases, communication from other people produces attitude change, whether by association, incentives, or increasing consistency, or whatever. These communications can occur in the mass media, such as when the president speaks on television, or in a direct interpersonal exchange, such as when your boyfriend tries to persuade you that smoking really is bad for your health. In contrast, the dissonance and attribution approaches describe your attitudes as changing because of your own behavior (regardless of whether the process is best described by dissonance or attribution theory). These two types of situations are sufficiently different that they need to be taken up separately. So attitude change resulting from communication is covered in the remainder of this chapter, and attitude change resulting from one's own behavior will be discussed in the next chapter.

A MODEL OF PERSUASION

In 1959, Carl Hovland and Irving Janis suggested a useful model of attitude change based on communication. Figure 10–3 presents a model based largely on theirs but simplified and changed to bring it more in line with recent work in this area. It begins with what Hovland called the "observable persuasion stimuli." There must be a *communicator* who holds a particular position on some issue and is trying to convince others to hold this position. To do so, he produces a *communication* designed to persuade people that his position is correct and to induce them to change their own positions in the direction of his. This communication is presented in a given *situation*. These, then, constitute the attack—the source, the communication, and the surroundings.

In the typical attitude-change situation, individuals are confronted with a communication in favor of a position different from the one they hold. They may have a negative attitude toward marijuana and someone tells them that it is really very good; they may be Democrats listening to a

FIGURE 10-3 Model of the attitude-change situation, showing examples of important factors at each stage. The amount of attitude change that occurs is determined by variables at each point in the process.

Republican campaign speech; they may be smokers reading the Surgeon General's report on cigarette smoking and cancer. Under these circumstances, stress is produced by the discrepancy between the individual's attitude and the attitude expressed in the communication. This stress has been called conflict, imbalance, or just inconsistency. Whichever we choose, there is general agreement that the individual feels pressured to resolve the discrepancy.

HOW THE TARGET RESISTS PERSUASION

When people are confronted with a discrepant communication, they generally want to resist its influence. People do not like to admit being influenced by others. In some research studies, subjects have been told that the point of the experiment is to persuade them, while others have been told that the experiment deals with something else entirely (such as testing for reading comprehension). Presenting the theme of the experiment as persuasion generally increases the subject's resistance to change (Kiesler & Kiesler, 1964; Watts & Holt, 1979). As an everyday example, college students often feel pressured to assert their political independence from their parents when it is questioned, even though their political attitudes usually are fairly similar.

Just *why* people want to resist being influenced is open to question. It might be reactance (Brehm, 1966), as discussed in Chapter 9. People turn stubborn when their freedom is threatened, and overt attempts to influence them may make them rebel in this way. People may also resist out of laziness; the principle of least effort makes them want to change as little as possible. Or perhaps their resistance is due more to a desire to "save face"; they just do not want to give the appearance of being easy to influence. At least under some circumstances people seem to feel that being

This determined effort to appear independent of influence is particularly characteristic of late adolescents who are striving to become independent of their parents. It shows up in many areas of life, and probably most often reflects a desire to *appear* independent rather than an active rebellion and repudiation of parental values, though of course we all know dramatic cases of rebellion. The need to appear independent was demonstrated in a simple way by Willick and Ashley (1971). They began with the familiar observation that adolescents normally reflect the political party preference of their parents (see Jennings & Niemi, 1974). They then asked students both their own party preference and those of their parents. But some had to give their own preference first, and others had to give their parents' first. They found that 62 percent differed from their parents when the parents' preference was measured first, and only 31 percent did when their own was given first. Presumably giving the parents' preference first set up pressures to assert independence from them. A student who says "My father's a Democrat" would want to add quickly, "but *I'm* an Independent." But if he first said, "*I'm* a Democrat," then it's all right to add, "And so's my Dad, probably (I don't really know or care what *he* thinks; I know what *I* think)."

influenced makes them look bad. Presumably there are occasions when it is appropriate to be influenced and foolish to resist it—when you are in a survival training course and learning what foods are poisonous, for example. But for most persuasion situations, people seem to be motivated to resist influence. So the real question is how they resist.

As we have indicated, a communication causes stress in the recipient when it is discrepant from the recipient's original position. If the recipient changes his attitude, reducing this discrepancy, then the stress ought to be reduced also. And indeed most research on attitudes has concentrated on this mechanism for reducing the stress; i.e., attitude change. People have a variety of ways of resolving the stress. The emphasis on so-called alternative modes of resolution is one of the important contributions of Carl Hovland's model of attitude change and of the cognitive consistency models.

One major problem for the communicator is to maximize the likelihood that targets will choose attitude change as their mode of resolution and to minimize or eliminate the use of alternative modes of resolution. Therefore, one of the critical factors in any attitude-change situation is whether or not alternative modes of resolution are present and, if they are, the extent to which they are used. Before discussing atittude change in detail, we shall describe briefly the most important alternative mechanisms the individual can use. That is, we need to consider how the person can resist persuasion and still reduce the stress created by a discrepant communication.

Generally speaking, there are two classes of resistance mechanisms. There are the mechanisms that follow from the simple consistency theories and involve changes in the evaluations of the communication, attitude, source, or perception of source's position. The other class of mechanisms follows broadly from incentive theories and involves more rational consideration of the arguments.

Consistency Mechanisms

BLANKET REJECTION A discrepant communication is inconsistent with one's prior attitude, so the most primitive (and perhaps most common) mode of resolution is simply to reject the communication point blank. Rather than refuting the arguments on logical grounds or weakening them by attacking their source, individuals often simply reject arguments for no apparent reason. A typical response by a smoker to a well-reasoned, logical attack on cigarette smoking is to say that the arguments are not good enough to make her stop. She does not answer them; she just does not accept them. When someone who believes in capital punishment is shown overwhelming evidence that it does not deter homicide, he tends to be unconvinced. He shrugs off the evidence, says he does not believe it, and continues to maintain his position. It often takes more than a good argument to convince people of something. Much of the time they respond in an illogical, nonrational manner to discrepant communications. They merely say "No, that's not right." We do not understand this mechanism very well but it is often employed in attitude-change situations.

DEROGATING THE SOURCE Someone who is faced with a discrepant communication can reduce the stress by deciding that the source of the communication is unreliable or negative in some other way. If we look at the balance model described earlier, we can see that there is nothing inconsistent about disagreeing with a negative source. In fact, people expect to disagree with a negative source. Thus, by deciding that the source is negative or the information unreliable, they can balance the system and remove all stress.

Such an attack on the source of a communication is common in politics, informal debates, courtroom trials, and partially every kind of adversary proceeding. The defense attorney in a trial tries to discredit the damaging witness when she cannot rebut his evidence. The politician calls his opponent a communist or a fascist or some other negative term when he finds it difficult to argue on the issues themselves.

This device is extremely effective because it not only eliminates the threat from the current argument, but also makes all future arguments from the opponent much less powerful. When an opponent has been discredited, anything he says carries less weight. Thus, attacking the source of the communication is an effective way of reducing the stress produced by a discrepant communication.

DISTORTING THE MESSAGE Another type of resolution is distorting or misperceiving the communication so as to reduce the discrepancy between it and one's own position. The Surgeon General says it is extremely dangerous to smoke because smoking has been shown to be a significant cause of lung cancer. The confirmed smoker reads this message and decides that the Surgeon General is recommending a decrease in smoking but that the evidence on lung cancer is not yet conclusive. The smoker may do this by a gross misperception of the article when he reads it, by distorting the article in his memory, or perhaps by reading only part of the article and reconstructing the rest of it in his own mind. However he accomplishes it, the result is the same—the message becomes considerably less discrepant.

Alternatively, he may exaggerate the extremity of the communication so as to make it ridiculous. Many environmentalists want to slow down the development of undeveloped lands and restrict the building of pollution-causing plants and buildings. Developers and many other businessmen naturally oppose these restrictions. It is fairly common for them to distort the positions taken by environmentalists, claiming they want to prevent the building of *all* new industrial plants and avoid *all* economic growth, which will cost the community many new jobs. The environmentalist position is made to appear so unreasonable that no thinking person would ever support it.

Hovland has suggested that message distortion follows certain rules. When a discrepant position is quite close to that of an individual, he perceives it as closer than it actually is. This is called **assimilation.** When it is quite far away, he perceives it as farther away than it is. This process is called **contrast.** We will discuss the conditions for these misperceptions later; for now it is enough to note that either could potentially reduce the stress in in attitude-change situation. Assimilating the discrepant position makes it seem closer than it actually is. This reduces the amount of discrepancy and, accordingly, the amount of stress. Contrasting an already distant communication makes the communication so extreme that it may seem ridiculous. Thus, both assimilation and contrast are effective means of reducing pressure caused by a discrepant communication.

**Refuting
the Arguments**

The consistency mechanisms describe a person who resists persuasion but who does not deal with the merits of the communication arguments. Sometimes, though, the recipient can resist by considering and actively attempting to refute the arguments contained in the discrepant communication. He can engage in a debate with the content of the communication and attempt to demonstrate to himself that his own position has more merit than the other one. This debate can be implicit or explicit, verbal or nonverbal, perhaps even conscious or unconscious. He can argue against the discrepant communication, produce evidence to support his own position, show how the other side is illogical or inconsistent, and in general do anything he can to weaken the impact of the communication. To the extent that he is able to refute these arguments, the stress should be reduced.

This process describes the recipient as actively relating the new arguments to his prior attitudes and beliefs. In so doing, the person rehearses his own attitudes as well as considers the details of the communication. The problem with this mode of resolution is twofold: usually recipients are rather lazy, and communicators are more motivated. Most people, most of the time, are not very motivated to analyze in close detail the pros and cons of complex arguments. Moreover, persuasive messages are usually designed to be difficult to reject on purely logical grounds. The authors of the communication naturally present as strong a case as they can and are generally better informed on the topic than the recipients. Therefore, although arguing against the discrepant communication is a rational mode of resolution, it is often difficult to employ.

With this background, we can turn to a consideration of the specific factors that increase or decrease the amount of attitude change produced by a persuasive communication after it has reached its target. Following the model in Figure 10–3, these factors are divided into several classes: those involving the communicator, the communication itself, the surrounding environment that is extraneous to the communication and the participants, and characteristics of the targets of the persuasive attempt.

THE SOURCE OF THE COMMUNICATION

One of the most straightforward and reliable findings in attitude change is that the higher a person's evaluation of a communicator, the more he is apt to change his attitude. This follows from any of the cognitive-consistency models. If a person thinks that marijuana is terrible but a friend says it is great, the system is imbalanced. He can reduce the imbalance by changing his attitude toward marijuana and agreeing with his friend. In contrast, if someone he dislikes has an attitude different from his, there is no imbalance and no pressure to change. Thus, the more favorably people evaluate the source of a discrepant communication, the more likely they will be to change their attitude. But there are several ways in which a communicator can be evaluated favorably, and not all of them yield exactly the same results.

Credibility

The dimension that has been studied most is credibility. By **credibility** we refer primarily to how expert the communicator is perceived to be in the area of concern, and also how much he is trusted by the individual receiving the communication (though we will consider trustworthiness separately). For example, when evaluations of a new medicine are attributed to a noted doctor, they are more persuasive than when they are attributed to a well-known comedian. If T. S. Eliot says that a certain poem is good, he should have more influence than a barber saying it is good.

This effect of credibility was demonstrated in a study by Hovland and Weiss (1952). Subjects heard communications concerned with four issues: the advisability of selling antihistamines without a prescription, whether the steel industry was to blame for the then-current steel shortage, the future of the movie industry in the context of the growing popularity of television, and the practicality of building an atomic-powered submarine. Each communication came from either a high-or low-credibility source. For example, the communication on atomic submarines was supposedly either by J. Robert Oppenheimer, a noted physicist, or from *Pravda,* the Russian newspaper. The results indicated that communications attributed to high-credibility sources produced more change than those from low-credibility sources.

In another study (Aronson, Turner, & Carlsmith, 1963), subjects were told they were in an experiment on esthetics and were asked to evaluate nine stanzas from obscure modern poems. They then read someone else's evaluation of one of the stanzas they had not liked very much. The communication argued that the poem was better than the subject had indicated. The crucial variable was that the communication was supposedly from either T. S. Eliot or Agnes Stearns, who was described as a student at Mississippi State Teachers College. After reading the communication, the subjects reevaluated the poems. There was more change with the high-credibility communicator than with the low-credibility one.

An interesting question, not yet answered, is whether an expert in one field can transfer the influence of his expertise to another field. If T. S. Eliot, who is highly respected in the field of poetry, had taken a stand on politics or education, would his opinion have carried more weight and produced more attitude change than someone less well known? Although there is little evidence on this question, it seems likely that an expert may be able to transfer some of his influence to *related* fields. For example, T. S. Eliot's comments on the teaching of English or even of music would probably be quite influential. However, as the area of concern became more different from his own area, the fact that he was an expert would matter less and he would be less able to transfer his power of persuasion. His comments on the teaching of music or on contemporary theater would also be quite persuasive; his comments on politics or ethics would be less persuasive; and his comments on space technology or submarine warfare would probably be more more persuasive than anybody else's. However, for the moment this is just speculation. The question of the transferability of prestige is an open one and should be more fully investigated in the future.

"Before I begin, I'd like to make a brief statement on American foreign policy."

Trustworthiness Regardless of the expertise of the communicator, it is extremely important for the listener to believe that he or she is unbiased. Even though someone may be the world's greatest expert on poetry, we would not be influenced by his writing reviews of his own poetry or of poetry written by a friend of his. We would not be concerned about his inherent ability to write accurately; we would be concerned about his objectivity and, therefore, his trustworthiness. As we saw in our discussions of attribution in general (Chapter 5) and ingratiation in particular (Chapter 6), to the extent that a communicator is not a disinterested observer, his trustworthiness may be in doubt and what he says will have less effect. If he is perceived as having something to gain from the position he is advocating or if he is taking that position for personal reasons, he would be less persuasive than someone perceived as advocating the position for entirely objective reasons.

A major problem for a communicator is how to convince an audience that he is a distinterested observer. One way to appear disinterested and trustworthy is to argue for a position that appears to be counter

BOX 10-3
COMPETING EXPLANATIONS FOR
THE CREDIBILITY EFFECT

Two main theoretical approaches —learning-by-association and Gestalt theory—have quite different explanations for the credibility effect. The associationists argue for a "transfer of affect" explanation: the positive affect associated with a positive communicator transfers to his message. You have the same solid, trusting feeling toward the doctor's recommendation as toward the doctor himself. The advertising industry and political campaigners have been acting on this assumption for some time. Television commercials are one example. They have recently been referred to as "one-minute movies," because they are so elaborate and so much care goes into making them as attractive and even enjoyable as possible. We are not simply shown a sleek car and told how powerful, quiet, and comfortable it is. Rather, while the message is being delivered, we are shown beautiful women, handsome men, and lovely children, with perhaps a couple of graceful horses or cute dogs cavorting around. The car may be endorsed by a famous athlete or movie star. Presumably, all this beauty, fame, and popularity become associated with the message, which is asking us to buy the car, and with the car itself. The hope is that this will increase our positive feelings toward the car and thus increase the likelihood that we will buy it.

To test this "transfer of affect" notion, Lorge (1936) presented American students with the following message: "I hold that a little rebellion, now and then, is a good thing, and as necessary in the political world as storms are in the physical." He showed that subjects agreed with the message when it was attributed to Thomas Jefferson, and disagreed with it when it was attributed to Lenin. He argued that the positive affect associated with Jefferson made the message more positive, and the reverse for Lenin—a simple transfer of affect.

But there is a competing explanation. The Gestalt "change of meaning" point of view, best expressed by Solomon Asch (1948), is that the message's association with the communicator gives it a different meaning. (We have already discussed this "change of meaning" idea in connection with context effects in impression formation, in chapter 4.) To test this notion, Asch got *his* subjects to explain what they thought the message meant in each case, and it was quite different. They understood Lenin as advocating revolution, as wanting to purge the old order and engage in a frightening overthrow of all that was familiar. Jefferson, they assumed, wanted continuous attention to reform and change, to keep politicians on their toes and uncomplacent, and to keep the citizenry alert and exercising their political rights. So the credibility effect could also be explained by assuming the message meant something different in each case.

This explanation did not settle the dispute, however. It could just as easily involve transfer of affect and rationalization. For example, Lorge could argue that subjects who thought the message came from Jefferson, and now believed the message to be good, would dredge up whatever arguments they needed in order to justify their position. But in his view these arguments are mere after-the-fact rationalizations, and have no force in their decision to go along with whatever the "good guy" (Jefferson) said. Asch, on the other hand, would still contend that the arguments themselves (the "changed meaning" of the message) determined the affects toward the message. While research has not settled the matter, the controversy illustrates the great differences between these two approaches to attitudes. The "transfer of affect" notion describes a reflexive, emotion-ridden, unthinking person, while the "change of meaning" notion describes a thoughtful, sensible, rather rational person.

to one's self-interest. A district attorney, whose main role is supposed to be procuring convictions, would be expected to argue in favor of greater power for law enforcement agencies. But if he does so, his credibility would be lessened, because he clearly has something to gain from this position. On the other hand, if he argues for greater protection of the rights of individuals and against strengthening law enforcement agencies—that is, if he argues against his self-interest—his credibility should be enhanced. We would expect that a district attorney would be more persuasive and produce more attitude change when he takes the latter rather than the former position. On the other hand, a convicted criminal ought to have most influence when arguing against *his* self-interest; e.g., in favor of stricter law enforcement. A study by Walster, Aronson, and Abrahams (1966) concerned the effects of communications from a prosecutor and a convicted criminal. When the criminal argued in favor of more individual freedom and against greater powers for the police, he produced virtually no attitude change. When he argued in favor of a stronger police force, he produced a great deal of attitude change. This is shown in Figure 10–5. Thus, even a low-prestige and highly doubtful communicator has a considerable amount of influence when he argues in favor of a position that would hurt rather than benefit him. And the prosecutor was somewhat more powerful arguing against his self-interest.

This study, however, does not distinguish between two different ways in which communicators can be biased. Their thinking can be biased (even though they report their attitudes honestly and faithfully); this has been called *knowledge bias* (Eagly, Wood, & Chaiken, 1978). Knowledge bias could happen for any of the reasons that people develop biased attitudes—e.g., they came from a very biased family, or they have been misinformed, or their general attitudes are so biased that they cannot see new facts for what they are. On the other hand, they may have really accurate and truthful underlying beliefs, but they do not communicate them to other people in an accurate and honest way. This is called

FIGURE 10–4 Although celebrities often support political causes, their effectiveness is uncertain. Often, their support for unpopular causes makes the celebrity less popular rather than helping the cause. However, Jane Fonda seems as popular as ever—perhaps because most people now support her anti-Vietnam position.

reporting bias. Reporting bias could also happen for any number of different reasons, some of which we have already discussed earlier in connection with ingratiation and conformity.

One implication of the reporting bias is people will be more influenced when they "accidentally" overhear a persuasive communication than when it is directed at them (Walster & Festinger, 1962). If the communicator knows people are listening, he may try to convince them and may not be entirely honest. If he does not know anyone is within earshot, it is

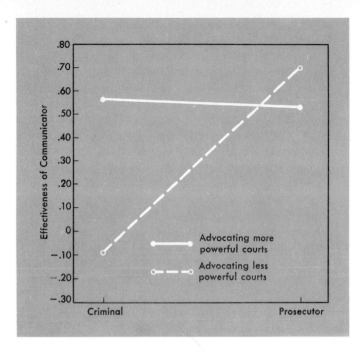

FIGURE 10–5 Effectiveness of communicators when advocating positions for and against one's own self-interest.

Source: Walter, Aronson, & Abrahams (1966), p. 333.

less likely that he is being dishonest. People are more likely to believe the message in the latter case and are therefore more likely to be convinced.

In most cases, though, it is clear that the communicator is trying to change one's attitude, and he is therefore already somewhat suspect. Trustworthiness is therefore crucial. Convincing an audience that one is a disinterested commentator is usually quite difficult. Politicians and advertisers therefore insist on their sincerity, basic integrity, and honesty.

Liking

As we discussed in Chapter 6, people have a strong tendency to like those whose views are similar to theirs. Similarly, as the consistency theories suggest, people change their attitudes to agree with the people they like. Hence anything that increases liking ought also to increase attitude change. For example, physical attractiveness increases liking; Chaiken (1979) has shown that more attractive communicators also are more persuasive. However, the psychological process by which liking produces attitude change is somewhat different from that by which credibility works. According to a theory proposed by Kelman (1961), liking produces attitude change because people try to identify with a liked communicator and thus tend to adopt that person's attitudes, tastes, modes of behavior, and modes of dress. His reasons or arguments for his attitudes are not very important. On the other hand, credibility produces attitude change because people pay more attention to an expert's arguments and consider them more seriously.

The implication of this theory is that good arguments are critical to an expert's persuasiveness, but should not be terribly important for a liked nonexpert. Norman (1976) tested this idea by using two sources: an unattractive expert and an attractive nonexpert. Since the topic was the number of hours of sleep required per night by the average person, the expert was a professor of physiological psychology who had just co-authored a book on sleep; the nonexpert was a twenty-year-old college student. Their pictures and other personal information were also presented, revealing the student to be an attractive, athletic young man recently elected to the student government, whereas the professor was middle-aged and not very attractive. In each case, half the subjects received extensive arguments on why people should cut down on their sleep, while the other half received the simple statement that they should cut down. Consistent with Kelman's theory, the addition of arguments significantly increased the expert's persuasiveness, but it did not affect the amount of attitude change produced by the attractive nonexpert.

As indicated in Chapter 6, *similarity* is one of the most important bases of liking. Not surprisingly, then, people tend to be influenced more by those who are similar to them than by those who are different. But similarity also increases influence because we assume people with backgrounds similar to our own share our general values and perspectives about things. So, suppose someone is similar to us in terms of national, economic, racial, and religious background. If he then says that he thinks drugs are bad, we would probably assume that he made this judgment on the same bases that we would. He is not using irrelevant or incorrect criteria—at least, not in our opinion. Accordingly, his judgment tends to carry considerable weight. Thus, in terms of both increased liking and shared perspectives, the greater the similarity between the source and recipient of a discrepant communication, the more attitude change is produced.

Reference Group

One of the strongest sources of persuasive pressure is a group to which an individual belongs. The group could be as large and inclusive as all American citizens or the middle class or a labor union or college students or all liberals or all blacks. It can also be a much smaller, more specialized group, such as a college fraternity, social psychologists, the Young Republicans, or the Elks Club. And it can be extremely small, such as a group of friends, an extended family, a bridge club, a discussion group, or just five people who happen to be in a room together.

As we have seen in Chapter 9, individuals have a strong tendency to go along with the group, particularly when everyone else in the group holds the same opinion or makes the same response. In these cases,

FIGURE 10–6 Members of an organized team usually look to each other for support and reference. They also accept their coach or captain as a source of information and attitudes.

Peter Southwick; Stock, Boston.

however, there is little actual change in the individual's opinions—he conforms to the group overtly but does not change his internal attitude. Nevertheless, the opinion of the group can also be an extremely persuasive force and can cause the individual to change his internal attitude on an issue. If the Young Republicans endorse a particular candidate, there is a tendency for all the members of the club to feel he is a good candidate. If our friends tell us they are in favor of student activism or like a particular movie, we probably are convinced by them. If most of the members of a fraternity think initiations are a good idea, the rest of the members will probably agree with them.

The reasons why reference groups are so effective in producing attitude change are those we have just discussed: liking and similarity. If people value a group, it is a highly credible, highly esteemed source of communication. When the group says something, each member tends to trust it and believe the message. In addition, because they consider themselves members of the group, they tend to evaluate themselves in com-

"And I thoroughly understand the problems of the caveman, because I'm a caveman myself."

parison with it. In essence, the group serves as the standard for their own behavior and attitudes. They want to be similar to the other members. When the other members express a particular opinion, each members thinks his own opinion wrong if it is different. Only when their opinion is the same as the group's would it be correct or "normal." Therefore, they tend to change their opinion to make it agree.

Attachment to the group can also serve to prevent somebody from being influenced by a communication from an outside source. If the group agrees with the individual's opinion, they provide him with strong support. Consider a fraternity member whose fraternity believes strongly in initiations. He may occasionally be exposed to an attack on initiations from someone outside the fraternity. Whenever he is so exposed, knowledge that his group agrees with him provides strong support and makes it easier for him to resist persuasion.

This dual effect of groups—changing a member's opinion to make it coincide with the rest of the group's opinion and supporting a member's opinion so he can resist persuasion from without—depends to some extent on how strong the individual's ties are to the group. The more he wants to be a member of it and the more likely he values it, the more he will be influenced by the group's beliefs. Kelley and Volkart (1952) demonstrated the effect of attachment to the group on members' resistance to outside influence. A communicator attempted to change some Boy Scouts' opinions on various issues that were closely related to their troop's norms. The more the Scouts valued their membership in the troop, the less effect the communicator had on their opinions.

Another way of demonstrating the potent effect of groups is to show how changes in the group's norms can pull people away from their own old positions. Kelley and Woodruff (1956) played subjects a tape recording of a speech arguing against their group's norm—they were education students, and the speech argued against "progressive education." The speech was interrupted periodically by applause which the experimenters attributed to faculty members and recent graduates of the college in one experimental condition ("members' applause"), or to an audience of college-trained people in a neighboring city, interested in community problems related to education ("outsiders' applause"). Attitude change toward the speech, away from old group norms, was much greater in the "members' applause" condition. This gives additional evidence of the potency of groups in producing or blocking attitude change; in this case, subjects confronted with an apparent change in their group's norm were likely to change their own attitudes to line up with the group's new position.

In general, any characteristic of the communicator which implies that he knows what he is talking about (is an expert), is being honest (has no ulterior motive), or is likeable increases the effectiveness of the communication. Since derogation of the source of the communication is one of the major ways of avoiding attitude change, these variables relating to the communicator are extremely important. Any disliking of the communicator, or lack of trust in his competence or credibility makes it relatively easy to reject the message by attacking him. In this way, the target frees himself from the pressure of worrying about the complex details of the message itself. Therefore, preventing this particular mode of resolution by emphasizing the honesty and expertise of the source of the communication is a major concern in the attempt to influence.

THE COMMUNICATION

Social psychologists tend to concentrate on factors that increase the effectiveness of a message rather than on the content of the message itself. This is because they are looking for general laws that determine the effectiveness of all messages. Naturally it is easier to sell something good than something less good. Crest toothpaste was successful in part because it offered protection against cavities; the automobile became popular because it was a very useful product; and some political candidates are more qualified than others. Given a particular product or opinion to sell, however, a number of variables in the communication itself have important effects on the amount of attitude change that is produced.

Discrepancy

As mentioned earlier, the major source of stress in any influence situation comes from the discrepancy between the target's initial position and the position advocated by the communication. The greater the discrepancy, the greater the stress. If someone who thinks Abraham Lincoln was a great president hears a communication arguing that he was only moderately successful, the individual's attitude is under pressure; if the communication argues that Lincoln was a terrible president, there is much more pressure. If on a scale there are 2 points of discrepancy, 2 points of attitude change are necessary to eliminate it. If there are 5 points of discrepancy, 5 points of change are necessary. An individual who changes his attitude under the pressure of a discrepant message must accordingly change it more with greater discrepancy. Therefore, within a wide range, there is more attitude change with greater discrepancy (Hovland & Pritzker, 1957).

However, the relationship between discrepancy and amount of change is not always this simple. There is more stress with greater discrepancy, but it does not always produce more change. There are two complicating factors. First, as discrepancy becomes quite great, the individual finds it increasingly difficult to change her attitude enough to eliminate the discrepancy. Moreover, an extremely discrepant statement tends to make individuals doubt the credibility of its source. So at high levels of discrepancy, the stress tends to be reduced more by source derogation than by attitude change.

Suppose a student thinks Lincoln was a very great president and is faced with a discrepant opinion from a history teacher, who says that most historians now think less favorably of him. What happens? If the teacher's message is at low discrepancy, and says he thinks Lincoln was not a great president but still a pretty good one, the student is likely to be somewhat influenced. There would be some pressure on her to change her opinion in the direction of the teacher's, and if the teacher presented a fairly persuasive argument, the student would probably do so. In this situation, it is difficult to reject the moderately credible communicator but easy to change one's opinion the little bit required to reduce the discrepancy.

As the discrepancy becomes extreme, however, it becomes much harder for individuals to reduce the stress by changing their opinion. It is extremely difficult for a student who thinks Lincoln was a great president to decide that he was a terrible one. At this point an important decision is made. The student whose teacher tells her that Lincoln was a terrible president now begins to doubt the teacher's credibility. She begins to think that the teacher does not know much about government or human beings. Two factors thus operate as discrepancy increases: attitude change becomes more difficult, and rejection of the communicator becomes easier. The result is that attitude change generally increases with greater discrepancy up to a point, and then it declines if discrepancy in-

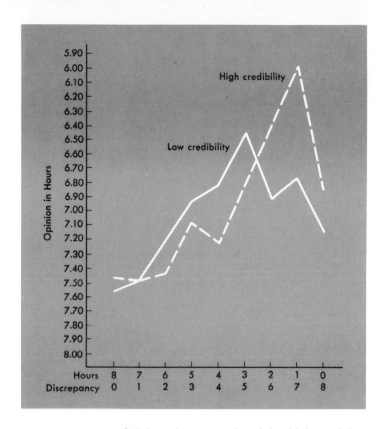

FIGURE 10–7 Opinion change produced by high- and low-credibility communicators at low, moderate, and high discrepancy.
Source: Bochner and Insko, 1966.

creases still further. This relationship between discrepancy and attitude change has been well documented (e.g., Freedman, 1964; Eagly & Telaak, 1972), and is shown in Figure 10–7.

Greater credibility, however, should allow communicators to advocate more discrepant positions with success, because they will not be rejected as easily. If one deeply respects the teacher who says that Lincoln was a terrible president, it is harder to decide that she does not know what she is talking about. (Only very extreme statements from her could make the individual come to this conclusion.) Therefore the greater the credibility of the communicator, the higher the level of discrepancy at which the maximum change occurs. Similarly, a lower-credibility source makes rejection relatively easy and the maximum point occurs at lower levels of discrepancy.

This relationship is nicely illustrated in Figure 10–7, which shows the effect of discrepancy and credibility on opinion change. Bochner and Insko (1966) had a Nobel Prize winner (high credibility) and a YMCA instructor (low credibility) give messages regarding the number of hours of sleep the average person requires per night. Each subject received one message from one source. Some subjects received a message saying eight hours were required, others a message saying seven hours were required and so on. Since the great majority of subjects initially thought eight hours was correct, these messages varied in discrepancy accordingly; zero discrepancy for the eight-hour message, one-hour discrepancy for the seven-hour message, and so on.

As you can see, there was more change at moderate levels of discrepancy than at higher levels. In addition, as expected, the optimal level of discrepancy was greater for the high-credibility source. The high-credibility source got the maximum attitude change by arguing that only one hour of sleep was really necessary, whereas the YMCA instructor did best by advocating three hours of sleep. But at best, the high-credibility source still could reduce the subjects' attitudes only from an average of eight hours per night to an average of about six. (By the way, you should probably ignore the slight superiority of the low-credibility source at low levels of discrepancy; it is probably a chance difference).

Thus, the level of credibility does not change the basic relationship between discrepancy and attitude change, but it does change the point at which maximum change occurs. A similar effect is produced by any other factor that affects the difficulty of rejection or the difficulty of changing. The more difficult it is to reject the communicator, the greater the discrepancy at which maximum change occurs; the more difficult it is to change one's attitude, the lower the discrepancy producing maximum change. This example illustrates how an interplay of forces determines which mode of resolution is adopted in a given situation and how the use of one mode implies less use of another.

Fear Arousal

Arousing fear is one of the most natural ways of trying to convince someone of something. A mother tells her young son that he will be run over if he crosses the street without her. Religious leaders frighten their followers with threats of eternal damnation and suffering. Political philosophers and candidates warn that if their opponents are elected, the country will be ruined, people will starve, and civilization will collapse. Advocates of population control warn of mass starvation. Environmentalists warn of mass lung disease, skin cancer, DDT in our vital organs, dying fish in our polluted oceans, lakes, and streams. Opponents of environmental improvements warn of rising tides of unemployment. Others try to scare us into energy conservation by painting a fearsome picture of imminent energy shortages. Given a particular argument in favor of a position, how does the amount of fear aroused affect the success of the argument?

The original study in this area was conducted by Janis and Feshbach in 1953. They showed high school students a film that emphasized the im-

BOX 10-4

DISCREPANCY AND MISPERCEIVING THE MESSAGE

The effect is heightened by the tendency to assimilate or contrast the position advocated in the discrepant communication. As mentioned earlier, discrepant positions that are close to the individual's are often seen as closer than they actually are, whereas those that are far away are seen as farther away than they are. Exaggerating the closeness of a discrepant position makes it easy to change enough to reduce the small discrepancy, or it may eliminate change by making the two positions essentially identical. Exaggerating the remoteness of a position makes it easier to attack the credibility of the person advocating it.

In order to test this notion, Hovland, Harvey, and Sherif (1957) asked subjects to rate communications designed to be similar to their views, moderately different, or extremely different. The issue chosen was one that the subjects felt strongly about—it was prohibition, and they were living in a "dry" state. Shortly before the study began, the state had voted, by a narrow margin, to retain the existing prohibition laws. The "dry" subjects consisted of members of the Women's Christian Temperance Union, a group of Salvation Army workers, and students in seminaries or in strict denominational colleges. Moderate positions were represented by college students in classes in journalism, speech, education, and chemistry. A group of "wet" subjects

was secured on the basis of personal knowledge of their views. (The experimenters did not describe how they obtained that personal knowledge).

All the subjects listened to a tape-recorded speech described as having been made by a proponent of the stand advocated. A "wet" (repeal) communication was presented to the extreme "dry" and moderate subjects. The "dry" (prohibition) communication was presented to the extreme "wet" and moderate subjects. And the moderate communication was presented to everyone. After listening to each communication, the subjects indicated where they thought it fell on a scale ranging from extreme dry to extreme wet.

The results supported the expectation that assimilation and contrast would occur. Subjects who held a strong wet position rated the moderate communication as much dryer than did the moderate subjects and subjects who held an extreme dry position rated it much wetter than did the moderates. In fact, the extreme dry subjects judged the moderate communication to be a wet communication, despite the fact that it was, by any objective criterion, not at all extreme. Both are examples of contrast. And the extreme dry subjects judged the moderate communication as much dryer than did the moderate subjects; that is, they assimilated the communication. These results are shown in Figure 10-8.

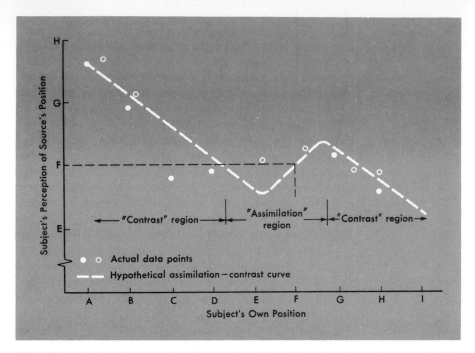

FIGURE 10–8 Average placements of position of moderately wet communication (F) by subjects holding various positions on the issue plotted against hypothetical assimilation-contrast curve.

Source: Hovland, Harvey, and Sherif (1957).

portance of brushing one's teeth three times a day, after every meal. The film described the dangers of not doing this and explained the advantages of good dental care. High fear was aroused by showing pictures of badly decayed teeth and gums, closeups of diseased teeth, mouths in which the gums had pulled away from the teeth, and so on. In the mild-fear condition, subjects saw less dramatic and less frightening pictures. And in the no-fear, or control, condition, the subjects saw no pictures of diseased teeth. The subjects in the high-fear condition reported being more impressed by the presentation and agreeing with it more. However, a week later it was found that the subjects in the no-fear condition had changed their behavior more than had subjects in either of the fear conditions. The authors concluded that the maximum effect was produced by the persuasive arguments without the fear-arousing slides.

This result has generally not been repeated in later experiments. Much of the work done in recent years has produced the opposite result. For example, a series of experiments conducted by Howard Leventhal and his colleagues at Yale University (see Leventhal, 1970) have shown that the arousal of fear tends to facilitate both attitude and behavioral change. In one study (Dabbs & Leventhal, 1966), college students were urged to get inoculations for tetanus. The disease was described in detail—it was pointed out how serious it was, that it was often fatal, and that it was easy to catch. In addition, the students were told that the inoculation was extremely effective and that it gave almost complete protection against the disease.

The message was delivered under several different conditions of fear arousal. In the high-fear condition, the descriptions of the disease were extremely vivid, the symptoms were made very explicit, and everything was done to make the situation as frightening as possible. In the second condition, a moderate amount of fear was aroused; and in the third, very little. Students were then asked how important they thought it was to get the inoculation and whether or not they intended to get one. The university health service, which was nearby, recorded how many of the students went for inoculations during the next month.

The findings (Table 10–1) are straightforward and impressive. The greater the fear aroused, the more the subjects intended to get shots. Perhaps more important, higher fear induced more subjects actually to go to the health service and receive inoculations. Thus, fear arousal not only produced more attitude change, but also had a greater effect on the relevant behavior.

Various other studies have used a wide range of issues, including automotive safety, atom bomb testing, fallout shelters, and dental hygiene, to study the effects of fear. Higbee (1969) has made a careful review of these many studies. He concludes the there is a predominant weight of evidence favoring the positive effect of fear. Only five studies clearly showed low fear having more effect, whereas over twenty experiments conducted by a number of diffrent experimenters have shown fear facilitating attitude change. Some studies, such as Dabbs and Leventhal (1966) and Evans and associates (1970), also indicated that high fear had a great effect on relevant action, although the evidence for this is somewhat less consistent. From all of this research, it seems clear that under most circumstances fear arousal increases the effectiveness of a persuasive communication.

TABLE 10–1
**Effects of Fear Arousal on Attitudes
and Behavior**

CONDITION	INTENTION TO TAKE SHOTS[a]	PERCENTAGE TAKING SHOTS
High fear	5.17	22
Low fear	4.73	13
Control	4.12	6

[a] The figures are ratings on a scale from 1 (lowest) to 7 (highest).
Source: Adapted from Dabbs and Leventhal (1966).

Mark Waters was a chain smoker. Wonder who'll get his office?

Too bad about Mark. Kept hearing the same thing everyone does about lung cancer. But, like so many people, he kept right on smoking cigarettes. Must have thought, "been smoking all my life... what good'll it do to stop now?" Fact is, once you've stopped smoking, no matter how long you've smoked, the body begins to reverse the damage done by cigarettes, provided cancer or emphysema have not developed. Next time you reach for a cigarette, think of Mark. Then think of your office—and your home.

American Cancer Society

"We'll miss ya, baby"

FEMME FATALE.
Cigarettes are part of the costume.
Next week she learns how to inhale.

MAN OF DESTINY.
Smokes because he thinks it's good
for his "image." Coughs a lot, too.

WISE GUY.
Likes to keep a cigarette in his mouth
when he talks. Very hard to understand.

ME-TOO.
Smokes because his friends do. Doesn't
know whether he likes it or not.

Cigarettes can kill you.
Keep smoking 'em and they may.
We'll miss ya, baby.

american
cancer
society ®

You cats have just one life. Why blow it?

*Here's where it's at, baby.
Cigarettes can kill you.
Smoke enough and, chances
are, they will. For real.
For good. And forever. You've
got just one life, pussycat.
Why blow it?*

american
cancer
society ®

There may be some situations, however, in which fear does reduce the effectiveness of a communication. Janis (1967) has suggested that the relationship between fear and attitude change depends on the level of fear involved. He argued that at low levels, greater fear produces more attitude change, but that at some point the fear becomes too intense, arouses defensive mechanisms, and thereby produces less change. This would explain the seemingly contradictory results that have been found because the studies have involved different amounts of fear. For example, high fear normally has had its strongest persuasive effects in experiments on tetanus, which is a simply prevented disease and rarely scares people much. However, high fear arousal is less often successful on lung cancer and smoking, probably because lung cancer causes too much fear and is too difficult for a lifelong smoker to prevent. Janis has reanalyzed a number of experiments in these terms, and although not all the data fit this model, most of the results appear to be consistent with it.

Even more specific theories about the conditions under which fear is effective have been developed by Leventhal (1970) and others (e.g., Rogers & Mewborn, 1976); these rest generally on an expectancy-value approach and view the individual as somewhat more cognitive and rational than does the Janis model. These theories take into consideration the noxiousness of the feared event, the person's vulnerability to the feared event, and the efficacy of the recommended preventive measures. They try to predict the special conditions under which fear will influence attitude change. For example, fear should increase attitude change if highly effective measures are recommended, but not if there is little or no remedy. These theories can also account for some of the data, though it seems clear that people do not uniformly calculate the most rational response in these situations.

To sum up, the evidence indicates that under most circumstances arousing fear increases the effectiveness of persuasive communications. But arousing too much fear may be disruptive. Causing a person to be too frightened can make him either so paralyzed that he is unable to act or so threatened that he tends to deny the danger and reject the persuasive communication. Aside from such cases, however, it appears that fear-arousing arguments are more effective in producing attitude change than are arguments that arouse little or no fear.

The Arousal of Aggression

One interesting explanation of the effect of motivational arousal on attitude change concerns the appropriateness of the motive aroused. In most of the studies on fear arousal, the persuasive communication contains information about a real danger such as cancer, tetanus, or reckless driving. When fear of cancer is aroused by vivid pictures, the fear is appropriate because it is realistic to be afraid of cancer. Perhaps more important, the messages are urging the subjects to take steps that would reduce the danger and the fear. If one takes a tetanus inoculation, one is, in fact, less liable to get tetanus and should no longer fear the disease. In situations such as these, the arousal of fear is appropriate to the attitude-change situation, and therefore the arousal should increase susceptibility to the message.

A study by Weiss and Fine (1956) on the arousal of aggression is relevant to this explanation of the effect of motivation. Some subjects were put through an annoying, frusrating experience designed to make them feel aggressive. Other subjects had the opposite experience—they went through a pleasant, satisfying experience. Then, both groups were exposed to a persuasive communication that took either a lenient or a punitive attitude toward juvenile delinquency. Thus, the experiment exposed aggressive and nonaggressive subjects to lenient or punitive persuasive communications.

The experimenters hypothesized that the subjects who had been made to feel aggressive would be more likely to accept the punitive communication than the lenient one and that the nonaggressive subjects would be more likely to accept the lenient communication. The rationale was that the punitive message would satisfy the motivational needs of the aggressive subjects by providing them with a way of displacing their aggression. The lenient message would be more likely to satisfy the relatively nonaggressive needs of the other subjects. The results were in line with these expectations—the aggressive subjects were more influenced by the punitive communication, and the nonaggressive subjects were more influenced by the lenient one. We have already seen in Chapter 7 how people displace aggression to new targets when the original source of frustration is too anxiety arousing or unavailable. This experiment suggests that displaced aggression occurs in our attitudes as well as in our behavior, but it requires an appropriate new target, one that is a natural channel for the expression of aggressive impulses. So personal frustrations might make a person more vulnerable to persuasive communications advocating military action, attacks on minorities, or harsh treatment of dissidents, but probably they would not increase susceptibility to environmentalist appeals, or charity campaigns.

CHARACTERISTICS OF THE TARGET

Even after a message from a particular source has reached the target, the problems of attitude change are not over. Various characteristics of individual personality and factors in immediate and past experience are important determinants of reaction to the message. These factors affect primarily the tendency to trust the message or its source, the ability to argue against the message, the motivation not to change an opinion, and the confidence in one's own position.

Commitment

An important aspect of attitude change is the strength of the target's commitment to an attitude. One of the many factors that affects the strength of commitment is action taken on the basis of the attitude. If a person has just bought a house, she is more committed to the belief that it is a fine house than if she had not yet bought it. Changing her opinion of the house has broader implications for her if she owns it than if she is only thinking about buying it.

Similarly, public statements of the attitude produce more commitment. Someone who has just stated on television that he thinks smoking is bad for health and is an evil, dirty habit is more committed to this attitude than if he had made these statements only to his wife or had kept them to himself. Changing his attitude is harder if he expressed it on television, because then the change would involve publicly admitting he was wrong. Whenever changing an attitude would cause the individual to give up more, suffer more, or change more of his other attitudes or behaviors, his commitment to his initial attitude increases and makes it more difficult for him to change it.

In addition, it appears that freely choosing a position produces a greater feeling of commitment than being forced. In a study on this problem (Freedman & Steinbruner, 1964), subjects were given information about a candidate for graduate school and asked to rate him, under cirumstances of either high or low choice. The subjects were made to feel either that they had made up their own minds and freely selected the particular rating or that they had virtually nothing to do with the decision and had been forced to select the rating. The subjects were then exposed to information that strongly contradicted their initial rating and were allowed to change their rating if they desired. Those who had made the first rating with a feeling of free choice changed less than did those in the low-choice condition.

A fourth factor affecting commitment is the extent to which the attitude is imbedded in other behaviors and attitudes. Someone in favor of fluoridation of drinking water may feel very strongly about it, but this feeling may not be related to any others she may have. Most people have taken no action on fluoridation and have few attitudes about it. Changing their attitude from favorable to unfavorable would therefore involve relatively few other changes in their cognitive systems. However, a dentist who has been fighting tooth decay for years, who has been coating teeth with fluorides, who has donated money to fluoridation campaigns, and who has read extensive literature supporting fluoridation would feel quite differently. Changing his opinion would involve many contradictions, inconsistencies, and changes in his cognitive and behavioral system.

Strong commitment of this kind reduces the amount of attitude change produced by a persuasive communication. Greater commitment makes it harder for the individual to change his attitude and means that he is more likely to use other modes of resolution instead. The exact mechanism of resistance is still not very clear. Greater commitment

makes people give more counterarguments when they are confronted with discrepant information (Petty & Cacioppo, 1979), but it is not clear whether they are necessary to this added resistance to change.

The joint effects of commitment and discrepancy on attitude change are similar to those of credibility and discrepancy. As described previously, the credibility of the source does not change the relationship between discrepancy and attitude change but does affect the point at which maximum change occurs—the higher the credibility the greater the discrepancy at which there is maximum attitude change. Commitment to an initial position also shifts the maximum point, but in the opposite direction. The harder it is to change position, the lower the discrepancy at which rejection of the source is easier than change. Therefore, the greater the commitment, the lower the discrepancy at which maximum attitude change occurs (Freedman, 1964; Rhine & Severance, 1970).

Inoculation

In the aftermath of the Korean War, William McGuire and others became very interested in reports of "brainwashing" of American prisoners-of-war by Chinese Communists. A number of POWs had given public speeches denouncing the American government, and several said publicly that they wished to remain in China when the war was over, rather than return to the United States. McGuire speculated that some soldiers might have been vulnerable to influence because they were being attacked on matters they were quite inexperienced and ignorant about—they had never been forced to defend the United States against the sophisticated Marxist attacks used against them by the Chinese.

So McGuire hypothesized that another source of resistance to change in the target comes from past experience with the issue. He and his associates conducted a series of experiments on the effects of giving people experiences designed to increase their ability to resist persuasion. He used a medical analogy to describe the influence situation. He pictured the individual faced with a discrepant communication as being similar to somebody being attacked by a virus or a disease. The stronger the persuasive message (virus), the more damage it would do; the stronger the person's defenses, the better able he is to resist persuasion (disease). There are two different ways of strengthening someone's defense against a disease. We can strengthen his body generally, by giving him vitamins, exercise, and so on; or we can strengthen his defenses against that particular disease by building up antibodies. McGuire argued that these two approaches are also applicable to the influence situation.

To begin with, he identified a number of *cultural truisms*—opinions so universally held in our society that they are almost never subjected to any kind of attack. One example is the belief that it is good to brush one's teeth after every meal. Probably almost everybody in the United States believes that this is basically a good idea in terms of dental health. And most people have never heard anything to the contrary. Thus, someone holding this opinion is analogous to an individual who has never been exposed to the smallpox germ. He has never been forced to defend himself from attack so has never built up any defense against attack.

One procedure that strengthens resistance is to build up the person's opinion directly by giving her additional arguments supporting her original position. If she believes that it is good to brush her teeth three times a day, she is shown a study by the United States Public Health Service which shows that people who do so have fewer cavities than those who brush their teeth less often or not at all. Giving individuals this kind of support for their position does, in fact, increase their resistance to a subsequent persuasive communication.

A different approach is to strengthen the individual's defenses against persuasion. McGuire has argued that, as with diseases, the most effective way of increasing resistance is to build up defenses. If a person is given a mild case of smallpox that he is able to fight off, his body produces antibodies, which in the future provide an effective and strong defense against more powerful attacks of smallpox. Similarly, if a particular opinion has never been attacked, it is extremely vulnerable because no defenses have been built up around it. When such an opinion is suddenly and surprisingly subjected to persuasive pressure, the individual does not have a set of defenses immediately available, and the opinion tends to be relatively easy to change. However, if the opinion has once been attacked and the individual has successfully defended herself, she should be better able to resist later attacks because she has built up a relatively strong defensive system around that opinion.

In other words, McGuire argued that it is possible to **inoculate** individuals against persuasive attacks just as we can inoculate them against diseases. This is accomplished by weakly attacking the individual's attitude. The attack must be weak or it would change his attitude and the battle would be lost. To be certain that this does not occur, the target is helped to defend himself against the mild attack. He is given an argument directed specifically at the attack or is told that the attack is not very good and he should be able to refute it.

One study by McGuire and Papageorgis (1961) used both the supportive and inoculation methods to build up defenses. There were three groups of subjects: one group received support for their position; one group had their position attacked weakly and the attack refuted (the inoculation condition); and the third group received neither of these procedures. Afterward, all groups were subjected to a strong attack on their initial position. Table 10–2 shows how much each group changed as a result of the attack. The supportive method helped subjects resist persuasion a little—the group receiving support changed a little less than the group that had no preparation. But the inoculation method helped a great deal; subjects receiving this preparation changed much less than the other subjects.

One implication would be that supportive defenses are best when

TABLE 10–2
Support, Inoculation, and Resistance to Persuasion

CONDITION	AMOUNT OF ATTITUDE CHANGE
Support	5.87
Inoculation	2.94
Neither	6.62

Source: Adapted from McGuire and Papageorgis (1961).

the target simply needs to be taught specific arguments. The inoculation defense would be better when the target has to be stimulated to thinking up his own defensive arguments. Consistent with this view later research has shown that support tends to be particularly effective when the subsequent attack contains arguments similar to the content of the supporting arguments, but it is relatively ineffective when new arguments are used. In contrast, inoculation is effective even when the attack includes new arguments.

The specific mechanism by which inoculation operates is not yet clear. It may be that in refuting the mild attack, the individual uses and therefore exercises all his defenses. He prepares arguments supporting his own position, constructs counterarguments against the opposing position, derogates the possible sources of opposing views, and so on. This would make each of the defensive mechanisms stronger and would provide the individual with a generally more effective position.

Personality Factors

Some people are generally more persuasible than others, regardless of the issue involved or the type of influence being attempted. Experiments have been conducted (Hovland & Janis, 1959) in which subjects were exposed to persuasive communications on a variety of issues with different types of appeals and arguments and in different attitude-change situations. They indicated that the subjects who were highly persuasible under one set of conditions tended to be highly persuasible under others. The effect is not very strong; it explains only a small percentage of the total variance. But considering the diversity of the situations and issues studied, the consistency found offers convincing support for the existence of the trait of general persuasibility. However, relatively little is known about the specific sources of this trait.

One fairly consistent finding has been that subjects with low self-esteem tend to be more persuasible than those with high self-esteem. The standard explanation is that low self-esteem people place a low value on their opinions just as they do on everything else about themselves. Since they do not value their own opinions, they are less reluctant to give them up and are more likely to change them when they are attacked. McGuire (1969) has added one complexity to this theory. Although he grants that low self-esteem should be related to acceptance of a message, he hypothesizes that it will at the same time be negatively related to comprehension of the message. Thus a low self-esteem person may be quite gullible, accept almost anything someone tells him, and thus be likely to show a great deal of attitude change. However, he may at the same time have trouble understanding complex communications, frequently miss the point of their arguments, and, as a result, show reduced attitude change. This hypothesis has been tested most directly by Zellner (1970). As expected, she found that low self-esteem was positively related to influence by simple arguments, while the reverse held for complex arguments. This provided support for the hypothesis that self-esteem affects persuasibility both by affecting the tendency to accept influence and by affecting comprehension of the communication.

It has also seemed likely to many people that individuals with high intelligence would be less persuasible than those with lower intelligence. Research has not generally supported this assumption. On the average, people of high intelligence are persuaded just as much as people of low intelligence. However, there is reason to believe that intelligence does have some effect on the kinds of persuasive appeals that are most effective. People of high intelligence are influenced less by inconsistent and illogical arguments than are people of lower intelligence, and the latter may be influenced less by complex, difficult arguments. It is important to note that the lack of an overall correlation between intelligence and persuasibility does not necessarily mean that intelligence is entirely unrelated to the influence process. Rather, it indicates that the relationship is complex.

Other than these few factors, there is little to support hypotheses about how personality affects persuasibility. There have been many suggestions (e.g., authoritarianism, richness of fantasy), but the evidence for any of these is rather weak at the moment.

SITUATIONAL FACTORS

The factors described thus far are concerned solely with the communicator, the message, and the target. Yet mass communications usually are delivered within a broader context in which other things are happening, and these also often prove to have decisive effects upon the success of persuasion attempts. Let us now consider some of the most important situational variables in attitude change.

**Forewarned
is Forearmed**

If someone is told ahead of time that he is going to be exposed to a discrepant communication on an issue he cares strongly about, he is better able to resist persuasion by that message. In a study by Freedman and

Sears (1965), teenagers were told ten minutes beforehand that they were going to hear a talk titled "Why Teenagers Should Not Be Allowed to Drive." Other teenagers were not told about the talk until just before the speaker began. Thus, one group had a ten-minute warning and the other group had no warning at all. Under these circumstances, those who had the warning were less influenced by the talk than were the others. In some way, the warning enabled them to better resist this very unpalatable message. Hass and Grady (1975) and others have found similar effects.

This is certainly a plausible finding, and it seems to be believed by many people in the business of persuasion. For example, we often hear an advertisement on radio or television with no warning that this is going to be an advertisement. Instead, the station sneaks in the ad before we are fully aware of what it is. A similar, although more altruistic example is the dentist who warns us that something is going to hurt. He seems to feel that we will be better able to withstand the pain if we are warned. In fact, there is some experimental evidence that subjects who are warned ahead of time that they are going to receive an electric shock report that it hurts less than do subjects who are not warned.

All this sounds plausible and reasonable, but why does it occur? Why does a ten-minute warning help people resist persuasion? It is important to keep in mind that all the subjects know that the speaker disagrees with them—the only difference is that some people know it ten minutes ahead of time and others know it only just before the speech. The greater

resistance shown by those with the longer warning is due to some process, some mechanism that goes on during those ten minutes between the warning and the speech.

Most likely, as with the inoculation procedure, the individual's defenses are in some way exercised or strengthened. Although there is little evidence that directly demonstrates how these defenses are strengthened, the individual probably employs all the defensive maneuvers and tactics we discussed previously. She constructs arguments that may come from the opponent. In the warning experiment, the teenagers probably say to themselves, "The message is going to present arguments against teenage driving. It will probably say that teenagers don't drive as well as adults. Well, that's not true. I know teenagers drive better, so that's a bad argument." The teenagers would also think about arguments in favor of teenage driving, such as "Old enough to fight, old enough to vote and drive." Indeed Petty and Cacioppo (1977) have shown the delay period between forewarning and exposure to the communication allows subjects to generate more counterarguments (though they had no way of determining whether this anticipatory counterarguing was necessary for the increased resistance).

Listeners also probably employ derogation of the discrepant source. As discussed above, the person who has been through the inoculation procedure has ample opportunity to derogate the opponent. Similarly, the forewarned person has ten minutes to convince himself that the communicator is unreliable, prejudiced, and misinformed.

In other words, the individual who is warned (or who, in the inoculation situation, has just experienced a mild attack) is like a fighter who has prepared for a match. He has been through training, so when the fight comes, he is in better shape and better able to meet his opponent. He also spends time convincing himself that his opponent is not very good and that he, himself, is great. This makes him more confident and better able to fight his best.

All this work has been done on situations in which the recipient was strongly committed to a position discrepant from the communicator's, however. When the listener is not very committed to his initial position, though, forewarning turns out to have the opposite effect—it actually facilitates attitude change. When the person is unlikely from the start to cling very tightly to his original attitude, the forewarning seems to operate as a cue to propel him along the road he was destined for sooner or later anyhow. For example, Apsler and Sears (1968) hypothesized that forewarning would facilitate attitude change among subjects who were not personally involved in the topic, whereas it would help block it among highly involved subjects. They gave subjects a persuasive communication advocating replacement of professors by teaching assistants in many upper-division courses, a change opposed by almost all subjects. Some subjects were told the change would come quickly, in time to affect their own education (high involvement); others were told it was several years

TABLE 10–3
Forewarning Increases Attitude Change with Low Involvement

| | MEAN ATTITUDE CHANGE | |
CONDITION	High Involvement	Low Involvement
Warning	1.5	2.4
No warning	1.8	0.7
Effects of warning	−0.3	1.7

Note: n = 20 in each cell. The larger the score, the greater the amount of change in the advocated direction on a 16-point scale.
Source: Apsler and Sears (1968), p. 164.

off and would not affect them (low involvement). Forewarning helped block change among the highly involved subjects, just as it had among the teenagers who were highly involved in the issue of teenage driving in the Freedman and Sears experiment. However, it facilitated change in the low-involvement condition. This is shown in Table 10–3.

These two effects of forewarning frequently can be detected even before the subject receives the communication. The highly committed person seems to begin to resist even before he is exposed to the forthcoming communication, while the uncommitted person seems to moderate his stand. In one experiment, subjects highly committed to their initial position became more extreme (and presumably more resistant to change) when forewarned of a forthcoming debate, while weakly committed subjects became more moderate (and presumably more receptive to change) while anticipating the debate (Sears, Freedman, & O'Connor, 1964). Cooper and Jones (1970) have shown that these anticipatory changes are due to the subjects' expectations of exposure to the communications and their likely effects, rather than just to the knowledge of their existence. Weakly committed subjects changed when forewarned of forthcoming exposure to the communication, but not when merely told that such a communication existed without any implication of forthcoming exposure.

There are still some controversies surrounding the exact nature of these responses to forewarning. For example, we do not know whether the increased resistance of highly committed persons is based on real thought and anticipation of arguments, or just increased blanket rejection of the communication, or source derogation. Forewarning does inspire more counterarguing, but that could just be an incidental byproduct of a stubborn, less thought-out refusal to give in. And some researchers suggest that the anticipatory attitude change among the uncommitted may be more apparent than real. That is, it may just be done to avoid looking like a compliant person, and may not be genuine attitude change at all. Finally, we do not mean to give the impression that all these maneuvers are done deliberately. Rather, people tend to think about the issue a little, go over some of the points in their minds, and in this way prepare for exposure. As far as we know, the process is all quite casual and almost accidental. But the effects are clear.

Distraction

In parts of our discussion, we have described the individual as actively fighting the persuasive message. Although he may sometimes be quite passive, the person whose opinions are attacked usually tries to resist changing. He counterargues, derogates the communicator, and generally marshals all his forces to defend his own position. One important implication of this is that the ability to resist persuasion is weakened by anything that makes it harder for the individual to fight the discrepant communication. In particular, **distracting** his attention from the battle may enable the persuasive message to get through without being fought.

A study by Festinger and Maccoby (1964) demonstrated this effect of distraction. Subjects listened to a speech against fraternities while watching a film. For some of the subjects, the film showed the person making the speech. For others, the film was "The Day of the Painter," a funny, somewhat zany satire on modern art. Presumably, those watching the irrelevant film were more distracted from the antifraternity speech than were those watching the person speak. Subjects who initially disagreed with the speech (who were in favor of fraternities) were more influenced in the distraction than the nondistraction condition. Taking the subjects' minds off the speech increased its effectiveness.

There is some debate about how reliable this finding is, and about the mechanism that is responsible for it. As indicated in a review of several subsequent studies, the results have been quite mixed, with as many failing to find distraction advancing attitude change as those finding it doing so (Osterhouse & Brock, 1970). It seems to occur primarily when the subjects are initially strongly opposed to the position being advocated, when they are quite familiar with the topic, when they attend to the distraction rather than to the message (Zimbardo et al., 1970), and when they have the opportunity to develop counterarguments in the absence of the distraction. Hence Petty, Wells, and Brock (1976) have shown that distraction fosters attitude change more when the message otherwise easily generates many counterarguments. So distraction would help persuasion much better on a familiar issue on which we know our own arguments (e.g., against a person advocating racially segregated schools) than on an issue we do not have ready arguments about (e.g., on some technical issue).

In any case, the effect must depend on the right amount of distraction. As usual, there is a conflict between getting the message through and getting it accepted. Obviously, too much distraction prevents the persuasive message from being heard at all and reduces its effectiveness to zero. Advertisers may want to distract television viewers from the main point of commercials by having irrelevant pictures and action going on during the speech. They do not, however, want to have the irrelevancies so fascinating or interfering that the message is lost. Having a beautiful girl in the background during a soap commercial may help sell soap; having her in the foreground may even help; but having her in the foreground singing so loud that the commercial can barely be heard would certainly reduce the effectiveness of the ad. Thus, the effect of distraction may work under limited conditions, but it is important that the distraction be not too great or the effect will be reversed.

ATTITUDE CHANGE OVER TIME

So far we have focused only on immediate responses to one-shot communications—that is, under what conditions does a televised speech, radio ad, or conversation with a friend *immediately* produce attitude change? In many cases, however, we want to know how attitudes change *over time.* We especially want to know the effects of repeated exposure to a message and what effects last when the exposure has ceased.

Repetition

Consider your reaction to seeing the same potato-faced athletes in a TV commercial downing the same brand of beer at the same bar week after week. Does the repetition reinforce your association between that brand of beer and the athletes? Or do you get so sick of the commercial you come to have both of them?

Recall the "mere exposure" research by Zajonc and others, which showed repetition increasing liking (see Chapter 6). This would imply repetition should generally increase attitude change. With persuasive communications, however, repetition apparently increases attitude change only up to a point. Cacioppo and Petty (1979) presented communications containing eight different arguments on increasing university expenditures (see Figure 10–11). Each communication was presented one, three, or five times. They found agreement increased with more exposure up to a point and then fell off. This inverted-U function occurred whether the communication advocated a low discrepancy, "desirable" position (increase the luxury tax) or a high discrepancy, "undesirable" one (increase tuition). They repeated the finding in a second experiment, which has also been corroborated by Belch's (1979) research on televised commercials. Cacioppo and Petty also found that high levels of repetition produced fewer favorable and more unfavorable thoughts, consistent with the notion that tedium or reactance sets in after a certain point. Exactly where this point occurs, or how much is "too much," is not known, but it probably depends on the pleasantness and novelty value of the stimulus,

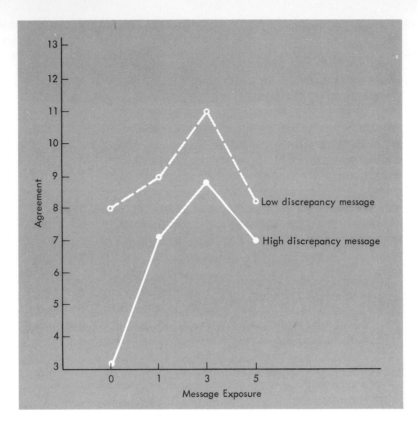

FIGURE 10–11 The effects of message position and message repetition on agreement.

Source: Adapted from Cacioppo and Petty (1979), p. 100. Effects of message repetition and position on cognitive response, in the *Journal of Personality and Social Psychology, 37*, 97–109. Copyright 1979 by the American Psychological Association. Reprinted by permission.

and the time intervals involved. In any case, there is clearly a limit to the value of repetition.

Spontaneous Attitude Change

Attitudes apparently get stronger the longer people hold them. Tesser (1978) has done a series of studies that compare thinking about an attitude object with being distracted and not thinking about it. He finds that thinking polarizes attitudes. So if you spend more than the usual amount of time thinking about your best friend, you will probably like her better, whereas if you think about your enemy more often, you will probably dislike her even more. According to Tesser, people review and rehearse their cognitions, and consistency pressures move them toward more evaluatively consistent clusters. So in thinking about your best friend, you might remember additional good qualities or enjoyable experiences you shared. And you might reinterpret some of your less pleasant memories to excuse your friend's behavior. The same could happen with your enemy: you would lengthen your list of offenses and find seamy motives for her apparently good and generous acts. Because the polarization process requires generating additional cognitions and reinterpreting existing ones, it presumably should be at its strongest with an established schema rather than with an attitude having little cognitive depth.

Attitudes also spontaneously move toward logical consistency over time, even in the absence of direct pressure to think about them. McGuire (1960) has shown that attitudes toward the premises and conclusions of logical syllogisms become more consistent over time. For example, if you believe that gasoline supplies are likely not to increase, and that people are not likely to reduce their consumption, then over time you are likely to come to expect shortages, even in the absence of any direct evidence of them. However, it is important to note that both Tesser and McGuire believe that only a limited amount of polarization or consistency is likely to result from thought and the passage of time, unless some new information is pumped into the system.

Persistence of Attitude Change

The last question concerns the persistence of attitude change over time, once it has been induced by a communication. It seems clear that, in general, memory for the details of an argument decays with time in a fashion resembling an Ebbinghaus forgetting curve—that is, decreases are rapid at first, then diminish later on. In general, though, the persistence of attitude changes is *not* necessarily dependent on retention of the details of arguments. A good bit of research finds memory for arguments of only secondary importance (McGuire, 1969). A host of other events that occur after the communication are of much greater significance.

The most important determinant of persistence is probably the kind of social support given the person after exposure to the communication. The best example is Newcomb's (1967) study of the long-term changes in political attitudes of girls attending Bennington College in the 1930s. Most girls became considerably more liberal while they were in college. Persistence depended on the attitudinal environment they established after graduating. Those surrounded by liberals stayed liberal; those surrounded by conservatives "regressed" to their precollege conservatism. We will discuss this study in more detail in Chapter 11.

Another factor is whether or not the recipient is later cued to remember the persuasion circumstances. Kelman and Hovland (1953), for example, manipulated source credibility and found the usual difference on an immediate posttest: the high-credibility source had produced more attitude change. Three weeks afterward, the credibility difference was gone. The low-credibility source's message was, by then, just as effective as the high-credibility source's. The original credibility difference could be reinstated, however, if the subject was reminded of the original source of the message. This study led to some controversy and considerable research. One possibility was that a *sleeper effect* had occurred in the low-credibility condition—attitude change increased as the association of message with low-credibility source was forgotten. A *discounting cue* hypothesis suggested that reinstating this degrading association would kill off that gradual increase in attitude change. Cook and Flay (1978) have concluded that such sleeper effects probably do happen, and that persistence of attitude change depends on the recipient's *not* being reminded that the message originally came from a low-credibility source.

Attitude change may also be artificially suppressed by warning the recipient about the communicator's persuasive intent. As we saw earlier, people become stubborn and refractory when they feel the source is trying to persuade them. But over time, such people seem to show increased attitude change, presumably as the discounting cue (of persuasive intent) is forgotten (Watts & Holt, 1979). In contrast, distraction seems to be an effective means of countering resistance, at least as assessed right after the communication. But it apparently interferes with initial learning. So attitude change decays more rapidly over time among initially distracted subjects than among the undistracted.

If there is a lesson in this, it may be that there is no such thing as a free lunch in the day of a persuader. A low-credibility source may get a message through, but the message is always vulnerable to its weak auspices' becoming salient again. Or, one may momentarily trick a person into changing by distracting or failing to forewarn him, but with time the persuasive impact will be lost. And a message can temporarily change a person's attitudes, but it needs to be consistent with his long-standing values, and with those of his friends, if it is going to endure. So it is a good idea to be skeptical of reports of sudden, dramatic changes of major attitudes. Unless they are supported by evidence, friends, and basic values, major attitude changes are likely to be short-lived.

Thus, many factors affect attitude change primarily by increasing the trust in the communication, by strengthening the persuasive message, and, in general, by determining how much the individual believes what is being said. An attempt to influence someone's opinion need not, however, be done in an entirely logical, unemotional, cognitive situation. The situation may, and often does, involve strong motivations, appeals to deep-seated needs, and a great many factors that are extraneous to the logical arguments contained in the message itself. An entirely rational, cognitive person would be influenced only to the extent that the arguments presented were logically sound. But since there are few, if any entirely rational beings, motivational and emotional factors are also important in determining the effectiveness of a persuasive communication.

1. Attitudes have a cognitive (thought) component, an affective (feeling) component, and a behavioral component.

2. "Facts" or "knowledge" differ from attitudes mainly in that they have no affective component.

3. Most people do not have very complex, broadly structured, or detailed attitudes about most things. Rather, like personality impressions, attitudes tend to be simple and are organized around the affective (or evaluative) dimension.

4. The conditioning and reinforcement approach views attitude formation and change as primarily a learning process. Attitudes are learned by association, reinforcement and imitation.

5. The incentive approach views attitudes in terms of the needs that the attitude satisfies for the person.

6. Cognitive consistency theories view a person as attempting to maintain consistency among his various attitudes, between his affects and his cognitions toward a given object, and between his attitudes and behavior.

7. A useful model of the attitude-change situation classifies possible influences upon the target in terms of communicator, communication, and situational and target variables.

8. The major mechanisms by which people resist persuasion include refutation of the communicator's arguments, simple blanket rejection of the message, derogating the communicator, and distorting the message.

9. The target's evaluation of the source of the communication is one of the most critical factors in the success of a persuasion attempt. More attitude change is likely if the source is viewed as credible, trustworthy, and is generally liked by the target.

10. A reference group with which the target identifies is another potent source of influence.

11. The most important aspect of the communication is how far its position differs from that already held by the target—that is, its discrepancy. The more discrepant the communication is, the more influence it has—up to a point, when it starts to fall off again. The point at which it falls off depends on source credibility and the target's commitment to this initial opinion. With high credibility and/or low commitment, the fall-off point occurs at higher levels of discrepancy.

12. Generally speaking, attitude change increases with greater fear arousal. But at very high levels of fear, when the message becomes too threatening or disruptive for the person, fear-arousing communications may become ineffective.

13. The degree of commitment to an opinion is a critical determinant of persuasion. With higher commitment, there is less persuasion.

14. A person can become inoculated against persuasion by being exposed to weak versions of the forthcoming persuasive arguments, and learning to combat them.

15. Forewarning of the position to be advocated tends to increase resistance to change when the listener is highly committed to a very discrepant position. But with weak commitment, forewarning can help to get the persuasion

process started, and attitude change occurs even before the full communication is heard.

16. Distraction can help create persuasion by reducing the listener's defenses against very discrepant messages.

SUGGESTIONS FOR ADDITIONAL READING

ABELSON, R. P., ARONSON, E., McGUIRE, W. J., NEWCOMB, T. M., ROSENBERG, M. J., & TANNENBAUM, P. E. *Theories of cognitive consistency: A sourcebook.* Chicago: Rand McNally, 1968. An extensive compilation of papers on almost every version of consistency theory, by almost everyone who ever wrote about it. Its nickname is TOCCAS.

EAGLY, A. H., & HIMMELFARB, S. Attitudes and opinions. In M. R. Rosenzweig and L. W. Porter (eds.), *Annual Review of Psychology.* Vol. 29. Palo Alto: Annual Reviews Inc., 1978. Every three years, the *Annual Review* has a comprehensive essay reviewing recent research on attitudes and opinions. Previous reviews have been compiled by Kiesler and Munson (1975), Fishbein and Azjen (1972), Sears and Abeles (1969), and McGuire (1966).

FISHBEIN, M., & AJZEN, I. *Belief, attitude, intention, and behavior: An introduction to theory and research.* Reading, Mass.: Addison-Wesley, 1975. A clear and systematic development of an approach strongly influenced by consistency theories.

HOVLAND, C. I., JANIS, I. L., & KELLEY, H. H. *Communication and persuasion.* New Haven, Conn.: Yale University Press, 1953. The original presentation of the best program in experimental studies of attitude change. Much of the rest of the work described in this chapter springs from work originally presented here.

KIESLER, C. A., COLLINS, B. E., & MILLER, N. *Attitude change: A critical analysis of theoretical approaches.* New York: John Wiley, 1969. A good overview of the several different approaches to attitude theory covered in this chapter.

LEVENTHAL, H., & NILES, P. A field experiment on fear arousal with data on the validity of questionnaire responses. *Journal of Personality,* 1964, *32,* 459–79. An ingeniously designed, realistic field experiment conducted at the New York City Health Exposition, on the effects of fear arousal regarding smoking and lung cancer.

McGUIRE, W. J. The nature of attitudes and attitude change. In G. Lindzey & E. Aronson (eds.), *Handbook of social psychology.* Vol 3. Reading, Mass.: Addison-Wesley, 1969. Pp. 136–314. The most complete review of attitude research and theory that has been written.

Attitudes and Behavior

© Bettye Lane; Photo Researchers, Inc.

The preceding chapter dealt only with the *attitudes* of the target of influence. The person's *behavior* is also sometimes implicated in an influence attempt, in one of two ways. A person's behavior might control his attitudes. Or the person's attitudes might control his behavior.

Take the first possibility. All the research in the preceding chapters has dealt with situations in which the target of influence is a more or less passive listener. This, of course, is the way much influence in our society takes place. Mass communications, such as TV commercials or PTA meetings, have that character. Even person-to-person exchanges or influence exerted in small groups frequently represent one-way communication. But in many other situations, the target of influence is very much involved in the process, as an active participant. So in this chapter we will deal with research that builds in the target's own behavior as an ingredient in predicting attitude change.

Second, as we have seen in Chapter 9, we are often interested in influencing an individual's overt behavior. And many techniques are highly successful in producing behavioral conformity or compliance. But most of the techniques we have discussed demand continuing surveillence by the influencer. For example, once the unanimous majority in the Asch line-judging experiment leaves the room, all influence over the lone, naïve subject is lost. The person's true attitudes were unaffected by the conformity pressures; only his overt behavior was influenced. So, we are often interested in producing attitude change because we assume it is a necessary first step in getting lasting changes in behavior. Only if we can persuade older, white middle-class grade school teachers to be less frightened and prejudiced will they be able to teach black children effec-tively. Only if we can inspire young soldiers to attitudes of patriotism or loyalty to their unit will they fight with courage and fearlessness.

And yet we know of many instances in which people's behavior does not follow from their attitudes. How many times have you seen people smile and say how pleased they are to meet someone when you know they are either bored stiff or hate them? The Watergate tapes revealed just how far Nixon's public behavior departed from his private attitudes. This raises a second question for this chapter. Do attitudes control behavior? Under what conditions?

THEORY OF COGNITIVE DISSONANCE

First let us take up the possibility that our behavior controls our at-titudes. Another way to put it is that our attitudes are sometimes just ra-tionalizations for what we have already done. Most of the research in this area has been inspired by the theory of cognitive dissonance. Like several other theories we have discussed, cognitive dissonance theory assumes that there is a tendency toward cognitive consistency. According to the theory, *dissonance* exists between two cognitions that are inconsistent with each other. Cognitions may be facts, beliefs, or opinions about anything, including one's own behavior. Any two cognitions are either *consonant*—that is, consistent with one another; *dissonant*, inconsistent; or irrelevant, where the existence of one implies nothing about the other.

Although it nominally can be applied to inconsistencies between any cognitions, cognitive dissonance theory has dealt most creatively with inconsistencies between behavior (or, more precisely, cognitions about one's own behavior) and attitudes. It has dealt with two particular kinds of behavior-attitude inconsistencies. Leon Festinger (1957), who developed cognitive dissonance theory, argued that making a decision or committing oneself to some course of action almost inevitably creates dissonance. No matter how perfect the choice, there are always some bad things about it (whether they are bad things about the chosen alternative, or good things about rejected alternatives). Negative attitudes toward these shortcomings are inconsistent with the act of making the decision itself, and that inconsistency produces dissonance.

There are also cases in which people engage in behavior which is counter to their attitudes, and these situations also create cognitive dissonance. Sometimes they are forced into it, because they have been drafted into the army, or because a hated regime has taken over their country. Sometimes they are simply seduced into it, or charmed into it; sometimes guilt makes them do it. In Chapter 9 we discussed a number of reasons why people do things they do not believe in. The point here is that engaging in behavior discrepant from attitudes leads to cognitive dissonance.

Dissonance creates psychological tension, and people feel pressured to reduce or remove it. Dissonance operates much like any other drive: if we are hungry, we do something to reduce our hunger; if we are afraid, we do something to reduce our fear; and if we feel dissonance, we do something to reduce it also. The main ways of reducing dissonance are to *add consonant* cognitions, or to *change dissonant* cognitions so they are no longer inconsistent. Since the magnitude of the dissonance depends on the number of consonant and dissonant elements, either of these methods should reduce the amount of dissonance.

By adding consonant elements to the system the relative number of dissonant elements can be reduced, which reduces the magnitude of the dissonance. The pacifist who joins the Marines probably finds it difficult to convince himself that either his pacifist attitudes or his act of joining the Marines is unimportant. But he can think of other consonant elements in the situation. He may decide that joining the Marines is a way of defending his country and the "free" world. This belief is consonant with the act of joining and would reduce the total amount of dissonance in the situation. If he has been offered a bonus of $10,000, special training in electronics, and a high rank, these also are good reasons for joining and are consonant with the behavior. His act is still inconsistent—dissonant—with his belief in pacifism, but the total amount of dissonance he feels is reduced. Alternatively, he can change one element no longer dissonant with the other. The pacifist who joins the Marines may decide that he does not believe in pacifism any more, that people are generally pretty brutal and selfish, so there is a need for a rugged national defense. Or he may change his attitude about the Marine Corps. Instead of thinking that the Marines are all killers, he may conclude that the surest way to avoid war is to have a strong military.

To summarize the major ideas of the theory of cognitive dissonance: (1) when a person holds two inconsistant cognitions, dissonance exists; (2) the greater the proportion of dissonant to consonant cognitions (and, obviously, the more important they are), the more dissonance is aroused; and (3) dissonance is unpleasant, and the individual tends to reduce it, usually by changing cognitions.

Postdecisional Dissonance

One behavior that almost always arouses dissonance is decision making. Whenever we must decide between two or more alternatives, whatever choice we make is to some extent inconsistent with some of our beliefs. After we decide, all the good aspects of the unchosen alternative and all the bad aspects of the chosen alternative are dissonant with the decision. If we decide to buy a Mercedes-Benz instead of a Honda, the Mercedes' speed, and stylishness, and the Honda's crampedness and homeliness, are consonant with the decision. But the Mercedes' price, and its penchant for expensive repairs, and the inexpensiveness and ease of upkeep of the Honda, are dissonant with the decision.

This dissonance can be reduced by changing our evaluations of the chosen and unchosen alternatives. Increasing the attractiveness and value of the chosen alternative reduces dissonance, because everything positive about it is consonant with the decision. Dissonance can also be reduced by lowering the evaluation of the unchosen alternative. The less attractive it is, the less dissonance should be aroused by choosing the other. Therefore, after someone has made a decision, there is a tendency for him to increase his liking for what he chose and to decrease his liking for what he did not choose. After choosing the Mercedes over the Honda we tend to rate the Mercedes even higher than we did before and the Honda even lower.

A study by Brehm (1956) demonstrated this effect. College women were shown eight products, such as a toaster, a stopwatch, and a radio, and were asked to indicate how much they would like to have each of them. They were then shown two of the eight products and told they would be given whichever they chose. After the objects were chosen and the subjects received the one they selected, they were asked to rate all the objects again. As shown in Table 11–1, on the second rating there was a

TABLE 11–1

Dissonance Reduction Following a Decision

CONDITION	RATING OF CHOSEN OBJECT	RATING OF UNCHOSEN OBJECT	TOTAL REDUCTION[a]
High dissonance (objects initially rated close)	+.32	−.53	.85
Low dissonance (objects initially rated far apart)	+.25	−.12	.37
No dissonance (gift— no choice)	.00	na	.00

[a] Figures are the increased evaluation of the chosen object plus the decrease in evaluation of the unchosen object.

Source: From Brehm (1956).

strong tendency for the women to increase their evaluation of the item they had picked and to decrease their evaluation of the other item.

A control group (shown on the bottom line in the table) shows that the effect was due primarily to dissonance reduction. These women made the first rating but, instead of next choosing between two items and receiving their preference, they were simply given one of the products they had rated high. When they rerated all the products, they showed no tendency to increase the evaluation of the object they owned. This demonstrated that the reevaluation was not simply due to pride of owner-ship—making the decision was the critical factor.

The tendency toward reevaluation is particularly strong when the two alternatives are initially rated close. If, before making a decision about which car to buy, we much prefer the Ford to the Toyota, we have little difficulty deciding and there is relatively little dissonance afterward. There are few reasons why we should have made the opposite choice and therefore few dissonant elements. Since there is little dissonance, there is relatively little change in our evaluations of the two alternatives. On the other hand, if the Ford and the Toyota were close in our estimation before we made the decision, it should arouse a great deal of dissonance. The more reason we had for choosing the Toyota, the more dissonance is aroused by picking the Ford. Thus, when two alternatives are close, a great deal of dissonance is aroused. After the decision is made, there are greater reevaluations of the two alternatives.

Brehm tested this notion also. He gave some women a choice be-tween a product they had ranked high and one they had ranked only one point below it. Other women were given a choice between a high-ranked product and one that was, on the average, two and one-half points below it. Thus, some had to choose between two products they liked approx-imately equally, and others had the easier choice between products that

FIGURE 11–2 People with religious beliefs, especially beliefs not generally accepted by the rest of society, often attempt to convert others to their views.

were quite different in their evaluation. As shown in Table 11–1, the two conditions differed considerably in the amount of dissonance reduction they produced after the choice. When the products were far apart initially (the low-dissonance condition), there was a total of .37 scale points of dissonance reduction; when the products were quite close (the high-dissonance condition), there was a total of .85 scale points of dissonance reduction. As the theory predicts, the closer the alternatives to begin with, the more dissonance aroused by the decision and the more attitude change after the decision is made.

Dissonance is often created when, having committed ourselves strongly to a course of action, we find the results to be inconsistent with what we expected. This was the reaction of a group who predicted the end of the world (Festinger et al., 1956). They thought that the world was going to end on a particular day but that they would be saved by a spaceship from outer space. The group kept to itself, avoided publicity, and in general was quiet about its beliefs. When the fateful day arrived and

BOX 11-2
POSTDECISION DISSONANCE AT POSTTIME

According to dissonance theory, making a decision produces dissonance and also produces attitude change that will help justify that decision. Knox and Inkster (1968) reasoned that bettors at a horse track ought to be susceptible to this process. After they have irreversibly put their money down on a horse at the betting window, they ought to be in a state of dissonance. To justive the bet, they should overestimate their horse's chances. So they interviewed one sample of bettors just before they reached the window, and another sample just after they had completed their bets. They found the postbet group was considerably more certain their horse would win than was the prebet group, as dissonance theory would predict. A control group was interviewed before making a bet and then again afterwards, to determine whether last-minute switches to the favorite might have explained the difference, but none had changed horses in the short time span between interviews. The authors conclude with a quote from one of the prebet subjects, who approached the postbet interviewer and volunteered this: "Are you working with that other fellow there?" (indicating the prebet experimenter who was by then engaged in another interview), "Well, I just told him that my horse had a fair chance of winning. Will you have him change that to a good chance? No, by God, make that an excellent chance."

passed without the world being destroyed, they were initially greatly shaken. Their response, however, was not to give up their beliefs and return to normal life. This would not have reduced the dissonance caused by all the effort they had put into their plans. Instead, they decided that the day was put off but that the end of the world was coming soon. In addition, they changed their style considerably. Instead of being quiet and avoiding publicity, they suddenly began to proselytize quite actively. They argued that their efforts had postponed the end of the world. And they became much more active in trying to get new supporters. Presumably, this helped reduce their dissonance by showing that their original beliefs were basically correct and that, in fact, more and more people were accepting them.

ATTITUDE–DISCREPANT BEHAVIOR

The other situation to which the theory of cognitive dissonance has been most often applied is that of **attitude-discrepant behavior.** Although this is probably the most interesting application of the theory, it is also the

most controversial, because dissonance theory comes into the most direct conflict with the incentive and attribution approaches to attitudes. We shall describe first the dissonance analysis and some of the work that has stemmed from it and later some conflicting interpretations of this situation.

The analysis in terms of dissonance is quite straightforward. When an individual holds a belief and performs an act that is inconsistent with it, dissonance is produced, because of the inconsistency between that belief and the knowledge that he has performed that particular behavior. If someone is a pacifist, he would not join the Marines. If he does so, he feels dissonance. He can reduce this dissonance by changing his attitude on pacifism. Someone who believes a task is dull and is then induced to tell someone else that the task is really enjoyable experiences dissonance. He can reduce this dissonance by evaluating the task more positively; if the task were enjoyable, his description would be accurate and no dissonance would be experienced.

Whenever someone performs an attitude-discrepant behavior, she should experience some dissonance and there should be a tendency for her attitude to change. Note that the other element in the situation (her knowledge that she performed the behavior) does not change readily. She has, in fact, performed the act and would find it difficult to convince herself that she did not. Accordingly, most of the pressure must be relieved by changing the attitude. This analysis explains why engaging in attitude-discrepant behavior produces changes in the relevant attitude. The discrepant act arouses dissonance that can be reduced most easily by changing the attitude to make it less discrepant from the behavior.

The next question is what determines how much attitude change will

Michael D. Sullivan.

FIGURE 11–3 Although most people believe that smoking is bad for their health, many smoke anyway. Exactly how they reduce the dissonance this causes, is unclear.

occur as a result of such behavior. The more dissonance aroused, the more attitude change will be necessary to reduce it. As discussed previously, the amount of dissonance aroused depends on the relative number of dissonant and consonant elements. So anything in the situation that puts pressure on the individual to perform the discrepant act or provides a reason for performing it is a consonant element and should reduce the amount of dissonance. If the pacifist is warned he will be jailed if he does not join the Marines, he will experience less dissonance than he would have otherwise.

On the other hand, there has to be enough pressure on the person to make him commit the counterattitudinal act. A person normally does not act in a way contrary to his attitudes unless there is some reason to do so. So imagine the person as being subjected to a certain level of pressure to perform the attitude-discrepant act. The pressure has to be sufficient to produce the act. Yet beyond that level, the more pressure is exerted, the less the dissonance, and thus the less the attitude change. The optimal level of pressure is thus a *barely sufficient* amount—enough to produce the behavior, but not enough to remove the dissonance. This assumption has led to interesting and provocative predictions regarding the effect of various factors on the amount of attitude change resulting from attitude-discrepant behavior in quite a number of different situations.

Perhaps the simplest way to get people to perform attitude-discrepant behavior is to pay them money. There is some minimum payment that is necessary to get the person to perform it. But beyond that minimal positive incentive, the more money someone is paid for performing an attitude-discrepant act, the less dissonance should be produced if he performs it. So paradoxically, after a certain point, the *more* money the person is paid, *the less* he will change his attitude to justify having done it. Suppose you are offered a menial summer job but the pay is extremely good. There is no dissonance—you are doing it for the good money— and so there is no pressure to reevaluate the job. But suppose you work at a minimum wage, say $3.00 an hour. Then dissonance is created, which you might reduce by reevaluating the job; perhaps you start to think that it is an educational experience, or that you meet very interesting people, or that you have plenty of freedom to do other things. The idea is that the *more* original pressure to perform the act (that is, the more consonant cognitions), the *less* the pressure to change your attitudes to make them consistent with the action.

The best early example of this point is found in a study by Festinger and Carlsmith (1959). Volunteers for an experiment worked on an exceedingly dull task. After they had completed the task, the experimenter said he needed their help because his usual assistant was unable to be there that day. He said that he was studying the effect of preconceptions on people's performance on a task. He was studying several groups of subjects who were told good things about the task ahead of time, bad things, or nothing. The next subject was supposed to receive favorable information about the task before performing it. The experimenter then asked the subject whether he would be willing to do this for him. All he would have to do is stop the next subject as he was coming into the room, talk to him briefly about the experiment, and tell him that the task was an exceedingly enjoyable one. In other words, he was supposed to pretend to be a regular subject who was just completing the experiment and to lie to the next subject about the dull task by saying that he had found it enjoyable.

At this point, the key experimental manipulation was introduced. Some subjects were told that the experimenter would pay them $1 for helping, and other subjects were told they would be paid $20. Virtually all the subjects agreed to the arrangement and proceeded to describe the task to the next subject as very enjoyable. There was also a control group, the members of which were not asked to lie. Soon afterward, the experimenter had all the subjects indicate how much they had actually enjoyed the task. Dissonance about telling the lie could be reduced by changing attitudes about the task—that is, by deciding that the task was quite enjoyable.

The key comparison was between the $1 and $20 conditions (Table 11–2). Those who were paid $1 rated the task more positively than those who were paid $20. This is what dissonance theory would predict. The

TABLE 11–2

Amount of Reward and Attitude Change

CONDITION	ENJOYED TASK	WILLING TO PARTICIPATE IN SIMILAR EXPERIMENTS
$1 reward	+ 1.35	+ 1.20
$20 reward	− .05	− .25
Control	− .45	− .62

Source: Adapted from Festinger and Carlsmith (1959).

larger amount of money served as an additional reason for performing the task; therefore it was a consonant element in the situation and reduced the overall amount of dissonance. The less dissonance, the less attitude change. Thus the more the subjects were paid for performing the discrepant behavior, the less attitude change they experienced.

Many similar experiments have used a variety of positive incentives. One factor is the amount of justification for performing a boring task. If someone voluntarily engages in an extremely dull activity, she generally feels dissonance, because knowledge that the task is dull is dissonant with the knowledge that she is performing it. Any reason she has for performing the task reduces this dissonance, if she thinks it is scientifically useful or will help somebody else, she would feel less dissonance than if she believes it is useless. So Freedman (1963) told subjects that his study concerned concepts of numbers and that the experimental method involved their writing a large number of random numbers. The amount of justification they received for doing the task was manipulated by telling some subjects that the work they did would be extremely useful, while others (the low-justification subjects) were told that all the necessary sessions had been conducted the previous week and the data were already being analyzed. These tests would be run because they had already been scheduled, but the data from their performance would not be included in the analysis of the results.

Then all the subjects performed the task, which was to write random numbers in the small squares on graph paper for twelve minutes. (This is an exceedingly dull, tedious task, and twelve minutes is about the limit of most people's endurance.) When the task was completed, the subjects were asked to indicate how much they had enjoyed it. Those who had been given low justification said they enjoyed it considerably more than those who had been given high justification. As found in the other work on this problem, the more reason one has for doing something, the less dissonance is aroused and the less need there is to reduce the dissonance by changing one's evaluation of the task.

BOX 11-3
COLD COOK, GREAT GRASSHOPPERS

Another factor that affects the amount of justification we have for engaging in a discrepant act is how much we like the person who is trying to get us to do it. If your best friend asks you to do something—lend him ten dollars, drive him to the airport, help him cheat on an exam—there is a considerable amount of pressure to agree. If someone you dislike asks you, you are under considerably less pressure. Under most circumstances, it is more difficult to refuse a friend. Thus, if you do something for someone, there should be more dissonance aroused if you dislike the other person than if you like him. The more you like the other person, the more justification you have for agreeing (for performing the discrepant act) and the less dissonance there will be. This, in turn, means that agreeing to perform a discrepant act for somebody you dislike produces more attitude change than performing the same act for someone you like.

This effect was demonstrated in a study (Zimbardo et al., 1965) in which subjects were persuaded by two different kinds of experimenters to eat grasshoppers. In one condition, the experimenter was pleasant, casual, relaxed, and friendly. He represented his arguments in an offhand manner and did his best to be as attractive as possible. In the other condition, the experi-menter was cold, formal, somewhat aggressive, and rather forbidding. In general, he did everything he could to be unpleasant. After the subjects who had chosen to eat the grasshoppers had done so, they indicated how much they liked them.

The analysis in terms of dissonance is straightforward. If a subject chose to eat the grasshoppers, dissonance existed if he disliked them. This dissonance could be reduced by making his evaluation of the grasshoppers more positive. To the extent that he liked the experimenter and was eating the grasshoppers as a favor to him, he had additional justification for performing the discrepant behavior. Therefore, the more he liked the experimenter, the less dissonance would exist and the less need he would have to decide that he really liked the grasshoppers.

The results were consistent with this analysis. Subjects who ate the grasshoppers when there was a nasty experimenter liked the grasshoppers more than those who ate the grasshoppers when there was a pleasant experimenter. The pleasant experimenter provided justification, which reduced the dissonance and therefore made it less necessary to reevaluate the grasshoppers.

Another direct, forceful pressure is threat. One way to try to get the individual to perform a disliked act is to threaten him with punishment. If he does not pay his income taxes, do his homework, wash behind his ears, or allow himself to be drafted into the army, he is penalized. Threats are also used to prevent people from doing things. If someone drives too fast, steals cookies from the cookie jar, plays with a forbidden toy, or smokes marijuana, he may be punished. The severity of the possible punishments varies enormously. He may get a mild reprimand, miss his dessert, be fined $100, spend five years in jail, or even face execution. Assuming the threat of punishment is strong enough to produce the desired behavior or suppress the wrong behavior, greater threat should produce less attitude change.

In experiments by Aronson and Carlsmith (1963) and Freedman (1965), children were shown a group of toys and then were forbidden to play with one of them. They were threatened with either mild or severe punishment if they played with that particular toy. Under these circumstances, if they obeyed and did not play with the toy, dissonance was aroused. The cognition "I would like to play with that toy" is dissonant with the cognition "I am not playing with it." If there were no other relevant cognitions, it would follow from liking the toy that they would play with it. In this situation, the threat served as a consonant element: "I will be punished if I play with it." The key point is that the more severe threat was a stronger consonant element, and should have resulted in less total dissonance.

If the children did not play with the toy, we would expect the dissonance aroused to produce some change in their attitude toward it. A convenient way to reduce the dissonance would be to decide that the toy was not attractive or to accept the belief that it was wrong to play with it. Either change would make their attitude less dissonant with their behavior. The greater the dissonance aroused, the more changes of this sort should occur. And because the greater the threat, the less the dissonance, there should be more attitude change with lower threats. Thus, the children would experience more attitude change when the mild threat was used to prevent them from playing with the toy than when the severe threat was used.

In these experiments, none of the children played with the toy, regardless of whether they were threatened with mild or severe punishment, because both threats were strong enough to prevent them. In the Aronson and Carlsmith study, the children rerated the toys at this point. In Freedman's study, several weeks after the first session another experimenter came and gave the children an opportunity to play with some toys if they wanted to. The previously forbidden toy was one of the toys and nothing was said about not playing with it; the children were free to play with it if they desired. In this second session, the only thing that would have prevented the children from playing with the toy was some

TABLE 11-3
Effect of Severity of Threat on Forbidden Behavior

CONDITION	PERCENTAGE DEVALUING FORBIDDEN TOY[a]	PERCENTAGE NOT PLAYING WITH FORBIDDEN TOY[b]
Mild threat	36	71
Severe threat	0	33

Source: [a] Aronson and Carlsmith (1963); [b] Freedman (1965).

feeling that it was wrong to play with it or that the toy was no longer desirable. The results of the two experiments are shown in Table 11–3. It can be seen that in the Aronson and Carlsmith study, the children reduced their evaluation of the forbidden toy more under mild threat than under severe threat. Similarly, in Freedman's study, fewer children in the mild-threat condition than in the severe-threat condition played with the toy when they were actually given the opportunity to do so. The greater threat presumably served as a consonant element in the situation and reduced the amount of dissonance produced by not playing with the toy in the first session. The greater dissonance in the mild-threat condition was reduced by either devaluing the toy or deciding it was wrong to play with it.

The implications of this relationship are very interesting. It strongly suggests that severe threats should be avoided whenever possible. The smaller the threat used, the more attitude change is to be expected. For example, if a parent wants to teach his child to be honest, he should try to do so without using strong threats. If he is successful when using only mild threats, the child is more likely to accept the *value* that honesty is good and stealing bad. If, instead, the parent uses strong threats, even if they seem to be successful in making the child behave honestly, it is less likely that the child will accept the value that honesty is inherently good. He may decide that honesty is the best policy if there is a chance of getting caught and therefore act honestly when his parent is present. When the threat (parent) is removed, he will have experienced little internal attitude change to make him sustain honest behavior.

Much of the legal system tries to induce law-abiding behavior on exactly this basis. It threatens people with punishments that are possible but not very likely, so that people will obey the law even when they are not under constant surveillance. There are not enough police to patrol every traffic light, and in fact the likelihood of being caught running a red light is not very great. Still, almost everyone stops at red lights. The threat of punishment is just sufficient to induce behavioral compliance, and we develop attitudes that make us stop at red lights even when no police are around at all. Similarly, most people obey the tax laws even though the chances of being audited are quite slight. And most marijuana smokers do not grow it in their backyards, even though the danger of being caught is slight. Given the costs of constant surveillance of illegal behavior, the legal system must rely on threats of punishment that are just barely sufficient to induce law-abiding behavior, and hope that attitudes justifying and supporting compliance with the law will develop.

CONDITIONS FOR DISSONANCE

We have identified two general situations in which our behavior may change our attitudes: decisions and attitude-discrepant behavior. Attitude change depends on the magnitude of dissonance, and dissonance theory specifies the conditions under which more or less dissonance will be created. The most obvious are *minimal positive incentives* or *minimal threats*. The maximum dissonance is created when a decision between two alternatives is very difficult (that is, when consonant and dissonant cognitions are relatively evenly balanced) or when there are barely sufficient incentives for engaging in counterattitudinal behavior. And the behavior must have *negative consequences*. A decision must involve giving up something desirable and/or acquiring something undesirable. Attitude-discrepant behavior must lead to undesirable consequences, such as losing money or being embarrassed or someone else being harmed or angry. We have considered both of these conditions in detail already. What are some of the others?

**Certainty of
Consequences**

An interesting aspect of the effect of decisions is that the reevaluation appears only when the result of the decision is certain. If the chances are that the Mercedes is not going to need much repair work in the first two or three years, the high cost of such repairs is not going to cause much dissonance.

IRREVOCABLE COMMITMENT One key, therefore, to attitude change as a dissonance-reducing mechanism is maintaining the person's commitment to the decision or behavior. As long as the person feels irreversibly committed to that course of action, dissonance promotes attitude change. But if the person feels that he can get out of the decision if it works out badly, or that he can do it half-heartedly, or that he may not have to go through with it at all, dissonance will not be present, and no attitude change may occur. Little dissonance will be created by paying $4,000 tuition if you know you can transfer to the state university after the first quarter and get most of it refunded.

FORESEEABLE CONSEQUENCES A related point is that a person must feel he could have anticipated the negative consequences of a decision, or no dissonance is produced. There should be nothing dissonant about making a choice or performing an act that turned out badly as long as there was no way for the individual to have anticipated this negative outcome. "Nobody's perfect" and nobody therefore expects to make the right decision every time. If, on the basis of all the available information, he makes a choice or performs an act, and then an entirely new and surprising negative event follows, the individual should not experience dissonance. If someone decides to walk to class on the left side of the street rather than the right side, and as he walks along a brick suddenly falls off a roof and hits him on the head, this is a terrible misfortune. But (if he lives) he should not experience dissonance. The cognition "I chose to walk on the left side of the street" is not dissonant with the cognition "a brick hit me on the head." For all intents and purposes, the two cognitions are not relevant to each other. On the other hand, if he knew that there was some chance that he would get hit on the head, perhaps because in the last week three other people had been hit on the head by bricks, then dissonance probably would be aroused.

This, then, suggests that dissonance arises from the negative consequences of a choice only when the negative consequences can be foreseen. This theoretical analysis has been supported in a series of very nice studies. In one of them, Brehm and Jones (1970) had subjects choose one of two records. There were additional positive or negative consequences to the choice: if the subject chose the correct record, she would also get free tickets to the local movie house, but if she chose the wrong one, she would get no tickets. The critical variation was whether these additional consequences of the choice were foreseen or not. In the "foreseen" condition, the experimenter told the subject about the possibility of the tickets before she made her choice, and said she could probably figure out which was the right record (i.e., the one with the free tickets attached to it) if she thought about it. In the "unforeseen" condition, subjects were told about the tickets only after making their choices. Then all subjects rated the original records. The dissonance prediction was that dissonance would be maximum when the person's choice had foreseen negative consequences, and much less with foreseen positive consequences, or unforeseen negative consequences. And this is how the data turned out, as shown in Table 11–4.

This indicates dissonance is caused by the consequences of an act that we have explicitly thought about and foreseen. Sometimes, however, an act has consequences we did not anticipate, but in retrospect we know we should have. Suppose you and your girlfriend graduate from the University of Wisconsin. You then enter law school at Stanford. She says she loves you forever but decides to stay at Wisconsin to get her MBA. You don't want to lose her, but you don't want to miss law school either. So you decide to go. You both promise to write and call and spend all vacations together, and you assume all will be well. In April you get an invitation to her June wedding to a senior law student at the University of Wisconsin. You are crushed. Do you have dissonance? You made your

TABLE 11–4

**Mean Dissonance Reduction, as a Function
of Consequences of Choice**

	FORESEEN	UNFORESEEN
Negative Consequences (got no tickets)	+1.73	+0.25
Positive Consequences (received tickets)	+0.38	+1.07

Note: Entry is sum of increased rating of chosen object and decreased rating of rejected object, following choice.
Source: Adapted from Brehm and Jones (1970), p. 427.

decision, but you did not foresee what would happen; you really believed all those promises. On the other hand, looking back on it, you can see it was a foreseeable consequence of your move; it is hard to maintain a close relationship at a great distance for a long time. So, do unforeseen, but *foreseeable,* bad consequences cause dissonance?

Goethals, Cooper, and Naficy (1979) predicted that *foreseeable* consequences, even if unforeseen, would produce dissonance and attitude change; only unforeseeable consequences would not. They had students at Princeton record speeches favoring the doubling of the size of the freshman class. That was a disagreeable possibility to the subjects, given Princeton's reputation as a relatively small, elite college. The possible negative consequence was that the speech might help bring about that undesirable change. Some (foreseen consequences) were told the speech might be given to the board of admissions, which was considering such an increase; others (foreseeable consequences) that it would be given to some other groups, but they were not named. Still others (unforeseeable consequences) were not told of any further use of the speech. After the speech was recorded, all were told of the negative consequences: their counterattitudinal speech would be given to the board of admissions. Under what circumstances did the subjects change their attitudes in the dissonance-reducing direction of their speech? It turned out that either foreseen or foreseeable consequences promoted attitude change, in line with the notion that either can produce dissonance. The answer is that you probably now believe the move to the Stanford law school has turned your future to gold, and you never liked your ex-girlfriend's loud laugh anyway.

**Personal
Responsibility**

CHOICE Another major contributor to dissonance is the feeling of choice about the behavior. If you feel you freely and of sound mind chose the Mercedes, you will have dissonance to reduce afterward. But many times we do not feel much sense of choice about what we do. Maybe the salesperson talked us into signing a contract and writing a check before we knew what was happening. Or maybe our old car had been wrecked and this was the only new one available. Without the feeling of choice, there is no dissonance.

Similarly, attitude-discrepant behavior creates dissonance only when the behavior is freely chosen (or at least the person feels it is freely chosen). This is shown quite clearly in two experiments by Linder, Cooper, and Jones (1967). Subjects wrote an essay that disagreed with their opinion on an issue. Some subjects were made to feel that they had free choice about whether or not they wrote the essay, whereas others were given no choice. Half the subjects in each condition were paid $2.50, and half were paid $0.50. The amount of attitude change in the four conditions for the two experiments is shown in Table 11–5.

With free choice, the typical dissonance effect appeared; there was more change with less reward. With no choice, the dissonance effect did not obtain; indeed, there was more change with greater reward. As we suggested earlier, perception of choice is necessary for the arousal of dissonance. When there is no choice, dissonance is not produced and the dissonance analysis does not apply.

RESPONSIBILITY FOR CONSEQUENCES   The importance of perceived choice is that it brings with it perceived responsibility for all consequences, whether or not it is "logical" to feel responsible for them. As we saw earlier in connection with attribution theory, people tend to make internal attributions whenever behavior is committed under free choice, and assign moral responsibility for that internally caused. A series of studies has shown this crucial role of the feeling of responsibility. For example, Collins and Hoyt (1972) approached student subjects in their dormitories and asked them to write essays against open visitation rights for the opposite sex (virtually all the subjects were in favor of open visitation rights). The design of the experiment was similar to many of the others discussed in this section on dissonance theory, so we can just focus on the particular set of conditions that seem to have produced dissonance, and

TABLE   11–5
Reward, Choice, and Attitude Change

CONDITION	FREE CHOICE	NO CHOICE
Experiment 1:		
$0.50 reward	2.96	1.66
$2.50 reward	1.64	2.34
Experiment 2:		
$0.50 reward	3.64	2.68
$2.50 reward	2.72	3.46

Note: The figures are ratings on a scale from 1 to 7. The higher the figure, the greater the attitude change.
Source: Adapted from Linder, Cooper, and Jones (1967).

consequent attitude change. These involved low incentive (50 cents paid to write the essay, rather than $2.50), high negative consequences (university administrators would use the essay in determining university policy, rather than filing it as a document of mere historical interest), and personal responsibility (the subject signed a form taking responsibility for the contents of the essay, rather than stating he was just following an assigned topic and was not responsible for the contents). Under these conditions, the subjects did change their attitudes toward the position consistent with their attitude-discrepant act. That is, they became more opposed to open visitation rights.

It turns out that even unforeseen negative consequences provoke dissonance, as long as the decision maker feels responsible for the consequences. If he feels no responsibility for the outcome, there is no dissonance regardless of how disastrous the result. If he does feel responsible, then dissonance occurs whether the consequence could reasonably have been foreseen or not. Pallak and his colleagues designed a series of studies to illustrate this point. In the first one (Pallak, Sogin, & Van Zante, 1974) a boring task was reevaluated in a more favorable direction, consistent with dissonance reduction, even when the negative consequences (learning that the task was just wasted time) were not known until after the task was completed—as long as the subject completed it under high perceived choice. In a second experiment, they found that perceived choice inspired more favorable evaluations of the task only when given unforeseen negative consequences, again consistent with a dissonance analysis. As they say, "initial volition may imply responsibility for unforeseen consequences." And in late work (Sogin & Pallak, 1976), they pinpointed the effect as depending on an internal attribution. If the negative consequences came about because of something the subject felt responsible for, a dissonance reevaluation would take place whether the effects were foreseen or unforeseen.

So the critical question regarding unforeseen negative consequences is whether or not the individual *feels* her own prior behavior was responsible for them. That is why perceived choice is so important. When a person chooses something that works out badly, she feels responsible for the outcome, and it creates dissonance for her.

And this is the importance of postmortems on political disasters, whether large ones like the Nazi mass murders of Jews, or relatively small ones like Watergate. The issue is whether the culprits were just "following orders" or not—that is, did they have free choice, and thus responsibility for the consequences? The importance of the dissonance approach to such problems is that when people feel they have no choice, they do not feel responsible for the consequences and therefore do not have to defend them. People who felt they were "just following orders" find it easier to criticize their own acts. But people who made the original decisions and felt free to do so have to defend their actions more strenuously.

These, then, are the main preconditions for cognitive dissonance, and for the attitude change that results from taking decisive action: minimum incentives, irrevocable commitment and foreseeable negative consequences, and personal responsibility for the consequences (usually indexed by perceived choice). This is a somewhat narrower set of conditions than originally proposed by dissonance theorists. Both postdecisional dissonance and dissonance inspired by attitude-discrepant behavior are not as common as had been believed in the earliest versions of dissonance theory. But they do occur fairly reliably, given this restricted set of circumstances.

ALTERNATIVE THEORIES

**Incentive
Theory**

Thus far, we have described the effect of attitude-discrepant behavior entirely in terms of cognitive dissonance. An alternative conceptualization of the situation has been made in terms of learning or incentive. Someone who engages in attitude-discrepant behavior tends to be exposed to information and experiences he otherwise would not be. And these may be convincing, all by themselves. A child who is induced to taste spinach, which he thinks he hates, will discover what spinach tastes like; a pacifist who joins the Marines will discover a lot more about the Marines than he knew before; and a police officer who is somehow induced to argue in favor of legalizing marijuana may think of some arguments he would not otherwise have heard or listened to. Exposure to this information may, in itself, change the individual's attitude. He may discover that spinach tastes good or that the Marines are a great group. Moreover, someone who argues against his own position may convince himself. If he tries to come up with the best possible arguments, he will be exposed to very persuasive communications. Thus, rather than dissonance reduction causing the attitude change, it may be due to the usual process of persuasion by effective arguments.

Although the two explanations are quite different, they are not completely inconsistent. Both play a role. Individuals do change their attitudes in order to make them consistent with the discrepant behavior; and people are to some extent influenced by their experiences while engaging in the discrepant behavior. Both processes usually work in the same direction. Operating together, they make the effect of discrepant behavior even stronger than it would be if one of them operated alone.

The one apparent contradiction involves the effect of incentives. Dissonance theory predicts that there is more change with less incentive, given the dissonance-arousing conditions cited earlier (irrevocable commitment and the feeling of responsibility for negative consequences). The learning explanation predicts that, under some circumstances, greater incentive for performing the discrepant act produces more attitude change than less incentive. This occurs when the added incentive in some way exposes the individual to more convincing information. For example, if someone is induced to make a speech defending a position opposite from his own, it might be expected that the more he is paid for doing so, the harder he would work and the better job he would do. Doing a better job means constructing better arguments and presenting them more forcefully. The better the arguments, the more convincing they are. This holds for the individual making the speech as well as for those listening to it. Therefore, if the larger sum of money caused the individual to make a better speech, he would convince himself more and we would expect more attitude change.

These two points of view can be reconciled rather neatly. More incentive should actually *increase* attitude change, due to greater learning, if dissonance is not created—for example, if the person does not feel responsible for any negative consequences. But more incentive should decrease attitude change if dissonance is created. An experiment by Carlsmith, Collins, and Helmreich (1966) demonstrates both these effects and supports this way of resolving the conflict. As in earlier experiments, subjects were induced to take a stand discrepant from their own opinion by having them take part in a dull task and then say that it was really fun, interesting, and exciting. Some subjects told the lie in a face-to-face situation to someone who was supposedly another experimental subject. This condition was expected to arouse a considerable amount of dissonance because it involved a public commitment to the lie and clear personal responsibility for its consequences. Other subjects were told to write an essay describing the task as enjoyable. However, these essays were to be anonymous, would never be shown to other subjects, and would be used only as sources of phrases and ideas for an essay the experimenter himself would eventually write. This condition was expected to arouse little or no dissonance, because the subject was simply performing an exercise and was in no way committing himself publicly to the discrepant message. Some subjects in each condition were paid $5.00 for performing the task; some were paid $1.50; and some were paid $.50. After performing the discrepant behavior, all the subjects were asked to rerate how enjoyable the original task had been.

The results are shown in Figure 11–4. It is apparent that they are consistent with the explanation above. In the role play condition, designed to arouse dissonance, there was more attitude change with less incentive. In the essay condition designed not to arouse dissonance, the opposite was found: there was more change with more money. Other studies have also demonstrated that the effect of rewards and other forms of justification depend on the particular conditions specified above. In general, greater incentives for performing a discrepant act result in less attitude change if dissonance is aroused, and that is most likely when the person feels a strong sense of responsibility for negative consequences of her act.

Note that we are referring only to change produced by attitude-

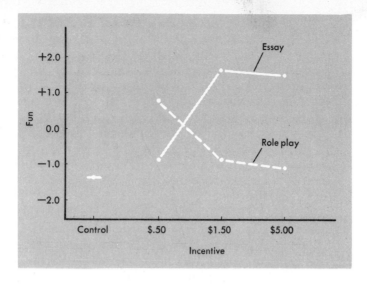

FIGURE 11–4 Forced compliance, incentive, and attitude change. When dissonance was aroused (the roleplay condition), greater incentive produced less attitude change; when dissonance was not aroused (essay condition), greater incentive produced more change.

Source: Carlsmith, Collins, and Helmreich, "Studies in forced compliance," *Journal of Personality and Social Psychology*, 1966, *4*, p. 9. Copyright 1966 by the American Psychological Association. Reprinted by permission.

discrepant behavior. In these circumstances the dissonance effect is usually the dominant one. Most of the research discussed in Chapter 10 did not refer to attitude change produced by attitude-discrepant behavior. When change is produced by a persuasive communication or information of any kind, the learning effect is dominant; then, the more incentive there is in the situation, the more attitude change we expect. Thus, the dissonance explanation is particularly relevant to the effect of discrepant behavior on attitudes, and the learning explanation is more relevant and powerful in the attitude-change paradigm involving discrepant communications from someone else.

Self-Perception Theory

Daryl Bem (1967) has offered an alternative explanation for the effects of attitude-discrepant behavior, in terms of self-perception. As we saw in Chapter 5, he argues that many of our attitudes are simply based on our perceptions of our own behavior. As he put it, "Individuals come to 'know' their own ... internal states partially by inferring them from observations of their own overt behavior and/or the circumstances in which this behavior occurs. ... the individual is functionally in the same position as an outside observer, an observer who must necessarily rely upon those same external cues to infer the individual's inner states,"

(Bem, 1972, p. 5). If we eat oranges and somebody asks us how we feel about oranges, we say to ourselves, "I eat oranges; nobody is forcing me to eat them; therefore I must like oranges." Accordingly, we tell the person that we like oranges. Similarly if we vote for a Republican, we assume that we have Republican attitudes; if we go to church, we assume that we are religious; and so on.

It is easy to see how this might apply to attitude-discrepant behavior. A subject is induced to tell someone that a particular task was very enjoyable. When the subject is subsequently asked how enjoyable he thought the task was, he says to himself, "I said that the task was enjoyable so I must think that it is." But there is more to the situation than that. If he has been paid one dollar to say that the task is enjoyable, he says to himself, "I said that the task was enjoyable and I was paid only one dollar. One dollar is not enough to make me lie, so I must really think that the task is enjoyable." On the other hand twenty dollars perhaps is a sufficient amount to tell a lie. So the subject then might say to himself, "I only said it was enjoyable to get the $20; I didn't really believe it." Thus this explanation makes the same predictions as dissonance theory: the more the subject is paid to make the discrepant statement, the less he will believe it. Similar explanations can be offered for virtually all dissonance phenomena. The major difference is that instead of the subject reducing cognitive inconsistency by genuinely changing his attitudes (as in dissonance theory), he bases his perception of his own attitude on his behavior in the situation.

It is difficult to design an experiment that will test between two plausible theories like dissonance and self-perception. Bem's original demonstration of his point involved presenting outside observers with a description of one of these dissonance experiments, and then asking them to predict how the real subjects would respond. If the real subjects responded on the basis of the same information the observers had (knowledge of the situation and of the subject's overt behavior), the observers ought to be able to duplicate their responses. Of course the real subjects had access to their own internal states, while the observers did not. If the observers could duplicate the real subjects' responses, it would mean that access to those internal states was not necessary to produce the kinds of attitude changes we have been discussing. Bem's (1967) observers did in fact replicate the real subjects' responses to a remarkable degree. Such data make the self-perception interpretation of these attitude-discrepant experiments quite plausible. But they do not rule out dissonance explanations, since the observers might simply be showing they have good hunches about how people are likely to behave in various specific situations.

Another line of attack on this controversy between these theoretical positions involves the dissonance theory contention that inconsistency is uncomfortable, that it acts as a drive much like hunger, and that the subject does what she can to reduce this discomfort. Bem's analysis is entirely cognitive and certainly would not expect these situations to arouse any kind of discomfort or drive. Fortunately, this difference between the theories is directly testable. One implication of the misattribution studies discussed in Chapter 5 is that subjective arousal states can be reduced to the extent that the person attributes them to other stimuli, such as a pill. This observation can help us determine whether dissonance depends on arousal or not. The theoretical reasoning is this: Dissonance is supposed to occur when one writes an attitude-discrepant essay under high-choice conditions. But if dissonance is really an aroused internal drive, then it can be reduced by reattributing the drive to a pill, as well as by changing attitudes to restore consistency. Telling subjects that they have been given an arousing pill therefore ought to substitute for attitude change. Hence attitude change should occur when the subject cannot reattribute his reactions to dissonance-arousing situations to an external cause like a pill, but not when the pill is present. One the other hand, the Bem self-perception analysis assumes no drive. Therefore, the presence or absence of a plausible external cause like a pill is irrelevant; if dissonance is not a drive, it should not matter what causes are available for attribution.

So the dissonance-as-drive idea holds that no attitude change should occur if arousal can be attributed to some cause other than inconsistency. To test this, Zanna and Cooper (1974) gave subjects a pill; in one condition they were told the pill would make them feel tense, in the other it would make them feel relaxed. Subjects were then induced to write counterattitudinal essays under either high- or low-choice conditions.

Subjects who were supposed to feel tense because of the pill showed no dissonance effect—that is, high choice produced no more attitude change than low choice. However when the pill was only supposed to make them feel relaxed, the high-choice condition produced more attitude change in the direction of the essay than did the low choice condition, in line with the usual dissonance effect. In other words, when the subject could attribute his arousal to the pill, there was no dissonance effect, and presumably no dissonance. When the subject could not attribute his arousal to the pill, the dissonance effect occurred, presumably because he still felt aroused. So this gives additional evidence for supposing that dissonance effects do depend on some kind of physiological arousal mechanism, which can be eliminated or reduced if the subject can attribute his arousal to some extraneous stimulus such as a pill.

The other side of this coin is that attitude change can occur even if no dissonance is created, if the person becomes aroused for some extraneous but unknown reason, and misattributes the arousal to his counterattitudinal behavior. That is, the person thinks the arousal comes from her actions and not from the true (but extraneous) cause, such as drugs or exercise. Cooper, Zanna, and Taves (1978) demonstrated this by giving subjects either arousing or tranquilizing drugs that were described as only milk powder pills. Then the subjects wrote essays supporting the pardon of Richard Nixon—a disagreeable position for almost all. The idea

TABLE 11–6
Agreement with Essay as a Function of Drugs and Choice

	DRUG CONDITION		
	Arousal	Neutral	Tranquilizer
High choice	20.2	14.7	8.6
Low choice	13.9	8.3	8.0
Dissonance effect	+6.3	+6.4	+0.6

Source: Cooper, Zanna, and Toves (1978).

was that the arousal caused by the arousing pill would be misattributed to the pro-Nixon essay, thus creating pro-Nixon attitude change even in a situation normally not producing dissonance (such as low choice). On the other hand, the tranquilizer would remove all arousal, so no attitude change would occur even in a situation normally producing it (such as high choice). These were in fact the results, as shown in Table 11–6. The standard dissonance effect, more attitude change with high choice than low choice, occurred in the control condition given the neutral milk powder pills. This was simply a replication of earlier dissonance studies. The arousing pill increased attitude change with both high and low choice, presumably because the arousal was misattributed to the writing of the ''bad'' essay. And the tranquilizer apparently removed any arousal due to dissonance, because the high and low choice conditions did not differ when a tranquilizer was given. So this study provides some evidence that dissonance is like a generalized arousal.

The general principle appears to be that situations involving commitments or counterattitudinal acts create tension under the conditions described: choice, foreseeable negative consequences, minimal external pressure, and so on. Attitude change as a response depends on having no other way to reduce the tension—e.g., by blaming it on external pressure, a drug-induced state (especially if unpleasant; see Higgins et al., 1979), or by revoking the behavior.

To some extent people probably do use attribution processes to infer their own attitudes from their own behavior and from their perception of the environment controlling it. But they do so only under circumstances in which their own attitudes are, as Bem says, vague and ambiguous. Most of the important and controversial issues that arise in the public domain are not of this kind. Almost everybody knows how he or she feels about busing, intervention in wars like Vietnam or the Second World War, abortion, and so on. Under these circumstances, self-perception theory seems unlikely to be very helpful. Self-perception theory, on the other hand, is very relevant to the kind of esoteric, uninvolving issues that are very common in laboratory experiments. So we would suggest that the two processes probably work best in these two different arenas; dissonance theory with more controversial, involving salient issues, and self-perception theory on more amorphous, vague, diffuse, uninvolving, minor issues.

ATTITUDES AND BEHAVIOR

Now it is time to consider the impact of attitudes on behavior. Originally it was simply assumed that a person's attitudes determined her behavior. A person who favors a certain politician is likely to vote for him; if she likes marijuana she is likely to smoke it; if she is prejudiced against blacks, she is unlikely to send her child to a school in which blacks are in the majority. Virtually all the interest in attitude change has been generated by the assumption that attitudes do affect behavior.

But this assumption has been questioned, and has become one of the important controversies in attitude research. In a classic study, LaPiere (1934), a white professor, toured the United States with a young Chinese student and his wife. They stopped at 66 hotels or motels and at 184 restaurants. Although at the time in the United States there was rather strong prejudice against Orientals, all but one of the hotels and motels gave them space, and they were never refused service at a restaurant. Sometime later, a letter was sent to the same motels and restaurants asking whether they would accept Chinese as guests. Of the 128 establishments replying, 92 percent said they would not. That is, the Chinese couple received nearly perfect service in person, but nearly universal discrimination in the subsequent letters. LaPiere, and many after him, interpreted these findings as reflecting a major inconsistency between behavior and attitudes. Almost all the proprietors *behaved* in a tolerant fashion, but they expressed an intolerant *attitude* when questioned by letter. A similar inconsistency between intolerant verbal attitudes and tolerant overt behaviors was found by Kutner, Wilkins, and Yarrow (1952). A group of two white women and one black woman was seated in all eleven restaurants they entered. But later they telephoned for reservations for a group that included blacks and were refused by six.

Part of the controversy centers on how typical these early studies were. Wicker (1969) conducted one widely cited review. He looked at studies testing for consistency between attitudes and behavior in the areas of race relations, job satisfaction, and classroom cheating. Summarizing thirty-one separate investigations, Wicker concluded: "It is considerably more likely that attitudes will be unrelated or only slightly related to overt behavior than that attitudes will be closely related to actions." Yet this conclusion has in turn been widely criticized as underestimating attitude-behavior consistency. Indeed, numerous studies show much higher degrees of consistency than Wicker reports. For example, in one study a large sample of Taiwanese married women was asked "Do you want any more children?" In the subsequent three years, 64 percent who had said "Yes" had a live birth, whereas only 19 percent who had said "No" had a child. Another example is voting behavior. Kelley and Mirer (1974) analyzed large-scale surveys conducted during the four presidential election campaigns from 1952 to 1964. Voters' partisan attitudes, as revealed in preelection interviews, were highly related to their actual voting behavior: 85 percent of the respondents showed a correspondence between attitude and behavior, despite the fact that the interviews took place over a two-month span prior to election day. Moreover, most (84 percent) of the inconsistencies occured for persons whose attitudes showed only weak preferences for either candidate or party.

Such studies led the most recent careful reviewers to the following conclusion: "Our review has shown that most attitude-behavior studies yield positive results. The correlations that do occur are large enough to indicate that important causal forces are involved, whatever one's model of the underlying causal process may be" (Schuman & Johnson, 1976, p. 199). But everyone acknowledges that there is substantial variation across different situations in just how consistent attitudes and behavior are. So in recent years, the major research effort has gone into trying to determine the conditions that yield greater or lesser degrees of consistency.

Strength and Stability of the Attitude

Clearly one set of important conditions concerns the attitude itself: it needs to be a *strong* and *clear* one. Inconsistencies can come from weak or ambivalent attitudes. As mentioned, Kelley and Mirer (1974) found that most attitude-vote inconsistencies came from voters with conflicted or weak attitudinal preferences to start with. Or consistent behavior may not follow when the affective and cognitive components of the attitude conflict with each other. Norman (1975) considered both the behavior of volunteering for a psychology experiment and a person's attitude about volunteering. He found attitudes and behavior to be closely related when both the cognitive and affective components of attitudes were consistent, but they were not closely related when the cognitive and affective components conflicted.

Anything that contributes to a strong attitude should increase attitude-behavior consistency, therefore. For example, it could be that we will have firmer attitudes about an attitude object when we have direct experience with it than when we only hear about it from someone else, or read about it. If so, attitudes should have the most effect on behavior when they have been formed through direct experience with the attitude object. Fazio and Zanna (1978) showed this with volunteers for psychology experiments. Their attitudes toward the value and pleasantness of participating in psychology experiments were most closely related to actual behavior (volunteering for experiments) among people who had had prior experience in experiments. And they showed that the reason was more confident and clear attitudes among prior participants.

Marc Anderson; Prentice-Hall, Inc.

FIGURE 11–5 Attitudes have a strong effect on political behavior. Women who favor free choice regulating abortion demonstrate in favor of abortion—they are extremely unlikely to demonstrate against abortion.

Another fairly obvious but critical point is that attitudes may change as time elapses between attitude measurement and behavior assessment. An original attitude will certainly not affect behavior as much as a current attitude. One would not expect to find a close relationship between a college girl's attraction to a boy and her dating behavior with him, if her attraction is measured when she is a freshman, and her behavior when she is a senior. Therefore, consistency between attitudes and behavior ought to be maximum when they are measured at about the same time. Kelley and Mirer (1974) found that errors in predicting the vote declined quite rapidly as the preelection interviews got closer to election day.

Partly these longer time intervals diminish the attitude-behavior correlation because attitudes change. But the person and the situation change in other ways as well. For example, a woman might continue not to want to have a child, but her husband may threaten her with divorce if she does not agree to have children. And the longer the interval between measuring the attitude and measuring the behavior, the more such unforeseen contingencies might have arisen. Indeed, in both of these studies, longer time delays in behavior measurement led to worse predictions by attitudes, quite aside from attitude change. So, when assessing whether or not someone "does what he says," make sure you don't try to hold him to something he said two years ago! Things may have changed.

Salience of Attitude

In most situations, perhaps, several attitudes are potentially relevant to behavior. Cheating on college examinations might be related to attitudes about honesty or about such career aspirations as getting into medical school. "White flight" behavior, putting one's child in a private school to avoid integrated schools, might be determined by general attitudes about equality or about the quality of education in integrated schools. A school superintendent's decision about letting a communist sympathizer address a high school assembly might be dictated by his favorable attitude toward the general principle of free speech or by his distaste for communism.

So one important determinant of attitude-behavior consistency should be the *salience* of the attitude we are studying. The consistency between intolerant attitudes and discriminatory behavior will probably be fairly low if the target person has another attitude in mind at the time of her action. Perhaps her restaurant has so little patronage she cannot afford to turn anyone away; she therefore shoves her dislike of minorities into the background and serves the Chinese couple. As a general matter, then, when any given attitude is made particularly *salient*, it is more likely to be related to behavior. Snyder and Swann (1976) assigned subjects to a mock jury situation and gave them a sex discrimination case. In one condition subjects' attitudes about affirmative action were made salient by instructing them to take a few minutes before the case to organize their thoughts on affirmative action. In the other, the "not salient" condition, the subjects were not given any warning that affirmative action was involved. When attitudes were made salient, they were highly related to jurors' verdicts in the case; but attitudes about affirmative action were not closely related to verdicts when they had not been made salient.

Specifically Relevant Attitudes

Finally, the more *specifically relevant* attitudes are to behavior, the more they will be correlated. Attitudes vary quite a bit in how specific they are to the behavioral act in question. LaPiere's asking a proprietor about his feelings about Orientals in general is plainly not as relevant as asking about his attitudes toward this particular Chinese couple (who happened to be quite well-dressed and dignified). In general, behavior tends to be more consistent with attitudes specifically relevant to it than with very general attitudes that apply to a much larger class of potential behaviors.

For example, several studies have asked subjects whether they believe in God or consider themselves religious, and then noted whether the subjects attended church. Typically there was only a weak relationship between the answers to those two questions and church attendance. But attending church is not directly related to a belief in God or even to being religious. Many people who believe in God and even consider themselves religious do not think that attending church is meaningful to them. Other people do not believe in God and may not even consider themselves religious, but attend church for a variety of reasons having nothing to do with these particular beliefs. That may be their one convivial, social outing of the week. Thus, it is not surprising that the answers to these two questions do not relate directly to church attendance. On the other hand, if the subjects were asked whether they thought attending church was a good idea, presumably the relationship to actual church attendance would be much stronger.

A good illustration of the importance of using attitudes specifically relevant to behaviors is a study done by Weigel, Vernon, and Tognacci (1974) on environmentalism. The behaviors concerned willingness to engage in various actions on behalf of the Sierra Club. They found that very general environmental attitudes were not significantly related to activist behavior but attitudes specifically toward the Sierra Club were (a correlation of .68).

This point is also very clear in a study of the predictors of oral contraceptive use (Davidson & Jaccard, 1979). Attitudes toward birth control in general correlated .08 with the use of oral contraceptives in the next two years, but attitudes toward using "the pill" in the next two years correlated .57 with actual behavior. Schwartz (1978) found the same to be true with regard to volunteering to tutor blind children: attitudes toward the behavior in question predicted it very well, even over several months' or years' time—but attitudes toward altruistic acts in general did not.

Situational Pressures

Whenever a person engages in overt behavior, she can be influenced both by her attitudes and by the situation she is in. In Chapter 9 we saw how powerful situational pressures can determine a person's overt behavior. When situational pressures are very strong, attitudes are not generally likely to determine behavior as strongly as when situational pressures are relatively weak. This is easy to see in the LaPiere study. Well-dressed, respectable-looking people asking for rooms are hard to refuse, despite feelings of prejudice against their ethnic group. The external pressures are even stronger when the law requires letting rooms to anyone who asks.

A later and more systematic example is found in the Snyder and Swann (1976) study of mock jury deliberations in the sex discrimination case mentioned above. Half the subjects expected to discuss the case with other subjects whose attitudes on sex discrimination generally differed from their own.. The other half expected to discuss the case with persons whose attitudes were unknown. Presumably, the expectation of being disagreed with is a strong situational pressure. And indeed, expecting disagreement reduced quite sharply the consistency between the subject's own attitudes and his verdict.

A similar dramatic impact of situational pressures on attitudes can be seen in a study of teenage marijuana smoking (Andrews & Kandel, 1979). Attitudes toward marijuana (whether or not it should be legalized, whether use causes physical harm) correlated about .50 with actual marijuana use. But situational forces, in this case peer pressure (as indexed by the number of friends using marijuana), had several times as large an effect. This balance between attitude strength and situational forces may change from one setting to another. In another study, teenagers' attitudes toward drinking beer, hard liquor, and wine were the best predictors of frequency of actual drinking of them, but only at parties. At home, actual drinking behavior was better predicted by perceptions of their parents' attitudes about drinking, a situational force (Schlegel et al., 1977). Obviously these predictions are not completely independent. Your friends probably influence your attitudes, you pick friends partly on the basis of attitude similarity, and your own attitudes influence your perceptions of your parents' views, as we saw in Chapters 6 and 10. Nevertheless, the situation introduces forces that strongly determine which attitudes are most influential.

We believe a great deal of evidence supports the idea that attitudes affect behavior. It seems correct to say that attitudes always produce pressure to behave consistently with them. However, external pressures and extraneous considerations can cause people to behave inconsistently with their attitudes. Any attitude or change in an attitude tends to produce behavior that corresponds with it, but this correspondence often does not appear because of other factors involved in the situation. The same is true for the influence of behavior on attitudes. Clearly behavior does influence attitudes in many situations, and consistency pressures do exist to change attitudes to align them with previous behavior. Yet such effects do not occur in all situations because of other factors. But in both cases many of these conditions are now known, so we can specify when such consistency pressures will be effective in inducing behavior or attitude change, and when they will not be.

SUMMARY

1. Dissonance exists when the opposite of one cognition follows from another cognition. The magnitude of dissonance is dependent on the proportion of cognitions that are inconsistent. Dissonance motivates behavior designed to reduce dissonance.

2. Dissonance is most commonly created by the individual's behavior. Dissonance arises following decisions and following behavioral acts contrary to the individual's attitudes.

3. Dissonance can be reduced in a variety of ways. If the behavior itself cannot be revoked, the most important alternative is attitude change to reduce attitude-behavior discrepancies.

4. Postdecisional dissonance is greatest when people remain committed to their decisions for a long time, if they have free choice in their decisions, if the consequences of the decisions are known in advance and are certain, and if they feel responsible for the consequences.

5. Dissonance following attitude-discrepant behavior depends upon barely suffcient incentives to commit the behavior. These incentives can be either minimal threat or minimal promised reward.

6. The maximum dissonance following attitude-discrepant behavior occurs with minimum incentive, negative consequences of the act, and clear personal responsibility for the consequence.

7. Alternative explanations for these dissonance effects have been generated by learning and attribution theorists. Research has generally supported dissonance theory explanations, except when people have rather vague, undefined attitudes. Under those circumstances behavioral acts may lead to fresh self-perceptions of attitudes, thus leading to attitude behavior consistency through an attribution rather than a dissonance-reduction process.

8. It is usually assumed that behavior arises from attitudes, but considerable research questions how consistent the two are with each other. Now it appears that behavior is consistent with attitudes only under certain conditions: strong, clear, specific attitudes, and with no conflicting situational pressures.

SUGGESTIONS FOR ADDITIONAL READING

BEM, D. J. Self-perception theory. In L. Berkowitz (ed.), *Advances in experimental social psychology.* Vol. 6. New York: Academic Press, 1972. The clearest and best statement of the self-perception approach to attitudes.

COLLINS, B. E., & HOYT, M. F. Personal responsibility for consequences: An integration and extension of the "forced compliance" literature. *Journal of Experimental Social Psychology,* 1972, *8,* 558–93. A good example of an experiment that attempts to maximize the conditions for dissonance arousal.

DAVIDSON, A. R., & JACCARD, J. J. Variables that moderate the attitude-behavior relation: Results of a longitudinal survey. *Journal of Personality and Social Psychology,* 1979, *37,* 1364–76. A sophisticated state-of-the-art study of attitudes and behavior.

FESTINGER, L. *A theory of cognitive dissonance.* Stanford, Calif.: Stanford University Press, 1957. The original statement of cognitive dissonance theory. It is elegant in its simplicity, and offers plausible speculations about a broad number of psychological phenomena.

FESTINGER, L., RIECKEN, H. W., & SCHACHTER, S. *When prophecy fails.* Minneapolis: University of Minnesota Press, 1956. A fascinating participant-observer study of a group that thought the world was coming to an end, and the social psychologists who joined the group hoping it would not.

LaPIERE, R. T. Attitudes versus actions. *Social Forces,* 1934, **13,** 230–37. The classic empirical test of the correlation between attitudes and behavior.

SCHUMAN, H., & JOHNSON, M. P. Attitudes and behavior. *Annual Review of Sociology, 1976, 2,* 161–207. The most comprehensive recent review of this literature.

Attitude Change in the Real World

12

Stan Wakefield.

Our earlier discussion of conformity and obedience suggested that people's overt behavior can be influenced rather readily. There are tried and true techniques of social influence (or other forms of power) that can produce behavior wholly contradictory to the person's attitudes, or even his perceptions of reality. Subjects freely administer shock to inoffensive people when they are told to, or express beliefs that wholly contradict their sense perceptions.

From the last two chapters it would appear that people's attitudes are equally susceptible to change. Whether induced through persuasive communication, as in Chapter 10, or through the individual's own behavior, as in Chapter 11, attitudes seem to change quite readily. But things turn out not to be so easy as that. As Hovland (1959) pointed out, the success of persuasion depends in part on whether it is attempted in an experimental laboratory or in the real world. In the controlled environment of a psychologist's laboratory, it is generally easy to change attitudes. Even a simple written essay can produce changes in attitudes toward foreign aid, atomic submarines, tuition rates in college, brushing teeth, cancer and cigarettes, the quality of a poem, and so on. A subject reads or hears a communication, is asked to state her own belief, and tends to agree with the communication more after she reads or hears it than she did before (or than does a control group that did not read or hear it). In contrast, attempts to change people's attitudes in the world outside the laboratory tend to be much less successful. It is well to contrast the ease of attitude or behavior change in the laboratory with the manifest difficulty of attitude change in real life, at least of attitudes that matter.

This is no trivial fact, because attitudes are the important matter in many situations. Because voting is an expression of attitude, attitudes determine who gets elected to public office, and therefore who runs all major government offices. Attitudes determine who gets hired and who gets fired, in large measure, whether it is the arbitrary judgment of a casting director in a large movie studio or the vote of a faculty meeting on a tenure decision, or the decision made by a civil service grievance panel. In court, attitudes determine who goes to jail and who goes free, whether it is from a jury's vote, a judge's decision, or the prosecutor's decision about whether or not to prosecute. Prejudices, when verbally expressed, can have a chilling effect upon members of minority groups who are attempting to exercise their equal rights; however courageous they may be, they are only human, and sometimes want to retreat from a place where "they are not wanted," as indicated by snide comments, upturned noses, and averted eyes. Public opinion polls have increasingly played a role in policy decisions by government officials, ranging from decisions about whether or not to reinstitute capital punishment, to legalize marijuana smoking, or to continue to pursue an aggressive military policy in Vietnam. In all these cases, people's attitudes have a major impact on other's lives—sometimes even on the lives of thousands or millions of other people—so the question of attitude change is of major social consequence.

This chapter is concerned with attempts to change such important attitudes. Most of its examples are from the worlds of politics and race relations, because that is where the best research has been done. But the same principles should hold for any other area of life as well—religion, health, advertising, education, or wherever people are trying to persuade others.

LIMITED MEDIA IMPACT

In general, campaigns conducted through the mass media are not successful in producing massive changes in attitudes. There are some exceptions. A high-powered, clever advertising campaign built around a grammatical error ("*like* a cigarette should") catapulted Winston cigarettes from a small seller to the most popular cigarette in the United States. A similarly successful campaign made Crest toothpaste (which, in contrast, did have something substantial to offer, in the way of protection from decay) one of the largest sellers after its introduction. Occasionally, a person who is virtually unknown at the beginning of a political campaign can win the election by virtue of intensive advertising and face-to-face contacts. Remember "Jimmy Who?" He became President Carter.

In spite of these exceptions, it is usually extremely difficult in a short

FIGURE 12–2 Although fortunes are spent on media advertising and publicity—the impact on attitudes is generally rather small.

period of time to produce any sizable change in people's opinions on any issue they really care about and are involved in. Most Americans know after the nominating conventions how they are going to vote in the presidential election in November, and the tens of millions of dollars spent during the intervening months does not produce much change. The results of surveys of American elections are shown in Table 12–1. The data show that the way people say they are going to vote early in the campaign is a good predictor of how they actually do vote in November.

Only 7 to 10 percent of those surveyed changed parties during the campaigns. True, those who have not decided in May may be influenced by a campaign, but these people did not yet have an opinion. The campaign, therefore, did not change an opinion—it *produced* one, which is

TABLE 12-1
Changes in Presidential Preferences During Election Campaign

YEAR OF SURVEY	FIRST POLL	LAST POLL	PERCENTAGE OF CHANGE
1940	May	November	8[a]
1948	June	August	8[b]
	August	October	3[b]
1960	August	November	7[c]
1964	August	November	10[c]

Sources: [a] Lazarsfeld, Berelson, and Gaudet (1948, pp. 65–66); [b] Berelson, Lazarsfeld, and McPhee (1954, p. 23); [c] Benham (1965).

quite a different matter. Of course, because the undecided votes often decide an election, the campaign can be extremely important. The 8 percent who do change their opinion can be decisive if more of them change in one direction than in the other. Nevertheless, the data indicate how difficult it is to change the opinion of those who have already made a decision.

There are other, similar, examples. Among the big media events in recent years have been televised debates between the major presidential candidates. In 1960 there were four televised debates between John F. Kennedy and Richard M. Nixon, each covered live, and whole, by all three major TV networks. Audience studies revealed that 55 percent of the adult population watched all four debates, and 80 percent watched at least one. Journalists widely ascribed Kennedy's narrow victory to his success in these debates. Yet careful survey research revealed that there were no substantial changes in vote preference (Kraus & Davis, 1976).

A simple graphic case of the limited persuasive power possessed by TV news coverage was the public reaction to the 1968 Democratic convention in Chicago. That convention featured violent and bloody confrontations in the streets between antiwar demonstrators and the Chicago police. The TV commentators covering the events were outspokenly shocked and horrified by the brutality of the police. Yet 57 percent of a national sample said that the police had used "not enough" or "the right amount" of force, whereas only 19 percent said they had used "too much force"; the others had not followed the events (Robinson, 1970). The mail to CBS ran 11 to 1 against the news commentators. Apparently TV news is not able to influence the attitudes of the public at its whim.

Other attempts at persuasion have had similarly meager effects. The campaigns to induce people to stop smoking are a case in point, at least in this country. There was a slight decrease in the amount of smoking immediately following each intensive antismoking campaign by the Public Health Service, but the changes evaporated quickly. In recent years the smoking rate has, if anything, been creeping upwards. Again, the National Safety Council's admonitions against unsafe driving and the warning that "The life you save may be your own" does not seem to have made people drive any more safely. The Johnson and Nixon Administrations tried everything they could think of to rally the American public behind the Vietnam War, only to see public support ebb away steadily through the late 1960s and early 1970s. Following the energy crisis of 1973–1974, caused by the Arab oil embargo, the government tried to keep public energy consumption down. But most indices of consumption (e.g., gasoline use) soared right back up again when the crisis was past. And let us not forget Richard Nixon's lack of success in trying to persuade the American public that he was "not a crook," despite the best of media consultants, and his unprecedented access to prime television time to make his pitch.

Similarly, the so-called brainwashing that occurred during the Korean War turns out to be another failure to influence opinions. American prisoners were subjected to an intensive long-term campaign to make them give up their belief in American democracy and adopt the principles of Chinese communism. The campaign did not have to fight counter-propaganda; and the Chinese could do just about anything they wanted, since the soldiers were held captive. The situation was ideal for changing attitudes. A great deal has been made of the fact that some Americans were influenced by this campaign and that a small number actually defected to Communist China. But in fact, the campaign was remarkably unsuccessful. Practically all the American soldiers—even the uneducated, unsophisticated, tired, weak, lonely, and perhaps not strongly pro-American ones—were able to resist the attempt to change their opinions.

Social and political commentators are often concerned about the possible incidental persuasive effects of information communicated to the public for ostensibly nonpersuasive reasons. For example, many worry about the effects of communicating the results of political polls to the public, some that polls will create a "bandwagon" sentiment that will make someone temporarily pacing the field into an insurmountably strong frontrunner, and others that an "underdog" sentiment will give an artificial boost to a candidate running behind. Again there is no evidence that either occurs; polls seem to have remarkably little effect on voter preferences. The same kind of anxiety has been expressed about early televised projections of a candidate's victory or defeat on election day; when Walter Cronkite says, at 5 P.M. Pacific Time, that a given candidate is losing, that may produce depressed apathy (or maybe frantic activity) among his potential supporters. Again it turns out, with careful research, that such broadcasts have remarkably little impact on anyone's voting behavior later in the day (see Mendelsohn & Crespi, 1970, on both points).

**Exposure
Interferences**

Why are the media apparently so ineffective? What are the major obstacles to attitude change in real life? Although our model of attitude change begins with a communicator, we shall first discuss the factors that intervene between the source and the target. To paraphrase a familiar expression, "what you don't hear can't change your attitude." If a message does not reach its target, for all intents and purposes no attitudes are changed. Thus, these intervening variables are the first hurdle that must be cleared in order to influence someone.

LOW LEVELS OF EXPOSURE People in the business of affecting public attitudes know that their most critical and difficult problem is reaching the people they want to influence. Advertisers, politicians, propagandists, and teachers must devote a considerable amount of their efforts to making sure that their messages reach the targets to which they are directed. Teachers have the least trouble in this respect, because they can require attendance in class. This does not guarantee that the students are listening, but at least the vibrations caused by the teachers' speech are striking the students' ears. This is a major advantage. An advertising man has to spend millions of dollars and use great ingenuity to accomplish the same thing. He must select some medium, say, television, find a program that people watch, and then try to keep them from leaving their seats or turning down the sound or switching channels during the ads. And even when all this is achieved, he reaches only a small percentage of his prospective audience—perhaps 30 percent of those owning sets *if* he selects the most popular program on the air.

A clear concrete example is the nightly national news programs on CBS, NBC, and ABC. One typical study found only 23 percent of the adult (age 18 and above) population watching those programs on an average weeknight, and most adults (53 percent) failed to watch even one such program in a two-week span (J. Robinson, 1971). Even these relatively few watchers seem not to have been watching very carefully. In a telephone survey in the San Francisco Bay Area of people who had watched one of the shows earlier in the evening, Neuman (1976) found that people could recall, on the average, only 1.2 of the 19.8 stories covered in the average program. Memory improved when the interviewer ran down the list of headlines: another 4.4 stories were remembered with supporting details, and 4.3 without, but still half the stories were completely forgotten. Similarly, the average newspaper editorial is only read by 25 percent of the newspaper's readers (Becker, McCombs, & McLeod, 1975). With so many people not in the audience, and such poor attention among those who do watch television, massive attitude change would seem to be unlikely.

The propagandist and political campaigner have even more difficult tasks. Very few people watch partisan presentations on television. One representative case is a twenty-hour telethon conducted in San Francisco by the Republican candidate for governor in 1958, the weekend before the election. Only 11.5 percent of the adults in the city watched any part of the telethon (Schramm & Carter, 1959). The main problem for most candidates is not persuasion or overcoming a negative image, but merely establishing "name recognition"—just getting any exposure at all.

FIGURE 12–3 Reaching an audience is one of the problems when trying to change attitudes. Not everyone can attract this kind of a crowd just to hear a speech.

The debates during the 1960 and 1976 presidential campaigns were remarkable and almost unique exceptions. Eighty million people watched at least one of these debates, but other political programs are lucky to get 8 million viewers. Many would not be watching television at all, and most of those who were would be watching other shows. Most viewers consider a football game, a western, or a good movie more interesting than a political speech.

Thus, getting through to people is exceedingly difficult and chancy. Particularly in politics and public affairs, people tend to be exposed very little to persuasive messages. And regardless of the topic, the percentage of the potential audience that is reached by any message is quite small.

TWO-STEP FLOW OF INFORMATION Some of the material does reach its intended audience through the mass media, but only indirectly. While most people do not watch public affairs programs or read editorials, some do—and they tend to be the most influential members of their community or group. Called **opinion leaders** because of their considerable impact on the attitudes of their associates, these people are exposed to persuasive information through the mass media and, to some extent, pass it on to their friends. By means of this two-step flow of communication, some persuasive material does eventually reach the people. Thus, reaching the opinion leaders is critical. If they hear a candidate's speech, many others will be exposed to the material it contained. Since generally the candidate cannot reach many people directly, this is one way of increasing exposure to his message. Overall level of exposure is still low, and the exposure that does exist tends to be through these relatively influential and informed members of society.

SELECTIVE EXPOSURE As difficult as the low level of exposure makes life for propagandists, they have other problems. When a message does get through, it is likely that the person it reaches already agrees with it. This is the phenomenon of **selective exposure.** Persuasive communications tend not to reach the people they are designed to influence. People tend to be exposed relatively less to information that disagrees with what they believe. Republicans hear talks mostly by other Republicans; nonreligious people hear talks against religion; and farmers tend to read articles in favor of farmers. For example, in the 1958 California Republican telethon mentioned earlier, only 10 percent of the Democrats watched any part of it, whereas more than twice as many Republicans did. And among those who watched, the Republicans watched twice as long. Thus, Senator Knowland spent twenty hours on television and failed to reach 90 percent of the Democrats he was trying to reach. It is clear he was not getting to most of the people whom he wanted to hear him. (He lost the governorship by over a million votes.) These examples could be multiplied almost indefinitely. People tend to be exposed disproportionately to opinions and information that they already agree with (Sears & Freedman, 1967). Why does selective exposure occur?

Some communications specialists have interpreted this pattern as reflecting a psychological preference for supportive information. That is, they assumed that individuals deliberately seek out supportive information and avoid nonsupportive information as a way of maintaining the consistency of their own attitudes. This has been called **motivated selectivity.** This is certainly a plausible idea, but selective exposure could arise for other reasons. Is it true that, given a free choice, individuals do tend to listen more to a speaker who agrees with them than to one who disagrees with them?

There has been a great deal of research on motivated selectivity in controlled situations, but unfortunately, the evidence is inconsistent. In an early study (Ehrlich et al., 1957), individuals who owned new cars were asked to choose among envelopes that contained advertisements on a variety of cars, including their own. It was found that people preferred to read material about their own car. This seems to indicate that people, at least in this situation, want to expose themselves primarily to information supporting their own decisions and actions.

But many other studies have failed to find any evidence of motivated selectivity. For example, during the great antiwar protests of the spring of 1968, many college students signed an antidraft petition called the "We Won't Go" pledge, and many others gave a great deal of thought to the possibility of it. It was an issue of great personal importance to young men who thought they might be drafted, and possibly killed, in a war they regarded as immoral. Janis and Rausch (1970) tested for selective exposure to propledge and antipledge communications among four different kinds of Yale students: those who immediately refused to sign the pledge, those who refused after some deliberation, those who favored the pledge and said they might sign, and those who had already signed it. Each student was given the titles of eight articles on the war, four of which supported the pledge and four opposed it. Each student then rated the articles for his interest in reading them. Selective exposure would have been reflected in a propledge student's greater interest in propledge than antipledge messages, with the reverse holding for antipledge students. In fact, however, Janis and Rausch found selective exposure in only one of the four groups (those who might sign but hadn't yet), while both groups opposed to the pledge were primarily interested in counterattitudinal information. Table 12–2 shows the results. So in this study, if anything, the general trend was for subjects to be interested in messages *opposing* their own position.

There are just about as many studies in this area producing a preference for supportive information as there are producing a preference for nonsupportive information, and a large number show no difference at all (Sears, 1968). The most likely conclusion from the research is that motivated selectivity is not a strong force in most situations. When a person is given a clear choice between negative and positive information, selective exposure does not operate strongly, if it operates at all.

But how can there be a general pattern of selective exposure in natural situations if people are not strongly motivated to ensure that incoming information will support their prior attitudes? It is obvious that there are many reasons for exposing oneself to a particular communication (or not exposing oneself to it) other than the attitudinal position being advocated. Few people decide to watch a particular program because it is advertising a particular product. They decide to watch it because they like the program or because it is at a convenient hour or for some other reason that is entirely irrelevant to the program's commercial message. Similarly, people choose a newspaper for a variety of reasons other than its political persuasion.

TABLE 12–2

Mean Scores on Interest in Being Exposed to Articles Pro and Anti the "We-Won't-Go" Pledge, Comparing Men Who Opposed and Favored the Pledge

| | OPPOSED TO PLEDGE | | IN FAVOR OF PLEDGE | |
Articles	Promptly refused to sign (*n* = 12)	Refused after deliberation (*n* = 16)	Might sign (*n* = 11)	Have already signed (*n* = 23)
Propledge	9.83	11.81	11.09	10.38
Antipledge	7.50	9.38	10.09	11.31
Selective exposure	−2.33	−2.43	+1.00	−0.52

Note: The ratings are of four articles, each on a five-point scale, so the total scale is from 4 (no interest) to 20 (great interest).
Source: Janis and Rausch (1970), p. 50.

BOX 12-2
THE COMPLIANT COMMUNICATOR

Another possible reason for selectivity is that communicators tailor their messages to their audiences. Since similarity in attitudes increases liking (see Chapter 6), speakers would stand to be evaluated more positively if they modified their messages to agree with their audience. This would make the audience *look* as if they were being selective, too, even though in reality the communicator is just trying to be ingratiating (Sears, 1968). To test this idea, Newston and Czerlinsky (1974) had moderates on the Vietnam War communicate their positions to hawks and to doves. In every case, the speakers significantly displaced their messages toward the positions they expected the audience to hold;

they communicated a more hawkish position to the hawks, and a more dovish position to the doves, than they actually held. To see if the same process works outside the laboratory, Miller and Sigelman (1978) content-analyzed Lyndon Johnson's speeches on the Vietnam War from mid-1967 to the end of his presidency in early 1969. They also coded the audiences either as hawkish (e.g., the Veterans of Foreign Wars or First Cavalry Division) or as "other" (Congress, American Milk Producers, Young Democrats). They found a substantial correlation ($r = .501$); more hawkish audiences attracted more hawkish speeches from President Johnson.

And it turns out that these other reasons produce selective exposure, almost as a by-product. Probably the most important factor producing selective exposure is the disproportionate *availability* of supportive information. Most people live in an environment that contains more information supporting than not supporting their attitudes. A Republican tends to live and work near other Republicans, to be sent Republican literature through the mails, and so on. The same would be true of an advocate of black power, opponents of nuclear power, and practically every other attitude.

Another important factor is *utility*. People tend to expose themselves more to useful information than to information that lacks these qualities. And apparently supportive information has more of these characteristics than nonsupportive information. The *Wall Street Journal* illustrates how utility tends to go along with supportiveness. The editors and reporters are interested in and concerned about business and tend to be Republican. The newspaper therefore contains financial news and has Republican editorials. The news is useful to other businesspeople, who tend to agree with the editorials. A liberal Democrat could publish the *Journal* or be a reporter on it, but he would be less likely to be interested in financial news and therefore less likely to be associated with that kind of news-paper. This is even more obvious with specialized journals such as the *American Psychologist,* which is actually edited by a psychologist.

Thus the work on selective exposure indicates that the communicator does not have to worry too much about the target person *deliberately* avoiding nonsupporting information. If the communicator can get his message near the targets and give them a clear choice as to whether or not to listen to it, the targets will not avoid it simply because they disagree with it. The difficulty of getting a message to people who disagree with it is due primarily to the sociology of life circumstances rather than to the narrow-minded preferences of individuals.

SELECTIVE ATTENTION AND SELECTIVE LEARNING Much research has also been done on other avoidance mechanisms, especially selective learning and selective retention: It could be that people avoid discrepant information by not learning it or by forgetting it quickly. Yet a number of careful studies done show that people do not learn supportive information more quickly than nonsupportive information, nor do they retain it longer or more completely (Smith & Jamieson, 1972).

The major exception to this lack of selectivity in information acquisition is **selective attention.** A number of clever experiments have been done in which the subject is given the opportunity to press a button to eliminate static masking a persuasive communication. Brock and Balloun (1967) found that subjects would be more likely to tune in to a supportive than to a nonsupportive message. And Kleinhesselink and Edwards (1975) took it a step further, finding that people would selectively attend even to dissonant, nonsupportive messages as long as they were easy to refute. But they would let the static block out nonsupportive messages that were hard to refute. The researchers selected students who were strongly pro marijuana or antimarijuana. Then they exposed all students to a speech urging the legalization of marijuana. But the strength of arguments was varied. In one condition, the students heard strong, difficult-to-refute arguments (e.g., prohibitions against popular drugs never work, is better for you than alcohol, present marijuana laws encourage criminality) or weak, easy-to-refute arguments (would bring the American family back together and make rock musicians less paranoid). When listening to the neutral speech, and to one of the marijuana speeches, the subject could press a button to eliminate static. As shown in Table 12–3, button-pressing (an index of full attention) went up for the difficult-to-refute supportive arguments, and for the easy-to-refute nonsupportive arguments. In other words, attention was highest for the arguments that would be least threatening to the subject's own position. These findings, that people will briefly attend or not attend to messages depending on their supportiveness, stand in contrast to the apparent lack of *motivated* selectivity in either exposure or learning.

TABLE 12-3

Attention (Button Pressing) to

Pro-Marijuana Message

	ARGUMENTS	
Subject	Difficult to Refute	Easy to Refute
Agrees with Message	11.93	8.24
Disagrees with Message	7.53	10.00
Selective Attention	+4.40	—1.76

Source: Kleinhesselink and Edwards (1975), p. 789.

Resistance to Persuasion

Assuming that the communicator has been successful in getting his message to the target, he is still a long way from changing the target's opinion, as could be expected from the research presented in Chapter 10. For example, both Democrats and Republicans watched the Kennedy-Nixon TV debates in 1960, but they differed enormously in their evaluation of them. The overwhelming journalistic consensus was that Kennedy had "won" the first debate. To the extent that impartial observers existed, they agreed with this evaluation. Yet, as you can see in Table 12–4, only 17 percent of pro-Nixon viewers thought Kennedy had won the debate. Consistency thus has a major impact. New information is interpreted in terms of existing attitudes as much as it is evaluated on its merits, and sometimes more so. This is even clearer in the case of the first 1976 Carter-Ford debate (Table 12–5). This seems to be a typical response to most such mass communications.

MODES OF RESOLUTION New information seems to be incorporated into existing attitudes without changing them very much. Why is this so? A large part of the reason is that people use modes of resolution

TABLE 12-4

Who Did the Better Job in the First Nixon-Kennedy Debate in 1960 as rated by Pro-Nixon, Pro-Kennedy, and Undecided Viewers

		KENNEDY	NO CHOICE	NIXON	TOTAL PERCENT
PRE-DEBATE PREFERENCE	Kennedy	71	26	3	100
	Undecided	26	62	12	100
	Nixon	17	38	45	100

Source: Adapted from Sears and Whitney (1973).

TABLE 12–5

Who Did the Better Job in the First Carter-Ford Debate in 1976, as Rated by Pro-Carter, Pro-Ford, and Undecided Viewers

		CARTER	NO CHOICE	FORD	TOTAL PERCENT
PRE-DEBATE PREFERENCE	Carter	62	32	6	100
	Undecided	25	47	28	100
	Ford	5	25	70	100

Source: Adapted from *The Ann Arbor News* (September 24, 1976), p. 1.

other than attitude change to restore cognitive consistency when it is upset by a discrepant persuasive communication.

For one thing, people are likely simply to reject outright arguments that are discrepant from their own previous attitude, as we saw in chapter 10. Pressures toward cognitive consistency cause the beliefs and values that fit into the already existing structure to be more easily accepted than those that do not fit in. For example, if someone had developed a negative attitude toward drugs, he would be more likely to accept negative statements about marijuana than he would be to accept positive ones. Similarly, if he considered himself a Democrat, he would be more likely to believe positive things about Democrats and negative things about Republicans. He would also be more likely to favor ideas proposed by Democratic politicians than to favor those proposed by Republicans.

Source derogation also takes place. When a politician takes a position on the unpopular side of a hotly contested issue, his own reputation suffers. George McGovern, in 1972, was on the "wrong" side of a whole series of issues, at least according to popular perceptions. Most people thought him too sympathetic to abortion, marijuana, reduced defense budgets, amnesty for draft resisters, busing, and campus unrest. As a consequence, voters did not change attitudes on these issues very much; rather, they derogated McGovern (Miller, Miller, Brown, & Raine, 1976). In general, political campaigns seem remarkably unsuccessful in changing the public's policy preferences. Instead, the candidate's evaluations became aligned with the voters' attitudes toward campaign issues and their perceptions of his positions.

Perceptual distortions follow the same pattern. In both 1968 and 1972, voters distorted the positions taken by the presidential candidates on issues like Vietnam to make them more consistent with their candidate preferences. Nixon supporters saw Nixon as agreeing with them more on Vietnam than he did in fact (an "assimilation" effect), and Humphrey and McGovern supporters also assimilated their positions to their own. Interestingly enough, in neither case was there much evidence of a "contrast" effect. That is, voters did not exaggerate their differences of opinion with the candidates they opposed, even when, in absolute terms, they evaluated such candidates negatively (Granberg & Brent, 1974). It has also been found that "unit relations" of the sort discussed in Chapter 6 contribute to these assimilation effects. Voters tend to assimilate the issue positions of the candidate they expect to win the election (Kinder, 1978), independent of whether they like or dislike him or plan to vote for him or not. It seems that people want to feel they agree with the president, even if they would prefer someone else in that office.

REINFORCEMENT The result is that the media mainly strengthen preexisting attitudes—that is, they reinforce the prior commitments of the audience. Televised debates usually strengthen prior preferences, as discussed above. Voters' preferences tend to get stronger the more media information they are exposed to. Predispositions are reinforced even when the events themselves are quite offensive. Mueller (1973) has pointed out that the popularity of the president generally increases when something bad happens to the country internationally. This "rally round the flag" phenomenon is due presumably to a reinforcement of patriotic and nationalistic sentiments. Even when media commentators themselves are outspokenly hostile to such flag waving, the media may reinforce it nevertheless. Another example is the newsmen at the 1968 Democratic convention in Chicago who denounced the police brutality over nationwide TV. The public, generally opposed to any kind of protest to begin with, therefore applauded the tough stance taken by the police. Apparently people are able to interpret what they see as generally supporting their prior beliefs, no matter how the announcers feel.

Some Real Media Effects

So much resistance to attitude change suggests that the attitudes in question must reflect fairly strong commitments. In fact, this is a major problem in achieving attitude change in real life situations. The communications that attract enough attention to get past all the exposure barriers happen also to encounter strong, highly committed attitudes in a great many people.

But the media are not totally ineffective. Indeed, in several clear ways they are quite important. The media can help in "setting the agenda" for people. That is, events given a great deal of media coverage tend to become the central foci of public attention. Media coverage of Watergate, especially the Senate committee hearings chaired by Senator Sam Ervin, at which John Dean made his sensational charges, helped bring that scandal to the forefront of public attention. The same was true of the moonshot program, the Vietnam War, the campus unrest of the late 1960s, the ghetto riots and assassinations of the 1960s, the Iranian takeover of the American embassy in Teheran in 1979, and so on (Comstock et al., 1978). Aside from very dramatic, unexpected, or remote events, however, the agenda-setting function of the media may be less striking. For example, careful studies of the 1974 and 1976 elections suggested the media played a small role in determining which issues most concerned people (Miller et al., 1979; Sears & Chaffee, 1979). But the media can focus mass attention on particular stimuli, if only briefly.

Second, some emotionally laden, deeply held, long-term attitudes are highly resistant to change, even though they can sometimes be influenced by long-term, powerful persuasion. But many other attitudes are quite susceptible to influence. The media do have a major persuasive impact when members of the audience are not especially committed to their prior attitudes. Attitude formation toward new attitude objects, like the Ayatollah Khomeini or Watergate or the early phases of the Vietnam War, may depend on media coverage. And the media may be more decisive in primary and nonpartisan elections than in general elections, because these elections involve fewer standing predispositions. The nearly unknown Jimmy Carter's meteoric rise in 1976 is a good example (Patterson, 1980).

Finally, the media are successful in providing information. The 1976 presidential debates somewhat increased voters' familiarity with the candidates' positions on campaign issues (Sears & Chaffee, 1979). Children learn a great deal from television, ranging from Sesame Street to weather forecasts (Comstock et al., 1978). And plainly the media are the major sources of information about the remote events cited above. As a consequence, a common contrast in the study of mass media is that between the increased factual information the media provide, and their relative impotence in creating attitude change on important issues. One of the earliest demonstrations of this is found in the wartime research done by Hovland, Lumsdaine, and Sheffield (1949). The Army commissioned them to evaluate the effectiveness of orientation films shown to incoming draftees and volunteers. These films were intended to explain the reasons for World War II, make new soldiers more sympathetic to the war effort, and turn them into enthusiastic fighters. The researchers did find markedly increased levels of information about the war as a result of viewing the films. For example, the films clearly communicated factual details about the Battle of Britain such as the relative sizes of the German and British air forces, the focusing of German bombings on ports and ships, and the fact that the Germans would have physically invaded England except for the resistance of the British air force. But opinions about the British and the war—such as whether the British were going all out, whether or not they would have given up with more bombing, or whether they would hold out to the end, along with attitudes toward the Germans and Japanese—were largely unaffected.

But even here it would be a mistake to expect too much impact from the media. Half the public heard of John Kennedy's assassination from a friend rather than from the media. In another national survey, J. Robinson (1972) found that people who watched TV news frequently were not significantly more familiar with the names of such public personalities as Ralph Nader, Martha Mitchell, and Bob Dylan than were people who

TABLE 12–6

The Impact of Network News Exposure on People's Issue Awareness During 1972 General Election

	NONREGULAR VIEWERS OF NETWORK NEWS	REGULAR VIEWERS OF NETWORK NEWS
	%	%
Nixon policies:		
Vietnam War	4	11
Government spending	14	3
Military spending	27	36
Busing	35	35
China	38	32
Russia	25	28
Foreign commitments	37	50
Taxes on upper incomes	7	0
Law and order	2	— 6
Jobs for the unemployed	15	16
Amnesty	41	49
Drugs	8	7
McGovern policies:		
Military spending	63	58
Vietnam withdrawal	38	67
Amnesty	38	31
Political corruption	— 4	9
Taxes on upper incomes	14	40
Jobs for the unemployed	45	45
Average on all issues	25	28

Note: Figures represent percent increase or percent decrease (—) in people's issue information during the 1972 general election.

Source: Patterson and McClure (1976), p. 50.

never watched TV news at all. And, since TV news tends to cover the "hoopla" aspects of elections and not the issues, regular viewers hardly knew any more about candidates' policies than nonviewers, as shown in Table 12–6.

In short, the places to look for relatively greater media impact are: agenda-setting, formation of attitudes on new attitude objects, and providing information. But we should not overestimate the magnitude of effects even here. As with media violence, it is much easier to document communication effects in the laboratory than in real life.

THE DEVELOPMENT OF ATTITUDES

To understand why some attitudes are almost impossible and others easy to change, we need to understand peoples' histories: why are they more or less committed to their positions? As mentioned earlier, attitudes are assumed to be learned in the same way as are any other dispositions.

TABLE 12-7
Relationship Between Party Preferences of Parents and Children

PARENT	HIGH SCHOOL SENIORS (N = 1852)			
	Democratic	Independent	Republican	Total
Democratic	32.6%	13.2%	3.6%	49.4%
Independent	7.0	12.8	4.1	23.9
Republican	3.4	9.7	13.6	26.7
Total	43.0	35.7	21.3	100.0

Source: Adapted from Jennings & Niemi (1974).

The basic processes of association, reinforcement, and imitation determine this acquisition. Children are exposed to certain things about the world. They are also reinforced for expressing some attitudes. In addition, imitation or identification is important in the learning process. Children spend a great deal of time with their parents and after a while begin to believe as they do simply by copying them—even when there is no deliberate attempt at influence. The same process works with peer groups, teachers, or any important figures in a child's life.

Parents and Peers

Children tend therefore to adopt the dominant attitudes of their environment. For young children, especially, and on some issues, this means the parents have a great deal of influence. For example, as shown in Table 12–7, a high percentage of high school seniors favored a given political party when both parents agreed on that party, with only about 10 percent having the opposite preference (Jennings & Niemi, 1974). The same national survey of high school seniors and their parents revealed that 83 percent agreed on a presidential candidate (in the 1964 campaign), and that there were similarly high levels of agreement regarding other partisan preferences.

However, parent-offspring agreement was much less in many other attitudinal areas. The extent of parent influence over their offspring's attitudes seems to depend most of all on the clarity and frequency of communication between them. Obviously parents are much more likely to communicate clearly and repeatedly their presidential preference in the heat of an election campaign than some subtle, relatively abstract aspect of their philosophy of life. In the same study, 92 percent of the students were able to report accurately which candidate their parent favored, but on other issues they were quite strikingly inaccurate—indeed, it often appeared they were simply guessing about their parents' beliefs (Niemi, 1974).

Within the family, this lack of communication leads to some predictable biases and misperceptions about one another's attitudes. One might be called a *generosity bias*. When they are ignorant of the truth children tend to attribute a socially desirable characteristic to the parent, such as having voted for the winning rather than the losing candidate. Another is the *self-directed bias*, in which a child falsely attributes the same attitude to the parent as he himself holds, a type of perceptual distortion we described earlier as an assimilation effect. On more diffuse and obscure issues, children and husbands and wives all seem to exaggerate terribly the extent to which they all agree (Niemi, 1974).

These biases, and the considerable gaps in communication they attempt to fill, limit the degree of influence parents have over their children's attitudes. Indeed, Tedin (1974) has shown that when the child accurately perceives her parents' attitudes, the parent has a high level of influence across a wide variety of the child's attitudes. There is a good bit of inaccuracy in adolescents' perceptions of their parents' attitudes about legalization of marijuana. Among adolescents who are uncertain of their parents' attitudes about marijuana, there is little agreement. But among offspring who are accurate, agreement is extremely high (Tedin, 1974).

More generally, friends are the dominant influence over adolescents' attitudes in a large number of areas that do not lend themselves to early, simple, repetitive, accurate communication of parental attitudes. One example is marijuana use. As shown in Table 12–8, adolescents' use of marijuana is highly correlated with friends' use, and hardly at all to their parents' drug use.

So the parents' influence tends to be more limited than many early observers originally felt (Jennings & Neimi, 1974). In general, they have their maximum influence on simple, concrete, recurrent issues like partisan choice, religious denomination, or prejudices against minority groups. They have relatively little influence on more diffuse, subjective, occasional issues, where communication is likely to be sporadic and

TABLE 12–8

Adolescent Marijuana Use Related to Best-School-Friend Use and Parental Psychoactive Drug Use

PARENT USED PSYCHOACTIVE DRUG?	HAS BEST SCHOOL FRIEND USED MARIJUANA?	
	No	Yes
No	13%	56%
Yes	17	67

Note: Entry is % in each category that use marijuana. Use patterns for each group are self-reported.

Source: Kandel (1974). "Inter- and Intragenerational Influences on Adolescent Marijuana Use," *JSI*, Vol. 30, No. 2, pp. 107–35. Copyright 1974 by the American Psychological Association. Reprinted by permission.

fuzzy, such as broad matters of religious philosophy, political cynicism, interpersonal trust, or civil liberties.

However, it should be noted that the child's friends normally do not communicate attitudes markedly different from his parents'. At this stage, various socioeconomic factors determine what he hears. His neighborhood, newspaper, school, church, and friends tend to be more homogeneous than the rest of the world. If he is wealthy, he would live in an expensive house and be relatively conservative politically. His neighbors would also have money and tend to be conservative. If he attended a public school, his classmates would come from his neighborhood and have attitudes similar to his. If he attended a private school, the similarity in financial and religious backgrounds (in parochial schools) would be even greater. His parents might read the *Wall Street Journal* to keep up with the financial news, and he would be exposed to its conservative views. And so on. All these factors would continue to present him with biased information that would be consistent with the attitudes he had already developed.

Thus, attitude formation begins primarily as a learning process. An individual is exposed to information and experiences relating to a particular object and forms an attitude toward that object by processes of reinforcement and imitation. Once the attitude begins to be formed, however, the principle of cognitive consistency becomes increasingly important. The individual is no longer entirely passive; she begins to process new information in terms of what she has previously learned. In particular, she strives to form a consistent attitude. She tends to reject or distort inconsistent information and to accept more readily consistent information. By and large, the information that continues to come to her tends to reinforce her prior attitudes—though frequently there is not much information that comes in

OVERCOMING OBSTACLES TO CHANGE

High commitment attitudes are very difficult to change, then, and frequently last for many years. But they must change sometimes. What are the occasions on which it is most likely to happen? To start with, there are, broadly speaking, two possible reasons for this lack of change. One is the low level of exposure to new information, especially to nonsupportive information. People's attitudes are only infrequently challenged. The other possibility is that people are so committed psychologically to their attitudes in these areas that even massive assaults are ineffective.

One way of assessing the relative strengths of these two factors is to look at cases in which the wall of selective exposure breaks down. Selectivity is of course never perfect, whether deliberate or accidental. Throughout his life and particularly as he grows older, an individual is exposed to some information that disagrees with his attitudes. The extent to which discrepant information reaches him varies greatly and is more prevalent for some issues than for others. For example, most people develop attitudes in favor of honesty, peace, and motherhood, and they are rarely exposed to information inconsistent with these attitudes. Similarly, a belief that democracy is the best political system is not often attacked in the United States. In contrast, a devout Catholic or a liberal Democrat would be more likely to be exposed to information that disagrees with their attitudes on religion or politics. Although they probably would be exposed to more supporting than nonsupporting information, they would have to face occasional disagreement.

The Bennington Study

A sudden exposure to conflicting opinions is a common effect of going to college. Students who have spent most of their years living in their parents' house and surrounded by childhood friends are introduced to an environment containing many different kinds of people with many different beliefs. Not surprisingly, this exposure has a profound effect on many of them. They change many attitudes they had held since childhood; they reevaluate other attitudes in the light of the new information; and, in general, much of their belief system may undergo considerable reorganization.

Bennington College is a small, exclusive women's college in Vermont that was started, with a very liberal faculty, in the early 1930s. In a famous study (1943), Newcomb traced the changes in attitudes that some students experienced during their college years. Most of the students came from affluent, conservative homes, yet there were large and marked changes toward liberalism as the women progressed through the school. Newcomb's careful analysis of these attitude changes shows that they were most common among women who identified most with Bennington, and who had the closest social relationships with the other students and faculty there. In other words, for these students, Bennington served as an important reference group, and their attitudes changed through the influence of the group.

Another interesting finding concerned the students' attitudes after they left school. Did their new-found liberalism persist or did they regress to their parents' conservatism? Newcomb and his associates (1967) studied the women twenty years later and found that their political views had remained remarkably stable. Those who left college as liberals were still liberals, and the conservatives were still conservatives. More precisely, the women's senior-year attitudes were better predictors of their ultimate attitudes than were their freshmen attitudes.

Newcomb attributed this stability to the social environments the women entered after college. He found almost perfect political agreement between the graduates and their husbands; these affluent-but-liberal women had found affluent-but-liberal husbands. Moreover, the occasional attitudinal regressions could be attributed to the fact that some

"They sent her to Bennington to lose her Southern accent, and then she turned her back on everything."

liberal women had married husbands in occupations such as banking or corporation law, in which they could be expected to move in a conservative world.

This study emphasized as an important determinant of individuals' opinions the attitudinal environment in which they live. Social acquaintances, family, spouse, and so on have a major impact on political views. The study also emphasized the malleability of the young, *if* they are placed in a sufficiently closed environment. However, it is a rare college that embodies the political homogeneity of the small, exclusive, isolated, and highly liberal Bennington campus (Newcomb's followup revealed that today even Bennington does not embody the same degree of liberalism).

The college experience is in some sense unique as an opportunity to be exposed to new ideas, because it is specifically designed to be just that. Most of society is not designed for this purpose, and in the past many people were never exposed to views that contradicted those they learned in childhood. They continued to be surrounded by people who held views similar to their own and never had an opportunity even to hear the other side of issues. It seems likely that, to some extent, the growth of television changed this. People often still do not hear both sides of unimportant issues or issues on which only a small minority disagrees. But on important, controversial issues, people are more likely to be exposed to both sides, at least to some minimal (and perhaps biased) degree.

The most important conclusion of the Bennington study, and indeed of this chapter, however, is that mere passive exposure to information will not be sufficient to change high-commitment attitudes. Intense, interpersonal contact such as that in the Bennington experience is necessary, and indeed may even be necessary for years afterwards if the change is to be maintained. Television cannot provide this interpersonal contact.

In general, then, attitudes that have been socialized early in life and to which the person is highly committed do not change very much in adulthood. There are some circumstances in which attitude change does occur more easily though. Low-commitment attitudes change once a communicator can break through the usual barriers of lack of interest, low levels of exposure, and selective exposure. As indicated in Chapter 10, a high-credibility communicator who makes a fairly low-discrepancy appeal probably can achieve small amounts of attitude change, though nothing very dramatic. The Bennington example illustrates that sometimes young adults can be strongly influenced by dominant social environment. Finally, of course, the early socialization of children can readily be influenced (though parents and school boards and other supporters of the status quo do strongly resist tampering with children). In short, exposure seems to be the greatest problem for children and adolescents, whereas the resistance born of commitment is also very important for adults.

PREJUDICE

Prejudice represents one category of high-commitment attitudes that is of particular importance to social psychologists, because it involves attitudes held by some people about some group of other people. Moreover, widespread antagonism toward members of social group has proven to be perhaps the most socially destructive type of attitude. All of us have read enough history to be aware of the tragic consequences of prejudice and discrimination against particular social groups. Over six million Jews were murdered by the Nazis in Germany in the 1940s, under the guise of "purifying" the European racial stock. Today only a fraction of that number of Jews remain in Europe. This is not the only recent example of group genocide. Millions of Armenians living in Turkey were massacred by the Turks in the early part of this century, as were thousands of Arabs in Zanzibar following decolonialization. The number of North American Indians dropped from an estimated 3 million in the 17th century to 600,000 today. The history of the Spanish genocide of Indians in Latin America is even more appalling.

Racial prejudice against blacks by whites has been one of the most tenacious social problems in American history. It has resulted in an enor-

FIGURE 12-4 This Nazi concentration camp for Jews is an extreme example of the mistreatment that prejudice can produce.

mous catalogue of social ills, ranging from the deterioration and near-bankruptcy of large cities to poverty, shorter life expectancy, high levels of crime and drug abuse, and human misery of all kinds among blacks themselves. It dates back at least as far as the earliest contact between English colonists and Africans in the fifteenth century, and was enormously exacerbated by the mass importation of Africans to the United States to serve as slaves. Since the Civil War and the emancipation of the slaves, it has been a long, hard struggle to provide genuine equality for black Americans. The harsh antiblack prejudices held by most, if not virtually all, white Americans have been difficult to eradicate. Whites today are much more accepting of formal equality than they were even twenty

FIGURE 12–5 Even though a drinking fountain is provided, limiting it to one group of people is a clear sign of discrimination. According to the United States Supreme Court such separate facilities are inherently unequal and illegal.

years ago; they strongly support blacks' rights to equal public accommodations, public offices, fair housing, and so on. But there is still strong resistance to blacks' progress toward full equality in other areas—for example, in cases of school integration and affirmative action (Campbell, 1971; Greeley & Sheatsley, 1971). In short, people readily adopt violent prejudices against other groups, and almost as readily engage in terrible acts against them. Racial prejudice is therefore a particularly important issue.

Components of Group Antagonism

Social psychologists generally distinguish three different components of group antagonism. These roughly correspond to the three components of any attitude presented in Chapter 10: the cognitive, affective, and behavioral.

Stereotypes are the cognitive aspect of group antagonism. They are a set of beliefs about the personal attributes shared by an entire group of people. This cognitive process starts with the way people are categorized in groups. Membership in a group is defined by arbitrary social norms; it is not anything that the person comes inherently stamped with at birth. In the racially segregated South during the century following emancipation, the definition of who was black and who was white varied a good bit. In some states a single drop of Negro blood classified a person as a Negro. The famous "separate-but-equal" Supreme Court decision in 1896, *Plessy vs. Ferguson*, condemned to an all-Negro segregated school a Louisiana pupil with one Negro great-grandparent and seven white ones. The Chinese who settled in Mississippi after the Civil War were designated as colored and were subject to the same restrictions as Negroes. But this gradually changed, and by World War II Chinese were largely treated as if they were white. The Nuremburg laws of the Nazi regime developed a complex and detailed definition of what a "Jew" was, but one Jewish grandparent generally sufficed.

Some examples of stereotypes are listed in Table 12–9. As mentioned in Chapter 4, stereotypes are one type of schema. Like any schema, they distort reality to achieve order and simplicity. Group stereotypes are not necessarily bizarre, deviant, or pathological. To some extent they are cognitive responses that are just as natural as the organized (although oversimplified) first impressions of a single individual. They become

TABLE 12–9
Stereotypes in Three Generations of College Students

TRAIT	% CHECKING TRAIT			TRAIT	% CHECKING TRAIT		
	1933	1951	1967		1933	1951	1967
Jews				Negroes			
Shrewd	79	47	30	Superstitious	84	41	13
Mercenary	49	28	15	Lazy	75	31	26
Industrious	48	29	33	Happy-go-lucky	38	17	27
Grasping	34	17	17	Ignorant	38	24	11
Intelligent	29	37	37	Musical	26	33	47
Ambitious	21	28	48	Ostentatious	26	11	25
Sly	20	14	7	Very religious	24	17	8
Loyal to family ties	15	19	19	Stupid	22	10	4
Persistent	13	—	9	Physically dirty	17	—	3
Talkative	13	—	3	Naïve	14	—	4
Aggressive	12	—	23	Slovenly	13	—	5
Very religious	12	—	7	Unreliable	12	—	6
Materialistic	—	—	46	Pleasure loving	—	19	26
Practical	—	—	19	Sensitive	—	—	17
				Gregarious	—	—	17
				Talkative	—	—	14
				Imitative	—	—	13

Note: Some traits were not asked at all three time points.
Source: Adapted from Karlins et al. (1969).

destructive when they ignore contrary evidence and are generalized excessively to all individuals.

Prejudice is the affective or evaluative aspect of group antagonism. It is an evaluation of a single individual that is based mainly on the person's group membership. It has the same predominant like-dislike quality of the affective or evaluative dimensions discussed earlier regarding impressions (Chapter 4) and attitudes (Chapter 10). But it has the additional quality of prejudgment, as the name implies. The perceiver evaluates other people on the basis of their social or racial category rather than on the basis of information or facts about them as individuals. In this sense prejudice is not very reasonable, and perhaps even illogical or irrational.

Discrimination is the behavioral component of group antagonism. This is the behavioral acceptance or rejection of a person based on (or at least influenced by) his or her group membership. The refusal to seating of Chinese and black customers in restaurants discussed in the last chapter is an example of discriminatory behavior. Affirmative action programs that support the hiring, admission, or promotion of workers and students based on their group membership are another example, though they are usually classified as "reverse discrimination" because they favor a minority group at the expense of the majority.

The three components of group antagonism are related but are not identical. Certainly unflattering stereotypes, prejudice, and discrimination go together. Some members of the majority will engage in all three more often than others. And some minority groups will bear the brunt of all three more than others. But to some extent the components of group antagonism are independent. Stereotypes of different groups can differ quite a bit in cognitive content, but yield equally strong negative prejudices. The contrasting stereotypes of Negroes and Jews in Table 12–9 show this vividly. Prejudice and discrimination are not always identical, as discussed in Chapter 11. A great deal of prejudice can exist with very little behavioral discrimination, if the situation is right.

THEORIES OF PREJUDICE

Theories of prejudice generally cluster around three different approaches. *Societal-level* theories focus on when and how prejudice develops in a particular society, culture, or group. They generally focus on groups instead of individuals; for example, they try to explain how Southern whites feel about blacks instead of being concerned with the attitudes of any particular individual. *Sociocultural-learning* theories deal with a particular individual's prejudice, but locate the causes in interpersonal interactions, such as those between parents and children. *Intrapersonal* theories also focus on an individual's prejudice but ascribe its origins to internal causes such as personality, other attitudes, and cognitive schemas.

These three approaches differ more in level of analysis than in any specific predictions they make. They do not compete with each other, but instead present alternative ways of looking at the same facts. For example, up until the late 1950s, most major American private universities restricted the number of Jewish students they would admit. The practice was informal, approximate, and unpublicized (though hardly secret); but it kept the number of Jewish students far below the levels attained in the years since the quotas were removed. Suppose that the admissions officer at Ivy University, himself an Episcopalian, had grown up in an upper class, exclusive area of New England in which anti-semitism was common, and he himself in fact had become quite prejudiced against Jews. Then suppose that years later, on the job at Ivy University, he looks at two applicants' records, one from a Jewish boy from the Bronx High School of Science, with a 4.0 GPA, very high test scores, and a father who owns a small neighborhood grocery store. The other, a white, Anglo-Saxon, Protestant ("WASP") boy from Phillips Exeter Academy, has a 2.0 GPA, mediocre test scores, and three previous generations of wealth in the family. The admissions officer reads the personal statements of both applicants and their recommendations, and decides that the Jewish boy is too aggressive and obnoxious, that he is likely to be unscrupulous and opportunistic, and would create trouble at Ivy. The WASP boy looks like an honest, upstanding, good American boy (he excelled in tennis and lacrosse), and is just what Ivy is looking for. So he accepts the WASP boy and rejects the Jewish boy. His prejudice, therefore, leads him to accept stereotypical perceptions and expectations about the Jewish boy, and to engage in discriminatory behavior against the boy in making the admissions decisions.

How would these three theoretical approaches interpret this act of discrimination and the prejudice and stereotypes that lie behind it? The societal-level theories would assert that older high-status WASP social groups are anxious to maintain their privileged sanctuaries and use private universities as mechanisms for conferring uniquely high status on their own sons and daughters, and for keeping their children apart from Jews so as not to be contaminated by "wrong" marriages. Sociocultural-learning theories might focus on the process of maintaining such a policy: they would examine who has influence over the admissions decisions, who hires admissions' officers, their socialization backgrounds, and so on. The intrapersonal theories would concentrate on trying to understand the admissions officer's action by looking at his attitudes, his perceptions, and his personality. Now let us take a closer look at these perspectives.

Societal-Level Theories

The main version of societal-level theories is the *realistic group conflict* theory. This theory argues that when two groups are in competition for scarce resources, they threaten each other, which creates hostility between them and thus produces mutually negative evaluations. So prejudice is a natural, inevitable consequence of a reality conflict. It is lamentable but not deplorable. Perhaps it can be minimized, but it cannot be eliminated altogether because it is created by unavoidable realities. The Palestinians and Israelis claim the same territory, so they hate each other. If blacks are hired on affirmative action programs, some whites are excluded from those jobs, so it is natural for whites to be angry at blacks. Jews cannot be admitted to Ivy University in anything like the numbers they deserve unless correspondingly fewer WASPS are admitted, so it is natural for WASPS to distrust and dislike Jews.

A version of this theory that is popular among Marxists is that powerful groups become prejudiced in order to justify the exploitation of weaker groups. If blacks are really lazier and less intelligent than whites, it is all right to have them in menial jobs, because they do not deserve and probably cannot handle anything better. For example, some historical analyses suggest Chinese and Japanese immigrants to the United States were well received as long as they did menial work no one else wanted to do. Only later, when they began to compete with Caucasians for jobs, did prejudice mount.

The realistic group conflict theory takes into account group interests; one group's interests are incompatible with those of another group, and antagonism follows from the conflict. Usually the analysis focuses on economic interests, such that most conflicts are over wealth, jobs, property, or territory (though sometimes the stakes concern issues of prestige, as in the Ivy University example). The theory does not deal with the mechanics of the process at the individual level. It shows a pattern of hostility and competition between groups and stops there. It does not try to determine if the most threatened individuals in each group are also the most hostile individuals. It would deal with the history and basis of friction between Jews and WASPS, but would ignore the particular members of either group.

Sociocultural Learning Theory

Another angle on prejudice views it as being transmitted interpersonally and therefore as being part of a larger package of norms acquired by sociocultural learning. This kind of analysis has four steps. The prejudice is a norm in the person's culture or subculture. It is acquired by the person in the process of his or her preadult socialization. The child acquires such prejudiced attitudes and expresses them, in order to gain acceptance by others. And, finally, the continued transmission and expression of the prejudice reinforces its role as a cultural norm (Ashmore & DelBoca, 1980). This approach emphasizes the mechanics of the individual's acquisition of prejudice, not the functions it serves for social groups or society as a whole.

So we might analyze our Ivy University registrar in this way. He grew up in the upper-crust WASP society of New England around the time of World War I, when some anti-semitism was quite acceptable. We would suspect that his family, their friends, and his friends shared it and passed it on to him. He perhaps would tell anti-semitic jokes and make slurring remarks about Jews he might see in shops or on the street, and his friends would laugh and contribute some of their own. That by itself would help to reinforce the anti-Semitism of his segment of society. But his later actions, as university registrar, would perpetuate even more powerfully the pattern of exclusion of Jews from privileged positions in American society.

It is easy to document the existence of such prejudiced social norms all over the world. For example, Table 12–10 shows the great stability of white North Americans' prejudice toward various national and ethnic groups through much of the twentieth century. The peoples of the British Isles are liked much the best, and those from Asia and Africa the least. World War II hurt the Germans, Italians, and Japanese, and the cold war

TABLE 12–10

**Rankings of 28 National and Ethnic Groups
by White Americans, 1926–1966**

TARGET GROUP	1926	1946	1956	1966
English	1.0	3.0	3.0	2.0
Americans (U.S., white)	2.0	1.0	1.0	1.0
Canadians	3.5	2.0	2.0	3.0
Scots	3.5	5.0	7.0	9.0
Irish	5.0	4.0	5.0	5.0
French	6.0	6.0	4.0	4.0
Germans	7.0	10.0	8.0	10.5
Swedish	8.0	9.0	6.0	6.0
Hollanders	9.0	8.0	9.0	10.5
Norwegians	10.0	7.0	10.0	7.0
Spanish	11.0	15.0	14.0	14.0
Finns	12.0	11.0	11.0	12.0
Russians	13.0	13.0	22.0	22.0
Italians	14.0	16.0	12.0	8.0
Poles	15.0	14.0	13.0	16.0
Armenians	16.0	17.5	18.0	19.0
Czechs	17.0	12.0	17.0	17.0
Indians (Amer.)	18.0	20.0	19.0	18.0
Jews	19.0	19.0	16.0	15.0
Greeks	20.0	17.5	15.0	13.0
Mexicans	21.0	23.5	26.0	26.5
Japanese	22.0	28.0	24.0	23.0
Filipinos	23.0	22.0	20.0	20.0
Negroes	24.0	27.0	25.0	26.5
Turks	25.0	23.5	21.0	24.0
Chinese	26.0	21.0	23.0	21.0
Koreans	27.0	25.0	28.0	25.0
Indians (India)	28.0	26.0	27.0	28.0

Source: Ehrlich (1973), p. 74; Entry is rank of "social distance," or degree of intimacy and understanding felt with each group.

hurt the Russians. Otherwise little has changed. If comparable data were available from other societies, they would doubtless show the same historic enmities, for example, between Vietnamese and Cambodians, or toward the "untouchables" in India, or tribal hatreds in Africa.

Like other high-commitment attitudes, these prejudices are acquired quite early in life. The most salient ones, like racial prejudice in this country, are acquired well before adolescence. White children simply learn, by being told and by observing the society in which they live, that blacks are socially inferior in a variety of ways. To show this, Goodman (1952) observed 103 black and white children intensively for a full year. She concluded that racial awareness was already present in many children at ages three and four, and that 25 percent of the four-year-olds were already expressing strongly entrenched race-related values. No white child ever expressed a wish to be like a black child, while the black children expressed much more conflict about their color.

Certainly by the early grade school years, most American children are aware of racial differences in our society and of the prevailing norms about the races, at least in some rough form. As children move through grade school, they increasingly perceive differences between the races, but often do not become more sensitive to differences among members of other races. The experiences children have during the grade school years are crucial, because by early adolescence, racial prejudice has crystallized and is much more difficult to break down. The consequences of this is that prejudice is considerably stronger in some areas of the society than in others. For example, it is stronger in the South than in other regions, it is stronger in the working class than in the middle class, it is stronger among older whites (who were brought up in a more segregationist period) than among younger whites, and so on (see Maykovich, 1975; Middleton, 1976).

Parents have a particularly important role in the child's acquisition of prejudice. There are consistent correlations between parents' and children's racial and ethnic attitudes (Ashmore & DelBoca, 1976). Parents often transmit these attitudes without directly instructing their children. As we saw in Chapter 10, attitudes can be learned by association or by imitation as well as by direct reinforcement. Children closely observe their parents' attitudes and behavior and pick up many nonverbal cues in their reactions to people of other races. But parents frequently are reluctant to express prejudice openly and freely. One result is that children are not perfectly accurate in the attitudes they attribute to their parents, particularly about matters not currently in the news and in the middle of controversy. As a result, as children grow older, peer groups become increasingly important. Normally peer groups mostly reinforce parents' views, because of the similarities in social background and values of people sharing a common community environment. But occasionally the parents' attitudes conflict with those dominant in the child's environment, children probably acquire prejudice both from a broad range of cues from their parents and a broad range of other people, as well.

The last general approach considers the inner dynamics of prejudice. What psychological processes *within* individuals cause them to hold prejudiced attitudes? This approach is the most "psychological" and has attracted the most attention from social psychologists. They have proposed several different variants.

COGNITIVE CONSISTENCY We have seen how pressures toward cognitive consistency cause changes in attitude or behavior. Cognitive consistency theories argue that people mold their attitudes and behavior to their preexisting dispositions. In the context of prejudice, they would suggest that people form prejudiced attitudes or engage in discriminatory behavior to promote consistency with other prior attitudes.

One example of consistency processes is the idea that "similarity breeds liking," as indicated in Chapter 6. We like a new person or group on the basis of consistency of their attitudes or values with our own. One provocative implication is that whites' prejudices against blacks do not arise because of their race per se, but because they assume blacks do not share similar values and attitudes. If that were true, people who hold similar values would be liked even if they were black. A series of studies (Byrne & Wong, 1962; Rokeach & Mezei, 1966; Stein et al., 1965) has compared the relative importance of racial and attitudinal similarity. In most of this work, subjects were given a description of another person who was either similar to them in attitudes and dissimilar racially or the reverse. Each subject was then asked how much he thought he would like the other person. The typical, although not unanimous, finding was that similarity of attitudes was more important in determining liking than belonging to the same racial group. These findings have been interpreted as showing that racial differences are relatively unimportant when compared to differences in attitude.

It would be nice to believe that this is true when real contacts are involved, for it would indicate that getting to know someone of another race and discovering that his attitudes are similar to one's own would make one like him regardless of the racial difference. The logical projection would be that a simple program of educating people about other races would reduce racial conflicts. However, these findings held only for relatively nonintimate relationships such as working together. Race was considerably more important than belief when closer relationships, such as dating or marriage, were concerned.

Similarly, behavior is determined by attitudes, at least in part, as we saw in the last chapter. Prejudiced people and those who hold negative stereotypes are therefore the most likely to engage in discriminatory behavior. That is, consistency processes also are responsible for a prejudiced person's behaving in a prejudiced or discriminatory manner.

The simplest examples demonstrate how powerfully prejudice (as an attitude) influences other attitudes and behaviors. In elections that pit one black candidate against a white candidate, a white voter's prejudice is the best predictor of which candidate he will support. This was true in Massachusetts when a black, Edward Brooke, ran his first victorious race for the United States Senate (Becker & Heaton, 1967). And it was true in Los Angeles when a black city councilman, Tom Bradley, twice challenged the incumbent white mayor, Sam Yorty (Kinder & Sears, 1980). Bradley lost the first time, and won the second. In all these elections, the overall level of whites' prejudice was low enough that Brooke and Bradley attracted many white votes. But the best predictor of which whites voted for them was prejudice. Prejudice is also the best predictor of how white people feel about busing schoolchildren for racial integration. The most prejudiced people are almost unanimously opposed to it, no matter what (Sears, Hensler, & Speer, 1979). So it is quite clear that the early acquisition of prejudice means that the person will later adopt unsympathetic or antiblack attitudes.

That prejudiced attitudes produce discriminatory behavior is perhaps such an obvious and familiar observation it needs little elaboration. But it can do so in some subtle, indirect ways that we are hardly aware of; for example, parents' prejudice can affect their children's interracial behavior. In one study, white children of prejudiced parents were less likely to engage in interracial social contact in integrated schools than were children of less prejudiced parents. The consequence was that their own racial tolerance was not increased as much as was that of children

Another type of consistency process is the halo effect. This, you will remember, involves attributing favorable characteristics and behavior to liked people. The opposite tendency (the "forked-tail effect") is to ascribe bad characteristics to disliked people. This is precisely what happens to the victims of prejudice. Ugwuegbu (1979) gave white college students at a midwestern university a description of a rape case, with instructions that it was a study of jury behavior and they were to act as if they were jurors. The case involved the alleged rape of a nineteen-year-old girl by a twenty-one-year-old male on the campus. The race of both victim and defendant were varied. Then the jurors were asked how much harm the defendant intended, how responsible he was for the rape, whether or not he was guilty, and what penalty he deserved. These responses were graded to form an index of perceived culpability. As can be seen below, the black defendant was seen as more culpable than the white, especially with a white victim. The strength of the evidence against the defendant was also varied: both the victim and an eyewitness could identify the assailant (strong evidence), or neither was sure (weak evidence). A middle or "marginal" condition pitted the victim's identification against the defendant's denials, and ambiguous reports by witnesses and police. The racial difference in defendant's culpability showed up only with marginal evidence.

PERCEIVED CULPABILITY OF THE
MALE DEFENDANT

Female Victim	Male Defendant	
	White	Black
White	13.5	17.2
Black	13.6	14.2

who engaged in more interaction with minority children (Stephan et al., 1978).

An even subtler process is that our stereotypes influence not only own behavior, but also the behavior of the *victims* of stereotyping when we interact with them. In this sense, a stereotype can be a self-fulfilling prophecy. If we think all Poles are bumblers, we are likely to interact with them as if we expected them to bumble at any opportunity. And, interestingly enough, this will increase the likelihood that they will behave in a bumbling, stereotype-confirming way. Snyder and Swann (1978a) showed this in an ingenious way. They told each subject (the "perceiver") he was going to interact with another subject (the "target") who was described either as hostile, liking contact sports, cruel, and insensitive, or as nonhostile, liking poetry and sailing, kind, and cooperative. This description set up the perceiver's stereotype of the target. Then the perceiver and target (who was also a naïve subject) engaged in a series of reaction time tests that allowed both to behave in a hostile way (by administering loud, painful, distracting noises to each other). Not surprisingly, it turned out that expecting a hostile partner led perceivers to administer more high-intensity noises. But the targets, completely ignorant of how they had been described to the other person, also administered more noise if they had been described as hostile, as shown in the top line of Table 12–11. Remember the targets had been described as hostile or nonhostile at random, so this higher level of hostile behavior had to be caused by the perceiver's expectations. And the perceivers, reasonably enough, saw the "hostile" target as more hostile than the "nonhostile" target, in view of his behavioral confirmation of their expectations. This is shown in the second line of the table.

The most interesting aspect of this experiment then followed. The target was then put through the same task with a new, completely naïve subject. Neither knew about the "hostile" or "nonhostile" description randomly assigned earlier to the target. Nevertheless the target continued to live up to expectations. The third row shows he gave more noise, and the fourth row, that he was regarded as more hostile in this new interaction.

So this experiment demonstrates that stereotypic expectations affect the stereotyper's own behavior toward the person, whose behavior then in return confirms the stereotype. Not only that, but the victim later behaves in a stereotype-confirming manner in other situations, even toward people who are completely ignorant of the stereotype. So even in neutral en-

TABLE 12–11
Effects of Perceivers' Expectations on Target Person's Behavior

	HOSTILE LABEL	NONHOSTILE LABEL
FIRST INTERACTION: WITH INFORMED PERCEIVER		
Hostile Behavior	4.12[a]	3.17
Perceiver's Impression of Target's Hostility	3.83	3.64
SECOND INTERACTION: WITH NAÏVE PERCEIVER		
Hostile Behavior	4.30	2.70
Perceiver's Impression of Target's Hostility	3.66	2.75

[a] The higher the number, the greater the hostility exhibited and perceived.
Source: Snyder and Swann (1978a), p. 155.

vironments, with people who do not share the stereotype, the victim of prejudice still tends to exhibit stereotype-confirming behavior. A later study by the same authors (Snyder & Swann, 1978b) made a similar point. Interviewers with clear (but randomly assigned) expectations about their interviewees' personality would selectively ask questions to confirm the expectation and elicit behavior that would also help confirm it. Consistency pressures work in a wide variety of ways to promote attitudes, behavior, and an interpersonal environment that all fit the same attitudinal expectations.

SOCIAL COGNITION We indicated earlier that certain systematic cognitive biases naturally accompany the process of impression formation. Perceivers try to develop a meaningful, structured impression of another person, which necessarily breeds certain distortions. And they overrespond to the most salient stimuli. By extension, stereotypes can be formed by such cognitive biases. Perceivers try to simplify a complex world by focusing their attention on its most salient aspects. Such efforts can, all by themselves, produce prejudice and stereotyping.

For example, perceivers naturally categorize other people into types: tall ones, pretty ones, jocks, obnoxious ones, foreigners, or whatever. This *categorization* process is highly functional. It helps the perceiver process information about a lot of individuals in an efficient way. But it turns out to have some negative consequences. It can lead the perceiver to blur the distinctions among the members of a particular group. For example, observers of group discussions including equal numbers of blacks and whites were more likely to confuse the contributions of people within a race than to confuse their contributions across race. It is easy to remember whether a black or a white said something, but not so easy to remember which one did (Taylor et al., 1970). Other experiments have been done in which people are *randomly* categorized into groups. This also led group members to blurred perceptions of people in other groups, and to showing favoritism toward members of their own group (Tajfel et al., 1971). In short, the categorization process is natural, normal, even unavoidable. But it does influence the information retained by the perceiver, the inferences made about the stimulus people, and behavior toward them.

Categorization is often based simply on some very prominent, salient cues. Skin color differentiates blacks and whites; body type, hair length, clothing, and voice differentiate men and women; accent differentiates foreigners from natives, and so on. This kind of salience has a number of predictable effects. We pay more attention to salient stimuli, so these differences tend to be on our mind when we encounter members of other groups, especially when they stand out in the environment. A white researcher in a ghetto school stands out; so did Jackie Robinson when he was the first black major league baseball player, or the female Chief Justice of the otherwise all-male California Supreme Court. And perceivers make more extreme evaluations of, and more confident and more dispositional attributions about, salient people—what Taylor and co-workers (1977) called "tokens." So, for example, we might be less likely to excuse flaws in a "token's" performance as due to situational forces than we might for members of the majority. If the "token" female executive is out of work because of illness periodically, we attribute it to her dispositions; she is "sickly," self-indulgent, or maybe even malingering. If a male is out, for the same reason we attribute his absence to an illness over which he has no control, perhaps extend more sympathy, and cover his workload.

Finally, if stereotypes are cognitive structures that consist of a set of expectations regarding a social group, they can be thought of as "schemas," with the same consequences we have already discussed in Chapter 4. Schemas affect other aspects of information processing, such as attention, memory, or filling in missing information. Stereotypes generally have the same effect. We are more likely to pay attention and remember behavior that fits our stereotypes than behavior that falls outside them. The big black athlete in the back of the class, who is a marginal student, is more likely to be remembered than the black secretary who does her work quietly and competently. However, this really does not apply when the nonconforming behavior is flagrantly inconsistent with the stereotype. If that same black athlete asks the most penetrating questions in the class and gets a strong A, he will be clearly noticed and remembered. Stereotypes are perpetuated, therefore, because we primarily attend to and remember behavior that is relevant to them, behavior that either confirms them or is a striking exception to them. Either way, stereotypes dominate our perception of the behavior.

Information inconsistent with schemas tends to be rejected. So if someone's behavior is inconsistent with our stereotype of that person, we should explain it as due to the situation, not the person. If there is no plausible situational cause, and we are forced to make an internal attribution, it probably will be to some temporary, unstable cause. A good example concerns whites' explanations for racial differences in socioeconomic status. Blacks, on the average, have always been lower in income, employment, educational level, and occupational status than whites. How do whites explain this? Years ago the main attribution for this relative lack of success was stable and internal; blacks were innately inferior in a variety of ways (e.g., intellectually). Whites have gradually surrendered this notion, however, as many public opinion surveys have shown. But the racial difference in status remains. So how do whites explain it now? Liberals invoke stable external obstacles: poverty, discrimination, prejudice, educational difficulties, and so on. These are analogous to "task difficulty," the main stable external cause in Weiner's model of success and failure (see Chapter 5). Conservatives invoke unstable internal causes, such as lack of effort and low aspirations (Ashmore & DelBoca, 1976).

PSYCHODYNAMIC THEORIES Finally, some intrapersonal theories of prejudice analyze it as an outgrowth of motivational tensions within the individual. One psychodynamic theory, for example, treats racial prejudice as displaced aggression. Displacement occurs when the source of frustration or annoyance cannot be attacked either because of fear or simple unavailability. If there is a depression and a man loses his job, he feels angry and aggressive, but there is no obvious person at fault. Under these circumstances, people look for a **scapegoat** whom they can blame for their difficulties and whom they accordingly can attack.

The choice of a scapegoat is determined by a number of the factors we have already discussed. Children learn early that it is safer to be aggressive toward someone who is smaller or weaker than they are. Thus, they learn that ideal scapegoats should be weak and unable to retaliate. In addition, children learn that certain groups are "socially approved" targets in their subculture. In the white working-class subculture of Cicero, Illinois, or Little Rock, Arkansas, blacks seem to be favorite objects of aggression. Elsewhere, Okies, Poles, Yankees, Kurds, Muslims, Hindus, or Huguenots would be targets of aggression.

Scapegoats typically have a distinguishable characteristic. This sets them off from the rest of the population and makes them perceptually distinctive. More important, people are generally suspicious of and somewhat antagonistic toward those who are different from themselves. As we have seen, dissimilarity breeds disliking. Group members treat other members better than they do nonmembers because they feel closer to the other members, know more about them, feel more loyal to them, and so on. But the suspiciousness and aggressiveness that is displayed toward people who are different seems to be more than a reaction to group loyalty. There seems to be a general tendency to mistreat people who are different. Ideal scapegoats are, therefore, weak, different, and easily distinguishable—qualities that seem to be characteristic of the groups that are the major targets of prejudice.

Another psychodynamic theory treats prejudice as a personality disorder, just like a phobia about snakes or a neurotic need for approval. The best-known example of this theory is found in work on the authoritarian personality (Adorno et al., 1950). This was generated by an impressive program of research, sponsored by the American Jewish Committee, motivated by their concerns about the rise of violent anti-Semitism in the 1930s and the compliant behavior of Germans toward Hitler. Antidemocratic, racist beliefs such as anti-Semitism were thought to develop from a particular personality syndrome called the authoritarian personality. This personality type is characterized by (1) rigid adherence to (and harsh punishment for deviation from) conventional values and patterns of behavior; (2) an exaggerated need to submit to, and identify with, strong authority; (3) generalized hostility; and (4) a mystical, superstitious cast of mind. This pattern was thought to stem from early rearing by a domineering father and a punitive mother who punished the child harshly for any disobedience. As an adult the individual repeats the whole experience, but now he is in the driver's seat. He too bullies and punishes people who are deviant or disobedient. People of other races and religions, the handicapped or weak of all kinds, those with unconventional life styles—all fall under the authoritarian's iron boot. Thus the authoritarian is *ethnocentric*—that is, he thinks his group is wonderful, and all other groups are disreputable and disgusting.

Research on authoritarianism quickly got caught up in methodological disputes about data interpretation, and the psychological analysis just presented became somewhat controversial. A central problem was that the research failed to distinguish adequately between sociocultural learning and personality factors in its explanation of ethnocentrism. For example, it found that working-class whites were disproportionately anti-Semitic. Was this because a disproportionate number of them had authoritarian personalities? It was easy to show that working-class parents demanded more submission from their children and dealt more harsh punishment than did middle-class parents (Lipset, 1960). Or was their anti-Semitism a product of an historical norm that got passed down from generation to generation? Many working-class families were only a generation or two removed from areas of Europe where violent anti-Semitism had reigned for centuries. So anti-Semitism could have stemmed from learning a traditional norm, and not from a personality obsessed with authority and domination.

Conclusions

These three broad theoretical approaches represent different *levels* of explanation of prejudice; the approaches are not competing at the same level. They could all be true, since they are not necessarily inconsistent with each other. Nevertheless, each cites different factors as causes of prejudice; and some factors are more important than others.

For example, normal cognitive processes of categorization and of special attention to salient stimuli can help promote stereotypes and discriminatory behavior. It is doubtful that they are sufficient to produce a consistent pattern of bias all by themselves, however. They require the backing of sociocultural learning that produces prejudice against particular groups, and specific stereotypical content. Blacks are stereotypically thought to be lazy and musical, and Chinese hard-working, though both are perceptually quite different from whites. But these cognitive processes may be necessary to get a pattern of group discrimination started, and they certainly help to maintain it.

In general, sociocultural learning has a major role in defining what is "appropriate" prejudice, what the "correct" stereotypes are, and what is acceptable behavior toward other groups and what is not. The wide variations in the treatment of any given group around the globe and across history testify to that, as do the major differences in the treatment of different groups within a society. In 1850, blacks could be bought and sold like cattle; today elaborate legal machinery protects their right to be treated like other people. Slavery never existed for other groups in this country, nor for blacks in most other societies. In most Muslim countries women must wear veils, do not engage in premarital or extramarital sexual relations, and do not compete with men for jobs. This is not so in the United States today, though in the nineteenth century American women were much less free than they are today. Personality tensions and cognitive biases therefore operate within a cultural framework that determines how much prejudice exists, when it can be expressed, and toward whom.

In one particular case, the implications of realistic group conflict theory contrast with those of sociocultural learning theory. If prejudice arises because two groups really threaten each other, then the threat ought to be the most potent psychological cause of prejudice within individuals as well as for groups. In other words, the most threatened *individuals* ought to be the most prejudiced. Whites who perceive their neighborhoods as being threatened with racial integration, or with crime by blacks, or with influxes of black children into the schools, ought to be the most prejudiced. Sociocultural learning theory, however, suggests that such reality threats in adulthood have very little to do with prejudice; the key factor is childhood learning.

This contrast has been tested in a number of studies by Sears and his colleagues (1979, 1980). They conclude that reality-based racial threats have surprisingly little direct impact on whites' prejudice levels or on their responses to government policies on racial issues. For example, whites' opposition to busing for racial integration is generally not based on concern about their own children. Parents of white children in school districts with busing (or threatened with busing) have about the same attitudes about busing as do nonparents or those who live in areas remote from any possibility of busing. In another study, they investigated the effects of direct racial threat in four areas: neighborhood desegregation, economic competition, busing, and crime (Kinder and Sears, 1980). Whites' fears that blacks might harm them in these areas had no effect upon their general racial attitudes. Nor did they influence whites' voting behavior in a hotly contested local (Los Angeles) mayoralty election pitting a black candidate against an incumbent white who was openly hostile toward civil rights.

Finally, realistic racial threats may have so little impact because racial prejudice just does not change very much, once it is initially acquired. Sears and Gahart (1980) assessed changes in the racial attitudes of a representative national sample of whites over a four-year period (1972–1976). The respondents' initial level of racial prejudice was a powerful predictor of how prejudiced they were four years later. Virtually no change had occurred. The natural fluctuations in any given white's vulnerability to racial threat (as their children enter and leave the public school system or their job status changes) had no important impact on their level of prejudice.

These investigators (Sears & McConahay, 1973; Kinder & Sears,

FIGURE 12–6 Although closer contact between blacks and whites may reduce prejudice eventually, it sometimes leads to heightened prejudice for a while as was the case with school busing.

1980) have coined the term **symbolic racism** to describe this phenomenon. Whites in the United States now overwhelmingly endorse the general principle of equal opportunity and oppose overt racial discrimination. But they are often quite opposed to racial progress at an abstract, symbolic level, when it violates their other values. Most do not like "forced" busing or "reverse" discrimination. And this opposition is not strongly based on their own self-interest or how racial issues might affect them personally. It seems to be a blend of primitive antiblack feeling, anxiety, hostility, and conservative sociopolitical values. Furthermore, it seems to be a long-standing attitude and probably dates back to much earlier sociocultural learning.

REDUCING PREJUDICE

As we have seen, high-commitment attitudes are quite difficult to change in real life. People tend to become surrounded by a social environment that supports and reinforces their attitudes. High-commitment attitudes allow them to withstand any contradictory information that does make its way through. So how can prejudice be changed?

Socialization

The obvious solution is to change people's early socialization. If people are not taught prejudice to start with, perhaps it will not develop later on. This is why desegregation experts emphasize the importance of positive interracial experiences in grade school rather than in high school. No single socialization experience takes place in a vacuum, however, and it is hard to change a child's entire life all at once. Many of the obstacles discussed earlier exist even for young children. Prejudiced parents may sabotage anything that happens at school; and as we saw, children of prejudiced parents engage in less interracial contact. Or prejudiced peers may sabotage the most earnest efforts of conscientious parents. In addition, the larger society sets a context that always makes change more difficult. Just think of the social obstacles faced by young interracial couples who are dating—the stares and strange looks, the awkward silences, the unspoken questions, the innuendoes and raised eyebrows, and so on.

Education has always been the great hope of those who wish for more interracial tolerance. They think it might help if people just were exposed to the facts, especially when they are young and their prejudice has not yet crystallized. And education does seem to help—at least at the higher levels. People who have been to college generally are less prejudiced than those who have not. But exactly why is less clear. Their greater tolerance is related to their educational level, not some other associated aspect of higher status (Campbell, 1971; Stember, 1961). Future college students are generally more tolerant than those not going on to college. And the best studies show that the college experience has very diverse effects that depend on many other variables (e.g., student's background, major, and type of college). Efforts to reduce prejudice with experimental curricula in the early years do not uniformly work (Katz, 1976b); this is hardly surprising, however, given the wide range of curricula, and the level of skills, prejudice, and motivation among teachers. Education may therefore help reduce prejudice, but its effects are not consistent, dramatic, or swift.

Psychodynamic theories hold that psychotherapy or quasitherapeutic experiences will reduce prejudice. Some experiments have shown that providing people with insight into the motives behind their prejudice helps a little. And occasionally group therapy or encounter group experiences can lessen prejudices (Ashmore, 1970). But those most attracted to such experiences tend to be the ones who least need them. People who are open and reasonably undefensive about their attitudes, and willing to examine them, are usually already the least prejudiced. So psychodynamic techniques are unlikely to prove useful on a large scale for prejudice reduction.

The media represent another possibility, but their persuasive impact is quite limited. And they have two additional liabilities in the case of minorities. First, minorities have traditionally been given relatively little attention in the media. For example, before television, magazines such as *Life* and *The Saturday Evening Post* reached very large national audiences. As of 1949–50, blacks were in only 0.5 percent of all ads, and in 2.5 percent of all nonadvertising material, despite the fact that they comprised about 10 percent of the population. And, second, even this coverage was highly stereotypical; 80 percent of the blacks in ads were maids, cooks, or servants for whites. Even in 1967, only 4 percent of all TV commercials used blacks. After 1967, this invisibility began to diminish somewhat. By 1973, 14 percent of the TV commercials were using blacks. But even this was tentative; blacks were shown mainly in groups of six or more (Greenberg & Mazingo, 1976). This invisibility and stereotypical treatment, together with the media's general ineffectiveness at persuasion, has made media exposure a weak way to reduce prejudice.

Contact

Another great hope for prejudice reduction has always been simple human contact. The belief has been that contact would help break down misinformed stereotypes, and that proximity and interaction would increase liking as it normally does. International student exchanges, the Olympic Games, international conference—all are predicated on this assumption. Does contact really work?

Since World War II, for a variety of reasons, America has gradually become desegregated. This development has given social scientists opportunities to test the effects of contact. Racial prejudice and antagonisms decreased in World War II, when black and white soldiers fought together (Stouffer et al., 1949). At the start of the war, military policy was to avoid racially mixed units. However, as time went by, white infantry replacements became in short supply. The Army allowed black volunteers to join previously all-white units. Surveys before this desegregation showed most white soldiers opposed it, but afterwards there was much less opposition. The greatest support came from those white soldiers who were most closely associated with the blacks. No realistic conflicts arose between the groups because instead of competing, they were fighting a common enemy. With this lack of conflict, unrealistic stereotypes decreased markedly because of the greater knowledge gained by the increased familiarity.

Some other early research also indicated that increased contact reduced antagonism, prejudice, and stereotypes. Studies on public housing have found less antagonism in both blacks and whites in integrated than in segregated areas. Deutsch and Collins (1951) compared two housing projects in which tenants were assigned to apartments without regard to race with two projects in which blacks and whites were kept in different buildings. White housewives in the integrated projects were less prejudiced and more likely to have a black as a "best friend" much more often. Similar results have been reported in studies on integrated working conditions. When blacks were hired to work in department stores in New York City, white clerks became progressively more accepting of them. White customers had similar positive reactions. Comparable results have been found among police officers and government workers. Thus, most of the research indicates that greater familiarity, even under trying conditions, leads to less antagonism.

The best recent reviews suggest, however, that mere contact is not invariably beneficial. For example, school desegregation by itself has not convincingly been shown to reduce prejudice in all cases. Surprisingly little research has been done on the question, but what there is does not show a strong pattern one way or the other (see Amir, 1976; Stephan & Rosenfield, 1978). The main problem is, as Pettigrew (1969) has pointed out, that desegregation is not the same as integration. Proximity by itself does not guarantee prejudice reduction, because putting children of different races in the same classroom does not guarantee positive interaction. Indeed, the development of interracial friendship turns out to be more important than mere contact in producing prejudice reduction (Ashmore, 1970).

In other words, the type of contact is the crucial factor, and *appropriate contact* has been found to reduce both bias and antagonism. There seem to be three necessary conditions: (1) close contact—it is not enough for people simply to coexist in the same geographical space; they must be brought together in close interaction. Desegregation in schools or at work often results in superficial contact. (2) Cooperative interdependence—whites and blacks need to be working together for common goals and to depend upon each others' efforts, as in World War II. (3) The contact must be of equal status—resentments build up if the traditional status imbalance is maintained, and stereotypes cannot easily be broken down. Contact occurs when a black clean-up man works for a Jewish businessman, but situations of this kind simply perpetuate the traditional stereotypes.

For example, Clore and co-workers (1978) ran an interracial summer camp, in which campers, administrative staff, and counsellors were all evenly divided between blacks and whites. The researchers tried to maximize: (1) intimate contact, by mixing the living arrangements by race; (2) superordinate goals, by creating primitive conditions that demanded cooperation such as fire building, cooking, and planning activities; and (3) equal status, by selecting campers from similar backgrounds. The one-week experience was successful in increasing the percentage of inter-racial choices campers made for partners in playing games.

Social psychologists today are quite active in trying to introduce such procedures into desegregated schools, with the idea that desegregation can reduce prejudice only if the right conditions prevail. Standard educational procedures have been compared with new procedures introducing interdependent "teams" that cooperate to complete classroom assignments. For example, Eliot Aronson and his colleagues have used what they call a "jigsaw" technique. Children are placed in small learning groups, usually consisting of five or six participants. They meet in the group for about an hour a day to focus on one particular lesson. Each person is assigned one portion of the day's lesson, and is responsible for teaching that material to the rest of the group. Since no one can put together the whole picture without the information contributed by others, the students are interdependent. Ultimately each student's learning is evaluated separately, but unless all cooperate in contributing their unique pieces of knowledge, none can do very well. Through this technique, the children get to know each other very well, and in addition they come to appreciate the abilities and contributions of all the other children. Aronson and his co-workers report good success with this technique in increasing peer liking across ethnic and racial groups, and in increasing the self-esteem of minority children (see Aronson and Osherow, 1980).

Close contact is not the only factor in reducing prejudice, though it may be the most important. *Successful* outcomes of cooperative efforts may be important. If people work together in wars, or games, or class-room jobs, and things go badly, they may get resentful of each other, and even more hostile. How important success is in this process is not yet clear, but it may be an important ingredient. And the *norms of the surrounding community* are very important. Even if the interracial experience is successful within one limited site, the people will quickly go back out into their normal lives, and if they are then surrounded by prejudiced people, they may quickly revert. This is one of the difficulties in trying to induce children of prejudiced parents to themselves not be prejudiced.

Using this theory, what kinds of situations would be likely to reduce prejudice, and what kinds would not? Mere desegregation would not be enough; integration would be required. And it would have to be done in such a way as to promote equal-status relationships between the races. Being teammates on a professional football team would. Being fellow conspirators in a prison break would. Having a black janitor in an office building, or a black maid in a middle-class household, would not. Having both races in a lecture class would not. Having interracial teams set up to solve homework problems in a statistics class would.

Are the most helpful kinds of situations common in our society? Unfortunately, through most of our history they have not been. Prior to the 1950s, American society was organized in a way that afforded almost no opportunities for equal-status, cooperative interdependent contact between blacks and whites. Almost all American institutions were segregated. There were white colleges, and there were black colleges. Only whites were permitted to play professional sports in the major leagues. Black athletes had to play on all-black teams in black leagues. Military units were either all-black or all-white. Most blacks lived in the South, and of course in the South segregation was the law in public accommodations, schools, transportation, politics, and every other social institution. At that time there were such gross differences between blacks and whites in income, education, and occupational status that the chance of widespread equal-status contact was minimal.

Today, contact of this type does generally occur in the armed forces, where blacks and whites fight together with more or less equal rank (at least among enlisted men), and in factories and stores in which members of the two races hold comparable jobs. But in many businesses, professions, and schools, interracial contact is often between people of different status. Integration frequently occurs by bringing blacks in at the bottom of the ladder, whether as students or apprentices, or in the least desirable jobs. They then have to interact with whites who outrank them; and so on. Under these circumstances, increased contact seems less likely to have a positive effect and may even have a negative effect on relations between blacks and whites.

One of the trickiest things to insure is continued intimate contact. There are many obstacles to it. As we have seen in the chapter on liking, people strongly prefer to associate with those similar to themselves. But this makes it especially difficult to get the most prejudiced people in contact with minorities, because they are extremely dissimilar in values and attitudes. The phenomenon of "white flight," whereby white children leave desegregated schools, illustrates how hard it is simply to insure any interracial contact at all, much less insuring that the circumstances of the contact will be helpful. This is why one of the most touchy aspects of desegregation is the relative proportions of each group; if the minority proportion is too high, the majority will flee, thereby diminishing the opportunity for contact. Furthermore, desegregation requires the full support of our political and judicial authorities. People have to be willing to overcome the temporary discomforts of association with unfamiliar people, and they are less likely to do so if they know they can easily escape.

Desegregation is therefore not a panacea for racial prejudice. The practical difficulties do not mean it should be abandoned, however. There are important moral and legal reasons for desegregation. But no single approach is going to solve the problem. Intergroup antagonism seems to be a fundamental aspect of the human condition. Every society in the world takes group membership into consideration when determining how it is going to treat any given individual. No culture is immune from prejudice. In a sense, the United States has set a higher standard for itself than most countries and has embarked on a highly ambitious program of group equality. The Bill of Rights and the later constitutional amendments (especially the Fourteenth) set up extremely idealistic guidelines. At the same time, the United States has tried to accommodate a bewildering variety of groups from all parts of the world, including Africans, Vietnamese, Hungarians, Mexican Indians, Russian Jews, and British Puritans. It is not surprising, therefore, that it should have failed to some degree. But is also well to remember the very considerable harmony and group tolerance that has allowed such a Noah's Ark of humanity to coexist and cooperate for so many years.

SUMMARY

1. Far-ranging attitude changes are rarely produced by such propaganda campaigns in the real world as advertising campaigns, presidential campaigns, presidential debates, and the Chinese "brainwashing."

2. Television news did not seem to have the effect attributed to it during the 1960s and early 1970s, of making the public more politically cynical.

3. One set of obstacles to attitude change in the real world is lack of exposure to discrepant information, because of low absolute levels of exposure and selective exposure.

4. Selective exposure can occur in the absence of any very general tendency for people to seek out supportive information (motivated selectivity).

5. Real-life propaganda also is often ineffective because it encounters highly committed attitudes, so any new information is selectively interpreted by the person to reinforce his prior attitudes.

6. The media can be effective, however, in "agenda-setting," providing information, or changing low-commitment attitudes.

7. These strong commitments frequently develop in childhood and adolescence. Although parents have an important part in the development of commitments, they are by no means the only, or even necessarily the most important, source of preadult attitude acquisition.

8. Mass attitude change can occur with low-commitment attitudes if there is a high level of exposure. Sometimes young adults can be swayed when they live in a social environment dominated by attitudes contrary to their preadult socialization.

9. Prejudice, stereotypes, and discrimination correspond to the affective, cognitive, and behavioral components of intergroup antagonism.

10. Societal-level theories view prejudice as stemming from realistic group conflicts; sociocultural learning, from preadult socialization; and intrapersonal theories, from application of the individual's predispositions.

11. Sociocultural learning is probably the strongest determinant of stereotypes and prejudices against minority groups.

12. Interracial contact is probably the most effective technique for reducing prejudice. But by itself it is not extremely effective. It is more likely to be successful if it involves close contact, cooperative interdependence, and equal status.

SUGGESTIONS FOR ADDITIONAL READING

ALLPORT, G. W. *The nature of prejudice.* Garden City, N.Y.: Doubleday Anchor (paperback), 1954. The classic sociopsychological treatment of prejudice. Covers all the theories.

COMSTOCK, G., CHAFFEE, S., KATZMAN, N., McCOMBS, M., & ROBERTS, D. *Television and human behavior.* New York: Columbia University Press, 1978. A useful current review of what is known about media effects of all kinds, from advertising and violence to politics.

HOVLAND, C. I. Reconciling conflicting results derived from experimental and survey studies of attitude change. *American Psychologist,* 1959, 14, 8–17. An influential early attempt to compare the findings of laboratory and field studies of attitude change.

KATZ, P. A. *Towards the elimination of racism.* Elmsford, N.Y.: Pergamon Press, 1976. An excellent collection of essays on many different aspects of racism.

PATTERSON, T. E. *The mass media election: How Americans choose their president.* New York: Praeger, 1980. An intensive investigation of the role played by the media in identifying viable candidates, how images are presented, and what the voters actually pick up.

SCHEIN, E. H. *Coercive persuasion.* New York: Norton, 1961. A fascinating account of the techniques used by the Chinese during the Korean War, and how they relate to social psychology.

SEARS, D. O. Political behavior. In G. Lindzey & E. Aronson (eds.), *Handbook of social psychology.* 2nd ed. Vol. 5. Reading Mass.: Addison-Wesley. A most complete account of research on public opinion concerning politics in the United States. Relates that research to the social-psychological principles discussed in this chapter.

Sex Roles

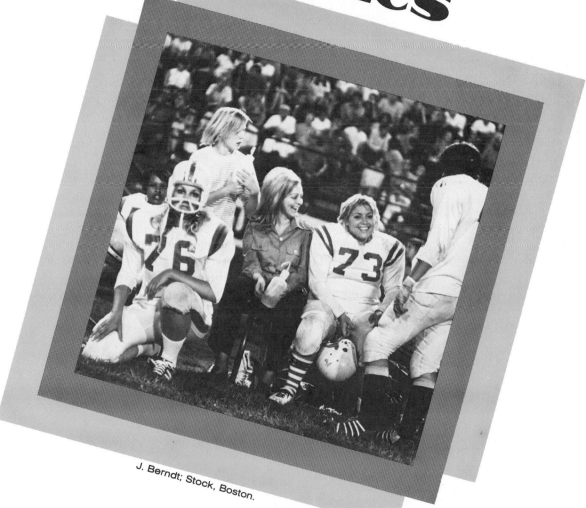

J. Berndt; Stock, Boston.

Each of us is either male or female. No other general distinction between individuals is quite so obvious or pervasive. From a biological perspective, the only difference that really matters is that females can bear young and males cannot. Yet, the biological function, together with some relatively minor physical differences, has given rise to the concept of sex roles, sexual discrimination, and the whole issue of how one's sex affects behavior. There is no doubt that our sex profoundly affects how we are perceived and treated by others, what others expect of us, and how we behave ourselves. This has probably been true of all human societies throughout history and is certainly true of current American society. Indeed, only in relatively recent years have we begun to seriously question sex roles and to investigate in detail how they develop, how they affect us, and whether they accurately reflect real differences between the sexes.

Before discussing the issues of how sex roles develop and their consequences, we must distinguish among sexual identity, sexual stereotypes, attitudes toward the sexes, and sex-typed behavior. **Sexual identity** refers to the knowledge that one belongs to a particular sex (i.e., am I female or male?) and also to the ability to recognize the sex of other people. **Sexual stereotypes** are beliefs about how the two sexes differ: what behavior, dress, appearance, and personality are typical of males and females. Sexual attitudes are similar to stereotypes except that attitudes are what people think *ought* to be the differences (if any) between the sexes and how they think men and women should act. Finally, and in the long run by far the most important question, is how all of the above affect an individual's behavior.

The simplest question concerning sexuality is whether someone is male or female. Usually this is easy to decide. At least from the point of view of society and the child's parents, sexual identity is determined entirely by the presence of male or female sex organs at birth. Assuming that the infant has normal sex organs, male genitals make the person a boy and female genitals make the person a girl.

Sexual identity is genetically controlled by one pair of chromosomes. Assuming normal development, if the pair consists of two X chromosomes (so called because of their shape), the person will be female; if the pair consists of one X and one Y, the person will be male. Unusual combinations, such as two X's and a Y (XXY), or one X and no Y (XO), often produce abnormalities in sexual identity and physical makeup (e.g., XO is female but without ovaries). The general rule, however, is that whenever at least one Y chromosome is present, the person is male; and the absence of a Y chromosome makes a female (see Box 13–1).

Children know their own sex at a very early age, usually by the time they are two (Thompson, 1975; Edelbrock & Sugawara, 1978). Most two-year-olds are aware that there are two sexes, that they belong to one of them, and that their father is male and their mother female. They are also able to identify the sex of other children and adults. Thus, sexual identity develops early in life.

On the other hand, children's understanding of sexual identity at this early age is far from complete. In the first place, they tend to identify sex by clothing, roles, or other superficial factors rather than by physical characteristics. Indeed, it is far from clear that children know that sex is defined in terms of the genitals. The notion that gender is constant, that someone is born female and stays female for life, seems to develop gradually and may not be fully developed until the age of five or six (De Vries, 1969; Emmerich et al., 1977; Marcus & Overton, 1978). In other words, by age two, children have learned their own sex and certain characteristics that distinguish the two sexes. But only later do they become aware of sexual identity in the full sense.

Sexual Stereotypes and Attitudes	Once sexual identity is established and understood, the next step (which may in fact overlap with the development of identity) is the development of beliefs and attitudes about the two sexes. As well as recognizing people's gender, we all have ideas about how the sexes differ and perhaps also about how they *should* differ. These are two quite distinct sets of beliefs. The first concerns sexual stereotypes—in general, how men and women differ in their behavior, personality, attitudes, responses, and so on. The second concerns how we think the ideal man should differ from the ideal woman. In reality, these differences may not exist; and they may not coincide with society's stereotypes about men and women. Instead, they are what the individual would like to see in the two sexes.

Sexual differentiation of the embryo occurs at about the seventh week of prenatal development and is determined by one chromosome pair. If a Y chromosome is present, the undeveloped gonads become testes; if no Y is present, they become ovaries. From this stage on, the development of additional sexual characteristics is determined in part by hormones that are secreted by the sex glands. The testes secrete two hormones, one of which promotes the development of male characteristics and the other prevents the development of female characteristics such as a uterus.

There are two fascinating aspects to this process. First, in any given embryo, the female characteristics must be suppressed in order for the embryo to develop into a male. That is, the testes must secrete an inhibiting hormone before male organs will develop. In contrast, no hormone needs to be secreted in order to suppress the development of male sexual organs and characteristics. For example, if the testes are removed early in the development of the embryo, female organs will develop. In contrast, if the ovaries are removed early, the embryo still develops female organs. In other words, a special substance is necessary to produce masculine characteristics, and another substance is necessary to suppress the production of female characteristics. In a sense then, development as a female is the normal course of things; development as a male comes about only by some active positive intervention of additional hormones.

The second important aspect of the developmental process is that all individuals possess both male and female physiological structures. A normal male possesses vestigial (undeveloped) female tissues that would have turned into female organs had not certain hormones intervened. Similarly a normal female possesses vestigial male organs. Thus, in a very basic sense all people retain within them some physical elements of the opposite sex. The physiological structure, therefore, supports the idea that the capabilities and qualities of the two sexes are far more similar than has been thought.

This is an important distinction that is often overlooked. It is entirely possible for someone to have a perfect understanding of traditional sexual stereotypes, but to prefer a different collection of differences. More to the point, someone who knows the standard sexual stereotype may believe that no such differences should exist in an ideal world. For example, as a psychologist I know that men tend to be more physically aggressive than women; but I do not by any means think that this is something toward which men and women should strive. Someone else might think that men and women are equally smart, but might believe that women *should* be less smart than men.

In a later section we shall describe current sexual stereotypes and discuss in detail how they affect our behavior and how we are treated by others. For the moment, the important point about sexual stereotypes and attitudes is that they are distinct from sexual identity. Stereotypes develop later and are more variable and complex. Knowledge of stereotypes and the development of sexual attitudes affect actual behavior—both one's own stereotypical behavior and also one's behavior toward others, depending on their sex. These effects are closely related to whether the individual forms a self-concept that involves a sex role. That is, does the person define his or her own behavior in terms of sex identity?

SEX ROLES

Sex roles originated a long time ago probably because of the basic physiological differences between men and women. In ancient primitive societies, the fact that women became pregnant, gave birth to children, and then nursed them had profound consequences. Unlike today, women were probably either pregnant or nursing most of their adult lives. Although healthy women can engage in most activities when they are pregnant, they are somewhat limited toward the end of pregnancy. Moreover, when they are nursing, they have to stay close to their children. When we add to this the somewhat greater physical strength and running speed of men, it is easy to see that tasks requiring traveling, strength, or endurance would tend to be done by men rather than women. Thus, men became the hunters, herders, and fighters, while the women stayed home, tended the children, farmed, and took care of the house.

This differentiation of roles came to extend to all aspects of life. Men in general came to be seen as courageous, strong, independent, and adventuresome (qualities needed for hunting and fighting), while women were seen as warm, passive, quiet, and nurturant (qualities useful at home and in caring for children). Today, the original reasons for sex roles have disappeared due to birth control methods, smaller families, and greatly reduced significance of differences in strength and speed. Nevertheless, these ancient sex roles persist and profoundly affect our lives.

Most people define themselves—at least in part—in terms of their gender. From the age of two on, most of us think of ourselves as either male or female, and we may pattern our behavior after what we think is appropriate for our sex. Of course, what we think is appropriate varies, and the extent to which we make clear sex-role distinctions does also. But people are either male or female, and most of us cannot entirely disregard this either for ourselves or for others.

However, the crucial question is how sexual identity and sex roles affect people. The traditional view has been that clear sexual identification and the acceptance of one's sex role are crucial to healthy development. According to this view, a male who cannot fully accept the fact that he is a man, or who wishes he were a woman, will not develop normally.

Likewise, a woman who tries to act like a man, who rejects her role as a woman, is considered to be psychologically unhealthy. Thus, traditional views insist that the child understand his or her sex role and behave accordingly.

A more recent view, however, distinguishes between sexual identity and sex roles. Since we are, in fact, one sex or the other, it is probably unhealthy not to accept our given sexual identity. Healthy adjustment may depend on our acknowledging our physical apparatus and biological heritage. A man who desperately wants to bear children or who wants fully developed breasts is doomed to frustration; a woman who desperately wants a penis or wants not to have a feminine shape or to menstruate is likely to be unhappy. Sex-change operations and sex hormones can alter some of these characteristics, but the treatment is drastic and can never fully transform one sex into the other. Thus, with some exceptions, people who cannot accept their own sexual identity are less likely to achieve happiness and healthy development than those who do accept their sexual identity.

Sex roles are an entirely different matter. Except for women's ability to give birth and to nurse children, there is nothing of substance that one sex can do that the other cannot. Sex roles, which sharply differentiate the behavior of the sexes, are arbitrary and limiting. There is no good reason why males should always be assertive and females passive; why females should be tender and males tough; why women should be sympathetic, warm, and sensitive, while men should be hard-boiled, cold, and insensitive. Although these values and expectations have developed over many generations, they are not rational. Moreover, they limit the development and possibilities of both sexes. Healthy adjustment does not require us to accept these values nor conform to them. Instead, each individual, regardless of sex, should behave in ways that come naturally and are satisfying and fulfilling; he or she should not worry about fitting into society's notions of sex-appropriate behavior. While it is helpful for us to know the stereotypes society believes in, we needn't accept them.

More to the point, any individual has qualities that are traditionally considered masculine as well as qualities that are traditionally considered feminine. Some people may be most happy and fulfilled if they are strongly feminine (in traditional terms), others strongly masculine, and others mixed. No one can decide what is best for any other person; and no mixture or lack of mixture is inappropriate to either sex.

Most psychologists now accept some version of this second view of sex roles. The work on androgyny (see Box 13–3) deals specifically with the combination of traditional masculine and feminine traits, and there is some indication that such combining leads to greater success and happiness than either sex type alone. However, we must recognize two limitations of this viewpoint. First, it is far from clear that the majority of the population accepts it. While most psychologists, college students, and so-called liberated men and women do, many others, perhaps a majority, either have serious doubts about this blending of traditional sex roles or reject it outright. Second, and following closely from the first point, most people may find it easier to succeed in our society if they adhere to the traditional sex roles. These roles are limiting in many respects, but they often produce less conflict and lead to less mistreatment than do mixed sex roles. This is not a value judgment; it is merely a statement of current reality.

The Development of Sex Roles

Children develop some knowledge of sex stereotypes and of sex roles at a very early age. By the age of five, most children demonstrate at least some sex-typed behavior. Shown a collection of toys, boys at this age will tend to choose "masculine" toys such as guns, trucks, or spaceships, while girls will show a preference for "feminine" toys such as dolls, tea sets, and houses. Five-year-olds are able to identify masculine and feminine toys, clothes, and even occupations (Garrett et al., 1977; Hartley, 1960; Masters & Wilkinson, 1976). Knowledge of sex-typed traits such as aggressiveness or warmth develop somewhat later, but these too are learned (Best et al., 1977). How do sex roles develop? Two general explanations have been offered. One emphasizes learning, while the other puts relatively greater stress on cognitive mechanisms.

LEARNING The social learning approach (Bandura, 1969) says in essence that sex roles and sex-role behavior are learned in the same way anything else is learned. Two major mechanisms are involved: First, children are reinforced by parents and others in society for behaving in sex-appropriate ways and are punished for behaving inappropriately. When a little boy chooses to play with a truck, his parents are pleased; they smile, they give him attention, and generally reinforce this choice. When he chooses to play with a doll, they may either punish him directly by making nasty statements, or take the doll away, or simply withhold rewards. In either case, the child eventually learns to choose the sex-typed toys instead of the others. Similarly, a little girl is rewarded for choosing dolls and avoiding guns. The same process operates with other behavior that conforms to traditional sex roles. The boy is encouraged to be assertive and aggressive, while the girl is rewarded more for being quiet and passive; the boy is rewarded for working hard on math and the girl for working hard on literature and art; and so on. Naturally this process works more successfully on some children than on others, some parents will care more about sex typing than others, and each parent will have a slightly different view of what is appropriate for each sex. But for virtually all children, so the theory says, there is differential reinforcement based on their sex.

Although the social learning approach sounds plausible, the research indicates that boys and girls are treated much more similarly than has been supposed. Parents spend the same amount of time with children of both sexes and do not seem to favor one sex over the other in the kind of attention they give (Beckwith, 1972; Pedersen & Robson, 1969). They are equally warm and affectionate to boys and girls (Kagan, 1971). Perhaps most surprisingly, there are no differences in the amount of independence allowed to the two sexes (Sears, Maccoby & Levin, 1957; Baumrind & Black, 1967), nor in parental reactions to children's aggressiveness or sexuality. Sons and daughters are often *described* in sex-typed terms by their parents, even when the children are very young and appear to behave identically (Rubin et al., 1974). But despite this, the treatment of the two sexes is remarkably similar.

On the other hand, some differences have emerged. The clearest is that parents are more "physical" with boys than with girls. They handle boys more roughly (Moss, 1967; Yarrow et al., 1972), respond more to motor behavior in boys (Lewis, 1972), and play with them more physically (Tasch, 1952). Parents also use more physical punishment with boys than girls (Minton et al., 1971; Newson & Newson, 1968). In addition, although parents do not punish children for choosing sex-inappropriate toys nor reward them directly for choosing appropriate ones, parents themselves are generally careful to select toys they think are correct for the sex of the child, especially for boys (Fling & Manosevitz, 1972).

There is also some evidence that boys are encouraged by their fathers (though not their mothers) to be achievement oriented and competitive (Block, 1977). This concern of the fathers centering on their sons seems to be a general phenomenon. Fathers are especially sensitive about their sons behaving in feminine ways, whereas mothers are less concerned about this, and neither parent cares as much if the daughter is somewhat masculine (Lansky, 1967). Maccoby and Jacklin quote from Goodenough (1957, p. 310), who asked a father whether he would be disturbed if his son appeared feminine. The father replied, "Yes, I would be, very, very much. I can't bear female characteristics in a man. I abhor them." This father may be an extreme case, but it is clear that many parents do worry whether their children are learning to behave appropriately for their sex. We can assume that this concern is communicated to children in indirect and subtle ways; even if specific rewards and punishments are not given, the children are reinforced by smiles, frowns, and other expressions of approval or disapproval that can be even more powerful.

The other major learning process involved in acquiring sex roles is imitation. As we have mentioned previously, children have a strong tendency to imitate other people. However, this imitation is not entirely random. Children tend to imitate powerful people more than weak people, and prominent people more than less prominent people. According to social learning theory, children tend to imitate the same-sex parent more than the opposite-sex parent, because the same sex-parent is for some reason seen as a more appropriate model. It may be that children are rewarded for imitating, and are rewarded more for imitating the same-sex

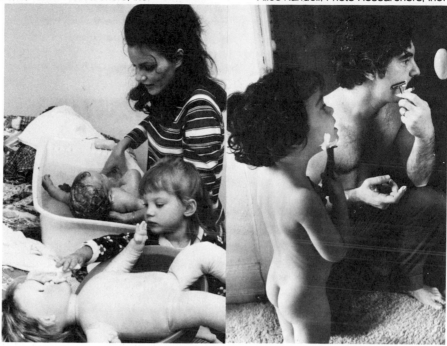

FIGURE 13-2 Imitation plays an important role in the development of sex-typed behavior. Children imitate their parents and tend to imitate the same-sex parent more than the opposite sex parent.

parent than the opposite-sex one. Whatever the reason (see Box 13–2), children do imitate their parents, and they imitate the same-sex parent more than the opposite-sex parent.

Obviously, this differential imitation will cause the children to behave more like the parent of the same sex than the parent of the opposite sex; and this in turn leads to sex-typed behavior. Again, as with the reinforcement process, the degree of imitation will vary from child to child, and the sex-typed behavior of the parents will vary considerably. Some fathers are more "masculine" than others, and some mothers are more "feminine" than others. It would follow from social learning theory that the more masculine the father, the more masculine the son should be; and the more feminine the mother, the more feminine the daughter should be. However, children have models other than their parents to imitate, including teachers in school, other parents, and other children. Assuming that children do tend to imitate, and that they are rewarded more for imitating same-sex people than others, regardless of the characteristics of their own parents, children should develop behavior that is to some extent sex-typed.

BOX 13-2
FREUD'S VIEW OF IDENTIFICATION

The social learning theorists' emphasis on the role of imitation in the formation of sex roles has much in common with Freud's view. Although the psychoanalytic description differs greatly from the learning description, and the two are often seen as strictly opposed to each other, they both stress imitation of the same-sex parent. According to Freud, a child develops a special relationship called **identification,** to the parent of the same sex, a relationship based on a combination of love and fear. The child is afraid of the same-sex parent, because the child is in some sense attracted to the opposite-sex parent and worries about the consequences of this attraction. A boy, for example, loves his mother and wants her for himself. Since the father obviously also wants her, the boy is afraid of and jealous of the father. He solves this by closely identifying with the father, being as similar to him as possible. This assures that the father will love the boy, and at the same time, makes the boy attain the qualities of his father so that eventually he can compete for his mother's affection (though actually, of course, only for the affection of other females). The same process applies to girls, who want their fathers, are jealous of their mothers, and therefore try to be like their mothers.

The identification process may not occur exactly as Freud described—that is, children may not always be jealous of the same-sex parent and attracted to the opposite-sex parent. The tendency of boys to imitate their fathers and girls their mothers is probably due to many factors. The learning approach explains this early sex-role behavior in terms of reinforcement and imitation. Freud puts it in more dramatic, emotional terms. Yet the result is the same. Children do tend to imitate the same-sex parent more than the opposite-sex parent, and this leads to sex roles.

In general, as noted above, the evidence for the influence of reinforcement and imitation on sex-role behavior is less consistent than we might have imagined. Differential reinforcement may occur, but it is usually quite subtle; children probably do imitate same-sex people more, but it is not entirely clear why they do. Nevertheless, the explanation has received some direct support and almost certainly is correct up to a point.

COGNITIVE VIEW The cognitive view of how sex roles develop adds another element to the process. According to this formulation (e.g., Kohlberg, 1966), the development of sex roles involves a kind of understanding and evaluation that are possible only when children reach a certain level of cognitive development. Children first learn their own

TABLE 13–1
Two Views of Sex-Role Development

LEARNING THEORY		COGNITIVE THEORY
Reinforcement	Imitation	
girl chooses: doll — gun ↓ ↓ mother — mother smiles — frowns ↘ girl learns to play with dolls, not guns	mother wears dresses ↓ girl imitates mother ↓ girl learns to wear dresses	girl learns she is female girl learns that females wear dresses and play with dolls, not guns ↓ girl wants to be feminine ↓ girl wears dresses and plays with dolls
girl learns specific sex-appropriate behavior through reinforcement and imitation		girl wants to act appropriately for her sex and does whatever she believes is right

sexual identity and then that of others. Next they learn the sexual stereotypes—what behavior is expected of the two sexes. Then they come to understand that they must act in accordance with the stereotype for their own sex. According to the cognitive theory, then and only then will they begin to act in sex-typed ways. Once they are striving to adopt the "correct" sex-role behavior, they do not need to be differentially reinforced for particular behaviors. They know when they are behaving appropriately and they *want* to behave in this manner. In a sense, they carry around with them their own rules about sex-appropriate behavior. Since they are already following these rules, there is no necessity for anyone else to reinforce them.

Some cognitive element clearly operates in the development of sex roles. Children not only learn to behave in sex-typed ways, but also learn the appropriate sex-role stereotypes. They must know that some behavior is more appropriate to their sex than other behavior and that it is desirable to behave in sex-typed ways. Thus, the learning explanation overemphasizes simple learning principles and ignores the role of understanding and comprehension. As we mentioned earlier, children recognize their own sexual identity very early but do not fully understand the notion of gender until they are old enough to have developed the cognitive capacity necessary to deal with the concept. Through a direct learning mechanism they may be able to say that they are boys or girls, but a more complex cognitive organization is required to know exactly what this means (see Table 13–1).

On the other hand, the available evidence runs directly counter to Kohlberg's rather rigid model of sex-role development. Since Kohlberg borrowed directly from Piaget's model, he is locked into a strict stage theory with specific ages. According to this model, childen should not be able to understand sex roles and sex-role stereotypes until the age of 5 or 6 and perhaps later, and should not show a preference for sex-appropriate behavior until then. However, research indicates that much younger children behave in sex-appropriate ways; they choose sex-appropriate toys, prefer clothing that is considered right for their sex, and understand that their behavior and the behavior of others can be classified according to sex stereotypes (see Ruble & Ruble, 1980, for a review). Anyone who has seen a four-year-old girl absolutely refusing to wear anything except pink dresses or a three-and-a-half-year-old boy already deeply committed to a career as a fireman understands that sex-typed behavior often appears very early in life. Thus, the details of Kohlberg's theory are almost certainly incorrect, even though the general idea that cognitive processes play a role in sex role development is well founded.

Social Factors that Reinforce Sex Roles

Many factors in society reinforce and to some extent teach sex roles. In addition to parents, other adults, peers, and teachers serve as sex models. And it is likely that these other people differentially reinforce sex-typed behavior, perhaps to a greater extent than parents do. For example, groups of young boys would probably tease another boy who wanted to play with dolls or play "girls'" games, but would encourage and reward him if he were good at sports. Thus, even if the parents do not try to teach sex-typed behavior, or deliberately avoid differential reinforcement, a child cannot escape being exposed to others who have more traditional views on sex roles.

Moreover, the media provide very clear sex-typed images. The books that are used in grade schools are typically extremely biased in their presentation of the sexes. Not only do they spend more time on boys and men than on girls and women, but they portray the sexes in stereotyped ways, with the stereotypes usually favoring the male. For example, in 554 stories in grade school readers, men and boys greatly outnumber females; and all the stories tended to be sex stereotyped (Graebner, 1972). In another study of 3,000 stories, boys were central characters more than twice as often as girls, adult males more than three times as often as adult females, and even male animals were described twice as often as female animals.

On television, males have been leading characters far more often than females, and they have usually been shown as aggressive, powerful, expert, and independent. Females, on the other hand, have been presented as emotional, submissive, and dependent; furthermore, they have usually been defined solely by their relationship with males, such as being the lead man's wife, friend, or assistant (Stein & Friedrich, 1975; McArthur & Eisen, 1976; Sternglanz & Serbin, 1974). Most women on television have been presented as either happily married but unemployed, unmarried with a career, or sometimes with a career but unhappily married (Manes & Melnyk, 1974). These stereotypes, however, are gradually changing. We

FIGURE 13-3 Views of the sexes are shaped and reinforced by magazines and other media. However, different magazines often give quite different views.

now see intelligent, career-oriented women on television, some of whom are married or at least maintain a good relationship with a man. Much more often than before, women are central characters and not only in silly situation comedies. And certainly in advertising many more successful, assertive women are being shown than before. Nevertheless, sex roles and sex stereotypes that children learn early in life are still reinforced by the media and by a variety of pressures in society.

SEX STEREOTYPES

Most children learn early in life that certain things are appropriate for one sex, and other things appropriate for the other sex. They learn that boys play with some toys, and girls with other toys; that the sexes wear different clothes, play different games, wear their hair differently, and generally act differently. And as they get older, children constantly add to their knowledge of sex stereotypes.

As adults most of us are familiar with the traditional stereotypes that our society has of the two sexes. We may or may not hold these views ourselves. Some of us may think that they are accurate descriptions of typical men and women; others may think that stereotypes are inaccurate; but we do agree on what the stereotypes are. In addition, as noted before, we can distinguish between the cultural stereotype of how men and

TABLE 13-2

Common Sexual Stereotypes

FEMALES	MALES
soft	hard
sensitive	insensitive
warm	cold
expressive	rigid
passive	active
dependent	independent
submissive	aggressive
modest	ambitious
weak	strong

women actually differ, and our view of how men and women should differ (if at all).

What are the common stereotypes? Table 13-2 lists some of the attributes that are typically used to describe men and women (e.g. Broverman et al., 1972). Naturally, what is characteristic of one sex is seen as uncharacteristic of the other because if it were characteristic of both, it would not distinguish them. Men are thought to be aggressive, self-reliant, independent, and ambitious—all relatively positive traits; women, on the other hand, are thought to be submissive, dependent, and retiring—all relatively negative traits. Women, however, are also seen as gentle, sensitive, and expressive, and men to be harsh, insensitive, and wooden. Although each stereotype contains some positive and some negative characteristics, by and large the masculine image represents strength and dominance, and the feminine weakness and submissiveness.

These stereotypes, however, differ considerably from most people's beliefs about the characteristics of the ideal man and woman. Spence, Helmreich, and Stapp (1975) asked people to describe typical men and women, and then asked what traits were desirable for each sex. They then divided the results into four types of traits: (1) those that were typically masculine but would be desirable for both sexes; (2) those typically feminine but desirable for both; (3) those typically masculine that were desirable only for men; and (4) those typically feminine that are desirable only for women. As shown in Table 13-3, most attributes that were good for one sex were thought also to be good for the other. Even though independence and ambition were thought to be typical of men and not women, these qualities ideally were desirable in both sexes. That is, a woman who was ambitious would be rated higher than one who was not. Similarly, while women were seen as gentle and kind, these traits would also be found in the ideal man. There are relatively few sex-specific traits—one that would be desirable for only one sex—but the list is infor-

BOX 13-3
ANDROGYNY

Although cultural stereotypes sharply separate feminine and masculine characteristics, most people in fact possess a mixture of the two. Several authors (Bem, 1974; Spence & Helmreich, 1978) have devised scales to measure the extent to which someone is androgynous—that is, has both male and female characteristics. For example, an androgynous woman can be sensitive, warm, open, and graceful but at the same time be strong, forceful, and logical. Note that this example includes only traits that are considered positive; the ideal androgynous personality, whether male or female, possesses the best characteristics of both sexes. But it is also possible for someone to have negative traits of both sexes. Thus an androgynous person could be insensitive, hard, and aggressive (stereotypical male traits) and at the same time, emotional, dependent, and illogical (stereotypical female traits).

As noted earlier, men who try to live up to the male stereotype suffer because they are prohibited from expressing their feelings, because they must appear strong and assertive at all times, and because they are under constant pressure to perform. Women who try to live up to the feminine stereotype suffer perhaps even more because they are required to be passive and dependent and are unable to use their talents fully or be as assertive as they might want. While all forms of androgyny may not be necessarily good, the idea that everyone has both kinds of traits is important because it solves some of the problems of sex stereotyping.

Androgynous people who have the positive traits of both sexes may be better off in many ways than more purely sex-typed individuals. Androgynous people rate their self-esteem higher (Bem, 1977; Helmreich, Spence, & Holohan, 1979), conform less to peer pressure (Bem, 1975b), and are more responsive to others (Bem et al., 1976). However, the results have not been totally consistent. In some studies, androgynous people fared no better than masculine-typed people (Bem, 1977; Heilbrun, 1977); and flexibility has been found to be more closely related to masculinity than to androgyny (Jones et al., 1978). Some have suggested that only masculine traits lead to satisfaction in our society, and that the reason androgynous women score higher than feminine women is simply that the former have more masculine traits. In contrast, masculine men score as high as, or higher than, androgynous men because our society values masculine traits more than it does feminine traits. For the moment, the relationship between androgyny and behavior is uncertain. The deeper question is not whether a particular combination of traits is more successful in our society than another, but whether in the long run people will conform to rigid sexual stereotypes or will be free to express whatever traits they naturally have.

TABLE 13–3

Desirable Traits for Males, Females, and Both Sexes

TRAITS TYPICAL OF MALES, BUT DESIRABLE FOR BOTH SEXES	TRAITS TYPICAL OF FEMALES, BUT DESIRABLE FOR BOTH SEXES	TRAITS DESIRABLE FOR ONLY ONE SEX	
		Males	Females
independent	considerate	aggressive	home-oriented
active	kind	dominant	needs security
outgoing	warm	mechanical	religious
ambitious	neat	aptitude	feelings easily
self-confident	tactful	sees self	hurt
good at business	creative	running show	cries easily
intellectual	likes children	likes math and	
acts as leader	understanding	science	
athletic	helpful		
adventurous	emotionally expressive		
interested in sex	devotes self to others		
courageous	expresses tenderness		

Source: Adapted from Spence, Helmreich, and Stapp (1975).

mative. Aggressiveness and dominance are desirable in men but not in women, while the need for security and being home-oriented are good only for women.

Table 13–3 indicates the gap between what people think is typical and what they think is desirable for the two sexes. Even though the stereotypes are far apart, the images of the ideal man and woman are quite close. Almost all traits that are desirable for one sex are also thought to be desirable for the other. Nevertheless, there are differences that focus on power (for men) and weakness and home-centeredness for women. Moreover, we should remember that most of the research has been done with college populations that tend to be relatively liberal regarding sex roles, and also that people may express less traditional opinions than they actually hold. The important point is that people still do have sharply contrasting sex stereotypes and that those beliefs undoubtedly affect how people act and are treated.

SEX DIFFERENCES

Males and females possess different genital organs, secondary sexual characteristics, and some general physical characteristics. Are there also differences in psychological processes such as intellectual functioning and social behavior? As we shall see, there are. Indeed, a few differences appear to be quite consistent. Research has found, however, that with a few exceptions, the evidence does not support the stereotypes: males and females are much more similar than is usually believed.

**Intellectual
Differences**

Research indicates quite convincingly that men and women do not differ in overall intellectual ability. They score approximately the same on all intelligence tests, on aptitude tests such as the SATs, and on various measures of ability. Moreover, there is no evidence for any sex differences in creativity, originality, or problem-solving ability. However, the sexes do seem to differ somewhat in where their abilities lie.

VERBAL ABILITY From a very early age, girls seem to be better than boys in verbal skills. This superior language ability appears as early as seventeen months (Clarke-Stewart, 1973). Girls also do better on various verbal tests during childhood (McCarthy & Kirk, 1963), and on tests of reading ability (Cotler & Palmer, 1971). Moreover, this superiority of females over males continues at least through adolescence and may even increase (Backman, 1972; Svensson, 1971).

QUANTITATIVE AND SPATIAL ABILITY In contrast, males seem to be better than females in quantitative and spatial ability. These differences appear only around puberty and become firmly established in adolescence. They show up on tests of spatial judgment, such as the rod and frame test, which requires the person to recognize a vertical line against a tilted background (Witkin, Goodenough, & Karp, 1967; Saarni, 1973), and in the imbedded figures test, in which the person has to pick out a design from a more complex pattern (Nash, 1973). The difference also occurs on tests of quantitative skills such as algebra, geometry, and mathematical reasoning (Droege, 1967; Bieri, Bradburn & Galinsky, 1958).

With these as well as all the other sex differences we shall describe, it is important to realize that the similarities between the sexes are much greater than the differences. Although there is a slight overall difference favoring females in verbal ability and males in quantitative ability, the scores of the two sexes are remarkably close. Many males are better than many females in verbal ability; many females are better than males in quantitative ability. That is, the overlap of scores is much greater than the difference in average scores.

The other point to consider is that these differences may be due not to innate differences in ability but rather to cultural and environmental factors. Certainly, in our culture boys are encouraged to go into scientific fields and are expected to be good at math; and girls are often expected to be poor in these areas. Girls who are good at math or science are often considered odd and may conceal their abilities in these areas or at least not develop them. In contrast, girls are more likely to be encouraged to be literary or artistic, whereas boys who are interested in such matters are thought to be sissies. In other words, the performance differences may be caused by social forces, not innate differences between the sexes.

Social Differences

Sex differences in social behavior are especially relevant for social psychology. In considering the differences that do appear, it is well to keep in mind that they are probably due largely or in part to sexual stereotypes and social pressures to conform to those stereotypes. That is, with the possible exception of differences in physical aggression, there is no evidence that any differences in social behavior are due to innate factors. This suggests that the differences are not inevitable. Nevertheless, real differences do exist and they play an important role in social interactions.

The sexual differences in social behavior revolve around two main dimensions: (1) power, dominance, and status; and (2) intimacy, expressiveness, and sensitivity. Both of these dimensions are important in our relations with other people. Any relationship can be described in terms of power (who is dominant, who has more status, who has more influence) and in terms of intimacy (how close are they, how much do they reveal of themselves). The dimensions are not entirely independent, and their importance varies depending on the particular social interaction, but together they are a major factor in social behavior. The various sex differences described below can all be considered in terms of the two overall dimensions of power and intimacy.

AGGRESSIVENESS The one clearest difference in social behavior is that males are more physically aggressive than females. This difference appears by the age of two or three (Pedersen & Bell, 1970; McIntyre, 1972), continues in early childhood (Omark, Omark, & Edelman, 1973), and persists through adolescence and adulthood (Titley & Viney, 1969; Shuck et al., 1971). When children are observed in schoolyards, the boys are much more likely to be involved in fights; adolescent males give more shocks in controlled laboratory studies (Kilham & Mann, 1974); males are much more likely to be involved in crimes of violence than females (though the number of teenage girls involved in crime is increasing dramatically); and husbands are much more likely to beat their wives than vice versa. It is important to realize that this difference occurs only in actual physical aggression. There is no evidence that females of any age are less aggressive verbally than males. But on virtually any measure, in any situation, at any age, males engage in more physical aggression than females.

DEPENDENCY AND CONFORMITY Although the cultural stereotype describes women as more dependent and conforming than men, evidence does not support this. Young boys and girls are about equally attached to their parents and feel equally free to wander from them. Older males and females do not seem to differ in terms of their tendency to be persuaded, to comply with requests, or to feel independent in general. A number of studies suggested that women conformed more than men in the Asch situation, but this is probably due largely to the fact that the materials used in the judgments were more male oriented than female (e.g., more mathematical or perceptual judgments were called for). When the items are equated in terms of familiarity to the sexes, differences in conformity disappear (see Box 13–4). In a lengthy review of work on suggestibility, Eagly (1978) concluded that males and females are equal.

LEADERSHIP AND GROUP BEHAVIOR Unfortunately, very few studies have compared the behavior of men and women in groups. For many years, social psychologists either studied only one-sex groups or did not pay attention to sex differences in analyzing the data when both sexes were included in the research. However, there is evidence that men and women act somewhat differently in group situations.

One incidental piece of evidence comes from research on the effects of crowding. In this work, groups of men and women were put into rooms that varied in size, so that some people were more crowded (had less space per person). Several studies indicated that men and women respond differently to crowding. In same-sex groups, men generally reacted negatively to increased crowding. They became more aggressive and liked other group members less. In contrast, women became less aggressive and liked each other more (Freedman et al., 1972). This research is discussed at greater length in chapter 16, where it is pointed out that this result may be due to cultural norms rather than more basic differences in response to space. But whatever the reason, this difference between the sexes occurs consistently.

Other studies suggest that men and women assume different roles in group interactions, with men directing and leading the work, while the women focus more on social interactions. Strodtbeck and Mann (1956) formed mock juries in the laboratory and recorded everything the group members said. They found that men were more likely to make so-called instrumental comments, such as asking for or giving information, whereas the women made expressive comments that dealt with the feelings of the group members, expressed tension, and so on. These results were replicated quite closely by Piliavin and Martin in 1974.

Although there is no evidence that women are any less capable as leaders than men or that women tend to be less powerful in relationships, it does appear that males are more concerned about power in social relationships and more likely to define the relationship in terms of who is stronger. Even boys as young as three years engage in more attempts than girls to influence other children's behavior (Sutton-Smith & Savasta, 1972; Whiting & Edwards, 1973). Boys also try more often to control adults' behavior (Emmerich, 1971). More generally, groups of boys are concerned about establishing dominance hierarchies and testing each other's strength, whereas girls of similar ages devote much less time to this (Omark et al., 1973; Anderson, 1939). In other words, although males do

BOX 13-4

BIASED MATERIAL AND CONFORMITY

For some time, women have appeared to be more conforming than men. Julian and co-workers (1966) found that women conformed 35 percent of the time, whereas men conformed only 22 percent of the time in identical situations. A later study (Julian et al., 1967) confirmed this difference, as did a variety of other experiments conducted during the 1950s and early 1970s.

However, as more research was done on sex differences, this finding began to be questioned because it was not consistent with other findings in slightly different situations. Psychologists then began to look more closely at the situation that had been used to test conformity. In a typical study, subjects were presented with a question to which there was a correct answer, but other "subjects" (actually confederates of the experimenter) gave incorrect answers. It was always assumed that the correct answer was so obvious that all subjects knew it, and that therefore, giving an incorrect answer was evidence of conformity. Yet, the materials used in these studies tended to involve perceptual judgments (seeing whether a given line is similar to a standard line) or questions of fact—usually about geography, science, or politics. Perhaps, it was reasoned, men were more familiar with these materials than women. Men would therefore be more certain of the correct answer and accordingly more willing to resist pressure to give another answer. Indeed, confidence in one's own knowledge does decrease conformity.

With this analysis in mind, Sistrunk and McDavid (1971) conducted a study in which the test materials were equalized. In particular, they chose some material that was generally masculine in that men were more familiar with it and more interested in it, some that was feminine, and some that was neutral. Then, in four separate experiments, high school and college students were asked questions that involved the three kinds of materials, and a "majority" response was indicated for each item. Conformity was measured by the extent to which each subject agreed with the majority responses.

As you can see in the figure, the type of material made a big difference. Women conformed more on the masculine items; men conformed more on the feminine items; and there was no differences between the sexes in amount of conformity on the neutral items, or overall. The findings of previous studies that women conform more was most likely due to the use of masculine materials. The male experimenters, who had done most of the work, probably did not deliberately choose items that would make women seem to be more conformist. Yet, because men were doing the research, they tended to choose items with which they were familiar, and thus they produced a biased situation. Presumably, in this and other research that is done in the future, psychologists will be more careful to make the situations equivalent for men and women.

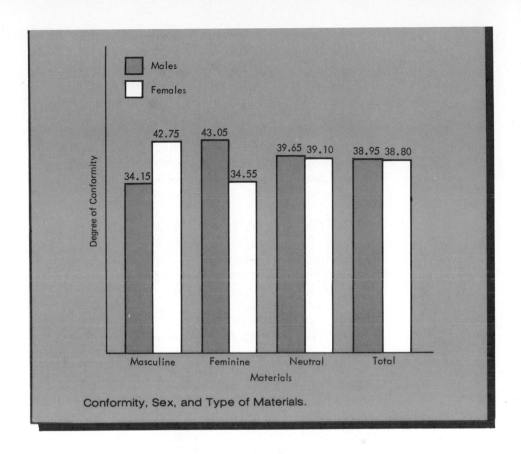

Conformity, Sex, and Type of Materials.

not seem to be generally dominant over females in social interactions, nor to be more independent in social situations, they are more concerned about this aspect of life.

Regarding sex differences in dominance, it is important to distinguish between individual men and women and the structure of society. The evidence based on individuals shows no basic differences, but in our society (as well as virtually all other societies) men tend to hold more dominant positions. With few exceptions, political leaders, heads of corporations and universities, union officers, and others who have institutionalized power are males. Moreover, at least until recently, our society insisted that men take the lead in relations between the sexes (they asked women out; they paid for dinner; they made sexual advances; they proposed marriage; married men kept their own name while women changed theirs; and so on). And men attempt to exert their dominance in countless ways. They initiate touching (including nonsexual touching), which is often a sign of dominance (Henley, 1973). Many business and professional men immediately call women by their first names or call them ''girl'' or ask them to make coffee or take notes even though they are supposed to be of equal status. Some of this is deliberate and some is not, but all of it puts women in an inferior, less powerful position. When actual status is equal, however, there is no evidence that any of this succeeds in giving men more power. For example, in marriage and other romantic relationships, men and women may have equal power, despite the cultural bias in favor of men in this respect. In one long-term study of male-female couples, more relationships were ended by women than by men, and there was some evidence that women were less involved and dependent than men (Rubin, Peplau, & Hill, 1980). Thus, even though men are more concerned about power in relationships, and our social structure gives men power, the sexes are remarkably equal in social interactions that are not directly affected by the existing power structure.

FRIENDSHIP AND INTIMACY Once again, the stereotypes appear to be inaccurate. It is widely believed that women are more socially oriented than males, more sensitive, have more and closer friendships, and reveal more about themselves. The evidence supports few of these assumptions. If anything boys are more sociable than girls, though women's friendships may be more intimate than men's. In fact, most of the work indicates little difference between the sexes.

The clearest difference to emerge is that boys are more sociable than girls in the sense of being oriented toward interactions with peers. Boys spend more time with other boys (McIntyre, 1972), give more affection and other reinforcements to other boys (Charlesworth & Hartup, 1967), welcome newcomers more warmly (Feshback & Sones, 1971), and are more accepting of disliked peers (Benton, 1971) than are girls.

The research with adults has produced inconsistent findings regarding friendship patterns. Booth (1972) reported that white-collar husbands had more friends than their wives, whereas there was no difference between blue-collar husbands and wives. Weiss and Lowenthal (1975) found that women had more friends than men. And male and female college students do not differ in number of friends (Caldwell & Peplau, 1980). Fischer (1980) perhaps resolving the issue, says that it depends on age and marital status. Unmarried men and women have about the same number of friends; among married young people, husbands tend to have more friends than their wives; but older married women have more friends than comparably aged married men. Most of the differences can probably be explained in terms of opportunity to meet people and time to spend with them. As long as married women stay home and take care of house and family, they are less likely than their husbands to make new acquaintances and less free to pursue those friendships they do make. Women with careers or with grown families have greater opportunities to make friendships.

Although the quantity of male and female same-sex friendships may not differ much, the nature of these friendships does. In the first place, boys tend to play in larger groups than girls (Laosa & Brophy, 1972; Omark et al., 1973). This may be due in part to the fact that boys engage in group sports more than girls (and therefore require larger groups for their activities), but it may also reflect differences in the intensity of the relationships. College-age men and women also differ in the way they spend time with friends. According to one study (Caldwell & Peplau, 1980), when they are with friends, most men (84 percent) prefer to engage in some activity (e.g., going to a movie or sporting event), whereas most women (57 percent) prefer just to talk.

It has often been suggested that men have difficulty with truly intimate relationships, especially with other men, and that male friendships are less rich and deep than female friendships. This may be true, but it is difficult to get convincing data to support the idea. Several studies report that women have more intimate friendships than men (Booth, 1972; Powers & Bultena, 1976); but other studies found no differences between the sexes in intimacy of friendships (e.g., Caldwell & Peplau, 1980). The difficulty with this research is that it usually depends on self-reports from the subjects, and what one person calls intimate, someone else might consider superficial.

One behavior that has been studied systematically without relying entirely on self-reports is self-disclosure—how much people reveal about themselves. Maccoby and Jacklin (1974) list seven attempts to find sex differences in self-disclosure, of which five found no difference, one found that males disclosed more, and one that females disclosed more. Some more recent studies have found that men and women do not differ in self-disclosure overall, but that women reveal more on intimate topics (Morgan, 1976) or at least on different kinds of topics (Rubin et al., 1980). In another review of this literature, Cozby (1973) concludes that although the results are inconsistent, when there is a difference, it almost always shows males revealing less than females.

Despite the inconsistency of the results, men and women appear to differ somewhat in the nature of their same-sex friendships and the role these friendships play in the lives. Men seem to rely on their friends for companionship, partnership in activities, and probably for support; whereas women are more likely to play the role of confidante, with whom one exchanges intimate feelings and concerns.

Nevertheless, the findings regarding intimacy and friendship suggest far less difference between the sexes than is generally assumed. Males are not less sociable than females, they do not have fewer friends, and there is no evidence that friends are less important to them. In addition, the few differences that have emerged may change rapidly with changes in attitudes toward sex-typed behavior, and especially toward the male stereotype of toughness.

EXPRESSIVENESS AND SENSITIVITY One particularly strong stereotype is that women are more expressive and sensitive than men—that is, women are supposed to be better at sensing what others are feeling and at indicating their own feelings. Although the data are inconsistent, to some extent this stereotype is accurate, at least for some kinds of emotions.

Certainly, our society gives women much more freedom than it does men to express emotions, especially feelings of sadness, fear, and other negative states (one exception may be anger which men may express more openly). Styles may be changing, but women are still much more likely to cry in public (and probably also in private), to cling to someone in fear, to blush, and so on. In addition, women are freer to express positive emotions of love and affection toward nonromantic partners. They are more likely to hug and kiss female friends, parents, and perhaps even children than are men. Two men who are friends usually avoid these open displays of affection. However, while this is true of American, Canadian, and Northern European cultures, it does not hold everywhere. Southern European men are much more expressive than their counterparts in North America and Northern Europe; and African, Asian, and Latin American men are even more expressive. Thus, this difference in expressiveness and interpersonal touching is strongly tied to cultural norms, not to innate sexual differences.

The evidence on sensitivity is less clear. There is no reason to believe that in general the sexes are any different in their concern for other people's feelings, or their ability to know what others are feeling. The only line of research that suggests some differences concerns the ability to express emotions nonverbally and to recognize such expressions in others. Work by Buck and his associates (1972, 1974) found that women could "send" their emotions better than men. That is, the women could show a particular recognizable emotion on their faces better than men. In contrast, the sexes did not differ in ability to identify emotions from facial expressions. Rosenthal and his colleagues claim to have found that women are better at recognizing expressions, but their work has many problems that make the conclusion questionable. Nevertheless, the differences that are found indicate women to be more sensitive than men and not vice versa. For the moment, we can say that in our society women are more expressive of their feelings than men, show affection for each other more openly than do men, and are better able to express emotions nonverbally; but there is some doubt whether there are any differences in the ability to recognize emotions in others.

OTHER PERSONALITY TRAITS There is no reason to believe that men and women differ in any other aspects of social behavior. It was thought for some time that women had less achievement motivation than men, and that women were actually afraid of success. However, in their review of this work, Maccoby and Jacklin conclude that males and females do not differ in achievement motivation, and most people are convinced that women show no greater fear of success than men. In school, males and females work equally hard on their tasks, show equal persistence, work toward similar goals, and want to achieve both for in-

TABLE 13–4
Some Sexual Stereotypes Compared to the Actual Findings

STEREOTYPE	FINDING
males more aggressive	yes, but only physically
females better verbally	yes
males better at math and spatial	yes, but not when very young
females more expressive	yes, but greater variability in men and women
males more dominant and better leaders	not generally when social factors are equated
females more sensitive to others' feelings	no good evidence
females more sociable	no
females more suggestible, conforming	no
females more self-disclosing	probably true, little evidence
females more passive and dependent	no evidence

trinsic feelings of satisfaction and extrinsic rewards. After school, however, more men achieve success in careers, science, the arts, and practically every other sphere outside the home. But this appears to be due not to differences in achievement motivation at a basic level, but in different expectations and opportunities, all of which tend to favor men over women.

The work on other personality traits also indicates that men and women do not differ. However, relatively little work has been done on most of these traits and the possibility remains that some differences will appear in the future. Nevertheless, with the few exceptions described earlier, the work on sex differences has generally shown that whenever a particular hypothesized difference is studied in detail, it disappears.

SEXUAL STEREOTYPES AND DISCRIMINATION

Almost any social stereotype leads to unequal treatment because the objects of the stereotype are treated as members of a uniform group rather than as individuals. To the extent that stereotypes are negative or limiting, they cause suffering. Both men and women suffer whenever they are treated according to stereotypes, but in most ways it is women who are the objects of discrimination, while men may actually benefit.

Discrimination against women has been described in considerable detail in many books, studies, anecdotes, and novels. Discrimination may assume subtle forms, in which women are treated graciously and courteously but their opinions are ignored, or more overt forms, such as asking the new woman but not the new man in the office to make coffee, or blatant forms such as when women who apply for training, jobs, or positions of leadership are rejected outright. Although discrimination occurs in many important areas of life, let us consider one—careers.

There is no question that some jobs are generally considered more appropriate for one sex or the other. Miner, auto mechanic, district attorney, criminal lawyer, and high official in government, university or corporation are all thought to be masculine positions; nurse, bank teller, fashion designer, decorator, and social worker are usually considered to be feminine positions. In addition, positions in police, fire, and sanitation departments are masculine; positions as secretaries, manicurists, and elementary school teachers are feminine. Clearly, many traditional men's jobs involve physical strength, mechanical ability, and leadership, while traditional women's work at best involves artistic ability or social sensitivity. As bad as it is to have jobs considered masculine or feminine, the negative effect of this stereotyping is that it actually determines who gets the jobs. In the first place, the evaluation of someone's performance appears to be affected somewhat by the person's sex. Goldberg (1968) gave college women a series of short articles that were signed by either male or female authors. Even though identical articles were used, the women rated those supposedly written by men higher than those by women. A more recent study by Cline, Holmes, and Werner (1977) produced somewhat different results. In this instance, each sex discriminated against the other. Men rated work by men higher than work by women, but women rated work by women higher than they rated work by men. And Mischel (1974) found that both sexes rated work higher when it was performed by the appropriate sex in the appropriate field. That is, work by women was rated higher than work by men in traditionally feminine fields; while the work by men was rated higher than that by women in masculine fields.

The difficulty with much of this research is that those doing the ratings are influenced by what they think are prevailing attitudes. College students today probably lean over backwards to avoid appearing sexist, and most of the studies involved college populations. It is possible that more extreme discrimination would appear with other groups of people, or that even college students would be less fair in their evaluations in a natural setting rather than a psychology experiment. But taking the results at face value, it is clear that, as with hiring, men and women are given better ratings if they maintain traditional roles.

The second finding from the research is that men are expected to outperform women; when women do succeed, their success is often attributed to luck and not to ability (Deaux, 1976; Frieze et al., 1978). However, even this effect appears to depend on whether the task is considered feminine or masculine. As shown in Figure 13–4, when a man succeeds on a masculine task (such as a mechanical or scientific task), he is thought to have ability, whereas when he succeeds on a feminine task (such as cooking or sewing) his success is thought to be due more to luck. The same is true, in reverse, for women. Success on a feminine task is at-

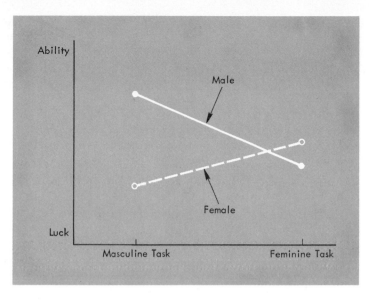

FIGURE 13–4 Perceptions of why men and women succeed. When a person succeeds on a sex-appropriate task, the success is attributed more to ability than when the task is not sex-appropriate. However, in general, men are thought to succeed because of their ability, whereas women's success is attributed more to luck.
Source: Adapted from Deaux and Emswiller (1974).

tributed more to ability than success on a masculine task. But, overall, any man's success is generally thought to be due more to ability than any woman's (Deaux & Emswiller, 1973). Given this point of view, it is hardly surprising that men are promoted more rapidly than women, even if their performances are identical. Ability is a quality one can count on in the future, whereas luck comes and goes.

Discrimination in hiring and on the job may be declining somewhat. It is illegal to discriminate on the basis of sex in hiring, in admittance to graduate and professional schools, and in promotions and pay. These laws have helped somewhat, and changing values have perhaps done even more good. For example, until recently medicine and law have been almost exclusively male professions. There have always been a few women in them, but the vast majority of doctors and lawyers were male. Moreover, the professional schools maintained this state of affairs by admitting very few women. However, entry to these professions is now open to women, who make up a large proportion of all admissions to medical and law schools in the United States. Women are also being admitted to business schools and scientific graduate schools, which were once mainly male preserves. The professions themselves may change only gradually, but the entrance of women should make a substantial difference eventually.

Similar changes may be taking place in other fields. Women are now on the police force of many cities, are beginning to be elected to top positions in corporations, and are becoming active in financial institutions. Just how fast the change will be, or even if it will continue is uncertain, but dramatic changes have come about over the past ten years.

CHANGING SEX ROLES IN A CHANGING SOCIETY

As we pointed out in the beginning of the chapter, sex roles developed because women gave birth to and nursed children, while men did not. For much of their lives women were either pregnant or were nursing the young, both of which rendered them less mobile than men. This, together with the fact that men tended to be stronger and faster than women caused a differentiation of roles. Men travelled more, hunted, did heavy work, and took major responsibility for protecting the group, while women stayed at home, cared for the young, and did domestic work.

In modern times, the decreased need for travel and hunting, and the industrial revolution, in which machinery replaced muscle, made differences in strength and mobility less important. But the demands and limitations of pregnancy and child care continued to reinforce sex-role differences. More recent changes in our society have largely eliminated the reasons for traditional sex roles, and these changes will no doubt have a dramatic effect in the next few decades.

The first and most important change is the availability of easy, reliable methods of birth control. The second is that women want fewer children than before. These two factors have resulted in greatly decreased family size. Not very long ago, women were pregnant just about every year of their adult lives until they reached menopause, and this is still true in some parts of the world. As recently as 1950, the average married American woman had more than three children. Now, however, in most of North America and Western Europe, the average family has fewer than two children. Thus, even though most women do marry and have children, they spend only a small part of their lives being pregnant and have only two or three children to care for.

Attitudes toward child care, women's roles, and work have also changed. In 1943, 50 percent of college women said that if they had a child, they would prefer to stay home and take care of it rather than get a job. In 1971, only 18 percent of college women expressed this preference (Komarovsky, 1973). And, sure enough, many more married women are working even if they have children. In 1950 only 11 percent of women with very young children held jobs and only 28 percent of those with older children. By 1960, the figures had risen to 18 percent and 39 percent, and by 1974, the comparable figures were 36 percent and 51 percent. Indeed, in 1980, over half of all married women held paying jobs outside the home and were thus a major portion of the work force.

FIGURE 13–5 Traditional sex roles at work and around the house seem to be changing somewhat. It is no longer only men who work on construction and women who cook.

Another change in our social structure that has had a profound effect on sex roles is the striking increase in the divorce rate. Divorce is no longer considered especially negative or unacceptable by most people; new laws have made divorce much easier than before, and have led to a steady increase in the number of marriages that end in divorce. In 1930, fewer than 15 percent of all marriages ended in divorce; now the figure is 50 percent. Although most people may still enter marriage wishing it to last forever, they are probably more disappointed than surprised if their marriage does not last. Attitudes toward marriage, therefore, are changing; a great many divorced people are raising children; and the family, though still important, is not as sacred as it once was. Women can no longer count on marriage providing them with a constant, secure, and unchanging life.

To be sure, most people are happier married than if they remain single (Freedman, 1978); this is true for both men and women (perhaps even more so for women than for men). Nevertheless, evidence indicates that many married women feel trapped by their marriages and wish they were freer to pursue their own interests. Thus, both men and women experience a constant conflict between the need for stability and security that marriage brings and the desire to express themselves and live freely. This conflict involves social life, careers, sexual intimacy, and personal expression in general. For the moment, the vast majority of men and women still expect to get married (and do), and to have children (though fewer than they used to). Even though many people live together before getting married, are sexually freer than their parents were, and are less certain they want to have children, the vast majority eventually follow the traditional pattern. A large number of people do get married, and most married couples have children. And if the marriage ends in divorce, over 80 percent of the divorced people remarry. Thus, despite changes in attitudes toward marriage, sex, and the family, and despite the great increase in the divorce rate, our society still consists largely of people who get married and have children. Thus, it is not so much the social institutions that have changed, but our attitudes toward them and the way we let them affect our lives.

SUMMARY

1. Sexual identity, knowledge of one's own sex and ability to recognize the sex of others, develops very early, perhaps as young as the age of two. However, true understanding that gender is determined by basic physical differences and cannot be changed comes later—around 5 or 6.

2. Knowledge of sexual stereotypes develops steadily. By 5 or 6 children are able to identify stereotypically masculine and feminine toys, dress, looks, and even occupations. Knowledge of personality traits associated with the two sexes comes later.

3. Sex roles involve behavior in accordance with rules regarding how the two sexes should behave. Children show some evidence of sex-role behavior quite young, often as early as 3 years.

4. One explanation of the development of sex roles is in terms of social learning. Sex roles are learned through reinforcement and imitation. Sex-appropriate behavior is rewarded; sex-inappropriate behavior is punished or rewarded less. Also, children tend to imitate adults, and to imitate the same-sex adult more than opposite-sex adult. This is consistent with Freud's idea of identification with same-sex adult, though the specific process by which it occurs is described in quite different terms by social learning and Freudian theories.

5. Although the social learning explanation is plausible, the evidence indicates much less differential reinforcement for the two sexes than might be expected. Boys and girls seem to be treated quite similarly in most respects. But fathers in particular are concerned about boys behaving in a masculine way, and they may communicate this to them in a subtle manner. Also, imitation of same-sex adult certainly does occur, perhaps because it is reinforced more than imitation of opposite-sex adult.

6. The other theory of sex role development introduces cognitive elements. According to Kohlberg, the child first learns its sex identity, then learns the appropriate behavior, but before being affected by this, must also decide that it is good to behave appropriately for its sex. Then it adopts sex role and differential reinforcement plays little or no role. Although cognitive elements probably enter into sex roles, children do seem to behave according to sex roles before they really understand sexual identity and long before they are supposed to have the intellectual capacity necessary for the cognitive model to operate.

7. Sexual stereotypes are widely held and there is considerable agreement as to how men and women differ. Generally, men are seen as more powerful, aggressive and ambitious; while women are more sensitive, expressive, and sociable.

8. These stereotypes lead to discrimination against those who do not fit them. Even if people are trying to be fair, they are affected by their expectations about the two sexes. For example, women who succeed are often seen as benefitting mostly from luck, while successful men are seen as having ability.

9. Actual sex differences are much less than represented in the stereotypes. The only differences that seem to be well supported by the evidence are that men are more aggressive, better at math and spatial tasks, while women are better at verbal tasks and more expressive of their emotions.

10. Androgyny is the mixing of the sexes in one individual. Clearly, since sex roles are arbitrary and sexual stereotypes mostly inaccurate, it is entirely possible for one person to have characteristics that are thought to be typical of both sexes. Women can be aggressive and ambitious as well as tender and expressive, etc. The evidence on the effects of androgyny is mixed. Androgynous females appear to be more successful, in many situations, but this may be due simply to their "masculine" traits rather than the mixture.

SUGGESTIONS FOR ADDITIONAL READING

DEAUX, K. *The behavior of women and men.* Monterey, Calif.: Brooks/Cole, 1976. Summarizes the research on many aspects of sex differences. Brief and to the point.

FRIEZE, I. H., PARSONS, J. E., JOHNSON, P. B., RUBLE, D. N., & ZELLMAN, G. L. *Women and sex roles: A social psychological perspective.* New York: Norton, 1978. A good introduction to many of the issues.

MACCOBY, E. E., & JACKLIN, C. N. *The psychology of sex differences.* Stanford, Calif.: Stanford University Press, 1974. A massive review of the literature on sex differences. Hard going, but complete.

RUBLE, D. N., & RUBLE, T. L. Sex stereotypes. In A. G. Miller (ed.), *In the eye of the beholder: Contemporary issues in stereotyping.* New York: Holt, 1980. A solid, reasoned discussion of sex stereotypes.

Group Structure and Leadership

14

Owen Franken; Stock, Boston.

Thus far we have been focusing on the individual in social situations. But individuals typically do not live, work, or play alone. We are members of groups that have enormous influence on our lives. In a complex society, most people belong to many groups—a family, a circle of friends, clubs, organizations, and political parties. These groups can be as small as two or three members such as a family or as large as millions, such as all Democrats or Protestants. Social psychologists are interested in two related aspects of groups: how being in a group affects the individual, and how the group as a whole functions. In this chapter we shall discuss the structure of groups and the one most important characteristic of structure—leadership. In the next chapter, we shall consider group dynamics, the processes of group action.

ASPECTS OF STRUCTURE

When a number of people are brought together in a group, they do not remain entirely undifferentiated. They develop patterns of behavior, divide tasks, adopt different roles, and so on; these structural aspects of the group have a profound effect on how it functions. Therefore, we shall begin our discussion of groups with two questions: What kinds of organization and structure appear in groups? How does a structure that is imposed on a group affect other aspects of its organization?

Communication Patterns

A characteristic of almost all groups is that some people talk a great deal and others say very little. The circumstances of the situation seem to have little effect on this pattern. It does not matter if the group is structured or unstructured, the problem they are discussing specific or general, the members friends or strangers. In a seminar with a permissive instructor, for example, there always seems to be one or two people who monopolize the discussion, regardless of the topic. They do most of the talking, and the rest say only an occasional word or two.

Probably the most striking aspect of this phenomenon is that it occurs despite the size of the group. Regardless of how many members there are, communication follows a fairly regular pattern that can be represented approximately by a logarithmic function. Figure 14–2 illustrates this pattern for groups of four, six, and eight. Note that in all cases one person does a great deal of talking, the next most talkative person does considerably less, and so on—the amount of talking done by each person drops at a logarithmic rate. In an eight-member group, two people contribute 60 percent of the conversation, one other contributes 14 percent, and the other five contribute only 26 percent among them. Clearly, the ex-

FIGURE 14–2 The amount of communication by members of a group follows a logarithmic or exponential curve. Regardless of the size of the group, the most talkative member does about 40 percent of the communicating and the amount of the other members' communication drops off sharply. The difference between the amount of communication drops off sharply. The difference between the amount of communication of the first and second most talkative people increases as the size of the group increases.

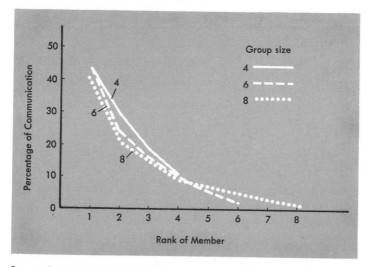

Source: Based on Stephan and Mishler (1952).

act percentage done by each person will vary from group to group. There may be some groups in which all members make equal contributions; but by and large, a pattern roughly similar to the one illustrated will appear in almost all groups.

Groups also develop other patterns of behavior even before a formal structure emerges. They adopt a wide variety of specific habits and traditions. Merei (1949) noted that after three or more meetings, groups of young children formed traditions such as where each child would sit in the room, who would play with which toy, what sequence of activities would be followed, and so on. Strong patterns of this type have also been observed in mental hospitals. Particular patients sit in particular chairs and follow certain sequences of action. For example, someone sitting in one spot might always have his cigarette lighted by another patient standing near him but might also lend cigarettes to someone else. Or the whole group might shift places at a particular time and in a set pattern. These examples are probably more extreme than those in most situations, but one can also notice that college students tend to take the same seats at each meeting of a class—even if they selected a poor one at the beginning of the term. This kind of organization of activity appears in all groups, although few members are consciously aware of it and most might be surprised if it were pointed out. Moreover, although the patterns are informal and unverbalized, they are generally firmly held and highly resistant to change.

The differentiation of communication and development of habits are the beginnings of structure. Each member has a somewhat separate function, some participate more than others, and some perform acts that others do not. This minimal structure is important because it anticipates a more explicit structure. The communication pattern is particularly crucial, because it is one of the key elements in the formation and identification of leadership in the group.

Leadership

Every group, both human and nonhuman, has leaders and followers. Groups of sled dogs, baboons, lions, elephants, and chickens all have leaders. Usually the strongest male asserts his dominance and then has the rights and responsibilities of leadership. He gets his pick of mates, food, and position but also must make decisions—such as where to find food—and must lead the defense of the group when necessary. Examples from nonhuman societies could be multiplied indefinitely—virtually all animals that live in groups appear to have leaders.

This is also true of human groups, though, of course, the leader need not be male and physical strength is not the main consideration. Teenagers standing on a street corner, men in a foxhole, a work gang, the United States Senate, and subjects gathered in a room to discuss a problem all tend to have leaders. Despite the fact that the purposes, structure,

FIGURE 14-3 In any group, some people seem to do most of the talking while others chiefly sit and listen.

and memberships of these groups are entirely different, they cannot truly function as groups unless they have some kind of leadership.

Although the terms **leader** and leadership are so commonly used that everyone probably has similar notions as to their meaning, there are two different ways of identifying the leader of a group. A straightforward approach, and in many ways the most reasonable one, is to ask the group members. If everyone agrees that a particular person is the leader (and they usually do in a group that has existed for any length of time), they must believe it and must look to that person when they want leadership. Thus, in a sense, he or she is the leader. This method avoids the tricky problem of constructing a formal definition, with which not everyone would agree entirely. True, the members of the group may disagree among themselves as to what they mean by leader, but as long as they agree on who the leader is, this is no problem. In fact, it is an advantage, because the person chosen fits all the implicit definitions that the different group members hold.

Although this makes good sense, to some extent it avoids the issue. We really want to say what we think makes a person a leader; we want to be able to tell someone how to identify the leader of a group. If we watch a juvenile gang, the United States Senate, or any other group, we want to be able to identify the leader ourselves without asking for a poll. This is partly because it is often quite an undertaking to ask a group who their leader is. A more basic problem, however, is that we want to be certain we know what we are talking about when we say someone is a leader.

The central attribute of leadership is *influence*. The leader is generally the person in the group who has the most influence on its activities and beliefs. He or she is the one who initiates action, gives orders, makes decisions, settles disputes between members, and makes judgments. Leaders are the ones who dispense approval and disapproval, offer encouragement, serve as inspiration, and are in the forefront of any activity. These functions are merely examples of the general influence the leader exerts over the group. Any particular leader may not perform all of them, but to be a leader, he must perform many. The members do, think, and feel according to the leader's wishes and directions to a greater extent than they do for any other member of the group.

In summary, there are two ways of defining a leader. He or she is the person whom the group says is the leader and/or the person who has the most influence on the group. Both definitions are workable and will usually result in the same person being selected. In fact, some research has shown that the members of a group agree quite closely with outside observers as to who is the leader. In one study (Stein, Geis, & Damarin, 1973) actual groups were videotaped. Later, people were shown the tapes and asked to rate each of the group members on leadership and to select the real leader of the group. Previously, the group had done the same thing while they were meeting. The two sets of ratings were very similar ($r = .82$). Thus, leadership tends to be seen in the same way by group members and objective observers—it may be difficult to define, but not to recognize or measure.

The rules governing dominance in animals are apparently quite simple compared to those in human groups. In virtually all animal groups, the males who have aspirations toward leadership fight, and the winner—the strongest—becomes dominant. There is also some evidence that occasionally leadership or dominance can be achieved by two animals cooperating so that they are stronger than any other single animal. Two male baboons might cooperate to achieve dominance even though neither of them is as big and strong as a single other male. According to Konrad Lorenz (1952), somewhat similar cooperation occurs among jackdaws (birds resembling crows), so presumably this behavior is not limited to primates. But even in these circumstances, leadership depends to a large extent on strength, which is determined in more or less open competition. Determinants of human leadership are considerably more complex.

Why do particular people become leaders? There are two facets to the question. The first deals with the kinds of situations, procedures, or other factors that make a person a leader; the second deals with the kinds of people who become leaders. That is, we can answer the question in terms of properties external to the individual or in terms of personality or other internal characteristics of the individual.

LEADERSHIP: EXTERNAL FACTORS

**Appointed
Leaders
and Legitimacy**

One way to become a leader is to be appointed by someone outside the group. An army lieutenant is the official leader of his company, and in some courts the person who happens to be selected as the first juror is the

FIGURE 14–4 In some circumstances, the leader is clearly established and the others must take orders from that person. But situations such as pictured here are rare in society, so that the authority of a leader is often questioned.

foreman. Simply being in a position of authority or being the person who is *supposed* to be the leader tends to make one the leader. This is obvious in the case of the army lieutenant, because he can give orders to the others in the company, but none of them can give orders to him. Almost automatically he is the leader. It is less obvious and more interesting in the case of the jury foreman, who has no more authority than any other juror, yet tends to lead the discussion and act as the leader of the group. In general, regardless of qualifications, someone who has the formal position of leader performs the functions of the leader.

There are often important differences, however, between leaders who have been appointed and those who have earned their position. In many cases, a group will not agree that an appointed leader deserves that position; they will not think he or she is the legitimate leader. This notion of **legitimacy** can be extremely important. In a study by Raven and French

(1958), leaders were either appointed by an outside agency or elected by the group. The elected leaders had considerably more influence and power than the appointed ones. Presumably, this was due to the fact that the elected leaders were seen as more legitimate and their power to lead was therefore recognized by the rest of the group (see Box 14–1).

However, even when a leader's position is considered legitimate, the members' reactions to a leader depend on many other factors in the situation. Studies by Michener (Michener & Burt, 1975a&b; Michener &

BOX 14-1
THE MANDATE PHENOMENON

Politicians often talk about having a mandate from the people. By this they mean that the people have expressed confidence in them and they have the right and the power to make decisions and to lead. Although almost all elected officials claim this kind of mandate, it is clear that it depends to some extent on the results of the election. An overwhelming victory in which a large percentage of the people voted for the winner indicates strong support and presumably a powerful mandate. In contrast, a narrow victory in which the winner just squeeks by with a bare majority of the votes obviously indicates much less support and no real mandate in the usual sense. The importance of the size of the victory seems to be reflected in the politician's confidence in his position, which in turn affects his freedom of action. Someone who has strong support from the voters is usually less concerned about being reelected, less worried about making unpopular decisions, and therefore freer to institute original or even unpopular programs. Someone who barely won and

who wants to be reelected often worries from the very beginning of the term about gaining more support or at least not losing what he has already.

A study by Clark and Sechrest (1976) demonstrated this effect in an experimental study. Small groups of subjects were set up in which the leaders in each would have full authority to make all decisions. This is similar to our political system, in which once the people have voted, the elected officials can make the decisions on their own. In these groups, leaders were chosen in three ways: by an apparently unanimous vote, by a majority vote, or by chance. The key question then was what kind of decisions would each kind of leader make. Sure enough, as suggested by observations of the political scene, those leaders who had been elected unanimously made riskier decisions than those who were elected by either a majority or randomly. Thus, a strong vote, in this case unanimous, does produce a mandate and allows a leader greater freedom in decision making.

Lawler, 1975) involved what determined the acceptance of leader's authority and demands. In the first place, a leader appears to be accepted more when the group is successful than when it is not. Furthermore, group members will be more accepting of a leader when they are rewarded even more than he is; they are also more accepting of a leader who is not permanent. Taking these three factors together, we can see that the typical political leader, at least in the United States, is in an extremely delicate situation. The political leader's authority and acceptance depend in part on how well the group (in this case the country) is doing—which is, of course, generally determined by many factors other than what the leader does. In addition, it seems important that the leader not reap more rewards than the people who elected her or him. Presumably, people who get rich in office should be aware of the consequences for their political futures. Finally, members do not seem to like permanent leadership and indeed are more likely to obey the commands of an impermanent leader. Anyone who has been in power for too long automatically begins to lose some authority; and indeed, most of the evidence from political science research suggests that the power of a leader increases with time in office up to a point and then begins to decline. There are many reasons for this, but one of them may simply be that people react negatively to the notion of permanency in leadership.

The other finding in this reasearch is that members will obey a leader most when he justifies his demands as being good for the group and when he has the power to punish noncompliance. Thus, a leader must be strong but must also explain his actions.

Although people generally prefer an elected leader to an appointed one, there are exceptions to this rule. One study (Kline, 1976) focused on groups with either elected or appointed leaders. Both kinds of groups were exposed to a simulated panic situation in which the stress was either low or high. When the stress was low, the elected leader was held more responsible for the state of the group than the appointed leader. In contrast, when the stress was high, the appointed leader was assumed to be more responsible for the outcome. Under high stress, the group preferred the appointed leader, perhaps because in this condition they wanted a very strong leader rather than one that they had elected in part for reasons of popularity and friendliness. In other words, under these special situations the normal preference reversed and the forceful, appointed leader was preferred despite his lack of legitimacy.

It is clear that being appointed leader does not guarantee that a person has the power that normally accrues to a leader. It does give him the nominal position, but only by legitimizing that position in some way can he guarantee that the group will follow his lead and that he will be effective. An appointed leader should do what he can to gain the support of the group—by demonstrating his ability, by becoming popular, or by using any other means at his disposal to convince the members that he deserves to be their leader.

"This daily metamorphosis never fails to amaze me. Around the house, I'm a perfect idiot. I come to court, put on a black robe and, by God, I'm it!"

Amount of Communication

One of the critical factors that determines leadership is amount of communication. Generally, the most active communicator is also the leader of the group. At the simplest level this is because the most active person will have the most influence on the group. He determines the course of conversation (most of what is said comes from him), he initiates interactions by asking questions, he receives the most replies, he makes the most suggestions and gives the most orders. Whatever the group is doing, he plays a central role. An outside observer would consider him the group leader, and the group concurs in this opinion.

This suggests that one way of influencing leadership is to influence communication. To make someone a leader, perhaps all that is necessary is to make him talk more. An experiment by Bavelas, Hastorf, Gross, and Kite (1965) demonstrated this effect. Subjects from industrial engineering classes, who did not know each other well, were recruited to participate in group discussions. They were divided into four-man groups, given a problem to discuss for ten minutes, and told that their discussions would be observed through a one-way mirror. An observer recorded the amount of time each subject talked and the number of times he talked. After the discussion session, all subjects filled out questionnaires in which they were asked to rank the other subjects on general leadership ability and a few other dimensions. Three such sessions were held.

Each subject had in front of him a small box containing a red and a green light, and only he could see his own lights. Before the second discussion session, some subjects were told they would receive feedback on their performance. If the red light went on, it would indicate that they had been hindering or interfering with the discussion; if the green light went on, it would indicate that their contribution was helpful. In other words, they would be punished or positively reinforced for what they said.

One subject who was at or near the bottom on both verbal output and others' rankings of his leadership potential was selected from each group. During the succeeding discussion period, he was positively reinforced (his green light was flashed) whenever he spoke, whereas the rest of the group was punished (with red lights) for most of their speeches. In control groups, members did not receive reinforcements of either kind. When the discussion period was over, all subjects filled out the rating forms again. Finally, a third discussion session was held without reinforcement and a third rating form was filled out. The results are shown in Table 14–1. During the second session, as one might expect, the positively reinforced subject began to talk more; conversely, the others talked less. After a while, the chosen subject was doing a much greater percentage of the talking than he had at the beginning. Moreover, this effect persisted during the third (nonreinforced) session, even though he was receiving no special encouragement.

At one level, it would be easy to say that the reinforced subject became more of a leader than before simply because he talked more. Impartial observers would see that he was taking an active, even dominant, role in the group and see him as being a leader. Another and perhaps more important test was the group's opinion of him. The striking result was that the group also rated him much higher on the leadership scale. In fact, he went from very low to very high.

Simple verbal activity therefore appears to be a critical factor in determining leadership. The more active a part a person takes, the more likely he is to be the leader.

It should be noted that this research was done in discussion groups, in which one might expect verbal activity to be particularly important. It may be that other kinds of activity are equally or more important in other kinds of groups. For example, the strong, silent athlete may be the captain of this team. We do know, however, that verbal behavior is extremely im-

TABLE 14–1

Effect of Reinforcement on Verbal Output and Reading as Leader

DISCUSSION PERIOD	VERBAL OUTPUT[a]	RANKING AS LEADER[b]
First (no lights)	15.7	1.77
Second (reinforcement)	37.0	3.30
Third (no lights)	26.9	2.70

[a] Figures are percentages of total group output.
[b] Figures are rankings on a scale from 1 (lowest) to 4 (highest).
Source: Based on Bavelas, Hastorf, Gross, and Kite (1965).

portant in many situations and that a person who talks a lot is for that reason alone perceived as a leader by the group.

But surely you would think that what people say should be more important than how much they talk. Although this sounds plausible, all the research on this issue indicates the opposite—quantity not quality is what counts in terms of leadership. Several studies (Regula & Julian, 1973; Sorrentino & Boutillier, 1975) compared these two characteristics of people's contributions to a group. They found that the perception of leadership was dependent almost entirely on quantity. The more someone talked, the more likely that person was to be seen as the leader regardless of how much of a contribution he or she actually made to the discussion. Quality does have an impact, but on other perceptions. For example, a group member who made high-quality statements was seen as more competent, more useful, and even more influential—all characteristics that would seem to be related to leadership. Yet, high quality did not relate directly to leadership. One study (Stang, 1973) did find that someone who talks a lot and says little may be heartily disliked, but that person is nevertheless considered high in leadership.

These surprising findings must be considered tentative in at least one respect. We know that quantity is very important; that seems clear. But no research has yet investigated the effect of quality over a long period. It may be that in ongoing groups eventually quality will begin to count more than it seems to in the relatively short-term groups that have been studied. However, for the moment, all the work indicates that the more you talk, the more you will be considered the leader, and that what you say (perhaps within some broad range) has relatively little effect.

Of course, as you would expect, groups do take factors other than talkativeness into account when choosing a leader. A study by Gintner and Lindskold (1975) indicates that amount of talking is important chiefly when there is no other good reason for selecting a leader. In this situation, a confederate of the experimenter deliberately talked either a great deal or a moderate amount and also posed either as an expert in the particular area with which the group was involved or as a nonexpert. As you can see in Table 14–2, the expert was chosen as the leader regardless of whether he talked a lot. His rate of participation had no effect on how likely he was to be made leader. Apparently, if you really have something to offer, the group will want you to lead. On the other hand, as in the previous studies, for the nonexpert, talking made a big difference and greatly increased the chance of being picked as leader.

Type of Communication

Although the amount of an individual's communication is one determinant of leadership, the type of communication is also important. Members of a group differ not only in the amount of talking they do, but also in the kinds of things they say. Analyzing the content of communications in a group is obviously much more complicated than measuring the quantity.

TABLE 14–2

Talking, Expertise, and Leadership Choice

	TALKS A LOT[a]	TALKS LITTLE
Expert	2.67	2.67
Nonexpert	1.67	0.17

[a] The higher the number, the more choices for leader.
Source: Based on Gintner and Lindskold (1975).

The latter can be done by simply recording how often and how long each person talks. The communications themselves can be recorded on tape or witnessed by trained observers. But separating communications into categories is more difficult. Fortunately, Bales (1950) has devised a system that makes it possible to analyze a complex communication in terms of a relatively small number of categories, and thereby to describe the interaction with a manageable number of measures.

Every communication—indeed, every interaction whether or not it is verbal—is placed into one of twelve broad categories: showing disagreement or agreement, tension or tension release, solidarity or antagonism; and giving or asking for suggestions, opinions, information. Note that the first six categories are emotional or reactive, whereas the latter six are cognitive. Each communication is broken down into distinct parts, and each part is scored separately. For example, consider the following interaction of a group trying to build a model airplane and its scoring. Member A: Where is the scotch tape? (Asks for information.) I think we need it. (Gives opinion.) Member B: Right. (Shows agreement.) Put it on the tail. (Gives suggestion.) Member C: Clumsy oaf. (Shows antagonism.) Member A laughs nervously (shows tension), and member B then tells a joke (shows tension release). Of course, this interaction is simple and most of the scoring is straightforward. But even in complex interactions, trained observers can use the Bales system with a high degree of reliability.

One point that should be made clear is that the system is designed to score only overt behavior. No attempt is made to deduce an individual's inner feelings during interaction. If someone says, "I agree with you," it is scored *shows agreement,* even if the individual appears to be angry at the other person. Although emotions are important elements in group interaction, they could not be scored accurately simply by observing the interaction. Therefore, the system deals with them only insofar as they are expressed openly. Despite this limitation, the system does specify the kinds of interactions taking place and the role each member is playing in the group.

Analyses of this kind indicate a marked difference in the communications of two kinds of people who do the most talking in a group.

One kind tends to make supportive, encouraging, conciliatory, friendly statements. He says such things as "This is a great group," "We're doing fine," "How do you think we should do this?" He is also the one who would tell a joke in order to release tension or amuse the group. In Bales's terms, this person initiates more interactions that fall into the categories of showing solidarity, tension release, and agreement than anyone else. He also asks more questions than the others—seeking information, opinions, or suggestions. The other kind of person comes to the fore when a task is being carried out. Her communications fall into the categories of giving suggestions, opinions, and information; and she is somewhat high on disagreements. She says such things as "Do it this way," "You work on that," "Let's get going," "That's the wrong way to do it." In general, one person concentrates more on the social aspects of the situation, keeping the group running smoothly and happily, whereas the other concentrates on getting the work done. Accordingly, the two have been labeled the **socioemotional** and **task leaders,** respectively.

The difference in function is most apparent when the group is working on a specific task or toward some goal, but it appears in other circumstances as well. One distinction is that the same person tends to be the social leader throughout the existence of the group, whereas the task leader can change according to the requirements of a particular task. When special skills are needed, someone who has them may assume this role temporarily. Generally, however, one person retains the role of task leader in most situations.

The emergence of the task leader during task-oriented activity and the difference in the types of communications made by the two active people make it seem as if groups actually have two different leaders. The social leader fulfills most of the roles we have described as being the job of the leader—he is the true leader, the one about whom the group revolves. But he may not have the particular skills necessary for a given task and may lack the general organizing skills necessary for carrying it out. If these skills reside in someone else, this person will take over certain aspects of leadership when the group is working. However, this task leader usually has a limited role—he controls, shapes, directs, and organizes the group in carrying out a specific task. Although he may have more influence than the social leader during the activity, his influence is limited to the particular job being done.

The qualities necessary for the two types of leaders are to some extent opposed. The social leader must be agreeable, conciliatory, concerned about the members' well-being and personal feelings, and generally socially oriented. The task leader must be firm, directive, efficient, and generally concerned about getting the job done. One person usually does not have all these qualities; someone who is conciliatory and agreeable ordinarily would not be firm and directive. The task leader would have to be particularly good in the area the group was working on; he would have special talents and abilities that the social leader lacked.

Therefore, most groups do have two leaders, with their relative importance depending on the kind of group, its goals, its degree of task orientation, and the degree to which specific skills are necessary for completion of its task. A group might be extremely task oriented, but if the task does not require special skills and needs a leader merely as a guide and decision-maker, the social leader probably would be dominant. For example, the task might be agreeing on a beauty contest winner, deciding on a movie to see, or simply choosing a topic and holding a meaningful and interesting discussion on it. On the other hand, if the task were to build a clubhouse or defeat a filibuster in the Senate, the person who had the necessary skills for the job would emerge as leader until the task was completed. In an extremely task-oriented group, the task leader might be quite dominant; his skills might be so important that he essentially would become the true leader. But the usual situation is for both leaders to coexist and cooperate with each other. The skills of one complement those of the other, with the relative dominance of the two depending on the group's situation at any particular time.

Communication Networks

We have been discussing groups as though every member were free to communicate with every other member. Although this is true in a discussion group, there are many groups in which communications are limited, and this limitation constitutes another important aspect of group structure that is intimately related to leadership. A series of experiments have studied groups having a variety of so-called communication networks. The basic idea is that communication is essential for leadership and that the person who can communicate most freely tends to be the leader.

The importance of communication has not escaped the notice of the revolutionaries of the world. One of the highest priority targets of any coup d'etat is a nation's radio stations. It is not uncommon to read that the rebellious forces of some general are fighting the premier's loyal troops for control of a country's radio stations or that the stations have been occupied and are broadcasting the news that the coup is successful despite the fact that well-informed sources report that fighting continues. The aim is to take over the communication system, tell everybody the coup has succeeded, and prevent the other side from saying it has won and from getting in touch with its troops. If one side can hold the stations long enough and assert its victory often enough, perhaps everyone will believe it and then it becomes true. The side that controls communication is not only in a strong position tactically but also has the evidence that it is the victor: the one who can communicate is, or is seen as, the leader. This is what strategists believe, and the research results indicate that, at least in small groups, it is true.

The typical study in this area consists of forming a group to work on some problem and imposing limits on the communication permitted among the members. This is accomplished by putting the subjects in

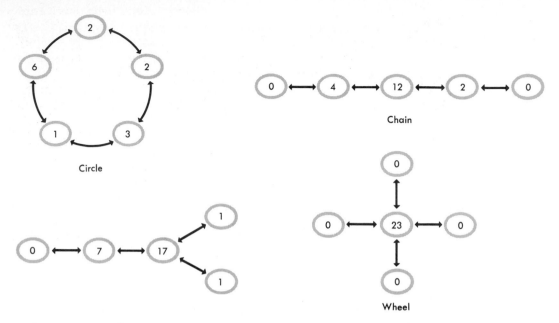

FIGURE 14–5 Communication networks and choice of leaders. The positions connected by a line can communicate directly to each other. The networks range in centrality of communication from the circle (least central, least restricted) to the wheel. The number at each position indicates the number of times the member at that position was considered the leader of the group. (Leavitt, 1951.)

separate rooms or booths and allowing them to communicate with each other only by written messages or an intercom system. In this way, the experimenters are able to control who can talk with whom, and a large number of different communication patterns can be imposed. By examining Figure 14–5, in which some of these patterns are represented for groups of five people, we can see that the structures determine freedom of communication. In the circle, all the members are equal—each of them can talk to his two neighbors and to no one else. In the chain, two of the members can each talk to only one person—obviously, in terms of communication, it is not advantageous to be at the end of a chain. The three other members are equal in terms of the number of persons they can talk to, but the person in the middle is more central. The two intermediate people are somewhat isolated from the opposite end. This progression is carried a step further in the Y-shaped structure. With three end members, only one of the others is able to talk to two people and the fifth member is able to talk to three. Finally, in the wheel, one member can talk to everyone else, but all the other members can talk only to the central one.

A study by Leavitt (1951) provided information on what happened when these types of groups were given a problem to work on—a problem that required communication in order to be solved. The more freedom the

FIGURE 14–6 The status of office workers is often apparent by how far they sit from the boss's office. Distance makes communication more difficult and limits the influence of those who are far away.

members had to talk, the more satisfied they were. The person who could talk to everyone was the most content, whereas those on the end of the chain, who could talk to only one other person, were the least content.

The networks also played a crucial role in producing a leader. When the members of all groups were asked if there was a group leader and to name him if there was one, the various groups differed markedly in their responses. There was a clear progression from circle to wheel in terms of the number of times a leader was named and in the agreement among members as to who the leader was. The number shown at each position in Figure 14–5 is the number of times the person at that position was named leader. Only half the members of circles named any leader at all and there was little agreement among them, whereas virtually all the wheel members named the central person as the leader. The other two structures fell in between on both counts. It appears that simply being in a position to control communication makes a person a leader.

An interesting sidelight on this type of analysis can be seen by examining the structures in Figure 14–7. As Alex Bavelas has pointed out, type B looks to many people to be an autocratic setup, whereas type A appears to be a typical business or hierarchical structure. A second look, however, reveals that the structures are identical, with one person able to talk to everyone else and the rest able to talk only to him.

The initial (mistaken) impression is caused by the assumption that the person who is on top in type A communicates down much easier than the others communicate up. The leader communicates primarily through

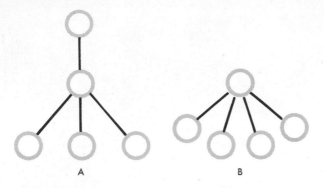

A   B

FIGURE 14–7 Hierarchical and autocratic communication networks. These structures are identical in terms of who can communicate to whom, as long as the direction of communication is ignored. The pattern on the left looks like a hierarchical structure, because we assume the man on top can communicate down easier than the others can communicate up.

a subordinate, and this seems to make it easy to communicate to the others and relatively difficult for them to communicate to him. Thus, he seems to be in a stronger position in terms of communications than they are.

Actually, the intermediary in A (equivalent to the top figure in type B) is the freest of all in terms of communication because he can talk to everyone, including the leader. He controls who sees the leader and, to some extent, whom the leader sees. Every communication must be relayed through him; not only does he pass on the leader's orders, he also controls communication up to the leader. A General Motors vice-president who wants to talk to the president has to ask the president's secretary. And, although theoretically the leader can communicate with anyone, he too must usually use the intermediary. This description immediately brings to mind the secretary who seems to run every department. Everyone fears him but is careful to remain on his good side, because he dispenses everything from paper clips to new typewriters. He is a very important and powerful person around an office.

Under these circumstances, the leader may relinquish some authority to the assistant. The latter knows the subordinates better, communicates with them more often, and finds it easier to give the orders. The leader will often let an able assistant make the routine decisions. After a while, the assistant knows more about what is going on and is considered by many of the subordinates to be the one in charge. Once this happens, of course, the "assistant" does have considerable power. Unless the leader is able to reassert his own authority, the assistant will emerge as the real leader. In extreme cases, the "boss" may actually lose power completely.

"Oh, I don't know   I just feel sort of out of things."

Of course, this picture is somewhat exaggerated. Most of the time the top person retains leadership. Although formally his communications are restricted, actually he can communicate with anyone whenever he wants to. The intermediary merely saves him the trouble by relaying his messages. If the president of General Motors wanted to talk to anyone in the organization, he would pick up the nearest phone and tell whomever answered to connect him with the person he wanted. It is difficult to imagine the president's assistant saying that he could not reach this person. As long as a leader remains the duly constituted authority, he can ordinarily exercise that authority whenever he desires.

However, the situation discussed above, in which the leader's assistant gradually takes over the leadership, is not merely a theoretical possibility; it happens even in important positions. For example, observers have suggested that for many months after President Eisenhower had his heart attack while in office, his assistant Sherman Adams was making most of the decisions in the White House. And at times it seemed as if

Kissinger, who talked to the press and met with many other political figures, had more power than Nixon, who often kept himself isolated. One cannot lead unless he can communicate with his followers and they can communicate with him. Thus, one who can communicate freely, particularly when others cannot, is in a strong position to become the leader—and often does.

LEADERSHIP: PERSONAL CHARACTERISTICS

Thus far in our discussion of leadership, we have been dealing with more or less external factors. What about the personal characteristics of people who become leaders?

Verbal Activity Level

We have seen that people who talk freely and easily tend to be leaders. As a personality factor, this is one of the most important qualities of a leader. At least in small groups, extroversion, garrulousness (perhaps even glibness), high activity level, and assertiveness characterize leaders.

Status

Some people are by nature more active than others in any circumstance. However, there are factors other than personality that tend to make someone more or less active and talkative. There is strong evidence, for example, that people of higher status talk more and have more influence than those of lower status. Stodtbeck, Simon, and Hawkins (1958) demonstrated this in a study in which people were selected from regular jury pools and asked to take part in mock trials. The participants listened to a recorded trial, debated, and returned a verdict—very much as in a real trial. After hearing the case, each jury chose a foreman. The members were given no criteria for their choice; they were completely free to pick whomever they pleased.

For our purposes, the major results are the effects of the members' occupational status on the selection of the jury foremen and the amount of participation in the deliberations of high- and low-status people. As shown in Table 14–3, there was a strong tendency to select as foremen people of relatively high status. Proprietors (i.e., professionals, managers, officials, engineers) were chosen almost twice as often as would be expected by chance, whereas laborers (i.e., semiskilled workers, servants, nonfarm laborers) were chosen half as often as would be expected by chance. In addition, high-status jurors participated considerably more than low-status jurors. Proprietors had a participation score of 11.8, laborers of only 6.4, and the other groups fell in between. This finding also holds when the amount of participation by the foremen is eliminated; proprietors still score highest and laborers lowest. Even in a democratic situation such as a jury, socioeconomic status is an almost perfect predictor of participation in discussions.

TABLE 14-3

Occupational Status, Participation, and Leadership

| Occupation | Elected Foreman[a] | PARTICIPATION[b] | |
		Including Foreman	Omitting Foreman
Proprietor	185	11.8	8.9
Clerical	100	9.2	7.0
Skilled	84	7.1	6.3
Labor	54	6.4	5.9

[a] Figures are the percentage of the expected value. A number greater than 100 indicates that members with that occupation were elected more than would be expected by chance.

[b] Figures are percentages of the total group participation. The figure expected by chance was 8.3.

Source: Adapted from Strodtbeck et al. (1958).

Although it is difficult to separate the effects of status and personality (a person's personality may affect his choice of job, and vice versa), it appears that status is an important determinant of leadership. A high-status person is likely to become a leader even though his status derives from factors entirely extraneous to the group.

Relation to the Rest of the Group

There is good reason to believe that to be chosen leader, someone must not be too different from the rest of the group. Particularly in small groups, members prefer their leader to be one of them—but the best of them. In street gangs, for example, leaders apparently must share most of the values of the rest of the group. They must not take too independent a stand on anything; they must not be deviates. When they make decisions they must make the choices that most of the group would have made. Leaders can have somewhat different ideas from the rest and can lead the members into new activities and attitudes, but the ideas must not be too different nor the new activities too sudden. If they cease to be "one of the gang," they risk losing their leadership and may, in fact, cease to be members of the group.

As we mentioned previously, deviancy is rarely accepted, especially in a position of leadership. Research indicates that a group avoids choosing a leader who holds deviant views. In a study by Schachter (1951), groups were set up to discuss a variety of problems. Several confederates were included in each group. One of the confederates (deviate) took a position on the first issue different from that taken by the rest of the group; another confederate (deviate-agreer) also took a deviant position but eventually changed so that he agreed with the group; and a third (agreer) agreed throughout. After the discussion, each group nominated members for the executive, steering, and correspondence committees,

TABLE 14–4

Liking and Treatment of Deviate, Changer, and Nondeviate

CONFEDERATE	LIKING [a]	ELECTION TO EXECUTIVE COMMITTEE (GOOD)[b]	ELECTION TO CORRESPONDENCE COMMITTEE (BAD)[b]
Deviate	3.89	−9.46	14.43
Changer	5.24	1.70	1.30
Nondeviate	5.53	−2.69	−6.92

[a] Figures are rankings of the confederate by the group members on a scale from 1 (lowest) to 9 (highest).

[b] Figures are percentages above and below those expected by chance.

Source: Adapted from Schachter (1951).

which varied in importance in that order. The executive committee was, in essence, the leadership branch of the government. The nominations for the deviate, deviate-agreer, and agreer are shown in Table 14–4. The confederate who took a consistently deviant position was nominated less often for the executive committee than anyone else. The confederate who began deviant and ended by agreeing was treated the same as the one who agreed all along. Thus, the group avoided making the deviate its leader but was willing to accept someone whom it could convince. Other research (Michener & Burt, 1975) shows that the leader is also very sensitive to deviancy in others. Members of the group who appeared deviant were punished by the leader, presumably to bring them into line and also because they were liked less. Thus, group members do not want their leader to be too different from them, but neither do they want him to be only average.

The study conducted by Merei mentioned earlier provides some interesting insights into the relationship between the leader and the group. Merei formed groups of young boys and girls and let each group meet for thirty or forty minutes on several successive days. At the end of this time, all the groups had adopted various habits and traditions. At this point, a somewhat older child who had previously shown evidence of being quite dominant, of having initiative, and of tending to be a leader was introduced into each group. The question was whether he would assume leadership of the already established group and, if so, how he would accomplish it.

The first finding was that, by and large, the new members were unable to change the traditions of the groups. Many tried, but eventually they had to accept these traditions themselves. In this sense, the new member proved weaker than the group. This does not mean that no one can ever enter a group and change it to fit his own values; this does occur sometimes with strong leaders and relatively weak groups. But in most cases, once a group has established some norms, these norms are resistant to change; someone who wishes to become the leader of such a group must, to some extent, accept the established system.

Despite this, most of the new members did manage to become the leaders of their respective groups. They were, after all, older and stronger than any of the individual members and therefore would be expected to play somewhat central roles in the groups. Although they were not able to change existing patterns or initiate many new activities, they were looked to as leaders, did make some decisions, and were more influential than any other single member. One way they attained their positions was to give orders that were in line with the traditions of the group. Instead of telling the members to do something new or different, the new leaders ordered them to do what they would have done anyway. If they knew at some point that the groups would begin playing with blocks, they said, "Okay, let's play with blocks now." Then, when the groups were about to stop, they said, "Let's stop now." And so on. Since these orders were consistent with what the groups wanted to do, they obeyed them. After a while, they looked to the new leader to see what they should do. He became their spokesman. He continued to give orders consistent with group traditions in order to maintain his position, but in a sense he had become the leader.

Many leaders operate this way. Certainly successful politicians often attempt to discover what the people want and then come out in favor of it. In one sense, this seems dishonest, since the politician is saying what he thinks the people want to hear rather than what he believes. In another sense, leaders are supposed to represent their constituency and this is one way to do it. The key point is that any leader must agree with his followers on most issues if he is to have any lasting power. Once he has achieved support, he can express some deviant views and perhaps then influence the others. Ideally, of course, the leader's attitudes should generally agree with the group's so that he can be honest and still be an effective leader.

Other than these relatively few pieces of information, we know little about the personality of leaders. There is some suggestion that leaders are more intelligent, more flexible, better adjusted, and perhaps more interpersonally sensitive than other members of groups. These variables, however, have relatively small effects. Someone who had them all would be somewhat more likely to be a leader than someone who had none of them, but they do not make a big difference. Some other factors we have mentioned seem to be more important. Leaders usually are more active, more talkative, more assertive, and not too different from the groups they lead.

Psychologists are still puzzled about the quality that is often described in the literature and elsewhere as "the ability to lead" or, more forcefully, as "charisma." Just what, if anything, this consists of is yet to be identified by controlled research. Some people make outstanding, forceful leaders, and the few qualities we have mentioned do not fully account for their ability. It may be that they simply have all the right qualities in large amounts, or it may be something more. At the moment, we do not know.

EFFECTS OF STRUCTURE ON GROUP PERFORMANCE

Let us now consider how various aspects of a group's organization and structure affect its functioning. As discussed above, many groups are so structured that there are certain limitations on communication. These limitations can take the form of poor communication (members are free to talk to each other but what they say may not get through) or actual restrictions (certain members are unable to talk to others). Both types of limitation affect a group's performance. In addition, there are different types of leaders. The style of leadership in a particular group is a major determinant of its performance.

Communication and Performance

As might be expected, the ability to communicate plays an important role in determining the performance of a group. To begin with, anything that interferes with communication among group members will hurt group performance. As we shall see below, it is not always necessary or even desirable for all group members to be able to communicate directly with one another. But if communication between two members is permitted, any ambiguities or restrictions in that communication, such as irrelevant noises or static, can have serious interfering effects. Obviously, if two members are trying to talk to each other and have trouble understanding each other's messages, they are unable to operate effectively.

Furthermore, if there is static in the system, it is crucial for the member who is sending a message to receive feedback from the recipient. Without feedback, member A can never be sure his message got through; he can only hope that B received it intact. Thus, A does not know whether he should repeat the message or go on to others. If the first message did get through, repeating it might confuse the situation. But if it did not get through and A does not repeat it, that piece of information is not available to B. If B can respond to A, this ambiguity is immediately removed; A can repeat the message until he is sure B understands it. When the lines of communication are freer, feedback is considerably less important, because A can be quite confident his message was received even without it. Thus, both clarity of message and the possibility of feedback are important, and feedback is particularly crucial when the messages themselves are not clear.

Knowledge that the other person has heard and understood is sometimes called **secondary information,** because it is data about the transmission of other data. An example of the importance of secondary information is provided by the "hot line" between Washington and Moscow, by which the president of the United States and the premier of the Soviet Union can call each other directly. One of the primary purposes of these calls is for each to explain to the other what he is planning to do. For example, during the June 1967 war between Israel and the Arabs, many such calls were supposedly made, with both men making it clear that they were not planning to intervene. At one point, the United States scrambled some planes to protect an American ship, and the president immediately called the Russian premier to explain why the planes were in the air and to assure him that they were not engaged in the war.

Thus, the "hot line" is a fast, efficient means of communication that enables each side to know what the other is doing. But one of the problems in setting it up was that the president and the premier speak different languages and must communicate through interpreters. This introduced difficulty in ascertaining that the messages got through as intended. Clear feedback was needed. It was provided by allowing the two interpreters to hear each other's translations. If the president said, for example, "Our planes are not attacking Cairo," the American translator would listen to the Russian translation so that he would know exactly what the premier heard. If the American thought the translation was incorrect, he could ask the president to clarify his statement to avoid the wrong meaning, innuendo, or connotation. The critical aspect of the "hot line" is that each man knows when the other has misunderstood him or heard the wrong message and is free to correct the communication until it is understood. In this way, possibly fatal misunderstandings can be avoided, or at least minimized.

The importance of secondary information can also be seen in confrontations between groups in our society, such as school administrators and students, or blacks and whites. In a typical situation, black students might ask administrators of a university to admit more minority group students. What the blacks are really asking for, however, is more complicated. They want a minority group member to be involved in admissions, and they want to have a part in running the university. But the white administrators think that all the students want is to have more blacks admitted. Both the blacks and the administrators think the administrators have understood. Then, when a program for admitting more black students through the normal admissions procedure is inaugurated, the administrators are surprised and upset that the black students feel they have been tricked because the old admissions procedures were used. Actually, neither side realized it had misunderstood the other. If either side had realized this, it could have asked for clarification and avoided unnecessary conflict.

**Communication
Networks
and
Performance**

Various communication patterns produce corresponding patterns of power and decision-making ability. The person at the center of the wheel, for example, is generally considered to be the leader of the group, and he is obviously in the best position to make decisions and see that the rest of the group agrees with them. Conversely, the circle structure, in which each person can talk only to her two neighbors, decentralizes communication and leadership. Thus, a highly centralized communication network produces a group with strong, centralized leadership and power.

The evidence on how these different kinds of networks affect group performance is not entirely consistent, but most of the data suggest that centralized groups are more effective when they work on simple problems, whereas decentralized groups are effective with more complex problems. In some studies, each member of a group was given a card with a number of geometric symbols written on it; the task was to discover which symbol was on all the cards. The solution was trivial—the problem was to get all the information in one place as quickly as possible. This problem is ideally suited to groups with highly centralized communication networks, in which all the information can be quickly given to one person. And as might be expected, they did better than decentralized groups. The leader simply collected the messages from the group members and discovered which symbol they all had.

In other studies, groups were given problems requiring a series of fairly complicated arithmetic manipulations. In order to solve this kind of problem efficiently, each group member should work on part of the problem by himself, at least one other member should check his solution, and all the information should be combined. The evidence suggests that decentralized groups are more effective on this kind of problem than are centralized groups.

The findings are due to several different effects of decentralization. On one hand, the more decentralized a group is, the less efficient it is in distributing information. The centralized group can quickly transmit all the information to the leader, who can then, if necessary, redistribute it to the members, also quite efficiently. The decentralized group must expend more effort and almost always must send more messages than the centralized group. Thus, because the centralized group provides more efficient, faster, and clearer communications, to the extent that transmission of information is for a solution, the centralized group should be superior.

The centralized group also has fewer distractions. As we shall see in Chapter 15, one of the characteristics of almost all groups is that they tend to be distracting. Since ordinarily not everyone needs to know everything in order for a group to solve a problem, many of the communications in decentralized groups are unnecessary distractions. The less free the communications, the fewer there are; and the fewer the people involved in decisions, the less distractions there are. The centralized group has less total communication and fewer members participating in decisions. Thus, it has the additional advantage of being less distracting. To the extent that concentration is important, then, it should be superior to a decentralized group.

On the other hand, the motivation of the group members is also critical. Members of decentralized groups tend to be happier and more satisfied with their positions and to like the group more. Satisfaction and morale are directly related to an individual's freedom of communication and his sense of participating actively in group decisions. Members who can communicate freely are more satisfied; those who can communicate least tend to be least happy in the group. Therefore, the wheel structure produces the least overall satisfaction, and the circle structure produces the most. The lower morale in the centralized groups tends to result in less production because the members work less hard. Thus, from this point of view, the decentralized group should be more effective.

The relative effectiveness of the various types of groups depends, therefore, on how important each of these factors is in a particular context. When a group is faced with a simple problem that primarily involves passing information from one member to another and performing easy operations on it, efficiency of communication and lack of distractions are normally the most important factors. In such cases, the centralized group is superior. When the problem is more complex and involves difficult operations or requires more intimate cooperation among group members, the morale of the individuals and their ability to communicate freely are more important, so the decentralized group performs better.

A somewhat different interpretation of the data is that the critical factor underlying the performance differences among groups with the various kinds of communication networks is the relative difficulty of organization. A group that is disorganized and has not yet worked out an efficient operating procedure obviously would do less well than one that is organized. And the simpler the group's communication structure, the simpler it is to organize. For example, the wheel is an exceedingly simple structure that allows only one reasonable organization. A group with this structure should find its organization easy to determine. In contrast, the circle and a group with no restrictions on communication (usually called an **all-channel** structure) are more complex and allow a variety of organizations. These groups have greater difficulties in setting up organizations. The effect of organization is most marked with simple problems for which a solution depends almost exclusively on the efficient passing of information. Group organization is relatively unimportant in solving complex problems for which a solution depends on considerable individual effort and a more creative combination of information.

Evidence for the effect of communication networks on group performance comes from a study by Guetzkow and Simon (1955). The first and most important finding is that differences in performance on simple tasks tend to disappear with time. After twenty trials the all-channel and wheel groups no longer differed; and although the circle groups continued to be somewhat less productive, the difference declined. Detailed analysis of the group organizations showed that by twenty trials, the all-channel groups had worked out an organization but the circle groups had not yet settled on one.

Another piece of relevant evidence is that the degree of organization is highly correlated with group performance. The groups that had organized satisfactorily did not differ in performance, regardless of their original structure. Well-organized wheel groups were no faster than well-organized all-channel or circle groups. The only difference was that most of the all-channel groups had not become well organized until after at least ten trials, and very few of the circle groups had produced a good organization even after twenty trials. Presumably, with more time, all the groups would settle on a good organization, and none would differ in performance. Nevertheless, the circle groups were harder to organize than the wheel groups; under many circumstances, circles might never achieve good centralized organization. Thus, although the structure of the groups did not fully determine their final organization, it did have an important effect. The more centralized the communication network, the more centralized the final organization. A group can overcome a particular structure, but there will still be some tendency for groups with less centralized structures to remain less centralized. Although the effect of communication networks is most apparent at the beginning of a group's meetings, to some extent it continues throughout the life of a group, unless for some reason the group overcomes the initial structure and imposes a different organization on itself.

Although most of the research on communication networks has been conducted in the laboratory, the kinds of networks studied there often play an important role in real groups in our society. For example, university communities vary greatly in their freedom of communication. Some have highly restricted communication networks, which might be called wheel-within-wheel structures. The top members of the administration talk only to one another and to their immediate subordinates. They in turn talk only to one another and their subordinates, and so on. In addition, the administration talks only to the most senior faculty members, who talk to the junior faculty, who talk to the students. Thus, the junior faculty forms the only link with the students. The students, in turn, are free to talk only to one another and to the junior faculty, but not to senior faculty or administrators. This structure is probably quite efficient in certain respects, but morale is low and dissatisfaction high. At present, many universities are moving toward less centralized structures, in which everyone is relatively free to talk to everyone else. This seems to lead to higher morale and to the feeling that everyone is participating in running the university, but it produces more distractions and is probably less efficient in handling straightforward problems. When everyone can take part in making simple decisions, it is difficult to make them quickly. Thus, this change to a more open communication structure has resulted in somewhat slower action on minor problems but increased satisfaction and more creative solutions to complex, important problems.

Type of Leader and Performance

There has been a considerable amount of discussion in the literature about the relative effectiveness of different types of leadership. In particular, psychologists have tried to compare the so-called democratic and authoritarian types of leadership. A **democratic leader** allows the group as a whole to make decisions, to choose the jobs they want to do; he generally issues few orders and serves primarily as a guide or chairman. In contrast, the **authoritarian leader** makes most of the decisions himself, issues a great many orders, and is generally a commander of the group. Part of the interest in the effectiveness of these two types of leaders stems from their correspondence to democratic and nondemocratic political organizations and societies. Of course, the effectiveness of leaders is also important in maximizing the efficiency of any group—in business, in government, and so on.

In a well-known study, Lippitt and White (1943) assigned adult leaders, who behaved in either a democratic or an authoritarian manner, to groups of ten-year-old boys. The authoritarian leaders determined policy, dictated the techniques and activities of the groups in such a way that future steps were uncertain, often assigned work tasks and work companions, tended to be personal in their praise and criticism of work, and remained aloof from active group participation. With democratic leadership, all policies were discussed by the group; the complete plan of action was detailed in advance; members were free to work on any task with whomever they chose; and the leaders were objective in their praise and criticism and tried to be regular group members in spirit. In a third condition, laissez-faire leaders allowed the group complete freedom and did not really act as leaders at all.

The findings of this study are somewhat mixed. There was some tendency for the quantity of work to be greatest in the autocratic groups and least in the laissez-faire groups. The motivation to work, however, seemed to be stronger in the democratic groups than in either of the other types. There was more aggression as well as more discontent expressed in the autocratic groups, and the members of the democratic groups seemed to be happier and more self-reliant than those in the autocratic groups.

This study has many important limitations. The leaders were imposed on the groups rather than elected by them and, pehaps more important, were adults whereas the group members were children. The groups were informal and not designed primarily to work on specific problems. In addition, the leaders were not free to provide the best possible kind of authoritarian or democratic leadership. They had to follow fairly strict patterns, which may or may not have been the most efficient for the given kind of leadership. For these and other reasons, the results are interesting but can be considered only suggestive.

Other research, however, has produced quite similar results (Lewin et al., 1939; Shaw, 1955). In these studies group members were generally happier and more satisfied with relatively democratic leadership, but often performed better with authoritarian leaders. And a number of authors (Gibb, 1969; Mulder & Stemerding, 1963) have suggested that even satisfaction may depend on the particular situation. When the group is under stress (as in wartime) or the situation is greatly disorganized (as in developing countries), groups seem to prefer strong, autocratic leadership,

BOX 14–2

GROUPTHINK

Sometimes a seemingly reasonable and intelligent group of people comes to a decision that in retrospect is obviously a serious mistake. Irving Janis (1972) has proposed that this may be the result of a process he calls **groupthink.** The process begins with the group feeling invulnerable and excessively optimistic; the group comes to a decision without allowing any member to express his doubts about it; group members shield themselves from any outside information that might undermine this decision; and finally, the group believes its decision to be unanimous, even with considerable unexpressed dissent. Under these circumstances, the group maintains extremely high morale, because of the extensive mutual support for the decision. But since disagreements both inside and outside the group are prevented, the group can sometimes delude itself into making terrible decisions.

Janis suggests that the groupthink process occurs most often in highly cohesive groups that are able to seal themselves off from outside opinions and that have very strong, dynamic leaders. These leaders propose a particular solution to a problem and argue strongly for it. Group members do not disagree partly because they are afraid of being rejected and partly because they do not want to lower the group's morale. According to Janis, skeptical members do not merely go along with the group, but actually convince themselves that their own doubts are not important and not worth expressing.

Janis claims that the groupthink process has contributed to several disastrous episodes in United States foreign policy. He cites the U.S.-sponsored Bay of Pigs invasion in Cuba, the crossing of the thirty-eighth parallel during the Korean War, the lack of preparation for the Japanese "surprise" attack on Pearl Harbor, and the escalation of the Vietnam War. In all instances, a small group of powerful politicians, generally led by the president, made a decision in isolation from potentially dissenting voices or from information that would have contradicted the eventual decision. For example, the Bay of Pigs plan called for the invaders to retreat into the Escambray mountains if the initial landing was unsuccessful. The group apparently thought this escape route was a good one since anti-Castro guerrillas who were in these mountains could assist the invaders. Incredibly, no one in the planning group bothered to look at a detailed map of the area. If he had, he would have realized that the Escambray mountains were separated from the landing area by eighty miles of swamps and marshes that no army could conceivably have gotten through. As it happened, the rest of the plan was also so badly conceived that the invading force was virtually wiped out before it could even consider a retreat.

Although Janis's notion of groupthink is fascinating, there is little evidence to support it. The one laboratory test of the idea (Flowers, 1977) produced results contrary to the original hypothesis. This was, of course, only a laboratory study, and it may be that groupthink occurs in true crisis situations but not in simulated ones. On the other hand, the more basic problem with Janis's proposal is that it does not specify in detail the situations in which groupthink will occur. Surely, many cohesive groups with strong leaders come to excellent decisions. Indeed, the various groups involved in these particular disasters often made reasonable decisions on other occasions. Both the Roosevelt and Kennedy administrations are thought by many to have been extremely effective in dealing with crisis situations, even though they also made the poor decisions described by Janis.

Under what conditions does a group exclude outside opinions and information? The groups in question had access to vast amounts of information and the opinions of a great' many intelligent and thoughtful people. In planning the Bay of Pigs invasion, the Kennedy group apparently did not seek outside information or opinions, but in most other instances it did. Lack of outside information and lack of internal dissent supposedly cause poor decisions, but nothing in the theory explains why these conditions obtained in some cases but not others. Thus, groupthink remains a fascinating, historical description of some important incidents in American foreign policy, but as yet has little scientific standing.

perhaps because it brings the order that is necessary. In contrast, the leader of an informal, socially oriented group such as an encounter group functions best when he becomes involved with the group members, interacts with them closely, and does not behave in an authoritarian manner.

An extensive series of studies by Fred Fiedler (1958, 1971) demonstrates how leader effectiveness is dependent on many factors in the situation. Fiedler began by distinguishing between two types of leaders on the basis of a personality test in which the key element was the person's feelings about the other group members. According to this test, the most important factor was how much esteem the leader felt for the group member he liked least. Stated somewhat differently, the test measured the minimum amount of esteem he felt for anyone in the group. Thus, the test was called the least preferred co-worker, or LPC, scale.

Someone high on this scale tends, in Fiedler's words, "to see even a poorer co-worker in a relatively favorable manner." A low LPC leader, on the other hand, perceives "his least preferred co-worker in a highly unfavorable, rejecting manner." More generally, high LPC leaders are permissive, passive, and considerate; they are more relaxed, friendlier, more compliant, less directive, and tend to reduce the group members' anxiety. Low LPC leaders are controlling, active, and structuring; they are less tolerant of irrelevant comments, produce less pleasant relationships within the group, are highly directive, and tend to induce anxiety. It can be seen that high and LPC leaders tend to correspond to certain aspects of democratic and authoritarian leadership, respectively.

A concerted attempt has been made to specify in detail the kinds of situations in which each type of leader is most effective. Although the research has not yet produced definitive answers, there are some findings in which we can have considerable confidence. Under most circumstances, a low LPC leader is more effective when the task is highly structured. With such a task, it is important to assign roles to individual members, to divide the work, and, in general, to organize efficiently. Interactions among the members, discussions, and interchange of ideas are relatively unimportant because the problem is straightforward. The low LPC leader is successful because he knows what has to be done, and the main problem is getting it done. Moreover, the rest of the group tends not to resent this kind of leader in this case, because his instructions increase efficiency and make the task easier for everyone. The one instance in which the situation does not hold is when the prior relationship between the leader and the group members is poor. Then, the group seems to react negatively to being ordered around and tends to be less efficient than it would be with the relatively warm, high LPC leader.

With unstructured tasks, the relationship is less clear. The strong, assertive, low LPC leaders also seem to do well in many unstructured situations. The exception is when the initial relations between the group and the leader are good but the leader's position is weak. This could be caused by a variety of factors, such as rotating leadership or the fact that the appointed leader was of lower status than the rest of the members. Under these conditions, a low LPC leader does quite poorly, for although the group likes him, they are unwilling to accept strong leadership from someone in a weak position.

Although Fiedler has presented a considerable amount of research supporting his theory, it has not fared too well in studies by other psychologists. For example, Schneier (1978) investigated the characteristics of people who emerged as leaders in groups and found little support for Fiedler's predictions. And Johnson and Ryan (1976) used structured and unstructured tasks, different styles of leadership, and varying degrees of power of the leader just as indicated in Fiedler's model. However, the interaction of the various factors provided no support at all for Fiedler's predictions. At the moment it seems that we can make two statements about Fiedler's general model: first, the specific details of the model are not precisely accurate; but, second, the general idea that the effect of leadership depends on the interaction of many factors involving characteristics of the leader and of the situation is almost certainly correct.

A study by Wilson, Aronoff, and Messe (1975) suggests that the critical factor is whether a particular kind of leadership and group structure is compatible with the goals of the group. They compared groups with hierarchical structures (a leader with power over the lower-ranked members) to egalitarian groups in which everyone was equal. When the goal of the group was to increase safety—a clear goal that required organization and cooperation—the hierarchical group was more successful. When the goal was to increase the members' self-esteem and their esteem for the group—a social goal that depends primarily on interpersonal factors—the egalitarian groups were better. Similarly, Shaw and Harkey (1976) found that the group is more effective when the leader acts in the way that group members expect. In other words, it is not so much what leadership style the leader adopts, but whether it fits in with the expectations of the members. And Downs and Pickett (1977) showed that group productivity and satisfaction depend on an interaction of leadership style and compatibility between the group members and the leader. All of this recent research supports Fiedler's basic idea that no one leader is best for all situations and the effectiveness of any leadership style depends on many factors. Recent work has stressed characteristics of members as much as those of leaders.

SUMMARY

1. The typical pattern of communication in a small group consists of one or two people doing most of the talking, regardless of the size of the group.

2. Almost all groups have leaders, people who are thought by the other members and by outside observers to have the most influence on the group.

3. A problem with leadership is legitimacy. Does the leader deserve his or her position? If the leader is appointed, he will often be seen as not legitimate and will have less influence and power.

4. Communication plays an important role in determining leadership. Someone who talks a lot is more likely to be the leader, regardless of the content of what he says. However, often two kinds of leaders emerge from within a group: a socioemotional leader who handles social aspects of the group, and a task leader who focuses on the job.

5. If communication is restricted, the person with the least restricted communication tends to be the leader and is also more satisfied.

6. Personal characteristics that produce leadership include verbal activity level, status, and lack of deviance from the group.

7. When communication is restricted, centralized structures (one person is allowed to talk to everyone, but the other people can talk only to the central person) are efficient for simple problem solving, but decentralized structures produce higher motivation and are probably superior for solving complex problems.

8. Authoritarian leaders seem to produce good performance, but lower member satisfaction when compared with democratic leaders. The effects of leadership style are complex, depending on the type of task and the strength of the leader's position.

SUGGESTIONS FOR ADDITIONAL READING

FIEDLER, F. E. *A theory of leadership effectiveness.* New York: McGraw-Hill, 1967. The clearest, most complete presentation of Fiedler's work. Difficult going nevertheless, but useful for those who are especially interested in leadership.

MACCOBY, M. *The gamesman.* New York: Simon & Schuster, 1977. One view by a psychoanalytically oriented researcher of who is successful in the business world.

WHYTE, W. H., JR. *The organization man.* New York: Simon and Schuster, 1956. A sociological discussion of how people operate in large organizations.

15

Group Dynamics

Someone is sitting alone in a room working on simple mathematical problems. He works steadily and makes a reasonable amount of progress. Then someone else comes into the room and begins to work on similar problems. The two people do not know each other; they do not talk to each other; they have little or nothing in common. Yet the presence of the second person has a profound effect on the first one. He begins to work harder, to solve the problems more quickly, and, in general, to be more productive. Merely having someone else in the room has increased the effectiveness of his work.

Three hundred people are having dinner in a restaurant. Suddenly there are cries of fire, and smoke begins pouring out of the kitchen. The crowd rushes for the exits and the first lucky few escape. But there are too many people trying to get through the narrow doorways. They block one another's progress so that no one can get through. The bodies pile up at the doorways within easy reach of safety.

In 1931, a young black man, accused of raping a white girl, is in a Southern jail. There is no evidence against him except that he was in the general vicinity of the crime. A crowd gathers outside the jail, builds up, and gets more and more excited and enraged. Members of the crowd talk of lynching, and before long the crowd has turned into an angry mob. It rushes the jail, breaks down the doors, and drags the prisoner from his cell. He is tortured and killed in a sadistic orgy of violence.

A large advertising company is trying to devise a new campaign for selling soap. The eight executives working on the account have been thinking about the problem separately for several weeks. They decide to have a **brainstorming** session. They all get together in a big, comfortable office to discuss their ideas. No one criticizes anyone, everyone is urged to say anything that could be helpful. They all talk freely and accumulate a large number of ideas. Afterward they feel they have accomplished a great deal they could not have done alone.

These examples illustrate the effects some groups have on their members. People are stimulated and distracted by being in a group. They respond to a wide variety of group norms and pressures. Being in a group or just in the presence of other people causes an individual to behave and think differently from when he is alone. This chapter concerns the effects of groups and the processes by which they are produced.

SOCIAL FACILITATION

For some time it was reported that people perform tasks better when they are in the presence of others than when they are alone. Although, as we shall see, not every kind of performance is improved, this effect—called **social facilitation**—occurs on many tasks. A number of studies conducted at Harvard by Allport (1920, 1924) used five tasks ranging from simple and trivial (crossing out all the vowels in a newspaper column) to somewhat more difficult (performing easy multiplications) and finally to fairly complex (writing refutations of a logical argument). On all of these, performance was better when there were five people in the room than when there was only one, even though in all cases the participants worked individually. Dashiell (1930) replicated these results; Travis (1925) found facilitation on a pursuit-rotor task; and many recent experiments (e.g., Zajonc & Sales, 1966; Martens, 1969) have demonstrated the social facilitation effect.

The phenomenon is not limited to humans. Chen (1937) compared the amount of sand dug by ants when they were alone or in pairs or in groups of three. He found that groups of two and three did not differ appreciably, but in both conditions the ants dug more than three times as much sand per ant as they did when the insects were alone. It is also worth noting that pairs of rats copulated less when there was a single pair in the cage than when there were three pairs (Larsson, 1956). Thus, for many different species and a number of different behaviors, the presence of another member of the same species has been shown to improve performance over that which occurs when an individual is alone.

Despite these impressive findings, it has become clear that under some circumstances the social facilitation effect does not occur. In fact, the presence of others can interfere with performance. In Allport's study (1924), subjects in the group condition wrote more refutations of the logical argument, but the quality of these refutations was lower than when the individuals were alone. Pessin (1933) found that the presence of a spectator reduced performance on a memory task, and Dashiell (1930) showed that more errors were made in simple multiplications when an audience was present. Recent research has also found that subjects in groups perform less well on certain kinds of tasks (which we will discuss in a moment) than they do when they are alone (e.g., Cottrell, Rittle, & Wack, 1967). This same inconsistent pattern holds for other animals. Cockroaches (Gates & Allee, 1933), parakeets (Allee & Masure, 1936), and green finches (Klopfer, 1958) all performed less well in groups than when alone. Thus, although most findings do demonstrate a social facilitation effect, a substantial body of evidence indicates that under some circumstances the presence of others can actually interfere with performance. How can these diverse results be explained?

Drive Arousal

Zajonc (1965) made a very interesting proposal that accounted for these diverse results. He suggested that being in the presence of another individual increases a person's drive or motivation, and this increased drive sometimes facilitates performance and sometimes interferes with it. It is well established that high drive improves performance on simple tasks in which the correct response is well known and dominant (i.e. the most common response); but hurts performance on more complex tasks for which the correct response is not dominant, or on learning tasks. Canceling the vowels in a newspaper, doing simple arithmetic, learning a simple list of words, or performing any other easy, repetitive tasks should be facilitated by an increase in drive level. In contrast, difficult arithmetic problems, complex logical deductions, memorizing a difficult list of words, or performing any other complicated tasks should be inhibited by increased drive. Although it is sometimes difficult to classify a particular task, most findings confirm this formulation. Allport's tasks were relatively simple, and he found a social facilitation effect. The one exception was the quality of the logical refutations, which is presumably a very complex task and should be performed less well with an audience. Digging sand and copulating are both fairly simple tasks for ants and rats, respectively, and are also highly dominant behaviors. Both were facilitated by the presence of other members of the species. Learning a maze is a difficult task for cockroaches and parakeets, and they did less well in the presence of others.

This explanation has been tested by more recent research. In an experiment by Cottrell, Rittle, and Wack (1967), subjects learned a list of word pairs either alone or in the presence of two other students. Some of the lists were designed to be easy and others to be quite difficult. The easy lists were composed of words that have the same meaning or are associated with each other—for example, adept-skillful and barren-fruitless. The other list contained items that had no meaning in common and accordingly had weak associations—for example, arid-grouchy and dessert-leading.

Of course, the difficult list would be harder to learn under any circumstances, but we are primarily interested in the effect of the social situation on learning. The results show that the easy list was learned somewhat better when there was an audience than when the subject worked alone, whereas the difficult list was learned much more slowly when an audience was present. The presence of other people improved performance on the simple task where the correct responses were dominant, and inhibited performance on the difficult task where the correct responses were not strong to begin with. See Figure 15–2.

Another study (Zajonc et al., 1969) tested this interpretation using cockroaches as subjects. High drive is expected to improve performance when the correct behavior is the dominant response, but interfere with performance when correct behavior is not dominant. In this study, cockroaches either alone or in pairs had to escape from a light by running down a straight alley or by learning a simple maze. In the alley, the dominant response would help the animals escape, but in the maze it would interfere. As shown in Table 15–1, pairs of roaches did worse in the maze but better in the runway. Apparently being with another animal increases drive and therefore strengthens the dominant response. A second study by the same authors demonstrated this effect even when roaches were alone in the runway or maze but were being observed by other roaches nearby.

Hunt and Hillery conducted a study similar to Zajonc's but used humans as subjects. Once again the task was to learn a maze that was easy or difficult either alone or in company. The results of the experiment

FIGURE 15–2 The effect of an audience on Learning. More errors occur on the hard list with an audience present than with no audience. The reverse tends to occur with an easy list.

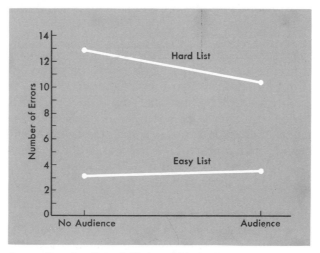

Source: Based on Cottrell, Rittle and Wack (1967).

TABLE 15-1

**Effect of an Audience and Task Difficulty
on Performance of Cockroaches and Humans**

	EASY TASK		HARD TASK	
	Alone	Audience	Alone	Audience
Cockroaches[a]	40.48[c]	32.96	110.45	129.46
Humans[b]	44.67	36.19	184.91	220.33

[a] Data on cockroaches adapted from Zajonc et al. (1969).

[b] Data on humans adapted from Hunt and Hillery (1973).

[c] The lower the number, the better the performance.

are also presented in Table 15–1. They are almost identical to previous results obtained from the experiments with roaches. People learn the easy maze faster when other people are present, but learn the difficult maze faster when alone.

Competition and Evaluation

The research thus offers strong support for Zajonc's hypothesis that the presence of others arouses drive. There is some question, however, as to exactly what kind of drive it is and the specific conditions that are necessary to produce the effect. It seems likely that at least for humans the presence of other people tends to arouse feelings of competition and also concerns about being evaluated. People tend to interpret virtually every social situation as competitive. As we shall see below, they compete with each other in a simple game even though they know they would win more by cooperating. Two people in a room may feel competitive with the other even when they have no explicit reason to feel so. They may think that there is an implied competition, that someone is comparing their performances, or that the other person is competing with them. Even ruling out these possibilities, the individual may compare his performance with the other person and want to do better, thus providing some sort of internal competition that does not depend on what the other person does.

Another and perhaps more important motive that is aroused by the presence of others is concern about being evaluated. We have already discussed the fact that in any social situation we tend to be worried about being rejected and want to be liked and accepted. Obviously, these motives are stronger when we are actually with another person. When someone else is in the room, there is always the possibility that he is judging you. He may be looking at your appearance, your behavior, or your performance on a particular task. The other person may actually be totally unconcerned with you, but there is a tendency to assume that he is to some extent evaluating you. This concern about evaluation raises the

Leo de Wys.

FIGURE 15-3 Competition among people seems to be natural. The presence of others often heightens the drive to compete and, in some cases, improves performance. A tug-of-war by yourself or with one other person isn't much fun.

drive level of the individual and produces the kinds of effects we have reported.

Two studies provide direct support for this idea. Henschy and Glass (1968) compared situations in which subjects thought they were being evaluated with others in which nothing was said about evaluation. Whenever subjects expected to be evaluated, the typical facilitation of dominant responses was observed. When no evaluation was expected, there was a much smaller difference between an alone condition and one in which nonevaluating spectators were present. Paulus and Murdoch (1971) conducted a similar study and found the facilitation effect only when evaluation was expected, with no difference between the alone and the spectator conditions.

On the other hand, an experiment by Hazel Marcus (1978) demonstrated that under some circumstances the mere presence of another person can cause the standard social facilitation effects. In this study subjects put on and took off their own shoes and various articles of clothing that either belonged to or did not belong to them. The explanation they were given of why they had to do this made it seem that the particular clothes they were wearing were only incidental to the situation. In other words, as far as the subjects were concerned, no one cared at all about how quickly they changed their clothes, as long as they eventually got into the appropriate clothing. This change of clothing took place under three conditions: with someone watching them, with someone in the room but not watching them, or alone. Note that the clothing was not intimate apparel, and the subjects did not under any circumstances disrobe. Rather they were simply putting on or taking off shoes and outer garments. The speed with which this changing of clothing occurred was timed unobtrusively by an experimenter who was hidden from the subject.

The point of the study was to compare the speed with which subjects performed well-learned tasks (defined as putting on and taking off their own clothing) with the speed with which they performed new tasks (defined as putting on and taking off unfamiliar clothing). The prediction was that the presence of another person would speed up the well-learned tasks and slow down the less-familiar tasks. Sure enough, the standard social facilitation effect occurred, even when the other person was not watching and therefore could not possibly have been evaluating the subject, and when feelings of competition must have been remote. Marcus interpreted this as indicating that the mere presence of another individual can cause social facilitation and that the effect does not depend on either competition or evaluation concerns.

At the moment it seems safe to say that the presence of others under most circumstances increases drive, which produces facilitation on simple tasks and interference on certain complex tasks. Concern about evaluation is usually the dominant drive aroused; but feelings of competition are also aroused under certain conditions, and sometimes other motives are involved.

Distraction

Although the arousal of drive is probably the most important mechanism activated by the presence of other people, another aspect of the minimal situation is that other people are usually somewhat distracting. When an individual works alone in a room, it is quiet (or perhaps some music is playing), and there is little to attend to except the work. Another person working in the same room may shift around in his chair, chew on a pencil, breathe heavily, and so on. Suddenly, there is much more going on in the room and more to attend to; it becomes difficult to devote full attention to the work. A good example of this is a college library. At certain times, it is an almost ideal place to study. There are empty tables to work on and little noise or activity. But just before an exam period, it is very crowded. The other people talk, move around, sit close together, bump against chairs. Under these circumstances, the presence of others is so distracting that performance is less efficient than if one were alone.

FIGURE 15—4 When other people are present, they are usually somewhat distracting. If you look at them, it will interfere with a task that requires concentration.

Evidence indicates that distractions caused by others are most annoying when one is trying to learn something new. Learning new material requires concentration on external stimuli (e.g., the contents of a book), and extraneous external stimuli interfere with that concentration. When taking an exam, external distractions are less bothersome; the material is already known and the ability to recall it is relatively unaffected.

Sanders has argued that, in fact, distraction is the major cause of social facilitation effects. Being distracted not only directly interferes with task performance, but also raises drive. Distraction threatens to interfere with an individual's performance, is therefore frustrating or annoying, and thus increases the individual's drive (Sanders et al., 1978). There is evidence that the presence of others is generally distracting (Baron et al., 1978), and this distraction can certainly interfere with performance. The argument that distraction is a source of drive is less clear, and the evidence for it is for the moment rather weak. The crucial question is whether distraction alone can not only interfere with performance on complex tasks but actually improve performance on simple ones. Sanders and the others who have studied this issue have found evidence that distraction can interfere, but have had difficulty demonstrating that distraction can improve performance. The idea that the presence of others arouses drive because it is distracting is not generally accepted. For now, let us say that the presence of others is distracting, and that this distraction can directly interfere with performance.

Certain behaviors may be increased primarily because they are almost entirely social in nature. These behaviors and responses depend on other people and rarely if ever occur when we are alone. Thus, being with other people will make these responses more likely. One example would be blushing, with the accompanying internal feelings of shame and embarrassment. We are almost never embarrassed when we are totally alone because this particular reaction depends on someone knowing what we have done. It is, of course, possible to blush when you are by yourself, but it is much more likely to happen in the presence of others. Similarly, though perhaps less clearly, we laugh more easily when other people are around. Again, we sometimes laugh by ourselves in response to something funny that we read or see on television, but being in an audience greatly increases laughter. This is true for children as young as seven (Chapman, 1973) and certainly holds for adults. Indeed, television producers know this well and therefore usually have shows performed in front of real audiences even if they are taped and shown later. The laughter of the real audience (or canned laughter if necessary) helps take the place of other people for the TV viewer.

Laughing, blushing, feeling embarrassed, and probably other behaviors occur mainly in social situations. They happen not because of any of the factors discussed in connection with social facilitation—dominant responses being strengthened, distraction, the arousal of competition or evaluation fears. Some actions are direct consequences of being with other people. When we are alone, the action does not occur (or is less likely to) because it is inherently connected to other people and needs their presence to be elicited.

COMPETITION VERSUS COOPERATION

In our discussion of social facilitation in a minimal social situation, we have been assuming that the people involved are not interacting directly but are merely in the same place at the same time. When they are not members of the same group but do interact, people often have the choice of cooperating or competing. In most games, one person's gain is another's loss. If you win a pot in poker, the other players lose. In Monopoly, if you land on Boardwalk with a hotel, you lose $2000 and someone else is that much richer. These are called **zero-sum games** because all the wins and losses add to zero. But in many real life situations, one side's gains need not be offset by the other's losses. They can both win or both lose. This is referred to as a **non-zero-sum game** (the total of gains and losses does not equal zero). In such a game, whether it involves interpersonal relationships, a business deal, or conflicts between nations, the players cooperate to maximize their total gains or they compete. What determines their actions?

It might be thought that people would in all cases try to maximize their rewards. If getting the most out of a situation requires cooperating, they would cooperate; if it requires competing, they would compete. As we shall see, this is not the case. Regardless of the complications in any situation, deal, or game, it is generally possible to specify the strategy that will produce the most profit. Mathematicians have developed what is called **game theory**—a mathematical analysis of games—which can be applied to complicated as well as simple games and which, in many cases, can tell individuals what to do at each step in order to maximize winnings. Game theory is an interesting and, in some contexts, useful exercise, but it is not applicable to our problem because people do not always follow ideal strategies. Even when it is obvious that cooperation is the best strategy, many—if not most—people compete rather than cooperate. The question, then, is not what is the best strategy, but what factors increase or decrease the tendency to compete.

The Trucking Game

Deutsch and Krauss (1960) conducted a classic experiment on this problem called the **trucking game.** Pairs of subjects engaged in a simple game. Each subject was asked to imagine that she was running a trucking company (either the Acme or the Bolt Company) and had to get a truck from one point to another as quickly as possible. The two trucks were not in competition; they had different starting points and different destinations. There was, however, one hitch—the fastest route for both converged at one point to a one-lane road, and they had to go in opposite directions. This is shown in Figure 15–5. The only way both could use the road would be for one of them to wait until the other had passed through. If either truck entered the road, the other could not use it; and if they both entered the road, neither of them could move at all until one had backed up. In addition, each player had a gate across the direct route that he could raise by pressing a button. The gate prevented the road from being used. Each truck was provided with an alternative route that did not conflict with the other's, but was much longer. In fact, the game was set up so that taking the alternate route was guaranteed to lose points, whereas taking the direct route would gain points for both sides, even if they alternated at the one-lane section of the road. The players were told that their goal was to earn as many points as possible for themselves. Nothing was said about earning more points than the other player.

The results of this experiment are quite striking. It was clear to the participants that the optimal strategy was to cooperate by alternating in using the one-lane road. In this way, they could both use the direct route and one would be delayed only a few seconds while the other was getting through. Despite this, there was little cooperation between the players. Instead of allowing each other to use the one-lane road, they fought for its use, raised their gates, and both of them ended up losing points. In a typical trial, both sides would try to use the road and would meet in the

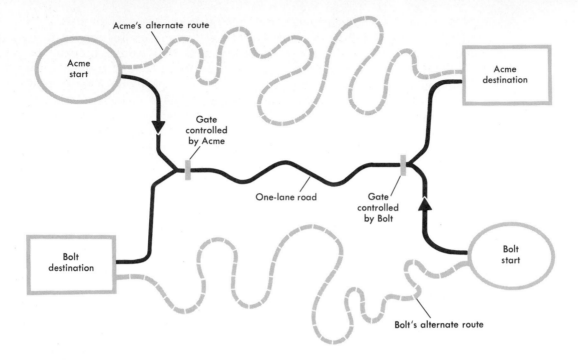

FIGURE 15–5 Road map of the trucking game. The players must get their truck to its destination as quickly as possible. Although they can do this efficiently only by cooperating and sharing the one-lane road, they often compete, particularly when gates are provided.

Source: Deutsch, M., and Krauss, R. M., "The effect of threat on interpersonal bargaining." *Journal of Abnormal and Social Psychology,* 1960, *61,* p. 183. Copyright 1960 by the American Psychological Association; reproduced by permission.

middle head on. They would stubbornly stay there for a while, each refusing to retreat. The players might laugh nervously or make nasty comments. Finally, one of them would back up, erect the barrier, and use the alternate route. On the next trial, they would do the same thing, and so it went. An occasional cooperative trial might be interspersed, but most of them were competitive.

Prisoner's Dilemma

The tendency to compete is not due to the particular characteristics of the trucking game. It also occurs in other non-zero-sum games, such as the **prisoner's dilemma,** so-called because it is based on a problem faced by two suspects at a police station. The district attorney thinks they have both committed a crime but has no proof against either one. The prisoners are put into separate rooms and told that they have two alternatives—to confess or not to confess. If neither of them confesses, they cannot be convicted of the major crime, but the district attorney tells them he can get them convicted of minor crimes and that they will both receive minor

DECISION MAKING IN JURIES

Research on group dynamics has been applied to jury deliberations. There has been considerable discussion in the legal system as to whether twelve-person juries are the ideal size, and whether it is essential that juries reach unanimous verdicts. Some courts have actually experimented with six-person juries for certain kinds of trials, and some civil cases (as opposed to criminal cases) do not require the jury to reach a unanimous decision. Most of the research on these issues has involved mock juries—that is, a group of people who do not actually attend the trial but listen to or read the material from a trial and pretend to be acting as a jury.

The research shows that the size of the jury has very little effect on the decisions that are reached. In one study (Davis et al., 1975) six-person and twelve-person mock juries did not differ at all in the number of guilty and not-guilty verdicts they reached. Other studies have found the same result. Apparently, simply having more people present does not change the final vote. Similarly, requiring unanimity did not change the verdicts. However, as might be expected, under unanimous rules the juries took much longer to decide and had much more conflict (Davis et al., 1976; Nemeth, 1977). And it should hardly be surprising to learn that when the juries have to be unanimous they are far less likely to reach a final decision. A final verdict is much more easily reached if it can be decided by a simple majority. Regardless of the size of the jury or the voting rule, however, the actual decisions did not change. This may not really tell us much about the operation of actual juries. It would be a mistake to conclude that the results of these mock juries, when no one's life or future is on the line, apply directly to real juries, in real cases. But for our purposes it does indicate that at least under some circumstances, neither the size of a group nor the voting rules affect group decisions.

punishments. If they both confess, they will be convicted of the major crime, but the district attorney says he will ask for leniency. But if one of them confesses and the other does not, the confessor will be freed for helping the state, whereas the other suspect will get the maximum penalty. The situation is diagramed in Figure 15–6.

Obviously, there is a conflict. If one suspect thinks his partner is going to confess, it is essential for him to confess also; on the other hand, the best joint outcome is for neither to confess and then for both to take the minor sentences. Thus, if the suspects trust each other, they should not confess. However, if one suspect trusts his partner and is convinced he will not confess, the first would do even better to confess and in that way be freed.

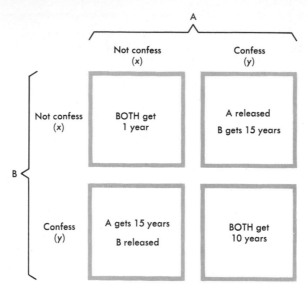

FIGURE 15-6 Prototype of Prisoner's Dilemma game. Two prisoners have the choice of confessing or not confessing. If they trust and support each other by not confessing, each receives a light sentence; if they both confess, they receive relatively heavy sentences; and if one confesses and the other does not, the former is released while the latter gets a very heavy sentence. The dilemma is that if either one has complete trust in the other, he would do best by being untrustworthy himself and confessing.

We do not know what real prisoners would do under these circumstances. In research on the problem, much of the drama is removed but the game is basically similar. Instead of playing for their freedom, subjects play for points or money. They play in pairs but usually are not allowed to talk to each other. Each player has a choice of two strategies, and each player's payoff depends both on what he does and on what his partner does. The exact pattern of payoffs varies; a typical one is shown in Figure 15–7. If both A and B choose X, they each get 10 points; if A chooses X and B chooses Y, the former loses 15 and the latter wins 15; and if both choose Y, they both lose 5. In other words, they can cooperate (choose X) and both win, or they can compete (one or both choosing Y) and try to win a lot but at the risk of losing.

The players are told that they are supposed to score as many points as they can. It is clear to virtually all of them that the way to have the highest score is for both to select X (the cooperative choice) on every trial. But just as with the trucking game, there is a strong tendency for them to compete. In a typical game, only about a third of the choices are cooperative. Moreover, as the game progresses (and the players are win-

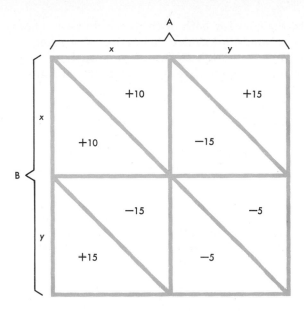

FIGURE 15–7 Typical Prisoner's Dilemma game matrix. The top figure in each square cell indicates A's payoff; the bottom indicates B's payoff. X is a cooperative choice, because it allows both members to win. The choice of Y is competitive, because only the one who chooses it has a chance of winning and both may lose. With this matrix there is a great deal of competition.

ning fairly few points), the number of cooperative choices actually goes down. The players choose the competitive strategy more and more, despite the fact that they know they can win more by cooperating.

It could be argued that in most of the prisoner's dilemma games, Y is the more rational choice, because the best single play is the competitive one. Let us analyze the game shown in Figure 15–5. If subject A selects the cooperative strategy, his payoff depends on what B does. If B chooses the cooperative strategy, A wins 10 points; if B chooses competitively, A loses 15 points. If A chooses the competitive strategy, once again his payoff depends on B. If B chooses the cooperative strategy, A wins 15 points; if B chooses competitively, A loses 5. Thus, in either case, A would do better by choosing the competitive strategy than he would by choosing the cooperative one. If B picks cooperatively, A wins 15 instead of 10; if B chooses competitively, A loses 5 instead of 15.

The dilemma is that over a long series of trials, A would be much better off if both he and B agreed to choose the cooperative strategy. They would both win on all trials rather than winning on some and losing on others. It is true that on any one trial, A would do better to pick the competitive strategy, regardless of what B picks. But over a long series of trials, the goal for both of them should be to choose cooperatively since doing so would maximize their gains. Nevertheless, particularly in a one-trial game, but even in longer games, there is strong pressure toward choosing the competitive strategy because it is the better one on any given trial.

This is not, however, an adequate explanation of why people choose competitively. Most of the players are bright enough to realize they would be better off if they and their partner could agree on picking cooperatively. The fact that they continue to pick competitively seems to indicate that they are, in fact, competing. This was forcefully demonstrated in a study (Minas et al., 1960) involving a game with the matrix shown in Figure 15–8.

This matrix is different from the others we have discussed because there is no rational reason for picking the competitive strategy. It is always better to pick the cooperative strategy, because it always results in a higher score. If player A chooses X, he would score more points than if

FIGURE 15–8 Matrix heavily favoring cooperative choices. Other than a desire to score more than the other person, there is no reason to choose Y. A player who chooses X scores more points than he would if he chose Y, regardless of what the other player selects. Nevertheless, players using this matrix make many competitive choices.

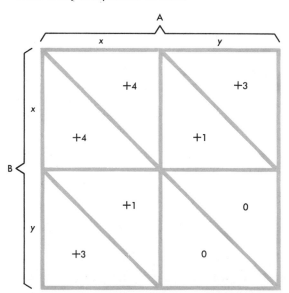

Source: This figure drawn from "Some Descriptive Aspects of Two-Person Non-Zero-Sum Games, II" by J. S. Minas et al. is reprinted from *Journal of Conflict Resolution* Vol. 4, No. 2 (June 1960), pp. 193–197 by permission of the Publisher, Sage Publications, Inc.

he had chosen Y, regardless of what player B does. If B chooses X also, player A wins 4; if B chooses Y, player A wins 1. Thus, depending on B's choice, player A wins either 4 or 1. In contrast, if A chooses Y, he would win either 3 or 0. From any point of view, both players should choose the cooperative strategy, because they would score more points that way.

The striking finding is that even with this kind of setup, subjects tend to compete a great deal, rather than pick the cooperative strategy and quietly gain 4 points on each trial. The only advantage of the competitive choice is that one player can score more than the other, even though he always scores less than he would have if both had picked the cooperative choice. When subjects in these studies were questioned about their reasons for behaving as they did, many of them reported that they wanted to "beat" the other player. This occurred despite the fact that the experimenter had told them that the aim of the game was to score as high as possible. Apparently, subjects are relatively unimpressed by a game in which the only incentive is to score points; they prefer to compete even if it means they do less well from the experimenter's point of view.

FACTORS AFFECTING COMPETITION

Incentive

The competitive tendency changes somewhat when the incentive for doing well is increased. In most of the studies, subjects were playing simply for points, for imaginary money, or perhaps for small stakes. They earned no more by doing well than by doing poorly. In an occasional study, they could earn a few extra cents by scoring a lot of points, but the subjects—not only those who were fairly affluent college students but even the not so affluent high school students and working women—were not impressed by the chance to earn an extra 15 or 20 cents. Therefore, their natural tendency to compete dominated their desire to earn the money. When the stakes were raised, however, and the subjects could earn as much as a few dollars, the desire to earn the money was relatively more important. Under these circumstances, there was a conflict between the competitive urge and the desire to maximize winnings. Yet the effect of incentive on competition is far from clear.

An experiment by Gallo (1966) demonstrated one effect of the size of rewards. Pairs of subjects played the trucking game, but half the pairs were paid off in real money, and the other half in points. With real money there was considerably more cooperation. Gallo and Sheposh (1971) obtained similar results when subjects who were given $10 to play with were compared to others who had only points. Once again, those with real money earned more. And a study involving negotiation (Kelly et al., 1970) compared money with points in several different countries. More agreements were reached and they were reached more quickly when money was involved.

FIGURE 15—9 The competitive urge. How do the stakes affect your reaction to games of this kind?

Other studies, however, have produced conflicting evidence on the role of monetary incentive. Gumpert, Deutsch, and Epstein (1969) found even more competition with real than with imaginary money in a prisoner's dilemma game. Oskamp and Kleinke (1970) conducted two experiments on this problem. In the first, each trial involved a range of payoffs from $.30 to $3, but the total earnings were based on a selection of trials and ranged only from $1.50 to $3. The second study had trials that were either no money (just points), pennies, or dimes with maximum earnings ranging from zero to $9. Although the effects of incentive were not strong, there was a consistent tendency for cooperation to be *greater* with lower payoff. Increasing the incentive actually decreased the amount of cooperative choices.

Finally, another study suggests that the absolute amount of money is not especially important but that people are sensitive to changes in their rewards (Friedland, Arnold, & Thibaut, 1974). As in the other work on this problem, subjects played a game with varying stakes. The amount of competition was unaffected by the amount of money involved. However, in other conditions the size of the reward changed during the course of the game, getting either larger or smaller. An increase made little difference, but decreasing the stakes reduced cooperation. Presumably, every player had two motives: winning money and beating the other person. When the stakes were suddenly decreased, the money motive became less important and subjects concentrated on seeking victory.

This research indicates that incentive does not have a simple effect on the amount of cooperation in these games. Sometimes it seems to increase cooperation, sometimes it decreases it, and sometimes it has little effect. A possible resolution of this seeming inconsistency is that people care more about winning when the stakes are greater, but greater stakes do not necessarily make them cooperate more. The temptation to make a competitive choice and possibly win a big bonus exists when points or money are involved. Increasing the incentive may cause some subjects to concentrate on winning money, but other subjects to maximize their winnings by competing. Knox and Douglas (1971) produced results that support this explanation. They compared subjects who were playing for pennies to those playing for dollars. The amount of cooperation was virtually identical for the two conditions, but there was three times as much variance when dollars were involved. Some players cooperated a great deal, others hardly at all. This suggests that the higher incentive caused some subjects to play more competitively and others more cooperatively. When you care more about winning, you choose a more consistent and more extreme strategy, but there is no evidence that you are necessarily more cooperative.

Even when the stakes are quite high, subjects make a large number of competitive responses. Apparently, the competitive urges are strong enough to cause people to compete despite the fact that it is to their disadvantage in terms of their total winnings. As we noted in our discussion of social facilitation, the presence of another person seems to arouse competitive feelings even when there is no realistic reason for competition. Our present findings reinforce this. Taken together, they seem to suggest that, at least in our society, one of the powerful, dominating factors in most interpersonal situations is the arousal of competitive feelings. This does not mean that people always compete nor that they feel competitive in all situations. But it does suggest that competition is a strong component in many interpersonal relationships even when the situation is structured to favor cooperation.

On the other hand, caution seems appropriate in interpreting this research. We must remember that the participants knew they were taking part in psychological experiments and were playing games. Moreover, even in games with the highest stakes, the amounts involved were pretty small for college students. Admittedly, it is nice to be able to win $9, but it is still not much money by most people's standards. Therefore, we should be careful about generalizing these results on incentive to situations involving substantial amounts of money or other rewards. We can legitimately question whether people would continue to compete if instead of playing for money they were playing to avoid severe electric shocks. Under these circumstances, would most people continue to concentrate on beating the other player (i.e., getting fewer shocks), or would they do anything possible to get the minimum number of shocks themselves? We do not know. For now, we do know that under the conditions of the studies we have described, many people are more concerned about doing better than the other person than they are about winning as much as possible.

Motivation

The evidence indicates that most people view the prisoner's dilemma game, at least in part, as a competitive situation. However, this competitive feeling can be influenced to some extent by what the subjects are told about the purpose of the game. The particular motive that is aroused helps determine the amount of cooperation. In a study by Deutsch (1960), subjects were given one of three different instructions: Cooperative instructions stressed concern for the other player's welfare; competitive instructions urged each player to win as much money as he could for himself and, in particular, to win more than the other player; and individualistic instructions stated that the only purpose was to win as much as possible and that the other player's outcome should be ignored.

The different instructions had a major impact on the amount of cooperation. The results are shown in the right-hand column of Table 15–2. Those subjects who were told to cooperate did so over 90 percent of their choices. In contrast, the individualistic instructions resulted in about 50 percent cooperation, and the competitive instructions produced only about 20 percent cooperation. Clearly, the tendency to view the game as competitive can be altered to a large extent by appropriate instructions.

The same kind of results are reported by Schulz and Pruitt (1978) in quite a different setting. They had subjects engage in bargaining and gave them instructions emphasizing either group or individual profit. In the former, the orientation focused on cooperation within the group so that the whole team would maximize its profit; in the latter the subjects were told that they should strive for maximum individual profit. As you might expect, regardless of whether communication was free or restricted, there was more cooperation with the team than with the individual orientation, and the total profit was also greater when emphasis was on cooperation. Clearly, once the view of the game has changed, the participants' behavior will change accordingly.

TABLE 15–2

Communication and Effects of Motivation on Cooperation

Motivation Instructions	PERCENTAGE OF COOPERATIVE CHOICES		
	No Communication	Communication	Average
Cooperative	89.1	96.9	93.0
Individualistic	35.0	70.6	52.8
Competitive	12.5	29.2	20.9

Source: Adapted from Deutsch (1960).

It should be noted that instructing subjects to compete or to cooperate affects their behavior in other situations as well. In several studies, groups that were working on problems were told either to maximize their individual efforts or to maximize the performance of the group as a whole. When they were urged to compete, there was less communication among the members, they had less influence on one another and accepted one another less, and there was less division of labor and poorer productivity. When they were supposed to cooperate, there was more mutual trust, and the productivity of the group as a whole went up. Thus, in many, if not all, kinds of social interactions, a cooperative goal produces more cooperation than a competitive one.

Threats

In some social situations, the people involved have no particular power over each other. If they are bargaining or playing some other social game, they compete or cooperate as equals and have no additional weapons at their disposal. In buying a car, you are trying to get it for the lowest possible price; the salesperson is trying to get the highest price. That's the whole story. If you agree on a price, the deal is closed; if you don't agree, the car stays in the showroom. Now imagine that you work for the local newspaper and threaten to write an unfavorable story about the dealer if he does not give you a good price. That threat may give you a big advantage. Or consider international negotiations on the price of oil. The United States and Saudi Arabia are trying to agree on a price. Each has certain bargaining cards, but they are playing the game by the usual rules. Now suppose the Americans say that if the Saudis do not agree on a reasonable price, their country will be invaded. This unilateral (one-sided) threat would obviously play an important role in subsequent bargaining. Knowing this, the Saudis reply that if there is no agreement, the oil fields will be blown up and no one will get any oil. This is hardly farfetched; a situation much like this occurred in the early days of the OPEC oil cartel. What effect do threats have on cooperation?

In variations of the trucking game, one, both, or neither players were provided with threats in the form of barriers that could be placed across the one-lane road. When only one player had a barrier to use, the condition was called **unilateral threat;** when both players had them, the condition was called **bilateral threat.** Note that the barriers in no way prevented cooperation. The players did not have to use them; they could take turns using the road and forget about the barriers.

The existence of the barriers made a sizable difference in the amount of cooperation between the players. The most cooperation occurred when neither one had a barrier to use. When one had a barrier, there was less cooperation and the holder of the threat tended to do better than the other. On a typical trial, the two trucks met in the middle of the road and the question was which would back up first. If the holder of the barrier backed up, she could erect the barrier and prevent the other from benefiting from the direct route. They both lost, but the one without the threat probably lost more. On the other hand, if the other backed up, no barrier had to be erected, and the first truck could roll through and gain a lot of points. Thus, the few cooperative choices tended to favor the one with the threat, and she therefore got a better score. Finally, the least cooperation occurred when both sides had a threat. The typical result was for both sides to erect their barriers and immediately take the long route. This was guaranteed to lose money but avoided the greater loss due to a stalemate at the narrow road.

Although threats sometimes interfere with maximal performance, a person who has a threat does seem to have a distinct advantage over someone who does not. In the trucking game, the possessor of a gate earns more points (or loses fewer) than the one without a gate. In prisoner's dilemma and other bargaining games, a player who has a threat of any kind is in a strong position. This is particularly true if he seems likely to carry out the threat (Guyer & Rapoport, 1970). Under these circumstances, he will usually get the better of the bargaining—win more points or money or whatever is involved. On the other hand, someone who has power and does not use it may be considered weak and will be taken advantage of. Swingle (1970) showed that subjects who have a threat and fail to use it are exploited more than subjects who have no threat in the first place. Apparently power is useful only when the other person is convinced that it may be used. Otherwise it may actually reduce the strength of a person's position by making him seem weak and ineffectual.

Black and Higbee (1973), however, found the situation even more complex, because male and female subjects differed in their response to threats. Females were especially cooperative when their partners had threats and did not use them, whereas males behaved differently depending on whether they perceived the other to be a powerful person. If the other was powerful, cooperative, and had no threats, males exploited him or her more than if the other was seen as weak. But if the other had threats, the males cooperated more with the powerful than with the weak.

Communication

Throughout our discussion of groups we have repeatedly stressed the importance of communication. The ability to talk to one's partner also plays a major role in determining the amount of cooperation between the two. In the study by Deutsch described above, some subjects with each kind of motivation were allowed to communicate with their partner before playing. The effect of this communication increased cooperation markedly, regardless of the kind of motivation that had been aroused (see Table 15–2). However, the effect of communication was most dramatic in the individualistic condition. When subjects were trying to maximize their own winnings and were supposed to ignore those of the other player, being able to communicate increased their percentage of cooperative choices from 35 to over 70.

The Deutsch and Krauss trucking study included three different types of communication conditions. Some subjects were not allowed to communicate; others were given the opportunity to talk if they wanted to; and a third group was required to communicate. The effect was similar to that in the prisoner's dilemma game. There was more cooperation when communication was allowed than when it was not allowed and still more when it was forced. The effect was particularly strong in the unilateral threat condition. When one player was provided with a barrier and not allowed to communicate, there was little cooperation; but when the players were forced to talk, the amount of cooperation increased dramatically.

This effect of communication was demonstrated even more convincingly by Wichman (1970). In a prisoner's dilemma game, some subjects were isolated from their partners; others could see their partners but could not talk to them; others could talk to their partners but could not see them; and still others could both see and hear each other. The amount of cooperation increased in that order. When there was no communication or only nonverbal communication, about 40 percent of the responses were cooperative. When verbal communication or both verbal and visual communication were allowed, cooperation occurred on more than 70 percent of the trials.

In order to have a beneficial effect, the communication must be relevant to the task at hand. Simply talking about irrelevant matters may make the job pleasanter, but there is no evidence that it increases cooperation. For example, in one study (Dawes, McTavish, & Shaklee, 1977) groups of eight subjects engaged in a modified prisoner's dilemma game. Some subjects were not allowed to communicate at all; some were allowed to talk before the game was played but not about the game itself; and others were allowed to talk about the game. Only when subjects could talk about the actual game did cooperation increase. But, talking about the game more than doubled the amount of cooperation.

The study included an additional interesting condition. Some of the subjects not only talked about the game but also announced publicly how they were planning to vote. These public announcements were not binding, but they were supposed to give an indication of the strategy followed by each of the subjects. Somewhat surprisingly, this unbinding vote resulted in no more cooperation than the condition in which the subjects merely discussed the game. Even though virtually all of the subjects said that they would vote in a cooperative manner, many of them lied; they altered their vote and chose a competitive strategy. It is also worth pointing out that even in the most cooperative condition, only 75 percent of the players made a cooperative choice. Looked at another way, in all instances at least 25 percent of the people chose the competitive strategy. Moreover, in the best condition, the voting resulted in no profit. Even though each person could have won as much as $10.50, the best actual result was an average of no gain at all.

Assuming there is any tendency to cooperate, knowledge of the other person and particularly of what he is planning to do should facilitate it. Since the optimal strategy in these games depends almost entirely on the degree of trust in the other person, the ability to communicate is especially helpful. There may, however, be other games in which trust is less important or in which the tendency to cooperate is weaker, in which case being able to communicate might have relatively little effect.

One of the obvious reasons that communication should increase the amount of cooperation is that the players in these games often misperceive the others' intentions. Kelly and Stahelski (1970) showed that it was difficult for individuals in a prisoner's dilemma game to know what the other person was planning to do. More important, someone who was intending to make a cooperative choice was misjudged more often than someone who was planning to be competitive. Apparently there was a general tendency to assume that the other person would make a competitive choice. One of the reasons for this misperception was that the player who was planning to make a cooperative choice was often unable to follow through on this intention. If his opponent consistently made competitive choices, the player who wanted to play cooperatively was eventually forced to protect himself by making the competitive choice also. Thus the misperception of the cooperative player's intentions turned out often to be consistent with what the player actually did. This is another case of the self-fulfilling prophecy, in which one player assumes the other player will be competitive. He accordingly chooses a competitive response, eventually forcing the other person to be competitive also. The net result is that his initial perception that the other person is competitive will turn out to be correct only because he has in fact forced the other person to behave that way. As usual, once you assume the other person is a dangerous character and start treating him as an enemy, he will start acting like one.

The possibility of misjudging the other player is greatly decreased when communication is possible. Accordingly, allowing or forcing players to communicate makes it considerably easier for them to cooperate. They can discuss their plans, urge each other to cooperate, make promises, convince each other they are trustworthy, learn something about each other, and so on. Assuming there is any tendency to cooperate, knowledge of the other should facilitate it.

On the other hand, a study by Smith and Anderson (1975) found that communication can sometimes have negative effects. Playing a game similar to the trucking game, subjects either had free communication or did not, and also either both had threats or neither did. In the nothreat condition, free communication led to more cooperation. In the bilateral threat condition, free communication actually led to somewhat less cooperation than when no communication was allowed. Apparently, these subjects used the opportunity to communicate to make threats and increase confrontation rather than resolve their mutual problem. Taking this finding along with the Deutsch and Krauss results suggests that communication is helpful chiefly when the players are equal, with neither having a threat, or when the communication can make it clear that one has the upper hand (unilateral threat) and allow the weaker player to compromise.

Maximizing Cooperation in Bargaining

We have seen that many factors, including motivation, threats, communication, the stakes, and perhaps also individual characteristics of the players, determine the outcome. Given a particular situation with particular people playing, are there any procedures or strategies that increase cooperativeness consistently?

One strategy that seems to work quite well is reciprocal concessions. The players take turns giving up a little. I'll go to the movie you want if you go to my favorite restaurant; I'll do the dishes if you cook. This is the traditional compromise solution to most conflicts. Each side starts with an extreme position and then retreats gradually until a common meeting ground is found. If one player makes a small concession and then waits for the other to do the same, there is indeed greater eventual cooperation (Esser & Komorita, 1975). However, a crucial element of this strategy is timing. If one person gives in too much, he may appear weak and the other will not reciprocate. The concessions must be gradual and sequential. In fact, according to Wall (1977) the most effective technique is to make reciprocal concessions that are slightly larger than those made by the other person. This reinforces the other's cooperation, and results in large concessions and quick agreement. In addition, obviously this does not work unless both sides are willing to cooperate to some extent. If one of them is totally competitive, the one who tries cooperating will only be taken advantage of and end up with a weaker position than before.

Perhaps a more general instance of this strategy is rewarding someone for cooperating in order to teach him to cooperate more in the future. There is evidence that, as you might expect, this does work (McNeel, 1973). Unfortunately, it works only for subjects who are initially trying to win as much as possible for themselves, not for those who are trying to "beat" the other player. Rewarding the latter for cooperating is ineffective because they are not interested in getting more points when the other person also gets the same number of points. Since in most games cooperating guarantees that both players earn the same amount, rewarding cooperativeness does not help. On the other hand, it would be possible to design a game so that cooperation of a certain kind helped one player even more than it helped the other, and then perhaps even the competitive player could be taught to cooperate.

Applicability of the Research Findings

Many psychologists have attempted to relate the findings of studies on non-zero-sum games to the world situation and relationships between countries. Countries, too, cooperate or compete. In many cases, they could maximize their gains if they would cooperate, and yet there seems to be a tendency for them to compete. It was hoped that the research on games would reveal some of the basic factors determining relationships between countries. However, the findings are more readily generalized to dealings between individuals. Friends, lovers, marriage partners, teachers and students, salespersons and buyers all engage in dealings that often involve the possibility of either competition or cooperation. Unlike some games, these interpersonal relationships typically do not require that one person's gain be at the expense of another's loss. On the contrary, as in the games we have discussed in this chapter, it is possible for people to cooperate to maximize gains for both parties.

In this context, the most significant research finding is that people are motivated to maximize their profits from several points of view. As we

BOX 15-3
ARE THE GAMES REALISTIC?

Most of the games described here have an unrealistic quality about them. Especially in the prisoner's dilemma game, the subjects are making simultaneous decisions with no feedback about what the other person is doing. There may be some occasions in the real world when this occurs, but usually we interact with other people over a period of time, each making decisions that affect the other. People gradually learn a considerable amount about each other and also come to realize that their actions affect the way the other person treats them. Thus, laboratory games in which people choose simultaneously and only once might seem to have little applicability to other situations.

However, some evidence suggests that the particular form of the game, the order in which decisions are made, and whether or not they are made at the same time have relatively little effect on the choices people make. Brickman, Becker, and Castle (1979) compared three kinds of situations that varied the time at which players made their decisions. In one case, two players made their decisions simultaneously. This is equivalent to the typical prisoner's dilemma situation. In a second case, the players alternated; first one would make a decision and then the other, and on the next choice they would reverse the order of decisions. But in both cases, the decision of one person was announced before the other had to decide. This might seem to give

undue power to the second person, but keep in mind that this is a continuous game involving a long series of decisions. In the third condition, the players again alternated, but the second choice became the first choice of the next decision. In other words, person A would choose, then person B, and the result of that particular game would be decided. Then, a second game would start and person B's previous choice would count as his or her choice for the second game. This continued for a series of interactions. The authors argued that this continuing condition was more like real life because interactions are typically not discrete. Rather, each response elicits a response in return. An interaction consists of a series of decisions, each of which carries over to the next interaction.

The important result for our purposes is that the particular structure of the game had relatively little effect on the amount of cooperation. The one effect that did appear was that alternating conditions resulted in more cooperation between males than any of the others. The structure of the game made no difference at all for female subjects. Thus, with the one small exception for the males, it appears that subjects play these games very much the same way, regardless of how the decisions are made. This implies that the games may have more generality than might appear, since small changes in the structure have little effect on the results.

would expect, in any bargaining or game situation, one of the strong considerations, and perhaps the dominant one, is to get as much as we can for as little as we can. But participants also want to maximize their gains in relation to other people. They want to "win" the exchange. Thus they might be willing to accept a slightly less advantageous deal if they felt it meant they were surpassing the other person. Some people refuse to accept a profitable arrangement merely because it means they would not win the exchange. Although they would be getting good value for their payment, the other person would receive equal value. Both accumulation of goods and competition motives are probably present in almost all bargaining situations.

One implication of this is well known to salespeople. Customers want to feel that they are getting a good deal, that they are somehow winning the exchange. Someone selling a used car tries to make us feel he has been talked into a deal he never wanted to agree to, that we are very good bargainers. In that way, we feel we have won the exchange, he feels (probably rightly) that he has won, and everyone is happy. In countries such as Mexico, where bargaining is a common mode of selling, this can be seen more clearly. If a vendor offers a rug for 200 pesos, the customer is not supposed to accept that price. It is deliberately high and the salesperson would be surprised if it were accepted. Part of the selling is the bargaining itself, and both parties enter into it determined to win the deal. Most of the time they settle on roughly the price the vendor had in mind to begin with, but by this bargaining process, both people enjoy the sale more. They feel they have not only gotten good value, but have also managed to beat the other person.

The same is true in relationships between friends and lovers. People do not always agree perfectly. Often they have different values and goals, and these differences give rise to conflicts. To the extent that each person is merely trying to get what he or she wants, the resolution of these conflicts simply requires compromise. As we mentioned earlier, each gives in on some points as long as the other gives in on others. And if the people care for each other, they will both want to find a resolution that gives both of them as much as possible.

Unfortunately, as we all know, the situation is not quite that simple. Many times people are not only trying to get something for themselves, they are also trying to "win" a dispute or "beat" the other person. Sadly, this occurs even between people who have warm and friendly feelings for each other. As the research has shown, competition is an important element in many conflicts. Thus, one reason why personal conflicts are not easily resolved is that each person wants to come out ahead of the other rather than settle for a solution that maximizes both their gains. If both want to win, obviously the resolution is difficult and will usually involve some hard feelings. One possible lesson from the research is that communication can often help. Talking about the conflict may make it easier to find a reasonable resolution and may even lead to cooperation rather than competition. Thus, the current popular emphasis on openness, honesty, and communication in relationships may lead to a more favorable resolution of the conflicts that inevitably arise.

Extending the work to relationships between countries seems to be even more speculative and should be done with great caution. Perhaps the surest conclusion is that in any conflict both sides want to look good and even like to think that they have won the exchange. Accordingly, the ideal treaty between countries is one that leaves each side thinking it has won the conference. Perhaps the hope that countries will cooperate is unrealistic; it seems more likely that they will always compete, as people do. The hope, then, should be for them to compete in selling cars, playing ping-pong, or in building more impressive dams rather than in armaments.

PROBLEM SOLVING BY GROUPS

How do groups compare with individuals in solving problems? We have seen that having another person present stimulates performance under some conditions but interferes with it under others. Stimulation and distraction also occur when a group is working on a problem together; and in this more complex situation, additional factors operate. We described above a common practice in business and government—the so-called brainstorming session. This is an unstructured, free type of group problem solving in which people get together and say anything that they think might be helpful. The idea is that they will stimulate one another into producing better ideas than each would produce alone. People also work together in more restricted types of groups. They can build a spaceship, design an experiment, solve a math problem, even write a novel in groups. In contrast, Thomas Edison invented the phonograph in virtual isolation; Albert Einstein devised the theory of relativity without discussing it with anyone; most novelists and artists work alone. Perhaps Edison would have been more effective in a work group at General Electric. Perhaps an advertising executive would think of a better slogan working alone than in a brainstorming group.

Although the question may seem to be straightforward and one that can be easily investigated, there is some difficulty in knowing just what to compare groups to. In some early studies, the same problem was given to groups of two, three, four, and five people and also to a number of individuals. The experimenters then compared the performance of the groups with the performance of each of the individuals. Examined in this way, the results are very clear: there is strength in numbers. By whatever criteria we choose, a group does better than a person working alone.

It quickly becomes apparent, however, that this is not the basic question. We really want to know whether four people working in a group would do better than four people working separately. To use the people we have most effectively, should we have them work in groups or alone?

In a classic study on brainstorming (Taylor, Berry, & Block, 1958), subjects were assigned at random to either five-person groups or the individual condition. (Those in the groups had met together several times before.) The people in both conditions were then given five problems and twelve minutes to work on each one. One problem, for example, was stated as follows: "Each year a great many American tourists visit Europe, but now suppose that our country wished to get many more European tourists to visit America during their vacations. What steps can you suggest that would get more European tourists to come to this country?" The subjects were told that their task was to consider the problems and to offer as many and as creative solutions as they could. There were obviously no "correct" solutions. The following rules, taken from Osborne (1957, p. 84), were outlined to the groups:

1. Criticism is ruled out. Adverse judgment of ideas must be withheld until later.
2. Freewheeling is welcomed. The wilder an idea, the better. It is easier to tame down than to perk up.
3. Quantity is wanted. The greater the number of ideas, the more likelihood of winners.
4. Combination and improvement are sought. In addition to contributing ideas of your own, you should suggest how ideas of others can be turned into better ideas or how two or more ideas can be joined into still another one.

Subjects in the alone condition were divided at random into five-person nominal groups. That is, although each of these subjects worked alone, for purposes of the analysis they were considered a group and their total production was compared to the production of the actual groups. In this way, Taylor compared five hours of work done by a five-person group with five hours done by five individuals working alone. This is the only meaningful way to compare the efficiency of the two procedures.

The results (presented in Table 15–3) can be considered in terms of the quantity of ideas produced and also in terms of their originality. Quantity consisted of the number of *different* ideas produced by the real and the nominal groups. If two members of a nominal group produced the same idea, it was counted as only one idea. As can be seen from the table, the nominal groups (individuals working alone) scored higher than the actual groups. The individuals produced an average of 68.1 ideas, whereas the groups produced only 37.5. Similarly, the nominal groups produced more unique, creative ideas (19.8 versus 10.8). In other words, five individuals working alone produced almost twice as many solutions and unique ideas as five comparable people did working together. Someone working alone can concentrate better than he can in a group and also

TABLE 15–3

Performance by Real and Nominal Groups

CONDITION	DIFFERENT IDEAS	UNIQUE IDEAS
Real groups	37.5	10.8
Nominal groups (five individuals working alone)	68.1	19.8

Note: Figures are number of ideas.
Source: Taylor et al. (1958).

does not have to worry about competing with other people in order to express his ideas. If the group did provide any mutual stimulation, it was apparently more than offset by the interfering and distracting effects of other people.

A study by Bray, Kerr, and Atkin (1978) found that groups solve more problems than individuals and that the larger the group the greater the advantage over one person working alone. However, as usual, the groups were less efficient than individuals because they solved fewer problems than the same number of separate individuals working by themselves. The important point that this study adds to the earlier ones is that the effects depended in part on the difficulty of the problems. As the problems got harder, the groups did less and less well compared to the individuals; in particular, the larger groups became less efficient. The authors argue that this is due to the fact that not everyone in a group actually participates in the problem solving. As we have mentioned before, in any group a few members do most of the talking. Even in larger groups, two or three people dominate the discussion. Thus, as a group increases in size, the percentage of the group that participates decreases. In a three-member group, everyone may take part; in a five-member group perhaps only three people; and in a ten-member group maybe four or five. Clearly, larger groups become less and less efficient and waste the time and talent of many of the members.

Limitations of the Research

Although the results of these studies showed that groups are inferior to individuals working alone, they have several limitations. For example, the most serious limitation of the Taylor study is that the groups had worked together for a relatively short time. It may be that people have to get to know each other and learn to work together before a group can become an effective unit. At least one study (Cohen et al., 1960) suggested that brainstorming in groups is quite productive when the individuals involved were specially selected to be compatible and were trained to work together.

Another question concerns the effect of dissimilarity of the group members on the quality of the solutions they produce. It appears that relatively heterogeneous groups, in which the personalities of the various members differ considerably, produce better solutions to most problems than do homogeneous groups. In a study by Hoffman and Maier (1961), the two kinds of groups were given problems that varied considerably in terms of whether or not there was an objective solution, the kinds of issues involved, and so on. For example, one problem required the group to think of a way for people to cross a heavily mined road, whereas another involved settling a simulated argument between two of the group's members. The results showed a large difference in the quality of the solutions offered to several problems. With other problems, the difference was considerably smaller. Overall, the results indicated that heterogeneous groups are superior to homogeneous groups on a wide variety of problems.

Another variable in this study was sex. Some groups were composed only of men, others of men and women. There was some indication that the groups containing both sexes produced higher-quality solutions than did the all-male groups. Thus, heterogeneity, in terms of both personality and sex, seems to improve the performance of groups.

A further limitation concerns the type of problem tackled. How to use foreign aid or what slogan to adopt for a new polka-dot toothpaste, questions that were discussed in the brainstorming research, cannot be resolved by a logical process. These questions have no "correct" or unique solution. It would seem that any stimulating effect a group might have on its members would be most beneficial and any distracting effect would be least harmful when such problems are considered. On the other hand, with problems that can be solved logically and that have unique, correct solutions (solving a math problem, building a spaceship, inventing the electric light, or solving a brainteaser), the stimulating effect of the group might be less important and the distraction more harmful. Groups do provide two important advantages: members can check one another's work, and they provide a variety of abilities that one individual would be unlikely to possess. However, because these characteristics are helpful only with certain types of problems, the relative effectiveness of groups and individuals depends on the kind of problem.

Groups are quite effective in working on problems that involve a large number of separate operations, such as complex arithmetic problems. In such cases, the ability of members to catch one another's mistakes is particularly important. A group provides a system of checks that is lacking when an individual works alone. On the other hand, with these problems, the group is not really working together; the individual members are working separately and then checking one another's work. This is quite different from brainstorming, but it does indicate that under some circumstances, groups perform better than individuals working alone.

It is obvious that problems requiring a number of separate skills tend to favor groups. If, in order to solve a problem, it is essential to know calculus, cellular biology, and organic chemistry, only an individual possessing all this knowledge would be able to find the solution. Even among individuals on a college faculty, it is unlikely that any one person would have all these skills. If, however, we form such a faculty into five-person groups, it is considerably more likely that a group of five professors would have, among them, the three necessary abilities. Thus in this admittedly specialized situation, groups would be better than individuals. It should be noted that many problems that require a number of skills can be worked on in stages. For example, the first stage may require a knowledge only of cellular biology; the second stage, a knowledge only of calculus; and the third, only of organic chemistry. With this kind of problem, it is not clear that groups are superior to individuals so long as we allow the individuals to work on the problem in stages and to distribute their findings at the end of each stage. Thus, the experiments in which groups have tended to be less effective than individuals may be somewhat misleading. We may conclude that groups set up at random and working together for a relatively short time almost certainly will be less effective than would the same individuals working alone. However, the possibility remains that properly constructed and well-trained groups may sometimes be more creative and efficient than individuals.

One final point should be made about group problem solving. Particular characteristics of any of the individuals may have an inhibiting or even a destructive effect on the rest of the group. One person may talk so much that no one else is able to say anything. Or someone may be so critical of everyone else's ideas that the rest of the group becomes reluctant to contribute. Another common phenomenon, discussed in detail in Chapter 14, is that persons of higher status in the group tend to have more influence than those of lower status.

In a study by Torrance (1955), airplane crews consisting of a pilot, navigator, and gunner worked on a series of problems together. A careful record was kept of the solutions suggested by each group member and of the final solution agreed on by the whole group. It was found that the group almost always unanimously approved the solutions suggested by the pilot, whereas it was rarely influenced by the contributions of the gunner (the lowest-status person). This is not surprising and by itself need not have had an adverse effect on the group's performance. The striking finding concerned the group's reaction when either the pilot or the gunner had the correct answer. Torrence found that when the pilot had the correct answer, the group went along with him 100 percent of the time. However, when the gunner had the correct answer, the group accepted it only about 40 percent of the time. This means that if the three men had been working separately, at least the gunner would have been correct the other 60 percent of the time that he knew the answer; but when they worked as a group, all three members were incorrect on those occasions when the pilot disagreed with the gunner. The same effect has been found (Riecken, 1958) when a clue is given to various members of a group. When it is

"J.B. has just had this marvellous brainwave—we'll use your idea!"

given to someone who talks a lot and is a leader, the group solves the problem; when the clue is given to a relatively silent member, the group often fails to use it. This research demonstrates that groups introduce all sorts of complex interactions, conflicts, and pressures that are not present when individuals work alone and that are often disruptive.

To sum up, under most circumstances, groups are less efficient than individuals working alone. Group members distract, inhibit, and generally tend to interfere with one another. Groups do provide a means of catching errors, and on certain types of problems, this might overcome their relative inefficiency. Also, when differing skills are needed for a solution, groups have a big advantage. Finally, as in minimal social situations, group members tend to motivate each other to work harder, and they probably do this to an even greater extent than in the minimal situations. If other incentives have not already produced a sufficiently high motivational level, this would be an advantage of working in groups.

Cohesiveness

Interactions and feelings among the group members play an important role in the group's performance. Groups in which there is a lot of internal fighting, disagreement, and lack of cooperation will obviously do poorly on tasks, whereas groups in which people generally agree and cooperate should do very well. In addition, groups in which all the members like each other and are strongly attracted to the group itself should do well. A group of this kind would have high morale, strong motivation, and strong pressures against conflicts that could interfere with performance. This quality of the group is called cohesiveness. The more the members are attracted to one another and to the group and the more they share the group's goals, the greater the group's cohesiveness.

These considerations suggest that highly cohesive groups are more effective than less cohesive ones and research has generally shown this effect (Husband, 1940; Berkowitz, 1956). However, it is important to take into account a group's norms and goals. The more cohesive a group, the more its members follow its goals. Thus, if the group's goal is to work hard and accomplish as much as possible, a highly cohesive group will be more productive than a less cohesive group. On the other hand, if for some reason the group's goals are to limit the amount of work, a highly cohesive group will be less productive than a less cohesive group (Schachter et al., 1951; Berkowitz, 1954). In other words, whatever the group as a whole decides to do, a cohesive group will do better.

Although it might seem that most groups would want to maximize their productivity, many groups deliberately limit production. A typical example is a union that places restrictions, formal or informal, on the amount of work each person is supposed to accomplish in a given period of time. The workers are expected to do that much and no more, and anyone who does more is considered a deviant and treated accordingly. Of course, in this situation the goal is set by an outside agency (the company management), and the group does not benefit directly from increased output. However, restricting productivity also occurs in more informal groups such as college fraternities and other living units. The members think that a certain amount of studying, for example, is appropriate, but anything more than that amount is "bad form." Someone who wants to study more than the accepted amount may be subjected to kidding, abuse, deliberate distractions, or even rejection. Thus, cohesive groups maintain performance at a set level better than do less cohesive groups, but the level of performance is not necessarily higher with greater cohesiveness.

EXTREMITY SHIFTS (THE "RISKY SHIFT")

One interesting effect that groups have on individuals' behavior concerns risk taking. People are often faced with a choice between a course of action that has only a small chance of working but the possibility of a large payoff and one that is more likely to work but would result in a much smaller payoff. For example, in roulette, betting $1 on red results in winning half the time (actually, slightly less than half the time because of the zeros, which are neither red nor black, but for this example we shall ignore them), with a payoff of $1. Betting $1 on a number results in winning about once in thirty-six times, with a payoff of $35. Thus, over many trials, the results would be equal. If either bet were made many times, the losses would be equivalent. The bets are, however, quite different in terms of expected gains and losses on any one trial. The first bet might be called conservative, because half the time the player wins a small amount. The second bet is risky, because the player loses over 95 percent of the time, but when he does win, he wins a lot. A more practical example, perhaps, would be the case of a college senior considering graduate work. She might have to choose between entering a university that has such rigorous standards that only a fraction of the degree candidates actually receive degrees and entering one that has less of a reputation but where almost everyone admitted receives degrees. Here again, there is a risky strategy (entering the more difficult university). The question is whether individuals and groups favor different strategies.

In a series of studies (Dion et al., 1970; Marquis, 1962; Stoner, 1961; Wallach & Kogan, 1965; Zajonc et al., 1972), a number of complex situations were described to the subjects. In each situation, a variety of choices, ranging from very high risk to very low risk, was available. The subjects were asked to consider the situations carefully and decide what recommendations they would make or which alternative they would prefer. One situation was described as follows:

> Mr. E. is president of a metals corporation in the United States. The corporation is quite prosperous and Mr. E. has considered the possibility of expansion by building an additional plant in a new location. His choice is between building another plant in the United States, where there would be a moderate return on the initial investment, or building a plant in a foreign country, where lower labor costs and easy access to raw materials would mean a much higher return on the initial investment. However, there is a history of political instability and revolution in the foreign country under consideration. In fact, the leader of a small minority party is committed to nationalizing, that is, taking over all foreign investments.
>
> Imagine that you are advising Mr. E. Listed below are several probabilities of continued political stability in the foreign country under consideration. Please check the *lowest* probability that you would consider acceptable in order for Mr. E.'s corporation to build in that country.
>
> > The chances are 1 in 10 that the foreign country will remain politically stable.
> >
> > The chances are 3 in 10 that the foreign country will remain politically stable.
> >
> > The chances are 5 in 10 that the foreign country will remain politically stable.
> >
> > The chances are 7 in 10 that the foreign country will remain politically stable.
> >
> > The chances are 9 in 10 that the foreign country will remain politically stable.
> >
> > Place a check here if you think Mr. E.'s corporation should not build a plant in the foreign country, no matter what the probabilities (Kogan & Wallach, 1967, pp. 234–35).

After listening to this problem, the subjects made individual decisions. They did not discuss the issue; they did not know that they were going to discuss it later. When they had made their decisions, they were brought into a group and asked to discuss the problem to reach a unanimous decision. Under these circumstances, there was a strong tendency for the group decision to involve higher risk than the average of the decisions made by the individuals. For example, in one group, two individuals were for 9 in 10, two for 7 in 10, and two for 5 in 10 when they made their decisions individually. After the group discussion, the unanimous decision was to endorse 5 in 10—a clear shift toward a risky strategy. Moreover, the strong overall tendency to favor riskier choices in groups held for both males and females.

This phenomenon has been referred to as the **risky shift.** It has been demonstrated with a wide variety of decisions involving quite different kinds of materials and with many different subject populations. The risky shift occurs with real life situations such as those just described. It also occurs when subjects have a selection of problems to work on that vary in difficulty and in the number of points they will get for solving them. This is the kind of choice a champion diver makes when he selects either very difficult dives which, if he does them well, will earn him many points, or somewhat simpler dives which are easier to do but will earn him fewer points even if he does them perfectly. And risky shifts also occur (although somewhat less consistently) in gambling situations where there is a choice between low-probability, high-payoff alternatives, and higher probability but lower payoff possibilities. Most of the research has involved subjects (usually students) in the United States and Canada, but the risky shift has also been demonstrated in England (Bateson, 1966), France (Kogan & Doise, 1969), Israel (Rim, 1963), and Germany (Lamm & Cogan, 1970). It is a stable, consistent finding that has attracted a great deal of research in recent years.

Although most of the work on group decisions indicated a shift toward riskier choices, careful analysis of some of the results and some additional findings (e.g. Frazer, Gouge, & Billig, 1971) indicate that sometimes the shift is in the conservative direction. Moreover, the direction of the shift is consistent for a particular decision; some cause most groups to become riskier than individuals, some produce conservative shifts. Thus, the term risky shift is not as appropriate as it first seemed. **Extremity shift** or *polarization* (a term favored by Moscovici & Zavalloni, 1969, and by Fraser et al., 1971) are more accurate.

We know that being involved in a group discussion of a decision causes people to shift their preferences, usually in a riskier direction, sometimes in a conservative direction. We also know that this occurs even when group members make their actual decisions individually and in private. How can we explain this effect of being in a group? A number of explanations have been offered; and the testing and changing of these explanations makes an interesting case history of research on an intriguing problem in social psychology. Therefore let us consider some of the most plausible explanations in detail.

Riskier People Are More Persuasive

One explanation is based on presumed differences between people who ordinarily favor risky choices and those who favor more conservative choices. If riskier people tend to be leaders of groups, participate more, play larger roles in group decisions, or be more persuasive for any reason, it would explain the risky shift. Obviously, if the group is more influenced by riskier people, the group as a whole will end up favoring riskier decisions after a discussion.

Although this is a plausible explanation, the evidence collected so far does not provide much support for it. There is some indication (Rim, 1964) that high-risk people value leadership more and are generally *perceived* as more persuasive by the other members of the group (Flanders & Thistlewaite, 1967; Wallach et al., 1962; Wallach, Kogan, & Burt, 1965). On the other hand, two studies (Nordhoy, 1962; Rabow et al., 1966) have shown that in situations where conservative shifts occur, high-risk people are seen as less persuasive. This indicates that the perception of how persuasive they are is probably not due to any inherent ability on their part, but rather to what happens in the group discussion. If the group is persuaded to be more risky, obviously those who initially favored high risk are seen as causing that shift; if the group ends up less risky, the conservative members of the group are seen as having caused the shift. Since there is no direct evidence that high-risk people are more persuasive, we are forced to conclude that the risky shift is not caused by any inherent differences in ability or persuasiveness among members of the group.

This conclusion is reinforced by the fact that several studies (Blank, 1968; Teger & Pruitt, 1967) have shown that the risky shift occurs without an actual discussion, but with only an exchange of preferences. When no discussion occurs, differences in persuasiveness cannot account for the results. The available evidence thus does not support this explanation of the risky shift, but the possibility remains that differences in persuasiveness may be a contributing factor in some situations, even though they are not the major reason for the effect.

Diffusion of Responsibility

Individuals in a group may sometimes feel less personal responsibility for their own acts than they would if they were alone. To some extent the decision is made by the whole group and the burden of responsibility is accordingly shared. Even if the person makes the decision on his own following a group discussion, he may feel he is less responsible for it because he is in a group. A second assumption is that most people would like to make risky decisions, but avoid them for fear of failure or other negative consequences. Being in a group reduces the feeling or responsibility, reduces the fear of negative consequences, and therefore allows people to pick riskier choices.

This is an interesting explanation of the risky shift because it conceives of it as a true group phenomenon. Being in the group would be a necessary condition for the effect because group feelings and the accompanying diffusion of responsibility are the crucial elements producing the risky shift. The test of this explanation depends on whether group membership is, in fact, a necessary condition for a risky shift. If the shift occurs without a discussion or even without the individual feeling that he is a member of a group, obviously it cannot be due to diffusion of responsibility. On the other hand, if giving the individual all the necessary information without actually having a group meeting does not produce a shift, it would suggest that diffusion of responsibility or some similar group phenomenon was the explanation. Unfortunately, the evidence on this point is somewhat inconsistent.

One study (Bem et al., 1965) demonstrated that having a discussion produced the effect, whereas merely anticipating a discussion but not having it did not. Similarly, Wallach and Kogan (1965) produced a risky shift when the group had a discussion with a group consensus, when there was a discussion without a group consensus, but not when there was consensus without an actual discussion. On the other hand, watching others discuss the issue seems to produce the effect (Kogan & Wallach, 1967); and, more damaging, some experimenters (Blank, 1968; Teger & Pruitt, 1967) have found the effect when the group knew one another's preferences but did not have a discussion. And making the group more cohesive, which might be expected to increase diffusion of responsibility, actually decreased the size of the risky shift (Dion et al., 1970).

None of these studies entirely rules out the diffusion of responsibility explanation. The crucial question—whether the effect occurs when the individual does not feel he is a member of a group—has never been fully tested. Even those studies that produced the effect without a group discussion did have groups, and perhaps simply being in a group is sufficient to reduce one's feeling of responsibility. Although we cannot confidently reject the explanation, the evidence in favor of it is somewhat questionable. No one has yet produced a study that directly demonstrates the feeling of reduced responsibility nor even that fear of failure is a basic reason for making conservative choices. Thus, although we cannot entirely rule out this explanation, at the moment the evidence in favor of it is not very convincing.

Cultural Value

An explanation that seems more consistent with the evidence is based on the assumption that under most circumstances risky decisions are valued more highly than conservative ones. In many situations and many cultures, people admire, respect, and value the tendency to take chances. Discussing a decision with other people or even knowing other people's choices makes this cultural norm more important and therefore causes the individual to select a riskier decision than he would if he were alone. In other situations, the culture may value caution. When this is so, the opposite effect should occur—following a group discussion, the choices should be more conservative than before. This explanation says in effect that the risky shift is not truly a group phenomenon, but rather that being in a group is one way in which these culture values can be made important and relevant. There would be other ways also, and they too would produce the risky shift. Thus, group discussion or even group membership is not absolutely crucial, but is merely one effective procedure for producing the phenomenon.

Most of the evidence bearing on this explanation is indirect. To begin with, it is clear that the research on the necessity of group discussion is consistent with this explanation. As we have said, some studies (e.g., Wallach & Kogan, 1965) demonstrated that discussion was necessary in order to produce the effect; others (e.g., Teger & Pruitt, 1967) found risky shift without discussion. In terms of the value hypothesis, we would expect that a discussion would be more likely to produce the effect and would produce a stronger effect, because it would make the cultural norms particularly salient. On the other hand, if the information given to subjects about others' preferences is detailed enough and is presented in such a way as to make these preferences important, the effect should occur even without a discussion. Yet, in several studies information about others' preferences was given to subjects in apparently considerable detail and yet no risky shift was found (e.g., Kogan & Carlson, 1969; Zajonc et al., 1970). If the effect is due entirely to the salience of cultural norms, this kind of information should produce a risky shift, and these studies in which it did not are somewhat damaging.

On the other hand, there is a considerable amount of supporting evidence from individuals' stated preferences. People tend to say they admire high-risk choices in situations that have in fact produced the risky-shift effect (Levenger & Schneider, 1969; Pilkonis & Zanna, 1969) and to rate fictitious risk-takers higher than more cautious people (Madaras & Bem, 1968). In situations that have produced shifts toward caution, people say they admire cautious responses (Levenger & Schneider, 1969; Pruit & Teger, 1967). In addition, people perceive themselves as riskier than their peers in situations that produce risky shifts (Baron et al., 1970) but see themselves as more cautious on items that produce a conservative shift (Levenger & Schneider, 1969). Thus, just as would be expected from the value explanation, when people value risk, the risky shift occurs; when they value caution, a conservative shift occurs. This is strong evidence that the effect is produced by evaluation of the situation rather than by differences in individual persuasiveness or the diffusion of responsibility.

Persuasive Arguments

Finally, there is an explanation in terms of the number of persuasive arguments offered in the group discussion. According to this view, proposed most forcefully by Burnstein and Vinokur (1975), the group discussion is an attitude change or persuasion situation. Each individual hears arguments presented by others. His own opinion is influenced by the quality and especially the quantity of those arguments. If there are more arguments in favor of a risky decision, the group members will shift in that direction; if there are more conservative arguments, there will be a conservative shift. This explanation requires no assumptions about some people being more persuasive, no deindividuation or cultural values. It relies entirely on the arguments that are proposed.

Quite a few studies have provided support for this position (e.g., Vinokur, Trope, & Burnstein, 1975; Vinokur & Burnstein, 1978; Madsen, 1978). However, it appears that being in a group may be a cruicial factor in producing the effect. Simply hearing other people's arguments, without being involved in any kind of discussion or group, does not generally result in polarization. Rather, the arguments have the effect only when the individual is forced to think about the arguments, to go over them in his mind, and essentially to take them seriously. In a careful and thoughtful review of the group polarization phenomenon, Myers and Lamb (1976) conclude that the effect is due to exposure to arguments, and that membership in a group is not absolutely essential. But, it is essential for the individual to think about the arguments, and being in a group discussion usually forces individuals to do this. Thus, group membership will generally produce the polarization effect whereas simply listening to the arguments will not.

DEPOLARIZATION AND POLARIZATION An interesting study by Vinokur and Burnstein (1978) demonstrates that being in a group can cause both polarization and depolarization of attitudes. They brought together people who held contrasting attitudes on a wide variety of issues. The group then engaged in a six-minute discussion of a particular issue, and afterwards the members' attitudes were measured a second time. This is a more or less standard procedure, and the typical effect of polarization was found. When initially most group members favored one position, the whole group moved in the direction of that position. For example, in groups where more members originally favored risky decisions, the whole group became riskier; whereas in groups where the majority initially favored a cautious decision, the whole group became more cautious. This, of course, is the standard polarization effect.

Vinokur and Burnstein then went one step further. They carefully analyzed all of the changes in attitudes that occurred within the group. They found a very strong tendency for all members to move closer together in their attitudes than they had been at the beginning. For example, consider a group in which the majority initially favors a risky decision. After the discussion, the risky subjects (those originally favoring the risky choice) actually move slightly toward a cautious decision. In contrast, the originally cautious subjects move strongly toward a risky decision. The same effect occurs when the majority initially favors a cautious decision. And perhaps most impressively, it occurs even on factual items such as the population of the United States in 1900. After a discussion, the whole group on average moves toward the position initially held by the majority; but those holding opposite views moved closer to each other.

This implies that people are more influenced by conflicting than supporting views. But the more arguments they hear on any given issue, the more they are influenced. In other words, two effects occur at the same time: polarization of the group as a whole because there are more arguments on one side than the other; and depolarization of the two opposing camps because each is influenced more by the other's arguments than by its own. This last finding sounds very much like a social comparison effect, in which, as we mentioned in Chapter 3, there is a general homogenization, a coming together of attitudes in feelings in a group. Thus, as Sanders and Baron (1977), Goethels and Zanna (1979), and others have argued, even though the number of arguments is a crucial factor in the extremity shift, social comparison also plays an important role.

GROUPS AS MOBS

Sometimes being in a group causes people to engage in behavior they would not engage in if they were by themselves. Such behavior may involve immoral or violent acts such as lynchings in the American South or urban riots, but it can also involve more moderate actions such as booing a poor speaker or tearing down goalposts after a football game. Whatever the particular behavior, under some circumstances, group members act not so much as individuals but as parts of a whole. Although such mob activity may not occur very often, it is the most striking and frightening phenomenon of groups, and various explanations of it have been offered.

We must distinguish, however, between the kind of effect just described and a less interesting effect of groups that is due simply to disorganization. The restaurant fire described at the beginning of the chapter provided the impetus for disorganized mob activity. Everyone wanted to get out of the burning restaurant, all or most of them could have if they had waited quietly and taken turns, but instead they rushed for the few exits and blocked them. They were not really doing anything that they would not have done if they were alone. Anyone in the restaurant, whether alone or in a group, would have gone as quickly as possible to an exit and tried to escape. What made this a tragedy was that the people were disorganized and rather than cooperating, they competed with each other.

With clouds of smoke billowing behind the diners, it was not surprising that they became frantic and disorganized. But this kind of phenomenon is not limited to such extreme circumstances. In the relatively placid setting of an experimental laboratory, each of a group of subjects was given one end of a string, the other end of which was attached to a small wooden spool (Mintz, 1951). The spools were placed in a large bottle, the neck of which was wide enough for only one spool to pass through at a time. The bottle then began to fill with water, and everyone was told to get his spool out before the water reached it. (The analogy to the restaurant fire is obvious.) The water rose slowly enough so that everyone could have gotten his spool out safely as long as only one person at a time

TABLE 15–4
Effect of Threat on Escape in a Situation Requiring Cooperation

THREAT	PERCENTAGE ESCAPING
Low	69
Medium	56
High	36

Source: Adapted from Kelley et al. (1965).

tried. The bottle was in plain sight, there was no bonus for getting one's spool out early, and, presumably, there was little or no actual fear of the water. Yet traffic jams almost always developed. Two or more people tried to get their spools through the bottle's neck at once, the spools got caught, and all those that were not already free were covered with water.

Harold Kelley and his associates (1965) repeated this study in a more controlled situation and, as shown in Table 15–4, got the same results. In addition, however, Kelley showed that increasing the actual level of fear (e.g., by threatening the subjects with electric shocks if they did not escape) produced more disorganization and more traffic jams. The main point of this research for our present purpose is that under even mild stress, a group sometimes acts in a disorganized, self-destructive manner, and that this tendency increases with higher stress.

Contagion and Deindividuation

That groups sometimes become disorganized is hardly surprising. But the more interesting phenomenon is that people in groups will behave in ways they would not by themselves. In 1895 Le Bon suggested that people in a mob tend to feel and behave the same way because the emotions of one person spread through the group. When one person does something, even if it would ordinarily be unacceptable to most of the group members, everyone else tends to do it also. He called this **contagion,** likening mob behavior to disease, like a cold spreading through members of a class. Both Le Bon and, somewhat later, Freud (1923) explained contagion in terms of a breakdown of the normal control mechanism that each person has internalized. Our actions are usually controlled by our moral sense, our value system, and social rules we have learned. In groups we sometimes lose a sense of responsibility for our own actions; we feel that the group and only the group is responsible. Thus, our own control system is weakened or breaks down completely. Moreover, once an individual's control mechanism is weakened, his primitive, aggressive, and sexual impulses are free to be expressed, and this results in violent, immoral acts.

More recently, Leon Festinger (Festinger, Pepitone, & Newcomb, 1952) and others have translated these ideas into more modern terms.

They propose that people in groups sometimes experience **deindividua-tion,** in which personal identity is lost and is replaced with a close identity with the goals and actions of the group. Deindividuation involves a loss of personal responsibility, as well as a heightened sensitivity to what the group is doing. It does not necessarily mean a release of aggressive impulses; rather, it is a submerging of the self in the group. In a sense, each person in the group thinks of his actions as being part of the group's behavior. This causes the person to feel less responsible for his own actions, and less concerned about their consequences.

One implication of deindividuation is that anything which makes the members of a group less identifiable increases the effect. The more anonymous the group members are, the less identifiable they are as individuals, the less they feel they have an identity of their own, and the more irresponsibly they may behave. In a mob, most of the people do not stand out as individuals. They blend together and, in a sense, do not have an identity of their own. Conversely, to the extent that they are identifiable and feel that they are, they retain their feeling of individuality and are less likely to act irresponsibly.

In an experiment by Singer, Brush, and Lublin (1965) to test this notion, some subjects were made easily identifiable and others were made more difficult to identify. In the former condition, everyone dressed in his normal clothes, which meant that each was dressed differently from the others. In addition, the subjects were called by name and everything was done to make each one stand out as an individual. In the latter condition, all the subjects put on identical, bulky lab coats. The experimenter

FIGURE 15–10 Uniforms such as these announce membership in a group. They may often tend to make the wearer more anonymous (since all wear about the same uniform) and thus lead to less concern about one's actions.

Esaias Baitel; Rapho Photo Researchers, Inc.

avoided using their names and, in general, tried to give the impression that their individual identities did not matter much. The group then discussed a variety of topics, including one that required the use of obscene language.

Groups in the low-identifiable condition showed much more freedom in all the discussions and, in particular, in the one involving obscene words. There were fewer pauses in the conversation, more lively discussions, and, most strongly, a greater willingness to use the obscene language that was necessary for a good discussion of the topic. Subjects who were more easily identified were much more constrained and appeared quite reluctant to use the taboo words.

A more dramatic effect of identifiability was provided in an experiment by Zimbardo (1970). Groups of four girls were recruited to take part in a study supposedly involving empathic responses to strangers. In one condition, the girls were greeted by name, wore name tags, and were easily identifiable. In another condition, the girls wore oversized white lab coats and hoods over their heads, were never called by name, and were difficult if not impossible to identify. All the groups were given an opportunity to deliver electric shocks to a girl not in the group. The subjects who were not identifiable gave almost twice as many shocks as the others. Apparently being less identifiable produced a marked increase in aggression, supporting the idea that loss of individuality is one cause of the violent, antisocial behavior sometimes exhibited by groups.

A clever demonstration of the deindividuation effect involved watching children who were trick-or-treating on Halloween. In this study (Diener et al., 1976), some of the children were first asked their names by the adults in the homes, while others were not. Then they were given the opportunity to steal extra candy when the adult was not present. Those who had been asked their names, and therefore were less anonymous, were less likely to steal, even though the chances of getting caught were virtually zero in all cases. And Watson (1973) reported that cultures in which warriers wear masks or otherwise disguise their faces are more likely to engage in especially aggressive acts during warfare than cultures in which warriers do not disguise themselves.

However, Johnson and Downing (1979) point out that almost all of the research subjects have worn disguises or masks that have negative implications. Zimbardo used Ku Klux Klan-like outfits; most Halloween masks are of monsters or ghosts; and, of course, warriors tend to paint their faces in lurid, ugly expressions, in part to scare their opponents. Perhaps it is not the anonymity that increases the violation of norms, but the implications of the particular disguise. To test this, anonymity was produced by having people wear either Ku Klux Klan outfits, or nurses' outfits consisting of white hats and coats. Those wearing outfits were compared to others wearing normal clothing. It was found that the Ku Klux Klan outfit had only a slight effect on the level of shock that subjects gave (thus not replicating Zimbardo's results); perhaps more important, the nurses' uniforms actually reduced the number of shocks given. Although anonymity probably produces increased aggression because it offers protection, this study indicates that people may also be influenced by the uniforms they wear. If the uniform implies positive, prosocial behavior, the wearer may behave accordingly. Thus, the notion that anonymity always produces more antisocial behavior appears to be incorrect.

The critical variable in all the research on individuation is not membership in a group but anonymity. That is, there is no evidence that simply being in a group produces deindividuation or increases antisocial behavior. For example, Diener (1976) observed young adults in a situation in which they were free to act aggressively towards someone who would not harm them in any way. In all conditions, the subjects first observed someone else acting aggressively toward the "victim" and thus had a model that might have increased their own tendencies to be aggressive. Yet, subjects who were alone with the victim were actually more aggressive than those who were in a group. In other words, being in a group decreased aggressiveness instead of increasing it. In summarizing the research on this issue, Diener (1977) concludes that the evidence does not generally support the idea that group membership increases antisocial behavior. Sometimes it does, but there is no reason to believe that in general people act more aggressively in groups than when they are alone.

Thus, the evidence for deindividuation is rather meager. We do know that people given the cover of anonymity will behave in more antisocial ways than when they can be recognized. We also know that sometimes being in a group tends to increase anonymity. But as yet there is no good evidence that group membership alone produces deindividuation.

Most mob behavior may be caused mainly by the fact that people in groups are less likely to be punished than if they acted individually. A person in a large group is anonymous and protected by the sheer number of other individuals. If one person throws a rock through a window or attacks a gathering of political opponents, he is likely to be identified and arrested. If five hundred people throw rocks or attack a political group, each of them is much less likely to be identified and arrested. Thus, much group behavior that appears to violate certain individual moral values may be entirely consistent with values that people are afraid to act on when alone. For the moment, there is no evidence that people in groups behave any more inconsistently with their beliefs than do individuals alone.

Some actions of groups are due to a strong collective belief in a cause or leader. The Jonestown episode, in which hundreds of people committed suicide, was probably due to both factors. The people at Jonestown shared religious beliefs and blindly followed a charismatic, powerful leader. While some suicides were enforced by threats, many were voluntary. Similarly, the Iranian students who took over the American embassy in Teheran were enflamed by religious and political feelings and were supported by their spiritual leaders. They were not acting against their moral codes; on the contrary, they claimed that they were acting from a higher morality. Thus, what sometimes appears to outsiders to be group immorality may actually arise from strongly held individual religious or moral beliefs. Such groups may engage in unusual and violent acts, but each individual is willing to take responsibility for them.

SUMMARY

1. Being with other people causes us to act differently from when we are alone. Even when there is no interaction with the other people, social facilitation usually occurs. Performance improves on simple tasks and declines on complex ones. The presence of others raises individual motivation, probably due to concerns about being evaluated. The presence of others can also make individuals feel competitive, or it can be distracting.

2. People have a tendency to compete even when they would improve their own performance and win more money or points by cooperating. Increasing incentive by raising the stakes does not have a consistent effect on the amount of competition.

3. Threats tend to reduce cooperation, especially when both sides have threats. If only one side has a threat, that side's outcome improves relative to the other's.

4. Communication usually increases cooperation by allowing the participants to make known their intentions.

5. Although a group can usually solve a problem faster and better than an individual, groups are not generally as good as the same number of individuals (i.e., a group of five versus five individuals working alone). However, this depends on many factors, including the number of different skills necessary to solve the problem and probably on how well the people know each other and can work together.

6. Groups typically make more extreme decisions than individuals where risks are involved; sometimes the decisions are more conservative and sometimes more risky. This has been called the risky shift, but would more appropriately be called the extremity shift because it occurs in both directions.

7. Several explanations of the risky shift effect have been offered: (a) Risky people are more persuasive; (b) responsibility is diffused in the group; (c) there is a cultural value to being risky (or for some choices conservative) and the group brings out this value; and (d) the number of arguments that are produced in a group tend to favor the extreme (either riskiness or conservatism), and the sheer number of these arguments persuades the group to change its opinion. The first two possibilities have generally been disproved. On the other hand, the cultural value and persuasive argument explanations are now generally accepted. Perhaps a combination of the two provides a full explanation.

8. Groups sometimes behave like mobs, committing acts that none of the individual members would commit if they were alone. The more identifiable the members of the group, the less likely mob behavior will occur. It has been suggested that this is due to deindividuation; each person loses his personality and sense of responsibility. Although anonymity does seem to increase "mob" effects, there is little evidence to support the idea of deindividuation. It is more likely that most of the effects are due to the protection and support provided by the group.

SUGGESTIONS FOR ADDITIONAL READING

LEBON, G. *The crowd.* London: Benn, 1898. Available in many modern editions. Despite the title, this is really a book on group dynamics, though admittedly it deals with large groups rather than small ones.

RAVEN, B., & RUBIN, J. *Social psychology: People in groups.* New York: John Wiley, 1976. This book provides thorough coverage of work on groups. It is rather slow going, but all the information is there.

ZAJONC, R. B. Social facilitation. *Science,* 1955, *149,* 269–74. A clear presentation of his theory of how the presence of others affects us.

16 Environmental and Urban Psychology

Donald C. Dietz; Stock, Boston.

Over the past ten or fifteen years, people have become more and more concerned about the environment. The environmental movement has focused attention on the quality of the air we breathe and the water we drink, on how new dam construction harms wildlife, and how strip mining devastates the landscape and causes floods. We are beginning to realize that virtually all aspects of the world around us can have profound and potentially negative effects on our health and well-being.

Social scientists, including psychologists, have also become concerned about how the environment affects us. Just as toxic chemicals in the air and the ground can damage physical health, so other characteristics of the environment can damage mental and social health. Noise, crowding, building design, and community structure all determine the quality of our lives and our day-to-day functioning. Researchers in social psychology and environmental psychology (a subfield of social psychology) have studied the effects of these environmental features, and we shall consider their findings in this chapter.

NOISE

Unless you are in a specially constructed sound-proof chamber, you are always exposed to noise. For those with normal hearing, sound is one of the most important means of knowing about and experiencing the world. A silent world is virtually impossible to imagine. However, psychologists are especially concerned about the effects of noise because so much of modern industrial life involves the production of noise, and because the amount of noise to which people are exposed in cities is often extremely high. Not only do traffic, construction, machinery of all kinds, and powerful stereo equipment produce noise of great intensity, but millions of people in a relatively small area create high noise levels. In fact, the most striking aspect of cities is their constant high noise levels, as compared to suburbs and rural areas. Country noises, or "natural" noises, are quite different from and usually less loud than city noises. Someone who moves from the city to the country or vice versa is immediately aware of the change in noise level, and both shifts can be disturbing. This is certainly true for those who move to the city, but it is also true for city dwellers who find themselves in the country. Just as it is difficult to get used to the sound of cars and trucks in the city, it is usually hard to sleep in the country either because it is too quiet or because the racket caused by crickets and birds is disturbing when you are not used to it. Thus, we know that we notice noises and are often quite sensitive to them. But what effect does noise have on us? The answer is that it has less effect than we might think.

Adaptation to Short-Term Noise

The most important finding from research on noise is that people adapt very quickly. When we are exposed to bursts of very loud noise, our initial reaction is strong. Everyone is familiar with one typical response—the so-called startle reflex. An unexpected loud noise causes us to jump, flex our stomach muscles, blink, and generally react physically. Even if we are expecting the noise, we respond physiologically with increased blood pressure, sweating, and other signs of arousal. In addition, loud noise interferes with our ability to perform tasks. We do less well on both simple and complex tasks when we are exposed to loud noise. Clearly, loud noise is upsetting, causes physiological arousal, and prevents us from functioning at our usual level.

However, these disruptive effects generally last only a short while. We quickly get used to (adapt to) even extremely loud noises. It takes only a few minutes for physiological reactions to disappear and for performance to return to normal. After ten minutes or less, people who are subjected to short bursts of extremely loud noise are virtually identical to people who hear moderate or low noise. This is true even for noise levels over 100 decibels, which is roughly equivalent to a big jet coming in low over your house or a huge truck rumbling by right next to you. As long as the noise is not so loud that it actually produces pain or physical damage, people adapt to it very quickly (Broadbent, 1971; Glass & Singer, 1972).

You can see this effect in a study by David Glass and Jerome Singer in which people were exposed either to background noise (no noise condition) or to a meaningless jumble of noise at 108 decibels in short bursts for twenty-three minutes. As shown in Figure 16–3, the loud noise did cause

FIGURE 16–2 Although the noice of construction can be almost deafening, brief exposure to it seems to have few negative consequences.

FIGURE 16–3 Physiological (GSR) response to loud noise. After a strong initial response, subjects adapt quickly.

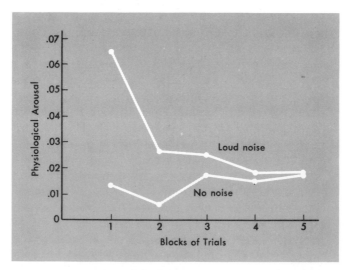

Source: Based on Glass and Singer (1972).

physiological arousal, but the arousal lasted only a few minutes. Moreover, after four minutes, all subjects did equally well on a variety of tasks including simple arithmetic, matching sets of numbers (i.e., deciding whether 68134 and 68243 are identical), anagrams, and higher level mathematics. Once they have gotten used to the noise, people perform almost any task as well with loud noise as they do in quieter environments.

There are a few important exceptions to this finding. Donald Broadbent (1968) and other researchers have shown that certain kinds of monitoring tasks are more difficult to do with loud noise. For example, if someone is required to watch three dials to be sure none of them goes over a certain point, high levels of noise interfere with performance. Similarly, it is apparently harder to do two tasks at the same time in a noisy environment. In one study (Finkelman & Glass, 1970), subjects had to repeat digits they heard over headphones while at the same time turning a steering wheel to track a moving line. Noise level did not affect the primary task, which was the tracking, but it made the subjects less accurate at repeating the digits. Presumably, noise is distracting and interferes with the performance of tasks that already strain our capacity to concentrate.

Most of the time we are only doing one thing at a time, so the effects of noise are probably quite limited. On the other hand, it is well to remember that some sensitive jobs do involve exactly the kinds of monitoring tasks that seem to be affected by loud noise. The pilot of a plane must watch many different dials while operating a variety of instruments; flight controllers have similar problems; and even the typical driver of a car has many things to attend to at once. (It is a little frightening to realize that all these jobs, especially those of pilot and flight controller, are performed under conditions of considerable noise.) With this potentially important exception, short-term exposure to loud noise appears to have little detrimental effect.

The Importance of Control

However, this is not the whole story. A series of experiments by Glass and Singer (1972) demonstrated that the adaptation to loud noise may take considerable effort that shows up later, after the noise is no longer present. In particular, this research indicated that these negative aftereffects occur when the noise is not under the control of the individual. If the noise is predictable (occurring every thirty seconds or only when there is warning) or if the person can turn off the noise, no bad effects occur. But if the noise seems to be totally out of the control of the person, certain kinds of performance suffer once the noise ceases.

The experiments were straightforward but ingenious. Subjects heard bursts of noise for a set period of time while they performed tasks. Then they performed other tasks with no noise. The crucial variation was that the circumstances under which the noise occurred either gave the person a sense of control or did not. In one study, people heard short bursts of

TABLE 16–1

Aftereffects of Predictable and Unpredictable Noise on Proofreading

CONDITION	NUMBER OF ERRORS
No noise	26.40
Soft Predictable	27.40
Soft Unpredictable	36.70
Loud Predictable	31.78
Loud Unpredictable	40.11

Source: Based on Glass and Singer (1972).

loud or soft noise. The crucial variation was that the noise bursts came either exactly one minute apart (and were therefore predictable) or at random intervals. Even though subjects heard just as much noise in the two conditions, the effects were entirely different. During the noise section of the study, all groups performed equally well regardless of how loud the noise was or whether it was predictable. But afterwards, as shown in Table 16–1, those who had heard the predictable noise performed better than those who had heard random noise. In fact, unpredictable soft noise caused more errors than predictable loud noise. This was true despite the fact that subjects reported finding the predictable and unpredictable noise equally annoying. In other studies, subjects were given a feeling of control by telling them they could stop the noise whenever they wanted to by pressing a button or by signaling their partner, who would then stop it. Even though subjects never did actually stop the noise, this feeling of control was apparently enough to eliminate the negative effects. There was no decline in performance either during or after the noise.

A later study (Sherrod, Hage, Halpern & Moore, 1977) replicated and extended these results. Subjects were allowed to start the noise, stop it, both start or stop it, or were allowed no control whatever. As in the earlier work, control reduced the negative effects of the noise. Moreover, the more control they had, the better the people performed. Also, in this study, unlike any previous work, the presence of uncontrollable noise actually caused subjects to do less well on a proofreading task while the noise was present. However, in line with the earlier work, the main result was that those exposed to controllable noise were more persistent in working on problems after the noise ended.

We do not know exactly why control is so important, but as we shall see, it may also play a role in reactions to other environmental factors. The importance of control may help us understand the effects of noise in the real world. Most of the noise in a city is fairly constant or predictable. There is the continuous noise of cars and trucks on the streets, periodic noise of trains in some communities, and the general din caused by many people. On the other hand, some noise is both unpredictable and uncontrollable. Jackhammers, firecrackers, backfiring cars, planes, and sudden loud music from radios fill the air with noise at random intervals and are therefore probably much more annoying than the usual background noise. It seems likely that the absolute level of the noise is less important than this unpredictability, and indeed, it is these kinds of noises that most people complain about.

Long-Term Constant Noise

Some research suggests that long-term exposure to loud noise can have detrimental effects of a very specific nature. A large apartment house in New York City is built over a highway, and because of the design of the building, the noise levels inside are quite high. Lower floors are almost always noisier than higher ones, and this situation provides an ideal setting for a natural experiment on the effects of long-term noise. Cohen, Glass, and Singer (1973) measured the reading achievement and ability to make auditory discriminations of children who had lived in the building for at least four years. As you can see in Figure 16–4, those who lived on lower floors did worse on both measures. The louder the noise on their floor, the less well they read and the poorer their auditory discriminations.

A study by Heff (1979) also indicates that long-term exposure to high levels of noise may be detrimental. The home environment of kinder-

FIGURE 16–4 Noise level in apartment and reading and auditory skills.

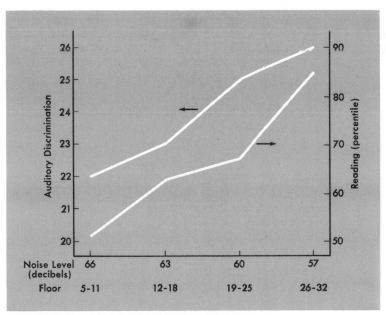

Source: Adapted from Cohen, Glass, and Singer (1973).

garten children was investigated carefully, and each home was rated in terms of general noise level. Then the children were given a task that involved searching for a particular stimulus. Those who came from noisier homes performed more poorly on this task than those who came from less noisy homes. The effects were not large; a noisy home seemed to make a small, but reliable difference, accounting for about 5 percent of the variation in scores. Part of the test involved measuring the effect of a loud, irrelevant noise on the distractibility of the children. Children from noisy homes performed much better than those from quieter homes—that is, living in a noisy environment apparently enabled the children to be less easily distracted by loud random noise. Thus, long-term exposure to loud noise may produce some deficits, but it may also enable people to ignore irrelevant and potentially distracting noises.

Far too little research on the effects of long-term exposure to noise has been done to produce any certain answers about its effects. There is, for example, no evidence that the hearing of people raised in cities (and therefore exposed to relatively high levels of noise all their lives) is any poorer than that of those who grew up in the country. Nor is there any indication that city people are less intelligent, discriminating, distractible, or for that matter different in any cognitive characteristics from rural or suburban people. The two studies described above raise the possibility that the effects of noise may be more serious than are suggested by experiments on short-term exposure, and this possibility should be explored further. But for now, most of the evidence suggests that the effects of noise are less severe than we might have imagined.

PERSONAL SPACE: PROXEMICS

Suppose you are standing by yourself in a physician's waiting room, and the nurse walks up to you. How close does she actually come? Three inches? Ten inches? Two feet? Suppose you are sitting on a park bench and a well-dressed man sits down immediately next to you. How does that make you feel? Would you feel any differently if he had sat down five feet away? As for yourself, how close to other people do you usually stand? Does it make any difference if they are friends, strangers, or members of your family? Does it make any difference if you are standing at a cocktail party, on a bus, or on line at the post office?

The use we make of the space around us is one of the most basic features of interpersonal behavior. The study of the personal use of space has been termed **proxemics** (Hall, 1959; Sommer, 1969); and research on it indicates wide differences, depending on nationality, ethnic background, and gender. Furthermore, how close to others we position ourselves indicates something about our feelings and intentions.

Ethnic Differences

If you have travelled much outside the United States, you have no doubt noticed that people in other countries differ in how close to each other they stand while talking. People in some cultures stand closer together than you are accustomed to, while people in other cultures maintain a greater distance. Research in this area has found that cultural norms determine typical personal space preferences. White North Americans, the English, and the Swedes stand the farthest apart; Southern Europeans stand closer; and Latin Americans and Arabs stand the closest (Watson & Graves, 1966; Hall, 1966; Little, 1968; Sommer, 1968). While much observation remains to be done in Africa, Eastern Europe, and Asia, it is clear that consistent differences exist all over the world.

There are also differences among ethnic groups within the United States. In general, blacks and whites do not differ much in the distances they choose. In early grades, black children seem to stand somewhat closer to each other than do white children, but the differences largely disappear by the fifth grade (Jones & Aiello, 1973). Blacks and whites of the same social class prefer the same distances (Scherer, 1974), but middle class people stand farther apart than lower-class people (Aiello & Jones, 1971). In contrast, Chicanos and other people from Latin America do stand closer than either whites or blacks (Baxter, 1970).

These ethnic differences might be considered a piece of interesting but trivial information if it were not for the fact that preferences in personal distance can sometimes have important consequences. People from cultures with different preferences may misinterpret one another's actions. For example, an American and a Pakistani have a problem when they stand next to each other to talk. The American likes to stand about three or four feet away, whereas the Pakistani would ordinarily stand much closer. Obviously, they cannot both have their way. If they are unaware of the cultural difference, they may execute a little dance around the room. The Pakistani feels uncomfortably far away and moves closer. The American feels uncomfortable and retreats, which in turn causes the Pakistani to move closer again. Moreover, as this is going on, the Pakistani may feel that the American is being cold and unfriendly, while the American thinks the other is being overly intimate and pushy. This is due to the fact that how close you stand does usually depend in part on your relationship to the other person.

Sex Differences

As you might have guessed, pairs of women stand closer than pairs of men (Horowitz et al., 1970; Sommer, 1959), although this difference seems to appear only when people are about twelve years old (Aiello & Aiello, 1974). In fact, women always tend to stand closer to whomever they are with (Hartnett et al., 1970; Leibman, 1970). On the other hand, mixed-sex pairs stand closer than same-sex pairs (Kuethe & Wingartner, 1964). This last finding, however, has not been demonstrated in a wide enough range of situations to be certain. As we shall see in a moment, the relationship between the people is extremely important and certainly affects how close the two people will stand.

In addition to these sex differences in interpersonal distance, males and females react somewhat differently to spatial arrangements. For example, when sitting at a table with someone they know and like, women tend to sit next to the person, whereas men choose seats opposite that person (Byrne et al., 1971). Jeffrey Fisher and Donn Byrne (1975) observed the reactions of people sitting alone at a table in a library when a stranger sat down across from them, one seat away, or right next to them. Regardless of the sex of the stranger, females appeared most bothered when the seat taken was next to them, but males disliked most having the opposite seat taken. Men also tried to protect themselves from intrusions by putting books in front of them, whereas women put their books and other possessions next to them. This is, of course, a special situation and may not hold in other contexts, but the sex differences seem quite consistent. As we shall see in the next section, sex differences also appear in responses to crowding.

BOX 16–1
TOUCHING AND HEALTH CARE

Although not dealing exactly with personal space, a study by Whitcher and Fisher (1979) provides additional evidence that men and women differ in their responses to interpersonal distance. In this case, patients and nurses in a hospital were observed over a long period of time. Nurses either deliberately touched patients whenever it was appropriate or carefully avoided touching them unless it was necessary. In the first condition, the nurses touched patients on their arms when giving them medicine, put their hand lightly on their backs when walking with them, and so on. The touching was not especially intimate or inappropriate.

Substantial differences were found in the reactions of male and female patients. Women responded more favorably to being touched than not being touched; whereas the reverse was true for men. Of course, being in a hospital is a special situation, and most of the nurses were women; it is therefore difficult to generalize from this one study.

Nevertheless, it is one more indication that there may be substantial sex differences in response to physical closeness, and that men in our society may tend to prefer less physical closeness than women. It also suggests that touching can have substantial benefits for some people, even improving their response to medical care when they are ill. The traditional rite of "laying on hands" for curative purposes may have real value when done in the right circumstances.

The Meaning of Distance	In addition to ethnic and sex differences in the use of personal space, there are substantial differences that depend on the relationship of the people involved. In general, the more intimate the relationship and the more friendly the people are, the closer they stand. Friends stand closer than strangers (Aiello & Cooper, 1972); people who want to seem friendly choose smaller distances (Lott & Sommer, 1967; Patterson & Sechrest, 1970); and people who are sexually attracted to each other stand close (Allgeier & Byrne, 1973). Although most people do not think much about personal space, we are all aware that standing close is usually a sign of friendship or interest. It may be one of the most important and easiest ways of telling someone you have just met that you like him or her. The other person is immediately aware of your interest, and if he is not interested, he will generally move away to make that clear.

Territoriality

The research on people's use of space and observations of animals in their natural habitats indicate that space is very important to us. It seems that we actually *need* a certain amount of space and that when less space is available than that required or when this minimum amount is invaded, the individual will become aggressive and defend his space. This need for space and the defense of it is sometimes called territoriality. Robert Ardrey (1966), one of the popularizers of the notion, claims that territoriality is instinctive in both animals and humans, that they are born with the need for space and automatically respond aggressively when there is too little. Although some animals may have such an instinct, most psychologists believe that humans do not. We do not require a fixed amount of space, and we do not always or automatically become aggressive even if we have very little space.

On the other hand, people do sometimes consider certain space or property their own and under some circumstances will defend that space from intrusions. As we discussed previously, various studies show that people respond negatively when others invade their space. Certainly, if you are alone in the library trying to study, it is usually annoying to have somebody sit down right next to you. This annoyance may be expressed as defensiveness, anger, or even outright aggression (Felipe & Sommer, 1966; Fisher & Byrne, 1975). We also often react negatively if a stranger stands closer to us than we consider comfortable or appropriate. In this case we would probably retreat if we were able, and if we could not retreat, we might become aggressive. We do have standards for interpersonal distance, we do claim possession of certain areas either temporarily or permanently, and any violations of these spaces produce defensive responses.

However, our need for space is by no means absolute. The amount we need and our reactions to incursions on it depend on the particular situation. In the library example, our response to someone joining us at a table would be quite different if it were the only remaining seat in the

FIGURE 16–5 People space themselves around the beach, marking off their spots with towels. By noticing the spacing, you can probably tell which people know each other and which are strangers.

library. We might have preferred to have the table to ourselves, but we would see that it was perfectly legitimate for the other person to take the seat if it was the only one free. She too is entitled to sit down. In contrast, if other seats are free, then the person is deliberately choosing to sit next to us and the act has more meaning. The "invader" might be interested in getting to know us, be planning to steal our books, or conceivably be taking his favorite chair in the library. But we would assume that his behavior was motivated—that he chose this seat rather than all the other free ones; and we are therefore more likely to respond to the invasion.

Even then, our reactions depend on other factors in the situation. For example, if you are bored by what you are reading, you might be pleased by the distraction. More to the point, if the other person is attractive, you may be flattered by the attention and perhaps interested in getting to know your new neighbor. True, it is still an invasion, but it may be a welcome one.

How we respond also depends on what is appropriate for a given situation. A study by Konečni (1975) involved having someone stand very close to a person who was waiting on a corner to cross the street. In this situation. A study by Konečni (1975) involved having someone stand very stand very close. Sure enough, people responded to this invasion by crossing the street much faster than usual in order to escape. Yet the same kind of close contact may be entirely appropriate or even desirable in other circumstances. At a large party people are expected to talk with one another, to meet strangers, and generally to interact in a friendly way. In

BOX 16-2
INVASIONS AND HELPING

As we discussed in Chapter 9, many factors influence the extent to which people are likely to offer help to someone in need. Among other considerations, the amount of helping depends on how urgently the individual actually needs the help. Under most circumstances we are more likely to give money to someone who is starving than to someone who is well fed. You will remember that in one study, people on a subway were more likely to help someone who fell down because he apparently suffered a heart attack than they were to the identical person when he fell down but seemed to be drunk. The heart attack victim presumably deserves help more than the alcoholic. Another factor that determines the amount of help given is how positive we feel towards the other person. Although there is little direct research on this, it seems highly probable that we are more likely to help someone whom we like or who seems likeable than someone whom we dislike or seems unpleasant. Thus, how much the person needs help and how likeable they seem should both affect how much help is offered.

Starting with the assumption that invasions of personal space generally produce negative reactions, Baron and Bell (1976) conducted a study in which requests for help were made from varying distances to the other person. The authors predicted that standing very close when asking for help would produce a negative reaction and would accordingly reduce the amount of helping. The study consisted of confederates approaching someone and asking them to serve as a subject in a psychology experiment. In half the conditions, the confederate stood a comfortable three or four feet from the other person—approximately the typical distance that North Americans stand from people they do not know. In the other half of the conditions, the confederate stood so that his face was from twelve to eighteen inches from the other person's face. This is extremely close by almost any standard and certainly is unusually close in our society. The results, however, were exactly opposite to what had been predicted. The close condition produced a great deal more helping than the distant condition. Even though standing a foot away from a stranger is unusual and might under some circumstances be interpreted as threatening or hostile, the confederates in that condition were helped more than when they stood at the more usual distance. The explanation of this effect is that the crucial element determining helping in this situation was the subject's interpretation of how urgently the confederate needed the help. Apparently, when the confederate stood very close, he was perceived as needing help more urgently than when he stood farther away. Regardless of the other implications of the two distances used, the effect is due to the subject's interpretation of the confederate's need.

such a gathering standing quite close to someone would be considered perfectly normal and friendly. If the person approached is not interested in being friendly, he or she is certainly free to move away. But approaching closely would not ordinarily be considered an aggressive act, nor would it produce an aggressive response.

In fact, it is unfortunate that psychologists have referred so often to "invasions" of personal space. This implies that whenever people sit or stand very close, they are trespassing on our personal property or at least getting closer than we want. Yet most of the research indicates that how we respond to someone coming close to us is largely determined by how we interpret the other person's behavior. Close contact can be either friendly and intimate or aggressive and intrusive. For example, Storms and Thomas (1977) observed what happened when male confederates sat either very close or at a normal distance to other males. The important additional factor in the situation was that the men who were sitting down acted either very friendly or quite unfriendly. Under these circumstances, the friendly men were liked more when they sat close than when they sat at a normal distance; but the unfriendly men were liked less if they sat close. In other words, once they were considered friendly, sitting close was considered an additional indication of their friendliness; but if they were considered unfriendly, then sitting close was interpreted as an additional negative characteristic.

In another experiment (Sundstrom & Sundstrom, 1977) confederates sat down on a bench either nine inches or eighteen inches away from a stranger. In all cases, the confederates were the same sex as the person on the bench. Before sitting down, however, half of the confederates asked permission—they asked whether it was OK if they sat down on the bench. The other half of the time, the confederates sat down without asking permission. Under these circumstances, it was clear that the "invasion" was interpreted differently by males and females and in both cases depended on whether or not permission was asked. When the confederate asked permission, women who were sitting on the bench got up and left sooner than when permission was not asked. In contrast, males who were asked permission stayed on the bench longer than when they were not asked. Once again males and females reacted in opposite ways to the situation. Apparently, women interpreted the request for permission as the beginning of an unwanted social contact and left in order to avoid it. When permission was not asked, women did not interpret the action as an invasion and did nothing to avoid it. Males, on the other hand, interpreted the action as a physical invasion unless permission was asked, and they therefore responded more negatively when the confederate sat down without asking.

All of this work, in addition to the study on helping that is described in Box 16–2, indicates that many of the initial ideas concerning personal space were somewhat simplistic. Hall (1959) assumed that under most circumstances standing very close would produce negative reactions. It would be interpreted as an aggressive invasion into the other person's territory. Indeed, Hall made a great deal of the idea that each person is surrounded by an imaginary bubble-shaped space and will respond immediately in a negative way whenever that space is violated. Clearly, our use of and interpretation of personal space is far more complex than this. We have seen that standing very close is a sign of intimacy and friendship much of the time. Far from being a hostile act, it is one of the most common ways of showing interest, attraction, and even love. Acquaintances stand closer than strangers, friends stand closer than acquaintances, and lovers stand closest of all. And even when a total stranger sits or stands extremely close to you, the act will sometimes be interpreted in a positive manner and sometimes in a negative, depending on circumstances and other actions by the "invader." Indeed, as the study described in the box indicates, we are sometimes more likely to offer help to someone who stands very close to us than to someone who keeps a more normal distance. Thus, there are no absolute rules about personal space, and there is certainly no reason to believe that standing very close will generally be interpreted as a hostile act.

CROWDING

One hundred million people every year; one billion people every ten years—that is the rate at which the population of the world is increasing. As you can see in Figure 16–4, it took tens of thousands of years for the world population to reach half a billion. Two hundred years passed before the population doubled and reached 1 billion. But the next doubling to 2 billion took only eighty years, and it doubled to 4 billion in only forty-five years. At the present rate of growth, the number of people on earth will double again and reach 8 billion in only thirty-five years.

Fortunately, we are beginning to see the first signs that the population explosion may be slowing down. The government of China, which has almost a quarter of the population of the world, is making a determined effort to reduce the birth rate. Other governments, including some in South America and Africa, which have traditionally had extremely high birth rates, are also beginning to encourage people to limit the size of their families. Probably the most promising sign is that women all over the world now seem to desire smaller families than they did in the past. Families in which women typically would have had seven or eight children twenty years ago now have only four or five. The difficulty is that women are not always able to achieve the reduction in family size that they desire. Even though many modern and traditional methods of birth control are available, an amazingly high percentage of women who would like to limit their family are not using any form of birth control. Moreover, in most instances this appears not to be caused by religious or moral conviction, but by ignorance of the techniques or simply their unavailability. Thus, although some optimistic signs have begun to appear, there is

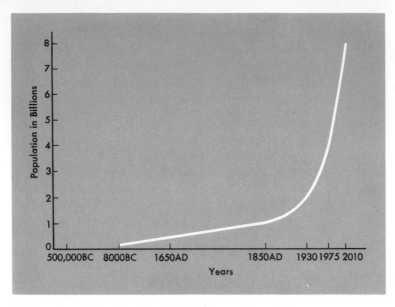

FIGURE 16–6 Growth of World Human Population

no question that, barring some catastrophe, the population of the world will continue to increase well into the twenty-first century and perhaps beyond that.

This population explosion has serious consequences for practically every aspect of our lives. It strains the economic resources of the world, exhausts natural resources, pushes up the cost of fuel, food, and every other necessary item, and leads to pollution. As populations increase, resources must be shared by more and more people. There is just so much good land, so much oil, so much wood for houses, and so on. In the United States, for example, the national parks are so crowded that it is practically "standing room only" in the more popular ones. They are still beautiful, but they are no longer a place to enjoy in solitude.

One of the consequences of the population explosion is that the concentration of people in and around cities is increasing steadily. Although the central cities have actually lost population over the past twenty or thirty years, the larger metropolitan areas have gained enormously. Most of the populations of the United States, Canada, and the other industrialized countries are concentrated in and around urban centers. Therefore, the question of how this might affect us is of more and more concern. Psychologists have become increasingly interested in this problem, to the point that in the past five years more research has been done on the effects of crowding on people than had been done in the previous fifty. Let us see what has been discovered.

It might not seem that we need to define what we mean by crowding, but it turns out to be quite important because the term has been used in two quite different ways. One is a feeling of being cramped and not having enough space. Obviously this feeling is unpleasant and is always negative. When we say that we are "crowded," we are almost always complaining. Moreover, this feeling of being crowded can occur regardless of the amount of space we actually have available. It is more likely to be aroused when we are cramped, but we sometimes feel crowded even when we have plenty of space around us. If you want to be entirely alone, the presence of even one other person would make you feel crowded. There are times when three is a crowd no matter how much space is available. If you like to swim at deserted beaches, the presence of a few other people may make you feel that the beach is overcrowded, whereas you would not feel crowded at a party even if there were fifty other people in a fairly small room. In other words, crowding sometimes refers to the psychological state of discomfort associated with wanting more space than is available regardless of the actual amount of space.

The other meaning of the term crowding concerns the physical situation itself. Crowding refers to the amount of space available per person. If there are ten square feet per person it is twice as crowded as when there are twenty square feet per person. This is a purely physical, objective definition and is often referred to as **density** or sometimes **spatial density** to distinguish it from the psychological state of feeling crowded. As Stokols (1972) and others have pointed out, it is essential to distinguish between crowding as a psychological feeling and crowding as a measure of the amount of space per person. While the former is a psychological state that is generally considered negative, the latter is a physical situation that is neutral. Indeed, as we shall see what effects density (crowding) has on people is an open question. Throughout this discussion, crowding will usually refer to physical density, the amount of space that is available, and not to a psychological state. When discussing the latter, we shall use the terms "perception of crowding" or "feeling crowded."

Crowding and Animals

Biologists and ethologists have done a great deal of research on how animals other than humans react to crowding. The work most well-known to psychologists consists of studies in which small groups of animals, usually rats or mice, are put in an enclosed space, provided with food, water, and other necessities, and otherwise left alone (Snyder, 1968; Southwick, 1955; Terman, 1974). Under these circumstances, a dramatic phenomenon occurs. The group behaves normally for a while and the population grows. Then, at some point, the population peaks and either stops growing or declines sharply. Instead of continuing to produce more offspring that survive, the animals sometimes cease reproducing at all or

BOX 16–3

THE NUMBER OF PEOPLE: SOCIAL DENSITY

Although most of the research on crowding has dealt with the amount of space available, a number of studies have concerned the number of people present rather than the amount of space they have. Regardless of the amount of space available, a situation in which only three or four people are present is quite different from one in which there are fifty. Having to interact with, or even be aware of, a large number of people is an important factor in any situation. This variable, the number of people present, is sometimes referred to as **social density.** Sometimes it is equated with crowding, or physical density, but this is an unfortunate confusion. Clearly the number of people present is quite a different concept from the amount of space each of them has.

Of course, in many situations we tend to have less space when more people are present. When ten people live in a house, the levels of both physical density and social density are higher than when only four people live in the same house. Increasing the number of people without increasing the amount of space results in less space per person as well as a larger number of people who have to intereact. However, physical density is often independent of the number of people present. Four people in a small house may have just as much space per person as eight people in a larger house. The number increases but the physical density remains constant. Similarly, a family of four will have less space per person in a small apartment than they will in a large one.

Thus, it is important to separate the effects of physical density from the number of people present. One of the few studies that has accomplished this was conducted by Nogami (1976), who had groups of either ten or four persons working in three rooms of different sizes. Because he varied both the size of the group and the amount of space, it was possible to look at the effect of physical density and group size separately. The results were that neither density nor group size had any effect on task performance, but that larger groups generally reacted more negatively to the situation than smaller ones. Actual physical density had little effect on any of the measures. However, only one study has obtained these results, and it would be a mistake to draw conclusions from it. Other work suggests that group size may be an important factor in social situations, but as yet there is too little research for us to know.

produce offspring that die very soon. In other words, the animals' normal reproductive functions are severely disrupted merely because they are enclosed in a limited area.

In addition, there is substantial evidence that animals living under conditions of high density, or simply being enclosed, suffer physiological damage. Their adrenal glands become enlarged (Christian, 1975; Christian, Flyger, & Davis, 1960; Terman, 1969; To & Tamarin, 1977). Their reproductive organs decrease in size or in activity (Davis & Meyer, 1973; Snyder, 1968; Southwick & Bland, 1959; Thiessen, 1964). And other, though less consistent glandular changes may occur (see Christian, 1975, for a review).

Finally, there is some evidence that social behavior is also affected. In a famous series of studies, Calhoun (1962) placed rats in cages that were specifically designed to produce very high densities in certain areas. The animals in these high-density central cages exhibited a wide range of abnormal behavior. They fought violently, mated indiscriminately, trampled nests and the young that were in them, and failed to build adequate nests in the first place. Calhoun called this phenomenon of anti-social and disruptive behavior a **behavioral sink.** Although other work (e.g., Terman, 1974) has failed to find these effects on aggressiveness, there is little doubt that under some circumstances high density does cause a breakdown in normal social behavior.

At first glance, these findings seem to indicate that the animals are being adversely affected by high density. Their reproductive behavior is reduced, their adrenal glands and sexual organs function abnormally, and they sometimes fight more than usual. Yet, the actual story is more complicated and less clear than it might seem. To begin with, most of the effects appear to be only marginally related to the amount of space available. The effects occur in both small and large cages, with the actual density mattering very little. Terman (1974) doubled the size of his cages and found no beneficial effects; Christian (1955) compared small cages with cages forty-two times as large and found no differences in the size of the adrenal glands. In both of these studies, the critical factors are that the animals are enclosed and that they are in groups. Animals alone in cages do not show these effects; but regardless of the size of the cages, animals in groups do suffer negative effects. Thus, within broad limits, it is not the physical density that causes the harm (though social density, the number of animals, may be the crucial variable).

On the other hand, density is not entirely unrelated to the negative effects. Clearly, the living space must be somewhat limited in order for the effects to appear. If the animals had been given a cage the size of Utah, presumably they would not have felt enclosed and there would be no harm done. That is, a certain degree of crowding is necessary for the negative effects to appear, but the relationship between density and these effects is not simple. At the extremes, density becomes important. When the animals are so crowded that they can barely move around, as in Calhoun's behavioral sink, negative effects almost always appear. This is an unnatural situation that almost never occurs in the real world, but it does indicate that density can be harmful if it is high enough. At the other extreme, when density is so low that the animals need not even interact, the presence of other animals is essentially irrelevant. Density, therefore, does not necessarily have negative effects on nonhuman animals, and when it does, the relationship between density and negative effects is complex (Freedman, 1979).

In any case, humans are not rats. We have much more complex social systems, higher levels of cognitive functioning, all sorts of rules and laws and customs with which to deal with the environment, and a flexible system of communication with other people. Generalizing from the results of work on other animals to humans is always both difficult and questionable. This is particularly true when complicated social factors and interpersonal relations are involved. As the noted biologist René Dubos has said:

> The readiness with which man adapts to potentially dangerous situations makes it unwise to apply directly to human life the results of experiments designed to test the acute effects of crowding on animals (1970, p. 207).

Thus, although this work on other animals is suggestive, we must look at research on humans to discover how they respond to crowding.

CROWDING AND PEOPLE

The effect of density on people has been one of the most active areas of research in social psychology over the past ten years. Fifteen years ago there was barely a handful of studies on this important topic; now there are literally hundreds of studies that have investigated the problem from many different points of view. The work by social psychologists has been supplemented by research done by urban sociologists and urban geographers, who have conducted some of the best large-scale studies. Although there are still many unanswered questions, we are now beginning to understand how density affects people. However, a considerable amount of controversy surrounds the interpretation of the findings in this area. Some psychologists believe that high density is generally harmful to people, while others strongly disagree. We feel that most of the evidence favors the latter position. Crowding is far less harmful than was previously imagined, and indeed, high density (within broad limits) is neither good nor bad for people. Rather, its effect depends on other factors in the situation. As with personal space, to which it is related, high density can have positive, negative, or even neutral consequences that are determined largely by the particular situation and the people involved.

**Crowding
in the
Real World**

Sociologists and social psychologists have investigated the relationships between living conditions and pathology in natural settings. The standard procedure is to obtain some measure of crowding—either the number of people per square mile or the amount of space available per person in the home—then get measures of various pathologies for the same communities or neighborhoods and see if high density is associated with high levels of pathology.

Several studies concentrated on the largest metropolitan areas of the United States. The measure of density was the number of people per square mile. In other words, this type of study was concerned simply with how many people lived within the boundaries of the city relative to the size of the city and how this measure of density correlated with the amount of crime committed in the cities. It was found (Freedman, Heshka, & Levy, 1973; Pressman & Carol, 1971) that there was a small but significant correlation between density and crime when only those two factors were considered (r = about .35). Of course, density tends to be highly correlated with other factors such as income, and it in turn is also highly correlated with crime rate. It is therefore impossible to tell from the simple correlation whether density causes crime or whether some other factor, such as income, leads to both higher density and higher crime rates. In order to assess this, it is necessary to control for income and other social factors and then look at the remaining relationship between density and crime. When this is done by the use of partial correlations or multiple regressions, the relationship between density and crime disappears. Across the major metropolitan areas in the country, once income is controlled, there seems to be little relationship between density and crime rate. For example, Los Angeles has one of the lowest densities but has one of the highest crime rates in the United States.

In addition, there have been studies of individual cities along much the same lines. Honolulu, Chicago, and New York have all been investigated to see whether density is associated with juvenile delinquency, mental illness, or any other kind of pathology. Although the results are not perfectly consistent, by and large they show the same patterns found across the metropolitan areas. In Honolulu (Schmitt, 1957, 1966), Chicago (Winsborough, 1965; Galle et al., 1972), and New York (Freedman, Heshka, & Levy, 1975), there were strong, simple correlations between population density and various measures of pathology. In these studies density was measured not only by population per acre but also by the number of rooms per person in their dwellings. Thus they were measuring not only the number of people that lived in a particular area, but also how much space people had in their own homes. However, no matter how density was measured, once income and other social factors were controlled, the relationships between density and pathology tended to disappear. The one exception was in Honolulu, where they remained substantial; but in all the other studies the partial correlations were essentially zero.

These studies all dealt with grouped data—they looked at large numbers of people at once. This is an efficient procedure, but there is always the chance that crowding is having serious effects on some people and not on others. Fortunately, two studies interviewed a great many people individually. Probably the most impressive research of this type was conducted by Mitchell (1971), who went into a vast number of homes in Hong Kong, one of the most crowded communities in the world. He measured the exact size of each family's living space, computed the density of the home, and took measures of anxiety, nervousness, and various other kinds of mental strain. He found no appreciable relationship between density and pathology. In a similar though less ambitious study, Booth and his associates (1974) focused primarily on physical measures but also obtained some indications of mental and social adjustment. Again, there were no appreciable consistent negative (or positive) effects of crowding. Thus, according to both survey and individual data, people who live in high-density communities or neighborhoods or who have little space in their homes are no worse off in terms of mental, social, or physical pathology than people who live under conditions of lower density.

This may seem surprising, but remember that a great many people, indeed most of the population of the industrialized world, does live under quite high density. New York, Chicago, Toronto, and other great North American cities have high population densities, and yet most of the people in these cities seem to function well. The incidence of mental disturbance is no higher in cities than in smaller communities (Srole, 1972; Schwab et al., 1972). People in cities are no more likely to commit suicide than people in smaller communities (Gibbs, 1971). In fact, urban people say that they are just as happy as people who live in suburbs, small towns, or rural areas (Shaver & Freedman, 1976). In a recent book on the urban experience, Claude Fischer writes that he found ". . . little evidence that urbanites are more stressed, disordered, alienated, or unhappy than ruralites" (1976, p. 177). As we shall see, there is reason to believe that some people do well in crowded conditions while others do poorly, and that under some circumstances, crowding can be harmful just as it can sometimes be beneficial. But crowding is not the generally harmful factor it is often thought to be.

However, it still seems to most people that being in a crowded environment is different from being in an uncrowded one. Psychologists have therefore attempted to discover how this difference affects behavior and reactions of all kinds. To do this, investigators have turned to more controlled experiments in laboratories or other settings.

Experimental Research: Short-Term Crowding

Although some cities are densely populated, very few people actually spend their whole lives under crowded conditions. They may live or work with many other people in a small area, but they also spend time on the street, in parks, and in other situations of relatively low density. Thus, even for people who live in the most crowded cities, such as New York or Hong Kong, exposure to really high levels of density occurs sporadically and for short periods. For example, a New Yorker may find himself in a crowded elevator or subway for a brief period, on a crowded sidewalk while going to work, or in a packed department store. These encounters are due to the high level of population density in the city. Yet, this high level makes itself felt primarily through these short incidents rather than through constant exposure to crowding. Therefore, experiments dealing with short-term crowding may be helpful in telling us how crowding in the real world affects us. In any case, this experimental approach is the only way at the moment to investigate the problem in detail.

The standard procedure for almost all the experimental work is to put some people in a small room, the same number of people in a large room, and look for any differences on a wide variety of measures. The one clear finding from this research is consistent with the results from survey studies described above: crowding is not generally harmful to people. Although the research has produced a complex pattern of results, virtually all the experiments show no overall negative effect of crowding. People in small rooms respond just as positively as people in larger rooms. Increasing the density does not lead to a decrement in any measure that has been taken. As we shall see, this does not mean that crowding is good for people, nor that it never has bad effects. What it means is that the effects are complicated and depend on the circumstances.

Task Performance

Quite a few studies have investigated task performance under crowded and uncrowded conditions. There are two reasons why this is an important question. The first is a practical one: people often work under high-density conditions, and we would like to know how this affects their performance. If it turned out that high density interfered with their work, presumably managers in factories, offices, and other workplaces would try to reduce density in order to improve performance. The second reason for studying this is theoretical: It is well established that when people are under stress or are aroused for any reason, they tend to do less well on difficult and complex tasks, though they often perform better on easy, familiar tasks. Thus, if people perform less well on complex tasks when they are crowded, this would indicate that high density is stressful or arousing. However, most of the research indicates that high density has little or no effect on task performance.

Freedman, Klevansky, and Ehrlich (1971) had hundreds of subjects of various ages and backgrounds work on many different tasks. Some subjects worked under very crowded conditions (as high as 3 to 4 square feet per person), whereas others had lots of space. There were no consistent differences of any kind. This finding has been repeated by many other experimenters (e.g., Griffitt & Veitch, 1971; Stokols et al., 1973; Nogami, 1976). Moreover, people who are totally isolated from the world under very high density for periods as long as twenty days also perform tasks perfectly well. Isolation studies of this sort have been conducted in connection with air raid shelters, submarine warfare, and the space program. Although not everyone who partipates enjoys the experience, and some cannot last the full time, most people do just fine and perform at a high level (Smith & Haythorn, 1972). This is hardly surprising, since we have dramatic proof of people's ability to function under these conditions from both submarines and the space program. The astronauts are obviously highly motivated and well trained. Nevertheless, it is worth noting that at least some members of our species can perform complex and tedious tasks while cooped up in a tiny capsule for many weeks.

However, one study (Paulus et al., 1976) did find that males performed less well under high density whereas females performed slightly better; and Evans (1979) also found negative effects on task performance. These results are at odds with virtually all of the other research. Nevertheless, they suggest that perhaps for some people high density will disrupt performance. In addition, the Paulus study raises the possibility that there may be important sex differences in response to crowding, a finding that we shall discuss in more detail later.

Although the work on task performance generally indicates little negative effect of high density, high density will sometimes interfere with a task. Whenever the particular job requires a lot of room or moving around, and whenever the presence of other individuals in a small space directly interferes with the performance of the task, performance will be hurt. Heller, Groff, and Sullivan (1977) demonstrated this; and McCallum and associates (1979) showed that when the resources available were inadequate for the number of people, performance suffered. Obviously, other people can get in the way if there is not enough space. You cannot play a good game of tennis if there are forty people on the court; nine people cannot play the same piano simultaneously (or at least they will not play it very well); and even reading a newspaper on a bus is difficult if you are so crowded that you cannot turn the pages. This is not a psychological effect in the usual sense of the word. Rather, it is a purely physical consequence of not having adequate space to perform a particular task. That is, these results do not indicate that high density is stressful or has any psychological effects on the individuals, which is really what we are interested in.

Physiological Effects

Although crowding is not usually a stressor, it can sometimes produce physiological arousal. Several experiments have taken physiological measures of people who are in high- and low-density situations. At least some of these studies have found that people are more aroused when they are crowded (Aiello et al., 1975; Evans, 1979).

How can we reconcile this with the lack of effect on performance in most studies? The answer seems to be that crowding may not usually be arousing, but can be under the right circumstances. In particular, in some of these studies the degree of crowding is extremely high—6 people in a room only 4 feet by 4 feet. In addition, the subjects were told that the study concerned their responses to the room and were given no explanation for being in such a tiny room. With their attention drawn to the room, with no reason for being in it, and with no social interaction among the subjects, the physical fact of being crowded becomes more important than it usually would be, and the people are annoyed or aroused by it. In other words, crowding can sometimes be unpleasant, and these experiments have managed to make it extreme enough to bring about this reaction. It is important to realize that crowding does not ordinarily produce arousal but that it can. Once again, the crucial question is when it has this effect and when it does not.

Social Effects

It seems that crowding would be more likely to affect social behavior than task performance. After all, when people are in close proximity to each other, their social relationships may change in response to the situation. Actually, research on this issue has found no consistent overall effects of density on social behavior. People in crowded conditions are not in general more aggressive, more friendly, more nervous, or less happy than people under less crowded conditions. In the isolation studies mentioned earlier (Smith & Haythorn, 1972), subjects who had less room were somewhat less hostile than others, but there were no major effects. Studies on adults (Freedman et al., 1972; Freedman, 1975; Nogami, 1976; Ross et al., 1973; Stokols et al., 1973) have found no consistent differences between high- and low-density conditions. The findings regarding children's reactions to variations in density are somewhat less consistent. Several studies (Ginsburg et al., 1977; Smith & Connelly, 1972) observed children in playgrounds or school playrooms. Ginsberg found that boys engaged in more fighting in smaller playgrounds, although the fights did not last as long as they did in larger areas. In contrast, a series of careful observations by Peter Smith indicated no effect of density on the amount of fighting. Rohe and Patterson (1974) suggest that as long as there are adequate facilities and toys, the amount of space makes little difference. This seems to have been supported by two studies (Loo & Kennelly, 1979; Loo & Smetana, 1978) that found little overall effect of density on aggressiveness, anger, happiness, or positive group interactions among preschoolers and ten-year-old boys.

Thus, with a few exceptions, this work indicates that generally there are few overall effects of variations in density on social behavior or mood. When less space is combined with reduced facilities, the effect may be negative. And we should remember that this often occurs in the world. People who have less space in their homes, for example, typically have fewer facilities as well. Children who are provided a tiny playroom in a poorly equipped school are probably also given relatively few toys to play with. But the negative consequences then are due mainly to the poor facilities, not to the lack of space. On the other hand, to return to a point made earlier, some games cannot be played in too small a space. Basketball and running games require a large play area. In these instances, high density will interfere with the games and may accordingly reduce the fun. However, as we shall see, high density does have substantial effects that depend on other factors in the situation.

Sex Differences   Several experiments have demonstrated that responses to high density may depend on the gender of the subjects. In two experiments (Freedman et al., 1972), all-male or all-female groups were put in high- or low-density conditions and various measures were taken of their competitiveness and the severity of sentencing they gave in a mock jury situation. It was found that men tended to respond more competitively and to give more severe sentences in the high-density condition than they did in the low-density condition. Women were actually less competitive and gave milder sentences under conditions of high density. Figure 16–7 shows the results of the jury study. In addition, the men in the group liked each other less under conditions of high than low density, and the women liked each other more under conditions of high density. In mixed-sex groups, there were no effects of density.

Other research has also found sex differences in response to crowding, but the effects are not entirely consistent. Most of the studies find that males are more sensitive to density than females, and that males tend to respond more negatively (Ross et al., 1973; Stokols et al., 1973; Paulus, 1976). However, at least one study showed that males reacted more

FIGURE 16–7 The effect of density on severity of sentences given by all male, all-female, and mixed-sex groups. Females give less severe sentences, males more severe in high-density situations. The effect in this study is much stronger for females than for males.

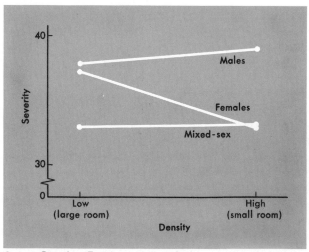

Source: Based on Freedman et al. (1972).

positively (Loo, 1972). In this experiment, groups of young children were put in same-sex groups in either large or small rooms and their behavior was observed. Girls were unaffected by the size of the room, whereas boys became less aggressive in a smaller room. But in another study by the same author (Loo & Kennelly, 1979) the pattern was almost exactly reversed; boys became slightly more aggressive in a small room, and girls slightly less aggressive. Finally, Marshall and Heslin (1975) found a very complex relationship between sex of the subjects, whether or not the sexes were mixed, and density. Thus, although there is a tendency for males to be somewhat more sensitive to density and to respond negatively whereas females respond positively to high density, there is considerable inconsistency. Accordingly, it seems likely that the effects are due not to some basic difference between the sexes in their response to density, but to some more general explanation.

THEORIES OF CROWDING

A number of explanations of crowding effects have been proposed. It is inaccurate to call them theories because they are tentative hypotheses rather than well-formulated explanations. But whatever they are called, they are attempts to come to grips with the findings we have described above.

**Sensory
Overload
and Stimulation
Level**

Stanley Milgram (1970) has discussed crowding in terms of what he calls **sensory overload.** Whenever people are exposed to too much stimulation, they experience sensory overload and can no longer deal with all the stimulation. Sensory overload is unpleasant and obviously would interfere with a person's ability to function properly. Therefore, people deal with overload by screening out some stimulation and attending only to what is most important. According to this notion, crowding is one source of stimulation and can sometimes produce overload. When it does, people are upset, under stress, and will "turn off" their attention.

Although Milgram has made no attempt to relate this idea to the results of crowding research, it might explain some of these findings. For example, men may be less able to deal with large amounts of stimulation than women. As density increases, the men are overloaded sooner and therefore respond more negatively. Similarly, high density may sometimes not reach the level where overload occurs and therefore may produce no negative effects. Unfortunately, this does not explain why high density sometimes produces positive effects nor why women generally respond positively. In addition, it says nothing about when overload will occur and when it will not. Perhaps additional research will relate this idea more closely to crowding effects. For the moment, it is a provocative notion with little or no research to support it.

On the other hand, a closely related idea does explain many of the crowding results. Assume that everyone has some level of stimulation that he or she finds pleasant and agreeable. Some people like high levels of stimulation—they like the radio blaring all the time, studying in busy rooms, and watching television while carrying on a conversation or doing the crossword puzzle. Others like low levels of stimulation. When they work, it has to be quiet; if they watch television they do not want any other distractions; and their idea of a perfect environment is a quiet spot somewhere. The high-stimulation people find high density pleasant and exciting; the low-stimulation people find it unpleasant and disruptive, simply because high density is the right level of stimulation for the former and too high for the latter. Although there is no direct support for this idea, one study (Loo & Smetana, 1978) provides some results consistent with it. Boys were classified as liking close or distant personal space and were then put in high- or low-density situations. Among strangers, those who liked close personal space reacted more positively in the small room than the large room, whereas the boys who liked distant space preferred the low- density large room. In other words, the density situation had different effects depending on preference for personal space.

These individual differences in preferences for high- and low-density situations may help us understand the diverse findings on the effects of crowding. Men and women may differ in the level of stimulation they prefer; different groups may have different preferences; and the preferences themselves may vary somewhat depending on the particular situation (e.g., someone hates distractions when working on a task but does not mind them if he is only engaging in social conversation). Once again, this idea does not specify when high density will have positive, negative, or neutral effects, but it does provide a framework in which to consider individual differences in response to crowding. It would also explain why some people like cities and others dislike them. Presumably, those who like high levels of stimulation will find cities exciting whereas those who like low levels will be bothered by the variety and the number of activities.

Density-Intensity

A different explanation of the various effects of crowding is that high density intensifies the usual reactions to a social situation. The idea (Freedman, 1975) is that the presence of other people is one stimulus in the situation and that increasing the density increases its importance. Just as turning up the volume on a hi-fi set magnifies our reaction to music, so increasing density magnifies our reaction to other people. If we are listening to music at a low volume, making it louder will intensify our reactions. If we dislike the music, we will dislike it more when it is loud than when it is soft; if we like it, we will like it more when it is loud. Similarly, whatever our response to other people who are near us, increasing density intensifies that response. If we like them, we will like them more; if we

A number of authors have suggested that one effect of high density is to make people feel that they have less control over their actions. The idea is that with so many people in a small space, each individual is less able to control the situation, to move around freely, to avoid contact if desired, and generally less able to determine for himself the level of social interaction that occurs. Since people usually want as much control as possible over their lives, a powerless feeling is a possible negative effect of being in a high-density situation. One study did show that people feel more crowded when they have less control (Rodin, Sullivan, & Metcalf, 1978); and another (Langer & Saegert, 1977) demonstrated that telling subjects that they might feel uncomfortable because of crowding reduces the negative effect of high density. Neither study is convincing, and certainly we should not expect that being aware of the number of people present will necessarily give a person greater sense of control.

However, as Sherrod and Cohen (1979) suggest, another aspect of control is how well a person can predict what the situation is going to be. Presumably if you find yourself in a situation that you did not expect, you may respond more negatively or at least be temporarily somewhat confused. With this in mind, Kline and Harris (1979) had subjects anticipate either a crowded or an uncrowded room and then either confirmed or did not confirm their expectations. The results were that the degree of crowding by itself had no effect. Instead, when subjects expected to be crowded and were crowded or expected not to be crowded and were not, they did better than if their expectations were not confirmed. In other words, there were no negative effects of being in a crowded room as long as it was anticipated.

dislike them, we will dislike them more. If we are afraid, nervous, angry, aggressive, friendly, or anything else under low density, we will feel more of it under high density.

According to this view, the sex differences would be due to different initial reactions to the situation. All-male groups in our society tend to be somewhat suspicious and competitive, so increasing density makes them more competitive and aggressive; all-female groups respond to each other with more friendliness and intimacy, and increasing density makes them friendlier and more cooperative. The inconsistent results are caused by differences in the specific situations. Some elicit negative responses by one sex or the other, and some produce no sex differences under low density. When density is increased, the usual reactions are magnified. But since the typical reactions vary, the effect of density also varies. Some

FIGURE 16–8 Not all crowds have bad effects. This game would be less exciting for the fans if there were many fewer people in the stands.

direct support for this view is provided by a series of studies by Freedman, Heshka, Levy, and staff (Freedman, 1975). In this work, situations are deliberately made either pleasant or unpleasant for both sexes. Increasing density should intensify the responses of both sexes, making the pleasant situation more pleasant and the unpleasant more unpleasant, regardless of sex of subject or whether the groups are mixed. That is what these studies show.

This explanation of the effect of crowding seems to fit quite nicely into our everyday experience. Sometimes crowding is unpleasant and sometimes it is pleasant, but generally it does appear to intensify the social situation. Riding a bus is not especially pleasant. If the bus is crowded, it usually becomes more unpleasant. More to the point, if there are six people in a bus, it does not matter too much who the other people are. They may be frightening or interesting, but scattered around a bus, they have little effect. Now imagine the same six people in a car. Their characteristics become much more important and our reactions are greatly magnified. If they are frightening, it is much more frightening to be in a car with them; if they are interesting, it is much nicer to be in the car. Or consider a party. If there are only twenty people in a huge room, the party tends to be flat, unexciting, and dull. In fact, under these circumstances people will usually collect in the kitchen or at one end of the room. The same twenty people in a small room will make a much better party, assuming of course that they are pleasant people. If they are unpleasant, the small room will produce a less pleasant experience than the large room. In other words, basically positive situations usually become more positive when density is increased; negative ones become more negative.

This density-intensity notion is consistent with most of the findings and seems to provide a plausible explanation. However, it is still in the speculative stage and much more work is necessary in order to test it. Also, the various theories we have described are by no means contradictory. It seems likely that crowding does sometimes cause overload or at least discomfort due to an inability to deal with the situation; that people do have different preferences for levels of stimulation and those who like high levels will respond more positively to high density; and that high density increases the importance of the other people and therefore intensifies our reactions to them. As with personal space, our reactions to crowding depend on the situation and our interpretation of it.

ARCHITECTURAL DESIGN

One of the most fascinating questions facing environmental psychologists is how the design of buildings, roads, and shopping centers affects us. Certainly the structures we produce, the so called "built environment," are an extremely important part of our world. And some of them seem to "work" better than others. Some houses are pleasant to be in and function smoothly, while others do not. Some stores minimize congestion and generally make the shopping experience relatively pleasant, while others have the reverse effect. And the same is true about virtually every other structure that we build. Architects are deeply concerned with making their designs work well, but by and large they have to rely entirely on their own intuitions and experiences. Until very recently there was no systematic research on how design affects people, and even now psychologists and sociologists are only beginning to study the problem seriously. But at least they are beginning to understand some of the ways in which design influences people, and perhaps soon they will be able to give some guidance to architects that is based on solid research. For the moment most of the reseach done by psychologists has been on the structure of dormitories (obviously of interest to many people at universities) and high-rise vs. low-rise housing.

**Dormitory
Design**

College dormitories generally are built according to two different designs. The more traditional type has single or double rooms located along a corridor, with social areas and bathrooms shared by all the residents on the corridor. Some newer dormitories have suites of rooms consisting of several bedrooms located around a common living room, usually with the residents of just these bedrooms sharing bathroom facilities. The amount of space available to each resident (and therefore the density) is approximately the same for the two designs. Yet the two kinds of designs seem to have different effects on the residents.

A series of studies (Baum & Valins, 1976; Baum et al., 1978) compared the corridor and suite arrangements. The research indicates that students who live in suite-type dormitories are more sociable and friendlier. At first glance, this seems obvious. Clearly, if you share a living room with, say, nine other people (five bedrooms with two people each), you will get to know these nine other students. In a sense, you have a "family" living situation. If you share a room with only one person, it takes greater effort to get to know other people on the floor. As we discussed in Chapter 6, proximity is one of the major factors in liking and friendship. The suite arrangement puts more people in close proximity and therefore should lead to more friendships. Thus far, this follows directly from our knowledge of the effects of proximity and certainly would be expected. The striking aspect of Baum's and Valins's work is that these sociability differences seem to carry over into the world outside the dormitory. When the students are observed in the psychology laboratory, the suite residents are friendlier than the corridor residents. For example, in one study a student arrived at the laboratory and was shown into a room in which another student (actually a confederate) was sitting. There were several chairs in the room and the question was how close to the other student the subject would sit. Suite residents tended to sit closer than corridor residents, and to initiate more conversations.

Baum and Valins have explained these results in terms of the degree of control that the residents have over their social contacts. They argue that in the corridor-design dormitories, the students are constantly being required to meet and interact with many others on their floor. When they walk to the bathroom or common lounge areas, they necessarily share the corridor and facilities with many others, most of whom are not friends and with whom they might prefer not to interact. Thus, they are overloaded with social contacts and have difficulty avoiding them. In contrast, those who live in suites have a self-contained living unit that they share only with people whom they get to know quite well. If they desire, they need have very little to do with anyone else on the floor. They therefore have much more control over their social interactions, which presumably increases their satisfaction with their residences and their general sense of control over their lives.

This is still a speculative idea. The explanation of the effects of dormitory design may be much simpler. For example, it might be argued that students simply prefer to have private bathrooms and livingrooms, not because of any sense of control, but merely because they want privacy and a sense of ownership over their living space. We know that people who stay in hotels generally prefer private baths to ones they share with others, and it seems likely that this preference is due to considerations other than control.

One of the difficulties with this kind of research (and the work on high-rise housing to be discussed next) is that the people in the two types of dormitories may be somewhat different even before they move in. Although assignment to dormitories at the college is supposed to be entirely random, it is hard to be certain of this. If, for any reason, more sociable people are placed in suite-type dormitories, obviously the differences Baum and Valins found would be due to the initial difference, not to the effect of the dormitory design. Although the authors have tried to eliminate this possibility, the one control study that deals with the problem is not entirely convincing. Thus, the possibility remains that the dormitories are not having the reported effects. Despite this problem, the research is exactly the kind we need to discover how architectural design affects people.

High-Rise Versus Low-Rise Housing

Although students are naturally quite concerned about dormitory design, a much more serious problem for our society is how high-rise housing affects people. During the 1950s and 1960s, a vast number of high-rise buildings were constructed for our rapidly expanding population. Some of these buildings are huge: thirty or forty stories with hundreds or even thousands of individual apartments; others are smaller. But all of them contrast sharply with one- or two-story private homes or four- or five-story apartment houses. It has become a matter of great social importance to determine whether high-rise housing of this sort is a good environment in which to live.

Some of these buildings have been failures. They have gotten run down, the halls have been defaced, the apartments have been allowed to deteriorate, crime and vandalism have made the buildings unsafe, and people have moved out whenever they were able. The most dramatic example of this kind of failure is the Pruitt Igoe project in St. Louis, which was eventually demolished by the city because no one was willing to live in it any more. This huge, multimillion dollar housing project was a total loss. Other buildings may not reach quite this point, but clearly some of them have not worked well. On the other hand, we know also that most of the buildings, both public and private, have been successful at least to the extent that people continue to live in them and function reasonably well. The issue is whether high- or low-rise buildings have different effects on the residents, and in particular whether high-rise housing is harmful.

Almost all the work on this question has been done by urban sociologists, but social psychologists are now beginning to become involved as well. The research results indicate that high-rise housing does not generally have any harmful effects. Studies by Holahan and Wilcox (1979) and by McCarthy and Saegert (1978) found negative effects of high-rise housing. Residents of high rises were generally less satisfied with their buildings and less happy with their social relationships with other tenants. A controversial study by Oscar Newman (1973) also found more crime in high-rise housing, but his study contains so many methodological errors and unsupported conclusions that serious scientists have generally rejected it.

FIGURE 16—9 High-rise housing often replaces run-down low-rise housing. It is difficult to assess the effects of type of house, because you are also comparing new with old.

In direct contrast with those negative findings, most studies have found no harmful effects of high-rise housing. A recent study by Larry Friedman (1979) compared residents of many high-rise and low-rise buildings in New York City and found very few differences. The few differences that did emerge tended to favor the high-rise rather than the low-rise buildings. In fact, high-rise residents felt safer, more content with various aspects of their buildings, liked the other people who lived in them more, and were more likely to rely on neighbors when they needed to borrow something such as food items.

Sociologists such as Michelson (1977), who have done large-scale studies of urban housing, generally conclude that there are few important differences between high-rise and low-rise living. As Barry Welman (1974), an expert on this issue, notes, "there is no convincing evidence that the experience of living in high-rise buildings is pathological. The residents of such dwellings are similar to other urbanites in their ability to form networks of social relationships, in their involvement in urban institutions, and in their mental health." Thus, despite some evidence to the contrary, it seems that there is no overall difference in health or general well-being between those who live in high-rise housing and those who live in low-rise housing.

On the other hand, it is important to keep in mind that high-rise housing (or for that matter any kind of housing) may not be suitable for everyone. Although none of the research produced consistent differences between high- and low-rise housing, there is no question that some people prefer one or the other. In particular, parents with young children often complain that high-rise housing presents great difficulties in supervising the children (Michelson, 1970). Someone who lives on the twentieth floor cannot watch a child in the playground on the street floor. Many parents are reluctant to let their young children ride elevators alone, so that even if they can play on the street, it is inconvenient to get them there. Perhaps because of this, residents of high-rise housing generally are less satisfied with their housing than are people who live in their own homes. Moreover, high-rise residents do not value the friendliness of their neighborhood as much (Wellman, 1974). None of these differences is large or related to any noticeable differences in health or general satisfaction, but the differences do exist. In other words, people complain more about high-rise housing even though the research has not shown any actual negative effects.

As with the dormitory design studies, work on high-rise housing faces enormous difficulty in equating the residents of the various kinds of buildings. People are not randomly assigned to housing in our society, so that residents of different buildings almost always differ in potentially important ways. For example, in Wellman's study high-rise residents were of a somewhat higher socioeconomic class than low-rise; in Michelson's study, people in high rises were generally younger than those who lived in their own homes. In cities like New York that have many high-rise apartments, upper, middle, and working-class families live in high-rise buildings. It is worth noting that many people who can afford to live anywere choose to live in a high-rise building in the middle of New York City. In other words, high-rise buildings are not only for low-income families. On the other hand, the middle and upper classes do generally have a choice, whereas the poorer families often are forced to live in a high-rise because it is the only housing available. This lack of choice may itself cause problems, and it should therefore probably be a matter of public policy to provide choice for all people. That is, if we continue to build high-rise apartments for low-income people, we should also provide the alternative of low-rise buildings for these same people. Although high-rise buildings may not have any negative effect, being forced to live in one (or to live anywhere with no choice) may be harmful. And it is probably no accident that most of the difficulty with high-rise housing has occurred in buildings that are entirely or primarily for low-income families.

LIFE IN THE CITY

As we said earlier, the United States and Canada are largely urban societies, with more than 70 percent of the population living in or around cities. It is therefore both relevant and important to ask how living in a city differs from living elsewhere. This question is especially appropriate now. In addition to financial problems, our cities are beset by high crime rates, rundown schools, heavy welfare rolls, unemployment, and generally low morale. Moreover, there appears to be, at least in the United States, a pervasive anticity feeling among many people. When I mention that I live in New York City, people often look at me with either sympathy or horror. They wonder how I can stand it and why I have not ended up in a mental hospital or the morgue. Yet, most of our population is urban and somehow most of us survive. In fact, as we shall see, living in a city has no negative psychological or physical effects on people. City life may be dangerous at times, it may not be to everyone's liking, but it is not harmful to mind or body.

The first point to make is to repeat what we said in the sections on crowding and noise. These two factors, so typical of cities, are the ones most often thought to be harmful, but they have few if any negative effects on people. High density, either in a neighborhood or a crowded apartment, has no overall harmful consequences (Freedman, 1975). It is not associated with higher rates of crime, mental illness, infant mortality, or any kind of disease. People who live in crowded conditions are just as healthy, physically, mentally, and socially, as people who live under less crowded conditions. Similarly, noise has a much less negative effect than most of us would have thought (Glass & Singer, 1972). Very loud noise does produce an immediate minor decrement in performance, but this soon disappears. Long-term exposure to loud noise may have some bad effects, but people generally adapt to loud noise quite easily.

On the other hand, we have noted that unpredictable and uncontrollable noise seems to be more irritating and might have long-term negative effects. This kind of noise occurs in some cities. If they are drilling the street outside your apartment, you are exposed to occasional bursts of very loud noise. The same is true if there is construction going on nearby, if you live on a quiet street that has a few trucks passing by, and so on. People who live in cities get used to a much higher level of noise than people who live in smaller communities, but it is probably the sudden changes from the usual level that are disturbing. However, we have no idea just how harmful this kind of noise can be, and there is little reason to believe that it has major effects.

The next point to make is that people who live in the city do not have any higher rates of mental disturbance than those who live in small towns, or even in rural communities (Srole, 1972). It might seem that there would be more stress in the city, but whether or not there is, it does not produce more disturbance. The rates of psychosis are about the same everywhere, including primitive societies; and there are no substantial differences in neurosis. Furthermore, city people do not feel any more anxious or unhappy than other people. In a survey of a large number of Americans (Shaver & Freedman, 1976), those who lived in cities said that they were just as happy and calm as those who lived in small towns or rural areas. The study found that the particular type of community, urban, suburban, town, or rural, mattered very little in terms of health, psychological well-being, or anything else.

It has been suggested that the large population and high density of cities make social relationships more difficult. The great sociologist Georg Simmel (1903) thought that city residents would be so overloaded by superficial social contacts that they would have fewer intimate friends than those who live in smaller communities. Other sociologists have agreed with this observation. However, the research findings directly contradict it. For example, a study by McCauley and Taylor (1976) compared residents of a large city with those of a small town and found that city residents had fewer personal conversations during the course of a day, but that they tended to be longer. In other words, it was the reverse of what Simmel predicted—the city people had a small number of long-standing contacts. The study found no difference in the intimacy of these conversations and found that city and town residents were equally satisfied with the number of friends that they had and the intimacy of their friendships. Other research has generally supported this finding. If anything, it appears that city people have more close friends than town people. Obviously a city resident sees more strangers during the course of a day than someone who lives in a small town. But social relationships seem to be fairly similar in either place, and there is no evidence that there are any important differences in satisfaction with friendship networks.

One characteristic of cities is that they tend to be more accepting of diversity than are smaller communities. We all know that cities tend to attract deviants of all kinds and also to treat these deviants better than smaller communities. (By **deviants** we mean only people who are different from the average of the community; we are not implying anything about their behavior, beliefs, or attitudes.) The fact of the matter is that the populations of small towns tend to be more homogeneous than those of big cities with respect to race, religion, ethnic background, sexual preference, political views, and just about anything else you can think of. This is not because cities produce deviancy, but rather they allow it and therefore deviants move to cities because they are more accepted there. There is also more open deviancy in cities than in small towns, where it must often remain hidden. In fact, one study (Hansson & Slade, 1977) demonstrated that city people are more altruistic toward deviants than are people in small towns. In this study, the experimenters dropped letters that were addressed to either an anonymous individual, someone who is apparently performing at something called the Pink Panther Lounge, or to the communist party headquarters. They then counted how many of each letter was returned. The town people returned somewhat more letters to the individual and to the Pink Panther Lounge, but many fewer to the communist party. Overall, the city and town barely differed in the number of letters returned. The authors concluded that there may be slightly higher rates of helping in the small town as long as the person being helped is within some acceptable category, but that city people were much more helpful toward deviants.

On the other hand, we all know that some people hate being in a city. They find the noise unpleasant, the crowds of people upsetting, the pace too fast, and the general atmosphere obnoxious. Many people prefer the quieter, more peaceful, slower life in the suburbs or better still in a small town or rural area. If they dislike cities so much, how can we say that cities are not harmful?

The answer is that reactions to the city depend on characteristics of the individual. Just as some people like high levels of stimulation while others do not, so some people like cities and some hate them. In fact, the critical factor may be the level of stimulation you prefer. Obviously, if you like a high level, cities are more likely to produce positive feelings than if you like lower levels. Similarly, if you like a high level of stimulation, you may dislike small towns. In the survey mentioned above (Shaver & Freedman, 1976), many people were not happy with their community. This was true of all kinds of communities. Some people who lived in rural areas were dissatisfied, as were people who lived in urban areas. The amount of dissatisfaction was about the same for all areas (actually slightly lower for the biggest cities than for any other type of community). But the important point is that people who did not like their community tended to be the least happy and healthy. Although the type of community in which people lived did not affect happiness, their satisfaction with their community did.

SUMMARY

1. Environmental psychology deals with how various factors in the environment affect people. Although practically anything could be considered part of the environment, the field has concentrated on the effects of noise, the use of space, crowding, the design of buildings, and cities in general.

2. Noise affects us less than we might think. As long as noise is not so loud that it causes physical damage, people adapt to it very quickly and with no harmful effects. Loud noise does, however, interfere with the performance of certain tasks.

3. Adaptation to noise takes some effort. If a noise is uncontrollable or unpredictable, effects show up after the noise has ceased. In this noise situation people do less well on tasks that require high motivation for good performance. Prolonged exposure to loud noise may have negative effects on hearing and reading comprehension.

4. Proxemics refers to how we use the space immediately surrounding us—sometimes called personal space. The distance we stand from other people depends on our ethnic background, our sex, and our relationship to the people. White Americans and Northern Europeans prefer the greatest distance, Southern Europeans stand closer, and Latin Americans and Arabs stand still closer. Blacks and whites in the United States have similar preferences. Women stand closer than men, and mixed-pairs closer than same-sex pairs.

5. Standing close has two quite different meanings. We stand closer to people we like, have close relationships with, or are sexually attracted to. But standing close can also be an aggressive act when it involves invading someone's space. On the other hand, there is no evidence that we have an innate need for a particular amount of territory.

6. Crowding has some negative effects on lower animals. It can produce a breakdown in normal social behavior, but it does not generally have negative effects on people. Crowding does not cause crime, pathological problems, or negative consequences either in the real world, or in the laboratory.

7. Under many circumstances, all-male groups respond badly to high density while all-female groups respond positively. Crowding, however, intensifies the usual reaction to the situation; it makes positive responses more positive, and negative ones more negative.

8. Another explanation of crowding effects is that some people like high levels of stimulation and others like low levels. Since high density involves higher stimulation, those who like high levels will respond positively while the others will respond negatively.

9. Architectural design seems to have some effects on people's behavior. Suite arrangements in dormitories appear to promote social interactions better than corridor designs. However, high-rise housing is not necessarily worse than low-rise housing.

10. Urban living is not generally less healthy than living in other kinds of communities. The effect of community type depends on the preferences and characteristics of each individual.

SUGGESTIONS FOR ADDITIONAL READING

BELL, P. A., FISHER, J. D., and LOOMIS, R. J. *Environmental psychology*. Philadelphia: W. B. Saunders, 1978. There are not yet any very good textbooks on environmental psychology, but this is better than most.

FREEDMAN, J. L. *Crowding and behavior*. San Francisco: W. H. Freeman, 1975. Presents all of the research on crowding up to that date, as well as the author's theory.

GLASS, D. C., & SINGER, J. E. *Urban stress*. New York: Academic Press, 1972. Focuses on the effects of noise. Presents lots of research as well as interesting theoretical discussions.

SOMMER, R. *Personal space: The behavioral basis of design*. Englewood Cliffs, N.J.: Prentice-Hall, 1969. Somewhat out of date, but still the best book on the subject.

Glossary

Affective Component Emotional feelings associated with beliefs about an attitude object; consists mainly of the evaluation of the object (like-dislike, pro-con).

Affiliation Tendency for people to be gregarious; to be in contact with others; to join with others.

Aggression Any action intended to hurt others; may also refer to internal state of wanting to hurt others (aggressive feelings).

Aggression Anxiety Anxiety about expressing overt aggression, usually with respect to a particular target.

All-Channel Type of communication network in which each member can communicate with each other member.

Altruism Performing acts intended to help another even though there is no expectation of reward.

Antisocial Aggression Aggressive acts such as murder that violate commonly accepted social norms.

Anxiety Worry based on the arousal of unconscious desires (Freud); being afraid when there is no real danger.

Applied Research Research designed to answer questions about specific, real-world issues, usually without concern for any general theoretical or scientific issues.

Archive Study Research technique based on the analysis of data already available in published records.

Assimilation Tendency to see discrepant or opposing positions on matters close to an individual as being closer than they actually are.

Association Linking different stimuli that occur together in place and time. Through pairing, evaluations of one stimulus become associated with those of the other; one of the basic processes by which learning occurs.

Assumed Similarity Tendency for people to believe that others are similar to them, particularly when they share demographic characteristics such as ethnic background, age, and education.

Attitude Enduring response disposition with a cognitive component, an affective component, and a behavioral tendency; we develop and hold attitudes toward persons, objects, and ideas.

Attitude-Discrepant Behavior Acts inconsistent with a person's attitudes. When an individual behaves in a way inconsistent with a belief, dissonance is produced and there is a tendency for the attitude to change.

Attribution Process by which people make inferences about the causes of attitudes or behavior. Attribution theory attempts to describe the principles by which these attributions are determined, and the effect they have.

Authoritarian Leader Leader who dictates group policies and activities, and who regulates members' work and selection of partners. This leadership style leads to highly productive groups with discontented members.

Autokinetic Phenomenon Visual illusion in which a single point of light seen in the dark appears to move even though it is stationary; used in Sherif's conformity experiments.

Averaging Principle Theoretical position according to which information used in forming impressions is averaged together. For example, a positive impression of another person would not be changed by new information that is also positive.

Balance Model or Theory Heider's theoretical model, in which unbalanced relationships (those with an odd number of negative relationships) between two persons and an object tend to change toward balanced ones.

Basic Principle of Learning The process by which the probability of engaging in any behavior is altered through the administration of rewards or punishments.

Basic Research Research designed to examine general relationships among phenomena rather than specific questions about particular issues.

Behavioral Sink A term used by Calhoun to describe an area of high population density, in which animals behave aggressively and suffer a breakdown in normal social behavior.

Bilateral Threat Trucking game condition in which both players have the option of blocking their opponent's path. Cooperation is very low under this condition.

Body Language Information transmitted about attitudes, emotions, and so on by nonverbal bodily movements and gestures, such as posture, stance, etc.

Brainstorming Unstructured group problem-solving technique in which the individual participants say anything they think might be helpful to stimulate the group to produce better ideas than any one person would produce alone.

Breakpoints The perceived starting or ending points of a behavioral act, as perceived by an observer.

Bystander Intervention The act of coming to the aid of a stranger in distress. Research indicates that a person is more likely to intervene when he or she is alone in the situation than when others are present.

Catharsis Freud's idea that the aggressive drive can be reduced by expressing and thus releasing aggression.

Centralized Communication Network Type of network in which only one person receives information from all the other members. These networks are effective for simple tasks and transmit information efficiently, but members tend to dislike the group.

Central Traits Extent to which a trait is central to an impression through being associated with the stimulus person's other characteristics. Traits such as warm or cold are considered central because they are important in determining impressions.

Cognitive Consistency Tendency for people to seek consistency among their beliefs; regarded as a major determinant of attitude formation and change.

Cognitive Dissonance Theory developed by Festinger according to which inconsistency (dissonance) between two cognitive elements produces pressure to make these elements consonant. It has been applied to a wide range of phenomena including decisions and attitude-discrepant behavior.

Cohesiveness The sum of all the factors that cause members of a group to want to maintain the group and their membership in it.

Commitment Extent to which a person is tied to, involved in, or for any reason finds it difficult to give up an attitude, judgment, or other kind of position. Higher commitment reduces conformity and attitude change.

Complementarity Tendency for people to be attracted to one another because they possess opposite qualities. For example, a dominant person may be attracted to a submissive person and vice versa.

Compliance Performance of an act at another's request.

Conformity Voluntary performance of an act because others also do it.

Contagion A term used by LeBon and others to refer to the spreading through a group, of the behavior or feelings of a small portion of the group.

Contrast Tendency to perceive attitudinal positions that are far from an individual's own position as being farther away than they actually are.

Counteraggression Aggression by a victim committed in retaliation for being aggressed against.

Credibility How expert a communicator is perceived to be in an area of concern, and how much he or she is trusted by the individual receiving the communication.

Crowding Psychological state of discomfort associated with wanting more space than is available; also, the physical state of being in a situation with little space (often called high density).

Cube Theory Kelley's model, according to which people base attributions on three independent kinds of information: distinctiveness, consistency, and consensus.

Deindividuation Loss of a sense of personal responsibility when in a group that leads people to do things they would normally not do when alone.

Democratic Leader Leader who discussed policies with the group, and allows members to work with whomever they choose. This style has been shown to produce groups that are not necessarily very productive but that have strong motivation to work and happier, more self-reliant members.

Density Physical measure of the amount of space available to each organism in an environment. High density is often called crowding.

Dependent Variable The behaviors or attitudes are measured in an experiment; responses to levels of the independent variable being manipulated.

Deviant Being seen as or actually being different from others.

Disinhibition Loosening of the tight control over anger in general by once releasing it under socially approved conditions; that is, once a person has committed a socially approved aggression, he or she has fewer inhibitions about aggressing under other conditions.

Displacement Expression of aggression toward a target other than the source of frustration or annoyance. Typically, it occurs because the original source is not available or because the reasons for restraining aggression against this other target are weaker.

Distracting Stimulus that draws attention away from a persuasive message. It sometimes in-

creases attitude change by making it harder for people to defend a position against the arguments in the message.

Empirical Research Research designed to gather information about a phenomenon, without regard to a particular theory or hypothesis. Often employs many measures at once.

Equity A sense that people should get what they deserve in terms of their contributions and efforts. Inequity is when people are not getting their fair share.

Evaluation Most important basic dimension underlying impression formation; the goodness or badness of another person, object, or concept.

Evaluative Component, *See* **Affective Component.**

Expectancy-Value Theory A theory of decision making that predicts the person will choose whatever is highest in goal desirability and probability of goal attainment.

Expected Utility The individual's perception of the anticipated gains and losses from a particular action.

External Validity Extent to which the results of an experiment are generalizable to other populations and settings.

Extremity Shift Move toward conservative or risky extremes when decisions are made by groups rather than individuals.

Fantasy Aggression Imagined act of aggression that tends to reduce direct aggression.

Fear Feeling of dread associated with realistic danger; found to be associated with increases in affiliative behavior in Schachter's experiments.

Field Experiment Study in which variables are systematically manipulated and measured in real-life, nonlaboratory settings.

Foot-in-the-Door Technique Method of increasing compliance with a large request by first getting the person to comply with a smaller request.

Gain-Loss Principle Tendency for people to like best those who show increasing liking for them, and to dislike most those who show decreasing liking. Aronson and Linder have explained this phenomenon in terms of changes in self-esteem that result from changes in others' evaluations.

Game Theory Mathematical analysis of games that makes it possible to determine which alternatives would maximize chances of winning.

Genetic Characteristics Any traits or qualities of

an individual that are inherited (i.e., that are controlled by their genes).

Gestalt The view that people form coherent and meaningful perceptions based on the entire perceptual field, so that the whole is different from the sum of its parts. In social perception, the implication is that the meaning of a trait is affected by its context.

Groupthink A term used by Janis to describe a group in which all members isolate themselves from outside opinions and information, try to please the group leader, and agree on a decision even if it is irrational.

Identification A term used by Freud to describe the strong attachment of a child with the same sex parent, and that results in sex-typed behavior.

Imitation Learning by watching what others do and doing the same; also applies to forming attitudes by modeling those of others, such as parents or teachers.

Incentive Size or value of the outcomes in a pay-off matrix in a prisoner's dilemma game. The effect of incentive in cooperation is mixed; sometimes it increases, sometimes it decreases, and sometimes it has little effect on cooperation. Also, what individuals have to gain or lose by embracing a particular position. When there are conflicting goals, individuals tend to adopt positions that maximize their gains.

Independent Variable Factor systematically manipulated by the experimenter in order to determine its effects on some behavior (the dependent variable).

Ingratiation Increasing others' liking for us by making positive responses such as expressing agreement with them, telling them we like them, and so on. Liking will not result when persons are perceived to have ulterior motives for these statements.

Inoculate McGuire's notion that people are more resistant to the effects of persuasive communications when they are exposed to weak counterarguments.

Leader Person in a group who has the greatest influence on its activities and the beliefs of members. Also, the person recognized by the group as its leader.

Learned Helplessness The feeling of helplessness and possible depression when people discover they have no control over their outcomes.

Legitimacy Extent to which leadership authority is recognized by members. Leaders who are elected tend to be seen as more legitimate than appointed leaders. Greater legitimacy usually results in more influence and authority.

Libido Freud's concept of sexual, creative energy.

Misattribution Assigning the cause of a particular behavior or emotional state to a stimulus other than the actual cause, such as thinking a lecture is exciting when actually you are excited by ten cups of coffee.

Motivated Selectivity Idea that people deliberately seek supportive information and avoid nonsupportive information as a way of maintaining the consistency of their own attitudes. The evidence indicates that this generally does not occur.

Naive Psychology The ordinary person's informal theories of what determines human behavior.

Negative Effect Tendency for impressions to be more influenced by negative traits than by positive traits. Hence positive impressions are more vulnerable to change than negative impressions.

Non-Zero-Sum Games Game in which the total of wins and losses does not necessarily equal zero; that is, both sides can win or lose. The trucking game and the prisoner's dilemma game are examples of non-zero-sum games.

Obedience Performing an action because of an order or request.

Opinion Leaders People who are most exposed to information in the mass media, and pass it along to their friends, thereby influencing their friends' opinions.

Paralanguage Information conveyed by variations in speech other than actual words and syntax, such as pitch, loudness, hesitations, etc.

Person Perception Process of forming impressions of others, making judgments about their personalities, and adopting hypotheses about the kind of persons they are.

Positivity Bias General tendency to express positive evaluations of people more often than negative evaluations. Also called the leniency effect.

Prejudice The affective component of group antagonism; disliking a group, or members of a group.

Prisoner's Dilemma Laboratory game designed to study the conditions under which people cooperate or compete. Despite the fact that the game is usually set up so that players can maximize their rewards by cooperating, they tend to compete in order to "beat" their opponent.

Prosocial Aggression Aggressive acts that support commonly accepted social norms, such as a parent spanking a disobedient child.

Prosocial Behavior Any act that helps or is designed to help others.

Proxemics Term used by Hall to describe persons' use of space and the kinds of social interaction that are appropriate at different interpersonal distances; the study of these phenomena.

Random Assignment Placement of subjects into experimental conditions in a manner which guarantees that the choice is made entirely by chance, such as by using a random number table; essential characteristic of an experiment.

Reactance Brehm's concept that people attempt to maintain their freedom of action; when this freedom is threatened, they do whatever they can to restore it: reactance is aroused, and compliance decreases.

Reciprocity Principle Predisposition toward liking others who are believed to like us.

Reinforcement The group's norm can act as a persuasive force leading to attitude change, or prevent change by supporting the individual's position when it is attacked.

Risky Shift Name given to the extremity shift when it was believed that groups made riskier decisions than individuals.

Sanctioned Aggression Aggression that is permissible (though not necessarily encouraged) according to the norms of the individual's social groups.

Scapegoat Person who, because he or she is weak, different, and easily distinguishable, tends to be selected as a target of displaced aggression.

Schema An organized system or structure of cognitions about some stimulus or type of stimulus, such as a person, personality type, group, role, event.

Secondary Information Information about information, such as knowing that a message was received and understood.

Selective Attention Tendency for people to pay more attention to a supportive message.

Selective Exposure Tendency for persuasive communications not to reach the intended audience because audience members tend to come into contact mostly with sources they agree with. Sometimes refers to a pressured psychological tendency to avoid nonsupportive information, but the evidence does not indicate such a tendency.

Semantic Differential Way of measuring attitudes by analyzing responses to an object on a series of bipolar (opposite) rating dimensions. Osgood has shown that much of the variance in attitudes (especially those involving people) is accounted for by a simple evaluative factor. The other two major factors are potency and activity.

Sensory Overload The notion that persons exposed to very high levels of stimulation cannot process all this information. The overloaded state is unpleasant, leading people to reduce overload by screening out less crucial sensory inputs. Milgram has suggested that this occurs during crowding or in urban environments, but no evidence has yet supported this idea.

Sexual Identity Knowing one's gender and being able to identify the gender of other people.

Sex Roles Behavior considered appropriate for one sex or the other. Also, behaving consistently with these roles.

Sexual Stereotypes Common beliefs within a culture as to the behavior and characteristics of the sexes.

Shift-of-Meaning Tendency for the connotations of a trait to change when placed in a different context.

Social Density The number of individuals present.

Social Facilitation Tendency for people (and some kinds of animals) to perform better on simple tasks when others are present than when they are alone.

Social Justice A belief that individuals should get what they deserve. Similar to equity.

Social Penetration Altman and Taylor's theory about the process by which people gradually attain closeness and intimacy with one another.

Socioemotional Leader Person who concentrates on keeping the group running smoothly and happily; typically, the same person tends to promote group solidarity.

Spatial Density, *See* **Density.**

Stereotype The cognitive component of group

antagonism; beliefs about the characteristics of group members.

Symbolic Racism Opposition progress of the blacks at an abstract level, especially when their progress would involve violations of traditional American values.

Task Leader Person who controls, shapes, directs, and organizes the group in carrying out a specific task; his or her influence is limited to the particular job being done.

Territoriality The idea that animals consider certain geographic places or areas as their own and defend them from intrusions. The evidence shows that territoriality occurs only for some animals and under some circumstances.

Thanatos Freud's concept of destructive, aggressive energy. These self-destructive forces or death wishes, can be turned inward, resulting in self-punishment, masochism, or suicide, or outward, resulting in aggression.

Theoretical Research Research designed to test hypotheses derived from a theory.

Trucking Game Simple laboratory game developed by Deutsch and Krauss to determine how conditions such as threats and communication affect cooperation and competition. Even though the game is set up so that it is to each player's advantage to cooperate, players tend to compete when they have the option of threatening one another.

Unilateral Threat Condition in the trucking game in which one player has the option of blocking his opponent's path.

Zero-Sum Game Game in which the total of gains and losses equals zero. That is, one person's gain is another's loss. Monopoly and poker are examples of zero-sum games.

References

Abel, E. L. 1977. The relationship between cannibis and violence: A review. *Psychological Bulletin, 84,* 193–11.

Abelson, R. P. 1976. Script processing in attitude formation and decision making. In J. S. Carroll and J. W. Payne (eds.), *Cognition and social behavior.* Hillsdale, N. J.: Lawrence Erlbaum.

Adams, J. S. 1963. Toward an understanding of inequity. *Journal of Abnormal and Social Psychology, 67,* 422–36.

Adams, J. S. 1966. Injustice in social exchange. In L. Berkowitz (ed.), *Advances in experimental psychology.* Vol. 2. New York: Academic Press.

Aderman, D. 1972. Elation, depression, and helping behavior. *Journal of Personality and Social Psychology, 24,* 91–101.

Adorno, T. W., Frenkel-Brunswik, E., Levinson, D. J., & Sanford, R. N. 1950. *The authoritarian personality.* New York: Harper & Row.

Aiello, J. R., & Aiello, T. 1974. The development of personal space: Proxemic behavior of children 6 through 16. *Human Ecology, 2,* 177–89.

Aiello, J. R., & Cooper, R. E. 1972. The use of personal space as a function of social affect. *Proceedings of the 80th Annual Convention of the American Psychology Association, 7,* 207–8.

Aiello, J. R., Epstein, Y. M., & Karlin, R. A. 1975. Effects of crowding on electrodermal activity. *Sociological Symposium, 14,* 43–57.

Aiello, J. R., & Jones, S. E. 1971. Field study of the proxemic behavior of young children in three subcultural groups. *Journal of Social Psychology, 19,* 351–56.

Ainsworth, M. D. S., & Bell, S. M. 1977. Infant crying and maternal responsiveness: A rejoinder to Bewirtz and Boyd. *Child Development, 48,* 1208–16.

Ajzen, I. 1977. Intuitive theories of events and the effects of base-rate in formation on prediction. *Journal of Personality and Social Psychology, 35,* 303–14.

Allee, W. C., & Masure, R. H. 1936. A comparison of maze behavior in paired and isolated shelf-parakeets (Melopsittacus undulatus Shaw) in a two-alley problem box. *Journal of Comparative Psychology, 22,* 131–55.

Allen, V. L., & Levin, J. M. 1971. Social support and conformity: The role of independent assessment of reality. *Journal of Experimental Social Psychology, 7,* 48–58.

Allgeier, A. R., & Byrne, D. 1973. Attraction toward the opposite sex as a determinant of physical proximity. *Journal of Social Psychology, 90,* 213–19.

Allport, F. H. 1920. The influence of the group upon association and thought. *Journal of Experimental Psychology, 3,* 159–82.

Allport, F. H. 1924. *Social psychology.* Boston: Riverside Editions, Houghton Mifflin.

Allport, G. W. 1935. Attitudes. In C. Murchison (ed.), *A handbook of social psychology.* Worcester, Mass.: Clark University Press.

Allport, G. W. 1954. *The nature of prejudice.* Garden City, N.Y.: Double-day Anchor.

Altman, I., & Haythorn, W. W. 1965. Interpersonal exchange in isolation. *Sociometry, 28,* 411–26.

Altman, I., & Taylor, D. A. 1973. *Social penetration: The development of interpersonal relationships.* New York: Holt, Rinehart & Winston.

Amir, Y. 1976. The role of intergroup contact in change

of prejudice and ethnic relations. In Katz, P. A. (ed.), *Towards the elimination of racism.* Elmsford, N.Y.: Pergamon Press. Pp. 245–308.

Anderson, H. H. 1939. Domination and integration in the behavior of kindergarten children in an experimental play situation. *Journal of Experimental Education, 8,* 123–31.

Anderson, N. H. 1959. Test of a model for opinion change. *Journal of Abnormal and Social Psychology, 59,* 371–81.

Anderson, N. H. 1965. Averaging vs. adding as a stimulus-combination rule in impression formation. *Journal of Experimental Psychology, 70,* 394–400.

Anderson, N. H. 1966. Component ratings in impression formation. *Psychonomic Science, 6,* 279–80.

Anderson, N. H. 1968a. Application of a linear-serial model to a personality-impression task using special presentation. *Journal of Personality and Social Psychology, 10,* 354–62.

Anderson, N. H. 1968b. Likableness ratings of 555 personality-trait words. *Journal of Personality and Social Psychology, 9,* 272–79.

Anderson, N. H., & Hubert, S. 1963. Effects of concomitant verbal recall on order effects in personality impression formation. *Journal of Verbal Learning and Verbal Behavior, 2,* 379–91.

Anderson, R., & Nida, S. A. 1978. Effect of physical attractiveness on opposite- and same-sex evaluations. *Journal of Personality, 46,* 401–13.

Andrews, K. H., & Kandel, D. B. 1979. Attitude and behavior. *American Sociological Review, 44,* 298–310.

Apple, W., Streeter, L. A., & Krauss, R. M. 1979. Effects of pitch and speech rate on personal attributions. *Journal of Personality and Social Psychology, 37,* 715–27.

Apsler, R., & Sears, D. O. 1968. Warning, personal involvement, and attitude change. *Journal of Personality and Social Psychology, 9,* 162–66.

Archer, D., & Akert, R. M. 1977. Words and everything else: Verbal and nonverbal cues in social interpretation. *Journal of Personality and Social Psychology, 35,* 443–49.

Archer, R. L., & Berg, J. H. 1978. Disclosure reciprocity and its limits: A reactance analysis. *Journal of Experimental Social Psychology, 14,* 527–40.

Ardrey, R. 1966. *The territorial imperative.* New York: Atheneum.

Arms, R. L., Russell, G. W., & Sandilands, M. L. 1979. Effects on the hostilty of spectators of viewing aggressive sports. *Sociometry, 42,* 275–79.

Armstrong, E. A. 1965. *Bird display and behavior: An introduction to the study of bird psychology.* 2nd ed. New York: Dover.

Aronson, E. 1972. *The social animal.* San Francisco: W. H. Freeman.

Aronson, E., & Carlsmith, J. M. 1963. The effect of the severity of threat on the devaluation of forbidden behavior. *Journal of Abnormal and Social Psychology, 66,* 584–88.

Aronson, E., & Linder, D. 1965. Gain and loss of esteem as determinants of interpersonal attractiveness. *Journal of Experimental Social Psychology, 1,* 156–71.

Aronson, E., & Osherow, N. 1980. Cooperation, social behavior, and academic performance: Experiments in the desegregated classroom. In Bickman, L. (ed.), *Applied Social Psychology Annual, Vol. 1.* Beverly Hills, CA: Sage Publications.

Aronson, E., Turner, J., & Carlsmith, J. M. 1963. Communicator credibility and communication discrepancy. *Journal of Abnormal and Social Psychology, 67,* 31–36.

Asch, S. E. 1946. Forming impressions of personality. *Journal of Abnormal and Social Psychology, 41,* 258–90.

Asch, S. E. 1948. The doctrine of suggestion, prestige, and imitation in social psychology. *Psychological Review, 55,* 250–76.

Asch, S. E. 1951. Effects of group pressure upon the modification and distortion of judgments. In H. Guetzkow (ed.), *Groups, leadership and men.* Pittsburgh, Pa.: Carnegie Press.

Asch, S. E. 1952. *Social psychology.* Englewood Cliffs, N.J.: Prentice-Hall.

Ashmore, R. D. 1970. Prejudice: Causes and cures. In B. E. Collins, Social psychology. Reading, Mass.: Addison-Wesley.

Ashmore, R. D., & DelBoca, F. K. 1976. Psychological approaches to understanding intergroup conflicts. In Katz, P. A. (ed.), *Towards the elimination of racism.* Elmsford, N.Y.: Pergamon Press. Pp. 73–124.

Ashmore, R. D., & DelBoca, F. K. 1980. Conceptual approaches to stereotypes and stereotyping. In Hamilton, D. L. (ed.), *Cognitive processes in stereotyping and intergroup behavior.* Hillsdale, N.J.: Lawrence Erlbaum (In press).

Bachman, M. E. 1972. Patterns of mental abilities: Ethnic, socioeconomic, and sex differences. *American Educational Research Journal, 9,* 1–12.

Bales, R. F. 1950. *Interaction process analysis: a method for the study of small groups.* Cambridge, Mass.: Addison-Wesley.

Bandura, A. 1969. Social learning theory of identificatory processes. In R. A. Goslin (ed.), *Handbook of socialization theory and research.* Chicago: Rand McNally.

Bandura, A., Ross, D., & Ross, S. 1961. Transmission of aggression through imitation of aggressive models. *Journal of Abnormal and Social Psychology, 63,* 575–82.

Barker, R. G., Dembo, T., & Lewis, K. 1941. Frustration and regression: An experiment with young children. *University of Iowa Studies in Child Welfare, 18,* No. 1.

Baron, R. A. 1971a. Magnitude of victim's pain cues and level of prior anger arousal as determinants of adult aggressive behavior. *Journal of Personality and Social Psychology, 17,* 236–43.

Baron, R. A. 1971b. Aggression as a function of magnitude of victim's pain cues, level of prior anger arousal, and aggressor-victim similarity. *Journal of Personality and Social Psychology, 18,* 48–54.

Baron, R. A. 1971c. Reducing the influence of an aggressive model: The restraining effects of discrepant modeling cues. *Journal of Personality and Social Psychology, 20,* 240–45.

Baron, R. A. 1972. Reducing the influence of an aggressive model: The restraining effects of peer censure. *Journal of Experimental Social Psychology, 8,* 266–75.

Baron, R. A. 1974. Aggression as a function of victim's pain cues, level of prior anger arousal, and exposure to an aggressive model. *Journal of Personality and Social Psychology, 29,* 117–24.

Baron, R. A. 1977. *Human aggression.* New York: Plenum Press.

Baron, R. A. 1978a. The influence of hostile and nonhostile humor upon physical aggression. *Personality and Social Psychology Bulletin, 4,* 77–80.

Baron, R. A. 1978b. Aggression-inhibiting influence of sexual humor. *Journal of Personality and Social Psychology, 36,* 189–97.

Baron, R. A. 1978. Invasions of personal space and helping: Mediating effects of invader's apparent need. *Journal of Experimental Social Psychology, 14,* 304–12.

Baron, R. A., & Ball, R. L. 1974. The aggression-inhibiting influence of nonhostile humor. *Journal of Experimental Social Psychology, 10,* 23–33.

Baron, R. A., & Bell, P. A. 1975. Aggression and heat: Mediating effects of provocation and exposure to an aggressive model. *Journal of Personality and Social Psychology, 31,* 825–32.

Baron, R. A., & Bell, P. A. 1976a. Aggression and heat: The influence of ambient temperature, negative affect, and a cooling drink on physical aggression. *Journal of Personality and Social Psychology, 33,* 245–55.

Baron, R. A., & Bell, P. A. 1976b. Physical distance and helping: Some unexpected benefits of "crowding in" on others. *Journal of Applied Social Psychology, 6,* 95–104.

Baron, R. A., & Bell, P. A. 1977. Sexual arousal and aggression by males: Effects of type of erotic stimuli and prior provocation. *Journal of Personality and Social Psychology, 35,* 79–87.

Baron, R. A., Dion, K. L., Baron, P., & Miller, N. 1970. Group norms, elicited values and risk-taking. Unpublished manuscript. University of Minnesota.

Baron, R. A., & Kepner, C. R. 1970. Model's behavior and attraction toward the model as determinants of adult aggressive behavior. *Journal of Personality and Social Psychology, 14,* 335–44.

Baron, R. A., Moore, D., & Sanders, C. S. 1978. Distraction as a source of drive in social facilitation research. *Journal of Personality and Social Psychology, 36,* 816–24.

Baron, R. A., & Ransberger, V. M. 1978. Ambient temperature and the occurrence of collective violence: The "long, hot summer" revisited. *Journal of Personality and Social Psychology, 36,* 351–60.

Bar-Tal, D., & Saxe, L. 1976. Perceptions of similarly and dissimilarly attractive couples and individuals. *Journal of Personality and Social Psychology, 33,* 772–81.

Bartlett, F. C. 1932. *Remembering.* Cambridge, England: Cambridge University Press.

Bassili, J. N. 1976. Temporal and spatial contingencies in the perception of social events. *Journal of Personality and Social Psychology, 33,* 680–85.

Bateson, N. 1966. Familiarization, group discussion, and risk-taking. *Journal of Experimental Social Psychology, 2,* 119–29.

Baum, A., Aiello, J.R., & Calesnick, L. E. 1978. Crowding and personal control: Social density and the development of learned helplessness. *Journal of Personality and Social Psychology, 36,* 1000–11.

Baum, A., & Valins, S. 1977. *Architecture and social behavior: Psychological studies of social density.* Hillsdale, N. J.: Lawrence Erlbaum.

Baumrind, D., & Black, A. 1967. Socialization practices associated with dimensions of competence in preschool boys and girls. *Child Development, 38,* 291–327.

Bavalas, A., Hastorf, A. H., Gross, A. E., & Kite, W. R. 1965. Experiments on the alteration of group structures. *Journal of Experimental Social Psychology, 1,* 55–70.

Baxter, J. C. 1970. Interpersonal spacing in natural settings. *Sociometry, 33,* 444–56.

Becker, J. F., & Heaton, E. E., Jr. 1967. The election of Senator Edward W. Brooke. *Public Opinion Quarterly, 31,* 346–58.

Becker, L. B., McCombs, M. E., McLeod, M. M. 1975. The development of political cognitions. In S. H. Chaffee (ed.), *Political communication: Issues and strategies for research.* Beverly Hills: Stage.

Beckwith, H. 1972. Relationships between infants' social behavior and their mothers' behavior. *Child Development, 43,* 397–411.

Belch, G. E. 1979. An Investigation of the Effects of Advertising Message Structure and Repetition Upon Cognitive Processes Mediating Message Acceptance. Unpublished doctoral dissertation, University of California, Los Angeles.

Bell, R. 1968. A reinterpretation of the direction of effects in studies of socialization. *Psychological Review, 75,* 81–85.

Bell, S. M., & Ainsworth, M. D. S. 1972. Infant crying and maternal responsiveness. *Child Development, 43,* 1171–90.

Bem, D. J. 1965. An experimental analysis of self-persuasion. *Journal of Experimental Psychology, 1,* 199–218.

Bem, D. J. 1967. Self-perception: An alternative interpretation of cognitive dissonance phenomena. *Psychological Review, 74,* 183–200.

Bem, D. J. 1972. Self-perception theory. In L. Berkowitz, (ed.), *Advances in experimental social psychology.* Vol. 6. New York: Academic Press.

Bem, D. J., Wallach, M. A., & Kogan, N. 1965. Group decision making under risk of aversive consequences. *Journal of Personality and Social Psychology, 1,* 453–60.

Bem, S. L. 1974. The measurement of psychological androgyny. *Journal of Consulting and Clinical Psychology, 42,* 155–62.

Bem, S. L. 1975. Sex-role adaptability: One consequence of psychological androgyny. *Journal of Personality and Social Psychology, 31,* 634–43.

Bem, S. L. 1977. On the utility of alternative procedures for assessing psychological androgyny. *Journal of Consulting and Clinical Psychology, 45,* 196–205.

Bem, S. L. Martyna, W., & Watson, C. 1976. Sex typing and androgyny: Further explorations of the expressive domain. *Journal of Personality and Social Psychology, 34,* 1016–23.

Benton, A. A. 1971. Productivity, distributive justice, and bargaining among children. *Journal of Personality and Social Psychology. 18,* 68–78.

Berelson, B. R., Lazarsfeld, P. F., & McPhee, W. N. 1954. *Voting: A study of opinion formation in a presidential election.* Chicago: University of Chicago Press.

Berkowitz, L. 1954. Group standards, cohesiveness, and productivity. *Human Relations, 7,* 509–19.

Berkowitz, L. 1965. Some aspects of observed aggression. *Journal of Personality and Social Psychology, 2(3),* 359–69.

Berkowitz, L. 1968. Responsibility, reciprocity, and social distance in help-giving: An experimental investigation of English social class differences. *Journal of Experimental Social Psychology, 4,* 46–63.

Berkowitz, L. 1970. The contagion of violence. In W. J. Arnold and M. M. Page (eds.), *Nebraska symposium on motivation.* Lincoln: University of Nebraska Press.

Berkowitz, L., & Alioto, J. T. 1973. The meaning of an observed event as a determinant of its aggressive consequences. *Journal of Personality and Social Psychology, 28,* 206–17.

Berkowitz, L., & Daniels, L. R. 1964. Responsibility and dependency. *Journal of Abnormal and Social Psychology, 66,* 427–36.

Berkowitz, L., & Frodi, A. 1979. Reactions to the child's mistakes as affected by her/his looks and speech. *Social Psychology Quarterly, 42,* 420–25.

Berkowitz, L., & Geen, R. G. 1900. Film violence and the cue properties of available targets. *Journal of Personality and Social Psychology, 3,* 525–30.

Berkowitz, L., & Geen, R. G. 1967. Stimulus qualities of the target of aggression: A further study. *Journal of Personality and Social Psychology, 5,* 364–68.

Berkowitz, L., & LePage, A. 1967. Weapons as aggression-eliciting stimuli. *Journal of Personality and Social Psychology, 7,* 202–7.

Berkowitz, L., & Rawlings, E. 1963. Effects of film violence on inhibitions against subsequent aggression. *Journal of Abnormal and Social Psychology, 66,* 405–12.

Berkowitz, W. R. 1970. Spectator responses at public war demonstrations. *Journal of Personality and Social Psychology, 14,* 305–11.

Bernstein, W. M., Stephan, W. G., & Davis, M. H. 1979. Explaining attributions for achievement: A path analytic approach. *Journal of Personality and Social Psychology, 37,* 1810–21.

Berscheid, E., Boye, D., & Walters, E. 1968. Retaliation as a means of restoring equity. *Journal of Personality & Social Psychology, 10,* 370–76.

Berscheid, E., Brothen, T., & Graziano, W. 1976. Gain-loss theory and the "Law of Infidelity": Mr. Doting versus the admiring stranger. *Journal of Personality and Social Psychology, 33,* 709–18.

Berscheid, E., Dion, K., Walster, E., & Walster, G. W. 1971. Physical attractiveness and dating choice: A test of the matching hypothesis. *Journal of Experimental Social Psychology, 7,* 173–89.

Berscheid, E., Graziano, W., Monson, T., & Dermer, M. 1976. Outcome dependency: Attention, attribution, and attraction. *Journal of Personality and Social Psychology, 34,* 978–89.

Berscheid, E., & Walster, E. 1967. When does a harm-doer compensate a victim? *Journal of Personality and Social Psychology, 6,* 435–41.

Berscheid, E., & Walster, E. 1974. A little bit about love. In T. L. Huston (ed.), *Foundations of interpersonal attractiveness.* New York: Academic Press.

Best, D. L., Williams, J. B., Cloud, J. M., Davis, S. W., Robertson, L. S., Edwards, J. R., Giles, H., & Fowles, J. 1977. Development of sex-trait stereotypes among young children in the United States, England, and Ireland. *Child Development, 48,* 1375–84.

Bickman, L. 1971. The effect of another bystander's ability to help on by-stander intervention in an emergency. *Journal of Experimental Social Psychology, 7,* 367–79.

Bieri, J., Bradburn, W., & Galinsky, M. 1958. Sex differences in perceptual behavior. *Journal of Personality, 26,* 1–12.

Birnbaum, M. H., & Stegner, S. E. 1979. Source credibility in social judgment: Bias, expertise, and the judge's point of view. *Journal of Personality and Social Psychology, 37,* 48–74.

Black, T. E., & Higbee, K. L. 1973. Effects of power, threat, and sex on exploitation. *Journal of Personality and Social Psychology, 27,* 382–88.

Blank, A. 1968. Effects of group and individual condition on choice behavior. *Journal of Personality and Social Psychology, 8,* 294–98.

Blehar, M. C., Lieberman, A. F., & Ainsworth, M. D. S. 1977. Early face-to-face interaction and its relation to later infant-mother attachment. *Child Development, 48,* 182–94.

Block, J. H. 1977. Another look at sex differentiation in the socialization behaviors of mothers and fathers. In J. Sherman and F. Denmark (eds.), *Psychology of women: Future of research.* New York: Psychological Dimensions.

Bochner, S., Insko, C. A. 1966. Communicator discrepancy, source credibility, and opinion change. *Journal of Personality and Social Psychology, 4,* 614–21.

Bond, M. H., & Dutton, D. G. 1975. The effect of interaction anticipation and experience as a victim on aggressive behavior. *Journal of Personality, 43(3).*

Bogardus, E. S. 1968. Comparing racial distance in Ethiopia, South Africa, and the United States. *Sociology and Social Research, 52,* 149–56.

Booth, A. 1972. Sex and social participation. *American Sociological Review, 37,* 183–93.

Booth, A., & Cowell, J. 1974. The effects of crowding upon health. Paper presented at the American Population Association Meetings, New York.

Borgida, E., & Nisbett, R. E. 1977. The differential impact of abstract vs. concrete information on decisions. *Journal of Applied Social Psychology, 7,* 258–71.

Boring, E. G., & Titchener, E. B. 1923. A model for the demonstration of facial expression. *American Journal of Psychology, 34,* 471–85.

Bowlby, J. 1969. *Attachment.* New York: Basic Books.

Bradley, G. W. 1978. Self-serving biases in the attribution process: A reexamination of the fact or fiction question. *Journal of Personality and Social Psychology, 36,* 56–71.

Bramel, D., Taub, B., & Blum, B. 1968. An observer's reaction to the suffering of his enemy. *Journal of Personality and Social Psychology, 8,* 384–92.

Braver, S. L., Linder, D. E., Corwin, T. T., & Cialdini, R. B. 1977. Some conditions that affect admissions of attitude change. *Journal of Experimental Social Psychology, 13,* 565–76.

Bray, R. M., Kerr, N. L., & Atkin, R. S. 1978. Effects of group size, problem difficulty, and sex on group performance and members reactions. *Journal of Personality and Social Psychology, 36,* 1224–40.

Brehm, J. W. 1956. Post-decision changes in desirability of alternatives. *Journal of Abnormal and Social Psychology, 52,* 348–89.

Brehm, J. W. 1966. *A theory of psychological reactance.* New York: Academic Press.

Brehm, J. W., & Jones, R. A. 1970. The effect on dissonance of surprise consequences. *Journal of Experimental Social Psychology, 6,* 420–31.

Brehm, J. W., & Sensenig, J. 1966. Social influence as a function of attempted and implied usurpation of a choice. *Journal of Personality and Social Psychology, 4,* 703–7.

Brickman, P., Becker, L. J., & Castle, S. 1979. Making trust easier and harder through two forms of sequential interaction. *Journal of Personality and Social Psychology, 37,* 515–21.

Brickman, P., Meyer, P., & Fredd, S. 1975. Effects of varying exposure to another person with familiar or unfamiliar thought processes. *Journal of Experimental Social Psychology, 11,* 261–70.

Brock, T. C., & Balloun, J. L. 1967. Behavioral receptivity to dissonant information. *Journal of Personality and Social Psychology, 6,* 413–28.

Brock, T. C., & Becker, Ł. A. 1965. Ineffectiveness of "overheard" counterpropaganda. *Journal of Personality and Social Psychology, 2,* 654–60.

Brockner, J., & Swap, W. C. 1976. Effects of repeated exposure and attitudinal similarity on self-disclosure and interpersonal attraction. *Journal of Personality and Social Psychology, 33,* 531–40.

Brothen, T. 1977. The gain/loss concept and the evaluator: First some good news, then some bad. *Journal of Personality and Social Psy-chology, 35,* 430–36.

Broverman, I. K., Vovel, S. R., Broverman, D. M., Clarkson, F. E., & Rosenkrantz, P. S. 1972. Sex-role stereotypes: A current appraisal. *Journal of Social Issues, 28,* 59–79.

Bruner, J. S., Shapiro, D., & Tagiuri, R. 1958. The meaning of traits in isolation and in combination. In R. Tagiuri and L. Petrullo (eds.), *Perso perception and interpersonal behavior.* Stanford, Calif.: Stanford.

Bruner, J. S., & Tagiuri, R. 1954. The perception of people. In G. Lindzey (ed.), *Handbook of social psychology.* Vol. 2. Reading, Mass.: Addison-Wesley.

Brunner, L. J. 1979. Smiles can be back channels. *Journal of Personality and Social Psychology, 37,* 728–34.

Bryan, J. H., & Text, N. A. 1967. Models and helping: Naturalistic studies in aiding behavior. *Journal of Personality and Social Psychology, 6,* 400–7.

Bryant, J., & Zillmann, D. 1979. Effect of intensification of annoyance through unrelated residual excitation on substantially delayed hostile behavior. *Journal of Experimental Social Psychology, 15,* 470–80.

Buck, R. W., Miller, R. E., & Caul, W. F. 1974. Sex, personality, and physiological variables in the communication of affect via facial expression. *Journal of Personality and Social Psychology, 30,* 587–96.

Buck, R. W., Savin, V. J., Miller, R. E. & Caul, W. F. 1972. Communication of affect through facial expressions in humans. *Journal of Personality and Social Psychology, 23,* 362–71.

Bulman, R. J., & Wortman, C. B. 1977. Attributions of blame and coping in the "real world": Severe accident victims react to their lot. *Journal of Personality and Social Psychology, 35,* 351–63.

Burnstein, E. 1967. Sources of cognitive bias in the representation of simple social structures: Balance, minimal change, positivity, reciprocity, and the respondent's own attitude. *Journal of Personality and Social Psychology, 7,* 36–48.

Burnstein, E., & Vinokur, A. 1973. Testing two classes of theories about group induced shifts in individual choice. *Journal of Experimental Social Psychology, 9,* 123–37.

Burnstein, E., & Vinokur, A. 1975. What a person thinks upon learning he has chosen differently from others: Nice evidence for the persuasive-arguments explanation of choice shifts. *Journal of Experimental Social Psychology, 11,* 412–26.

Buss, A. H. 1961. *The psychology of aggression.* New York: John Wiley & Sons.

Buss, A. H., Booker, A., & Buss, E. 1972. Firing a weapon and aggression. *Journal of Personality and Social Psychology, 22,* 296–302.

Byrne, D. 1961. Interpersonal attraction and attitude similarity. *Journal of Abnormal and Social Psychology, 62,* 713–15.

Byrne, D., Baskett, G. D., & Hodges, L. 1971. Behavioral indicators of interpersonal attraction. *Journal of Applied Social Psychology,* 137–49.

Byrne, D., Ervin, C. R., & Lamberth, J. 1970. Continuity between the experimental study attraction and real-life computer dating. *Journal of Personality and Social Psychology, 16*(1), 157–65.

Byrne, D., & Nelson, D. 1964. Attraction as a function of attitude similarity-dissimilarity: The effect of topic importance. *Psychonomic Science, 1,* 93–94.

Byrne, D., & Wong, T. J. 1962. Racial prejudice, interpersonal attraction and assumed dissimilarity of attitudes. *Journal of Abnormal and Social Psychology, 65*, 246–53.

Cacioppo, J. T., & Petty, R. E. 1979. Effects of message repetition and position on cognitive response, recall, and persuasion. *Journal of Personality and Social Psychology, 37*, 97–109.

Caldwell, M. A., & Peplau, L. A. Sex differences in same-sex relationships. *Sex Roles.* (in press)

Calhoun, J. B. 1962. Population density and social pathology.*Scientific American, 206*, 139–48.

Campbell, Angus. 1971. *White attitudes toward black people.* Ann Arbor: Institute for Social Research.

Campbell, A., Converse, P. E., Miller, W. E., & Stokes, D. E. 1960. *The American voter.* New York: John Wiley & Sons.

Campbell, D. T., & Stanley, J. C. 1963. *Experimental and quasiexperimental designs for research.* Chicago: Rand McNally.

Cantor, J. R., Zillmann, D., & Bryant, J. 1975. Enhancement of experienced sexual arousal in response to erotic stimuli through misattribution of unrelated residual excitation. *Journal of Personality and Social Psychology, 32*, 69–75.

Cantor, N., & Mischel, W. 1977. Traits as prototypes: Effects on recognition memory. *Journal of Personality and Social Psychology, 35*, 38–48.

Carlsmith, J. M., & Anderson, C. A. 1979. Ambient temperature and the occurrence of collective violence: A new analysis. *Journal of Personality and Social Psychology, 37*, 337–44.

Carlsmith, J. M., Collins, B. E., & Helmreich, R. L. 1966. Studies in forced compliance: I. The effect of pressure for compliance on attitude change produced by face-to-face role-playing and anonymous essay writing. *Journal of Personality and Social Psychology, 4*, 1–13.

Carlsmith, J. M., Ellsworth, P., & Whiteside, J. 1968. Guilt, confession and compliance. Unpublished manuscript, Stanford University.

Carlsmith, J. M., & Freedman, J. L. 1968. Bad decisions and dissonance: Nobody's perfect. In R. Abelson et al. (eds.), *Theories of cognitive consistency.* Chicago: Rand McNally.

Carlsmith, J. M., & Gross, A. E. 1969. Some effects of guilt on compliance. *Journal of Personality and Social Psychology, 11*, 232–39.

Carlsmith, J. M., Lepper, M., & Landauer, T. K. 1969. Two processes in children's obedience to adult requests. Unpublished manuscript. Stanford University.

Carroll, J. S. 1978. Causal attributions in expert parole decisions. *Journal of Personality and Social Psychology, 36*, 1501–11.

Carver, C. S. 1974. Facilitation of physical aggression through objective self-awareness. *Journal of Experimental Social Psychology, 10*, 365–70.

Carver, C. S. 1979. A cybernetic model of self-attention processes. *Journal of Personality and Social Psychology, 37*, 1251–81.

Cater, D., & Strickland, D. 1975. *TV violence and the child.* New York: Russell Sage.

Chaikin, A. L., & Derlega, V. J. 1974. Liking for the norm-breaker in self-disclosure. *Journal of Personality, 42*, 112–29.

Chaiken, S. 1979. Communicator physical attractiveness and persuasion. *Journal of Personality and Social Psychology, 37*, 1387–97.

Chapman, A. J. 1973. Social facilitation of laughter in children. *Journal of Experimental Social Psychology, 9*, 528–41.

Charlesworth, E., & Hartup, W. W. 1967. Positive social reinforcement in the nursery school peer group. *Child Development, 38*, 993–1002.

Chen, S. C. 1937. Social modification of the activity of ants in nest-building. *Physiological Zoology, 10*, 420–36.

Christian, J. J. 1955. Effect of population size on the adrenal glands and reproductive organs of male white mice. *American Journal of Physiology, 181*, 477–80.

Christian, J. J. 1975. Hormonal control of population growth. In B. E. Eleftheriou & R. L. Sprott (eds.), *Hormonal correlates of behavior (Vol. 1).* New York: Plenum Press.

Christian, J. J., Glyger, V., & Davis, D. 1960. Factors in the mass mortality of a herd of sika deer *Carvus nippon. Chesapeake Science, 1*, 79–95.

Cialdini, R. B., Bickman, L., & Cacioppo, J. T. 1979. An example of consumeristic social psychology: Bargaining tough in the new car showroom. *Journal of Applied Social Psychology, 9*, 115–26.

Cialdini, R. B., Braver, S. L., & Lewis, S. K. 1974. Attributional bias and the easily persuaded other. *Journal of Personality and Social Psychology, 30*, 631–37.

Cialdini, R. B., Cacioppo, J. T., Bassett, B., & Miller, J. A. 1978. Low-ball procedure for producing compliance: Commitment then cost. *Journal of Personality and Social Psychology, 36*, 463–78.

Cialdini, R. B., Levy, A., Herman, P., & Evenbeck, S. 1973. Attitudinal politics: The strategy of moderation. *Journal of Personality and Social Psychology, 25*, 100–8.

Cialdini, R. B., Vincent, J. E., Lewis, S. K., Catalan, J., Wheeler, D., & Darby, B. L. 1975. Reciprocal consessions procedure for inducing compliance: The door-in-the-face technique. *Journal of Personality and Social Psychology, 31*, 206–15.

Citrin, J. 1974. Comment: The political relevance of trust in government. *The American Political Science Review, 68*, 973–88.

Clark, M. S., & Mills, J. 1979. Interpersonal attraction in exchange and communal relationships. *Journal of Personality and Social Psychology, 37*, 12–24.

Clark, R., & Sechrest, L. B. 1976. The mandate phenomenon. *Journal of Personality and Social Psychology, 34*, 1057–61.

Clark, R. D., III, & Word, L. E. 1974. Where is the apathetic bystander? Situational characteristics of the emergency. *Journal of Personality and Social Psychology, 29*, 279–87.

Clarke-Stewart, K. A. 1973. Interactions between mothers and their young children: Characteristics and consequences. *Child Development, 38*, 153.

Cline, M. F., Holmes, D. S., & Werner, J. C. 1977. Evaluations of the works of men and women as a function of the sex of the judge and type of work. *Journal of Applied Social Psychology, 7,* 89–93.

Cline, V. H., Croft, R. G., & Courrier, S. 1973. Desensitization of children to television violence. *Journal of Personality and Social Psychology, 27,* 360–65.

Clore, G. L., Bray, R. B., Itkin, S. M., & Murphy, P. 1978. Interracial attitudes and behavior at a summer camp. *Journal of Personality and Social Psychology, 36,* 107–16.

Clore, G. L., Wiggins, N., & Itkin, S. 1975. Gain and loss in attraction: Attributions from nonverbal behavior. *Journal of Personality and Social Psychology, 31,* 706–12.

Cochran, S. D., & Peplan, L. A. 1979. The interplay of attachment and autonomy in love relationships: A comparison of men and women. Paper given at Western Psychological Association meeting, April.

Cohen, D., Whitmyre, J. W., & Funk, W. H. 1960. Effect of group cohesiveness and training upon creative thinking. *Journal of Applied Psychology, 44,* 319–22.

Cohen, S., Glass, D. C., & Singer, J. E. 1973. Apartment noise, auditory discrimination, and reading ability in children. *Journal of Experimental Social Psychology, 9,* 407–22.

Coleman, J. F., Blake, R. R., & Mouton, J. S. 1958. Task difficulty and conformity pressures. *Journal of Abnormal and Social Psychology, 57,* 120–22.

Collins, B. E., & Hoyt, M. F. 1972. Personal responsibility-for-conse-quences: An integration and extension of the "forced compliance" literature. *Journal of Experimental Social Psychology, 8,* 558–93.

Comstock, G., Chaffee, S., Katzman, N., McCombs, M., & Roberts, D. 1978. *Television and human behavior.* New York: Columbia University Press.

Comstock, G., Christen, F. G., Fisher, M. L., Quarles, R. C., & Richards, W. D. 1975. *Television and human behavior: The key studies.* Santa Monica: Rand Corporation.

Cook, S. W. 1970. Motives in a conceptual analysis of attitude-related behavior. *Nebraska Symposium on Motivation, 18,* 179–231.

Cook, T. D., & Flay, B. R. 1978. The persistence of experimentally induced attitude change. In Berkowitz, L. (ed.), *Advances in experimental social psychology.* Vol. II. Pp. 2–59. New York: Academic Press.

Cooper, J., & Jones, R. A. 1970. Self-esteem and consistency as determinants of anticipatory opinion change. *Journal of Personality and Social Psychology, 14,* 312–20.

Cooper, J., Zanna, M. P., & Taves, T. A. 1978. Arousal as a necessary condition for attitude change following induced compliance. *Journal of Personality and Social Psychology, 36,* 1101–6.

Costanzo, P. R., & Woody, E. Z. 1979. Externality as a function of obesity in children: Pervasive style or eating-specific attribute? *Journal of Personality and Social Psychology, 37,* 2286–96.

Cotler, S., & Palmer, R. J. 1971. Social reinforcement, individual difference factors, and the reading performance of elementary school children. *Journal of Personality and Social Psychology, 18,* 87–104.

Cottrell, N. B., Rittle, R. H., & Wack, D. L. 1967. Presence of an audience and list type (competitional or noncompetitional) as joint determinants of performance in paired-associates learning. *Journal of Personality, 35,* 425–34.

Cozby, P. C. 1973. Self-disclosure: A literature review. *Psychological Bulletin, 79,* 73–91.

Crano, W. D. 1970. Effects of sex, response order, and expertise in conformity: A dispositional approach. *Sociometry, 33,* 239–252.

Crano, W. D., & Cooper, R. E. 1973. Examination of Newcomb's extension of structural balance theory. *Journal of Personality and Social Psychology, 27,* 344–53.

Crockett, W. H. 1974. Balance, agreement, and subjective evaluations of the P–O–X triads. *Journal of Personality and Social Psychology, 29,* 102–10.

Cronbach, L. J. 1955. Processes affecting scores on "understanding of others" and "assumed similarity." *Psychological Bulletin, 52,* 177–93.

Croner, M. D., & Willis, R. H. 1961. Perceived differences in task competence and symmetry of dyadic influence. *Journal of Abnormal and Social Psychology, 62,* 705–8.

Curran, J. P., & Lippold, S. 1975. The effects of physical attraction and attitude similarity on attraction in dating dyads. *Journal of Personality, 44,* 528–39.

Dabbs, J. M., Jr., & Leventhal, H. 1966. Effects of varying the recommendations in a fear-arousing communication. *Journal of Personality and Social Psychology, 4,* 525–31.

Daher, D. M., & Banikiotes, P. G. 1976. Interpersonal attraction and rewarding aspects of disclosure content and level. *Journal of Personality and Social Psychology, 33,* 492–96.

Dashiell, J. F. 1930. An experimental analysis of some group effects. *Journal of Abnormal and Social Psychology, 25,* 190–99.

Davidson, A. R., & Jaccard, J. J. 1979. Variables that moderate the attitudebehavior relation: Results of a longitudinal survey. *Journal of Personality and Social Psychology, 37,* 1364–76.

Davis, G. J., Meyer, R. K. 1973. FSH and LH in the snowshoe hare during the increasing phase of the 10-year cycle. *General Comparative Endocrinology, 20,* 53–60.

Davis, J. D. 1976. Self-disclosure in an acquaintance exercise: Responsibility for level of intimacy. *Journal of Personality and Social Psychology, 33,* 787–92.

Davis, J. D. 1977. Effects of communication about interpersonal process on the evolution of self-disclosure in dyads. *Journal of Personality and Social Psychology, 35,* 31–37.

Davis, J. H., Kerr, N., Atkin, R., Holt, R., & Meek, D. 1975. The decision process of 6 and 12 person mock juries assigned unanimous and two-third party majority rules. *Journal of Personality and Social Psychology, 32,* 1–14.

Davis, J. H., Stasser, G., Spitzer, C. E., & Holt, R. W. 1976. Changes in group members' decision preferences during discussion: An illustration with mock juries. *Journal of Personality and Social Psychology, 34,* 1177–87.

Dawes, R. M., McTavish, J., & Shaklee, H. 1977. Behavior, communication, and assumptions about other people's behavior in a common dilemma situation. *Journal of Personality and Social Psychology, 35,* 1–11.

Deaux, K. 1976. *The behavior of women and men.* Monterey, Calif.: Brooks/Cole Publishing.

Deaux, K., & Emswiller, T. 1973. Explanations of successful performance on sex-linked tasks: What is skill for the male is luck for the female. *Journal of Personality and Social Psychology, 28,* 360–67.

Deci, E. 1971. Effects of externally mediated rewards on intrinsic motivation. *Journal of Personality and Social Psychology, 18,* 105–11.

Dengerink, H. A., & Myers, J. D. 1977. The effects of failure and depression on subsequent aggression. *Journal of Personality and Social Psychology, 35,* 88–96.

Dengerink, H. A., Schnedler, R. W., & Covey, M. K. 1978. Role of avoidance in aggressive responses to attack and no attack. *Journal of Personality and Social Psychology, 36,* 1044–53.

DePaulo, B. M., Rosenthal, R., Eisenstat, R. A., Rogers, P. L., & Finkelstein, S. 1978. Decoding descrepant nonverbal cues. *Journal of Personality and Social Psychology, 36,* 313–23.

Deutsch, M. 1960. The effect of motivational orientation upon trust and suspicion. *Human Relations, 13,* 122–39.

Deutsch, M., & Collins, M. E. 1951. *Interracial housing: A psychological evaluation of a social experiment.* Minneapolis: University of Minnesota Press.

Deutsch, M., & Gerard, H. B. 1955. A study of normative and informational social influences upon individual judgment. *Journal of Abnormal and Social Psychology, 51,* 629–36.

Deutsch, M., & Krauss, R. M. 1960. The effect of threat on interpersonal bargaining. *Journal of Abnormal and Social Psychology, 61,* 181–89.

Deutsch, M., & Krauss, R. M. 1965. *Theories in Social Psychology.* New York: Basic Books, Inc.

DeVellis, R. G., DeVellis, B. M., & McCauley, C. 1978. Vicarious acquisition of learned helplessness. *Journal of Personality and Social Psychology, 36,* 894–99.

DeVries, V. 1969. Constancy of generic identity in the years three to six. *Child Development, 34*(3).

Diener, E., & DeFour, D. 1978. Does television violence enhance program popularity? *Journal of Personality and Social Psychology, 36,* 333–41.

Diener, F. 1976. Effects of prior destructive behavior, anonymity, and group presence on deindividuation and aggression. *Journal of Personality and Social Psychology, 33,* 497–507.

Diener, F. 1977. Deindividuation: Causes and consequences. *Social Behavior and Personality, 5,* 143–55.

Diener, F., Fraser, S. C., Beaman, A. L., & Kelem, Z. R. T. 1976. Effects of deindividuation variables on stealing among Halloween trick-or-treaters. *Journal of Personality and Social Psychology, 33,* 178–83.

Dienstbier, R. A., & Munter, P. O. 1971. Cheating as a function of labeling of natural arousal. *Journal of Personality and Social Psychology, 17,* 208–13.

Dion, K., Baron, R. S., & Miller, N. 1970. Why do groups make riskier decisions than individuals? In L. Berkowitz (ed.), *Advances in experimental social psychology.* Vol. 5. New York: Academic Press.

Dion, K., Berscheid, E., & Walter, E. 1972. What is beautiful is good. *Journal of Personality and Social Psychology, 24,* 285–90.

Dion, K. K. 1972. Physical attractiveness and evaluations of children's transgressions. *Journal of Personality and Social Psychology, 24,* 285–90.

Dion, K. K., & Stein, S. 1978. Physical attractiveness and interpersonal influence. *Journal of Experimental Social Psychology, 14,* 97–108.

Dittes, J. E. 1959. Effect of changes in self-esteem upon impulsiveness and deliberation in making judgements. *Journal of Abnormal and Social Psychology, 58,* 348–56.

Dohrenwend, B. P., & Dohrenwend, B. S. 1974. Social and cultural influences on psychopathology. *Annual Review of Psychology, 25,* 417–52.

Dollard, J., Doob, J., Miller, N., Mowrer, O., & Sears, R. 1939. *Frustration and aggression.* New Haven, Conn.: Yale University Press.

Donnerstein, E., & Barrett, G. 1978. Effects of erotic stimuli on male aggression toward females. *Journal of Personality and Social Psychology, 36,* 180–88.

Donnerstein, E., Donnerstein, M., & Evans, R. 1975. Erotic stimuli and aggression: Facilitation or inhibition. *Journal of Personality and Social Psychology, 32,* 237–44.

Donnerstein, E., & Hallam, J. 1978. Facilitating effects of erotica on aggression against women. *Journal of Personality and Social Psychology, 36,* 1270–77.

Doob, A. N., & Climie, R. J. 1972. Delay of measurement and the effects of film violence. *Journal of Experimental Social Psychology, 8,* 136–42.

Doob, A. N., & Macdonald, G. E. 1979. Television viewing and fear of victimization: Is the relationship causal? *Journal of Personality and Social Psychology, 37,* 170–79.

Doob, A. N., & Wood, L. 1972. Catharsis and aggression: The effects of annoyance and retaliation on aggressive behavior. *Journal of Personality and Social Psychology, 22,* 156–62.

Dorfman, D. D., Keeve, S., & Saslow, C. 1971. Ethnic identification: A signal detection analysis. *Journal of Personality and Social Psychology, 18,* 373–79.

Dornbusch, S. M., Hastorf, A. H., Richardson, S. A., Muzzy, R. E., & Vreeland, R. S. 1965. The perceiver and the perceived: Their relative influence on the categories of interpersonal cognition. *Journal of Personality and Social Psychology, 1,* 434–40.

Downs, C. W., & Pickett, T. 1977. An analysis of the effects of nine leadership-group compatibility contingencies upon productivity and member satisfaction. *Communication Monographs, 44,* 220–30.

Driscoll, R., Davis, K. E., & Lipetz, M. E. 1972. Parental interference and romantic love: The Romeo & Juliet effect. *Journal of Personality and Social Psychology, 24,* 1–10.

Droege, R. C. 1967. Sex differences in aptitude maturation during high school. *Journal of Counselling Psychology, 14,* 407–11.

Duncan, S., Jr. 1972. Some signals and rules for taking speaking turns in conversations. *Journal of Personality and Social Psychology, 23,* 283–92.

Duncan, S., Jr., & Fiske, D. 1977. *Face-to-face interaction.* Hillsdale, N.J.: Erlbaum.

Dutton, D. G., & Aron, A. P. 1974. Some evidence for heightened sexual attraction under conditions of high anxiety. *Journal of Personality and Social Psychology, 30,* 510–17.

Duval, S., & Wicklund, R. A. 1972. *A theory of objective self-awareness.* New York: Academic Press.

Duval, S., & Wicklund, R. A. 1973. Effects of objective self-awareness on attribution of causality. *Journal of Experimental Social Psychology, 9,* 17–31.

Dyck, R. J., & Rule, B. G. 1978. Effect on retaliation of causal attributions concerning attack. *Journal of Personality and Social Psychology, 36,* 521–29.

Eagly, A. H. 1978. Sex differences in influenceability. *Psychological Bulletin, 85,* 758–73.

Eagly, A. H., & Telaak, K. 1972. Width of the latitude of acceptance as a determinant of attitude change. *Journal of Personality and Social Psychology, 23,* 388–97.

Eagly, A. H., Wood, W., & Chaiken, S. 1978. Causal inferences about communicators and their effect on opinion change. *Journal of Personality and Social Psychology, 36,* 424–35.

Ebbesen, E. B., Duncan, B., & Konecni, V. J. 1975. Effects of content of verbal aggression on future verbal aggression: A field experiment. *Journal of experimental social psychology, 11,* 192–204.

Edelbrock, C., & Sugawara, A. I. 1978. Acquisition of sex-typed preferences in preschool aged children. *Developmental Psychology, 14,* 614–23.

Edwards, W. 1954. The theory of decision-making. *Psychological Bulletin, 51,* 380–417.

Ehrlich, D., Guttman, I., Schonbach, P., & Mills, J. 1957. Post-decision exposure to relevant information. *Journal of Abnormal and Social Psychology, 54,* 98–102.

Ehrlich, H.J. 1973. *The Social Psychology of Prejudice.* New York: John Wiley & Sons.

Eisen, S. V. 1979. Actor-observer differences in information inference and causal attribution. *Journal of Personality and Social Psychology, 37,* 261–72.

Ekman, P., & Friesen, W. V. 1971. Constants across cultures in the face and emotion. *Journal of Personality and Social Psychology, 17,* 124–29.

Ekman, P., & Friesen, W. V. 1974. Detecting deception from body or face. *Journal of Personality and Social Psychology, 29,* 288–98.

Ekman, P., Friesen, W. V., & Scherer, K. 1976. Body movements and voice pitch in deceptive interaction. *Semiotica, 16,* 23–27.

Ellsworth, P., & Carlsmith, J. M. 1973. Eye contact and gaze aversion in an aggressive encounter. *Journal of Personality and Social Psychology, 28,* 280–92.

Ellsworth P., Carlsmith, J. M., & Henson, A. 1972. The stare as a stimulus to flight in human subjects: A series of field experiments. *Journal of Personality and Social Psychology, 21,* 302–11.

Ellsworth, P. C., Friedman, H. S., Perlick, D., & Hoyt, M. E. 1978. Some effects of gaze on subjects motivated to seek or to avoid social comparison. *Journal of Experimental Social Psychology, 14,* 69–87.

Emmerich, W. 1971. Structure and development of personal-social behaviors in preschool settings. *Educational Testing Service—Head Start Longitudinal Study.*

Emmerich, W., Goldman, K. S., Kirsh, B., & Sharabany, R. 1977. Evidence for a transitional phase in the development of gender constancy. *Child Development, 48,* 930–36.

Epstein, S., & Taylor, S. P. 1967. Instigation to aggression as a function of degree of defeat and perceived aggressive intent of the opponent. *Journal of Personality, 35,* 265–89.

Esser, J. K. & Komorita, S. S. 1975. Reciprocity and concession making in bargaining. *Journal of Personality and Social Psychology, 31,* 864–72.

Ettinger, R. F., Marino, C. J., Endler, N. S., Geller, S. H., & Natziuk, T. 1971. Effects of agreement and correctness on relative competence and conformity. *Journal of Personality and Social Psychology, 19,* 204–12.

Evans, G. 1979. Behavioral and physiological consequences of crowding in humans. *Journal of Applied Social Psychology, 9,* 27–46.

Evans, R. I., Rozelle, R. M., Lasater, T. M., Dembroski, T. M., & Allen, B. P. 1970. Fear arousal, persuasion, and actual versus implied behavioral change: New perspective utilizing a real-life dental hygiene program. *Journal of Personality and Social Psychology, 16,* 220–27.

Fazio, R. H., & Zanna, M. P. 1978. Attitudinal qualities relating to the strength of the attitude-behavior relationship. *Journal of Experimental Social Psychology, 14,* 398–408.

Feldman, N. S., Higgins, E. T., Karlovac, M., & Ruble, D. N. 1976. Use of consensus information in causal attributions as a function of temporal presentation and availability of direct information. *Journal of Personality and Social Psychology, 34,* 694–98.

Felipe, N. J., & Sommer, R. 1966. Invasions of personal space. *Social Problems, 14,* 206–14.

Fenigstein, A. 1979. Does aggression cause a preference for viewing media violence? *Journal of Personality and Social Psychology, 37,* 2307–98.

Feshbach, N. D., & Sones, G. 1971. Sex differences in adolescent reactions toward newcomers. *Developmental Psychology, 4,* 381–86.

Feshbach, S. 1955. The drive-reducing function of fantasy behavior. *Journal of Abnormal and Social Psychology, 50,* 3–12.

Feshbach, S. 1961. The stimulating versus cathartic effects of a vicarious aggressive activity. *Journal of Abnormal and Social Psychology, 63,* 381–85.

Feshbach, S. 1970. Aggression. In Musser (ed.), *Carmichael's manual of child psychology.* Vol. 2. New York: John Wiley & Sons.

Feshbach, S. 1972. Reality and fantasy in filmed violence. In J. P. Murray, E. A. Rubinstein, and G. A. Comstock (eds.), *Television and social behavior.* Vol. 2. Washington, D.C.: Government Printing Office.

Feshbach, S., & Singer, R. D. 1970. *Television and aggression.* San Francisco: Jossey-Bass.

Festinger, L. 1954. A theory of social comparison processes. *Human Relations, 7,* 117–40.

Festinger, L. 1957. *A theory of cognitive dissonance.* Stanford, Calif.: Stanford University Press, 1957.

Festinger, L., & Carlsmith, J. 1959. Cognitive consequences of forced compliance. *Journal of Abnormal and Social Psychology, 58,* 203–10.

Festinger, L., & Maccoby, N. 1964. On resistance to persuasive communications. *Journal of Abnormal and Social Psychology, 68,* 359–66.

Festinger, L., Pepitone, A., & Newcomb, T. 1952. Some consequences of deindividuation in a group. *Journal of Abnormal and Social Psychology, 47,* 383–89.

Festinger, L., Riecken, H. W., & Schachter, S. 1956. *When prophecy fails.* Minneapolis: University of Minnesota Press.

Festinger, L., Schachter, S., & Back, K. 1950. *Social pressures in informal groups: A study of human factors in housing.* New York: Harper & Row.

Fiedler, F. 1958. *Leader attributes and group effectiveness.* Urbana: University of Illinois Press.

Fiedler, F. 1971. *Leadership.* New York: General Learning Press.

Filter, T. A., & Gross, A. E. 1975. Effects of public and private deviancy on compliance with a request. *Journal of Experimental Social Psychology, 11,* 553–59.

Finkelman, J. M., & Glass, D. C. 1970. Reappraisal of the relationship between noise and human performance by means of a subsidiary task measure. *Journal of Applied Psychology, 54,* 211–13.

Firestone, I. J., Kaufman, I. K., & Russell, I. C. 1973. Anxiety, fear and affiliation with similar-state versus dissimilar-state others: Misery sometimes loves nonmiserable company. *Journal of Personality and Social Psychology, 26,* 409–14.

Fischer, C. S. 1976. *The urban experience.* New York: Harcourt Brace.

Fish, B., Karabenick, S., & Heath, M. 1978. The effects of observation on emotional arousal and affiliation. *Journal of experimental social psychology, 14,* 250–65.

Fisher, J. D., & Byrne, D. 1975. Too close for comfort: Sex differences in response to invasions of personal space. *Journal of Personality and Social Psychology, 32,* 15–21.

Fiske, S. T. 1978. How do I know thee: A review of interpersonal information processing. Unpublished manuscript. Harvard University.

Flanders, J. P., & Thistlewaite, D. L. 1967. Effects of familiarization and group discussion upon risk-taking. *Journal of Personality and Social Psychology, 5,* 91–97.

Fling, S., & Manosevitz, M. 1972. Sex typing in nursery school children's play interests. *Developmental Psychology, 7,* 146–52.

Flowers, M. L. 1977. A laboratory test of some implications of Janis's groupthink hypothesis. *Journal of Personality and Social Psychology, 35,* 888–96.

Folkes, V. S., & Sears, D. O. 1977. Does everybody like a liker? *Journal of Experimental Social Psychology, 13,* 505–19.

Frager, R. 1970. Conformity and anticonformity in Japan. *Journal of Personality and Social Psychology, 15,* 203–10.

Fraser, C., Gouge, C., & Billig, M. 1971. Risky shifts, cautious shifts, and group polarization. *European Journal of Social Psychology, 1,* 7–30.

Freedman, J. L. 1963. Attitudinal effects of inadequate justification. *Journal of Personality, 31,* 371–85.

Freedman, J. L. 1964. Involvement, discrepancy, and change. *Journal of Abnormal and Social Psychology, 64,* 290–95.

Freedman, J. L. 1965. Long-term behavioral effects of cognitive dissonance. *Journal of Experimental Social Psychology, 1,* 145–55.

Freedman, J. L. 1965. Preference for dissonance information. *Journal of Personality and Social Psychology, 2,* 287–89.

Freedman, J. L. 1975. *Crowding and behavior.* New York: Viking Press.

Freedman, J. L. 1978. *Happy people.* New York: Harcourt Brace Jovanovich.

Freedman, J. L. 1979. Reconciling apparent differences between the responses of humans and other animals to crowding. *Psychological Review, 86,* 80–85.

Freedman, J. L., & Fraser, S. C. 1966. Compliance without pressure: The foot-in-the-door technique. *Journal of Personality and Social Psychology, 4,* 195–202.

Freedman, J. L., Heshka, S., & Levy, A. 1973. Population density and pathology: Is there a relationship? *Journal of Experimental Social Psychology, 11,* 539–52.

Freedman, J. L., Klevansky, S., & Ehrlich, P. 1971. The effect of crowding on human task performance. *Journal of Applied Social Psychology, 1,* 7–25.

Freedman, J. L., Levy, A. S., Buchanan, R. W., & Price, J. 1972. Crowding and human aggressiveness. *Journal of Experimental Social Psychology, 8,* 528–48.

Freedman, J. L., & Sears, D. O. 1965. Warning, distraction and resistance to influence. *Journal of Personality and Social Psychology, 1,* 262–65.

Freedman, J. L., & Steinbruner, J. D. 1964. Perceived choice and resistance to persuasion. *Journal of Abnormal and Social Psychology, 68,* 678.

Freedman, J. L., Wallington, S., & Bless, E. 1967. Compliance without pressure: The effect of guilt. *Journal of Personality and Social Psychology, 7,* 117–24.

French, J. R. P., Jr. 1944. Organized and unorganized groups under fear and frustration. *University of Iowa studies: Studies in child welfare.* Iowa City: University of Iowa.

Fried, R., & Berkowitz, L. 1979. Music hath charms . . . and can influence helpfulness. *Journal of Applied Social Psychology, 3,* 199–208.

Friedland, N., Arnold, S. E., & Thibaut, J. 1974. Motivational bases in mixed-motive interactions: The effects of comparison levels. *Journal of Experimental Social Psychology, 10,* 188–99.

Friedman, H. 1976. Effects of self-esteem and expected duration of interaction on liking for a highly rewarding partner. *Journal of Personality and Social Psychology, 33*(6), 686–90.

Friedman, L. 1979. The relationship of some architectural variables to the social behavior of building residents. Dissertation. Columbia University.

Friedrich, L. K., & Stein, A. H. 1973. Aggressive and prosocial television programs and the natural behavior of preschool children. *Child Development, 38*(4, Serial No. 151).

Frieze, I. H., Parsons, J. E., Johnson, P. B., Puble, D. N., & Zellman, G. L. 1978. *Women and Sex Roles: A Social Psychological Perspective.* New York: Norton.

Frodi, A., Macauley, J., & Thome, P. R. 1977. Are women always less aggressive than men? A review of the experimental literature. *Psychological Bulletin, 84,* 634–60.

Fromkin, H. L., Goldstein, J. H., & Brock, T. C. 1977. The role of "irrelevant" derogation in vicarious aggression catharsis: A field experiment. *Journal of Experimental Social Psychology, 13,* 239–52.

Gage, N. L. 1952. Judging interests from expressive behavior. *Psychology Monographs, 66*(18, Whole No. 350).

Gahart, M. T., & Sears, D. O. 1980. Attitude stability through the life cycle: Racial prejudice as a function of environmental consistency. Paper presented at the annual meeting of the Western Psychological Association, Hawaii.

Galle, O. R., Gove, W. R., & McPherson, J. M. 1972. Population density and pathology: What are the relations for man. *Science, 176,* 23–30.

Gallo, P. S. 1966. Effects of increased incentives upon the use of threat in bargaining. *Journal of Personality and Social Psychology, 4,* 14–20.

Gallo, P. S., & Sheposh, J. 1971. Effects of incentive magnitude on cooperation in the prisoner's dilemma game: A reply to Gumpert, Deutsch, and Epstein. *Journal of Personality and Social Psychology, 19,* 42–46.

Gardner, G. T. 1978. Effects of federal human subjects regulations on data obtained in environmental stressor research. *Journal of Personality and Social Psychology, 36,* 628–34.

Garrett, C. S., Ein, P. L., & Tremaine, L. 1977. The development of gender stereotyping of adult occupations in elementary school children. *Child Development, 48,* 507–12.

Gates, M. F., & Allee, W. C. 1933. Conditioned behavior of isolated and grouped cockroaches on a simple maze. *Journal of Comparative Psychology, 15,* 331–58.

Geen, R. G., & O'Neal, E. C. 1969. Activation of cue-elicited aggression by general arousal. *Journal of Personality and Social Psychology, 11,* 289–92.

Geen, R. G., & Pigg, R. 1970. Acquisition of an aggressive response and its generalization to verbal behavior. *Journal of Personality and Social Psychology, 15,* 165–70.

Geen, R. G., & Quantz, M. B. 1977. The catharsis of aggression: An evaluation of a hypothesis. In Berkowitz, L. (ed.), *Advances in experimental social psychology.* Vol. 10. Pp. 2–39. New York: Academic Press.

Gerard, H. B. 1963. Emotional uncertainty and social comparison. *Journal of Abnormal and Social Psychology, 66,* 568–73.

Gerard, H. B., & Rabbie, J. M. 1961. Fear and social comparison. *Journal of Abnormal and Social Psychology, 62,* 586–92.

Gerard, H. B., Wilhelmy, R. A., & Connolley, E. S. 1968. Conformity and group size. *Journal of Personality and Social Psychology, 8,* 79–82.

Gerbner, G., Gross, L., Eleey, M. F., Jackson-Beeck, M., Jeffries-Fox, S., & Signorelli, N. 1977. Television violence profile no. 8: The highlights. *Journal of Communication, 27,* 171–80.

Gergen, K. J. 1978. Toward generative theory. *Journal of Personality and Social Psychology. 36,* 1344–60.

Gergen, K. J., Ellsworth, P., Muslach, C. & Seipel, M. 1975. Obligation, donor resources, and reactions to aid in three cultures. *Journal of Personality and Social Psychology, 31,* 390–400.

Gibb, C. 1969. Leadership. In G. Lindzey and E. Aronson (eds.), *Handbook of social psychology.* 2nd edition. Vol. 4. Reading, Mass.: Addison-Wesley.

Ginter, G., & Lindskold, S. 1975. Rate of participation and expertise as factors influencing leader choice. *Journal of Personality and Social Psychology, 32,* 1085–89.

Ginsburg, H. J., Polman, V. A., Yanson, M. S. & Hope, M. L. 1977. Variation of aggressive interaction among male elementary school children as a function of chances in spatial density. *Environmental Psychology and Nonverbal Behavior, 2,* 67–75.

Glass, D. C., & Singer, J. E. 1972. *Urban stress.* New York: Academic Press.

Goethals, G. R., Cooper, J., & Naficy, A. 1979. Role of foreseen, foreseeable and unforeseeable behavioral consequences in the arousal of cognitive dissonance. *Journal of Personality and Social Psychology, 37,* 1179–85.

Goethals, G. R., & Zanna, M. P. 1979. The role of social comparison in choice shifts. *Journal of Personality and Social Psychology, 37,* 1469–76.

Goldberg, L. R. 1978. Differential attribution of trait-descriptive terms to oneself as compared to well-liked, neutral, and disliked others: A psychometric analysis. *Journal of Personality and Social Psychology, 36,* 1012–28.

Goldberg, P. 1968. Are women prejudiced against women? *Transaction, 5,* 28–30.

Goldman, W., & Lewis, P. 1977. Beautiful is good: Evidence that the physically attractive are more socially skillful. *Journal of Experimental Social Psychology, 13,* 125–30.

Goldstein, J. H., & Arms, R. L. 1971. Effects of observing athletic contests on hostility. *Sociometry, 34,* 83–90.

Goldstein, J. H., Davis, R. W., & Herman, D. 1975. Escalation of aggression: Experimental studies. *Journal of Personality and Social Psychology, 31,* 162–70.

Goodman, M. E. 1952. *Race awareness in young children.* Cambridge, Mass.: Addison-Wesley.

Goranson, R. E., & Berkowitz, L. 1966. Reciprocity and responsibility reactions to prior help. *Journal of Personality and Social Psychology, 3,* 227–32.

Goranson, R. E., & King, D. 1977. Rioting and daily temperature: Analysis of the U.S. riots in 1967. Unpublished manuscript. York University, Toronto, 1970. Cited in R. A. Bacon and D. Byrne, *Social psychology.* 2nd edition. Boston: Allyn-Bacon.

Gould, R., & Sigall, H. 1977. The effects of empathy and outcome on attribution: An examination of the divergent-perspectives hypothesis. *Journal of Experimental Social Psychology, 13,* 480–91.

Grager, D. A. 1976. Press and TV as opinion resources in presidential campaigns. *Public Opinion Quarterly, 40,* 285–303.

Graebner, D. B. 1972. A decade of sexism in readers. *Reading Teacher, 26,* 52–58.

Gramza, A. F. 1967. Responses of brooding nighthawks to a disturbance stimulus. *Auk, 84*(1), 72–86.

Granberg, D., & Brent, E. E., Jr. 1974. Dove-Hawk placements in the 1968 election: Application of social judgment and balance theories. *Journal of Personality and Social Psychology, 29*(5), 687–95.

Granberg, D., Cooper, H. M., & King, M. 1979. Cross-lagged panel analysis of the relation between attraction and perceived similarity. Unpublished manuscript. Center for Research in Social Behavior, University of Missouri, Columbia.

Graziano, W., Brothen, T., & Berscheid, E. 1978. Height and attraction: Do men and women see eye-to-eye? *Journal of Personality, 46,* 128–45.

Greeley, A. M., & Sheatsley, P. B. 1971. Attitudes toward racial integration. *Scientific American, 223,* 13–19.

Greenbaum, P., & Rosenfeld, H. M. 1978. Patterns of avoidance in response to interpersonal staring and proximity: Effects of bystanders on drivers at a traffic intersection. *Journal of Personality and Social Psychology, 36,* 575–87.

Greenberg, B. S., & Mazingo, S. L. 1976. Racial issues in mass media institutions. In Katz, P. A. (ed.), *Towards the elimination of racism.* Elmsford, N.Y.: Pergamon Press. Pp. 309–40.

Greenberg, J. 1978. Effects of reward value and retaliative power on allocation decisions: justice, generosity, or greed. *Journal of Personality and Social Psychology, 36,* 367–79.

Greenberg, J. 1978. Equity, equality, and the Protestant ethic: Allocating rewards following fair and unfair competition. *Journal of Experimental Social Psychology, 14,* 217–26.

Greenberg, M. S., & Frisch, D. M. 1972. Effect of intentionality on willingness to reciprocate a favor. *Journal of Experimental Social Psychology, 8,* 99–111.

Greenwald, A. G. 1968. Cognitive Learning, Cognitive Response to Persuasion, and Attitude Change. In Greenwald, A. G., Brock, T. C., and Ostrom, T. M. (eds.), *Psychological Foundations of Attitudes.* New York: Academic Press, pp. 147–70.

Greenwald, A. G., & Sakumura, J. S. 1967. Attitude and selective learning: Where are the phenomena of yesteryear? *Journal of Personality and Social Psychology, 7,* 387–97.

Griffit, W., & Veitch, R. 1971. Hot and crowded: Influences of population density and temperature on interpersonal affective behavior. *Journal of Personality and Social Psychology, 17,* 92–98.

Gross, A. E., & Crofton, C. 1977. What is good is beautiful. *Sociometry, 40,* 85–90.

Gruder, C. L., Romer, D., & Korth, B. 1978. Dependency and fault as determinants of helping. *Journal of Experimental Social Psychology, 14,* 227–35.

Grusec, J. E., & Skubiski, S. 1970. Model nurturance, demand characteristics of the modeling experiment and altruism. *Journal of Personality and Social Psychology, 14,* 353–59.

Grush, J. E., McKeogh, K. L., & Ahlering, R. G. 1978. Extrapolating laboratory exposure research to actual political elections. *Journal of Personality and Social Psychology, 36,* 257–70.

Guetzkow, H., & Simon, H. A. 1955. The impact of certain communication nets upon organization and performance in task-oriented groups. *Management Science, 1,* 233–50.

Gumpert, P., Deutsch, M., & Epstein, Y. 1969. Effect of incentive magnitude on cooperation in the prisoner's dilemma game. *Journal of Personality and Social Psychology, 11,* 66–69.

Gurwitz, S. B., Panciera, L. 1975. Attributions of freedom by actors and observers. *Journal of Personality and Social Psychology, 32,* 531–39.

Guyer, M., & Rapoport, A. 1970. Threat in a two-person game. *Journal of Experimental Social Psychology, 6,* 11–25.

Hall, E. T. 1959. *The silent language.* Garden City, N.Y.: Doubleday.

Hall, E. T. 1966. *The hidden dimension.* Garden City, N.Y.: Doubleday.

Hall, K. R. L. 1960. Social vigilance behavior of the Chacma baboon (*Papio ursinus*). *Behaviour, 16*(3, 4), 261–94.

Hamilton, D. L. 1979. A cognitive-attributional analysis of stereotyping. In Berkowitz, L. (ed.), *Advances in experimental social psychology.* Vol. 12. New York: Academic Press.

Hamilton, D. L. (ed.) 1980. *Cognitive processes in stereotyping and intergroup behavior.* Hillsdale, N.J.: L. Erlbaum, 1980.

Hamilton, D. L. 1980. Cognitive representations of persons. In Higgins, E. T., Herman, C. P., and Zanna, M. P. (eds.), *Social cognition: The Ontario symposium on personality and social psychology.* Hillsdale, N.J.: Lawrence Erlbaum.

Hamilton, D. L., & Fallot, R. D. 1974. Information salience as a weighting factor in impression formation. *Journal of Personality and Social Psychology, 30,* 444–48.

Hamilton, D. L., & Zanna, M. P. 1972. Differential weighting favorable and unfavorable attributes in impressions of personality. *Journal of Experimental Research in Personality, 6,* 204–12.

Hamilton, D. L., Zanna, M. P. 1974. Context effects in impression formation: Changes in connotative meaning. *Journal of Personality and Social Psychology, 29,* 649–54.

Hansen, R. D., & Donaghue, J. M. 1977. The power of consensus: information derived from one's own and others' behavior. *Journal of Personality and Social Psychology, 35,* 294–302.

Hansson, R. O., & Slade, K. M. 1977. Altruism toward a deviant in city and small town. *Journal of Applied Social Psychology, 7,* 272–79.

Harachiewicz, J. M. 1979. The effects of reward contingency and performance feedback on intrinsic motivation. *Journal of Personality and Social Psychology, 37,* 1352–63.

Harlow, H. F., & Zimmermann, R. R. 1959. Affectional responses in the infant monkey. *Science, 130,* 421–32.

Harrison, A. A. 1977. Mere exposure. In Berkowitz, L. (ed.), *Advances in experimental social psychology.* Vol. 10. Pp. 40–76. New York: Academic Press.

Harrison, A. A., & Saeed, L. 1977. Let's make a deal: An analysis of revelations and stipulations in lonely hearts advertisements. *Journal of Personality and Social Psychology, 35,* 257–64.

Hartley, R. 1960. Children's concepts of male and female roles. *Merrill-Palmer Quarterly, 6,* 83–91.

Hartman, D. P. 1969. Influence of symbolically modeled instrumental aggression and pain cues on aggressive behavior. *Journal of Personality and Social Psychology, 11,* 280–88.

Hartnett, J. J., Bailey, K. G., & Gibson F. W., Jr. 1970. Personal space as influenced by sex and type of movement. *Journal of Psychology, 76,* 139–44.

Hass, R. G., & Grady, K. 1975. Temporal delay, type of forewarning and resistance to influence. *Journal of Experimental Social Psychology, 11,* 459–69.

Hastorf, A. H., Northcraft, G. B., & Picciotto, S. R. 1979. Helping the handicapped: How realistic is the performance feedback received by the physically handicapped. *Personality and Social Psychology Bulletin, 5,* 373–76.

Heberlein, T. A., & Black, J. S. 1976. Attitudinal specificity and the prediction of behavior in a field setting. *Journal of Personality and Social Psychology, 33,* 474–79.

Heff, H. 1979. Background and focal environmental conditions of the home and attention in young children. *Journal of Applied Social Psychology, 9,* 47–69.

Heider, F. 1958. *The psychology of interpersonal relations.* New York: Wiley.

Heider, F., & Simmel, M. 1944. An experimental study of apparent behavior. *American Journal of Psychology, 57,* 243–59.

Heilbrun, A. B., Jr. 1977. Measurement of masculine and feminine sex-role identities as independent dimensions. *Journal of Consulting and Clinical Psychology, 1977, 44,* 183–90.

Heller, J. B., Groff, B. D., & Solomon, S. H. 1977. Toward an understanding of crowding: The role of physical interaction. *Journal of Personality and Social Psychology, 35,* 183–90.

Helmreich, P., Spence, J., & Holahan, C. 1979. Psychological androgyny and sex role flexibility: A test of two hypotheses. *Journal of Personality and Social Psychology, 37,* 1631–44.

Henchy, T., & Glass, D. C. 1968. Evaluation apprehension and the social facilitation of dominant and subordinate responses. *Journal of Personality and Social Psychology, 10,* 446–54.

Henley, N. M. 1973. The politics of touch. In P. Brown (ed.), *Radical psychology.* New York: Harper and Row.

Higbee, K. L. 1969. Fifteen years of fear arousal: Research on threat appeals, 1953–1968. *Psychological Bulletin, 72,* 426–44.

Higgins, E. T., Rhodewalt, F., & Zanna, M. P. 1979. Dissonance motivation: Its nature, persistence, and reinstatement. *Journal of Experimental Social Psychology, 15,* 16–34.

Hodges, B. H. 1974. Effect of valence on relative weighting in impression information. *Journal of Personality and Social Psychology, 39,* 378–81.

Hokanson, J. E. 1961. Vascular and psychogalvanic effects of experimentally aroused anger. *Journal of Personality, 29,* 30–39.

Hokanson, J. E., & Burgess, M. 1962. The effects of three types of aggression on vascular processes. *Journal of Abnormal and Social Psychology, 64,* 446–49.

Holmes, D. S. 1972. Aggression, displacement and guilt. *Journal of Personality and Social Psychology, 21,* 296–301.

Homans, G. C. 1961. *Social behavior: Its elementary forms.* New York: Harcourt Brace.

Homans, G. C. 1965. Group factors in worker productivity. In H. Proshansky and L. Seidenberg (eds.), *Basic studies in social psychology.* New York: Holt.

Homicide in Canada: A Statistical Synopsis. (Ottawa: Statistics Canada, 1979).

Hopkins, J. R. Sexual behavior in adolescence. *Journal of Social Issues, 1977, 33,* 67–85.

Horowitz, M. J., Duff, D. F., & Stratton, L. O. 1970. Personal space and the body buffer zone. In H. Proshansky, W. Ittelson, & L. Rivlin (eds.), *Environmental psychology: Man and his physical setting.* New York: Holt, Rinehart & Winston.

Hovland, C. I. 1959. Reconciling conflicting results derived from experimental and survey studies of attitude change. *American Psychologist, 14,* 8–17.

Hovland, C. I., Harvey, O. J., & Sherif, M. 1957. Assimilation and contrast effects in reactions to communication and attitude change. *Journal of Abnormal and Social Psychology, 55,* 224–52.

Hovland, C. I., & Janis, I. L. 1959. Summary and implications for further research. In Hovland, C. I., & Janis, I. L. (eds.), *Personality and persuasibility.* New Haven: Yale University Press.

Hovland, C. I., Lumsdaine, A. A., & Sheffield, F. D. 1949. *Experiments on mass communication.* Princeton: Princeton University Press.

Hovland, C. I., & Pritzker, H. A. 1957. Extent of opinion change as a function of amount of change advocated. *Journal of Abnormal and Social Psychology, 54,* 257–61.

Hovland, C. I., & Sears, R. R. 1940. Minor studies in aggression: VI. Correlation of lynchings with economic indices. *Journal of Personality, 9,* 301–10.

Hovland, C. I., & Weiss, W. 1952. The influence of source credibility on communication effectiveness. *Public Opinion Quarterly, 15,* 635–50.

Hunt, P. J., & Hillery, J. M. 1973. Social facilitation at different stages in learning. Paper read at the Midwestern Psychological Association Meetings, Cleveland, Ohio.

Husband, R. W. 1940. Cooperative versus solitary problem solution. *Journal of Social Psychology, 11,* 405–9.

Insko, C. A., & Wilson, M. 1977. Interpersonal Attraction as a Function of Social Interaction. *Journal of Personality and Social Psychology, 35,* 903–11.

Isen, A. M. 1970. Success, failure, attention, and reaction to others: The warm glow of success. *Journal of Personality and Social Psychology, 15,* 294–301.

Isen, A. M., Horn, N., & Rosenhan, D. L. 1973. Effects of success and failure on children's generosity. *Journal of Personality and Social Psychology, 27,* 239–47.

Isen, A. M., & Levin, P. F. 1972. Effect of feeling good on helping: Cookies and kindness. *Journal of Personality and Social Psychology, 21,* 384–88.

Jaffe, Y., Malamuth, N., Feingold, J., & Feshbach, S. 1974. Sexual arousal and behavioral aggression. *Journal of Personality and Social Psychology, 30,* 759–64.

Janis, I. L. 1972. *Victims of groupthink.* Boston: Houghton Mifflin.

Janis, I. L., & Feshbach, S. 1953. Effects of fear-arousing communications. *Journal of Abnormal and Social Psychology, 48,* 78–92.

Janis, I. L., Kaye, D., & Kirschner, P. 1965. Facilitating effects of "eating-while-reading" on responsiveness to persuasive communications. *Journal of Personality and Social Psychology, 1,* 181–06.

Janis, I. L., & Mann, L. 1965. Effectiveness of emotional role-playing in modifying smoking habits and attitudes. *Journal of Experimental Research in Personality, 1,* 84–90.

Janis, I. L., & Rausch, C. N. 1970. Selective interest in communications that could arouse decisional conflict: A field study of participants in the draft resistance movement. *Journal of Personality and Social Psychology, 14,* 46–54.

Janoff-Bulman, R. 1979. Characterological versus behavioral self-blame: Inquiries into depression and rape. *Journal of Personality and Social Psychology, 37,* 1798–809.

Jennings, M. K., & Niemi, R. G. 1974. *The political character of adolescence.* Princeton: Princeton University Press.

Johnson, P. B., Sears, D. O., & McConahay, J. B. 1971. Black invisibility, the press, and the Los Angeles riot. *American Journal of Sociology, 76,* 698–721.

Johnson, R. D., & Downing, L. L. 1979. Deindividuation and valence of cues: Effects of prosocial and antisocial behavior. *Journal of Personality and Social Psychology, 37,* 1532–38.

Johnson, R. W., & Ryan, B. J. 1976. A test of the contingency model of leadership effectiveness. *Journal of Applied Social Psychology, 6,* 177–85.

Jones, E. E. 1964. *Ingratiation.* New York: Appleton-Century-Crofts.

Jones, E. E. 1979. The rocky road from acts to dispositions. *American Psychologist, 34,* 107–17.

Jones, E. E., & Davis, K. E. 1965. From acts to dispositions. In L. Berkowitz (ed.), *Advances in experimental social psychology.* Vol. 2. New York: Academic Press.

Jones, E. E., & Harris, V. A. 1967. The attribution of attitudes. *Journal of Experimental Social Psychology, 3,* 1–24.

Jones, E. E., & Nisbett, R. E. 1972. The actor and the observer: Divergent perceptions of the causes of behavior. *Attribution: Perceiving the causes of behavior.* Morristown, N.J.: General Learning Press.

Jones, E. E., & Sigall, H. 1971. The bogus pipeline: A new paradigm for measuring affect and attitude. *Psychological Bulletin, 76,* 349–64.

Jones, E. E., Worchel, S., Goethals, G. R., & Grumet, J. F. 1971. Prior expectancy and behavioral extremity as determinants of attitude attribution. *Journal of Experimental Social Psychology, 7,* 59–80.

Jones, S. C. 1973. Self and interpersonal evaluations: Esteem theories versus consistency theories. *Psychological Bulletin, 79,* 185–99.

Jones, S. E., & Aiello, J. R. 1973. Proxemic behavior of black and white first-, third-, and fifth-grade children. *Journal of Personality and Social Psychology, 25,* 21–27.

Jones, W. H., Chernovetz, M. E., & Hansson, B. C. 1978. The enigma of androgyny: Differential implications for males and females? *Journal of Clinical and Consulting Psychology, 46,* 298–313.

Jourard, S. M., & Friedman, R. 1970. Experimenter-subject "distance" and self-disclosure. *Journal of Personality and Social Psychology, 15,* 278 82.

Julian, J. W., Regula, C. R., & Hollander, E. P. 1967. *Effects of prior agreement from others on task confidence and conformity.* Technical Report 9, ONR Contract 4679. Buffalo, N.Y.: State University of New York.

Julian, J. W., Ryckman, R. M., & Hollander, E. P. 1966. *Effects of prior group support on conformity: An extension.* Technical Report 4, ONR Contract 4679. Buffalo, N.Y.: State University of New York.

Kagan, J. 1971. *Change and continuity in infancy.* New York: Wiley.

Kahn, A., & McGaughey, T. A. 1977. Distance and liking: When moving close produces increased liking. *Sociometry, 40,* 138–44.

Kahneman, D., & Tversky, A. 1973. On the psychology of prediction. *Psychological Review, 80,* 237–51.

Kandel, D. 1974. Inter- and intragenerational influences on adolescent marijuana use. *Journal of Social Issues, 30,* 107–35.

Kanouse, D. E., & Hanson, Jr., L. R. 1972. Negativity in evaluations. In *Attribution: Perceiving the causes of behavior,* pp. 47–62.

Kaplan, K. J., Firestone, I. J., Degnore, R., & Morre, M. 1974. Gradients of attraction as a function of disclosure probe intimacy and setting formality: On distinguishing attitude oscillation from attitude change—Study One. *Journal of Personality and Social Psychology, 30,* 638–46.

Kaplan, M. F. 1971. Context effects in impression formation: The weighted average versus the meaning-change formulation. *Journal of Personality and Social Psychology, 19,* 92–99.

Kaplan, R., & Singer, J. E. 1976. Violence and viewer aggression: A reexamination of the evidence. *Journal of Social Issues, 32,* 35–70.

Karaz, V., & Perlan, D. 1975. Attribution at the wire: Consistency and outcome finish strong. *Journal of Experimental Social Psychology, 11,* 470–77.

Karlins, M., Coffman, T. L., & Walters, G. 1969. On the fading of social stereotypes: Studies in three generations of college students. *Journal of Personality and Social Psychology, 13,* 1–16.

Karlins, R. A., McFarland, D., Aiello, J. R., & Epstein, Y. M. 1976. Normative mediation of reactions to crowding. *Environmental Psychology and Nonverbal Behavior, 1,* 30–40.

Karniol, R., & Ross, M. 1977. The effects of performance relevant and performance irrelevant rewards on children's intrinsic motivation. *Child Development, 48,* 482–87.

Kassin, S. M. 1979. Consensus information, prediction, and causal attribution: A review of the literature and issues. *Journal of Personality and Social Psychology, 37,* 1966–81.

Katz, D., & Braly, K. W. 1933. Racial stereotypes of 100 college students. *Journal of Abnormal and Social Psychology, 28,* 280–90.

Katz, D. 1960. The functional approach to the study of attitudes. *Public Opinion Quarterly, 24,* 163–204.

Katz, P. A. 1976a. The acquisition of racial attitudes in children. In Katz, P. A. (ed.), *Towards the elimination of racism.* Elmsford, N.Y.: Pergamon Press. Pp. 125–56.

Katz, P. A. 1976b. Attitude change in children: Can the twig be straightened? In Katz, P. A. (ed.), *Towards the elimination of racism.* Elmsford, N.Y.: Pergamon Press. Pp. 213–44.

Kelley, H. H. 1950. The warm-cold variable in the first impressions of persons. *Journal of Personality, 18,* 431–39.

Kelley, H. H. 1967. Attribution theory in social psychology. In D. Levine (ed.) *Nebraska Symposium on Motivation.* Lincoln: University of Nebraska.

Kelley, H. H. 1972. Attribution in social interaction. In Jones, E. E., et al. *Attribution: Perceiving the causes of behavior.* Morristown, N.J.: General Learning Press.

Kelley, H. H., Condry, J. C., Dahlke, A. E., & Hill, A. H. 1965. Collective behavior in simulated panic situation. *Journal of Experimental Social Psychology, 1,* 20–54.

Kelley, H. H., & Michela, J. L. 1979. Attribution theory and research. *Annual Review of Psychology, 31,* 1–79.

Kelley, H. H., & Michela, J. 1980. Annual Review of Psychology, Vol. 31.

Kelley, H. H., Shure, G. H., Deutsch, M., Faucheuz, C., Lanzetta, J. T., Moscovici, S., Nuttin, J. M., Rabbie, J. M., & Thibaut, J. W. 1970. A comparative experimental study of negotiation behavior. *Journal of Personality and Social Psychology, 16,* 411–38.

Kelley, H. H., & Stahelski, A. J. 1970. Errors in perception of intentions in a mixed-motive game. *Journal of Experimental Social Psychology, 6,* 379–400.

Kelley, H. H., & Volkart, E. H. 1952. The resistance to change of group-anchored attitudes. *American Sociological Review, 17,* 453–56.

Kelley, H. H., & Woodruff, C. 1956. Members' reactions to apparent group approval of a counter-norm communication. *Journal of Abnormal and Social Psychology, 52,* 67–74.

Kelley, S., Jr., & Mirer, T. W. 1974. The simple act of voting. *American Political Science Review, 68*(2), 572–91.

Kellogg, R. & Baron, R. S. 1975. Attribution theory, insomnia, and the reverse placebo effect: A reversal of Storms and Nisbett's finding. *Journal of Personality and Social Psychology, 32,* 231–36.

Kelman, H. C. 1961. Process of opinion change. *Public Opinion Quarterly, 25,* 57–78.

Kelman, H. C., & Hovland, C. I. 1953. "Reinstatement" of the communicator in delayed measurement of opinion change. *Journal of Abnormal and Social Psychology, 48,* 327–35.

Kendon, A. 1967. Some functions of gaze-direction in social interaction. *Acta Psychologica, 26,* 22–63.

Kendrick, D. T., Baumann, D. J., & Cialdini, R. B. 1979. A step in the socialization of altruism as hedonism: Effects of negative mood on children's generosity under public and private conditions. *Journal of Personality and Social Psychology, 37,* 747–55.

Kendrick D. T., & Cialdini, R. B. 1977. Romantic attraction: Misattribution versus reinforcement explanations. *Journal of Personality and Social Psychology, 35,* 381–91.

Kenrick, D. T., & Johnson, G. A. 1979. Interpersonal attraction in aversive environments: A problem for the classical conditioning paradigm? *Journal of Personality and Social Psychology, 37,* 572–79.

Kerckhoff, A. C., & Davis, K. E. 1962. Value and need complementarity in mate selection. *American Sociological Review, 26,* 295–303.

Kiesler, C. A., & Kiesler, S. B. 1964. Role of forewarning in persuasive communications. *Journal of Abnormal and Social Psychology, 68,* 547–49.

Kilham, W., & Mann, L. 1974. Level of destructive obedience as a function of transmitter and executant roles in the Milgram Obedience Paradigm. *Journal of Personality and Social Psychology, 29,* 696–702.

Kimble, C. E., Fitz, D., & Onorad, J. R. 1977. Effectiveness of counteraggression strategies in reducing interactive aggression by males. *Journal of Personality and Social Psychology, 35,* 272–78.

Kinder, D. R. 1978. Political person perception: The asymmetrical influence of sentiment and choice on perceptions of presidential candidates. *Journal of Personality and Social Psychology, 36,* 859–71.

Kinder, D. R., & Sears, D. O. 1980. Prejudice and politics: Symbolic racism versus racial threats to the good life. Unpublished manuscript, Yale University.

Kingdon, J. W. 1967. Politicians' beliefs about voters. *The American Political Science Review, 61,* 137–45.

Kleck, R. E., & Rubenstein, C. 1975. Physical attractiveness, perceived attitude similarity, and interpersonal attraction in an opposite-sex encounter. *Journal of Personality and Social Psychology, 31,* 107–14.

Klein, A. L. 1976. Changes in leadership appraisal as a function of the stress of a simulated panic situation. *Journal of Personality and Social Psychology, 34,* 1143–54.

Klein, K., & Harris, B. 1979. Disruptive effects of disconfirmed expectancies about crowding. *Journal of Personality and Social Psychology, 37,* 769–77.

Kleinhesselink, R. R., & Edwards, R. E. 1975. Seeking and avoiding belief-discrepant information as a function of its perceived refutability. *Journal of Personality and Social Psychology, 31,* 787–90.

Klopfer, P. H. 1958. Influence of social interaction on learning rates in birds. *Science, 128,* 903–4.

Knox, R. E., & Inkster, J. A. 1968. Postdecision dissonance at post time. *Journal of Personality and Social Psychology, 8,* 319–23.

Knox, R. E., & Douglas, R. L. 1971. Trivial incentives, marginal comprehension, and dubious generalization from prisoner's dilemma studies. *Journal of Personality and Social Psychology, 20,* 160–65.

Koenig, K. 1973. False emotional feedback and the modification of anxiety. *Behavior Therapy, 4,* 193–202.

Koffka, K. 1935. *Principles of Gestalt psychology.* New York: Harcourt Brace Jovanovich.

Kogan, N., & Carlson, J. 1968. Group risk-taking under competitive and noncompetitive conditions in adults and children. *Journal of Educational Psychology, 60,* 158–67.

Kogan, N., & Doise, W. 1969. Effects of anticipated delegate status on level of risk-taking in small decision-making groups. *Acta Psychologica, 29,* 228–43.

Kogan, N., & Wallach, M. A. 1967. Risk taking as a function of the situation, the person, and the group. In G. Mandler (ed.), *New directions in psychology.* Vol. III. New York: Holt.

Kohlberg, L. 1966. A cognitive-developmental analysis of children's sex-role concepts and attitudes. In B. E. Maccoby (ed.), *The development of sex differences.* Stanford, Calif.: Stanford University Press.

Komarovsky, M. 1973. Cultural contradictions and sex roles: The masculine case. *American Journal of Sociology, 78,* 873–84.

Konečni, V. J. 1972. Some effects of guilt on compliance: A field replication. *Journal of Personality and Social Psychology, 23,* 30–32.

Konečni, V. J., & Doob, A. N. 1972. Catharsis through displacement of aggression. *Journal of Personality and Social Psychology, 23,* 379–87.

Konečni, V. J., & Ebbesen, E. B. 1976. Disinhibition versus the cathartic effect: Artifact and substance. *Journal of Personality and Social Psychology, 34,* 352–65.

Kraus, S., & Davis, D. 1976. *The effects of mass communication on political behavior.* University Park, Penn.: Pennsylvania State University Press.

Krauss, R. M., Geller, V., & Olson, C. 1976. Modalities and cues in the detection of deception. Paper presented at American Psychological Association meetings, September.

Kraut, R. E. 1973. Effects of social labelling on giving to charity. *Journal of Experimental Social Psychology, 9,* 551–62.

Kraut, R. E. 1978. Verbal and nonverbal cues in the perception of lying. *Journal of Personality and Social Psychology, 36,* 380–91.

Kraut, R. E., & Johnston, R. E. 1979. Social and emotional messages of smiling: An ethological approach. *Journal of Personality and Social Psychology, 37,* 1539–53.

Krebs, D., & Adinolfi, A. A. 1975. Physical attractiveness, social relations, and personality style. *Journal of Personality and Social Psychology, 31*(2), 245–53.

Krech, D., and Crutchfield, R. A. 1948. *Theory and Problems of Social Psychology,* New York: McGraw-Hill.

Krech, D., Crutchfield, R. S., & Ballachey, E. L. 1962. *Individual in society.* New York: McGraw-Hill.

Kuethe, J. L., & Weingartner, N. 1964. Male-female schemata of homosexual and nonhomosexual penitentiary inmates. *Journal of Personality, 32,* 23–31.

Kuiper, N. A., & Rogers, T. B. 1979. Encoding of personal information: Self-other differences. *Journal of Personality and Social Psychology, 37,* 499–514.

Kulik, J. A., & Brown, R. 1979. Frustration, attribution of blame, and aggression. *Journal of Experimental Social Psychology, 15,* 183–94.

Kutner, B., Wilkins, C., and Yarrow, P. 1952. Verbal attitudes and overt behavior involving racial prejudice. *Journal of Abnormal and Social Psychology, 47,* 649–52.

Lamm, H., & Kogan, N. 1970. Risk-taking in the context of intergroup negotiation. *Journal of Experimental Social Psychology, 6,* 351–63.

Landy, D. 1972. The effects of an overheard audience's reaction and attractiveness on opinion change. *Journal of Experimental Social Psychology, 8,* 276–88.

Landy D., & Aronson, E. 1969. The influence of the character of the criminal and his victim on the decisions of simulated jurors. *Journal of Experimental Social Psychology, 5,* 141–52.

Landy, D., & Sigall, H. 1974. Beauty is talent: Task evaluation as a function of the performer's physical attractiveness. *Journal of Personality and Social Psychology, 29,* 299–304.

Lane, I. M., & Messé, L. A. 1972. Distribution of insufficient, sufficient, and over-sufficient rewards: A clarification of equity theory. *Journal of Personality and Social Psychology, 21,* 228–33.

Langer, E. J. 1975. The illusion of control. *Journal of Personality and Social Psychology, 32,* 311–28.

Langer, E. J., & Imber, L. G. 1979. When practice makes imperfect: Debilitating effects of overlearning. *Journal of Personality and Social Psychology, 37,* 2014–24.

Langer, E. J., & Rodin, J. 1976. The effects of choice and enhanced personal responsibility for the aged: A field experiment in an institutional setting. *Journal of Personality and Social Psychology, 34,* 191–98.

Langer, R., & Saegert, S. 1977. Crowding and cognitive control. *Journal of Personality and Social Psychology, 35,* 175–82.

Lansky, L. M. 1967. The family structure also affects the model: Sex-role attitudes in parents of preschool children. *Merrill-Palmer Quarterly, 13,* 139–50.

Laosa, L. M. & Brophy, J. E. 1972. Effects of sex and birth order on sex-role development and intelligence among kindergarten children. *Developmental Psychology, 6,* 409–415.

LaPiere, R. 1934. Attitudes versus actions. *Social Forces, 13,* 230–37.

Larsson, R. 1956. *Conditioning and sexual behavior in the male albino rat.* Stockholm: Almqvist & Wiksell.

Latané, B., & Darley, J. M. 1968. Group inhibition of bystander intervention in emergencies. *Journal of Personality and Social Psychology, 10,* 215–21.

Latané, B., & Rodin, J. 1969. A lady in distress: Inhibiting effects of friends and strangers on bystander intervention. *Journal of Experimental and Social Psychology, 5,* 189–202.

Lau, R. R. 1979. Negativity in person perception with applications to political behavior. Doctoral dissertation. University of California, Los Angeles.

Lazarsfeld, P. F., Berelson, B., & Gaudet, H. 1948. *The people's choice.* 2nd ed. New York: Columbia University Press.

Leak, G. K. 1974. Effects of hostility arousal and aggressive humor on catharsis and humor preference. *Journal of Personality and Social Psychology, 30,* 736–40.

LeBon, G. 1895. *The Crowd.* London: F. Unwin.

Leavitt, H. J. 1951. Some effects of certain communication patterns on group performance. *Journal of Abnormal and Social Psychology, 46,* 38–50.

Leibman, M. 1970. The effects of sex and race norms on personal space. *Dissertation Abstracts International, 31,* 3038–39.

Lepper, M. R. 1970. Anxiety and experimenter valence as determinants of social reinforcer effectiveness. *Journal of Personality and Social Psychology, 16,* 704–9.

Lepper, M., Greene, D., & Nisbett, R. 1973. Undermining children's interest with extrinsic rewards: A test of the "overjustification hypothesis." *Journal of Personality and Social Psychology, 28,* 129–37.

Lerner, M. J. 1965. The effect of responsibility and choice on a partner's attractiveness following failure. *Journal of·Personality, 33,* 178–87.

Lerner, M. J. 1974. The justice motive; "equity" and "parity" among children. *Journal of Personality and Social Psychology, 29,* 539–50.

Leventhal, G. S., & Anderson, D. 1970. Self-interest and the maintenance of equity. *Journal of Personality and Social Psychology, 15,* 57–62.

Leventhal, G. S., & Lane, D. W. 1970. Sex, age and equity behavior. *Journal of Personality and Social Psychology, 15,* 312–16.

Leventhal, G. S., Michaels, J. W., & Sanford, G. 1972. Inequity and interpersonal conflict: Reward allocation and secrecy about reward as methods of preventing conflict. *Journal of Personality and Social Psychology, 23,* 88–102.

Leventhal, H. 1970. Findings and theory in the study of fear communications. In Berkowitz, L. (ed.), *Advances in experimental social psychology.* Vol. 5. Pp. 120–86. New York: Academic Press.

Levinger, G., & Schneider, D. J. 1969. Test of the "Risk is a value" hypothesis. *Journal of Personality and Social Psychology, 11,* 165–70.

Lewin, K., Lippitt, R., & White, R. K. 1939. Patterns of aggressive behavior in experimentally created social climates. *Journal of Social Psychology, 10,* 271–99.

Lewis, M. 1972. State as an infant-environment interaction: An analysis of mother-infant behavior as a function of sex. *Merrill-Palmer Quarterly, 18,* 95–121.

Linder, D. E., Cooper, J., & Jones, E. E. 1967. Decision freedom as a determinant of the role of incentive magnitude in attitude change. *Journal of Personality and Social Psychology, 6,* 245–54.

Lippitt, T. R., & White, R. K. 1943. The "social climate" of children's groups. In R. G. Barker, J. S. Kounin, and H. F. Wright (eds.), *Child behavior and development.* New York: McGraw-Hill.

Lipset, S. M. 1960. *Political man.* Garden City, N.Y.: Doubleday.

Little, K. B. 1968. Cultural variations in social schemata. *Journal of Personality and Social Psychology, 10,* 1–7.

Long, G. T., & Lerner, M. J. 1974. Deserving, the "personal contact," and altruistic behavior by children. *Journal of Personality and Social Psychology, 29,* 551–56.

Loo, C. M. 1972. The effects of spatial density on the social behavior of children. *Journal of Applied Social Psychology, 2,* 372–81.

Loo, C., & Kennelly, D. 1979. Social density: Its effects on behaviors and perceptions of preschoolers. *Environmental Psychology and Nonverbal Behavior, 3,* 131–46.

Loo, C., & Smetana, J. 1978. The effects of crowding on the behavior and perception of 10-year-old boys. *Environmental Psychology and Nonverbal Behavior, 2,* 226–49.

Lorenz, K. 1966. *On aggression.* New York: Harcourt, Brace, & World.

Lorenz, K. Z. 1952. *King Solomon's Ring.* London: Methuen.

Lorge, I. 1936. Prestige, suggestion, and attitudes. *Journal of Social Psychology, 7,* 386–402.

Lott, D. F., & Sommer, R. 1967. Seating arrangements and status. *Journal of Personality and Social Psychology, 7,* 90–95.

Lynch, J. G., Jr., & Cohen, J. L. 1978. The use of subjective expected utility theory as an aid to understanding variables that influence helping behavior. *Journal of Personality and Social Psychology, 36,* 1138–51.

McArthur, L. A. 1972. The how and what of why: Some determinants and consequences of causal attribution. *Journal of Personality and Social Psychology, 22,* 171–93.

McArthur, L. A. 1976. The lesser influence of consensus than distinctiveness information on causal attributions: A test of the person-thing hypothesis. *Journal of Personality and Social Psychology, 33,* 733–42.

McArthur, L. Z. & Eisen, S. V. 1976. Achievements of male and female storybook characters as determinants of achievement behavior by boys and girls. *Journal of Personality and Social Psychology, 33,* 467–73.

McArthur, L. Z., & Post, D. L. 1977. Figural emphasis and person perception. *Journal of Experimental Social Psychology, 13,* 520–35.

McCallum, P., Pusbult, C. E., Hong, C. K., Walden, T. A., & Schopler, J. 1979. Effects of resource availability and importance of behavior on the experience of crowding. *Journal of Personality and Social Psychology, 37,* 1304–13.

McCarthy, D., & Saegert, S. 1978. Residential density, social overload, and social withdrawal. *Human Ecology, 6,* 253–72.

McCarthy, J. J., & Kirk, S. A. *The construction, standardization, and statistical characteristics of the Illinois Test of Psycholinguistic Abilities.* Urbana: University of Illinois Press.

McCauley, C., & Taylor, J. 1976. Is there overload of acquaintances in the city? *Environmental Psychology and Nonverbal Behavior, 1,* 41–55.

Maccoby, E. E., & Jacklin, C. N. 1974. *The Psychology of Sex Differences.* Stanford, Calif.: Stanford University Press.

McCord, J. 1979. Some child-rearing antecedents of criminal behavior in adult men. *Journal of Personality and Social Psychology, 37,* 1477–86.

McDonald, R. A. P., Jr. 1970. Anxiety, affiliation and social isolation. *Developmental Psychology, 3,* 242–54.

McGuire, W. J. 1960. Cognitive consistency and attitude change. *Journal of Abnormal and Social Psychology, 60,* 345–53.

McGuire, W. J. 1969. The nature of attitudes and attitude change. In G. Lindzey and E. Aronson (eds.), *The handbook of social psychology.* Vol. 3. 2nd ed. Reading, Mass.: Addison-Wesley. Pp. 136–314.

McGuire, W. J. & Papageorgis, D. 1961. The relative efficacy of various types of prior belief-defense in producing immunity against persuasion. *Journal of Abnormal and Social Psychology, 62,* 327–37.

McIntyre, A. 1972. Sex differences in children's aggression. *Proceedings of the 80th annual convention of the APA, 7,* 93–94.

McNeel, S. P. 1973. Training cooperation in the prisoner's dilemma. *Journal of Experimental Social Psychology, 9,* 335–48.

Madaras, G. R., & Bem, D. J. 1968. Risk and conservatism in group decision making. *Journal of Experimental Social Psychology, 4,* 350–66.

Madsen, D. B. 1978. Issue importance and group choice shifts: A persuasive arguments approach. *Journal of Personality and Social Psychology, 36,* 1118–27.

Malof, M., & Lott, A. J. 1962. Ethnocentrism and the acceptance of Negro support in a group pressure situation. *Journal of Abnormal and Social Psychology, 65,* 254–58.

Manes, A. L., & Melnyk, P. 1974. Televised models of female achievement. *Journal of Applied Social Psychology, 4,* 365–74.

Mann, L. 1977. The effect of stimulus queues on queue-joining behavior. *Journal of Personality and Social Psychology, 35,* 437–42.

Mann, L., & Janis, I. L. 1968. A follow-up study on the long-term effects of emotional role-playing. *Journal of Personality and Social Psychology, 8,* 339–42.

Marcus, D. E., & Overton, W. F. 1978. The development of cognitive gender constancy and sex-role preferences. *Child Development, 49,* 434–44.

Marcus, H. 1977. Self-schemata and processing information about the self. *Journal of Personality and Social Psychology, 35,* 63–78.

Marcus, H. 1978. The effect of mere presence on social facilitation: An unobtrusive test. *Journal of Experimental Social Psychology, 14,* 389–97.

Marquis, D. G. 1962. Individual responsibility and group decisions involving risk. *Industrial Management Review, 3,* 8–23.

Marshall, G. D., & Zimbardo, P. G. 1979. Affective consequences of inadequately explained physiological arousal. *Journal of Personality and Social Psychology, 37,* 970–88.

Marshall, J. E., & Heslin, R. 1975. Boys and girls together: Sexual group composition and the effect of density and group size on cohesiveness. *Journal of Personality and Social Psychology, 3,* 952–61.

Martens, R. 1969. Effect of an audience on learning and performance of a complex motor skill. *Journal of Personality and Social Psychology, 12,* 252–60.

Masters, J. C., & Wilkinson, A. 1976. Consensual and discriminative stereotypes of sex-type judgments by parents and children. *Child Development, 47,* 208–17.

Matlin, M., & Stang, D. 1978. *The Pollyanna Principle: Selectivity in language, memory, and thought.* Cambridge, Mass.: Schenkman.

Mausner, B. 1954. The effect of prior reinforcement on the interaction of observer pairs. *Journal of Abnormal Social Psychology, 49,* 65–68.

Mausner, B. 1954. The effect of one's partner's success in a relevant task on the interaction of observer pairs. *Journal of Abnormal and Social Psychology, 49,* 557–60.

Maykovich, M. K. 1975. Correlates of racial prejudice. *Journal of Personality and Social Psychology, 32,* 1014–20.

Mendelsohn, H., & Crespi, I. 1970. *Polls, television, and the new politics.* Scranton, Penn: Chandler Publications.

Merei, F. 1949. Group leadership and institutionalization. *Human Relations, 2,* 23–29.

Mettee, D. R. 1971a. Changes in liking as a function of the magnitude and effect of sequential evaluations. *Journal of Experimental Social Psychology, 7,* 157–72.

Mettee, D. R. 1971b. The true discerner as a potent

source of positive affect. *Journal of Experimental Social Psychology, 7,* 292–303.

Meyer, J. P., & Pepper, S. 1977. Need compatibility and marital adjustment in young married couples. *Journal of Personality and Social Psychology, 35,* 331–42.

Meyer, T. P. 1972. The effects of sexually arousing and violent films on aggressive behavior. *Journal of Sex Research, 8,* 324–33.

Michelson, W. 1970. *Man and His Urban Environment: A Sociological Approach.* Reading, Mass.: Addison-Wesley.

Michelson, W. 1977. *Environmental choice, human behavior, and residential satisfaction.* New York: Oxford University Press.

Michener, H. A., & Burt, M. R. 1975. Components of "authority" as determinants of compliance. *Journal of Personality and Social Psychology, 31,* 606–14.

Michener, H. A., & Burt, M. R. 1975. Use of social influence under varying conditions of legitimacy. *Journal of Personality and Social Psychology, 32,* 398–407.

Michener, H. A., & Lawler, E. J. 1975. Endorsement of formal leaders: An integrative model. *Journal of Personality and Social Psychology, 31,* 216–23.

Middleton, R. 1976. Regional differences in prejudice. *American Sociological Review, 41,* 94–117.

Milgram, S. 1961. Nationality and conformity. *Scientific American, 205,* 45–51.

Milgram, S. 1963. Behavioral study of obedience. *Journal of Abnormal and Social Psychology, 67,* 371–78.

Milgram, S. 1965. Some conditions of obedience and disobedience to authority. *Human Relations, 18,* 57–76.

Milgram, S. 1970. The experience of living in cities. *Science, 167,* 1461–68.

Milgram, S., Bickman, L., & Berkowitz, L. 1969. Note on the drawing power of crowds of different size. *Journal of Personality and Social Psychology, 13,* 79–82.

Milgram, S., & Shotland, R. L. 1973. *Television and antisocial behavior: Field experiments.* New York: Academic Press.

Miller, A. G. 1976. Constraint and target effects in the attribution of attitudes. *Journal of Experimental Social Psychology, 12,* 325–39.

Miller, A. H. 1974. Political issues and trust in government: 1964–1970. *American Political Science Review, 68,* 951–72.

Miller, A. H., Goldenberg, E. N., & Erbring, L. 1979. Type-set politics: Impact of newspapers on public confidence. *American Political Science Review, 73,* 67–84.

Miller, A. H., Miller, W. E., Brown, T. A., & Raine, A. S., 1976. A majority party in disarray: Policy polarization in the 1972 election. *American Political Science Review, 70,* 753–78.

Miller, D. T. 1977. Altruism and threat to a belief in a just world. *Journal of Experimental Social Psychology, 13,* 113–24.

Miller, D. T., & Ross, M. 1975. Self-serving biases in the attribution of causality: Fact or fiction? *Psychological Bulletin, 82,* 213–25.

Miller, L. W., & Sigelman, L. 1978. Is the audience the message? A note on LBJ's Vietnam statements. *Public Opinion Quarterly, 42,* 71–80.

Miller, N., & Campbell, D. T. 1959. Recency and primacy in persuasion as a function of the timing of speeches and measurements. *Journal of Abnormal and Social Psychology, 59,* 1–9.

Mills, J., & Mintz, P. M. 1972. Effect of unexplained arousal on affiliation. *Journal of Personality and Social Psychology, 24,* 11–13.

Minard, R. D. 1952. Race relationships in the Pocahontas coal field. *Journal of Social Issues, 8,* 29–44.

Minas, J. S., Scodel, A., Marlowe, D., & Rawson, H. 1960 Some descriptive aspects of two-person non-zero-sum games, II. *Journal of Conflict Resolution, 4,* 193–97.

Minton, C., Kagan, J., & Levine, A. 1971. Maternal control and obedience in the two-year-old. *Child Development, 42,* 1873–94.

Mintz, A. 1946. A reexamination of correlations between lynchings and economic indices. *Journal of Abnormal and Social Psychology, 41,* 154–60.

Mintz, A. 1951. Nonadaptive group behavior. *Journal of Abnormal and Social Psychology, 46,* 150–59.

Mischel, H. 1974. Sex bias in the evaluation of professional achievements. *Journal of Educational Psychology, 66,* 157–66.

Mischel, W. 1979. On the interface of cognition and personality: Beyond the person-situation debate. *American Psychologist, 34,* 740–54.

Mita, T. H., Dermer, M., & Knight, J. 1977. Reversed facial images and the mere-exposure hypothesis. *Journal of Personality and Social Psychology, 35,* 597–601.

Mitchell, R. E. 1971. Some social implications of high-density housing. *American Sociological Review, 36,* 18–29.

Monson, T. C., & Snyder, M. 1977. Actors, observers, and the attribution process: Toward a reconceptualization. *Journal of Experimental Social Psychology, 13,* 89–111.

Moreland, R. L., & Zajonc, R. B. 1979. Exposure effects may not depend on stimulus recognition. *Journal of Personality and Social Psychology, 37,* 1085–89.

Morgan, B. S. 1976. Intimacy of disclosure topics and sex differences in self-disclosure. *Sex-Roles, 2,* 161–67.

Morgan, C. J. 1978. Bystander intervention: Experimental test of a formal model. *Journal of Personality and Social Psychology, 36,* 43–55.

Morgan, C. J., & Leik, R. K. 1979. Simulation theory development: The bystander intervention case. In R. B. Smith & B. Anderson (eds.), *Social science methods, Vol. 3: Theory Construction.* Halstead Press.

Moriarty, T. 1975. Crime, commitment, and the responsive bystander: Two field experiments. *Journal of Personality and Social Psychology, 31,* 370–76.

Morris, W. N. & Miller, R. S. 1975. The effects of consensus-breaking and consensus-preempting partners on reduction in conformity. *Journal of Experimental Social Psychology, 11,* 215–23.

Morse, S. J., Gruzen, J., & Reis, H. 1976. The "eye of the beholder": A neglected variable in the study of physical attractiveness? *Journal of Personality, 44,* 209–25.

Moscovici, S., & Zavalloni, M. 1969. The group as a polarizer of attitudes. *Journal of Personality and Social Psychology, 12,* 125–35.

Moss, H. A. 1967. Sex, age, and state as determinants of mother-infant interaction. *Merrill-Palmer Quarterly, 13,* 19–36.

Mueller, C., & Donnerstein, E. 1977. The effects of humor-induced arousal upon aggressive behavior. *Journal of Research in Personality, 11,* 73–82.

Mueller, J. E. 1973. *War, presidents, and public opinion.* New York: Wiley.

Mulder, M., & Stemerding, A. 1963. Threat, attraction to group and need for strong leadership. *Human Relations, 16,* 317–34.

Murphy, G., Murphy, L. B., & Newcomb, T. N. 1937. *Experimental social psychology* (rev. ed.). New York: Harper.

Murray, H. A. 1933. The effect of fear upon estimates of the maliciousness of other personalities. *Journal of Social Psychology, 4,* 310–29.

Murstein, B. I. 1972. Physical attractiveness and marital choice. *Journal of Personality and Social Psychology, 22,* 8–12.

Myers, D. G., & Lamb, H. 1976. The group polarization phenomenon. *Psychological Bulletin, 83,* 602–27.

Nash, S. C. 1973. Conceptions and concomitants of sex-role stereotyping. Unpublished doctoral dissertation. Columbia University.

Nemeth, C. 1977. Interaction between jurors as a function of majority vs. unanimity rules. *Journal of Applied Social Psychology, 7,* 38–56.

Neuman, W. R. 1976. Patterns of recall among television news viewers. *Public Opinion Quarterly, 40,* 115–23.

Newcomb, T. M. 1943. *Personality and social change.* New York: Holt.

Newcomb, T. M. 1961. *The acquaintance process.* New York: Holt.

Newcomb, T. M. Persistence and regression of changed attitudes: Long-range studies. *Journal of Social Issues,* 1963, 19, 3–14.

Newcomb, T. M. 1968. Interpersonal balance. In Abelson, R. P. et al. (eds.), *Theories of cognitive consistency: A sourcebook.* Chicago: Rand, McNally.

Newcomb, T. M., Koenig, K. E., Flacks, R., & Warwick, D. P. 1967. *Persistence and change: Bennington College and its students after 25 years.* New York: John Wiley & Sons.

Newman, O. 1973. *Defensible space.* New York: Macmillan.

Newson, J., & Newson, E. 1968. *Four years old in an urban community.* Harmondworth, Eng.: Pelican Books.

Newtson, D. 1973. Attribution and the unit of perception of ongoing behavior. *Journal of Personality and Social Psychology, 28,* 28–38.

Newtson, D., & Czerlinsky, T. 1974. Adjustment of attitude communications for contrasts by extreme audiences. *Journal of Personality and Social Psychology, 30,* 829–37.

Newtson, D., Engquist, G., & Bois, J. 1977. The objective basis of behavior units. *Journal of Personality and Social Psychology, 35,* 847–62.

Newtson, D., & Rindner, R. J. 1979. Variation in behavior perception and ability attribution. *Journal of Personality and Social Psychology, 37,* 1847–58.

Newtson, D., Rindner, R., Miller, R., & Lacross, K. 1978. Effects of availability of feature changes on behavior segmentation. *Journal of Experimental Social Psychology, 14,* 379–88.

Nickel, T. W. 1974. The attribution of intention as a critical factor in the relation between frustration and aggression. *Journal of Personality, 42,* 482–92.

Nie, N. H., Verba, S., & Petrocik. 1976. *The changing American voter.* Cambridge: Harvard University Press.

Niemi, Richard, G. 1974. *How family members perceive each other.* New Haven: Yale University Press.

Niemi, R. G., Ross, R. D., & Alexander, J. 1978. The similarity of political values of parents and college-age youths. *Public Opinion Quarterly, 42,* 503–20.

Nincic, M., & Russett, B. 1979. The effect of similarity and interest on attitudes toward foreign countries. *Public Opinion Quarterly, 43,* 68–78.

Nisbett, R. E. 1973. Behavior as seen by the actor and as seen by the observer. *Journal of Personality and Social Psychology, 27*(2), 154–64.

Nisbett, R. E., & Borgida, E. 1975. Attribution and the psychology of prediction. *Journal of Personality and Social Psychology, 32,* 932–43.

Nisbett, R. E., Borgida, E., Crandall, R., & Reed, H. 1976. Popular induction: Information is not necessarily informative. In J. S. Carroll and J. W. Payne (eds.), *Cognition and social behavior.* Hillsdale, N.J.: Lawrence Erlbaum.

Nisbett, R. E., Caputo, C., Legant, P., & Marecek, J. 1973. Behavior as seen by the actor and as seen by the observer. *Journal of Personality and Social Psychology, 27,* 154–64.

Nisbett, R. E., & Ross, L. 1980. *Human inference: Strategies and short-comings of social judgment.* Englewood Cliffs, N.J.: Prentice-Hall.

Nisbett, R. E., & Schachter, S. 1966. Cognitive manipulation of pain. *Journal of Experimental Social Psychology, 2,* 227–36.

Nisbett, R. E., & Wilson, T. D. 1977a. Telling more than we can know: Verbal reports on mental processes. *Psychological Review, 84,* 231–59.

Nogami, G. Y. 1976. Crowding: Effects of group size, room size, or density? *Journal of Applied Social Psychology, 6,* 105–25.

Nordhoy, F. 1962. Group interaction in decision-making under risk. Unpublished master's thesis. School of Industrial Management, Massachusetts Institute of Technology.

Norman, R. 1975. Affective-cognitive consistency, attitudes, conformity, and behavior. *Journal of Personality and Social Psychology, 32,* 83–91.

Norman, R. 1976. When what is said is important: A

comparison of expert and attractive sources. *Journal of Experimental Social Psychology, 12,* 294–300.

Omark, D. R., Omark, M., & Edelman, M. 1973. Dominance hierarchies in young children. Paper presented at the International Congress of Anthropological and Ethnological Science.

Orvis, B. R. 1977. The bases, nature, and affective significance of attributional conflict in young couples. Dissertation. University of California, Los Angeles.

Orvis, B. R., Kelley, H. H., & Butler, D. 1976. Attributional conflict in young couples. In Harvey, J. H., Ickes, W., and Kidd, R. F. (eds.), *New Directions in Attribution Research.* Vol 1. Pp. 353–86. Hillsdale: Erlbaum.

Osborn, A. F. 1957. *Applied imagination.* New York: Scribners.

Osgood, C. E., Suci, G. J., & Tannenbaum, P. S. 1957. *The measurement of meaning.* Urbana: University of Illinois Press.

Oskamp, S., & Kleinke, C. 1970. Amount of reward as a variable in the prisoner's dilemma game. *Journal of Personality and Social Psychology, 16,* 133–40.

Osterhouse, R. A., Brock, T. C. 1970. Distraction increases yielding to propaganda in inhibiting counterarguing. *Journal of Personality and Social Psychology, 15,* 344–58.

Ostrom, T. M. 1967. Meaning shift in the judgment of compound stimuli. Unpublished manuscript. Ohio State University.

Page, M. M., & Scheidt, R. J. 1971. The elusive weapon effect: Demand awareness, evaluation apprehension, and slightly sophisticated subjects. *Journal of Personality and Social Psychology, 20,* 304–18.

Pallak, M. S., & Pittman, T. S. 1972. General motivational effects of dissonance arousal. *Journal of Personality and Social Psychology, 21,* 349–58.

Pallak, M. S., Sogin, S. R., & Van Zante, A. 1974. Bad decisions: Effect of volition, locus of causality, and negative consequences on attitude change. *Journal of Personality and Social Psychology, 30,* 217–27.

Parke, R. D., Berkowitz, L., Leyens, J. P., West, S. G., & Sebastian, R. J. 1977. Some effects of violent and nonviolent movies on the behavior of juvenile delinquents. In Berkowitz, L. (ed.), *Advances in Experimental Social Psychology.* Vol. 10. Pp. 136–73. New York: Academic Press.

Patterson, M. L., & Sechrest, L. B. 1970. Interpersonal distance and impression formation. *Journal of Personality, 38,* 161–66.

Patterson, T. E. 1980. *The mass media election: How Americans choose their president.* New York: Praeger.

Patterson, T. E., & McClure, R. D. 1976. *The unseeing eye.* New York: G. P. Putnam's Sons.

Paucer, S. M., McMykkwb, L. M., Kabatoff, B. A., Johnson, K. G., & Pond, C. A. 1979. Conflict and avoidance in the helping situation. *Journal of Personality and Social Psychology, 37,* 1406–11.

Paulus, P. B., Annis, A. B., Seta, J. J., Schkade, J. K., & Matthews, R. W. 1976. Density does affect task performance. *Journal of Personality and Social Psychology, 34,* 248–53.

Paulus, P. B., & Murdoch, P. 1971. Anticipated evaluation and audience presence in the enhancement of dominant responses. *Journal of Experimental Social Psychology, 7,* 280–91.

Pedersen, F. A., & Bell, R. Q. 1970. Sex differences in preschool children without histories of complications of pregnancy and delivery. *Developmental Psychology, 3,* 10–15.

Perlman, D., & Oskamp, S. 1971. The effects of picture content and exposure frequency on evaluations of negroes and whites. *Journal of Experimental Social Psychology, 7,* 503–14.

Pessin, J. 1933. The comparative effects of social and mechanical stimulation on memorizing. *American Journal of Psychology, 45,* 263–70.

Pettigrew, T. F. 1969. Racially separate or together? *Journal of Social Issues, 25,* 43–69.

Petty, R. E., & Cacioppo, J. T. 1977. Forewarning, cognitive responding, and resistance to persuasion. *Journal of Personality and Social Psychology, 35,* 645–56.

Petty, R. E., & Cacioppo, J. T. 1979. Issue involvement can increase or decrease persuasion by enhancing message-relevant cognitive responses. *Journal of Personality and Social Psychology, 37,* 1915–26.

Piliavin, J. A., & Martin, R. R. 1974. The effects of the sex composition of groups on style of social interaction. Unpublished manuscript. University of Wisconsin.

Piliavin, I. M., Rodin, J., & Piliavan, J. A. 1969. Good Samaritanism: An underground phenomenon? *Journal of Personality and Social Psychology, 13,* 289–99.

Pilkonis, P. A., & Zanna, M. P. 1969. The choice-shift phenomenon in groups: Replication and extension. Unpublished manuscript. Yale University.

Pittman, N. L., & Pittman, T. S. 1979. Effects of amount of helplessness training and internal-external locus of control on mood and performance. *Journal of Personality and Social Psychology, 37,* 39–47.

Pliner, P., Heather, H., Kohl, J., & Saari, D. 1974. Compliance without pressure: Some further data on the foot-in-the-door technique. *Journal of Experimental Social Psychology, 10,* 17–22.

Powers, E. A., & Bultena, G. L. 1976. Sex differences in intimate friendships in old age. *Journal of Marriage and the Family, 38,* 739–47.

Pressman, I., & Carol, A. 1969. Crime as a diseconomy of scale. Talk delivered at the Operations Research Society of America Convention.

Priest, R. F., & Sawyer, J. 1967. Proximity and peership: Bases of balance in interpersonal attraction. *American Journal of Sociology, 72,* 633–49.

Rabow, J., Fowler, F. J., Jr., Bradford, D. L., Hofeller, M. A., & Shibuya, Y. 1966. The role of social norms and leadership in risk-taking. *Sociometry, 29.*

Rands, M., & Levinger, G. 1979. Implicit theories of relationship: An intergenerational study. *Journal of Personality and Social Psychology, 37,* 645–61.

Raven, B. H., & French, J. R. P., Jr. 1958. Group support, legitimate power, and social influence. *Journal of Personality, 26,* 400–9.

Regan, D. T., & Totten, J. 1975. Empathy and attribution: Turning observers into actors. *Journal of Personality and Social Psychology, 32,* 850–56.

Regan, D. T., Williams, M., & Sparling, S. 1972. Voluntary expiation of guilt: A field experiment. *Journal of Personality and Social Psychology, 24,* 42–45.

Regula, R. C., & Julian, J. W. 1973. The impact of quality and frequency of task contributions on perceived ability. *Journal of Social Psychology, 89,* 115–22.

Rhine, R. J., & Severance, L. J. 1970. Ego-involvement, discrepancy, source credibility, and attitude change. *Journal of Personality and Social Psychology, 16,* 175–90.

Riecken, H. W. 1958. The effect of talkativeness on ability to influence group solutions of problems. *Sociometry, 21,* 309–21.

Riemer, B. S. 1975. Influence of causal beliefs on affect and expectancy. *Journal of Personality and Social Psychology, 31(6),* 1163–67.

Rim, Y. 1963. Risk-taking and need for achievement. *Acta Psychologica, 21,* 108–15.

Rim, Y. 1964. Interpersonal values and risk-taking. Paper presented at the First International Congress of Psychiatry, London.

Robinson, J. P. 1970. Public reaction to political protest: Chicago, 1968. *Public Opinion Quarterly, 34,* 1–9.

Robinson, J. P. 1971. The audience for national TV news programs. *Public Opinion Quarterly, 35,* 403–5.

Robinson, J. P. 1972. Mass communication and information diffusion. In F. G. Kline and P. J. Tichenor (eds.), *Current perspectives in mass communication research.* Beverly Hills, Calif.: Sage.

Robinson, M. J. 1976. Public affairs television and the growth of political malaise: The case of "the selling of the pentagon." *American Political Science Review, 70,* 409–32.

Rocha, R. F., & Rogers, R. W. 1976. Ares and Babbitt in the classroom: Effects of competition and reward on children's aggression. *Journal of Personality and Social Psychology, 33(5),* 588–93.

Rodin, J. 1975. Causes and consequences of time perception differences in overweight and normal weight people. *Journal of Personality and Social Psychology, 31,* 898–904.

Rodin, J., & Langer, E. J. 1977. Long-term effects of a control-relevant intervention with the institutionalized aged. *Journal of Personality and Social Psychology, 35,* 897–902.

Rodin, J. Solomon, S. K., & Metcalf, J. 1978. Role of control in mediating perceptions of density. *Journal of Personality and Social Psychology, 36,* 988–99.

Rogers, R. W., & Mewborn, C. R. 1976. Fear appeals and attitude change: Effects of a threat's noxiousness, probability of occurrence, and the efficacy of coping responses. *Journal of Personality and Social Psychology, 34,* 54–61.

Rogers, T. B., Kuiper, N. A., & Kirker W. S. 1977. Self-reference and the encoding of personal information. *Journal of Personality and Social Psychology, 35,* 677–88.

Rohe, W., & Patterson, A. 1974. The effects of varied levels of resources and density on behavior in a day care center. In D. Carson (ed.), *EDRA V,* Pp. 161–71.

Rokeach, M., & Mezei, L. 1966. Race and shared belief as factors in social choice. *Science, 151,* 167–72.

Rosenberg, M. J. 1960. Cognitive reoganization in response to the hypnotic reversal of attitudinal affect. *Journal of Personality, 28,* 39–63.

Rosenberg, S. 1977. New approaches to the analysis of personal constructs in person perception. In A. W. Landfield (ed.), *Nebraska symposium on motivation, 1976.* Lincoln: University of Nebraska Press.

Rosenberg, S., & Jones, R. 1972. A method for investigating and representing a person's implicit theory of personality: Theodore Dreiser's view of people. *Journal of Personality and Social Psychology, 22,* 372–86.

Rosenberg, S., Nelson, C., & Vivekananthan, P. S. 1968. A multidimensional approach to the structure of personality impressions. *Journal of Personality and Social Psychology, 9,* 283–94.

Rosenhan, D. L., Underwood, B., & Moore, B. 1974. Affect moderates self-gratification and altruism. *Journal of Personality and Social Psychology, 30,* 546–52.

Rosenthal, R. 1966. *Experimenter effects in behavioral research.* New York: Appleton-Century-Crofts.

Ross, A. S. 1971. Effect of increased responsibility on bystander intervention: The presence of children. *Journal of Personalty and Social Psychology, 19,* 306–10.

Ross, L. 1977. The intuitive psychologist and his shortcomings: Distortions in the attribution process. In L. Berkowitz (ed.), *Advances in experimental social psychology,* Vol. 10. New York: Academic Press.

Ross, L., Bierbrauer, & Polly, S. 1974. Attribution of educational outcomes by professional and nonprofessional instructors. *Journal of Personality and Social Psychology, 29,* 609–18.

Ross, L. D., Amabile, T. M., & Steinmetz, J. L. 1977. Social roles, social control, and biases in social-perception processes. *Journal of Personality and Social Psychology, 35,* 485–94.

Ross, L., Greene, D., & House, P. 1977. The "false consensus effect": An egocentric bias in social perception and attribution processes. *Journal of Experimental Social Psychology, 13,* 279–301.

Ross, M., Layton, B., Erickson, B., & Schopler, J. 1973. Affect, facial regard, and reactions to crowding. *Journal of Personality and Social Psychology, 28,* 69–76.

Ross, M., & Sicoly, F. 1979. Egocentric biases in availability and attribution. *Journal of Personality and Social Psychology, 37,* 322–36.

Rubin, J. Z., Provenzano, F. J., & Luria, Z. 1974. The eye of the beholder: Parent's views on sex of newborns. *American Journal of Orthopsychiatry, 44,* 510–19.

Rubin, Z. 1973. *Liking and loving: An invitation to social psychology.* New York: Holt, Rinehart, Winston.

Rubin, Z. 1975. Disclosing oneself to a stranger: Reciprocity and its limits. *Journal of Experimental Social Psychology, 11,* 233–60.

Rubin, Z., Hill, C. T., Peplau, L. A., & Dunkel-Schetter, C. Self-disclosure in dating couples: sex roles and the ethic of openness. *Journal of Marriage and the Family*, 1980, 42(2), 305–17.

Rubin, Z., Peplau, L. A., & Hill, C. T. Loving and leaving: Sex differences in romantic attachments. *Sex Roles* (in press).

Rubin, Z., & Shenker, S. 1978. Friendship, proximity, and self-disclosure. *Journal of Personality*, 46, 1–22.

Ruble, D. N., & Feldman, N. S. 1976. Order of consensus, distinctiveness, and consistency information and causal attributions. *Journal of Personality and Social Psychology*, 34, 930–37.

Ruble, D. N. & Ruble, T. L. 1980. Sex stereotypes. In A. G. Miller (ed.), *In the eye of the beholder: Contemporary issues in stereotyping*. New York: Holt.

Saarni, C. I. 1973. Piagetian operations and field independence as factors in children's problem-solving performance. *Child Development*, 44, 338–45.

Saegert, S., Swap, W., & Zajonc, R. B. 1973. Exposure, context, and interpersonal attraction. *Journal of Personality and Social Psychology*, 25, 234–42.

Sakagami, S. F., & Akahira, Y. 1960. Studies on the Japanese honeybee, *Apis cerana, cerana Fabricius*: 8, two opposing adaptations in the post-stinging behavior of honeybees. *Evolution*, 14, 29–40.

Salancik, G. R., & Conway, M. 1975. Attitude inferences from salient and relevant cognitive content about behavior. *Journal of Personality and Social Psychology*, 32, 829–40.

Sampson, E. E. 1977. Psychology and the American ideal. *Journal of Personality and Social Psychology*, 35, 767–82.

Sanders, G. S., & Baron, R. S. 1977. Is social comparison irrelevant for producing choice shifts? *Journal of Experimental Social Psychology*, 13, 303–14.

Sanders, G. S., Baron, R. S., & Moore, D. L. 1978. Distraction and social comparison as mediators of social facilitation effects. *Journal of Experimental Social Psychology*, 14, 291–303.

Sarnoff, I., & Zimbardo, P. G. 1961. Anxiety, fear, and social affiliation. *Journal of Abnormal and Social Psychology*, 62, 356–63.

Schachter, S. 1951. Deviation, rejection and communication. *Journal of Abnormal and Social Psychology*, 46, 190–208.

Schachter, S. 1959. *The psychology of affiliation*. Stanford, Calif.: Stanford.

Schachter, S. 1971. Some extraordinary facts about obese humans and rats. *American Psychologist*, 26, 129–44.

Schachter, S., Ellertson, N., McBride, D., & Gregory, D. 1951. An experimental study of cohesiveness and productivity. *Human Relations*, 4, 229–38.

Schachter, S., & Rodin, J. (eds.) 1974. *Obese humans and rats*. Washington, D.C.: Erlbaum/Halsted.

Schachter, S., & Singer, J. E. 1962. Cognitive, social and physiological determinants of emotional state. *Psychological Review*, 69, 379–99.

Scheier, M. F., Fenigstein, A., & Buss, A. H. 1974. Self-awareness and physical aggression. *Journal of Experimental Social Psychology*, 10, 264–73.

Scherer, S. E. 1974. Proxemic behavior of primary school children as a function of their socioeconomic class and subculture. *Journal of Personality and Social Psychology*, 29, 800–5.

Schiffenbauer, A. 1974. Effect of observer's emotional state on judgments of the emotional state of others. *Journal of Personality and Social Psychology*, 30, 31–35.

Schiffenbauer, A., & Schiavo, R. S. 1976. Physical distance and attraction: An intensification effect. *Journal of Experimental Social Psychology*, 12, 274–82.

Schmitt, D. R., & Mmarwel, G. 1972. Withdrawal and regard reallocation as responses to inequity. *Journal of Experimental Social Psychology*, 8, 207–21.

Schmitt, R. C. 1957. Density, delinquency and crime in Honolulu. *Sociology and Social Research*, 41, 274–76.

Schmitt, R. C. 1966. Density, health, and social disorganization. *Journal of American Institute of Planners*, 32, 38–40.

Schneider, D. J., Hastorf, A. H., & Ellsworth, P. C. 1979. *Person perception*. 2nd ed. Reading, Mass.: Addison-Wesley.

Schneider, D. J., & Miller, R. S. 1975. The effects of enthusiasm and quality of arguments on attitude attribution. *Journal of Personality*, 43, 693–708.

Schneider, F. W. 1970. Conforming behavior of black and white children. *Journal of Personality and Social Psychology*, 16, 466–71.

Schneier, C. E. 1978. The contingency model of leadership: An extension to emergent leadership and leader's sex. *Organizational Behavior and Human Performance*, 21, 230–39.

Schramm, W., & Carter, R. F. 1959. Effectiveness of a political telethon. *Public Opinion Quarterly*, 23, 121–26.

Schultz J. W., & Pruitt, D. G. 1978. The effects of mutual concern on joint welfare. *Journal of Experimental Social Psychology*, 14, 480–92.

Schulz, R. 1976. The effects of control and predictability on the psychological and physical well-being of the institutionalized aged. *Journal of Personality and Social Psychology*, 33, 563–73.

Schulz, R., & Hanusa, B. H. 1978. Long-term effects of control and predictability-enhancing interventions: Findings and ethical issues. *Journal of Personality and Social Psychology*, 36, 1194–1201.

Schuman, H., & Johnson, M. P. 1976. Attitudes and behavior. *Annual Review of Sociology*, 2, 161–207.

Schwab, J. J., McGinnis, N. H., & Warheit, G. J. 1973. Social psychiatric impairment: Racial comparisons. *American Journal of Psychiatry*, 130, 183–87.

Schwartz, S. H. 1978. Temporal instability as a moderator of the attitude-behavior relationship. *Journal of Personality and Social Psychology*, 36, 715.

Schwartz, S. H., & Clausen, G. T. 1970. Responsibility, norms, and helping in an emergency. *Journal of Personality and Social Psychology*, 16, 299–310.

Sears, D. O. 1968. The paradox of de facto selective exposure without preferences for supportive information. In R. P. Abelson, et al. (eds.), *Theories of cognitive consistency: A sourcebook*. Chicago: Rand-McNally.

Sears, D. O. 1969. Political behavior. In G. Lindzey and E. Aronson (eds.), *Handbook of social psychology.* Vol. V. Reading, Mass.: Addison-Wesley.

Sears, D. O. 1975. Political socialization. In F. I. Greenstein & N. W. Polsby (eds.), *Handbook of political science.* Vol. II. Reading, Mass.: Addison-Wesley.

Sears, D. O. 1976. *Positivity biases in evaluations of public figures.* Paper presented at annual meeting of American Psychological Association, Washington, D.C.

Sears, D. O. & Chaffee, S. H. 1979. Uses and effects of the 1976 debates: An overview of empirical studies. In S. Kraus (ed.), *The great debates, 1976: Ford vs. Carter.* Bloomington, Ind.: Indiana University Press.

Sears, D. O., & Freedman, J. L. 1967. Selective exposure to information: A critical review. *Public Opinion Quarterly, 31,* 194–213.

Sears, D. O., Freedman, J. L., & O'Connor, E. F., Jr. 1964. The effects of anticipated debate and commitment on the polarization of audience opinion. *Public Opinion Quarterly, 28,* 615–27.

Sears, D. O., Hensler, C. P., & Speer, L. K. 1979. Whites' opposition to "busing": Self-interest or symbolic politics? *American Political Science Review, 73,* 369–84.

Sears, D. O., & McConahay, J. B. 1973. *The politics of violence: The New uban blacks and the Watts riot.* Boston: Houghton Mifflin.

Sears, D. O., & Whitney, R. E. 1973. Political persuasion. In I. deS. Pool, W. Schramm, et al (eds.), *Handbook of communication.* Chicago: Rand McNally.

Sears, R. R., Whiting, J. W. M., Nowlis, V., & Sears, P. S. 1953. Some child-rearing antecedents of aggression and dependency in young children. *Genetic Psychological Monographs, 47,* 135–236.

Sears, R. R., Maccoby, E., & Levin, H. 1959. *Patterns of child rearing.* Evanston, Ill.: Row, Peterson.

Segal, M. W. 1974. Alphabet and attraction: An unobstrusive measure of the effect of propinquity in a field setting. *Journal of Personality and Social Psychology, 30*(5), 654–57.

Segal, M. W. 1979. Varieties of interpersonal attraction and their interrelationships in natural groups. *Social Psychology Quarterly, 42,* 253–61.

Seligman, C., Bush, M., & Kirsch, K. 1975. Relationship between compliance in the foot-in-the-door paradigm and size of first request. *Journal of Personality and Social Psychology, 33,* 517–20.

Seligman, M. E. P. 1975. *Helplessness: On depression, development, and death.* San Francisco: Freeman.

Shanab, M. E., & Yahya, K. A. 1977. A behavioral study of obedience in children. *Journal of Personality and Social Psychology, 35,* 530–36.

Shanteau, J., & Nagy, G. F. 1979. Probability of acceptance in dating choice. *Journal of Personality and Social Psychology, 37,* 522–33.

Shaver, P., & Freedman, J. L. 1976. Happiness. *Psychology Today* (August).

Shaw, M. E. 1955. A comparison of two types of leadership in various communication nets. *Journal of Abnormal and Social Psychology, 50,* 127–34.

Shaw, M. E., & Harkey, B. 1976. Some effects of congruency of member characteristics and group struc-

ture upon group behavior. *Journal of Personality and Social Psychology, 34,* 412–18.

Sherif, M. 1935. A study of some social factors in perception. *Archives of Psychology,* No. 187.

Sherif, M., Harvey, O. J., White, B. J., Hood, W. R., & Sherif, C. W. 1961. *Intergroup conflict and cooperation: The robbers' cave experiment.* Norman, Okla.: University Book Exchange.

Sherrod, D. R., Hage, J. N., Halpern, P. L., & Moore, B. S. 1977. Effects of personal causation and perceived control on responses to an aversive environment: The more control, the better. *Journal of Experimental Social Psychology, 13,* 14–27.

Shotland, R. L. & Straw, M. K. 1976. Bystander response to an assault: When a man attacks a woman. *Journal of Personality and Social Psychology, 34,* 990–99.

Shuck, S. Z., Shuck, A., Hallam, E., Mancini, R., & Wells, R. 1971. Sex differences in aggressive behavior subject to listening to a radio broadcast of violence. *Psychological Reports, 28,* 921–26.

Sicoly, F., & Ross, M. 1977. Facilitation of ego-biased attributions by means of self-serving observer feedback. *Journal of Personality and Social Psychology, 35,* 734–41.

Sigall, H., & Landy, D. 1973. Radiating beauty: The effects of having a physically attractive partner on person perception. *Journal of Personality and Social Psychology, 28,* 218–24.

Sigall, H., & Ostrove, N. 1975. Beautiful but dangerous: Effects of offender attractiveness and nature of the crime on juridic judgment. *Journal of Personality and Social Psychology, 31,* 410–14.

Silverman, B. I. 1974. Consequences, racial discrimination, and the principle of belief congruence. *Journal of Personality and Social Psychology, 29,* 497–508.

Silverman, I. 1971. Physical attractiveness and courtship. *Sexual Behavior, 22*–25.

Simmel, G. 1903. *Sociology of Georg Simmel.* New York: Macmillan, 1950. Translation of German edition.

Singer, J. E., Brush, C., & Lublin, S. D. 1965. Some aspects of deindividuation: Identification and conformity. *Journal of Experimental Social Psychology, 1,* 356–78.

Sistrunk, F., & McDavid, J. W. 1971. Sex variable in conforming behavior. *Journal of Personality and Social Psychology, 17,* 200–7.

Smith, M. B., Bruner, J. S., & White, R. W. 1956. *Opinions and Personality.* New York: John Wiley & Sons.

Smith, P. K., & Connelly, K. 1972. Patterns of play and social interaction in preschool children. In N. B. Jones (ed.), *Ethological Studies of Child Behavior.* Cambridge, Eng.: Cambridge University Press.

Smith, R. E., Smythe, L., & Lien, D. 1972. Inhibition of helping behavior by a similar or dissimilar nonreactive fellow bystander. *Journal of Personality and Social Psychology, 23,* 414–19.

Smith, S., & Haythorn, W. H. 1972. Effects of compatibility, crowding, group size, and leadership seniority on stress, anxiety, hostility, and annoyance in isolated groups. *Journal of Personality and Social Psychology, 22,* 67–79.

Smith, W. P., & Anderson, A. J. 1975. Threats, communication and bargaining. *Journal of Personality and Social Psychology, 32,* 76–82.

Sniderman, P. M., & Brody, R. A. 1977. Coping: The ethic of self-reliance. *American Journal of Political Science, 21,* 501–22.

Snyder, A., Mischel, W., & Lott, B. 1960. Value, information, and conformity behavior. *Journal of Personality, 28,* 333–42.

Snyder, M., & Cunningham, M. R. 1975. To comply or not comply: Testing the self-perception explanation of the "foot in the door" phenomenon. *Journal of Personality and Social Psychology, 31,* 64–67.

Snyder, M., & Jones, E. E. 1974. Attitude attribution when behavior is constrained. *Journal of Experimental Social Psychology, 10,* 585–600.

Snyder, M., & Swann, W. B., Jr., 1976. When actions reflect attitudes: The politics of impression management. *Journal of Personality and Social Psychology, 34,* 1034–42.

Snyder, M. & Swann, W. B., Jr. 1978a. Behavioral confirmation in social interaction: From social perception to social reality. *Journal of Experimental Social Psychology, 14,* 148–62.

Snyder, M., & Swann, W. B., Jr. 1978b. Hypothesis-testing processes in social interaction. *Journal of Personality and Social Psychology, 36,* 1202–12.

Snyder, M., & Uranowitz, S. W. 1978. Reconstructing the past: Some cognitive consequences of person perception. *Journal of Personality and Social Psychology, 36,* 941–50.

Snyder, M. L., Stephan, W. G., & Rosenfeld, D. 1976. Egotism and attribution. *Journal of Personality and Social Psychology, 33,* 435–41.

Snyder, R. L. 1968. Reproduction and population pressures. In. E. Steller and J. M. Sprague (eds.), *Progress in physiological psychology.* New York: Academic Press.

Sogin, S. R. & Pallak, M. S. 1976. Bad decisions, responsibility, and attitude change. Effects of volition, foresee-ability, and locus of causality of negative consequences. *Journal of Personality and Social Psychology, 33*(3), 300–6.

Sommer, R. 1959. Studies in personal space. *Sociometry, 22,* 247–60.

Sommer, R. 1969. *Personal space: The behavioral basis of design.* Englewood Cliffs, N.J.: Prentice-Hall.

Sorrentino, R. M., & Boutiller, R. G. 1975. The effect of quantity and quality of verbal interaction on ratings of leadership ability. *Journal of Experimental Social Psychology, 11,* 403–11.

Southwick, C. H. 1955. The population dynamics of confined house mice supplied with unlimited food. *Ecology, 36,* 212–15.

Southwick, C. H., & Bland, V. P. 1959. Effect of population density on adrenal glands and reproductive organs of CFW mice. *American Journal of Physiology, 197,* 111–14.

Spence, J. T., Helmreich, R., & Stapp, J. 1975. Ratings of self and peers on sex-role attributes and their relation to self-esteem and conceptions of masculinity and feminity. *Journal of Personality and Social Psychology, 32,* 29–39.

Srole, L. 1972. Urbanization and mental health: Some reformulations. *American Scientist, 60,* 576–83.

Srull, T. K., & Wyer, R. S., Jr. 1979. The role of category accessibility in the interpretation of information about persons: Some determinants and implications. *Journal of Personality and Social Psychology, 37,* 1660–72.

Stang, D. J. 1972. Conformity, ability, and self-esteem. *Representative Research in Social Psychology, 3,* 97–103.

Stang, D. J. 1973. Effect of interaction rate on ratings of leadership and liking. *Journal of Personality and Social Psychology, 27,* 405–8.

Staub, E. 1971. Helping a person in distress: The influence of implicit and explicit "rules" of conduct on children and adults. *Journal of Personality and Social Psychology, 17,* 137–44.

Stayton, D. J., & Ainsworth, M. D. S. 1973. Individual differences in infant responses to brief, everyday separations as related to other infant and maternal behaviors. *Developmental Psychology, 9,* 226–35.

Steele, C. M. 1975. Name-calling and compliance. *Journal of Personality and Social Psychology, 31,* 361–69.

Stein, A. H., & Friedrich, C. K. 1975. The impact of television on children and youth. In H. M. Hetherington (ed.), *Review of child development research.* Chicago: University of Chicago Press.

Stein, D. D., Hardyck, J. A., & Smith M. B. 1965. Race and belief: An open and shut case. *Journal of Personality and Social Psychology, 1,* 281–89.

Stein, R. T., Geis, F. L., & Damarin, F. 1973. Perception of emergent leadership hierarchies in task groups. *Journal of Personality and Social Psychology, 28,* 77–87.

Stember, C. H. 1961. *Education and attitude change.* New York: Institute of Human Relations Press.

Stephan, F. F., & Mishler, E. G. 1952. The distribution of partication in small groups: an exponential approximation. *American Sociological Review, 17,* 598–608.

Stephan, W. G., & Rosenfield, D. 1978. Effects of desegregation on racial attitudes. *Journal of Personality and Social Psychology, 36,* 795–804.

Sternglanz, S. H., & Serbin, L. A. 1974. Sex-role stereotyping in children's television programs. *Developmental Psychology, 10,* 710–15.

Stokols, D. 1972. On the distinction betwen density and crowding: Some implications for future research. *Psychological Review, 79,* 275–77.

Stokols, D., Rall, M., Pinner, B. & Schopler, J. 1973. Physical, social, and personal determinants of the perception of crowding. *Environment and Behavior, 5,* 87–115.

Stoner, J. A. F. 1961. A comparison of individual and group decisions involving risk. Unpublished master's thesis. School of Industrial Management.

Storms, M. D. 1973. Videotape and the attribution process: Reversing actors' and observers' points of view. *Journal of Personality and Social Psychology, 27*(2), 165–75.

Storms, M. D., & Nisbett, R. E. 1970. Insomnia and the

attribution process. *Journal of Personality and Social Psychology, 16,* 319–28.

Storms, M. D., & Thomas, C. C. 1977. Reactions to physical closeness. *Journal of Personality and Social Psychology, 35,* 412–18.

Stouffer, S. A., Lumsdaine, A. A., Lumsdaine, M. H., Williams, R. M., Jr., Smith, M. B., Janis, I. L., Star, S. A., & Cottrell, L. S., Jr. 1949. *The American soldier combat.* Princeton, N.J.: Princeton.

Strodtbeck, F. L., James, R. M., & Hawkins, C. 1958. Social status in jury deliberations. In E. Maccoby, T. Newcomb, & E. Hartley (eds.), *Readings in social psychology.* New York: Holt.

Strodtbeck, F. L., & Mann, R. D. Sex-role differentiation in jury deliberations. *Sociometry, 19,* 3–11.

Stroebe, W., Insko, C. A., Thompson, V. D., & Layton, B. D. 1971. Effects of physical attractiveness, attitude similarity, and sex on various aspects of interpersonal attraction. *Journal of Personality and Social Psychology, 18,* 79–91.

Sundstrom, E., & Sundstrom, M. G. 1977. Personal space invasions: What happens when the invader asks permission? *Environmental Psychology and Nonverbal Behavior, 2,* 76–82.

Surgeon General's Scientific Advisory Committee 1972. *Television and growing up: The impact of televised violence.* (Report to the Surgeon General, U. S. Public Health Service, Department of Health, Education, and Welfare Publication N. HSM 72–9090). Rockville, Md: National Institute of Mental Health.

Sutton-Smith, B., & Savasta, M. 1972. Sex differences in play and power. Paper presented at the annual meeting of the Eastern Psychological Association.

Svensson, A. 1971. *Relative achievement: School performance in relation to intelligence, sex, and home environment.* Stockholm: Almqvist and Wiksell.

Swingle, P. G. 1970. Exploitative behavior in non-zero sum games. *Journal of Personality and Social Psychology, 16,* 121–32.

Taifel, H., Billig, M. G., Bundy, R. P., & Flament, C. 1971. Social categorization and intergroup behavior. *European Journal of Social Psychology, 1,* 149–78.

Tasch, P. J. 1952. The role of the father in the family. *Journal of Experimental Education, 20,* 319–61.

Taylor, D. W., Berry, P. C., & Block, C. H. 1958. Does group participation when using brainstorming facilitate or inhibit creative thinking? *Administrative Science Quarterly, 2,* 23–47.

Taylor, R. B., De Soto, C. B., & Lieb, R. 1979. Sharing secrets: Disclosure and discretion in dyads and triads. *Journal of Personality and Social Psychology, 37,* 1196–203.

Taylor, S. E. 1975. On inferring one's attitudes from one's behavior: Some delimiting conditions. *Journal of Personality and Social Psychology, 31*(1), 126–31.

Taylor, S. E. 1980. The interface of cognitive and social psychology. In J. Harvey (ed.), *Cognition, social behavior, and the environment.* Hillsdale, N.J.: Lawrence Erlbaum.

Taylor, S. E., & Crocker, J. 1980. Schematic bases of social information processing. In Higgins, E. T., Hermann, P., and Zanna, M. P. (eds.). Social Cognition: *Cognitive Structure and Processes Underlying Person Perception.* Hillsdale, N.J.: Lawrence Erlbaum.

Taylor, S. E., Crocker, J., Fiske, S. T., Sprinzen, M., & Winkler, J. D. 1979. The generalizability of salience effects. *Journal of Personality and Social Psychology, 37,* 357–68.

Taylor, S. E., & Fiske, S. T. 1975. Point of view and perceptions of causality. *Journal of Personality and Social Psychology, 32,* 439–45.

Taylor, S. E., & Fiske, S. T. 1978. Salience, attention, and attribution: Top of the head phenomena. In Berkowitz, L. (ed.), *Advances in Experimental Social Psychology, Vol. 11.* New York: Academic Press, pp. 249–88.

Taylor, S. E., Fiske, S. T., Close, M., Anderson, C., & Ruderman, A. 1977. Solo status as a psychological variable: The power of being distinctive. Unpublished manuscript. Harvard University.

Taylor, S. E., Fiske, S. T., Etcoff, N. L., & Ruderman, A. J. 1978. Categorical and contextual bases of person memory and stereotyping. *Journal of Personality and Social Psychology, 36,* 778–93.

Taylor, S. E., & Koivumaki, J. H. 1976. The perception of self and others: Acquaintanceship, affect, and actor-observer differences. *Journal of Personality and Social Psychology, 33,* 403–8.

Taylor, S. P., & Gammong C. B. 1975. Effects of type and dose of alcohol on human physical aggression. *Journal of Personality and Social Psychology, 32,* 169–75.

Tedin, K. L. 1974. The influence of parents on the political attitudes of adolescents. *American Political Science Review, 68,* 1579–92.

Tegin, A. I., & Pruitt, D. G. 1967. Components of group risk-taking. *Journal of Experimental Social Psychology, 3,* 189–205.

Teichman, Y. 1973. Emotional arousal and affiliation. *Journal of Experimental Social Psychology, 9,* 591–605.

Terman, C. R. 1969. Pregnancy failure in female prairie deermice related to parity and social environment. *Animal Behavior, 17,* 104–8.

Terman, C. R. 1974. Behavioral factors associated with cessation of growth of laboratory populations of prairie deermice. *Research in Population Ecology, 15,* 138–47.

Tesser, A. 1978. Self-generated attitude change. In Berkowitz, L. (ed.), *Advances in experimental social psychology, Vol. 11.* Pp. 290–338. New York: Academic Press.

Thibaut, J. W., & Riecken, H. W. 1955. Some determinants and consequences of the perception of social causality. *Journal of Personality, 24,* 113–33.

Thiessen, D. D. 1964. Population density, mouse genotype, and endocrine function in behavior. *Journal of Comparative and Physiological Psychology, 57,* 412–16.

Thomas, M. H., & Drabman, R. S. 1975. Toleration of real-life aggression as a function of exposure to televised violence and age of subject. *Merrill-Palmer Quarterly, 21,* 227–32.

Thomas, M. H., Horton, R. W., Lippincott, E. C., & Drabman, R. S. 1977. Desensitization to portrayals of real-life aggression as a function of exposure to television violence. *Journal of Personality and Social Psychology, 35,* 450–79.

Thompson, D. F., & Meltzer, L. 1964. Communication of emotional intent by facial expression. *Journal of Abnormal and Social Psychology, 68,* 129–35.

Tilker, H. A. 1970. Socially responsible behavior as a function of observer responsibility and victim feedback. *Journal of Personality and Social Psychology, 14,* 95–100.

Tillman, W. S., & Carver, C. S. 1980. Actors' and observers' attributions for success and failure: A comparative test of predictions from Kelley's Cube, self-serving bias, and positivity bias formulations. *Journal of Experimental Social Psychology, 16,* 18–32.

Titley, H. W., & Viney, W. 1969. Expression of aggression toward the physically handicapped. *Perceptual and Motor Skills, 29,* 51–56.

To, L. P., & Tamarin, R. H. 1977. The Relation of population density and adrenal gland weight in cycling and noncycling voles (Microtus). *Ecology, 58,* 928–34.

Toda, M., Shinotsuka, H., McClintock, C. G., & Stech, F. L. 1978. Development of competitive behavior as a function of culture, age, and social comparison. *Journal of Personality and Social Psychology, 36,* 825–39.

Torrance, E. P. 1955. Some consequences of power difference on decision making in permanent and temporary three-man groups. In A. P. Hare, E. F. Bogatta and R. F. Bales (eds.), *Small groups: Studies in social interaction.* New York: Knopf.

Travis, L. E. 1925. The effect of a small audience upon eye-hand coordination. *Journal of Abnormal and Social Psychology, 20,* 142–46.

Turner, C. W., & Layton, J. F. 1976. Verbal imagery and connotation as memory-induced mediators of aggressive behavior. *Journal of Personality and Social Psychology, 33,* 755–63.

Turner, C. W., Layton, J. F., & Simons, L. S. 1975. Naturalistic studies of aggressive behavior: Aggressive stimuli, victim visibility, and horn honking. *Journal of Personality and Social Psychology, 31,* 1098–1107.

Tyler, T. R., & Sears, D. O. 1977. Coming to like obnoxious people when we must live with them. *Journal of Personality and Social Psychology, 35,* 200–11.

Ugwuegbu, D. C. E. 1979. Racial and evidential factors in juror attribution of legal responsibility. *Journal of Experimental Social Psychology, 15,* 133–46.

Valins, S., & Ray, A. A. 1967. Effects of cognitive desensitization on avoidance behavior. *Journal of Personality and Social Psychology, 7,* 345–50.

Valle, V. A., & Frieze, I. H. 1976. Stability of causal attributions as a mediator in changing expectations for success. *Journal of Personality and Social Psychology, 33,* 579–87.

Vinokur, A., Trope, Y., & Burnstein, E. 1975. A decision-making analysis of persuasive argumentation and the choice-shift effect. *Journal of Experimental Social Psychology, 11,* 127–48.

Vinokur, A., & Burnstein, E. 1978. Depolarization of attitudes in groups. *Journal of Personality and Social Psychology, 36,* 872–85.

Wagner, R. V. 1975. Complementary needs, role expectations, interpersonal attraction, and the stability of working relationships. *Journal of Personality and Social Psychology, 32,* 116–24.

Wallach, M. A., & Kogan, N. 1965. The roles of information, discussion, and consensus in group risk taking. *Journal of Experimental Social Psychology, 1,* 1–19.

Wallach, M. A., Kogan, N., & Bem, D. J. 1962. Group influence on individual risk taking. *Journal of Abnormal and Social Psychology, 65,* 75–87.

Wallach, M. A., Kogan, N., & Burt, R. B. 1965. Can group members recognize the effects of group discussion upon risk taking? *Journal of Experimental Social Psychology, 1,* 379–95.

Wallington, S. A. 1973. Consequences of transgression: Self-punishment and depression. *Journal of Personality and Social Psychology, 28,* 1–7.

Walster, E., Aronson, E., & Abrahams, D. 1966. On increasing the persuasiveness of a low prestige communicator. *Journal of Experimental Social Psychology, 2,* 325–42.

Walster, E., Aronson, V., Abrahams, D., & Rottman, L. 1966. Importance of physical attractiveness in dating behavior. *Journal of Personality and Social Psychology, 4,* 508–16.

Walster, E., Berscheid, E., & Walster, G. W. 1973. New directions in equity research. *Journal of Personality and Social Psychology, 25,* 151–76.

Walster, E., & Festinger, L. 1962. The effectiveness of "overheard" persuasive communications. *Journal of Abnormal and Social Psychology, 65,* 395–402.

Walster, E., Walster, G. W., & Traupmann, Jane 1978. Equity and premarital sex. *Journal of Personality and Social Psychology, 36,* 82–92.

Ward, C. 1967. Own height, sex, and liking in the judgment of the height of others. *Journal of Personality, 35,* 381–401.

Warr, P. 1974. Inference magnitude, range and evaluative direction as factors affecting relative importance of cues in impression formation. *Journal of Personality and Social Psychology, 30,* 192–97.

Waters, E. 1978. The reliability and stability of individual differences in infant-mother attachment. *Child Development, 49,* 483–94.

Watson, O. M. & Graves, T. 1966. Quantitative research in proxemic behavior. *American Anthropologist, 68,* 971–85.

Watson, R. I. Jr. 1973. Investigation into deindividuation using a cross-cultural survey technique. *Journal of Personality and Social Psychology, 25,* 342–45.

Watts, W. A., & Holt, L. E. 1979. Persistence of opinion change induced under conditions of forewarning and distraction. *Journal of Personality and Social Psychology, 37,* 778–89.

Weigel, R. H., & Newman, L. S. 1976. Increasing attitude-behavior correspondence by broadening the scope of the behavioral measure. *Journal of Personality and Social Psychology, 33,* 793–802.

Weigel, R. H., Vernon, D. T. A., & Tognacci, L. N. 1974. Specificity of the attitude as a determinant of attitude-behavior congruence. *Journal of Personality and Social Psychology, 30,* 724–28.

Weigel, R. H., Wiser, P. L., Cook, S. W. 1979. The impact of cooperative learning experiences on cross-ethnic relations and attitudes. *Journal of Social Issues, 1,* 219–44.

Weiner, B. 1974. *Achievement motivation and attribution theory.* Morristown, N.J.: General Learning Press.

Weinstein, A. G. 1972. Predicting behavior from attitudes. *Public Opinion Quarterly, 36,* 355–60.

Weisbrod, R. A. 1965. Looking behavior in a discussion group. Unpublished term paper. Ithaca, N.Y.: Cornell University.

Weiss, L., & Lowenthal, M. F. 1975. Life-course perspectives on friendship. In M. F. Lowenthal, M. Thurnher, & D. Chiriboga (eds.), *Four stages of life.* San Francisco: Jossey-Bass.

Weiss, W. A., & Fine, B. J. 1956. The effect of induced aggressiveness on opinion change. *Journal of Abnormal and Social Psychology, 52,* 109–14.

Wellman, B., & Whitaker, M. 1974. High-rise, low-rise: The effects of high-density living. Ministry of State, Urban Affairs, Canada, B. 74.29.

Wells, G. L., & Harvey, J. H. 1977. Do people use consensus information in making causal attributions? *Journal of Personality and Social Psychology, 35,* 279–93.

Wells, G. L., & Harvey, J. H. 1978. Naïve attributors' attributions and predictions: What is informative and when is an effect an effect? *Journal of Personality and Social Psychology, 36,* 483–90.

Wells, W. D. 1973. Television and aggression: Replication of an experimental field study. Unpublished manuscript, Graduate School of Business, University of Chicago.

Weyant, J. M. 1978. Effects of mood states, costs, and benefits on helping. *Journal of Personality and Social Psychology, 36,* 1169–76.

Whitcher, S. J., & Fisher, J. D. 1979. Multidimensional reaction to therapeutic touch in a hospital setting. *Journal of Personality and Social Psychology, 37,* 87–96.

White, G. M. 1972. Immediate and deferred effects of model observation and guided and unguided rehearsal on donating and stealing. *Journal of Personality and Social Psychology, 21,* 139–48.

White, L. A. 1979. Erotica and aggression: The influence of sexual arousal, positive affect, and negative affect on aggression behavior. *Journal of Personality and Social Psychology, 37,* 591–601.

Whiting, B., & Edwards, C. P. 1973. A cross-cultural analysis of sex differences in the behavior of children aged three through eleven. *Journal of Social Psychology, 91,* 171–88.

Whiting, B., & Pope, C. A cross-cultural analysis of sex differences in the behavior of children aged three to eleven. *Journal of Social Psychology,* 1974.

Whyte, W. H., Jr. 1956. *The organization man.* New York: Simon and Schuster.

Wichman, H. 1970. Effects of isolation and communication on cooperation in a two-person game. *Journal of Personality and Social Psychology, 16,* 114–20.

Wicker, A. W. 1969. Attitudes versus action: The relationship of verbal and overt behavioral responses to attitude objects. *Journal of Social Issues, 25,* 41–78.

Wiesenthal, D. L., Endler, N. S., Coward, T. R., & Edwards, J. 1976. Reversibility of relative competence as a determinant of conformity across different perceptual tasks. *Representative Research in Social Psychology, 7,* 319–42.

Wilder, D. A. 1977. Perception of groups, size of opposition, and social influence. *Journal of Experimental Social Psychology, 13,* 253–58.

Wilder, D. A., & Allen, V. L. 1973. Veridical dissent, erroneous dissent, and conformity. Unpublished master's thesis.

Wilhelmy, R. A. 1974. The role of commitment in cognitive reversibility. *Journal of Personality and Social Psychology, 30,* 695–98.

Willick, D. H., & Ashley, R. K. 1971. Survey question order and the political party preferences of college students and their parents. *Public Opinion Quarterly, 35,* 189–99.

Wilson, E. O. 1971. *The insect societies.* Cambridge, Mass.: Belknap Press of Harvard University Press.

Wilson, E. O. 1975. *Sociobiology, the new synthesis.* Cambridge, Mass.: Harvard University Press.

Wilson, J. P., Aronoff, J. & Messe L. A. 1975. Social structure, member motivation, and group productivity. *Journal of Personality and Social Psychology, 32,* 1094–98.

Wilson, L., & Rogers, R. W. 1975. The fire this time: Effects of race of target, insult, and potential retaliation on black aggression. *Journal of Personality and Social Psychology, 32,* 857–64.

Wilson, P. R. 1968. Perceptual distortion of height as a function of ascribed academic status. *Journal of Social Psychology, 74,* 97–102.

Wilson, W. R. 1979. Feeling more than we can know: Exposure effects without learning. *Journal of Personality and Social Psychology, 37,* 811–21.

Winsborough, H. H. 1965. The social consequences of high population density. *Law and Contemporary Problems, 30,* 120–26.

Witkin, M. A., Goodenough, D. R., & Karp, S. A. 1967. Stability of cognitive style from childhood to young adulthood. *Journal of Personality and Social Psychology. 7,* 291–300.

Wober, J. M. 1978. Televised violence and paranoid perception: The view from Great Britian. *Public Opinion Quarterly, 42,* 315–21.

Wolfson, M. R., Salancik, G. R. 1977. Observer orientation and actor-observer differences in attributions for failure. *Journal of Experimental Social Psychology, 13,* 441–51.

Won-Doornink, M. J. 1979. On getting to know you: The

association between the stage of a relationship and reciprocity of self-disclosure. *Journal of Experimental Social Psychology, 15,* 229–41.

Woodworth, R. D. 1938. *Experimental psychology.* New York: Holt.

Worchel, S., Hardy, T. W., & Hurley, R. 1976. The effects of commercial interruption of violent and nonviolent films on viewers' subsequent aggression. *Journal of Experimental Social Psychology, 12,* 220–32.

Wortman, C. B. 1975. Some determinants of perceived control. *Journal of Personality and Social Psychology, 31,* 282–94.

Wortman, C. B. 1976. Causal attributions and personal control. In Harvey, J. H., Ickes, W., and Kidd, R. F., (eds.), *New directions in attribution research.* Vol. 1. Pp. 23–52. Hillsdale, N.J.: Erlbaum.

Wrightsman, L. S. 1960. Effects of waiting with others on changes in level of felt anxiety. *Journal of Abnormal and Social Psychology, 61,* 216–22.

Wrightsman, L. S. 1977. *Social psychology.* 2nd ed. Monterey, Calif.: Brooks-Cole.

Wyer, R. S., Jr. 1974. Changes in meaning and halo effects in personality impression formation. *Journal of Personality and Social Psychology, 29*(6), 829–35.

Yorrew, L. J., Rubenstein, J. L., Pedersen, R. A., & Jankowski, J. J. 1972. Dimensions of early stimulation and their differential effects on infant development. *Merrill-Palmer Quarterly, 18,* 205–18.

Zajonc, R. B. 1965. Social facilitation. *Science, 149,* 269–74.

Zajonc, R. B. 1968. Attitudinal effects of mere exposure. *Journal of Personality and Social Psychology,* Monograph supplement, Part 2, 1–29.

Zajonc, R. B. 1968. Cognitive theories in social psychology. In G. Lindzey and E. Aronson (eds.), *Handbook of social psychology.* 2nd ed. Vol. 1. Reading, Mass.: Addison-Wesley.

Zajonc, R. B., Heingertner, A., & Herman, E. M. 1969. Social enhancement and impairment of performance in the cockroach. *Journal of Personality and Social Psychology, 13,* 83–92.

Zajonc, R. B., & Sales, S. M. 1966. Social facilitation of dominant and subordinate responses. *Journal of Experimental Social Psychology, 2,* 160–68.

Zajonc, R. B., Wolosin, R. J., & Wolosin, M. A. 1972. Group risk-taking under various group decision schemes. *Journal of Experimental Social Psychology, 8,* 16–30.

Zajonc, R. B., Wolosin, R. J., Wolosin, M. A., & Loh, W. D. 1970. Social facilitation and imitation in group risk-taking. *Journal of Experimental Social Psychology, 6,* 26–46.

Zanna, M. P. & Cooper, J. 1974. Dissonance and the pill: An attribution approach to studying the arousal properties of dissonance. *Journal of Personality and Social Psychology, 29,* 703–9.

Zanna, M. P., and Hamilton, D. L. 1977. Further evidence for meaning change in impression formation. *Journal of Experimental Social Psychology, 13,* 224–38.

Zellner, M. 1970. Self-esteem, reception, and influenceability. *Journal of Personality and Social Psychology, 15,* 87–93.

Zillmann, D., & Bryant, J. 1974. Effect of residual excitation on the emotional response to provocation and delayed aggressive behavior. *Journal of Personality and Social Psychology, 30,* 782–91.

Zillmann, D., & Cantor, J. R. 1976. Effects of timing of information about mitigating circumstances on emotional responses to provocation and retaliatory behavior. *Journal of Experimental Social Psychology, 12,* 38–55.

Zillmann, D., & Sapolsky, B. S. 1977. What mediates the effect of mild erotica on annoyance and hostile behavior in males? *Journal of Personality and Social Psychology, 35,* 587–96.

Zimbardo, P. G. 1970. The human choice: Individuation, reason and order versus deindividuation, impulse and chaos. In N. J. Arnold and D. Levine (eds.), *Nebraska symposium on motivation, 1969.* Lincoln: University of Nebraska Press.

Zimbardo, P. G., & Formica, R. 1963. Emotional comparison and self-esteem as determinants of affiliation. *Journal of Personality, 31,* 141–62.

Zimbardo, P. G., Snyder, M., Thomas, J., Gold, A., & Gurwitz, S. 1970. Modifying the impact of persuasive communications with external distraction. *Journal of Personality and Social Psychology, 16,* 669–80.

Zimbardo, P. G., Weisenberg, M., Firestone, I., & Levy, B. 1965. Communicator effectiveness in producing public conformity and private attitude change. *Journal of Personality, 33,* 233–56.

Ziv, A., Kruglanski, A. W., & Shulman, 1974. Children's psychological reactions to wartime stress. *Journal of Personality and Social Psychology, 30,* 24–30.

Zuckerman, M. 1979. Attribution of success and failure revisited, or: The motivational bias is alive and well in attribution theory. *Journal of Personality, 47,* 245–87.

Zuckerman, M., Lazzano, M. M. & Waldgeir, D. 1979. Undermining effects of the foot-in-the-door technique with extrinsic rewards. *Journal of Applied Social Psychology, 9,* 292–96.

Indexes

Author Index

Friedman, R., 217
Friedrich, C. K., 498
Friedrich, L. K., 274
Friesen, W., 108
Frieze, I. H., 131, 512
Frisch, D. M., 299
Frodi, A., 257, 263

Gahart, M. T., 477
Galinsky, M., 503
Galle, O. R., 621
Gallo, P. S., 569
Gammon, C. B., 260
Garrett, C. S., 493
Gates, M. F., 556
Geen, R. G., 240, 243, 253, 254, 267, 268
Geis, F. L., 524
Gerard, H. B., 79, 81, 82, 327, 331
Gergen, K. J., 20, 299
Gibb, C., 547
Ginsburg, H. J., 625
Gintner, G., 530
Glass, D. C., 559, 603, 605, 607, 636
Goethals, G. R., 420, 594
Goldberg, P., 512
Goldman, W., 190
Goldstein, J. H., 254, 276
Goodenough, D. R., 494, 503
Goodman, M. E., 468
Goranson, R. E., 298, 300
Gouge, C., 589
Grady, K., 393
Graebner, D. B., 498
Gramza, A. F., 287
Granberg, D., 209, 452
Graziano, W., 199, 206
Greeley, A. M., 462
Greenbaum, P., 102
Greenberg, B. S., 480
Greenberg, J., 297
Greeenberg, M. S., 299
Greene, D., 120
Griffitt, W., 623
Groff, B. D., 624
Grofton, C., 189
Gross, A. G., 189, 300, 528
Gruder, C. L., 294
Grusec, J. E., 334
Grush, J. E., 196
Gruzen, J., 189
Guetzkow, H., 545
Gumpert, P., 570
Guyer, M., 575

Hage, J. N., 606
Hall, E. T., 608, 609, 614
Hall, K. R. L., 287
Hallam, J., 277, 278
Halpern, P. L., 606
Hamilton, D. L., 94, 95, 118
Hansen, R. D., 160
Hanson, L. R., Jr., 95
Hansson, R. O., 637
Harachiewicz, J. M., 339
Harkey, B., 551
Harlow, H. F., 61
Harris, B., 629

Harris, V. A., 138, 139, 153
Harrison, A. A., 213
Hartley, R., 493
Hartnett, J. J., 609
Hartup, W. W., 508
Harvey, J. H., 159
Harvey, O. J., 381
Hass, R. G., 393
Hastorf, A. H., 106, 528
Hawkins, C., 538
Haythorn, W. H., 624, 625
Haythorn, W. W., 216
Heath, M., 72
Heather, H., 342
Heaton, E. E., 470
Heff, H., 607
Heider, F., 11, 129, 132, 149, 153, 155,
    170, 201, 359, 360
Heilbrun, A. B., Jr., 501
Heller, J. B., 624
Helmreich, R., 424, 500, 501
Henley, N. M., 507
Henschy, T., 559
Hensler, C. P., 470
Herman, D., 254
Heshka, S., 621, 630
Heslin, R., 627
Higbee, K. L., 383, 575
Higgins, E. T., 428
Hill, C. T., 508
Hillery, J. M., 557
Hodges, B. H., 95
Hokanson, J. E., 250
Holmes, D. S., 512
Holohan, C., 501
Holt, L. E., 363, 400
Homans, G. C., 293, 337
Hopkins, J. R., 189
Horn, N., 305
Horowitz, M. J., 609
House, J., 120
Hovland, C. I., 236, 356, 362, 364, 368,
    378, 381, 391, 399, 438, 453
Hoyt, M. F., 421
Hubert, S., 355
Hull, C., 5, 8
Hunt, P. J., 557
Husband, R. W., 587

Imber, L. G., 120
Inkster, J. A., 410
Insko, C. A., 183, 379
Isen, A. M., 305, 306
Itkin, S., 199

Jaccard, J. J., 433
Jacklin, C. N., 494, 509, 510
Jaffe, Y., 277, 278
Janis, I. L., 358, 362, 380, 391, 405, 446,
    447, 548
Janoff-Bulman, R., 168–69
Jennings, M. K., 455, 456
Johnson, G. A., 197
Johnson, M. P., 430
Johnson, P. B., 260
Johnson, R. D., 597
Johnson, R. W., 550

Jones, E. E., 50, 138, 139, 153, 154, 155,
    156, 158, 170, 200, 210, 421
Jones, R. A., 395, 419
Jones, S. E., 609
Jones, W. H., 501
Jourard, S. M., 217
Julian, J. W., 506, 530

Kagen, J., 494
Kahneman, D., 123, 160
Kandel, D. B., 434
Kanouse, D. E., 95
Kaplan, K. J., 217, 218
Kaplan, R., 269
Karabenick, S., 72
Karaz, V., 165
Karniol, R., 339
Karp, S. A., 503
Katz, D., 116
Katz, P. A., 479
Kelley, H. H., 11, 93, 132–35, 137, 148,
    149, 156, 160, 164, 376, 377, 569,
    576, 595
Kelley, S., Jr., 430, 431
Kellogg, R., 145
Kelman, H. C., 373, 399
Kendon, A., 101
Kennelly, D., 625, 627
Kenrick, D. T., 197, 223, 305, 306
Kepner, C. R., 245
Kerckhoff, A. C., 213
Kerr, N. L., 583
Kiesler, C. A., 363
Kiesler, S. B., 363
Kilham, W., 504
Kimble, C. E., 233
Kinder, D. R., 452, 470, 477
Kingdon, J. W., 162
Kirk, S. A., 503
Kirsch, K., 342
Kite, W. R., 528
Kleck, R. E., 191, 210
Kleinhesselink, R. R., 449
Kleinke, C., 570
Klevansky, S., 623
Kline, K., 629
Klopfer, P. H., 556
Knight, J., 193
Knox, R. E., 310, 571
Koenig, K., 146
Koffka, K., 5, 11
Kogan, N., 588, 589, 590, 591, 592
Kohl, J., 342
Kohlberg, L., 496, 498
Köhler, W., 5, 11
Koivumaki, J. H., 163, 165
Komarovsky, M., 514
Komorita, S. S., 578
Konečni, V. J., 249, 251, 252, 253, 302,
    612
Korth, B., 294
Kraus, S., 441
Krauss, R. M., 104, 563, 575, 577
Kraut, R. E., 104, 345
Krebs, D., 189
Krech, D., 329, 351
Kuethe, J. L., 609
Kuiper, N. A., 119

Subject Index